The Law Relating To Hindu And Mahomedan Religious Endowments: With Commentaries On The Religious Endowments Act

Pudukota R. Ganapathi Iyer

THE LAW

RELATING TO

HINDU AND MAHOMEDAN RELIGIOUS ENDOWMENTS

WITH

COMMENTARIES

ON THE

RELIGIOUS ENDOWMENTS ACT

(Act XX of 1863)

AND

BENGAL AND MADRAS REGULATIONS

(XIX of 1810 and VII of 1817).

BY

P. R. GANAPATHI IYER, B.A., B.L.,

High Court Vakil,

and First Assistant Professor, Law College, Madras.

Madras:

PRINTED AT THE SCOTTISH PRESS, BY GRAVES, COOKSON AND CO.

1905.

TO

SIR S. SUBRAHMANIA AIYAR, K.C.I.E.,

THIS BOOK

IS

(BY KIND PERMISSION)

RESPECTFULLY DEDICATED.

PREFACE.

IN the course of my professional practice I formed the idea of writing a commentary on the Religious Endowments Act. The task of collecting materials necessarily took some time, and when I found that a large number of cases were cropping up of late upon the subject, I thought I might usefully deal as well with the General Law relating to Religious Endowments. This readily took shape when I was invited in 1902 by the proprietors of the Madras Law Journal to write articles for their Journal. My thanks are due to them for their kindness in allowing me to print in their Journal articles relating to this subject, and to reprint them with such modifications as I deemed necessary for the purposes of a book. Owing to limitations of time and space, only some articles could be printed in the Journal. At the outset one would feel whether there would be enough matter for a book on this subject. But with the enormous mass of decisions which have cropped up in half a century upon the subject of Religious Endowments, the question that must be felt would be how best to curtail the matter. The task of collecting cases and making brief notes thereof had to be gone through, and in this and in correcting some of the proofs I was to a certain extent assisted by my friend M. R. Ry. K. Subramania Sastri Avergal, B A., B. L, High Court Vakil, to whom I hereby express my thanks. The ever increasing growth of Reports with their attendant 'myriad of precedent' taxes most one's memory. But with all that the practitioner will often find that his memory is in a great many instances the best guide to find whether the cases upon any given point are exhausted. The head notes of cases are often misleading. Besides, many cases are reported without the facts although the decisions themselves are unintelligible without the facts. One is often led to think, under these circumstances, whether it cannot be arranged to publish a new series of authorized reports (containing only important cases) which should alone be treated as authoritative. This would save a great deal of the lawyer's time and labour. Then again there is hardly any attempt made in the reports to adopt an uniform spelling of the Indian names. As it is the same names are made to appear differently. It will be useful if the several High Courts take steps to remedy this defect. The art of digest-making has not yet attained its perfection at any rate in India and one does not, therefore, derive material assistance from the digests in collating the decisions. I need hardly state that I derived much assistance in several portions of my book from such standard treatises as Lewin on Trusts and Tudor on Charitable Trusts. It is the fervent hope of all well-wishers of our religious institutions that the law relating to them will be placed on a better footing than it is now.

MYLAPORE,
1st January 1905.

P. R. Ganapathi Iyer.

CONTENTS.

ADDENDA ET CORRIGENDA.

INTRODUCTION.

p. iii, note (1) For "1836" read "1837."

p. v, (1) For *Lady Hewley's Charity* read *Lady Hewley's Charity*[2].
and read the following as foot note:—
"(2) S. C. *Shore* v. *Attorney General*, (1842) 9 Cl. Fin. 355: S. C. 8 Eng. Rep. 450."

p. x, note (4) add at the end:—"See also *Free Church of Scotland* v. *Overtoun*, [1904] A. C. 515 (617)."

p. xv, note (1) add at the end:—See *Rani Bhagwan Kuar* v. *Bose*, (1903) L. R 30 I. A., 249 (252 to 257): S. C. I. L R., 31 C. 11 (29 to 33).

p. xvii, margin for "revocations gift" read "revocation of gift."

p. „ note (5) for "15 B. 612" read "15 B. 625."

p. xxi, note (2) Add at the end:—"See also *Dakhni Din* v, *Rahim-un-nissa* (1891) I. L. R. 16 A 412 (414)."

p. xxx, note (4) read at the end:—"See also *Syed Asheeroddeen* v. *Sremutty Drobo Moyee*, (1876) 25 W. R. C. R. 557."

„ note (5) read at the end:—"See *Montgomerie and Co., Limited* v. *Wallace-James*, [1904] A. C. 73 at p. 77."

p. xxxiv, note (1) For "Mirdal" read "Mirdad" and for "5 S. D. A." read "5 B. S. D. A."

p. xxxv, note (1) add at the end:—"But merely building a temple and planting a grove will not amount to a setting apart. *Dakhni Din* v. *Rahim-un-nissa*, (1894) I. L. R. 16 A. 412 (415)."

p. xxxviii, note (1) add:—"See also *Parbati* v. *Ram Barun*, (1904) I.L.R. 31 C. 895."

p. xl, line (21) for "I" read "It."

p. xliii, note (3) for "12 B. 122" read "6 B. 122"

p. xlix, note (1) for "10 R. R." read "48 R. R."

„ note (6) read at the end:—"See also *Rajender Dutt* v. *Shamchund Mitter*, (1880) I. L. R., 6 C. 106 and *Ranjit Singh* v. *Jajannath Prosad Gupta*, (1885) I. L. R., 12 C. 375."

„ „ for "*Goswami Shr*" read "*Goswami Shree*."

p. liv, note (2) For "Jogeysh" read "Jogesh" and read at the end:—"See *Muhammad Yussub* v. *Sayad Ahmud*, (1861) 1 B. H. C. app. xviii."

p. lviii, note (5) for "states *gana* that means" read "states that *gana* means."

p. lx, note (4) add at the end:—"*Mercer* v. *Denne*, [1904] 2 Ch. 534 (552). Custom is not unreasonable although prejudicial to the interests of a private individual if it is for the benefit of the commonwealth. The period for ascertaining whether a custom is reasonable or not is at its inception. Ibid at p. 557."

p. lxiv, note (1) for "17 I. A. 137" read "16 I. A. 137." and also read at the end:—"See also *Montgomerie & Co., Limited* v *Wallace James*, [1904] A. C. 73 (77), and *Mercer* v. *Denne*, [1904] 2 Ch. 534 (556)"

„ note (3) add at the end:—"No presumption will be made in favor of the legal obligation of an immemorial burthen. Per *Heath*, J. in *Steel* v. *Houghton*, (1788) 1 H. B. 51 (60): S. C. 2 R. R. 715 (718); per Lord *Macnaghten* in *Simpson* v. *Attorney General*, [1904] A.C. 476 (491). Cf. *Neill* v. *Devonshire*, (1882) L. R. 8 A. C. 135 (156)."

p. lxvi, note (1) for "I. R. Eq., read "I. R. (I). Eq.,"

p. lxix, line (11) for "contitute" read "constitute."

p. lxx, note (1) for "1 Blis" read "1 Bligh."

p. lxxix, note (1) For "Naziram" read "Nazirun."

p. lxxxvi, note (5)	for "B. L. R, (O. C. J.) 23" read "4 B. L. R., (O. C. J.) 231"
p. xcvi, margin	for "jurisdic" read "juristic."
p. xcix, note (5)	add at the end "; *Nallayappa Pillan* v. *Ambalavana Pandara Sannadhi*, (1903) I. L. R., 27 M. 465 (472). But see *Dattagiri* v *Dattatraya*, (1902) I. L. R., 27 B. 363 at p. 368."
p. c, note (1)	after "14 M. L. J. R., 105 (120)" and before "See also Ghose" read "S. C. I. L R., 27 M. 435 (449 to 451); *Nallayappa Pillian* v. *Ambalavana Pandara Sannadhi*, (1903) I. L. R., 27 M. 465 (472, 473)."
p. cx, line (23)	For "Bombay Presidency" read "Bombay Presidency[4]" and read the following as footnote:—"4. But see *Dattagiri* v. *Dattatraya*, (1902) I. L. R., 27 B. 363 at p. 368."
p. cxii, note (5)	*dele* '5' after "(1893)" and before "I. L. R."
p. cxxi, note (5)	For "5. B. S. D. A. 136" read "5 B. S. D. A. 133."
p. cxxxvii, note (1)	*dele* "I" after "(1830)" and "at" after "I. L. R." and before "11 A"
p. cxxxix, note (4)	add at the end:— "See Macnaghten Ch. X. Endowments (Principles) 2."
p. cxli, note (1)	for "9 I. A. 33" read "9 I. A. 86."
p. cxlvi, note (4)	line 3 for '369' read "396."
" note (6)	for "5 B. S. D. A. 136" read "5 B. S. D. A. 133."
p. cliv, note (4)	add at the end:— "In the American Digest (Century Edition) Vol. VII p. 1471 under title "Religious Societies" it is said that when there is no limitation as to time in the order of appointment of a trustee the presumption is that the person appointed remains in office until duly removed."
p. clix, line (8)	for "Ch. II, S. 3 and S. 43" read "Ch. III, S. ii, § 43."
" note (5)	for "4 B. S. D. A. 213" read "4 B. S. D. A. 337."
p. clx, note (3)	read at the end:—"See also *Poorun* v. *Kasheessuree* (1865) 3 W.R. C. R. 180, where a woman was held competent to hold the office of *Adhikaree*."
p. clxi, note (2)	add at the end:—"But where the right to management is not appurtenant to the Raj the rule governing the succession to the Raj will not necessarily apply to the devolution of the right to sheba. *Jaggannath* v. *Ram Gobind*, (1880) 4 Ind. Jur. 529 (530)."
" note (5)	for "*Rujah Vurma*." read "*Rajah Vurmah*."
p. clxii, note (2)	for "*Gopal Ghunder*" read "*Gopal Chunder*."
" note (4)	for "13 M. 287" read 13 M. 293."
" "	for "22 I A" read "21 I. A."
p. clxiii, note (4)	line 6 *dele* "I" after "(1890)."
p. clxiv, margin	for "sucsion" read "succession."
p. clxxi, note (4)	for "*Swaroohathil*" read "*Swaroopathil*"
p. clxxii, note (7)	for "147" read "471."
p. clxxxiv, margin	for "Wukf" read "Wakf."
p. clxxxvi, note (3)	for "133" read "136."
p. cxcvi, line (15)	for "ordinarliy" read "ordinarily."
" note (9)	add at the end "772."
p. cxcix, margin	for "hy" read "by."
p. cc, note (4)	for "Tangoce" read "Tanjore" and for "384" read "334."
p. ccii, note (5)	read at the end "But see *Muthappa* v. *Muttu Palani*, (1903) I. L. R., 27 M. 80."

p. ccv, note (1) for "*Greedhareejee*" read "*Greedharreejee*" and for "*Romanlol-jee*" read "*Rumanlolljee.*"

p. ccvi, note (2) for "336 note" read "337 (note)." and after "(662)" and before "See also" add "; *Satianama Bharati* v. *Saravanabaji Ammal*, (1894) I. L. R., 18 M. 266 (272, 273)."

p. ccxi, note (2) add at the end :—" See also *Kannan* v. *Pazhniandhi*, (1901) I. L. R., 24 M. 438."

p. ccxx, note (3) for "20 B. 49" read "20 B. 495"

p. ccxxiv, note (2) add at the end:- " See also *Mariya Pillai* v. *Govinda Pillai*, (1860) M. S. D. A 285."

p. ccxxvi, note (10) for "9 B 195" read "9 B 198."

p. ccxxxiv, note (3) for "376 (377)" read "377 (378)".

p. ccxxxix, margin for "mutwalli power of lease." read "mutwalli's power to lease."

p. ccxli, note (6) add at the end: —" A person whose title is extinguished may not mortgage endowed property. *Subbaramayyar* v. *Nigamadulla Saheb*, (1895) I. L. R.. 18 M. 342".

p. ccxlix, note (8) Add at the end :—" As to the creditor's right to stand in the place of the trustee in the case of private trusts, see *In the matter of* M. *A Shard*, (1901) I. L. R 28 C. 574; and *Bridge* v. *Madden*, (1904) I. L. R. 31 C. 1084."

p. cclii, note (4) For "5 M. 312" read "5 M. 313"

p. ccliv, note (3) add at the end: —" See notes to S 7 of Act XX of 1863 p. 50 note (5). Cf. *Vijiaragava* v. *The Secretary of State for India*, (1884) I. L. R.. 7 M. 466."

p. cclvi, note (3) read at the end :—" See also *Free Church of Scotland* v. *Overtoun* [1904] A. C. 515 (617)."

p. cclxvii, note (7) for "1903 p. 8" "read "1903 p. 68."

p. cclxxx, line (13) for "party aggrieved." read "party aggrieved 7a". and add as footnote before note (8) the following:—
"7a. *Vengamuthu* v. *Pandaveswara*, (1882) I. L. R., 6 M. 151; *Anandarav* v. *Sankara Daji*, supra; *Jagannath Churn* v. *Akali Dassia*, (1893) I. L. R., 21 C. 463".

" note (5) line 3 before "*Srinivasa*" add "*Thanakoti* v. *Munappa*, (1885) I. L. R., 8. M. 496;"

p. ccxci, note (1) add at the end :—" The dispute must, however, be of a public nature. See *Monijan Beebee* v. *Khadem*, (1904) 9 C. W. N. 151 (153)".

p. ccciii, note (3) after "Hyragange," add "v. Kapabhat."

p. cccvii, note (4) for "78" read "278."

p. cccx, note (5) *dele* "1" after "(1899)"

NOTES.

p. 32, line (13) for "suggestion" read "suggestion[a]" and read the following as footnote :—" (*a*) *Gyananda Asram* v. *Kristo Chandra Mukherji*, (1901) 8 C. W. N. 404."

p. 33, note (2) add at the end:—" See per *Banerji*, J. in *Gyanananda Asram* v. *Kristo Chandra Mukherji*, (1901) 8 C. W. N. 404."

p. 37, line (26) for "it" read "the office"

p. 45, note (5) add at the end:—"See *Muthusami Pillai* v. *Queen Empress*, (1895) I. L. R., 26 M 678 : S. C. 6. M. L. J. R. 14".

p. 50, note (5) add at the end:—"See also *Chinna Rangaiyangar* v. *Subbraya Mudali*,(1867) 3 M. H. C. 334; *Ramanuja* v. *Devanayaka*, (1885) I. L. R., 8 M. 361. See further Ch. XIV, p. ccliv".

p. 59, note (1) read at the end:—" But see *Subbramaniya Sastri* v. *Meenakshi Naidu*, (1882) 6 Ind. Jur. 128 affd. on review. Ibid 632; and *Gandavathara Devanayaga*, (1883) I. L. R., 7 M. 222 (224)."

p. 64, line (24) for "regretable" read "regrettable."

" note (2) after "Looe." add "(1825)" and before "685" add "677 at p."

p.	65, line (7)	for "elecion" read "election."
p.	69, line (10)	add at the end:—"Such a suit is virtually a suit to set aside an order and is governed by Art. 13 and not Art. 120 of the Limitation Act. See Introduction Chapter XVI p. cccxxii"
p.	71, note (2)	add at the end:—": S. C. L. R. 31 I. A. 83: S. C I. L. R., 27 M. 391."
p.	76, line (12)	after "S. 9" add "of the Specific Relief Act."
	,, note, (1)	for "1 & B. 246" read "1 B& B 226 (246)."
p.	80, line (21)	for "may" read "will."
p.	93, note (8)	for "15 D" read "15 B"
p.	94, note (1)	for "(1870) 4" read "(1870) 2."
	,, note (5)	add at the end:—"But see *Narasimha* v. *Ayyan*, (1888) I. L.R., 12 M 157 and Introduction Chapter XV."
p.	97, note (3)	add after "22 M. 223" the following:—"See also *Sheik Abool Khalek* v. *Foran Bibee*, (1876) 25 W. R. C. R. 542 (548)."
p.	101, note (2),	add after "13 M. L. J. (Rec. Cas.) 59" the following:—"S. C. *Chinnammal* v. *Madarsa Rowthar*, (1903) I. L. R., 27 M. 480."
p.	105, note (22)	add at the end:— "or a suit involving the rival claims of parties as managers[8]." and read the following as footnote "8. *Kishore Bon Mohunt* v. *Kalee Churn Giree*, (1874) 22 W. R. C. R. 364."
p.	115, note (5)	after "365" read ": S. C. I. L. R, 22 C. 92."
p.	118, note (6)	add at the end:— "See also *Jaafar Mohi-u-Din* v. *Aji Mohi u-Din*, (1864) 2 M. H. C. 19 (20)."
p.	124, note (3)	for "Court Fee" read "Court Fees."
	,, note (5)	add at the end:— "See also *Kalidas Jivram* v. *Gor Parjaram Hirji*, (1890) I. L R., 15 B. 309 (315)."
p.	134, note (2)	for "26 M 461" read "26 M. 361."
p.	137, note (5)	for "14 I. A. 86" read "14 I. A. 160."
p.	159, note (1)	for "(1840) 2 M. I. A. 30." read "(1841) 2. M. I. A. 390."
p.	162, note (1)	for "1872" "read 1867"
p.	185, note (1)	for "15 B. R." read "15 B. L. R."
p.	193, note (a)	for "inclusive" read "inclusive of."
p.	199, line (20)	for "155a" read "155[a]."
	,, ,, (22)	for "presidency" read "Presidency."
	,, ,, (24)	for "1864b" read "1864b."
p.	207, ,, (38)	for "signed fr" read "signed for."
	,, foot note	for "Nc" read "No"

TABLE OF CASES.

A

D

E

H

PAGE.

N

Y

Z

INTRODUCTION.

THE

LAW RELATING TO HINDU AND MAHOMEDAN RELIGIOUS ENDOWMENTS.

CHAPTER I.

JURISDICTION OF BRITISH COURTS OVER NATIVE RELIGIOUS ENDOWMENTS.

WE propose to discuss some of the questions relating to the law governing Hindu and Mahomedan religious endowments and foundations, their nature and origin. The statute law that we have to deal with is extremely meagre, and the decisions of the courts can hardly be said to have cleared up many of the difficulties and obscurities in which the whole subject is involved.

Jurisdiction of British Indian Courts during the days of East India Company.

The first question that had to be faced by the courts of British India was whether they had jurisdiction to try suits relating to these endowments. Of course so long as the East India Company was only a commercial body, the question could not well arise. Even where native inhabitants dwelt in the factories built by the Company and the Company came to have courts of their own in the said factories exercising jurisdiction over Europeans and other persons resident in such factories, such a question was not likely to have arisen. For, the policy of the Company was, undoubtedly, not to create suspicion among the natives who were left in the enjoyment of their own laws and customs and were given their own courts to decide disputes among themselves. In fact, there was an implied, if not express, agreement when the natives came to live with the Europeans in the factories that they would be left in the undisturbed enjoyment of their rights and that their laws, &c., would be respected and given effect to.

The truth seems to be, as Mr. Cowell puts it, (Cowell's History and Constitution of Courts in India, page 8) that during the period prior to, and shortly after, the battle of Plassey "wherever the English settled, except in the island of Bombay, which had been ceded in full sovereignty to Charles II, the general character of their position was that it was obtained by leave of the *Native* Government. In Bengal especially their settlements were founded and their factories fortified with that leave, in districts purchased from the owners of the soil by permission of that Government, and held under it by the Company as subjects owing obedience, as tenants rendering rent, and even as officers exercising by delegation a part of the authority of the Native Government.

The ordinary consequence of this state of things would have been to render the English subject to the Native Government and amenable to its laws. They could not, however, be governed by the law of the Koran, and therefore from necessity they remained subject to their own law, and were obliged to take measures for introducing and administering it. Before the English assumed sovereign powers and independence of native authority, their position was extremely anomalous. Though their factories were part of the dominion of the Mogul, their own law was administered in them, and their own national character was imparted to them as completely as if they were parts of English territory. A foreigner residing in them and carrying on trade was held to take his temporary national character not from the Mogul dominion to which they were subject, but from the British possessions.

Necessity for legislative and judicial authority.

Under these circumstances, it became necessary in very early days of the existence of the Company that the Crown should grant to them certain legislative and judicial authority to be exercised in their East Indian possessions. That authority, however, it seems clear, was only intended to be exercised over their English servants and such native settlers as placed themselves under their protection."

At page 11 of his book Cowell says, "With regard to the grant of the judicial authority to be exercised, we might reasonably expect that it would be called for and required before the necessity arose for establishing any legislative authority. The actual decision of disputes in an infant society is of practical importance long before the necessity of a body of rules is felt. Moreover, the English were supposed to bring with them such of their own laws as were applicable to them in the circumstances in which they were placed. And factories established amongst races alien in religion, habits and customs have always been deemed by the law of nations which has prevailed in Christendom to be so far exclusive possessions, or at least privileged places, that all persons during their residence within them have been considered for most purposes to be clothed with the national character of the State to which the factory has belonged." He then mentions how treaties were obtained from the Mogul Government, securing for the English factories at Surat and other places the privilege of deciding disputes between the English only and how the servants of the Company bribed the Kazi, the person sent by the Nabob to administer justice to natives, to refrain from doing so.[1]

For the history of the legislative and judicial authority of the Company, and the history and constitution of the courts administering civil and criminal justice in the early days of the Company, reference may be made to Cowell's History and Constitution of Courts in India, pp. 12 to 59.

When the Company claimed to acquire territory and shook themselves free from their dubious role of tradesmen and exchanged the character of subjects for that of sovereign over the territories they occupied, and when, therefore, British Courts came into existence owing their origin to a sovereign power which was Christian in its profession and faith, the question whether such British Courts had jurisdiction over the Hindu and Mahomedan religious institutions within their territories had to be met face to face and had to be decided one way or other. Common sense and policy required that the answer to the question should be in the affirmative. We find, therefore, in some of the early cases that the decision was based partly, if not solely, on the difficulty which the courts felt if a contrary decision was to be arrived at.

Early cases relative to validity of gifts to idols.

Thus in *Ramtonoo Mullick* v. *Ramgopal Mullick*[2] a Hindu testator authorised his executors (two of his sons) to perform his and his wife's obsequies out of his estate and provided that any

1. Vide *Mayor of Lyons* v. *East India Company* (1836) I. M. I. A.. 175, at p. 273.

2. (1829), 1 Knapp., 245; S. C. 12 Eng. Rep. P. C., p. 312; S. C. I. Ind. Rev. Rep., p. 513.

objection by his other sons as regards such expense was inadmissible, but the testator did not provide the particular amount that was to be expended. He also directed by his will that they should build a temple at Ombica and consecrate the same, that they should make a ghaut at the Ganges and that they should do some work at Sri Brindabun and at Juggernaut. The Master of the Supreme Court at Fort William reported that the expense made by the executors was proper under the terms of the will, that the temple at Ombica should be built and consecrated, that a temple at Brindabun should also be built and consecrated, and that the ghaut at the Ganges should also be made and consecrated. This was accepted by the High Court. On appeal to the Privy Council it was objected that the expense was not reasonable and proper and that the testator in mentioning that some work should be done at Brindabun could not have meant a temple to be built and consecrated seeing that he mentioned the building of such temple expressly wherever he meant it and that the consecration of the ghaut was unnecessary. The Privy Council held that the Master's report should be affirmed as regards the building of the temple at Ombica, and that as regards the other two matters his report was based on insufficient materials and could not be supported. They directed that the testator not having himself fixed any sum as regards the performance of the obsequies, enquiry should be made as regards the usage of families similarly circumstanced as regards the expenses to be incurred on such occasions and that the Master should report whether there were any other cheaper religious buildings than temples that could be built at Brindabun and whether ghauts if made or erected should necessarily be consecrated. In the course of their judgment they observed at p. 247 of Knapp's Report : "The interest of sovereigns as well as their duty will ever incline them to secure as far as lies in their power the *happiness* of those who live under their Government, and no person can be *happy* whose religious feelings are not respected. If this were a case between Europeans and Hindus, we would not take a step without the assistance of some persons from India who are acquainted with the usages of that Company with regard to the ceremonies that ought to be observed and the rites that ought to be performed on the death of opulent natives, for we should fear, lest by the judgment which we might advise His Majesty to pronounce, the feelings of the people of Hindustan might be wounded."

There are many cases in the early reports upholding the validity of gifts to an idol and some of these are to be found cited in Morley's Digest (*vide* I Morley's Digest. Tit. 'Religious Endowment,' pp. 550 and 551 under the sub-heading of 'Bequest.')

The Advocate-General *v.* Vishvanath Atmaram.

So late as 1855, however, it was objected in the Bombay Sudder Court in the case of *The Advocate-General* v. *Vishvanath Atmaram,*[1] that if questions regarding Hindu temples were decided by Civil Courts, it would virtually amount to propagating the Hindu religion and that such questions were, therefore, not within the pale of Civil Courts. The Bombay Sudder Court (consisting of *Yardley*, C. J., and *Jackson*, J.) in deciding against that contention and holding that the Supreme Court had jurisdiction to interfere in cases of Hindu and Mahomedan charities and religious institutions observed: "Then it is said that by granting the prayer of this information we shall be propagating the Hindu religion, but that is not the case. If property were left by a testator with general directions to apply the same for the benefits of the natives and we were to build a Hindu temple or place of worship out of such property, the case would be different; but this fund is not open; it is already appropriated to Hindu religious purposes, and we only act ministerially in carrying out the wishes of the donors, subscribers and testators."

In the same case, in disposing of the contention that the Advocate-General had no right to inform or interfere in the case of public charities of a religion other than that of the State, *Jackson*, J., held that the statute 53 Geo. III, Ch. 155, S. 3, conferred powers on the Advocate-General similar to those of the Attorney-General in England and observed: "The Attorney-General, notwithstanding the State religion is a different one, can undoubtedly inform the Court on behalf of a dissenting charity: *Vide Lady Hewley's charity* and *John Wesley's case*. There have

1. (1855) 1 B. H. C. R. app. 9.

been enquiries into the change of religion in sects. The Attorney-General interfered in all these cases without question. The corresponding officer of the Crown in another country in different circumstances is surely justified in interfering in cases of a *different* but *lawful* religion. Where there is a religion *tolerated* by the State, the Crown will see that that religion is enjoyed, though it may be strongly at variance with the State religion in doctrine, as in the case of Roman Catholic aud Unitarian charities. I agree that the Hindu religion is more amply recognised here than the religion of Dissenters in England."

Analogy of English Law as to Dissenters and Roman Catholics.

In fact the history of English Law as to Dissenters bears a strong analogy to the case in hard. In England previously to the Toleration Acts, the Courts of Chancery would not carry out trusts for Protestant Dissenters. Those Acts permitted them to exercise their religion, but did not direct the Court of Chancery to aid them in such trusts; yet ever since those Acts were passed, trusts for the religious purposes of such Dissenters have been enforced by the Court (Boyle on Charities, p. 42).

Maintenance of a Protestant Dissenting Chapel has been held to be a charitable purpose[1]. Bequest for the assistance of a Unitarian congregation has also been held valid in the English courts[2]. A bequest to enable persons professing the Jewish religion to observe its rights has been held to be good; but a bequest not merely for the *maintenance* but also for the *advancement* of religion was bad prior to 9 & 10 Vict. C. 59[4]. Roman Catholic trusts have also been carried out since the Catholic Emancipation Acts[1].

No state church in India.

Such being the view of the English Courts as regards dissenting religious bodies in England where there exists side by side a

1. *Attorney-General* v. *Fowler*, (1808) 15 Ves. 85; *Attorney-General* v. *Cock*, (1751) 2 Ves. sen., 273 (276); *Attorney-General* v. *Lord Dudley*, (1815) Coop. G. 146, S. C. 14 R. R., 226; *Attorney-General* v. *Molland*, (1832) Younge, 562. S. C. 34 R. R.. 294.

2. *Shrewsbury* v. *Hornby*, (1846) 5 Hare 406; *Shore* v. *Attorney-General*, (1842) 9 Cl. & F., 355.

3. *In Re Bedford Charity*, (1819) 3 Swans, 470, S. C. 19 R. R., 107; and *DeCosta* v. *DePaz*, (1743) 2 Swans, 487 *n*. S. C. 19 R. R., 104.

4. *Bradshaw* v. *Tasker*, (1834) 2 My. & K., 221, S. C. 39 R. R., 187; *West* v. *Shuttleworth*, (1835) 2 My. & K., 685, S. C. 39 R. R., 327; and *Attorney-General* v. *Gladstone*, (1842) 13, Sim. 7.

State church, it must be admitted that in India where there exists no State church and where the Hindu and Mahomedan religions are more amply recognised[1], civil courts cannot refuse to interfere in cases of Hindu and Mahomedan charities and religious institutions and there exists a stronger reason for British Indian courts exercising jurisdiction over matters connected with such charities and religious institutions than for English courts over dissenting charities.

Test of jurisdiction.

The *ratio decidendi* of all the above English and Indian cases bearing upon this point is that in order to give civil courts jurisdiction, it is enough if the religion is one recognised or tolerated by the law. The courts in exercising such jurisdiction are not enforcing the particular religion to which the charities in question may appertain. They are merely enforcing civil and secular rights in favour of the professors of a religion tolerated by the State.

Manohar Ganesh Tambekar v. Lakshmiram Govindram.

In the famous *Ranchhod Temple case*[2], *West* and *Birdwood*, JJ., observed: "Civil courts have jurisdiction to enforce trusts for charitable and religious purposes, having connection with Hindu and Mahomedan foundations and to prevent fraud and waste in dealing with religious endowments, though incidentally it has to take cognizance of religious or caste questions. The religion of the Hindu population being *jurally* allowed, the duties and services connected with it must be deemed objects of public concern and at least as to their physical and secular elements enforceable like other obligations."

This case went up to the Privy Council[3] and though this question was not specifically raised, yet the judgment of the Judicial Committee affirming the decision as a whole involved a decision upon this point impliedly. For the Judicial Committee in this case held

---

1. Vide *Vasudev* v. *Vamnaji*, (1880) I. L. R., 5 B. 80; *Narayan* v. *Chintamani*, (1881) I. L. R., 5 B. 393; and *Venkatachalapati* v. *Subbarayadu*, (1890) I. L. R., 13 M. 293 at p. 305.

2. *Manohar Ganesh Tambekar* v. *Lakhmiram Govindram*, (1887) I. L. R., 12 B. 27.

3. *Chotalal* v. *Manohar Ganesh*, (1899) I. L. R., 24 B. 50: S. C. 26 I. A. 199.

that there was a religious foundation (Hindu) for which the court had power to frame a scheme, and this could not be done if the court could not interfere as contended by the counsel in the *Shri Vithoba temple case*[1] already referred to.

Duty of Courts to protect trusts.

The objection on the score of the propagation of a false or heathen faith not being thus available, civil courts in British India have ample jurisdiction over Hindu temples and other native religious institutions, and this jurisdiction is given not because courts want to interfere with the Hindu and other religions, but because courts are bound to protect all trusts, and it is, as already stated, the duty of the sovereign to protect his subjects in the enjoyment of their religion. When once it is shown that the jurisdiction of civil courts cannot be gainsaid, it cannot equally be gainsaid that courts have jurisdiction to try all matters which are merely ancillary to the general jurisdiction, for it is only by exercising jurisdiction over these ancillary or incidental matters that the courts can effectively exercise over these endowments the right of protection and control which vests in them as representative of the Sovereign who has a general superintending power over the public interests.

Questions of ritual-Competency of courts to try.

It is in this way courts are competent to deal with questions of ritual though they deal with the same only incidentally. Of course no Court, at any rate, no Court constituted in British India, will try and determine a suit merely to determine what is the ritual of a particular sect. But if a decision on questions of ritual is necessary for the decision of any relief awardable by the civil courts, the courts must enquire into the same and give a decision and cannot deny justice by refusing to entertain such questions on the mere ground that they ought not to interfere in matters of religion.

Right to office

Thus where a right to a certain office is claimed and it is necessary to determine what exactly is the nature of the office claimed, a court of justice will not stay its hand[2] on the ground that a determination as to ritual or religious tenets is necessarily involved in such enquiry.

---

1. (1855) 1 B. H. C. R., App. p. 9.

2. *Krishnama* v. *Krishnamachari*, (1879) L. R. 6 I. A. 120; S. C. I. L. R., 2 M 62; *Krishnasami* v. *Krishnama*, (1882) I. L. R., 5 M. 313.

A simpler and commoner case is where a trustee of a temple fails to perform a certain festival which it has been the usage of the temple to perform and it is either sought to remove the trustee for breach of trust or to compel the trustee to do the act. In this case the court has clearly the jurisdiction to try such a suit, and in deciding it, it must try the question whether there has been the usage set up, for it is the duty of the court to compel the execution of the trusts of the institution and not to permit the trustee to divert the trust funds from the purposes for which they are intended[1].

Trustee's failure to celebrate festivals.

Again, suppose a muttawalli of a mosque pronounces the word "*Amen*" in a loud or low tone when engaged in prayer, and it is objected that this is contrary to the usages of the institution, courts must try whether, according to the usage of the institution and the Mahomedan Law on which it may be based, any particular form of ritual is binding on the Muttawalli and whether the pronouncing of the word "*Amen*" in any particular tone is contrary to the usage[2].

Muttawalli pronouncing "Amen."

Similarly where the question is as to the persons that are the objects of a religious charity, civil courts are clearly competent to try the same, though a decision on the same may involve inquiry into religious matters. Where the plaintiffs assert that they alone have the right to enter the *sanctum or garbha* in a Hindu temple and to worship there as being the members of a certain class, and that the defendants are not members of that class and not entitled to enter such *sanctum*, it has been held by the Bombay High Court that the civil courts have jurisdiction to entertain and decide such questions.[3]

Objects of a religious charity.

Similarly where a person is expelled from caste either by the caste at a meeting,[4] or by a religious superior,[5] or where a person

Effect of expulsion from caste or remarriage.

1. *Subbaraya* v. *Chellappa*, (1881) I. L. R., 4 M. 315; *Elayalwar Reddiyar* v. *Namberumal Chettiar*, (1899) I. L. R., 23 M. 298.

2. Vide *Fuzul Karim* v. *Mowla Buksh*, (1891) L. R., 18, I. A., 59: S. C. I. L. R., 18 C. 448.

3. *Anandrav Bhikaji Phadke* v. *Shankar Daji Charya*, (1883) I. L. R., 7 B. 323.

4. Vide *Krishnasami Chetti* v. *Virasami Chetti*, (1886) I. L. R., 10 M. 133; *Lalji Shamji* v. *Walji Wardhman*, (1895) I. L. R., 19 B. 507; *Jagannath Churn* v. *Akali Dassia*, (1893) I. L. R., 21 C. 463; and *Keshav Lal* v. *Bai Girja*, (1899) I. L. R., 24 B. 13.

5. Vide *Murari* v. *Suba*, (1882) I. L. R., 6 B. 725; *The Queen* v. *Sankara*, (1883) I. L. R., 6 M. 381; *Ganapati Bhatta* v. *Bharati Swami*, (1894) I. L. R., 17 M. 222; *Basumati Adhikarini* v. *Budram Kolita*, (1894) I. L. R., 22 C. 46; and *Appaya* v. *Padappa*, (1898) I. L. R., 23 B. 122.

2

marries a widow, and it is alleged that, by reason of such expulsion or of such re-marriage, such person had not the right to enter a temple or has lost certain benefits which he would otherwise be entitled to, the courts have jurisdiction to try whether the individual in question has been duly expelled according to caste usage, and whether the expulsion or re-marriage results in the consequences alleged.[1]

Conflicting claims of dissident parties.

In *The Advocate-General Ex relatione Daya Muhammad* v. *Muhammad Husen Huseni*,[2] *Arnold*, J., held that where a court in the exercise of its charitable jurisdiction is called upon to adjudicate between conflicting claims of dissident parties in a community distinguished by some religious profession, the rights of the parties would be regulated by a reference to what upon an enquiry might turn out to have been the religious tenets held by the community in its origin or foundation[3] and that a minority, however small, holding fast by these tenets[4] would be entitled to prevail against the majority, however numerically large, which could be shown to have receded from or renounced them. And hence in that case the court went into the question what the original tenets were and what the tenets of the seceders were in order to determine who were entitled to the benefits therein contended for.

It is not intended here to discuss fully the limits of the jurisdiction of the court in religious matters. We may have to consider such limits hereafter, but we trust it is clear that both on principle and according to precedents, the courts are bound to carry and protect the trusts made in favour of Hindu and Mahomedan religious and charitable endowments.

---

1. *Venkatachalapati* v. *Subbarayadu*, (1890) I. L. R., 13 M. 293.
2. (1866) 12 B. H. C. 323.
3. Per *Samuel Romilly*, *M. R.*, in *Attorney-General* v. *Calvert*, (1857) 23 Beav. 248 and approved by *Stirling*, J., in *In Re Perry Almshouses*, (1898) 1 Ch. 391, affirmed by C. A. in (1899) 1 Ch. 21. Cf. *Augustine* v. *Medleycott*, (1892) I. L. R., 15 M. 241; and *Chinnasami Mudali* v. *Advocate-General*, (1894) I. L. R., 17 M. 406.
4. *Attorney-General* v. *Welsh*, (1844) 4 Hare 572.

CHAPTER II.

WHAT IS A RELIGIOUS ENDOWMENT?

Religious endowment—primary and secondary significations.

We shall have next to consider what a religious endowment is and in what it consists. An endowment in its primary signification is the creation of a perpetual provision out of lands or money for any institution or person. In a secondary and more general sense it is used to denote wealth applied to any person or use[1]. The term is also more technically used in England and is then applied to any provision for the officiating minister of the church, the provision consisting in the setting apart of a portion of lands for his maintenance. Thus in Browne's Law Dictionary[2] it is said: "In ancient times the Lord of a manor, when he built a church on his demesne lands, usually endowed it with a piece of land called the *glebe*. But at the present day many endowments exist and for many very diverse objects, and may consist either in land or money or consols simply, which private individuals have given to trustees in trust for charity." In Webster's Dictionary, the term 'Endowment' is stated, among others, to mean: "That which is bestowed or settled on a person or constitution; property, fund or revenue permanently appropriated to any object." This corresponds with the secondary signification stated above. According to this signification the word means wealth, (whether in the form of money, land, produce of land, or any other moveable or immoveable property), set apart permanently as a provision for any object or purpose. This is apparently the meaning of the word as used in the term 'Religious Endowment' occurringi n Act XX of 1863 and in Regulations XIX of 1810 (Bengal) and VII of 1817 (Madras). Religious endowments must, therefore, mean wealth set apart permanently for a religious purpose, *e. g.*, a religious establishment, foundation, or institution.

---

1. Wharton's Law Lexicon, p. 269.

2. *Page* 200.

Religious establishment, foundation, institution, meaning of.

We shall next proceed to consider, what is meant by a religious establishment, foundation or institution, as these words are used in the aforesaid Act and Regulations and occur so frequently in Indian cases on this subject. "*Religious Foundation*" has, among others, two meanings. (1) A donation or legacy appropriated to support a charitable institution. In this sense the word is synonymous with the term "Religious Endowment" in its secondary sense. But this is not the meaning of the word as used in the context we are now considering. (2) That which is founded or established by endowment. "*Establishment*" has also various meanings. In the Century Dictionary we find the meaning of this term is given to be "that which has been established or set up for any purpose" This corresponds with the second meaning of "*foundation*" as given above. Another meaning that is given in the same book is this: "The authoritative recognition by a State of a church, as the national church, hence, also, the religious body thus recognized by the State, and maintained and more or less supported as the State church." The church is accepted in England by the State as the religious body which is the legitimate possessor of all property set apart for religious uses. But in India there is no State church and hence, though a religious establishment in India is regarded under certain circumstances as a fictitious but legal entity, there is no use in considering this aspect of the term. An "*institution*" is said to be in the Century Dictionary: "an establishment for the promotion of some object; an organized society or body of persons, usually, with a fixed place of assemblage and operation, devoted to a special pursuit or purpose."

Distinction between religious endowment and establishment, &c.

Thus it will be seen that the above three terms have among their various meanings one common signification. In that sense they are synonymous and must be taken to be "that which is established by an endowment for a religious purpose." It is in this sense that we find these terms used in the Act and the Regulations aforesaid. The distinction between a religious endowment and a religious establishment, foundation, or institution should be carefully borne in mind. A religious endowment is wealth set apart permanently for a religious purpose, *i. e.*, a religious establishment. A religious establishment, foundation or institution is that for which a religious endowment is founded, constituted or established.

Religious endowments &c., are chiefly Hindu and Mahomedan.

In every society, that is certainly not atheistic, there must always exist religious institutions to which endowments must necessarily attach for their maintenance and support. In India, where people of various nationalities, tribes, sects, and sub-sects exist side by side under one common rule, these religious institutions are to be found in a greater degree than elsewhere. Religious institutions, establishments or foundations as well as the endowments, if any, attached thereto are in India chiefly two *viz.*, (*a*) Hindu, and (*b*) Mahomedan[1]. We exclude, of course, those of the Christians.

Hindu, meanings of.

The term Hindu, is rather vague and indefinite though it is frequently used. It would not have been absolutely necessary to discuss the various applications of the term, and there could have been no objection in simply saying that we would use the term in a particular sense, but for the fact that the term is to be found in the Act and the Regulations already adverted to. It is therefore necessary to see in what sense the term is used in that Act and those Regulations.

1*st*—Etymologically it means an inhabitant of India.

2*nd*—A person who is a Hindu not by birth merely but by religion also[2].

3*rd*—It is used to denote a person who is governed by Hindu Law.

These are not, however, the meanings in which the term 'Hindu' is apparently used in the Religious Endowments Act and the older Regulations. In order to arrive at a correct signification of the term, we may adopt the division into three classes of the population of India given by Dr. Banerjee in his book on "Marriage and Stridhan" for another purpose (*i. e.*, for finding out who are governed by Hindu Law).

---

1. See *Krishnarav Ganesh* v. *Rangrav* (1867), 4 B. H. C. A. C. J. 1 at p. 7; and *Narayan* v. *Chintaman* (1881), I. L. R., 5 B. 393 at p. 396.

2. Vide *Abraham* v. *Abraham* (1863), 9 M. I. A., p. 199, where the Judicial Committee held that when the Civil Courts Regulation III of 1802, Madras, provided that the Hindu Law should govern the Hindus and the Mahomedan Law, the Mahomedans, it was intended that Hindus and Mahomedans should respectively, be Hindus and Mahomedans, not by birth merely, but by religion also. See the question discussed in *Bhagwan Kuar* v. *Jogendra*, (1903) L. R., 30 I. A. 249.

First :—The descendants of the aboriginal tribes who have more or less avoided complete conversion to the Brahminical religion ;

Second :—The descendants of the early Aryan settlors and of such aboriginal races as have been completely absorbed in the Aryan community ;

Descendants of aboriginal tribes.

Third :—Modern settlors of various religious persuasions, such as Mahomedans, Christians and Parsis.

The *first* class, according to Dr. Banerjee, comprises "considerable portions of the population of the Madras Presidency and Central India (the Jats) and the hill tribes of various other parts of India. Their customs and their religion differ widely from those of the Hindus properly so called. They have no Codes of Law, but in some instances they have adopted much that is Hindu in their customs and religion, and some of these tribes, such as the Koch and others, have been described by Dalton as the 'Hinduised aborigines of India'." Dr. Banerjee then contends that "these races ought not to be held to be governed by Hindu Law," and it may be so. But for our present purpose, it is enough to say that these *semi-Hindu races* have been sometimes regarded as Hindus. Though this class may not be governed by Hindu Law as contended by Dr. Banerjee, yet there are many among them who call themselves Hindus. Their title to be called Hindus has never been denied though they may not be governed by Hindu Law. Thus it appears from the Census Report[1] of the North-West Provinces, 1891 that "Hinduism includes a fluctuating mass of beliefs, opinions, usages and observances, social and religious ideas, the exact details of which it is impossible to reduce to anything like order, and in the most aspects of which it is impossible to recognise anything that is common. A belief in the religious superiority of Brahmans, veneration for the cow and respect for the distribution of castes are the elements of Hinduism, which are most generally recognised as fundamental. But each and all of these has been rejected, or is rejected by tribes, castes or sects whose title to be included amongst Hindus is not denied." It will, therefore, be seen that this class comes under the term 'Hindu', and their religious endowments must also be classed as 'Hindu' and come within the purview of the Religious Endowments Act and the Regulations.

---

1. Cited in Mayne's Hindu Law, page 12.

As regards the *second* class, *viz.*, the descendants of the early Aryan settlors and of such aboriginal races as have been completely absorbed in the Aryan community, there can be no doubt that the members comprised under this class come within our purview and are 'Hindus.' They are not merely 'Hindus' but are also governed by Hindu Law. The Buddhists, Jains, Sikhs and Brahmos come under this class. The religious endowments of this class fall within the purview of the Act and the Regulations. In *Dhurrum Singh* v. *Kissen Singh*[1], it was held that a Sikh religious institution came within the purview of the Religious Endowment Act. In *Thackersey Dewraj* v. *Hurbhum Nursey*[2], a Jain religious institution was in question.

Aryan settlors and Aboriginal races absorbed in the Aryan community.

As regards the *third* division we have the following:—

(1). *Christians*:—These are not within our province. The prevalent opinion is that their religious institutions are not within the purview of Act XX of 1863 or of the earlier Regulations.

(2). *Parsis*:—These cannot be said to be Mahomedans in the strict sense of the term, but it cannot be said that their religious institutions do not fall under Act XX of 1863 or the old Regulations VII of 1817 and XIX of 1810.

(3). *Mahomedans*:—This is sufficiently descriptive.

A Hindu religious endowment is ordinarily a grant to an idol[3] and is either *Devasthan* or *Sevasthan*, while a Mahomedan religious endowment which is known in Mahomedan Law as *wakf*, is either a Mosque, Durga, or Khankah, &c.[4] Hindu religious institutions are usually temples, mutts, &c. According to Hindu Law, an idol[5] or, for the matter of that, any religious foundation is a juridical subject or person capable of holding and enjoying property. An idol is a *caput mortuum*[6]. It is only in an ideal sense that property can belong to an idol; and the possession and manage-

Idol and grant to idol.

1. (1881) I. L. R., 7 C. 767.
2. (1884) I. L. R., 8 B. 432.
3. *Ananthatirtha Chariar* v. *Nagamuthu Ambalagaren*, (1881) I. L. R., 4 M. 200.
4. *Narayan* v. *Chintaman*, (1881) I. L. R., 5 B. 393 at p. 396.
5. *Syud Shah Alleh Ahmed* v. *Mussamut Bibee Nuseebun*, (1874) 21 W. R. 415.
6. *Kumara Asima Krishna Deb* v. *Kumara Kumara Krishna Deb*, (1868) 2 B. L. R. O. C. J. 11 at p. 47.

ment of it must in the nature of things be entrusted to some person as Shebait, or Manager[1], and property dedicated to the idol is *res-sacra.* In *Thackersey Dewraj* v. *Hurbhum Nursey*[2] *Scott*, J., observed at p. 456 :—"In short the deity of the temple is considered in Hindu Law as a sacred entity or an ideal personality possessing proprietary rights. The managers hold these rights as trustees and any alienation or infringement is a kind of sacrilege. The money once entered in the temple books is dedicated to the god and becomes *res-sacra.*"

Idol :—human entity.

In a case where the validity of a court sale of debutter lands in execution of a personal decree against the trustee was in question, the Bombay High Court observed[3]: "The idol itself is looked on 'as a kind of human entity,' the religious services of which are allowed by Hindu Law to be provided for in perpetuity." In the leading case of *Manohar Ganesh* v. *Lakhmiram*[4], *West*, J., observed: "The Hindu Law recognises not only corporate bodies with rights of property vested in the corporation apart from its individual members, but also the juridical subjects or persons called foundations." On the same principle it was held in *Shri Ganesh Dharnidhar* v. *Kulgavkar*,[5] familiarly known as the *Chinchavad Devasthan case*, that the idol was a fictitious legal entity owning property.

Foundations :—Juridical subjects.

Idol :—fictitious legal entity.

Calcutta view.

The same view has been held in Calcutta. Thus in *Tayubunnissa Bibi* v. *Sham Kishore Roy*[6], where the validity of a patni lease of property endowed to an idol was in question it was held that the idol must be considered in law as the owner of the endowed property. Again in *Nilmony Singh* v. *Jagabandhu Roy*[7], where the question was whether possession of the alienee could be adverse as against the idol so as to

---

1. *Prosunno Kumari Debya* v. *Golab Chand Baboo*, (1875) L. R., 2 I. A. 145 (152); and *Nilmony Singh* v. *Jagabandhu Roy*, (1896) I. L. R., 23 C. 536.

2. (1884) I. L. R., 8 B. 432.

3. *Rupa Jagshet* v. *Krishnaji Govind*, (1884) I. L. R., 9 B. 169.

4. (1887) I. L. R., 12 B. 247 at p. 264.

5. (1890) I. L. R., 15 B. 625.

6. (1871) 7 B. L. R., 621 ; S. C. 15 W. R. C. R. 228.

7. (1896) I. L. R., 23 C. 536.

bar the trustee from recovering property alienated by his predecessor in office it was observed: "The idol is a juridical person capable of holding property and the possession of the defendants (alienees) who profess to derive title not from the idol but ignoring its rights, must be taken to have become adverse to the idol from the dates of the alienations." In *Girijanund Dattajha* v. *Saila Janund Dattajha*,[1] the above principle was again re-affirmed and it was held that an idol in Hindu Law, as symbolical of religious purposes, was capable of being endowed with and of holding property.[2]

When once property is devoted to the service of an idol, the donor cannot revoke the gift. This is a principle applicable to all cases of gifts and trusts[3]. Property so endowed cannot be alienated save in the interests of the idol[4]. In Bombay the rule as to inalienability of the corpus is absolute though the income may be charged[5]. The Shebait has no legal ownership in the same but has only the title of Manager of a religious endowment[6]. No revocations gift.

Grants of inams for religious or charitable purposes are frequently found to be of great antiquity, and evidenced by inscriptions on copper plates. They were granted by former sovereigns[7]. A royal grant for Hindu religious purposes is never temporary. It is perpetual and irresumable. No act on the part of a Hindu prince or sovereign would have been more disgraceful than the resumption of such a grant. A religious penalty is also attached to such resumption under Hindu Law.[8] Royal grants.

1. (1896) I. L. R., 23 C., 645.

2. Vide *Bhuggobutty Prosonno Sen* v. *Gooroo Prosonno Sen*, (1897) I. L. R., 25 C. 112. But see *Raghubar Dial* v. *Kesho Ramanuj Das*, (1888) I. L. R., 11 A. 18.

3. *Ghulam Hussain* v. *Aji Ajam*, (1868) 4 M. H. C. 44; *Collector of Ratnagiri* v. *Vyankatrav*, (1871) 8 B. H. C. (A. C. J.) 1; *Doyal Chand Mullick* v. *Keramut Ali*, (1871) 16 W. R. 116; *Ram Narain Sing* v. *Ramoon Paurey*, (1874) 23 W. R. 76; *Subramanya* v. *The Secretary of State*, (1888) I. L. R. 6 M. 361; and Transfer of Property Act, S. 126.

4. *Tayibun-nissa Bibi* v. *Sham Kishore Roy*, (1871) 7 B. L. R. 621; *Prosunno Kumari Debya* v. *Golab Chand Baboo*, (1875) L. R. 2 I. A. 145; *Konwar Doorganath Roy* v. *Ram Chunder Sen*, (1876) L. R. 4 I. A. 52: S. C. I. L. R. 2 C. 341; *Thackersey Dewraj* v. *Hurbhum Nursey*, (1884) I. L. R. 8 B., 432 at p. 456; *Sheo Shankar Gir* v. *Ram Shewak*, (1896) I. L. R., 24 C. 77; *Parsotam Gir* v. *Dat Gir*, (1903) I. L. R., 25 A. 296. See *Maharanee Shibessouree Debia* v. *Mothooranath Acharjo*, (1869) 13 M. I. A. 270.

5. Vide *Narayan* v. *Chintaman*, (1881) I. L. R., 5 B. 393; *The Collector of Thana* v. *Hari Sitaram*, (1882) I. L. R., 6 B. 546 F. B.: *Shri Ganesh Dharnidar* v. *Krishna Rav Kulgarker* (1890) I. L. R., 15 B. 612; and *Parsotam Gir* v. *Dat Gir*, supra.

6. Vide *Maharanee Shibessouree Debia* v. *Mothooranath Acharjo*, supra; *Prosunno Kumari Debya* v. *Golab Chand Baboo*, supra; and *Thackersey Dewraj* v. *Hurbhum Nursey*, supra.

7. *Krishnarav Ganesh* v. *Rang Rav*, (1867) 4 B. H. C., A. C. J. 1 at p. 7.

8. *The Collector of Thana* v. *Hari Sitaram*, supra.

We shall discuss the history of Mutts and other religious institutions and the right of Shebaits, &c., in a later chapter.

Wakf :— 2 views.

The nature of a mosque is also similar in Mahomedan Law. "Wakf" in its primary sense means detention.[1] There are two views taken with reference to the nature of a *wakf*. According to Haneefa, a *wakf* "in the language of the law signifies the appropriation of any particular thing in such a way that the appropriator's right in it shall continue and the advantage of it go to some charitable purpose, in the manner of a loan"[2]. According to the two disciples, "*wakf*" signifies "the appropriation of a particular article in such a manner as subjects it to the rules of divine property, whence the appropriator's right in it is extinguished, and it becomes a property of God, by the advantage of it resulting to his creatures. The two disciples, therefore, hold appropriation to be absolute, though differing in this that *Aboo Yoosuf* holds the appropriation to be absolute from the moment of its execution, whereas *Mahomed* holds it to be absolute only on the delivery of it to a Muttawalli and, consequently, that it cannot be disposed of by gift or sale, and that inheritance also does not obtain with respect to it"[2].

Primary objects of wakf.

Wakf is a bequest or gift for religious or charitable purposes, or an appropriation of a pious or charitable nature, *to wit*, the service of God in such a way that it may be beneficial to men[3]. The primary objects for which lands may be endowed under Mahomedan Law are to support a mosque and to defray the expenses of the worship conducted in that mosque[4].

Jawahra v. Akbar Hussain.

In *Jawahra* v. *Akbar Husain*[5] a Full Bench of the Allahabad High Court had to consider the nature of a mosque. *Petheram*, C. J., observed in that case : "According to Mahomedan custom, the property in a mosque and in the land connected with it is vested in no one, and is not the subject of *human ownership*, but all the members of the Mahomedan community are entitled to use it for

1. Hamilton's Hedaya, Vol. II, p. 334, Ch. XV—Wakf; *Jewun Doss Sahoo* v. *Shah Kubeer-Ood-Deen*, (1841) 2 M. I. A. 390; and *Abdul Ganne Kasam* v. *Hussen Miya Rahimtula*, (1873) 10 B. H. C. 7.

2. *Jewun Doss Sahoo* v. *Shah Kubeer Ood-Deen*, supra.

3. *Abdul Ganne Kasam* v. *Hussen Miya Rahimtula*, supra.

4. *Muzhurool Huq* v. *Puhraj Ditarey Mohapattur*, (1870) 13 W. R., C. R., 235.

5. (1884) I. L. R., 7 A. 178.

purposes of devotion whenever the mosque is open." *Mahmood, J.*, observed in the same case that it was the rule of Mahomedan Law that when any person "has resolved to devote his property to religious purposes, as soon as his mind is made up and his intention declared by some specific act, such as delivery, &c., an endowment is immediately constituted; his act deprives him of all the ownership in the property, and to use the technical language of Mahomedan lawyers vests it in God 'in such a manner as subjects it to the rules of divine property, when the appropriator's right in it is extinguished and it becomes a property of God by the advantage of it resulting to his creatures'."

No dedication to a particular school or sect.

According to the Mahomedan Law, a mosque cannot be dedicated or appropriated exclusively to any particular school or sect of Sunni Mahomedans. It is a place where all Mahomedans are entitled to go and perform their devotions as of right according to their conscience. No one sect or portion of the Mahomedan community can restrain any other from the exercise of this right. It was therefore held by a Full Bench of the Allahabad High Court[1] that members of the Muhammadi or Wahabi sect are Mahomedans and as such are entitled to perform their devotions in a mosque, though they may differ from the majority of Sunni Mahomedans in respect of particular points of ritual.

Public mosque.

This, however, will be the case only where the mosque is a public one when it is open to all Mahomedans without distinction of sect, and a Mahomedan pronouncing the word 'Amen' in a loud tone according to the tenets of his sect in the *bona-fide* exercise of his religious devotion does nothing contrary to the Mahomedan ecclesiastical law and does not commit any offence or actionable wrong[2]. "It is a fundamental principle of Mahomedan Law that when a mosque is built and consecrated by public worship, it ceases to be the property of the builder and vests in God, to use the language of the Hedaya, 'in such manner as subjects it to the rules of divine property'." A mosque once so consecrated cannot in any case revert to the founder, and every Mahomedan has a legal right to enter and perform devotions according to his own tenets so long as the form of worship is in accordance with the recognised rules of

1. *Ataul-lah* v. *Azimullah*, (1889) I. L. R., 12 All. 494.
2. *Jangu* v. *Ahmadullah*, (1889) I. L. R., 13 All. 419.

Mahomedan ecclesiastical law[1]. A mosque when public is not the property of a particular individual or even of a body or corporation or of any other human organisation which in law has a personality. In the eye of the Mahomedan Law, a mosque is the property of God and must be regarded as such.

Use of wakf not material.

There may be a valid disposition as *wakf* without the use of the word *wakf*. If the intention of the donor was to constitute a *wakf* and the document can be so construed, the absence of the word *wakf* is immaterial[2]. So the mere use of the word *wakf* is not conclusive. The mere fact that the word '*wakf*' is used in a grant without there being a destination of the property to religious and charitable uses does not constitute a valid *wakf*.[3]

Wazifa graut.

A *Wazifa* grant may be a religious endowment, but this is neither necessarily nor generally its nature. *Marifa* is the same as *Wazifa*[4].

An appropriation of property for the expenses of the repairs of mosques, wages of the muzzin, expenses of the 2 Eeds and lighting and taking care of fakirs and travellers is a *wakf* and is an endowment for religious and charitable purposes or uses[5].

We shall discuss about the objects which can properly constitute a valid *wakf* and the origin and nature of durgas or khankahs, &c., later on.

---

1. Per *Mahmood*, J., in *Jangu* v. *Ahmadullah*, (1889) I. L. R., 13 A. 419; *Doyal Chund Mullick* v. *Syud Keramut Ali*, (1871) 16 W. R. C. R., 116; and *Fatma Bibi* v. *The Advocate General of Bombay*, (1881) I. L. R., 6 B. 42.

2. *Jewun Doss Sahoo* v. *Shah Kubeer-Ood-Deen*, (1841) 2 M. I. A. 390: S. C. 6 W. R., (P. C.) 3; and *Piran* v. *Abdool Karim*, (1891) I. L. R., 19 C. 203 (216); *Abul Fata Mahomed* v. *Rasarmaya*, (1894) I. L. R., 22 C. 619: S. C. L. R. 22 I. A. 76; *Saliq-Un-Nissa* v. *Mati Ahmad*, (1903) I. L. R., 25 A. 418, (420). *See* Pothier on Obligations, Vol. 1, 22.

3. *Abdul Ganne Kasam* v. *Hussen Miya Rahimtula*, (1873) 10 B. H. C. 7.

4. *Sayad Mahomed Ali* v. *Sayad Gobar Ali*, (1881) I. L. R., 6 B. 88.

5. *Sheik Abdool Khalek* v. *Poran Bibee*, (1876) 25 W. R. C. R. 542.

CHAPTER III.

CONSTITUTION AND PROOF—DEDICATION.

Dedication, real or apparent.

We shall now consider how religious endowments may be constituted. In this connection the first question that arises is, whether there is a dedication, and, if so, whether there is a real or apparent dedication. Indeed the two questions are one and the same, and an answer to the one will serve the other equally.

Onus on party asserting dedication.

The onus lies on the party who sets up the case that the property has been inalienably conferred upon an idol to sustain its worship to prove such case. Very strong and clear evidence of such an endowment ought to exist[1]. Hence in a suit by a shebait to recover possession of properties as endowed, it is on the plaintiff to prove the title which gives him the right to recover possession of the property just as it would be if he were seeking to recover upon a secular, instead of a quasi-religious title[2]. In one case[3] the Privy Council held that the plaintiff who sued the defendant to recover certain lands perpetually demised to the latter's ancestor by the plaintiff's predecessors in title on the ground that the lands being Devaswom a lease of the same was not binding, must shew that such lands were in fact Devaswom and that as no attempt was made to show when, by whom, or in what way the land was dedicated, the plaintiff's suit must be dismissed. If a trust for a religious endowment is once established, the onus lies on on the party alleging that it has become ordinary property (which can only be in the case of private religious trusts) to show that there has been some subsequent legal conversion of the lands to the ordinary uses[4].

Real dedication.

Where the intention to set apart for religious uses is clear and there is a transfer of property to such uses, then there is a real dedication.[5]

---

1. *Konwar Doorganath Roy* v. *Ram Chunder Sen*, (1876) I. L. R., 2 C. 341 (P. C.).

2. *Nund Pandah* v. *Gyadhur*, (1868) 10 W. R. (C. R.) 89.

3. *Venkatesvara Iyan* v. *Shekhari Varma*, (1881) I. L. R., 3 M. 384 at pp. 395 and 396 : S. C. L. R. 8 I. A. 143.

4. *Juggut Mohini Dossee* v. *Mussumat Sokheemoney Dossee*, (1871) 14 M. I. A. 289 (303).

5. *Jivan Dass Sahoo* v. *Shah Kubeer-Ood-Deen*, (1841) 2 M. I. A. 390; *Piran* v. *Abdool Karim*, (1891) I. L. R., 19 C. 203 (216).

Apparent dedication, what is.

An *apparent* dedication consists in the ostensible title to certain property remaining with the idol or religious foundation, while the person who is said to have endowed remains the real owner. If the endowment, therefore, is merely *nominal,* and is not *bona-fide,* the property will not be treated as set apart for religious purposes[1].

Apparent dedication—Benami.

A case of an apparent dedication arises where the property is purchased in the name of an idol, but is enjoyed by the person who advanced the money, and is neither really intended to be devoted to the idol nor is intended to be a gift to the idol. In such a case though the property is taken or purchased in the name of the idol, it is merely a benami transaction. The person who is the real owner is the person who advanced the money.

Benami held applicable to idol.

In *Gopeekrist Gosain* v. *Gungapersaud Gosain*[2], the Privy Council held that where a Hindu purchases property in the name of his son, the property is not vested in the son, but remains vested in the father who has paid the consideration, the English theory of advancement not obtaining in India either in the case of Hindus or Mahomedans. This principle was held by the Privy Council to be also applicable to the case of an idol in *Maharanee Brojosoondery Debia* v. *Ranee Luchmee Koonwaree*[3], where the facts were that one Maharaja Ramnath bought property a certain Zemindary in Rajshahye Zilla) in the name of an idol (named Sham Soonder Thakoor) which was kept in his family house, but dealt with the funds or income of the Zemindary as his own property. The Privy Council in holding that the transaction was only benami or nominal and that the principle of benami purchases enunciated in *Gosain* v. *Gosain*[2] applied to the case of an idol, observed: "If a man merely purchases property in the name of his own idol, whom no one, except himself, has the power or right to worship, the property is not the property of the idol, but the property of the person who purchased."

Benami doctrine too well settled.

It is now too late to question the benami doctrine enunciated by the Judicial Committee so long ago as 1854[4] in *Gosain's case*[2] and

1. *Juggurnath Roy Chowdhry* v. *Kishen Pershad Surmah,* (1867) 7 W. R., C. R. 266.

2. (1854) 6 M. I. A., 53 : S. C. 4 W. R. (P. C.) 46.

3. (1873) 15 B. L. R., 176 (note): S. C. 20 W. R. (P. C.) 95.

4. If the case of *Dhurm Das Pandey* v. *Mussumat Shama Soondri Dibiah,* (1843) 3 M. I. A. 229, be also taken into consideration, it will be 1843 really.

re-affirmed in more cases than one[1] by that august tribunal especially when it is remembered that the doctrine has received legislative sanction in sections 81 and 82 of the Indian Trusts Act (II of 1882). It is unfortunate that even the admitted exceptions to this doctrine obtaining in England[2] should not be held applicable in India. Whether these exceptions are not held applicable in this country either because the principles founded on them are opposed to natural justice or because they are inconsistent with some supposed theory said to obtain in the Hindu Law regarding the propriety of making unequal distribution, it is at least open to grave doubt whether the mere fact of the purchase money having been advanced by another is of itself sufficient to show that the purchase is really intended for such person when the person in whose name the conveyance has been taken is either the wife or son of the person advancing the money. At any rate the fact of the person in whose name the conveyance appears standing in such relationship (or as it is called in *loco parentis*) is a circumstance from which it may be inferred that the transaction is intended for the benefit of the transferee (or other person in whose name the conveyance is taken) and the *onus* is upon the person asserting the transaction to be *benami* to prove his case. This view receives support from the wording of sections 81 and 82 of the Trusts Act and by illustration (*d*) to section 81.

Motives of people in making gifts to idols.

In the case of wives, children and other persons similarly circumstanced there is a motive in people intending to give a beneficial interest in property transferred to them or taken in their names. In India the motives of the people in making gifts to idols, temples, or other religious establishments are stronger than in England. In *Thackersey Dewraj* v. *Hurbhum Nursey*[3], *Scott*, J. observed : "It is also to be borne in mind that the orthodox Hindu, whether Jain or Brahminical in his faith, has a stronger motive for charity

---

1. *Lokhee Narain Roy Chowdhry* v. *Kalypuddo Bandopadhya*, (1875) L. R. 2. I. A 154; *Dharani Kant Lahiri Chowdhry* v. *Kristo Kumari Chowdhrani*, (1886) L. R. 13 I. A. 70 ; *Imambandi Begum* v. *Kumleswari Pershad*, (1886; L. R. 13 I. A. 160; *Uman Parshad* v. *Gandharp Singh*, (1887) L. R. 14 I. A. 127 ; *Musammut Thakro* v. *Ganga Pershad*, (1887; L. R. 15 I. A. 29 (S. C.), I. L. R. 10 A. 197; *Nawab Ibrahim Ali Khan* v. *Ummutul Zohra*, (1896) L. R. 24 I. A. 1; *Prince Suleman Kadar Bahadur* v. *Nawab Mehndi*, (1897) L. R. 25 I. A. 15; *Muhammad Imam Ali Khan* v *Sardar Husain*, (1898) L. R. 25 I. A. 161; and *Pandit Ram Narain* v. *Maulvi Muhammad Hadi*, (1898) L. R. 26 I. A. 38..

2. See *In re A Policy No. 6402 of the Scottish Equitable Life Assurance Society*, (1902) 1 Ch. 282 for the latest pronouncement of the law on this subject.

3. (1884) I. L. R., 8 B. 432 at p. 451.

than an Englishman. The desire to perpetuate a name or to render some great service to his fellow creatures has been the chief cause of great public charitable gifts in the West. The propitiation of heaven may also have been an object, but it is only a secondary one. But here in India the importance of the motives is reversed." These observations receive some support from the case of *Surendro Keshub Roy* v. *Doorga Soondery Dossee*[1], where in considering the question whether there was an absolute dedication of certain property to the idol or only a charge or trust in favor of the idol with a beneficial interest in the surplus to the trustee or donee, the Privy Council observed: "The testator shows no intention save that which may be reasonably attributed to a devout Hindu gentleman, *i. e.*, to secure that his family worship shall be conducted in the accustomed way, by giving his property to one of the Thakoors whom he venerates most. But the effect when the estate is large is to have some beneficial interest undisposed of." In such cases, therefore, we must look to the intention as expressed in the document prompted as it is by the strong motives already described and regard the transaction as not *benami* unless the party asserting the contrary is able to prove his assertion by circumstances. Indeed "courts could act only on public acts of parties, and purchasers have a right to bind parties by such public acts. Courts ought not to credit readily assertions of hidden and fraudulent intentions which made today for one purpose may be abandoned or denied tomorrow for the assertion of another and inconsistent purpose"[2].

Apparent dedication—Wakfs—Veil for family aggrandisement.

A frequent case of an apparent dedication is to be found in the case of settlements made by Mahomedans in the nature of *wakfs*. For, one feature of Mahomedan settlements is the prominence given by the settlor for the aggrandisement of the family. To a Mahomedan mind, settlements made to the family are but natural. An anxiety to keep the family above want and the preservation of the family prestige by tying down the property in the family, are the prime considerations guiding a Mahomedan. The family is the first object of charity. In fact it is the settlor's chief solicitude to keep the family always in an influential position and at any rate out of poverty. As the Privy Council observed quite recently[3]:

1. (1892) I. L. R., 19 C. (P.C.) 513: S. C. 19 I A 108.
2. *Srimati Sukhimani Dasi* v. *Mahendra Nath Dutt*, (1869) 4 B. L. R. (P.C.) 16: S. C. 13 W. R. (P. C.) 14.
3. *Mujib-un-nissa* v. *Abdul Rahim*, (1900) L. R., 28 I. A. 15: S. C. I. L. R. 23 A. 233 at p. 245.

'The theory..........seems to be that the creation of a family endowment is of itself a religious and meritorious act, and that the perpetual application of the surplus income in the acquisition of new properties to be added to the family estate is a charitable purpose." They added that "it is superfluous in the present day to say that is not the law." Hence it has been held that where there has been no substantial dedication to *wakf*, but the object is, in the *guise of a wakf*, to tie up the property perpetually in the family, the whole settlement is invalid. Where, therefore, there has been no substantial dedication of the property for religious and charitable uses, but the settlor uses the form of a *wakf* as a veil, under cover of which he attempts to aggrandise the family, it has been held in a series of cases that the settlor is attempting to do what the law does not permit him to do openly and that, therefore, effect cannot be given to the transaction[1].

Apparent dedication—Gift of man's whole property.

It may be said that in the case where a person gives the whole of his property to charity or an idol (as is frequently the case in wills, &c., made by Bengalis) a question of apparent dedication also arises[2]. It is possible that such a question may arise. Unless of course it can be shewn that the whole thing is a nominal transaction and that the transaction is not what it purports to be or unless the testator has done it in mere jest or has been deceived or has not understood the nature and effect of the transaction, it cannot be said that a gift or devise of the whole of a man's property to an idol or charity cannot be given effect to. If the donor is an idiot or is weak-minded and advantage is taken of his position, the gift or devise of his whole property may be said to be proof of such weak-mindedness or idiocy. Otherwise it cannot be seen why effect should not be given to the transaction. Of course though an endowment may be found to have been established, where the nature and extent of the endowment itself is in question and a gift of all the owner's property (declared orally at his death) is alleged, strong proof of the same is required[3].

---

1. See *Sheik Mahomed Ahsan-ula Chowdhry* v. *Amarchand Kundu*, (1889) L. R., 17 I. A. 28; S. C. I. L. R. 17 C. 498; *Abdul Gafur* v. *Nizamudin*, (1892) L. R. 19 I. A. 170; S. C. I. L. R. 17 B. 1; *Mujib-un-nissa* v. *Abdur Rahim*, (1900) L. R., 28 I. A. 15; S. C. I. L. R., 23 A. 233; and *Hamid* v. *Mujawar*, (1902) I. L. R., 24 A. 257.
2. *Promotha Dossee* v. *Radhika Persaud*, (1875) 14 B. L. R. 175.
3. *Bipro Prosad* v. *Mussamut Kenae Doyee*, (1865) 3 W. R., (C. R.) 165.

Apparent dedication—gift to idol or charity for defeating creditors.

The last case of an apparent dedication arises where the donor in order to defeat his creditors disposes of the whole or other substantial part of his property to an idol or charity. In this case it may have been intended at the time by the donor that no effect ought to be given to the endowment at all but merely that the transaction should operate as a nominal transaction in order to prevent property from being attached by his creditors. In such a case, of course, there is no endowment in fact[1]. In *Ramchandra Mukerjee* v. *Ranjit Singh*[2], it was observed by the Calcutta High Court: "Where a deed of endowment is made to defeat the claims of creditors, it is not valid and can only be treated as nominal and colorable." This is, however, stating the proposition too broadly. For, it may have been intended by the donor at the time to operate as a real transaction, but the effect of it may be to operate to delay or to hinder creditors. In such a case the transaction is voidable as against creditors. For, an idol being a mere volunteer, such a gift will not be valid as against creditors[3]. Of course where a person has got ample property and has also debts and devotes some property to charity or an idol, the fact that he has debts will not vitiate the transaction if the remainder of the property still possessed by the donor is amply sufficient to satisfy the claims of the creditors. Thus in *Deoki Prasad* v. *Inayit-ullah*[4], it was held by the Allahabad High Court that where a settlor had other property besides that settled in *wakf*, enough to pay the creditors, the existence of debts did not incapacitate him from making a gift of the portion of the property as wakf.

Clear dedication—mere suspicion will not affect.

Where the dedication is a fact and is clearly proved, a mere suspicion that the deed, giving property to an idol, may have been executed with the object of defeating creditors or may possibly affect some future creditors or claimants, will not invalidate the gift. Thus in *Radha Mohun Mundul* v. *Jadoomonee Dossee*,[5] the facts

1. *Juggurnath Roy Chowdhry* v. *Kishen Pershad Surmah*, (1867) 7 W. R. (C. R.) 266; and *Srimati Sukhimani Dasi* v. *Mahendra Nath Dutt*, (1869) 13 W. R. (P. C.) 14: S. C. 4 B. L. R. 16.

2. (1899) I. L. R., 27 C. 242.

3 Vide *Soshikishore Bundopadhya* v. *Ranee Chooramoney Putto Mohadabee*, W. R, (1864) (C. R.) 107.

4. (1892) I. L. R., 14 A. 375.

5. (1875) 23 W. R. (P. C.) 369.

were that the plaintiff as widow and heiress of her husband sued for a share of certain property, some of which (a Talooka, certain Government pro-notes for 2 lakhs and odd and certain other Government pro-notes for 14,000 Rs.) she claimed in her right as the heiress of her husband and as appertaining to his estate, while the rest she claimed as the joint shebait of certain idols, being debuttur property. The Sub-Judge gave the plaintiff a decree as regards some of the debuttur lands claimed by her and also awarded possession of her share in Government pro-notes for Rs. 14,000, provided she furnished security for the latter against waste. As regards her claim for the Talooka and the Government pro-notes for 2 lakhs and odd, the Sub-Judge held that such property did not appertain to the family estate, but was *debuttur* property belonging to the idol Sreedhur, and that, as plaintiff's suit was not framed in this way, he could not give her a decree in her right as shebait. On appeal the High Court held that the objection of the Sub-Judge (*viz.*, that the plaintiff only claimed in her own personal right) for refusing to give relief to plaintiff on the findings come to by him was one of form rather than of substance, and that the plaintiff would be entitled to relief as shebait if the property were found to be debuttur. A decree for the Talooka was given, but the High Court held, however, that the agreement among the members of the family constituting 2 lakhs and odd Government pro-notes as debuttur was not valid as it was fraudulent and collusive to defeat the rights of some widows of the family. The Privy Council agreed with the Subordinate Judge on the question of fact but concurred with the High Court that the objection taken by the Subordinate Judge was one of form rather than of substance, and that the same ought not to be allowed to prevail. They held that as no question was raised as to the genuineness of the agreement and as the same was acted upon for a long time, that as there were accounts (which were produced) relating to its application in pursuance of the agreement, and that as a temple had been in fact built for the idol at great cost, the arrangement evidenced by the agreement was a real transaction and must, therefore, be given effect to. Their Lordships observed: "The mere suggestion that the amount set aside was an exorbitant amount, and that there might possibly have been some intention to defraud widows or other persons is not enough to outweigh the evidence of conduct. It is not upon mere speculations of this sort that an agreement proved by evidence so strong to have been not merely executed but acted upon for a number of years can in their Lordships' judgment be properly set aside."

T. P. Act, S. 53—principle applies to idols and wakfs.

It is now enacted by section 53 of the Transfer of Property Act (IV of 1882) that "every transfer of immoveable property, made with intent to defraud prior or subsequent transferees thereof for consideration, or co-owners or other persons having an interest in such property, or to defeat or delay the creditors of the transferor, is voidable at the option of any person so defrauded, defeated or delayed. Where the effect of any transfer of immovable property is to defraud, defeat or delay any such person, and such transfer is made gratuitously or for a grossly inadequate consideration, the transfer may be presumed to have been made with such intent as aforesaid. Nothing contained in this section shall impair the rights of any transferee in good faith and for consideration." Section 2, cl. (*d*) of the same Act enacts that "nothing in the second chapter of this Act shall be deemed to affect any rule of Hindu, Mahomedan, or Buddhist Law." Section 53 is in the second chapter, but there is no rule of Hindu, Mahomedan or Buddhist Law that lays down anything contrary to the principle enunciated in the section. In *Abdul Hye* v. *Mir Mohamed Mozuffer Hossein*[1], the Privy Council held that the principles laid down in 13 Elizabeth, ch. 5, were given effect to by the High Courts of India and properly guided their decisions in administering law according to equity and good conscience. It, therefore, follows that section 53 of the Transfer of Propery Act applies to all gifts made by a Hindu donor in favor of an idol or by a Mahomedan donor in the nature of wakfs.

Endowments real or nominal—tests in finding out.

There are several tests laid down in the cases to see whether a transaction which purports to be a religious endowment is real or nominal. From the several tests to be presently mentioned, it will be seen how difficult it is to lay down general rules on a question of fact which must more or less be left to be decided by the court upon a consideration of the circumstances of each case. One strong test in considering whether an endowment is *bonâ fide* or *nominal*, is to see how the property has been enjoyed and how its

Enjoyment.

1. (1883) L. R. 11, I. A. 10 at pp. 17 and 18: S. C. I. L. R. 10 C. 616. In *Deoki Prasad* v. *Inhyit-Ullah*, (1892) I. L. R., 14 A 375 the question whether S. 53 of the T. P. Act applied to *wakfs* was raised but not decided.

income has been utilised, or how the founder himself and his descendants have dealt with the same[1]. The manner in which the property is held and enjoyed is always an important point for consideration. Thus in *Ramchandra Mukerjee* v. *Ranjit Singh*[2] the Calcutta High Court finding that the properties there in question were not debuttur, and that there was only a nominal or colorable dedication, observed : "In dealing with the question whether an endowment is real or nominal only, the manner in which the dedicated property is held and enjoyed is the most important point for consideration. Now, in the present case, there is no reliable and sufficient evidence to show how, during the few months for which the donor lived after the dedication, the income of the properties in dispute was spent; nor is there any such evidence in respect of any period subsequent to his death. It is true there is some vague oral evidence that Rani Anandamoyi all along performed the worship of the idol * * but the idol being a family idol, she would perform its worship, as every Hindu does, whether there is any endowment in favour of the idol or not." If no accounts which every rich and respectable donor will be expected to have, are produced showing how the income of the properties in dispute has been spent, the evidence as to dedication must be treated with great suspicion. For aught it may be, the income may have gone into the general accounts relating to the estates of the family[3].

Application of income.

Where, however, accounts are produced showing that rents have been separately collected and applied for the worship of the idol, it is some evidence of a prior endowment[3], and where there is good evidence going back for more than half a century that certain land has been given to an idol, proof that from that time the proceeds have been so expended will be strong corroborative evidence of such gift[4]. On this principle, the Privy Council upheld an agreement by which a certain Hindu family endowed for its idol Government paper worth two lakhs and odd, finding that the agreement was in fact executed, that the same had been acted upon for a long time

1. *Gunga Narain Sircar* v. *Brindabun Chunderkur Chowdhry*, (1865) 3 W. R. (C. R.) 142; *Watson* v. *Ramchand*, (1890) L. R., 17 I. A. 110.

2. (1899) I. L. R., 27 C. 242.

3. *Konwar Doorganath Roy* v. *Ram Chunder Sen*, (1876) I. L. R., 2 C. (P. C.) 341; and *Ram Chandra Mukerjee* v. *Ranjit Singh*, (1899) I. L. R. 27 C. 242.

4. *Muddun Lal* v. *Sreemutty Komul Bibee*, (1867) 8 W. R. C. R. 42.

and that accounts were produced relating to the application of the interest accruing on the same in pursuance of the agreement[1].

Family conduct.

The application of rents for the purposes of the endowment and accounts produced to show such application can only be relevant as evidence showing the conduct of the donor or his family[2] and as such may be negatived by the conduct of the donor or his family in claiming a partition of the property or otherwise treating it as separate property[3].

Personal appropriation—when breach of trust, and when proof of no endowment.

Where the dedication is clearly proved and there is in fact an endowment, mere breach of trust on the part of the donor or trustee in not applying the income of the trust property for the purposes of the trust would not invalidate the trust or alter the original nature of the grant[4]. But where the question to be determined is whether certain property is trust property or belongs to the trustee in his own right, instances of appropriation by the alleged trustee to his own use, if numerous and extending for a long period, will be good evidence of his right, but if the instances are recent or occasional, they are of no value and will be treated as mere abuses of trust[5]. In *Juggut Mohini Dossee* v. *Mussumat Sokheemoney Dossee*[6], the Privy Council observed: "A former abuse of trust, in another instance, cannot be pleaded against a trustee who seeks to prevent a repetition of abuse, even if he were formerly implicated in the same indefensible courses against which he is seeking to protect the property, though it would be a reason for excluding him from the administration of the property as shebait. The court would not with any propriety say 'we will decline to protect the property' and 'leave it further exposed to loss' and decline to make a declaration that it was trust property, merely because they would not trust the plaintiff with its administration."

---

1. *Radha Mohun Mundul* v. *Jadoomonee Dossee*, (1875) 23 W. R. (P. C.) 369.

2. See cases cited in page 29 note (3) and in note (1) *supra*.

3. See cases cited in page 29 note (3). See also *Bibee Kuneez Fatima* v. *Bibee Saheba Jan*, (1867) 8 W. R. C. R. 313.

4. *Muddun Lal* v. *Sreemutty Komul Bibee*, (1867) 8 W. R. C. R. 42; *Juggut Mohini Dossee* v. *Mussumat Sokheemoney Dossee*, (1871) 14 M. I. A. 289; *Luchmiput Singh* v. *Amir Alum*, (1882) I. L. R., 9. C. 176; *Girijanund Dattajha* v. *Saila Janand Dattajha*, (1896) I. L. R., 23 C. 645; *Ramchandra Mukerjee* v. *Ranjit Singh*, (1899) I. L. R., 27 C. 242 at pp. 251 and 252; and *Suppammal* v. *The Collector of Tanjore*, (1889) I. L. R., 12 M. 387.

5. *Girijanund Dattajha* v. *Saila Janund Dattajha*, (1896) I. L. R., 23 C. 645 at 654; See also *Ramchandra Mukerjee* v. *Ranjit Singh*, (1899) I. L. R. 27 C 242.

6. (1871) 14 M. I. A. 289 at pp. 306 and 307.

Paper dedication.

If there is only a paper dedication and there is no evidence that the income has been utilised for the idol or, on the contrary, there is evidence that the income has been utilised by the appropriator himself, and the latter purports to deal with the property as his own, then the endowments cannot be said to be real[1]. If it could be shown that at the time of the paper dedication the appropriator had heavy debts, it would be almost conclusive to show that the real object was not the creation of any real and valid endowment, but that the object was only, in the guise of a dedication to the idol, to defeat creditors[2].

Proceeds applied—no endowment necessarily.

The mere fact of the proceeds of any lands being used for the support of an idol is no proof that those lands are debuttur and constitute an endowment for that purpose[3]. For, that by itself does not constitute an endowment where previously there is none or where there is no proof of a prior endowment. The mere fact of applying the income for the use of an idol is consistent with the case of no endowment. A person may give out of his personal funds some money to another person and may be in the habit of so giving for some continuous period, but that by itself gives no right of action to the donee to compel the donor to give for ever. If the donee be an idol, the position is exactly the same. Even if a person pay from the proceeds of certain property belonging to him certain sums to another and has been in the habit of so doing for a long time, no right of action accrues to the latter to compel the person paying to give for ever when in fact there is no gift of the property. It is just the same if the donee be an idol. In all such cases the contribution is voluntary and the person so contributing has at any time a right to stop it if he be so minded[4].

---

1. *Suppammal* v. *The Collector of Tanjore*, (1889) I. L. R., 12 M. 387; *Muhammad Aziz-Ud-Din* v. *The Legal Remembrancer*, (1893) I. L. R., 15 A. 321 (322).

2. *Sookheemoney Dossee* v. *Mohendro Nath*, (1869) 4 B. L. R., (P. C.) 16.

3. Vide *Muddun Lal* v. *Sreemutty Komul Bibee*, (1867) 8 W. R. C. R. 42; *Mussamut Shurfoonnissa* v. *Mussamut Koolsoom*, (1876) 25 W. R. C. R. 447; *Konwar Doorganath Roy* v. *Ram Chunder Sen*, (1876) I. L. R., 2 C. 341 (P. C.); *Ganapati Ayyar Savithri Ammal*, (1897) I. L. R., 21 M. 10.

4. See *Muddun Lal* v. *Sreemutty Komul Bibee*, (1867) 8 W. R. C. R. 42; *Ram Pershad Doss Adhikaree* v. *Sreehuree Doss Adhikaree*, (1872) 18 W. R. C. R. 399; *Mussamut Shurfoonnissa* v. *Mussamut Koolsoom*, (1876) 25 W. R. C. R. 446; and *Ganapati Ayyan* v. *Savithri Ammal*, supra.

Private chapels—In England no private charitable trust—India different.

The principles applicable to private chapels in England proceed on the same footing. A lord of the manor or any other who generally keeps a private chapel in his own mansion or house, is at full liberty to divert or otherwise use the chapel at his own sweet will and pleasure. Of course in England there is no such thing as a private charitable trust, *i. e.*, property cannot be so perpetually dedicated to a private chapel as to be inalienable. In fact, in England, the rule against perpetuities will apply universally to all gifts unless the gift be to a public charitable purpose. We shall refer to this matter more fully hereafter. In India, of course, the rule is different. At any rate, the Hindu Law recognises a gift to a family idol and any property can be dedicated in perpetuity for the worship of the idol or other religious purpose so as to be inalienable. But where there is no such dedication, the effect is the same as that of a private chapel in England. The position is, as has already been pointed out, exactly the same when a person merely makes a payment to a charity or spends for an idol out of his income or out of the income from a particular fund or property without dedicating the fund or property for the purpose[1]. This principle is well enunciated by the Privy Council in *Mussumat Ameeroonnissa Khanum* v. *Mussumat Ashrufoonissa*[2]. There the facts were one Bekessonissa Begum owned large properties and among them, an Imambara. She was betrothed to her cousin, but separated and lived with one Velayet Hussain as husband and wife. The latter used to style himself as Shahjada of the Imambara. The Privy Council held that " there was no existing Imambara in the sense of any place of worship which might be said to have its property belonging to it, as distinct from the ownership of the Begum, that it was a sort of lay Imambara, and that, although he may have called himself Shahjada, it was really more a title of honor which he had assumed or a nominal appointment of Shahjada than any *real status* which he had, or anything which would put him in the position of a trustee for an Imambara as distinguished from any property which his wife had. The property of the Imambara belonged to the Begum as her other property would do."

---

1. *Muddun Lal* v. *Srimutty Komul Bibee*, *Ram Pershad Doss Adhikaree* v. *Sreehuree Doss Adhikaree* and *Mussamut Shurfoonnisa* v. *Mussamut Koolsoom*, *supra*, p. 31 note (4).

2. (1872) 14 M. I. A. 433

Value or extent of property.

The value or extent of the property endowed will sometimes be a material factor in considering whether there has been a real or apparent dedication. For instance, in the case of settlements made by Mahomedans in the nature of wakfs, the test of finding whether there has been a substantial dedication of the property as wakf is to see whether the extent of the property given is large enough to meet the charitable and religious purposes mentioned in the settlement; but if it is inconsiderably small, then it will be regarded only as a veil under cover of which it is attempted to create a perpetuity in the family which the law will not allow[1]. In the case of settlements or endowments made for the purpose of defeating creditors, the test is rather the reverse. If the property conveyed for religious purposes is small and does not impair or diminish the rights or security of the creditors, the transaction may be regarded as real and may even be upheld as against creditors. But if the value or extent of the property conveyed is large or where a donor conveys away all his property for religious purposes without making any provision even for his own maintenance, then surely his object is only to defeat the creditors and not to create a real transaction. Where, therefore, a deed purports to create a religious trust, but the transaction is not intended to be real or is a mere cloak for the aggrandisement of the family benefit under the pretence of a gift for religious purposes (idol), it cannot be enforced or given effect to[2].

Presence or absence of priests.

The presence or absence of priests will also be a valuable test. Thus where no priests are employed for the worship of the family idol and the idol itself remains in the family house which may be sold away to strangers, it is some evidence to negative a regular endowment and the property will not be debuttur[3]. In *Brojosoondery Debia's case*[4], the Privy Council observed: "This was not an endowment for the benefit of the public. The idol was not set up for the benefit of the public worship. There are no priests appointed, no Brahmins who have any legal interest whatever in

1. See *Muhammad Munawar Ali v. Rasulan Bibi*, (1899) I. L. R., 21 A. 329.

2. *Juggut Mohini Dossee v. Sokheemoney Dossee*, (1871) 14 M. I. A. 289 at p. 302.

3. *Maharanee Brojosoondery Debia v. Ranee Luchmee Koonwaree*, (1873) 15 B. L. R. 176 (note): S. C. 20 W. R. (P. C.) 95; *Kunwar Doorganath Roy v. Ram Chunder Sen*, (1876) I. L. R., 2 C. 341 (P. C.).

4. (1873) 15 B. L. R. 176 (note).

the fund. It is not like a temple for the support of Brahmins, for the purpose of performing religious service for the benefit of any Hindu who might please to go there." The Privy Council followed an earlier case (*Madhub Chunder's case*[1]) in which it was held that where an endowment was merely nominal and indications of personal appropriation and exercise of proprietary rights were found, there was no endowment and a sale of property alleged to be endowed under such circumstances was valid. The above observations of the Judicial Committee, however, should be taken with the facts of that case and should not be taken as negativing the existence of the numerous classes of cases frequently to be found in Bengal and Northern India, *viz.*, those of private religious endowments, *i. e.*, endowments in favor of family idols. Where, however, the idol has a temple of its own, the mere fact that no regular priests are appointed will not negative the endowment[2]. For, if a person be the owner of an idol as shebait (which will be so in the case of private religious endowments in favour of family idols), he will be entitled to appoint anybody he likes to perform the puja, and even the fact that another and his ancestors have been allowed to perform it for a long period of time will create no right in his favour[3] though if the idol be a public idol, such fact will be evidence of an hereditary right to perform the worship. Even in the latter case (*i. e.*, of a public idol) there may be no hereditary priests and the dharmakarta may appoint any one he chooses to perform the worship of the idol. The existence of regular priests may be strong if not conclusive evidence of endowment, but the non-existence of regular priests ought not to be pressed much as negativing the endowment, especially when there is other evidence of dedication.

Strangers not taking part in management.

The fact that the possession and management of the properties endowed by a family may have been transmitted from one of its members to another, no strangers having taken part in the management, is not inconsistent with its being an endowment. For the trusteeship may remain with the donor and his family by the constitution of the endowment[1].

Property set apart for religious purposes.

If property is set apart for religious purposes, that constitutes dedication and such property must be treated as partaking of a trust

1. *Mahatab Chand* v. *Mirdal Ali*, (1833) 5 S. D. A. 268.
2. *Radha Mohun Mundul* v. *Jademonee Dossee*, (1875) 23 W. R. (P. C). 369.
3. *Maharanee Indurjeet Kooer* v. *Chundemun Misser*, (1871) 16 W. R. C. R. 99.
4. *Goosaeen Sree Chowndawalle Bahooalee* v. *Girdhareeji*, (1868) 3 Agra H.C. 226.

or religious endowment[1]. There is of course a great difference between a testator saying that he sets property apart for providing an income for religious purposes, and his merely saying that the ceremonies are to be paid out of the income and shall be performed in the family dwelling house in which the idol is located[1]. In the latter case it depends upon the intention of the testator to be gathered from the instrument and the surrounding circumstances to say whether such a gift of the income is really a gift of the corpus and is capable of being enforced[2].

Formal document not necessary before T. P. Act.

Before the Transfer of Property Act, documentary proof or a specific grant by deed was not necessary to establish an endowment[3]. For, under the Hindu Law, a man may by mere word of mouth constitute an endowment. Thus *West*, J., in the famous *Rancchod Temple case*[4] observed: "A Hindu who wishes to establish a religious or charitable institution may, according to his law, express his purpose and endow it, and the ruler will give effect to the bounty, or at least protect it." This position was also affirmed by the Calcutta High Court in *Bhuggobutty Prosonno Sen* v. *Gooroo Prosonno Sen*[5], which was, however, a case of devise. *Sale*, J., there observed: "Under Hindu Law, an idol, as symbolical of religious purposes, is capable of being endowed with property, but no express words of gift to such an idol in the shape of a trust or otherwise are required to create a valid dedication."

T. P. Act, S. 123.

But, now by the Transfer of Property Act, S. 123, it is enacted that for the purpose of making a gift of immovable property, the transfer of property must be effected by a registered instrument signed by or on behalf of the donor, and attested by at least two witnesses. The same section goes on to provide that "for the purpose of making a gift of movable property, the transfer may be effected either by a registered instrument signed as aforesaid or by delivery. Such delivery may be made in the same way as goods sold may be delivered."

Whether endowments are trusts or gifts—Necessity of writing and registration.

If the transaction creating a religious endowment should be treated and viewed as a trust, then S. 123 of the Transfer of Property Act does not apply, and the Trusts Act not being applicable

1. *Anath Nath Day* v. *A. B. Mackintosh*, (1871) 8 B. L. R. 60; *Piran* v. *Abdool Karim*, (1891) I. L. R. 19 C. 203 (216).
2. *Shook Moychunder Dass* v. *Manohari Dossi*, (1881) I. L. R., 7 C. 269; and *WaeChandler's case*, (1873) L. R. 6 H. L. 1 at p 21 approved by Lord *Selborne* in *Goodman* v. *Mayor of Saltash*, (1882) 7 A. C. 633 (642).
3. Vide *Muddun Lal* v. *Sreemutty Komul Bibee*, (1867) 8 W. R. (C. R.) 42.
4. *Manohar Ganesh* v. *Lakhmiram*, (1887) I. L. R., 12 B. 247.
5. (1897) I. L. R., 25 C. 112.

to public or private religious endowments[1], there is no provision in any express enactment requiring such transaction to be compulsorily evidenced by a writing registered. Of course, if there is a writing, S. 17 of the Registration Act requires such writing to be compulsorily registered. Otherwise, the writing cannot be given in evidence. If the transaction be viewed as a trust and endowments in favour of an idol are no doubt regarded as such, then there is no statutory provision requiring endowments to be compulsorily evidenced by a writing registered. In favor of this view, it may be said, that the policy of the Legislature and of Government in keeping a strict neutrality over religious matters, and in not interfering with native religious endowments points to the conclusion that the Legislature never meant to interfere, as by a sidewind, with the Hindu Law relating to the mode of constituting religious endowments. On the other hand, it may be observed in favor of the view that the transaction is a gift, that an idol or a religious establishment is regarded in the eye of law as a fictitious person capable of holding property symbolically though it may be, and that endowments in favor of idols &c., should be regarded as gifts to a volunteer, so that if the transaction is not complete the gift cannot be enforced. But the recent case of *Pallayya* v. *Ramavadhanulu*[2] holds that S.123, Transfer Property Act, applies only to gifts to ascertained persons and that a transaction by which a public religious endowment is constituted does not come under the section as the gift is only to the public or unascertained body of persons. Whether this is the true legal theory may be doubtful. The idol is the owner. The public may be interested in it. But the gift is not directly to any human personage. If the view laid down in the above case be correct result may be different in the case of a private religious endowment.

Delivery of possession not essential under Hindu Law.

Under Hindu Law, delivery of possession is not absolutely necessary to validate a gift of immoveable property, and hence such delivery will also not be necessary in the case of a gift to an idol[3]. Possession remaining with the donor will not of itself invalidate the gift to debuttur; especially when the gift is followed by mutation of names pursuant to its terms[3].

1. S. 1 of Act II of 1882.

2. (1903) 13 M. L. J. R. 364

3. Vide *Ramchandra Mukerjee* v. *Ranjit Singh*, (1899) I. L. R., 27 C. 242. In *Dharmodas Das* v. *Nistarini Dasi*, (1887) I. L. R., 14 C. 446 and *Phulchand* v. *Lakkhu* (1903) I.L.R., 25 A. 358, it was held that the rule of Hindu Law, if any, as to necessity of possession for validating a gift of immoveable property was abrogated by S. 123.

T. P. Act, S. 123, does not apply to wakfs.

It may be pointed out that S. 123 is made applicable notwithstanding the same may contravene any provision of the Hindu Law, but no mention is made of Mahomedan Law. Hence the provisions of the Mahomedan Law relating to the mode of constituting property as wakf are not affected. No deed is necessary, S. 123 not applying. We shall advert to this matter later on.

Perfect trusts cannot be defeated.

If a trust has been once perfectly created, it cannot be defeated by any subsequent act of the donor[1], or by the retirement of the trustee from his office, or by the refusal of the trustee to accept the office, or by the inability of the trustee to discharge his duties properly[2]. But if the trust be imperfect, as where the donor expresses his intention to create one but contemplates some further act for its completion, courts will not raise a trust and there is no trust to be enforced[3].

Rule of Chancery Courts in carrying out indefinite trusts.

Of course, courts in this country should act in conformity with the practice of the English Courts of Chancery in carrying out charitable bequests, the Courts of Chancery departing from their ordinary rule in such cases and undertaking to see them carried into execution, however indefinite they might be[4]. But where a testator directs his brothers to give alms for his spiritual benefit according to their judgment, such a direction or bequest is vague and is void for uncertainty; for even the English Courts will not ascertain or undertake to enquire what giving of alms will or will not be for the testator's spiritual benefit[1].

Instances where courts uphold *objects* as trusts or treat them as void—(*a*) Charitable purpose, (*b*) Dharm or charitable and benevolent objects.

A gift to Government for such charitable and philanthropic purposes, as it may think proper, has been held to be good[4], but a bequest by a testator that his property shall be disposed of in a pious and charitable way as his executors think proper is bad[5]. A gift to *Dharm* is held void,[6] as it embraces many objects of benevolence not recognised as charitable (such as giving feast to

---

1. *Sir Jamsetji Jijibhai* v. *Sonabai*. (1865) 2 B. H. C. (O. C. J.) 133.
2. *Banur Gartner* v. *Stephenson*, (1868) 3 Agra H. C. 321.
3. *Joseph Ezekiel Judah* v. *Aaron Hye Nusseem Ezekiel Judah*, (1870) 5 B. L. R. (O. C. J.) 433.
4. *Hori Dasi Dabi* v. *The Secretary of State for India in Council*, (1879) I. L. R., 5 C. 228. But see *In re Macduff*, (1896) 2 Ch. 451 where, however, the gift was to charitable *or* philanthropic purposes.
5. Apparently on the ground that the words are merelyr ecommendatory. See *Nanalal Lallubhoy* v. *Harlochand Jugusha*, (1889) I. L. R., 14 B. 476, where the point was apparently not decided.
6. Vide *Gangbai* v. *Thavur Mulla*. (1863) 1 B. H. C. (O. C. J.) 71; *Cursandas Govindji* v. *Vundravandas Purshotam*. (1889) I. L. R., 14 B. 482; *Ranchordas* v. *Parvatibai*, (1899) I. L. R., 23 B. 725; S. C. L. R. 26 I. A. 71.

Brahmins). A gift to *Dharm* is regarded on the same footing as a gift to charitable and benevolent objects which is held void in England though gifts for charitable and religious purposes without the addition of the word 'benevolent' are there held valid.[1]

Trust for maintenance of idols—no amount fixed.

A bequest of immoveable property to some of the testator's heirs subject to the trust for the maintenance of the worship of the family idols will be regarded as valid though no amount is fixed by the testator himself. Here the fund is pointed out and the provision satisfies the other requisites of a precatory trust. The court will enforce such provision and direct enquiry into the amount required for such expenses[2]. The court will be guided in such enquiry by the amount usually expended by the testator in such matters. That is a reasonable amount to be fixed[3]. Where, however, a testator bequeathed his property to his 3 sons in trust, so that the latter should, out of the rents and profits (after payment of expenses of management), perform and celebrate the Doorgapujah and the Kalipuja and other religious ceremonies and festivals and the worship of the family idol at an expense and on a style the testator usually was doing and that the surplus should go for the maintenance of his 5 sons, it was held by *Wilson, J.*, in *Chundramoney Dossee* v. *Motilal Mullick*[4], that such bequest was void for uncertainty, the object of the testator being only to establish a permanent endowment for the testator's benefit and the so-called religious trusts being only trusts for their worship and perpetual trusts for the family and not gifts to idol or to charity.

Precatory trusts.

These are all cases known to the English Chancery Law as precatory trusts and the principle of these decisions have been followed in India. The principle laid down in the English cases is that a court of equity cannot act when there is only a power given to the executors or other persons generally to do certain things which they refuse to exercise[5], but if the power is coupled with a trust, then courts of equity will enforce such a power coupled

---

1. *Baker* v. *Sutton*,(1836) 1 Keen 224 : S.C. 44 R.R. 65 ; *Townsend* v. *Carus*,(1844) 3 Hare 257; *Morice* v. *Bishop of Durham*, (1804) 7 R. R. 232; *James* v. *Allen*, (1817) 17 R. R. 4 ; *Leavers* v. *Clayton*, (1878) 8 Ch. D. 584 ; *In Re Macduff*, (1896) 2 Ch. 463 ; *Hunter* v. *Attorney General*, (1899) A. C. 309 (323, 324.)

2. *Kally Prosono Mitter* v. *Gopee Nauthkur*, (1880) 7 C. L. R., 241 ; and *Asutosh Dutt* v. *Doorgachurn Chatterjee*, (1879) L. R. 6, I. A. 182.

3. See also *Jamnabai* v. *Khimji Vullabdass*, (1889) I. L. R., 14 B. 1.

4. (1879) 5 C. L. R., 496.

5. *Keates* v. *Burton*, (1808) 14 Ves. 434 ; 9 R. R. 315.

with a trust[1]. A trust is not created unless the words are imperative, and the subject and objects are certain[2]. It was, therefore, held in a Madras case[3] that where a testator directed that out of the income of his property ten persons should be fed daily and that one day's *'Ubhayam'* should be performed during a certain festival in Arunachallesvara Swami Covil in Black Town, there was a valid charge created for such purposes. But a direction in the same will that the executors should, according to their wishes, pay the testator's brothers, their wives and children was held in the same case not to create any trust and that the words were merely recommendatory as they gave a discretion to the executors.

It is not possible within the limits of this work to go through the entire ground taken by the English Courts as regards precatory trusts. The reader is referred to the standard works upon Trusts and especially to Lewin on Trusts[4].

Dedication—no assent of State required.

If there is a dedication of property for religious purposes (or for idols), the assent of the State is not necessary to render it valid Thus in *Juggut Mohini Dossee* v. *Mussumat Sokheemoney Dossee*[5], where the suit was to set aside an alienation of endowed property alleged by the plaintiff to have been made for purposes not binding on the endowment and to recover possession, the Privy Council observed: "It was argued that such dedications of property without the assent of the State should be regarded as merely revocable appropriations, of which the founders might vary the use. No authority whatever was adduced in support of this position which strikes at the root of most modern endowments of the like nature"[6].

We shall in the following chapter refer to the various kinds of dedications where a perfect trust is admitted or proved.

---

1. *Brown* v. *Higgs*, (1803) 8 Ves. 561-569; 4 R. R. 323.

2. *Knight* v. *Knight*, (1844) 3 Beav. 148: 52 R. R. 74. See also *Mussoorie Bank* v. *Raynor*, (1882) L. R. 9 I. A. 70; *Kumarasami* v. *Subbaraya*, (1886) I. L. R., 9 M. 325 at p. 326; *Gookool Nath Guha* v. *Issur Lochun Roy*, (1886) I. L. R., 14 C. 222 (233).

3. *Kumarasami* v. *Subbaraya*, supra.

4. pp. 140 to 149.

5. (1871) 14 M. I. A. 289.

6. Their Lordships referred with approval to the cases collected in Norton's Leading Cases on Hindu Law, Part II, p. 106. See also *Manohar Ganesh* v. *Lakhmiram*, (1887) I. L. R., 12 B. 247.

CHAPTER IV.

DIFFERENT KINDS OF DEDICATION.

Having considered what constitutes dedication we shall next refer to the different kinds of dedication. Where the dedication is complete and the trust is perfect different considerations will arise, and the nature of the trust constituted will be different according to the nature of the dedication.

Idol holding lands—practice of vesting in trustees.

It has been already observed in a former chapter that the idol in Hindu Law is an ideal subject or person capable of owning property; though at the same time it has been said that it is only in an ideal sense that property can belong to an idol and that the possession and management of it must, in the nature of things, be entrusted to some person as shebait or manager.[1] The dictum of *Straight, J.*, in *Raghubar Dial* v. *Kesho Ramanuj Das*[2] that "an idol cannot itself hold lands" is explicable in this sense, *viz.*, that an idol can hold lands legally but that physically it cannot hold and manage the same. It is, therefore, the practice in such cases "to vest the lands in a trustee for the religious purpose or to impose upon the holders of the lands a trust to defray the expenses of worship" (Per *Straight, J.*, in *Raghubar Dial* v. *Kesho Ramanuj Das*[2].). Sometimes the donor himself is the trustee. It may, however, be observed that a dedication in favor of a religious establishment is not invalid even though no trustee is appointed; for, under the Hindu Law, "no express words of gift to such an idol in the shape of a trust or otherwise are required to create a valid dedication."[3]

Property endowed or personal—question of construction.

The practice being to vest the lands in a trustee, the question arises whether property is given for the religious purpose, or is given to the trustee for the latter to enjoy at his pleasure. This greatly depends upon the intention of the parties and the construction of the document, if any, under which the property is claimed as an endowment[4].

---

1. Vide Ch. II., pp. 15, 16 and 17 ante and the cases therein cited.

2. (1888) I. L. R., 11 A. 18. See also Mayne, para. 437, 5th edition.

3. *Bhuggobutty Prosonno Sen* v. *Gooroo Prosonno Sen*, (1897) I. L. R., 25 C. 112. Vide also *Manohar Ganesh Tambekar* v. *Lakhmiram Govindram*, (1887) I. L. R., 12 B. 247 at p. 263.

4. *Ranjit Singh* v. *Jagannath Prosad Gupta*, (1885) I. L. R., 12 C. 375. See also cases cited in 44 notes (4) and (5).

Offerings to idol—endowment.

It may be observed that in the English Law a gift placed on the altar of God suffices to convey the lands or other property so placed to the church[1]. Similarly where offerings are made by a devotee to a Hindu idol, the gift is to the idol and the shevaks or other trustees of the idol have no title or interest in the same. Indeed it cannot be contended that the idol has got a potentiality or separate existence for the purpose of bringing in offerings and vouchsafing blessings, but is, with reference to the property in such gifts and offerings, a mere block having no potentiality and subject to the ownership of the trustee or the archaka. As Mr. Justice *West* observed in the famous *Ranchhod Temple case*[2], "It is indeed a strange, if not wilful, confusion of thought by which the defendants set up the Sri Ranchhod as a deity for the purpose of inviting gifts and vouchsafing blessings, but, as a mere block of stone, their property for the purpose of their appropriating every gift laid at its feet. But if there is a juridical person, the ideal embodiment of a pious or benevolent idea as the centre of the foundation, this artificial subject of rights is as capable of taking offerings of cash and jewels as of land." It was, therefore, held in that case that the *Shevaks* were not the owners of the offerings and were responsible for their due application for the purposes of the foundation[3].

Offerings, when not idol's.

The above, however, is true of an idol which is an ancient one permanently established for public worship and the offerings are more or less of a generally permanent character. There are, however, some cases in which this general rule may not be applicable. These are:—(1) where the idol is set up temporarily for worship, or where the offerings are of a perishable nature or are of a temporary character; and (2), where an usage is proved or the donor's intention is that such offerings whether permanent or otherwise should go to the shevaks or archakas or trustees.

First exception, no regular endowment.

The former part of the first heading presupposes a case of no regular endowment. The idol is the private property of the person owning the same. If, however, it is a family idol which has endowments of its own, though it is not a public institution and not set apart for public worship so that only persons who are members of the family or its shebaits are entitled to worship and

1. Pollock and Maitland's History of the English Law Vol. I, pp. 481 to 484.
2. *Manohar Ganesh Tambekar* v. *Lakhmiram Govindram*, (1887) I. L. R., 12 B. 247 at p. 265.
3. Vide also *Thackersey Devraj* v. *Hurbhum Nursey*, (1884) I. L. R., 8 B. 432.

have the right to exclude the public from worship, yet if such persons permit outsiders to worship the idol temporarily or otherwise, any offerings made by such outsiders will not necessarily go to the members of the family or the shebaits in their personal character[1]. As regards offerings of a perishable nature, from the very necessity of things, they cannot be preserved. It would seem that, in such cases, the intention of the devotee is taken to be that they should be used by the Archakas.

Girijaunund Datta Jha's case.

The above principles are well illustrated n *Girijanund Datta Jha* v. *Sailajanund Datta Jha*[2]. It was there observed : "Where an idol is set up temporarily for worship or where the offerings are of a perishable nature, such as articles of food, the priest in attendance as the nearest Brahmin available generally appropriates the offerings, and the same is the case where the idol itself is the private property of a priest, but where the idol is an ancient one permanently established for public worship, and the offerings are more or less generally of a permanent character, being coins or other metallic articles, in the absence of any custom or express declaration by the donor to the contrary, they are, as they ought to be, taken to be intended to contribute to the maintenance of the shrine with all its rights, ceremonies and charities, and not to become the personal property of the priests."

Rajah Varmah v. Ravi Vurmah.

In *Rajah Vurmah Valia* v. *Ravi Vurmah*[3], the pagoda was not a pagoda in the ordinary sense of the word but a mere platform in the middle of the forest upon which, once in every year, certain ceremonies were taking place in honour of a particular idol, and it was apparently assumed that the considerable presents and offerings made by the worshippers belonged to the idol. In this case the idol apparently had been permanently established.

Goosaeen v. Gridhareejee.

In *Goosaeen Sree Choundawalee Bahooalee* v. *Girdhareejee*[4] where the suit was for the establishment of the plaintiff's right to the office of Gaddinashin of the temples at Nathdwara and Gokul and for possession of the temples and their endowments, the Agra High Court in holding that such properties were public religious endowments and not the private properties of the trustee

1. But see judgment of High Court referred to in *Srimati Kamini Debi* v. *Asutosh Mookerjee*, (1888) L. R. 15 I. A. 159 (164 and 165) : S. C. I. L. R., 16 C. 103.
2. (1896) I. L. R., 23 C. 645. See also *Dhadphale* v. *Gurav*, (1881) I. L. R., 6 B. 122.
3. (1876) I. L. R., 1 M. 235 : S. C. L. R., 4 I. A., 76.
4. (1868) 3 Agra H. C. 226.

observed: "Such properties and the funds arising from the offerings of the devotees, not being devoted to the mere private uses of the recipient, are regarded substantially as partaking of a trust or religious endowment and are not private properties, though the trust may not be clearly defined and may be such as not wholly to exclude some personal enjoyment or profit."

Second exception usage.

As regards the second exception stated above, *viz.*, the one founded on usage and intention the principle is intelligible. The rule obtaining in all cases of endowments is primarily to be found in the intention expressed by the founder and, in the absence of such, the usage obtaining in the institution. Usage is, however, given effect to not as overruling or contravening the intention of the founder but as an index of such intention[1].

Original intention perverted by usage.

It is, however, difficult to say whether the usage now obtaining in some of these ancient religious institutions, by which trustees archakas or both distribute among themselves the offerings offered to the deity is well-founded and legal. There is not strictly the question of the founder's intention in such a case. The offerings are made by the public for the propitiation of the deity and on account of its worship. No doubt the offerings may be received by the trustees[2] but that does not entitle them to distribute the same among themselves. It is perfectly possible that in some cases the offerings are intended for the *pujaris* for the work they do[3]. But in the absence of any such intention the *prima facie* inference is that such offerings are made by the devotees not for the benefit of the God-server but for God. It appears to us that the usage on the part of trustees appropriating the offerings now prevailing in some of the religious establishments, is not altogether correct. The usage can be justified only upon the unwarranted assumption that such offerings when made are intended for the benefit of the *managers* of the religious establishment. This usage having grown up for a long time, the intention of devotees in making these offerings is not adverted to at all. This practice has, moreover, now

---

1. Vide *Greedharee Doss* v. *Nundokissore Doss Mohunt*, (1867) 11 M. I. A., 405 at 428; *Gossain Dowlut Geer* v. *Bissessur Geer*, (1873) 19 W. R. 215; *Rajah Muttu Ramalinga Setupati* v. *Perianayagum Pillai*, (1874) L. R. 1, I. A. 209; *Rahumtulla Sahib* v. *Mahommed Akbar Sahib*, (1875) 8 M. H. C. 63; *Venkatachalapati* v. *Subbarayadu*, (1890) I. L. R., 13 M. 293 at 299; *Ramalingam Pillai* v. *Vythilingam Pillai*, (1893) I. L. R., 16 M. 490: S. C. L. R. 20 I. A. 150.

2. *Durga Bibi* v. *Chanchal Ram*, (1881) I. L. R., 4 A. 81.

3. *Dhadphale* v. *Gurav*, (1881) I. L. R., 12 B. 122; *Kashichandra Chuckerbutty* v. *Kailash Chandra*, (1899) I. L. R., 26 C. 356.

become so inveterate that any attempt to enforce the trust on behalf of the idol with reference to the said offerings be looked upon as trenching upon vested rights. Of course where an intention to give the offerings for the shevaks is clear the latter are entitled to the same. But where the offerings are intended for the idol the trustees or shevaks have no right to such offerings. It may be justifiable where the archakas or pujaris take the offerings as the same may be in return for the work they do. But there seems to be no justification for the Dharmakartas taking the offerings except when such offerings are expressly intended for them.

Property in offerings.

The general principle that the offerings made by devotees are *prima facie* for the benefit of the idol and not for its shevaks, is recognised in many of the Bombay and Calcutta cases[1], where it has been held that the shevaks are neither owners of temples nor owners of offerings. It is not easy to reconcile the principle laid down in such cases with the usage obtaining in some temples in Madras by which Dharmakartas appropriate the whole or part of the offerings.

Grants to trustees—capable of double construction

Grants made to trustees are also capable of this double construction. The reason is that a trustee has a dual capacity. The one is his own personal right[2]. The other is the right of the person for whom, or of the estate for which, he is trustee. In these two capacities he must be treated as different persons[3]. It must, therefore, be a question of construction whether a particular grant is intended for the trustee's private benefit and is made in his individual right, or whether it is intended for the benefit of the person or estate represented by him and is made in his capacity as trustee. A mere description of the legatee as holder of an office will not do[4]. The test is to look to the intention of the donor as appearing from the grant and the surrounding circumstances of the case[5].

1. *Thackersey Dewraj* v. *Hurbhum Nursey*, (1884) I. L. R., 8 B. 432 ; *The Advocate-General of Bombay* v. *David Haim Devakar*, (1886) I.L.R., 11 B. 185 ; *Manohar Ganesh* v. *Lakhmiram*, (1887) I.L R., 12 B. 247 ; *Chintaman* v. *Dhondo*, (1888) I. L. R., 15 B. 612 ; *Kalidas Jivram* v. *Gorparjaram*, (1890) I. L. R., 15 B. 309 ; *Girijanund Datta Jha* v. *Sailajanund Datta Jha*, (1896) I. L. R., 23 C. 645.

2. *Manohar Ganesh* v. *Lakhmiram*, supra ; *Kalidas Jivram* v. *Gorparjaram*, supra ; *Chintaman* v. *Dhondo*, supra ; *Goosaeen Sree Choundawalee Bahooalee* v. *Girdhareeji*, (1868) 3 Agra H. C. 226 ; and *Rupa Jagshet* v. *Krishnaji Govind*, (1884) I. L. R., 9 B. 169.

3. Vide *Ramanathan Chettiar* v. *Levvai Marakayar*, (1899) I. L. R., 23 M. 195 ; See also *Daoud Ali Beg* v. *Nadir Hossein*, (1869) 11 W. R C. R. 388.

4. *Doe* v. *Aldridge*, (1791) 2 R. R. 379 ; *Donnellan* v. *O'Neil*, (1870) L. R. 3 Eq. 523 ; and *Conoley* v. *Quick*, (1902) 2 Ch. 642.

5. *Thornber* v. *Wilson*, (1855) 3 Drew 245 : (1858) 4 Drew 350; and *Conoley* v. *Quick*, supra ; *Asheerooddeen* v. *Drobo Moyee*, (1876) 25 W. R. C. R. 557 ; *Annaji* v. *Narayan*, (1896) I. L. R., 21 B. 556.

Thus where, by a sanad, a sovereign prince (Mahratta) granted to a trustee of the Chinchavad Sevasthan certain properties on account of the worship &c., in honor of the Shri (deity), it was held in *Shri Ganesh Dharnidhar Maharaj Dev* v. *Keshavrav Govind Kulgavkar*[1], that it was a question of construction of the sanad, whether the grant was to the grantee as trustee of a religious endowment or to him for his private benefit and that, according to such construction, the grant in the particular case was made for the religious establishment. **Grants to idol-cases.**

Similarly in *Ranjit Singh* v. *Jagannath Prosad Gupta*[2], it was held that the gift to the trustee was not to his personal benefit or individual capacity but must enure for the benefit of the idol of which he was the trustee.

In *Ram Doss* v. *Moheeur Deb Missree*[3], however, it was held that the grant by a Raja of Assam was not to the idol but to the religious fraternity of an already existing 'Tharo' or temple though for the purpose of keeping up certain religious ceremonies[4]. **Grant to fraternity.**

Grants of land or other property made to the trustee of a mutt are governed by the same principles. They are not grants of secular property intended for the trustee or Matadhipati of the mutt, but they are endowments in trust for the mutt and the charities connected therewith[5]. In *Khusalchand* v. *Mahadevgiri*[6], it was held by the Bombay High Court that a grant by a sovereign to a Gosavi and his disciples in perpetual succession was not equivalent to a grant to a man and his heirs and was intended by the grantor to be a perpetual fountain of merit producing benefit to himself and that his intention would be defeated by the diversion of the gift at the will of the grantor or his successors to purely secular uses. **Grants to trustees of mutt.**

On the same principle it was held by the Madras High Court in *Sathianama Bharati* v. *Saravanabagi Ammal*[7] that where there was a grant to the head of a Gosavi Mutt to be enjoyed from generation to generation, and it was provided by the grant that the grantee was to improve the mutt and maintain the charity

1. (1890), I. L. R., 15 B. 625
2. (1885), I. L. R., 12 C. 375.
3. (1867), 7 W. R. C. R. 446.
4. *Cf. Rajah Nursing Deb* v. *Roy Koylasanath*, (1862) 9 M. I. A. 55.
5. *GoosaeenSree Choundawalee Bahooalee* v. *Girdhareeji*, (1868) 3 Agra H.C. 226; and *Kolandai Mudali* v. *Sankara Bharadhi*, (1882) I. L. R., 5 M. 302. See also cases cited in Ch. VIII.
6. (1875), 12 B. H. C. 214.
7. (1894). I. L. R., 18 M. 266.

and be happy, the grant was an endowment in trust for the mutt and the charities connected therewith, though what might remain after the due execution of the trust was intended to be applied for the maintenance of the grantee and his descendants and that it was not merely a grant of private property to the original grantee[1].

Grantor's motive immaterial.

The motive actuating the grantor would be immaterial if in fact the grant was intended by him for the private benefit of the grantee. Thus where a person granted certain properties to another on account of his pious and religious nature, the grant was really for his individual benefit and the motive of the grantor in making the grant did not convert it into a religious endowment[2]. So, the direction in a grant that the donee and his issue should pray for the perpetuity of the then existing Government stands on the same principle and is no more than an inculcation of gratitude for the gift[3].

In *Bibee Kuneez Fatima* v. *Bibee Saheba Jan*[4], it was held by the Calcutta High Court that where a grant was made by the Nabobs to a certain person (Syed Mahomed Meer) because he had a large family to support and had to defray the expenses of the Khankah, and his income had not been sufficient for these and for meeting the expenses of the abwabs and other heavy cesses which were accordingly remitted, there was no dedication to God or to any religious or charitable purposes and that the grant was personal to the grantee and in his own right for furnishing the means of subsistence. The court observed: "The motive of the grantor in making the grant might be the charitable disposition of the grantee. But his grant was not for charitable purposes."

Grants to Muttawallis.

Grants made to Muttawallis also rest on the same principle. A grant may be made to a person named because the grantor thought he was a pious man and charitably disposed. But the motive in making a gift is immaterial[5] as already stated. The test is only what the intention of the donor is. Does he intend the person named to be the object of the gift or does he intend the

1. Vide *Sammantha Pandara* v. *Sellappa Chetti*, (1879) I. L. R., 2 M. 175.
2. *Anantha Tirtha Chariar* v. *Nagamuthu Ambalagaren*, (1881) I.L.R., 4 M. 200.
3. *Sayad Mahomed Ali* v. *Sayad Gobar-Ali*, (1881) I. L. R., 6 B. 88.
4. (1867) 8 W. R. C. R., 313.
5. See cases in notes 2, 3 and 4.

religious establishment or religious service to be the object of the gift? This is apparently the reasoning upon which the case of *Sayad Mahomed Ali* v. *Sayad Gobar Ali*[1] proceeds. It was held in this case that a grant to a man and his children without restriction as to names for his and their maintenance was not a wakf though the donee should engage for himself and his issue to pray for the perpetuity of the then existing Government and that such a direction in a grant meant no more than an inculcation of gratitude for the gift. Such a direction was not a condition, and neither neglect to fulfil the direction, nor the downfall of the Government would have worked a forfeiture or avoidance of the grant.

If the grant be in favor of a religious institution or establishment, the next question that has to be considered is whether the dedication is absolute in favor of the religious establishment or whether it amounts only to a charge in its favor, *i. e.*, whether the gift in favor of the religious establishment extends to the whole of the property conveyed or is only limited to a part of it as where a part of the income only is appropriated for the religious service or establishment. Grant to institution—absolute or bare charge.

The question that has to be considered in this class of cases is, whether from the nature and terms of the gift, the intention of the donor to confer on the grantee a beneficial and alienable interest in property to be utilized for the idol may be inferred, or whether an intention to preserve the worship and endowments in the family, and to make the gift solely to the idol may be inferred. The *prima facie* presumption of Hindu Law is that endowments of this kind are of the latter class, *i. e.*, that they are made usually with the object of preserving the *Sheba* in families, rather than of conferring a benefit on individuals[2]. In *The Collector of Moorshedabad* v. *Ranee Shibessuree Dabea*[2], their Lordships of the Privy Council observed: "It is more consonant with the genius and spirit of Hindu Law and usage that endowments of this kind should be made to a family, by whose members in succession, the worship might be performed, than to an individual who might sell or give them to a stranger". But in the absence of any Intention essential.

---

1. (1881) I. L. R., 6 B. 88.

2. *The Collector of Moorshedabad* v. *Ranee Shibessuree Dabea* and *Rajah Chundernath Roy* v. *Kooar Gobindnath Roy*, (1872) 11 B. L. R., 86: S. C. 18 W. R. (P. C.) 221 (226).

language denoting the intention of the donor that the gift is to belong to the idol and that the worship is to remain in the family, this presumption will not be sufficient, of itself, to impress that construction upon the deed.

Beneficial interest in surplus.

At the same time, however, it must be observed that in the case of a private religious endowment, *i. e.*, where a Hindu donor makes a bequest or gift of his property for his family idol, a large beneficial interest is usually given to the members of the family who are constituted shebaits of the idol[1], though it is of course competent to the donor to make an absolute dedication of his property to the idol without leaving any beneficial interest or without a gift over of a beneficial interest in the surplus to the members of his family or to any one else. Upon this point, the Privy Council in *Surendro Keshub Roy* v. *Doorga Soondery Dossee*[2] observed: "The testator shows no intention save that which may be reasonably attributed to a devout Hindu gentleman, *i. e.*, to secure that his family worship shall be conducted in the accustomed way, by giving his property to one of the Thakoors whom he venerates most. But the effect when the estate is large is to have some beneficial interest undisposed of."

Wakf—absolute or bare trust.

A land is said to be absolutely wakf where the whole of the profits arising from it is devoted to religious purposes[3]. There are many cases in which it has been held that an absolute wakf exists and not simply a grant burdened with a trust[4]. It is always a question of construction whether a deed makes property absolutely wakf so that the Muttawalli has no proprietary interest except in his character as Muttawalli, or whether it is a gift to a person named subject to certain trusts or conditions, in which case the person will have the proprietary interest but takes the property subject to the condition[5]. Of course, even where the estate is constituted as wakf, the donor may give a portion of the income of such estate as an allowance for the trustee, in which case the property is still wakf, but there is a charge in favor of the trustee[6]. For, it

---

1. *Radha Jeebun Moostuffy* v. *Taramonee Dossee*, (1869) 12 M. I. A., 380: S. C. 2 B., L. R. 4; S. C. 11 W. R. (P. C.) 1.
2. (1892) I. L. R., 19 C. 513; S. C. L. R. 19 I. A. 108.
3. *Futtoo Bibee* v. *Bhurrut Lall Bhukut*, (1868) 10 W. R. C. R. 299.
4. *Doyal Chund Mullick* v. *Keramut Ali*, (1871) 16 W. R., 116; *Nallathambi Battar* v. *Nellakumara Pillai*, (1873) 7 M. H. C. 306; *Juggodumba Dossee* v. *Puddomoney Dossee*, (1875) 15 B. L. R., 318; *Syud Asheerooddeen* v. *Sreemutty Drobomoyee*, (1876) 25 W. R. 557.
5. *Sheik Abdool Khalek* v. *Poran Bibee*, (1876) 25 W. R., 542 at p. 546.
6. *Bishenchand Basawat* v. *Nadir Hossein*, (1887) I. L. R., 15 C. 329: S. C. L. R., 15 I. A. 1.

is open to the donor at the time of the dedication to impose or annex any condition he pleases, and the donee must take it subject to that condition[1] though no condition can be imported after the gift or dedication[2]. A religious establishment or institution is no exception to this rule.

Idol—Absolute gift or bare trust.

All these principles are equally applicable to the case of an idol. Even there it is a question of intention of the parties whether there has been an absolute dedication to the idol or there has been a gift of the property subject to some trusts in favor of the idol[3]. In *Rajender Dutt* v. *Shamchund Mitter*[4] it was held that there was an absolute dedication.

Trustees to reside—still absolute.

It is consistent with the case of an absolute dedication if the donor should provide that the trustee should live in a portion of the trust property. Thus it was held in *Bhuggobutty Prosonno Sen* v. *Gooroo Prosonno Sen*[5] that the provision that the testator's family should live did not give any beneficial interest in the property to such members and did not make the transaction a bare charge in favor of the idol, but was only consistent with the dedication being absolute[6]. As to the extent of this right of residence in such a case, it is reasonable, in the absence of express provision, to look to the mode of living adopted by the testator during his life for himself and his members[5].

Charge in favor of an idol.

Of course, as has already been observed, the donor may, without making an absolute dedication, either create a charge in favor of the idol or religious establishment leaving the beneficial interest in favor of a private person, who will then take the property burdened with the trust or the donor may grant a part of the property or of its income to the idol or religious establishment leaving the surplus to others to hold as private property. These cases must be distinguished from another class of cases already adverted to, *viz.*,

1. *Marquis of Stafford* v. *Coyney*, (1827) 7 B. & C. 257; *Davies* v. *Stephens*, (1836) 7 C. & P. 570; S. C. 10 R. R. 820; *Poole* v. *Huskinson*, (1848) 11 M. & W. 827; *Fisher* v. *Prowse*, (1862) 2 B. & S. 770; *Mercer* v. *Woodgate*, (1869) L. R., 5 Q. B. 26; *Morant* v. *Chamberlin*, (1870) 6 H. & N. 541; *Arnold* v. *Blaker*, (1871) L. R., 6 Q. B. 433; *Arnold* v. *Holbrook*, (1873) L. R., 8 Q. B. 96. See Pratt on Highways (14th Edn.), pp. 15 to 20, and Carson on Real Property Statutes 53. Cf. *Gossami Sree Giridhariji* v. *Romau Lalji*, (1889) I. L. R., 17 C. 3 (P. C.)

2. *Ram Surup* v. *Bela*, (1883) L. R., 11 I. A. 44; *Fisher* v. *Prowse*, (1862) 2 B. & S. 770; and Pratt on Highways (14th Edn.), pp. 15 to 20.

3. *Ramcoomar Paul* v. *Jogendernath Paul*, (1878) I. L. R., 4 C. 56; S. C. 2 C. L. R. 310.

4. (1880), I. L. R., 6 C. 106.

5. (1897), I. L. R., 25 C. 112.

6. See also *Natesa* v. *Ganapati*, (1890) I. L. R., 14 M. 103; *Gossami Shr Giridhariji* v. *Madhowdas Premji*, (1893) I. L. R., 17 B. 600.

where the estate is given to the idol, subject, however, to some charge or allowance created in favor of the trustee.

In *Ashutosh Dutt* v. *Doorgachurn Chatterjee*[1], the Privy Council held that where a Hindu lady bequeathed to her sons certain property to support the daily worship of an idol and to defray the expenses of certain religious ceremonies with a provision that in the event of there being a surplus after these uses had been satisfied out of the revenue, such surplus should be applied for the support of the family, there was no absolute dedication but that there was a valid trust in favor of the idol and the surplus remained private property.

There are several cases in the reports in which it was held that there was a trust with reference to an idol[2] and with reference to wakfs[3], while there are others in which it was held that there was only a charge in favor of the idol or religious purposes[4] or wakf purposes[5] and the beneficial interest in the whole property vested in private owners.

Dedication four kinds.

Thus it will be seen that a transaction of this sort may be of four kinds :—

(1). An absolute dedication in which the entire beneficial interest is with the idol or religious establishment. (2). A dedication to the idol or religious establishment, but a charge is created as to a part of the income in favor of a private person. (3). A gift as to a part of the income in favor of the idol or reli-

---

1. (1879), L. R. 6 I. A. 182: S. C. I. L. R., 5 C. 438 : S. C. 5 C. L. R., 296.

2. *Sonatun Bysack* v. *Sreemutty Juggut Soondree Dossee*, (1859) 8 M. I. A. 66; *Kumara Asima Krishna Deb* v. *Kumara Kumara Krishna Deb*, (1868) 2 B. L. R. O. C. 11 at p. 39 (Per *Peacock, C.J.*); *Mohamaya Dossee* v. *Bindoo Bashinee Dossee*, (1872) 19 W. R. C. R. 35; *Nallathambi Battar* v. *Nellakumara Pillai*, (1873) 7 M. H. C. 306; *Juggadumba Dossee* v. *Puddomoney Dossee*, (1875) 15 B. L. R. 318; *Kally Prosono Mitter* v. *Gopee Nauth Kur*, (1880) 7 C. L. R. 241; *Thackersey Dewraj* v. *Hurbhum Nursey*, (1884) I. L. R., 8 B. 432; *Girijanund Dattajha* v. *Saila Janund Dattajha*, (1896) I. L. R., 23 C. 645; *Bhuggobutty Prosonno Sen* v. *Guru Prosonno Sen*, (1897) I. L. R., 25 C. 112.

3. *Futto Bibee* v. *Bhurrut Lall*, (1868) 10 W. R. C. R. 299; *Gulam Hussain Saib Saiyad* v. *Aji Ajam Tadallah Saib Kuraishi*, (1868) 4 M. H. C. 44; *Doyal Chund Mullick* v. *Keramut Ali*, (1871) 16 W. R. C. R. 116; and *Kazi Hassan* v. *Sagun Bal Krishna*, (1899) I. L. R., 24 B. 170 (Per *Ranade*, J).

4. *Radha Jeebun* v. *Taramoney*, (1869) 12 M. I. A. 380; *Mohesh Chunder* v. *Koylash Chunder*, (1869) 11 W. R. C. R. 443; *Horidasi Davi* v. *The Secretary of State for India*, (1879) I. L. R., 5 C. 228; *Kally Prosono Mitter* v. *Gopee Nath Kur*, supra; *Shookmoy Chunder Dass* v. *Monohari Dassi*, (1881) I. L. R., 7 C. 269; *Kumarasami* v. *Subbaraya*, (1886) I. L. R., 9 M. 325; and *Surendro Keshub Roy* v. *Doorga Soondery Dossee*, (1892) I. L. R., 19 C. 513 : S. C. L. R. 19 I. A. 108.

5. *Futto Bibee* v. *Bhurrut Lall*, supra; *Syed Asheeroodden* v. *Drobo Moyee*, (1876) 25 W. R. C. R. 557; *Pathukutti* v. *Avathala Kutti*, (1889) I. L. R., 13 M. 66. (Per *Shephard*, J., *Parker* and *Muthusawmi Iyer*, JJ., however, held in this case that the wakf was invalid as the gift to wakf depended on a contingency); and *Bikani Mia* v. *Shuk Lal Poddar*, (1892) I. L. R., 20 C. 116; and Per *Starling*, J., in *Sagun Balkrishna* v. *Kaji Hussen*, (1903) I. L. R., 27 B. 500 (514 and 515).

gious establishment so that there is a trust to that extent while the surplus is given to the trustee in his private capacity. (4). The whole property is given to a certain person, but there is a charge created in favor of the idol or religious establishment as regards a portion of the income.

The legal effect of these different kinds of dedication has next to be considered, and the distinction is only important with reference to the different legal effects produced[1].

Absolute property—inalienable

In the first class of cases, *i. e.*, where there is an absolute dedication, the property cannot be sold or alienated by the trustee or manager except for certain purposes recognised by law. Such alienation will be altogether invalid[2] and it follows that the property is not divisible among the trustees[3].

Endowment subject to charge—inalienable.

Even in the second case the property is not alienable. Thus in *Bishen Chand Basawut* v. *Syed Nadir Hossein*[4], the question arose whether property constituted as wakf (under a wakfnama by which property was given to the donor's grandson in trust for the performance of certain religious ceremonies, &c., subject to allowances in favor of the trustee, the donor's son and daughter) was attachable either in whole or in part in execution of a personal decree against the trustee and their Lordships of the Privy Council in holding that such property was not attachable altogether, observed: "If the whole property is to be sold, it must be taken out of the hands of the trustee altogether and put into the hands of a purchaser. That purchaser might be a Christian, he might be a Hindu, or he might be of any other religion. It surely cannot be contended that property, devised by a Mahomedan lady to a Mahomedan trustee with the object of providing for certain Mahomedan religious duties, could be taken out of the hands of that trustee and sold to a person of any other religion and that the purchaser should become

1. *Raghubar Dial* v. *Kesho Ramanuj Das*, (1888) I. L. R., 11 A. 18.

2. *Futtoo Bibee* v. *Bhurrut Lall Bhukut*, (1868) 10 W. R. C. R. 299; *Basoo Dhul* v. *Kishen Chunder Geer Gossain*, (1870) 13 W. R. C. R. 200; *Golak Chunder Bose* v. *Raghoonath Sree Chunder Roy*, (1872) 17 W. R. C. R. 444: S. C. 11 B. L. R. 337 note; *The Collector of Moorshedabad* v. *Ranee Shebessuree*, (1872) 11 B. L. 86: S. C. 18 W. R. 221 P. C.; *Bunwaree Chand Thakoor* v. *Mudden Mohun Chuttoraj*, (1873) 21 W. R. C. R. 41; *Sheik Abdool Khalek* v. *Poran Bibee*, (1876) 25 W. R. 542 (546); *Ramcoomar Paul* v. *Jogendernath Paul*, (1878) I. L. R., 4 C. 56; *Durga Bibi* v. *Chanchal Ram*, (1881) I. L. R., 4 A. 81.

3. *Mushurool Huq* v. *Puhraj Ditarey*, (1870) 13 W. R. C. R. 235; *Bunwaree Chand Thakoor* v. *Mudden Mohun Chuttoraj*, supra; *Ram Coomar Paul* v. *Jogendernath Paul*, (1878) I. L. R., 4 C. 56: S. C. 2 C. L. R. 310.

4. (1887) L. R. 15 I. A. 1: S. C. I. L. R 15 C. 329.

the trustee for the purpose of performing or seeing to the performance of those religious duties. If property is to be sold and alienated from the trustee whom this lady appointed, or the trustee who was subsequently appointed by him to succeed as trustee, the purchaser, of whatever religion he might be, would have to see to the execution of the trusts. Is it possible that the law can be such that a Hindu might become the purchaser of the property for the purpose of seeing to the performance of certain religious duties under the Mahomedan Law? For example, that a Hindu might be substituted for a Mahomedan trustee for the purpose of providing funds for the Mohurrum and taking care that it should be duly and properly performed, when it is well known what disputes and bitter feelings frequently exist between Hindus and Mahomedans at the time of the Mohurrum. * * * The corpus of the estate cannot be sold, nor can any specific portion of the corpus of the estate be taken out of the hands of the trustee, because there may be a margin of profit coming to him after the performance of all the religious duties. Under section 266, C. P. C., a judgment-creditor can only attach property over which his judgment-debtor has disposing power, and if there was any surplus in the trustee's hands for the benefit of the judgment-debtor, it would not entitle the judgment-creditor to attach and sell the whole or any specific portion of the corpus of the estate."

Charge for endowment—alienable.

The third and fourth classes of cases are similar. In such cases the property may be sold or alienated subject to the trust or charge and the property is held to be divisible among the members.[1]

---

1. *Sonatun Bysack* v. *Sreemutty Juggut Soondree Dossee*, (1859) 8 M. I. A. 66; *Futtoo Bibee* v. *Bhurrut Lall Bhukut*, (1868) 10 W. R. C. R. 299; *Basoo Dhul* v. *Kishen Chunder Geer Gossain*, (1870) 13 W. R. C. R. 200; *Golak Chunder Bose* v. *Raghoonath Sree Chunder Roy*, (1872) 17 W. R. C. R. 444; S. C. 11 B. L. R 337 note; *The Collector of Moorshedabad* v. *Ranee Shebessuree*, (1872) 18 W. R. P C. 221: S. C. 11 B. L. R. 86; *Mohamaya Dossee* v. *Bindoo Bashinee Dossee*, (1872) 19 W. R. C. R. 35; *Bunwaree Chand Thakoor* v *Mudden Mohan Chuttoraj*, (1873) 21 W. R. C R. 41; *Sheik Abdool Khalek* v. *Poran Bibee*, (1876) 25 W. R. C. R. 542, 546; *Ramcoomar Paul* v. *Jogendernath Paul*, (1878) I. L. R., 4 C. 56; *Ashutosh Dutt* v. *Doorgas Churn Chatterjee*, (1879) L. R. 6 I. A. 182: S. C. I. L. R., 5 C. 438; *Shookmoy Chunder Dass* v. *Monohari Dassi*, (1881) I. L. R., 7 C. 269; *Rajender Dutt* v. *Shamchund Mitter*, (1880) I. L. R., 6 C. 106; *Raghubar Dial* v. *Kesho Ramanuj Das*, (1888) I. L. R., 11 A. 18 F. B.; *Suppammal* v. *The Collector of Tanjore*, (1889) I. L. R., 12 M. 387: and *Bhuggobutty Prosonno Sen* v. *Gooroo Prosonno Sen*, (1897) I. L. R., 25 C. 1[illegible].

CHAPTER V.

CUSTOMARY RIGHT CASES.

Gift of whole land.

We shall now advert to a class of cases which we may, for convenience, style as the customary right cases and discuss the principles upon which such rights have been recognised. If the whole land is given for the religious establishment or institution, the whole constitutes a religious endowment. So also where the land is described as yielding a certain amount of income and the land so described is constituted as the religious endowment, the fact that in course of time the land yields more income and the donor has not taken this into account will not constitute the surplus income as private property. The endowment is still the entire land yielding the larger income and not simply that portion of the land yielding the income mentioned in the grant [1].

Right to do certain acts on land.

On the other hand, the land may not have been constituted as an endowment. The donor may have granted the right to enter upon his land and do certain things, as, for instance, to burn the *Holi*, to place the *tazia*, or to bury the dead. In all these cases the land is not constituted as an endowment, but the public or others interested have the right to do certain things upon the land and nothing more. Where no specific grant can be proved, but the public or others interested are using the land for a certain purpose for a long period of time though on specific occasions, or are exercising for a considerable period the right which they claim (*viz.*, of burning the *Holi* or placing the tazia, &c.), then either a lost grant may be inferred to do those things or a customary right may be said to have been established. In such cases, the right which a person has is that he may do the act and that others may not interfere with his doing the act. He can have no cause of compalint if others use the land for other purposes, provided such user does not invade or obstruct the enjoyment of his limited right. Moreover where a right is invaded, the suit must be against persons actually interfering with it; otherwise there will be no cause of action. Where, therefore, there was a ghat known as *Pushto jha* at the Ganges and there was attached to it a *Sangat* and the plaintiff, the Mahant and manager of the *Sangat*, finding that some Mahomedans came to bathe and desecrated the ghat brought a suit for injunction against a number of Mahomedans without

1. *Jagatmoni Chowdrani* v. *Ranjani Bibee*, (1884) I. L. R., 10 C. 533.

alleging that they in any way interfered with the rights of the plaintiff and the other Hindus, it was held in *Shah Muhammad* v. *Kashi Das*[1], that such a suit was not sustainable and that there could be no injunction against the whole world[1].

Long user—presumption.

Every presumption ought to be made in favor of such user. Where there has been such long continued user in assertion of a right, such right must be presumed to have had a legal origin if such a legal origin was possible, and the Courts will presume that those acts were done and those circumstances existed which were necessary to the creation of a valid title[2]. Such a right may be very reasonable and necessary[3] at the time though the reason and necessity may not be apparent now.

Grant of right of passage or of ownership in soil —Intention.

These questions arise very frequently in connection with the bathing ghats near the sacred rivers. Thus in *Jaggamoni Dasi* v. *Nilmoni Ghosal*[4], the plaintiff's father owned a site upon which he built a temple, a bathing ghat and a room called Ganga Jathri Ghar. It was customary to remove persons, when on the point of death, to this ghat for certain ceremonies being performed. The Court held that the question which had to be considered in such cases was, whether the plaintiff's father when he erected the room and the ghat intended to grant a mere right of passage over this property to the Hindu community, so that the ownership of the soil might still remain with him, or to transfer the ownership in the ghat and the soil to the said community.

Appointment of trustee—presumption.

The test for finding out such intention is to see whether a trustee or shebait has been appointed. If one had been appointed, then the reasonable presumption might be that the ownership was transferred to such trustee or shebait. But if no trustee or shebait had been appointed, then it would be reasonable to suppose that the ownership of the soil continued in the owner.[4]

---

1. (1884) I. L. R., 7 A. 199.

2. *Doe* v. *Wilson*, (1855) 10 Moo. P. C. 502 (527 and 528); *Johnson* v. *Barnes*, (1872) L. R. 7 C. P. 592: (1873) L. R., 8 C. P. 527; *Goodman* v. *Mayor of Saltash*, (1882) 7 A. C. 633 at pp. 639 and 647; *Attorney-General* v. *Horner*, (1885) 11 A. C. 66; *Phillips* v. *Halliday*, (1891) A. C. 228 at p. 231; *Simpson* v. *Mayor of Godmanchester*, (1896) 1 Ch. 214 (218); *Attorney-General* v. *Wright*, (1897) 2 K. B. 318; *Attorney-General* v. *Copeland*, (1902) 1 K. B. 690 (693); *Brocklebank* v. *Thompson*, (1903) 2 Ch. 344 at p. 350; *Clippens Oil Company* v. *Edinburgh and District Water Trustees*, (1904) A. C. 64. See also *Rameshur Pershad* v. *Koonj Behari*, (1878) L. R. 6 I. A. 33; S. C. I. L. R., 4 C. 633; *Maharani Rajroop Koer* v. *Syed Abdul Hossein*, (1880) L. R. 7 I. A. 240 (247); S. C. I. L. R., 6 C. 394; *Madhub* v. *Jogeysh*, (1902) I. L. R., 30 C. 281; *Ismail Khan Mahomed* v. *Aghore Nath Mukerjee*, (1903) 7 C. W. N. 734; *Bholanath* v. *Watson*, (1904) 8 C. W. N. 425.

3. *Jones* v. *Waters*, (1835) 40 R. R. 694; *Wilcox* v. *Steel*, (1904) 1 Ch. 212 (220).

4. (1882) I. L. R., 9 C. 75.

The right in question is not an easement[1]. Nor is it a customary easement within the meaning of S. 18 of the Easements Act for the latter section implies some right of ownership or occupation or habitation of some particular place[2]. It is a customary right or a right by custom which is preserved by S. 2 of the Easements Act[3]. The nature of the right enjoyed in such cases by the general public or a limited portion thereof in the absence of a grant is well discussed in the case of *Ashraf Ali* v. *Jagan Nath*[4]. The inhabitants of a certain village were using a plot of land in the said village for the purpose of burning the holi and celebrating the ceremonies incident thereto at the time of the Holi festival. Adjacent to this was a house which came to be owned by a Mahomedan. The latter for the first time caused a tazia to be placed on the land. The plaintiffs, the inhabitants of the village, sued for restraining the defendant from interfering with their right. The Allahabad High Court held that the plaintiff had no proprietary interest in the land, that the claim they asserted was not an easement as there was no dominant heritage for the servitude to attach, and that the right claimed was a customary right.

Nature of right—customary right.

The claim in such cases not being based on any allegation of right in the soil of the land in question or in any other soil to which the user of the ghat may be appurtenant the infringement will depend upon the nature of the right. In *Ashraf Ali* v. *Jagan Nath*[4] the High Court held that the right of the inhabitants was to burn the Holi only on certain days, that they had no right on other days, that the placing of the tazia by the defendant at other times could not interfere with plaintiff's rights, and that as it was not proved that the defendant's act desecrated the place, the plaintiffs had no cause of action.

In *Jaggamoni* v. *Nilmoni*[5] the defendant was using the ghat and room as a place for landing goods. This was held to be

1. *Kuar Sen* v. *Mamman*, (1895) I. L. R., 17 A. 87; *The Municipal Board of Cawnpore* v. *Lallu*, (1898) I. L. R., 20 A. 200; and *Mohidin* v. *Shivalingappa*, (1899) I. L. R., 23 B. 666. The opinion of Mr. Justice *Aikman* in *Mamman* v. *Kuarsen*, (1895) I. L. R., 16 A. 178, reversed in I. L. R., 17 A. 87 is not sustainable.

2. *The Municipal Board of Cawnpore* v. *Lallu*, supra.

3. *The Municipal Board of Cawnpore* v. *Lallu*, supra; and *Mohidin* v. *Shivalingappa*, supra.

4. (1884) I. L. R., 6 A. 497.

5. (1882) I. L. R., 9 C. 75.

an obstruction of the plaintiff's right on the assumption or finding that as the ownership of the soil had vested in the plaintiffs, the defendant's act would be wrongful and would constitute an interference of his right of ownership. If there was a complete dedication, then the user by the Hindu community for any other purpose than that intended by the donor was clearly not warranted, and the representative of the donor would have the undoubted right to maintain a suit which should have for its object not to resume the grant but to effectuate the grantor's intention by preserving the property for the uses for which he presumably granted it.

Dedication of highway.

Cases of dedication of highway also stand on the same footing. Thus in the case of *St. Mary Newington* v. *Jacobs*[1], it was held that the owner who dedicated a portion of his land to the public as a highway parted with no other right than a right of passage to the public, and might exercise all other rights of ownership not inconsistent with such dedication; and the appropriation made to and adopted by the public, of one part of the street to one kind of passage and another part to another, would not deprive him at common law of any rights as owner of the land not inconsistent with the right of passage by the public.

Lade v. Shephard.

The case of *Lade* v. *Shephard*[2], also proceeds on the same principle. In this case the owner of land who had built a street upon it and dedicated the street to the public, was nevertheless held entitled to maintain an action of trespass against the owner of the adjoining land who laid a bridge over a ditch, so as to rest the end on the highway.

Freehold in owner.

The principle of these decisions is that the property or the freehold of the soil in a highway remains in the owner or the representative of the dedicating owner, subject to an easement or right of passage for the benefit of the public, so that if the street or highway is used for any other purpose than the one for which it is dedicated, the owner has a right to interdict such use[3].

---

1. (1871) L. R., 7 Q. B. 47.

2. (1729) 1 Str. 1004.

3 *Dovaston* v. *Payne*, (1795) 3 R. R. 497: S. C. 2 Sm. L. C. 157; and *Harrison* v. *Duke of Rutland*, (1893) 1 Q. B. 142; *Hickman* v. *Maisey*, (1900) 1 Q. B. 752. See also Pratt on Highways, pp. 44 and 46, and Theobald's Law of Land, pp. 137 and 140.

Where the question is as to the dedication of a highway proof must be given of the owner's intention to dedicate of which the user by the public is *evidence* and no more[1]. So also where some rights of user are claimed by a community in the soil of another, such rights are upheld either upon proof of express grant or, in its absence, upon proof of the owner's intention to dedicate his land for the purposes claimed of which the user by the public or the community concerned is evidence and no more.

There seems, however, to be a distinction in English Law which may not well apply to India. Thus in *Poole* v. *Huskinson*[1] it was observed by *Parke*, B., that though there might be a dedication to the public for a limited purpose, as for a footway, horseway or driftway, there could not be a dedication to a limited part of the public (as to a parish)[2]. It is difficult, however, to appreciate the distinction or limitation suggested. It is not easy to understand why there can be no dedication to a limited part of the public. Probably the way ought not to be called a highway. But there can be no reason to suppose that when such a dedication is made the persons for whom it is intended acquire no rights altogether. On the other hand, the observations of *Heath*, J., in *Woodyer* v. *Hadden*[3], are very pertinent. He cites the following passage from Hawkins' Pleas of the Crown, Book 1 c. 76, s. 1:—"A way to a parish church, or to the common fields of a town, or to a private house, or perhaps to a village, and which terminates there and is for the benefit of the particular inhabitants of such parish, house or village only, may be called a private way, but not a highway, because it belongeth not to all the King's subjects, but only to some particular persons, and each of which, as it seems, may have an action on the case for a nuisance therein." He then says "the authorities he cites are exactly in point."

It is, however, said that it is a well settled principle of English Law that profits a prendre cannot be acquired by a fluctuating body. *A profit a prendre* is not a corporeal right, *i. e.*, not a right **Profits a prendre-Fluctuating bodies**

---

1. *Rugby Charity* v. *Merryweather*, (1790) 11 East 375*n*; S. C. 10 R. R. 528; *Rex.* v. *Lloyd*, (1808) 1 Camp. 260: S. C. 10 R. R. 674; *Poole* v. *Huskinson*, (1843) 11 M. & W. 827: S. C. 63 R. R. 702.

2. See also *Bermondsey Vestry* v. *Brown*, (1865) L. R. 1 Eq. 204; *Stafford* v. *Coyney*, (1827) 7 B. & C. 257: S. C. 31 R. R. 186; and notes to *Dovaston* v. *Payne* in 2 Sm. L. C. at p. 169.

3. (1813) 5 Taunt 125; S. C. 14 R. R., 706.

to any part of the soil but an incorporeal one. It is a right merely to enter and take some indefinite part or product of the soil. It is a right similar to an easement as it is merely a right to enter the land and do certain acts. It is distinguishable from an easement in 3 respects :—(1) *Profit a prendre* entitles a person not only to enter the land but to take something from it for his own use. An easement only entitles the dominant owner to enter his neighbour's land and make some use of it but without taking any tangible profit from the soil or prevent the neighbour from doing something on his own land. (2). A person may be entitled to a *profit a prendre* irrespectively of any estate in land so that *profits a prendre* may be had in gross. But easements can only exist in connection with and for the benefit of a dominant estate. (3) Easements and certain rights possessed by bodies of persons in gross, such as the rights of inhabitants of a place to sport or walk over land, may be claimed by custom ; *profits a prendre* cannot, except in the case of manorial customs. There are several reasons assigned for this in *Gateward's case*[1].

Rights of fluctuating bodies in India.

But the principle that profits a prendre cannot be acquired by fluctuating bodies cannot have application to the cases we are considering. The rights we are considering are not *profits a prendre*[2] but rights by custom and the principle does not apply to a custom.[3] Moreover it is doubtful whether the principle holds good in India. Rights are claimed by the whole or part of a Hindu Community[4] and from the nature of some of these rights other classes such as Mahomedans are excluded from their benefit. A fluctuating body of persons such as a village community is even capable of owning property according to Hindu Law[5]. The burning of the Holi[6] or the placing of the tazia[7] or the doing of any other act of

1. (1606), 6 Coke's Reports 59. See also *Fitch* v. *Rawling*, (1795) 3 R. R. 425 ; and *Allgood* v. *Gibson*, (1876) 34 L. T. 883.

2. *Corporation of Truro* v. *Rowe*, (1901) 2 K. B. 870 (878).

3. *Gateward's case*, (1606) 6 Co. Rep. 59*b* ; *Brocklebank* v. *Thompson*, (1903) 2 Ch. 344 (348).

4. *Jaggamoni Dasi* v. *Nilmoni Ghosal*, (1882) I. L. R., 9 C. 75.

5. Yajnawalkya, Ch. II, verses 187 and 190. In commenting upon v. 187 the author of the Mitakshara states *gana* that means *a collective body of villagers and others*. See also *Sivaraman Chetti* v. *Muthia Chetti*, (1888) L. R., 16 I. A. 48 : S. C. I. L. R., 12 M. 241 ; and *Navroji Manakji Wadia* v. *Dastur*, (1908) I. L. R., 28 B. 21 at pp. 49 and 50.

6. *Ashraf Ali* v. *Jagan Nath*, (1884) I. L. R., 6 A. 497.

7. *Mamman* v. *Kuar Sen*, (1893) I. L. R., 16 A. 178 and on appeal *Kuar Sen* v. *Mamman*, (1895) I. L. R., 17 A. 87.

religious worship[1] is necessarily personal to the members of a certain religious persuasion. Burying the dead[2] and performing certain religious services at their tombs[3] are of a similar nature.

Customs, general and public.

Customs may be public or general. A public custom is one which applies to the whole community or all the members of a state. We are not concerned with such customs. A general custom is one which is common not to all the members of a state but to a considerable class of persons. The rights we are considering are only common to the members of a particular religious persuasion.

Proof of customs.

The most cogent evidence of custom is not that which is afforded by the expression of opinion of competent persons as to their existence but by the enumeration of instances in which the alleged custom has been acted upon and by the proof afforded by judicial or revenue records[4]. What the law requires before an alleged custom can receive the recognition of the Court is satisfactory proof of usage so long and invariably acted upon in practice as to show that it has, by common consent, been submitted to as an established governing rule of the particular family, class, district or country[5]. The nature of the evidence will depend upon the kind and nature of custom set up. As regards local customs they must be proved by reliable evidence of such repeated acts openly done, which have been assented and submitted to, as leads to the conclusion that the usage has, by agreement or otherwise, become the local law of the place in respect of the person or things which it concerns[6]. No fixed period of enjoyment is necessary to prove a valid customary right[7]. From modern usage for a series of years an immemorial existence of the right ought to be presumed[8].

---

1. *Dhunput Singh* v. *Paresh Nath*, (1893) I. L. R., 21 C. 180; *Baiju Lal Parbatia* v. *Bulak Lal*, (1897) I. L. R., 24 C. 385; *The Municipal Board of Cawnpore* v. *Lallu*, (1898) I. L. R., 20 A 2:0; *Dino Nath Chuckerbutty* v. *Pratap Chandra Goswami*, (1899) I. L. R.. 27 C. 30
2. *Mohidin* v. *Shivlingappa*, (1899) I. L. R., 23 B. 666.
3. *Ramrao* v. *Rustumkhan*, (1901) I. L. R., 26 B. 198 (200).
4. *Lachman Rai* v. *Akbar Khan*, (1877) I. L. R., 1 A. 440.
5. *Sivananja Perumal Sethurayar* v. *Muttu Ramalinga*, (1866) 3 M. H. C. 75 (77).
6. *Mohidin* v. *Shivlingappa*, (1899) I. L. R., 23 B. 666. See also *Tekaet Doorga Pershad* v. *Tekaetnee Doorga Kooeree*, (1873) 20 W. R. C. R. 154.
7. *Narasayya* v. *Sami*, (1888) I. L. R., 12 M. 43; *Palaniandi Tevan* v. *Puthirangonda Nadan*, (1897) I. L. R., 20 M. 389; *Bealey* v. *Shaw*, (1805) 6 East 208: S. C. 8 R. R. 466: *Rex* v. *Joliffe*, (1823) 2 B. & C 54|: S. C. 26 R. R. 264; *Brocklebank* v. *Thompson*, (1903) 2 Ch. 344 (350). In these cases 20 years' user was held sufficient.
8. *Jenkins* v. *Harvey*, (1835) 40 R. R. 769; *Earl de la Warr* v. *Miles*, (1881) 17 Ch. D. 535; *Brocklebank* v. *Thompson*, (1903) 2 Ch. 241. See also cases cited in p. liv note (2).

Certainty in custom.

Customs to have the effect of excluding or limiting the operation of general rules of law must be certain[1] and reasonable. As regards the requisite of certainty, the circumstances of each case must be looked to and courts must not be too easily led to hold that a custom is bad because the parties have failed in their pleadings to define i with accuracy. As observed by *Cleasby*, B., in *Hall* v. *Nottingham*[2]: "Looking to the nature and origin of such customs, it would be unreasonable to expect any precise certainty as to what should be enjoyed as a matter of right. If at the present time the inhabitants all meet to discuss and determine such a matter, it would be unreasonable to expect them to be very precise as to the enjoyment which they were to have."

Reasonableness in custom.

As regards reasonableness, a custom may be good though no reason for its origin can be assigned. It may be good though it is contrary to any rule of the common law. The test of reasonableness must be according to the Hindu or Mahomedan standard[3] as the case may be. A custom may also be good though its exercise may have the effect of depriving the owner of the soil of the whole use and enjoyment of his property. For instance a right to bury the dead in another man's land may be good and the mere possibility that after many years the number of tombs may increase to such an extent as to deprive the owner of the use of his field is too remote to describe the custom (*viz.*, burying the dead near a durga) as unreasonable[4]. In *Mohidin* v. *Shirlingappa*[4] where the validity of this custom was in question the Bombay High Court observed: "Amongst all races that bury their dead, this right of burial in a particular locality is one that is most clearly prized, and although the plaintiff's land may be rendered

1. They must be invariable and established by clear and unambiguous evidence. *Ramalakshmi Ammal* v. *Sivanantha Perumal Sethurayar*, (1872) 14 M. I. A. 570: S. C. 12 B. L. R., 396.

2. (1875) 1 Ex. D. 1 approved in *Mohidin* v. *Shivlingappa*, (1899) I. L. R., 23 B 666.

3. *Kamalam* v. *Sadagopa Sami*, (1878) I. L. R., 1 M 356; *Venku* v. *Mahalinga*, (1888) I. L. R., 11 M. 393; *Tara Naikin* v. *Nana Lakshman*, (1889) I. L. R., 14 B 90; But see *Chinna Ummayi* v. *Tegarai Chetti*, (1876) I. L. R., 1 M. 168; *Mathura* v. *Esu*, (1880) I. L. R., 4 B. 545; *Ghasite* v. *Umrao Jan*, (1893) I. L. R.. 20 I. A. 193. But it must not be immoral or contrary to public policy.

4. *Mohidin* v. *Shivlingappa*, (1899) I. L R., 23 B. 666. See also *Corporation of Truro* v. *Rowe*, (1901) 2 K. B. 870.

practically useless, if these tombs are multiplied exceedingly, the contingency seems too distant to justify the courts in summarily putting an end to the right............If a custom which allows all lawful games to be played on another person's land at all times of the year is not an unreasonable custom[1], it seems impossible to hold that the limited custom established by these defendants is bad." The right not being a *profit a prendre* the principle that no right to a profit can be acquired which has the effect of depriving the owner of the soil of the whole use and enjoyment of his property has no application[2].

Requisites of custom.

It will be too much common place to discuss the several requisites of a valid custom and the cases dealing with the matter. It is enough to say that in all cases of this class where a custom excluding the operation of a general rule (*viz.*, that the proprietor or other person lawfully in possession whose rights are not controlled by statute law, grant, or contract, has an exclusive right to the use of his land for all purposes) is alleged, it is necessary that those setting up such a custom, should be put to strict proof thereof, and a court cannot decide that it exists unless such court is satisfied of its reasonableness, its certainty as to its extent and application, and is further satisfied that the enjoyment of the right has not been by leave granted or by stealth or force, and that it has been openly enjoyed for such a length of time as to suggest that, the usage has, by agreement or otherwise, become a customary law of the place[3].

Analogy of English cases.

The nature of these customary rights is often compared to a class of customary rights noted in the English cases of which *Mounsey* v. *Ismay*[4] is the leading instance. Such rights were held not to be easements within the meaning of the English Prescription Act (Lord Tenderden's Act, 2 & 3 Will. IV. C. 71, S. 2.) In the report of that case in 32 L. J. 94 it was held that a

---

1. *Hall v. Nottingham*, (1875) 1 Ex. D. 1.

2. *Lord Rivers v. Adams*, (1878) 3 Ex. D. 361; *Corporation of Truro v. Rowe*, (1901) 2 K. B. 810. See Clerk and Lindsell 284 and S. 18 of the Easements Act.

3. *Kuar Sen v. Mamman*, (1895) I. L. R., 17 A. 87. See also *Sivananja Perumal v. Muttu Ramalinga*, (1866) 3 M. H. C. 75 (77)

4. (1863) 32 L. J. (Ex. N. S.) 94; (1865) 34 L. J. (Ex. N. S.) 52.

custom for all the freemen and citizens of a neighbouring city (Carlisle) to hold horse races over the close of the plaintiff (Mounsey) in the hamlet of Kingsmoor on Ascension day every year was good, and that in pleading the custom which was claimed for a day certain, it was not necessary to allege that the day was a reasonable day. In the report of the same case in 34 L. J. 52, it was held that such a right was not an easement within the meaning of the Prescription Act. The Court observed: "To bring the right within the term 'easement' in the 2nd section, it must be one analogous to that of a right of way which precedes it and a right of water-course which follows it, and must be a right of utility and benefit and not one of mere recreation and amusement. It was never within the contemplation of Lord Tenderten to include within the Act such customary rights as entering land to enjoy rural sports as in *Millichamp* v. *Johnson*[1], or to dance upon a green as in *Abbot* v. *Weekly*[2], by analogy to which we held this alleged customary right to run horse races a lawful one at common law[3]. What we think he contemplated were incorporeal rights incident and annexed to property for its more beneficial and profitable enjoyment, and not customs for mere pleasure."

Customary rights in India.

The above principle does not cover all the customary rights upheld in the Indian Courts, for in many cases customary rights are enjoyed by people in respect of their religious avocations. The right to place the *tazia* in the case of Mahomedans or the right to bathe in the bathing ghats of the sacred rivers or even to burn the *holi* is not a custom for mere pleasure. But as already observed, there can be no doubt that all such customs are valid and are not within the scope of the Easements Act, there being no dominant heritage for the servitude to attach.

Claim of person interested to exclude.

In the case of customary rights in which several persons as belonging to a class (sect) or community are interested, it has been held that it is not competent for a single person to assert an exclusive right, *i. e.*, a right as against the rest of the public or community. Thus in the case of *The Municipal Board of Cawnpore* v. *Lallu*[4], the two plaintiffs, Gangaputras, sued for a declaration of their exclusive right to sit whenever they pleased at their old cus-

1. Willes 206 *n*.
2. (1677) 1 Levins 176.
3. (1863) 32 L. J. (Ex. N. S.) 94.
4. I. L. R., (1898) 20 A. 300.

tomary seats at certain spots at the Sarsayya Ghat on the bank of the Ganges in Cawnpore and to attend to their Jajmans at the time of bathing and other religious ceremonies and to receive their dues and presents &c , as usual. Their complaint was that the Municipality was arranging seats to be occupied by the Gangaputras at such places as the Municipality thought proper and that this was an illegal interference of their right. The Allahabad High Court held that though there had been at some remote time a dedication of the ghat to the use of pilgrims desiring to perform their spiritual ablutions in the sacred river and, for the proper performance of those ablutions, the services of Gangaputras would be required, yet the latter could not assert an exclusive right or a right as against the public and that, unless the Gangaputras could show a right to the soil of the ghat or any portion thereof, they could not in law maintain a claim to the exclusive use of the ghat for the purpose of collecting alms or fees to the exclusion of other persons.

Ownership of soil.

In order that such exclusive right may be established, it is held in some of the cases that the plaintiff asserting such exclusive right must allege some right to the soil of the ghat or any portion thereof[1]. The principle seems to be, as in cases of dedication, that the mere use or enjoyment of a right in common with others will not be an adverse user by the one as against the others[2].

User, evidence of prior dedication—conditions annexed.

But it is not easy to see why a right in the soil or ghat should be shewn to establish such exclusive right. That may no doubt be one instance in which an exclusive right may be set up. It may also be that one of a number of persons cannot gain by prescription an adverse title by mere user as against the rest of the community. But user in the way indicated may be proper evidence of a prior dedication, *i. e.*, that at the time when the dedication was made to the public or to the class, the person dedicating clothed a certain person with a higher right and there can

1. See *Husain Ali* v. *Matukman*, I. L. R., (1883) 6 A. 39 ; and *The Municipal Board of Cawnpore* v. *Lallu*, (1898) I. L. R., 20 A. 200.

2. *Reg. v. Johnson*, (1859) 1 F. & F. 657 ; *Turner* v. *Ringwood Highway Board*, (1870) L. R. 9 Eq. 418.

be no doubt that the person dedicating is competent to annex any conditions at the time of dedication[1].

Test as to contributions being voluntary or otherwise.

In the case of certain customary payments to a temple it must be remembered that persons accustomed to worship in the temple will ordinarily continue a payment as an act of piety and, therefore, *prima facie* such contributions are voluntary. The question in all such cases is whether a legal origin is to be assigned to the claim on behalf of the temple or institution or whether the payment is merely voluntary. If the payment is voluntary, the mere fact that the payments have been made for a long series of years does not convert the voluntary nature of the payment into one of legal obligation[2]. A legal obligation to pay dues of this nature, as a customary payment to Mariamman temple in a village on occasions of marriage will probably be held to exist in a case in which the evidence shows presumably that it has been customarily contributed from time immemorial by the community residing within a village for the enjoyment of the benefits attached to the right of worshipping in the temple and attendance at its ceremonials and the services rendered to them by the managers and other officers of the temple. In such a case there will be a consideration of advantage to which to ascribe the origin and continuance of the custom, sufficient probably to make it valid and binding[3].

Judgments relevant.

In all such cases judgments obtained by trustees &c, against others affirming the right will be relevant under S. 13 as being evidence of instances in which the right claimed has been asserted or under S. 42 of the Evidence Act as relating to matters of a public nature.

---

1. *Morant* v. *Chamberlain*, (1861) 6 H. & N. 541; *Fisher* v. *Prowse* (1862) 2 B. & S. 770; *Mercer* v. *Woodgate*, (1869) L. R. 5 Q. B. 26; *Gossamee Sree Greedhareejee* v. *Romanloljee Gossamee*, (1889) I. R. 17 I. A. 137: S. C. I. L. R., 17 C. 3. An exclusive right of fishery in the fishermen of a particular village in derogation of the public right of fishery in a public river has been recognised. See *Viresa* v. *Tatayya*, (1885) I. L. R., 8 M. 467; and *Narasayya* v. *Sami*, (1888) I. L. R., 12 M. 43.

2. *Ramasami* v. *Apparu*, (1887) I. L. R., 12 M. 9. See also Chapter III, p. xxxi.

3. *Maadan* v. *Erlandi*, (1870) 5 M. H. C. R. 471.

CHAPTER VI.

PUBLIC AND PRIVATE RELIGIOUS ENDOWMENTS.

Having considered the nature and kinds of dedication, we next advert to a distinction which obtains in Indian Law between public and private religious endowments. It is difficult to lay down general principles from the application of which it may be said whether in any given case an endowment or trust is public or private. It is useful to refer to the English Law where also the difference between public and private trusts is to be found though the incidents respectively attaching to them under the two systems are very dissimilar.

Trusts public and private.

"Public trusts" are stated in the Century Dictionary (Title, 'Public') to be trusts "constituted for the benefit either of the public at large or of some considerable part of it answering to a particular description," while "Private trusts" are stated to be (see Century Dictionary, Title, 'Private') "those trusts wherein the beneficial interest is vested absolutely in one or more individuals who are or within a certain time may be definitely ascertained, and to whom, therefore, collectively, unless under some legal disability, it is competent to control, modify or determine the trust[1]." In Perry on Trusts[2] it is stated: "Again trusts are either public or private. Private trusts concern only individuals or families, for private convenience and support. Public trusts are for public charities or for the general public good. They concern the general and indefinite public." Mr. Lewin on this division of trusts into *public* and *private* observes[3]: "Another division of trusts is into public and private. By *public* must be understood such as are constituted for the benefit either of the public at large or of some considerable portion of it answering a particular description. To this class belong all trusts for charitable purposes, and indeed public trusts and charitable trusts may be considered in general as synonymous expressions. In private trusts the beneficial interest is vested absolutely in one or more individuals who are, or within a certain time may be, definitely ascertained, and to whom, therefore, collectively, unless under some legal disability, it is, or within

1. See Bispham, Principles of Equity, para 58.
2. Para 22.
3. Lewin on Trusts, p. 18

the allowed time will be, competent to control, modify, or determine the trust. The duration of trusts of this kind cannot be extended by the will of the settlor beyond the bounds of legal limitations, *viz.*, a life or lives in being with an engraftment of 21 years. A public or charitable trust on the other hand, has, for its objects, the members of an uncertain and fluctuating body, and the trust itself is of a permanent and indefinite character and is not confined within the limits prescribed to a settlement upon a private trust[1]."

Evan v. The Corporation of Avon.

In *Evan* v. *The Corporation of Avon*[2], *Lord Romilly* observed: —"A trust may be of two characters: it may be of a *general* character or of a *private* and individual character. A person might leave a sum of money to a corporation in trust to support the children of A. B. and pay them the principal at 21. That would be a private and particular trust which the children could enforce against the corporation, if the corporation applied the property to its own benefit. On the other hand, a person might leave money to a corporation in trust for the benefit of the inhabitants of a particular place or for paving or lighting the town. That would be a public trust for the benefit of all the inhabitants and the proper form of a suit, in the event of any breach of trust, would be an *information* by the Attorney-General at the instance of all or some of the persons interested in the matter. If there was a particular trust in favor of particular persons, and they were too numerous for all to be made parties, one or two might then sue, on behalf of themselves, and the other *cestuis que trustent* for the performance of the trust."

Public and charitable trusts synonymous

Public and charitable trusts are synonymous in English Law as, according to the English decisions, every public trust is a charitable trust[3]. We shall have, therefore, to consider the tests of a charity.

Charity, meaning of.

Before considering these tests, it may be observed at the outset, that the term 'charity' has a technical meaning in the English.

---

1. Vide *Christ's Hospital* v. *Grainger*, (1849) 1 M. & G. 460; *Stewart* v. *Green*. 5 I. R., Eq. 470; *In Re Tyler*, (1891) 3 Ch. 252 (C. A.); and *In Re Bowen*, (1893) 2 Ch. 491.

2. (1860) 29 Beav. 144 at p. 149.

3. *Jones* v. *Williams*, (1767) Amb. 651: S. C. 27 Eng. Rep. 422; *Attorney-General* v. *Aspinall*, (1837) 2 My. & Cr. 623: S. C. 45 R. R. 142 (149); Per *Earl Cairns* in *Goodman* v. *Mayor of Saltash*, (1882) 7 A. C. 633 (650); and *Re Christ Church Inclosure Act*, (1888) 38 Ch. D. 532.

In a general sense it means good-will or the good affections which men ought to feel towards one another (see Century Dictionary, Title, Charity). But this is not the sense in which the word is understood in English Law. Thus *Grant*, M. R., observed in *Morice* v. *Bishop of Durham*[1]: "That word (charity) in its widest sense denotes all the good affections men ought to bear towards each other; in its most restricted and common sense, relief of the poor. In neither of these senses is it employed in this court. Here its signification is chiefly derived from the Statute of Elizabeth (43 Eliz. Ch. 4, now repealed[2]). Those purposes are charitable which the Statute enumerates, or which by analogies are deemed within its spirit or intendment; and to some such purpose every bequest to charity generally shall be applied." In this technical sense charity is defined as a gift to a general public use which extends to the poor as well as to the rich[3] though there can be no objection to a charity being confined to a particular class as shall be pointed out hereafter.

Purposes within the purview of the statute of Elizabeth.

Several purposes are mentioned by the Statute of Elizabeth as charitable; but gifts for the advancement of religion are not mentioned in the Statute. The reason for this is stated in Perry on Trusts to be that it was intended to avoid confiscations in case the Reformation went backwards. But be this as it may, such gifts have been held by analogy to be charitable within the equity of the Statute[4]. Thus Tudor in his book on Charitable Trusts mentions that "bequests for the good[5], the reparation, furniture or ornaments[6] of a parish church or for building and endowing a church[7] or for keeping in repair a chancel or a window or a

1. (1804-5) 9 Ves. 405: S. C. 7 R. R. 232. See Act VI of 1890 and *The University of Bombay* v. *The Municipal Commissioner for the City of Bombay*, (1891) I. L. R., 16 B. 217.

2. See, The Mortmain Charitable Uses Act 1888 (51 and 52 Vict. Ch. 42).

3. *Jones* v. *Williams*, (1767) Amb. 651: S. C. 27 Eng. Rep. 422; *Attorney-General* v. *Heelis*, (1824) 2 S. & S. 67: S. C. 25 R. R. 158; *British Museum* v. *White*, (1826) 2 S. & S. 594: S. C. 25 R. R. 270.

4. Tudor on Charitable Trusts, p. 6; and Perry on Trusts, Vol. II, paras 701 and 708.

5. *Wingfield's Case*, Duke 80.

6. *Attorney-General* v. *Ruper*, (1722) 2 P. Wms. 125: S. C. 24 Eng. Rep. 667; *Attorney-General* v. *Vivian*, (1826) 1 Russ. 226; *Attorney-General* v. *Love*, (1856) 23 Beav. 499; and *Re Palatine Estate Charity*, (1888) 39 Ch. D. 54.

7. *Re Parker*, (1859) 4 H. & N. 666.

monument in a church[1] or any part of the fabric of a church are charitable."

Four objects of Charity.

Though it is true that the term 'charity' or 'charitable purpose' technically and in the eye of a Court of Equity has a meaning so extensive as to include everything which is expressly described in the Statute of Elizabeth or is within what has been called the equity of the statute, there is perhaps not one person in a thousand who knows what the technical and the legal meaning of the term 'charity'[2] is. There were four objects of charity stated by *Sir Samuel Romilly* in his argument as counsel in *Morice* v. *Bishop of Durham*[3]: (1) relief of poor, (2) advancement of learning, (3) advancement of religion and (4) advancement of objects of general public utility. This was adopted by *Lord Macnaghten* with a slight qualification as to the fourth in *Commissioners for the Special Purposes of Income-tax* v. *Pemsel*[4]. This division, however, has really no practical value in deciding whether a gift is charitable or otherwise[5].

Religious uses.

Religious uses or purposes are uses or trusts for the propagation of religion, of religious institutions or the performance of religious rites. All religious uses are charitable uses, *i. e.*, such uses as will sustain a gift or bequest as a charity[6]. A bequest of property "to the following religious societies" (but which were not named) was held to be a valid bequest for charity[6] though there might exist religious societies which were not charitable[7]. A *religious* or *pious* use must be distinguished in English Law from a *superstitious* use. Superstitious uses were such religious uses as were condemned by the English Law at or after the Reformation as maintaining superstition in which were included the providing of masses for the dead. There is, however, no statute making gifts for superstitious uses void generally. The statute of Edward VI applied only to certain superstitious gifts (*i. e.*, gifts to superstitious

Superstitious uses.

1. Per *Kindersley*, V-C. in *Hoare* v. *Osborne*, (1866) L. R. 1 Eq. 585 (588).
2. *Dolan* v. *Macdermot*, (1868) L. R., 3 Ch. App. 676, (678). See also Per *Lindley*, L. J. in *Macduff* v. *Macduff*, (1896) 2 Ch. 451 (464).
3. (1804-5) 9 Ves. 405: S. C. 7 R. R. 232.
4. [1891] A. C., 531 (583).
5. Per *Lindley*, L. J. in *Macduff* v. *Macduff*, (1896) 2 Ch. 451 (466).
6. Per *Lindley*, L. J. in *In Re White—White* v. *White*, (1893) 2 Ch. 41 (52).
7. *Cocks* v. *Manners*, (1871) L. R. 12 Eq. 574.

uses then existing or created before the statute)[1]. A bequest to Roman Catholic priests and chapels by a testatrix that she might have the benefit of their prayers and masses was held to be void[1]. In construing a will, it must always be remembered that the court must not lean on the side of avoiding the will in order to gain money for the family, nor, on the other hand, strain to support the will to gain money for the charity[2]. But this rule, however, does not enable us to ascertain the distinction between public and private trusts.

Extensiveness of a charity.

With reference to the tests of a charity, it may first be observed that it is the extensiveness which will constitute a charity a public one and it has been observed that "the Charter of the Crown cannot make a charity more or less public, but only more permanent than it would otherwise be[3]." In the case in which these remarks were made[3] it was held that a devise to the poor of a parish was a public charity and *Lord Hardwicke*, Chancellor, observed : "I am rather of opinion that the word public was meant only by way of description of the nature of them, and not by way of distinguishing one charity from another, for it would be almost impossible to say which are public and which are private in their nature."

A sum to be disposed of by a testator's executors at their discretion among poor house-keepers falls under the category of public charity. For, as observed by Lord Chancellor *Hardwicke* in *Attorney-General* v. *Pearce*[3] : "Where testators have not any particular person in their contemplation, but leave it to the discretion of a trustee to choose out the objects, though such person is private, and each particular object may be said to be private, yet in the extensiveness of the benefit accruing from them they may very properly be called public charities.'

Purposes of institution.

In ascertaining whether an institution is a public charity we ought to consider the general character or in other words the

1. *West* v. *Shuttleworth*, (1835) 2 Myl. & K. 684 : S. C. 39 R. R. 327.

2. Per *Lord Selborne*, L. C. in *Goodman* v. *Mayor of Saltash*, (1882) 7 A. C. 633 (642).

3. *Attorney-General* v. *Pearce*, (1740) 2 Atk. 87 (88).

constitution of the institution and the purposes for which it is constituted. The purposes are the main questions to be considered[1].

Particular or limited class-Number of objects no test.

There may be a public charity the purposes of which are confined to a particular class. The question whether the charity is 'public' does not necessarily depend on its being universal for a charity is not deprived of its public character merely because its objects are confined to a particular class[2]. So also a bequest is not the less a (public) charitable bequest from the fact that it is given for the benefit of a limited class of persons or is not confined to a class at large but is only confined to some of the members of a particular class who are subject to grievances[3]. The principle is that it is not the number of objects which make the distinction between a public and a private charity[3]. In the case in which the above principles were held[3] the charitable bequest was contained in the following words of the testatrix: "I direct my executors to pay unto Messrs. Drummonds, bankers......... a clear yearly sum of £100, for the sole use and benefit of the ministers and members of the Churches now forming upon the apostolical doctrines brought forward originally by the late *Edward Irving*, who may be persecuted, aggrieved, or in poverty for preaching or upholding those doctrines, or half the sum may be appropriated for the benefit of the church founded by the late *Edward Irving* in Newman Street." Vice-Chancellor *Shadwell* held that the bequest was a good charitable bequest and was not a private trust and that the alternative nature of the bequest did not vitiate it[3]. There are public charities the purposes of which are confined to a particular class, as for instance, the institutions for the deaf, dumb and blind. Thus it was held in *Hall* v. *Derby Sanitary Authority*[4] that an orphanage

1. *Attorney-General* v. *Brown*, (1818) 1 Swans 265 (307 and 308); *Attorney-General* v. *Dublin*, (1827) 1 Blis. N. S. 312: S. C. 30 R. R. 43; *Attorney-General* v. *Eastlake*, (1853) 11 Hare 221; *Governors of Charity* v. *Sutton*, (1860) 27 Beav. 651; Per *Manisty*, J. in *Hall* v. *Derby Sanitary Authority*, (1885) 16 Q. B. D. 163 (171); *In re St. Botolph Without Bishopsgate Parish Estates*, (1887) 35 Ch. D. 142 (150); *In re Christ Church Enclosure Act*, (1888) 38 Ch. D. 520.

2. *Governors of Charity* v. *Sutton*, (1860) 27 Beav. 651; Per *Manisty*, J. in *Hall* v. *Derby Sanitary Authority*, (1885) 16 Q. B. D. 163 (171); and *In Re Christ Church Enclosure Act*, (1888) 38 Ch. Div. 520.

3. Per *Shadwell*, V. C. in *Attorney-General* v. *Lawes*, (1849) 8 Hare 32 (41).

4. (1885) 16 Q. B. D. 163. See also *In Re Wall*, (1889) 42 Ch. D. 310, where it was held that a gift to aged persons who might be Unitarians and attendants at a certain chapel was held to be a charitable gift; and *Administrator-General of Madras* v. *Money*, (1892) I. L. R., 15 M. 448.

founded and used for the purpose of boarding, lodging, clothing and educating the children of deceased servants was a "public charity" being open to an extensive class of Her Majesty's subjects (the Railway servants all over England) and that, therefore, it was exempt from rateability under the Local Improvement Act (6 Geo. iv C. 132, S. 103).

A gift subject to a condition or trust for the benefit of the inhabitants of a parish or town or of any particular class of such inhabitants, is a charitable trust[1] (*i. e.*, a public charity). In fact charity is generally understood and used in English decisions as a public charity[2], and as already observed every public purpose is a charitable purpose though, at the same time, it may be observed that there is no uniformity in the use. In *Dolan* v. *Macdermont*[3] where it was held that a bequest of personalty "for such charities" and other public purposes as lawfully might be in the parish of Tadmarton was a good charitable gift, *Cairns*, L. C. observed[3]: "It would be shutting our eyes deliberately to the plain and simple meaning of words if the court were to construe the words in the will otherwise than as a gift to trustees of money to be laid out in such charities and other public purposes as they think fit *for the benefit of the parish of Tadmarton*; for, I take it that a gift to trustees to be laid out in charities in the parish of A is a gift to trustees to be laid out in charities for the benefit of the parish of A * * It is clear that this testator when he used the word 'charities' did not point to private charities, because he accompanies the terms with the words 'and other public purposes' evidently implying that the word first used meant public charities."

Trust for residents of a parish or town.

It may, however, be observed that the mere fact of a gift to a Municipal Corporation will not of itself make the gift to be one for a public charitable purpose. Thus in *In the matter of Oxford Charities*[4], it was held that property appropriated by a Municipal corporation for the maintenance of lecturers to preach before the

1. Per *Lord Selborne*, L. C. in *Goodman* v. *Mayor of Saltash*, (1882) 7 A. C. 633 (642). See *Attorney-General* v. *Comber*, (1824) 2 S. & S. 93: S. C. 25 R. R. 163, where it was held that a bequest to the widows and orphans of a particular parish was a good charitable bequest.

2. See cases cited in note (2) lxvi; and *White*, v. *White* (1893) 2 Ch 41.

3. (1868) L. R. 3 Ch. App. 676.

4. (1837) 3 My. & Cr. 239: S. C. 45 R. R. 259.

corporation was not property held by the corporation upon a charitable bequest within the meaning of S. 71 of Act 5 & 6 Will, 4 C. 76. The ground of the decision was that there was no provision that the sermons should be preached in any particular church, that the corporation might say that the sermons should be preached to themselves with closed doors and that the trust was, therefore, exclusively for the benefit of the corporation.

In a case in 3 *Atkins*[1] there was a voluntary society entered into with the intention of providing by a weekly subscription for such of the members as should become necessitous and their widows and it was held by *Lord Hardwicke* that it was only a private charity. In *Cunnack* v. *Edwards*[2] it was held by *Chitty*, J., that a society whose object was to raise a fund by the subscriptions, &c., of its members to provide annuities for the widows (whether rich or poor) of its respective members is not a charitable gift. In *Ommaney* v. *Butcher*[3] however, it was held, that a bequest of personalty for "private charity" was altogether bad. The Court held that private charity was an object too indefinite to give the Crown jurisdiction or to enable the court to execute the trust. The next of kin were held entitled to take.

Right of control.

Apparently the test observed in the above cases was to see whether any person had the right of control over the fund and to direct it in the way he liked.

Failure of objects.

It is no objection to a charity being public that the objects of a testator's or donor's bounty may at some time fail or are certain to fail in the near future. For, where a charitable bequest is once established, Courts of Chancery have jurisdiction to administer the fund *cypres* if the objects happen to fail and will not permit it afterwards to drop for want of objects[4].

---

1. *Anon*, (1745) 3 Atk. 276.

2. (1895) 1 Ch. 489 affirmed by the Court of Appeal upon this point in *Cunnack* v. *Edwards*, (1896) 2 Ch. 679. See, however, *Bruty* v. *Mackey*, (1896) 2 Ch. 727, where *Kekewich*, J. held that a friendly society established to provide by subscriptions, contributions, &c., which were invested for relief of members, their widows &c., if in distressed circumstances, is a charitable society.

3. (1823) Tur. & Russ. 260: S. C. 24 R. R. 42.

4. *Attorney-General* v. *Lawes*, (1849) 8 Hare 32 (41).

The test of a public charity is not the source from which the income is derived[1]. In *Attorney-General* v. *Heelis*[2], however, it was held by *Sir John Leach*, V. C., that the test of public charity was the source from which the funds were derived and not the mere purposes to which they were dedicated. This would seem to have been also the view of *Smith*, J., in *Hall* v. *Derby Sanitary Authority*[3]. But this view can scarcely be maintained at the present day[4]. So that a charity maintained by voluntary subscriptions or contributions from the public would be a public charity. In India in the case of public religious institutions, voluntary contributions are usually made[5] but this will not be a decisive or conclusive test[6].

Source of income no test.

The mere fact that permission to worship in a church or chapel was subject to good behaviour does not make the chapel a private one. Good conduct is a condition imposed on all votaries in every place of worship[7]. If a certain person is entitled to exclude any person at any time during the celebration of divine worship and to charge for admission or if a person is entitled to close it at any time owing to want of funds or other reason, then the chapel is either proprietary[8] or private. So that in the case of public temples or churches the trustee or manager cannot close the same; nor can he make a rule that worshippers shall only be admitted upon payment of certain fees. The right of entrance into a public temple or church is a free right. So that a rule as to admission upon payment will be illegal and not binding upon the

Good conduct condition.

---

1. See cases cited in note (2) p. lxx.
2. (1824) 2 S. & S. 67 (77): S. C. 25 R. R. 153.
3. (1885) 16 Q. B. D. 163.
4. *Attorney-General* v. *Brown*, (1818) 1 Swans 265 (307 and 308); *Attorney-General* v. *Dublin*, (1827) 1 Blis. N. S. 312: S. C. 30 R. R. 43; *Attorney-General* v. *Eastlake*, (1853) 11 Hare 221; Per *Manisty* J. in *Hall* v. *Derby Sanitary Authority*, (1885) 16 Q. B. D. 163 (171); *In re St. Botolph Without Bishopsgate Parish Estates*, (1887) 35 Ch. D. 142 (150).
5. Per *Subramania Iyer*, J., in *Elayalwar Reddiar* v. *Numberumal Chettiar*, (1899) I. L R., 23 M 298 (303). See also W. & B. Dig. of Hindu Law (3rd Edn.) 201. Such contributions include not only annual subscriptions but donations. *Governors of Charity* v. *Sutton*, (1866) 27 Beav. 651.
6. Per *Kekewich*, J., in *Bruty* v. *Mackey*, (1896) 2 Ch. 727 (733).
7. Per *Scott*, J., in *Thakersey Dewraj* v. *Hurbhum Nursey*, (1843) I. L. R., 8 B. 432 (459).
8. *Bosanquet* v. *Heath*, (1860) 9 W. R. 35.

worshippers. But this will not prevent the trustee from making rules for good order and decency of worship and for preventing over-crowding[1].

Distinction between public and private endowments important in India.

This distinction between public and private religious endowments is more important in India. For instance, if an endowment is only private and not public, the Religious Endowments Act will have no application[2]. It is, therefore, useful to turn to the Indian cases on the point.

Delroos Banoo Begum v. Ashgur Ally.

In *Delroos Banoo Begum* v. *Nawab Syed Ashgur Ally Khan*[3], a *public* endowment for *religious uses* was defined as "one which distributes its benefits to *all men* of *all classes* professing a *defined form* of religion : a similar endowment for pious and charitable purposes generally would include all members of a community who chose to avail themselves of the means afforded to them by the appropriator ; every one would have an equal right to participate, and that, at all times and at all seasons." In this case one Banoo Begum executed a waqfnama and under the terms of that deed a large part of the income was to be spent on certain ceremonies according to family usage such as fatiahas of Mahomed and the twelve Imams, expenses of the *first* ten days of the Mohurram, and repairs of an imambara and of certain tombs (her mother's tomb being one). The Begum was never interfered with by Government under the Bengal Regulation. The suit was to remove the Begum from her muttawalliship after leave obtained under section 18 of the Pagoda Act. It was contended, among others, that the Act of 1863 had no application and that the Begum did not intend to constitute a present waqf. The High Court held that Act XX of 1863 did not apply to the case as the endowment by the Begum was not for any public purpose and that the said Act only applied to cases of endowments to which the old Regulations were applicable.

---

1. *Kalidas Jivram* v. *Gorparjaram Hirji*, (1890) I. L. R., 15 B. 309.

2. *Delroos Banoo Begum* v. *Nawab Syed Ashgur Ally Khan*, (1875) 23 W. R. 453 ; S. C. 15 B. L. R. 167 affirmed by P. C. in I. L. R., 3 C. 324 ; *Sathapayyar* v. *Periasawmi*, (1891) I. L. R., 14 M. 1 ; *Protap Chandra Misser* v. *Brojanath Misser*, (1891) I. L. R., 19 C 275. See further notes to Ss. 1 and 14.

3. (1875) 15 B. L. R. 167 ; S. C. 23 W. R. C. R 453.

Now, under S 15 of the Regulations which referred to the classes of cases to which the Regulations were applicable, the question that had to be considered was whether the appropriation of lands was for public purposes. Upon this question *Glover*, J. observed in *Delroos Banoo Begum* v. *Ashgur Ally*[1]: "It seems to me that there is nothing in the tauliatnama that contemplates an appropriation for the general benefit, whilst the defendant's object in making it is further explained in her deposition. It was to perpetuate certain ceremonies in commemoration of her mother's death according to the custom of the family (which was of the Shiah sect). * * The prayers, &c., to be recited were not to be made in any mosque or regular place of worship but in the *defendant's own imambara* (a dwelling admittedly within the precincts of her dwelling house), and the expenses of the first ten days of the Mohurram were matters of an *essentially private* character. Mahomedans of both sects are in the habit of performing these ceremonies according to their means......... but these ceremonies are personal matters only, and the general public have no right to take part in them. An imambara, moreover, is not a public place of worship as is a mosque or temple, but an apartment in a private house set apart, no doubt, for certain Mahomedan ceremonies, but no more open to the general public than a private oratory in England would be. As a matter of fact, strangers are ordinarily excluded from these celebrations. Doles of a particular kind of provision are no doubt distributed at this time to the fakirs and beggars in attendance, but this is a matter of individual charity; there is no general distribution in which all the poor have a claim to share. It appears to me that the appropriation Delroos Banu Begum was not of a public character, and that Act XX of 1863 does not apply to it." Upon appeal the Judicial Committee[2] while affirming the High Court's decision on another point expressly stated that they did not see anything to disagree with the High Court's judgment on the construction of Act XX of 1863 and on the nature of the appropriation in the case.

Test of public purposes-general benefit.

---

1. (1875) 15 B. L. R., 167: S. C. 23 W. R. C. R. 453.

2. *Ashgar Alli* v. *Delroos Banoo Begum*, (1877) I. L. R., 3 C. 324.

Absence of control by Board under Regulations.

Under Regulations XIX of 1810 (Bengal) and VII of 1817 (Madras), the Board of Revenue and the local agents had the powers of control and supervision over public religious or charitable endowments and where a particular religious endowment did not come under the control of the Board of Revenue it was held that that was an indication of the endowment being private[1]. The absence of the control and supervision by the Board can only be regarded as at best a piece of evidence to show that the endowment may not be public but is neither a conclusive nor a decisive test.

Gift by former Rulers—Charter of Crown.

In *Trimbak* v. *Lakshman*[2] it was observed by the Bombay High Court that where a gift was made by former rulers of this country and confirmed by the British Government, the endowment should be held to be a public endowment. But as observed by *Lord Hardwicke* in *Attorney General* v. *Pearce*[3], "the charter of the Crown cannot make a charity more or less public, but only more permanent than it would otherwise be." In the generality of cases, however, former Governments of this country made grants because of the extensiveness of the charity (including in this a religious purpose) and it was because of the public nature of the endowments the British were pleased to confirm all such endowments and did not resume them when they became rulers either by occupation, cession or conquest. In certain cases the British Government also allotted a certain tasdik or mohini allowance in favor of certain public temples. The granting of such allowance would show that the institution was an ancient one[4].

Inams.

It is useful to look to the language employed in describing these grants. An 'inam' is "a gift, a benefaction in general, a gift by a superior to an inferior." These inams may be divided into two classes: (1) inams granted by the State called "*Sanadi-inams*," and (2) inams granted by the village community called "*Gaon nisbat inams*." The former are divisible into many classes, one of which consists of inams which are denominated *chakaria*

---

1. *Bibee Kuneez Fatima* v. *Bibee Saheba Jan*, (1867) 8 W. R. C. R., 313; *Delroos Banoo Begum* v. *Nawab Syed Ashgur Ally Khan*, (1875) 15 B. L. R., 167: S. C. 23 W. R. C. R. 453. See also notes to Ss. 1, 3 and 14.
2. (1895) I. L. R., 20 B. 495. See also *Chintaman* v. *Dhondo*, (1888) I. L. R., 15 B. 612.
3. (1740) 2 Atk. 87 (88) followed in *Thackersey Dewraj* v. *Hurbhum Nursey*, (1884) I. L. R., 8 B. 432.
4. *Appasami* v. *Nagappa*, (1884) I. L. R., 7 M. 499.

and held on the condition of discharging some obligation or trust or as *Khairat* or *Khayra*: in case the duty or trust to be fulfilled be charitable or religious (and more especially where such grants are given by or to Mohamedans). The latter are also called *altamgha* inams. An *altamgha* inam is "a royal grant under the seal of some of the former native princes of Hindustan and recognised by the British Government and conferring an hereditary title" (*altamgha* being derived from the word *al* red, and *tamgha* a stamp or impression)[1]. Grants of inams for religious or charitable purposes are frequently found to be of great antiquity, and evidenced by inscriptions on copper-plates[2].

General public having no interest in maintenance of mutt.

Where the general public or any section of the people had no interest either in the erection and maintenance of the mutt or where there is no intention to confer a benefit either upon the people in general or upon any class of sectarians the grant is not a public but a private endowment. In *Sathappayyar* v. *Periasami*[3] where this point arose the facts were that the plaintiff's ancestor a Zemindar of Sivaganga, founded an institution which came to be known as Sathappayyar's Mutt and gave what was called a charity grant (Dharma Sasanam). Appellant was the paradesi or representative for the time being of the said mutt. The suit was brought by the Zemindar in the Sub-Court to remove the appellant from the headship of the mutt on account of misconduct or breach of trust and to recover possession of the properties for the benefit of the person to be appointed by the Zemindar in the place of the appellant. Under the deed of grant the then Zemindar gave some properties to his then Guru or preceptor "so that a mutt may be built thereon, that *Siva oga Nishtai*[4] and other penance may be performed by the Guru and that the expenses of the establishment may be paid," and other properties were given for the performance of the annual *gurupuja*[5] and for *dehapuja*[6]. The document also pro-

1. *Jewan Dass Sahoo* v. *Shah Kubeer-ood-deen*, (1841) 2 M. I. A. 390.

2. *Krishnarav Ganesh* v. *Rangrav*, (1867) 4 B. H. C. A. C. J. 1.

3. (1890) I. L. R., 14 M. 1. See also *Delroos Banoo Begum* v. *Ashgar Ally*, (1875) 15 B. L. R. 167.

4. It is in substance a form of worship and prayer.

5. Annual ceremony by the head of a Mutt in honor and for the spiritual benefit of his guru.

6. Self-support of a person who has a sacred or religious status.

vided for the distribution of food among paradesis or Sudra ascetics and others whenever *gurupuja* was performed (but this, it must be observed, was not an independent trust but only the accompaniment or incident of *gurupuja*). There was also a trust for opening and keeping up a water-shed in the mutt for the supply of drinking water to the poor during the hot season, but this was not contained in the document but depended on custom. The High Court held that the Subordinate Judge had jurisdiction. Upon this question of jurisdiction Mr. *Justice Muthusami Iyer* observed :—"The contention regarding jurisdiction is that under Act XX of 1863 the District Court is the proper forum. This would be so if the institution is endowed and dedicated to any section of the public either as a place of worship, such as a temple, or religious establishment where religious instruction is to be had like a public mutt. For Act XX of 1863 only replaced Regulation VII of 1817 so far as religious institutions are concerned, which, as shown by its preamble and its provisions dealt with trusts, express or implied, created for public purposes. But the grant in the case before us discloses no intention to confer a benefit either upon the people in general or upon any class of sectarians; on the other hand the grantor desired only to perpetuate the spiritual family of his guru. * * Neither the general public nor any section of the people had an interest either in the erection and maintenance of the mutt, or in the performance of the prescribed religious duties, the motive for the grant being the grantor's conviction that the performance of such services in perpetuity by the class of persons named by him in the mutt and with the aid of funds provided by him was an act of religious charity which would ensure the prosperity of his family. The original grantor and his descendants are the only persons interested in seeing that the institution is kept up for their benefit in accordance with the intention of the grantor. Although a few paradesis and others are fed when Gurupuja is performed and a water-pandal is maintained in the mutt during the hot season, these were not contemplated as independent charities in which any class of the public was to have a direct and independent interest. * * I am of opinion that the Subordinate Judge is well-founded in holding that the trusts of the institution concerned in this litigation are in the nature of *private trusts*."

Conversely it will follow that a trust for the benefit of a considerable portion of the public answering a particular description is a public trust[1]. A trust for the feeding of wayfarers and travellers is a public charitable purpose[1]. When the whole Hindu community is interested in the worship of an idol, it is a trust for a public religious purpose[2]. The user by the public is the test in such cases[3]. So also where an endowment was created for a sect known as Bhagawatas (who are devoted to the cult of Vishnu) such endowment would be a public religious one[4].

Trust for a considerable portion of the public.

Perhaps the only case in India which attempts to deal with the principles bearing upon the subject is that of *Thackersey Dewraj* v. *Hurbhum Nursey*[5] decided by *Scott*, J. The following are the tests to be gathered from his judgment:—(1) the nature of the objects and purposes of the funds; (2) the nature of the dedication *i. e.*, whether it is to the public or whether it is open generally to a class of the community[6]; (3) the authority, if any, of the donors to divert the fund and to condone maladministration; and (4) the existence or otherwise of any present or reversionary right of the donor individually or anybody of donors collectively in the endowed funds.

Tests laid down in Thackersey Dewraj v. Hurbhum Nursey.

In holding that the institution there in question was a public one, *Scott*, J., observed on the *first* point: "What, then, are the objects and purposes of the funds now in question? Are they charitable, or religious, or both? The funds are three in number, each different in character. The *Mahajan* fund is a purely secular fund. It is made up partly of subscriptions from the caste members, partly of fees and fines paid by them, partly of payments made for the use of caste pots. The other two funds, the *Darasa* and the *Sadaran*, are really made up, as I have already shown, of

Objects of fund.

1. *Lutefunnissa Bibi* v. *Naziam Bibi*, (1884) I. L. R., 11 C. 33. See also *Jaggamani Dasi* v. *Nilmoni Ghosal*, (1882) I. L. R., 9 C. 75.

2. *Sajedur Raja* v. *Baidyanath Deb*, (1892), I. L. R., 20 C. 397.

3. *Jugal Kishore* v. *Lakshmandas Raghunathdas*, (1899) I. L. R., 23 B. 659. See also *Rajah Vurma* v. *Ravi Vurma*, (1876) L. R. 4 I. A. 76: S. C. I. L. R., 1 M. 235; *Natesa* v. *Ganapati*, (1890) I. L. R., 14 M. 103 (109).

4. *Kanhaya Lal* v. *Salig Ram*, (1894) A. W. N. 159. No distinction is made by the Court of Chancery in England between one sort of religion and another or between one sect and another. See *Thornton* v. *Howe*, (1862) 31 Beav. 14 (19) where it was held that a bequest for the purpose of propagating the sacred writings of Joanna Southcote was a good charitable bequest.

5. (1884) I. L. R., 8 B. 432.

6. See also per *Straight*, J. in *Raghubar Dial* v. *Kesho Ramanuj Das*, (1888) I. L. R., 11 A. 18.

donations intended for pious as well as charitable purposes. The maintenance of the temple and gifts to other temples are express objects of the temple funds just as the benefit of *Sadhus* and poor Jains is one of the express objects of the *Sadaran* fund. Those who are entrusted with the administration of such funds are undoubtedly administering a public religious endowment as well as a public charitable trust. No caste line of demarcation is drawn either with regard to the temples to be assisted or the poor to be relieved. The terms would cover all Jain temples and all the Jain poor. These two funds, therefore, differ widely from the *Mahajan* fund, whose object is narrowed to the supply of the needs of the caste as a social institution."

Temple open to a community.

As regards the *second* point he observed: "It was also contended that the temple belonged to the caste and therefore its funds were equally caste property. I do not think this argument bears examination. The temple itself was erected primarily, perhaps, for the convenience of the caste, but it was also built for purposes of ordinary worship, and has always been open to all the Jain community. Permission to worship there was subject to good behaviour, but it was not shown to have been closed to any one who came to do homage or worship. The *good-conduct* condition is imposed on all votaries in every place of worship; it does not make the temple a private temple. It is a condition imposed on the right of attendance in this Court, but it does not make the Court any the less a public place."

No diversion —No condonation.

As regard the *third* and *fourth* points he observed: "All such institutions (public religious and charitable) are under the superintendence of the Crown as *parens patriae*, and those who manage them can at any time be called to account for their management. Story reviews all the authorities and says: 'The King, as *parens patriae*, has a right to guard and enforce all charities of a public nature by virtue of his general superintending power over the public interests.' * * It is not enough to show that the gifts........ were irrevocably made for charitable or religious purposes. It must also be shown that the charitable purposes were public in character; that the gifts were not made merely in the interest of the Dossa Oswall caste who, if they rank as sole beneficiaries of this as a private charity, may condone any mal-administration. If the gifts were to a public charity, or to a religious endowment, there would be no doubt of the incapacity of the caste to interfere by way of condonation. Mismanagement of any public trust is a distinct contravention of the law, and is a case for the intervention of the State. * * This rule is embodied in the maxim *pacta privata juri publico derogare non possunt.*"

The case of *Chintaman* v. *Dhondo*[1] is the next and the last case that may usefully be considered in this connection as laying down any principle. The case is familiarly known as the *Chinchavad Sevasthan case.* The Bombay High Court in holding that it was a public religious and charitable trust within the meaning of S. 539, C. P. C., observed: "The long established practice of treating the entire income of the endowments as constituting one fund for the support of the several shrines the *use* which the *public generally* have made of the shrine for the purposes of worship and devotion, differing in no important particular from what obtains in other temples admittedly public, and lastly the active part taken by individuals outside the Dev (founder's) family in the festivals of the deity and the votive offerings from the same class of persons are all irreconcileable with any other conclusion than that it was not only the intention of the governing power (in 1744 when a grant was made by the Peshwa) that thenceforth the sevasthan consisting of the above shrines would be a *public devasthan* but that it has always, as a fact, been regarded as such by the managing members of the Dev family and the public generally for more than a century and a half." Chinchavad Sevasthan Case—User by general public-Votive offerings.

The fact that the property of an institution is described in the Inam title-deed as "*devadayam*" is a test to show that the institution is public[2]. Devadayam.

There are many other cases in which it has been held that the trusts in question were public trusts, charitable or religious or both. But it is unnecessary to refer to them as they do not lay down any principle[3].

---

1. (1888) I. L. R., 15 B. 612. See also *Shri Dhundiraj Ganesh Dev v. Ganesh* (1893) I. L. R., 18 B. 721.

2. *Muhammad Jafar* v. *Muhammad Ibrahim*, (1900) I. L. R., 24 M. 243 (245).

3. *Jeewun Doss Sahoo* v. *Shah Kubeer Ood-deen* (1841), 2 M.I.A. 390; *Rahumtulla Sahib* v. *Mahommed Akbar Sahib* (1875), 8 M. H. C. 63; *Huseni Begam* v. *The Collector of Moradabad* (1897), I. L. R., 20 A. 46, where a trust for the up-keep of mosque, for expenses of an annual 'urs' and for feeding the poor at 'urs' was held to be a public charitable and religious trust; *Alagappa Mudaliar* v. *Sivaramasundara Mudaliar* (1895), I. L. R., 19 M. 211, where a choultry in Vachakarapatti intended for travellers was held to be a public charity.

CHAPTER VII.

DISTINCTION BETWEEN PUBLIC AND PRIVATE RELIGIOUS ENDOWMENTS.

Distinctions between public and private.

Having considered the several tests that are useful in ascertaining whether a trust is public or private, we shall advert to the distinctions obtaining in England and India between a *public* and a *private* trust. The distinction between a public and a private trust obtaining in England is succinctly stated in Perry on Trusts[1] : "Private trusts which concern individuals are limited in their duration. Being for individuals they must be certain and the individual or individuals must be identified within a limited period. They can endure only for a life or lives in being, and 21 years and the period of gestation in addition. On the other hand, public trusts or charities, existing for the general and indefinite public, may continue for an indefinite period[2]. It must be kept in mind, however, that this rule against perpetuities only applies to cases in which the power of alienation is suspended, and that the creation of a trust does not necessarily result in such suspension."

This, however, is not exhaustive. We shall, therefore, proceed to state in detail, the distinctions obtaining in English Law :—

Perpetuities.

(1) A private trust though charitable is subject to the rule of perpetuities[3] ; but a public charitable trust is not subject to this rule[4]. So that a bequest for the perpetual maintenance and repair of a private chapel or private monuments or tombs except in churches is bad[5]. Even then a gift to a charity subject to a defeasance clause (*i. e.*, failure to fulfil the condition of repairing a tomb) with a gift over to another charity will be valid[6].

---

1. Para 231.

2. *Christ's Hospital* v. *Grainger*, (1849) 1 Mac & G. 460; and *In re Tyler*, (1891) 3 Ch. 252 ; *Lloyd Phillips* v. *Davis*, (1893) 2 Ch. 491 (which contains the exceptions to the doctrine that a transfer of property in a certain event from one charity to another is not subject to the rule of perpetuities). See, however, *Anon*, (1745) 3 Atk. 277.

3. *Hoare* v. *Osborne*, (1866) L. R., 1 Eq., 585. See Perry on Trusts, paras 23 and 737.

4. Per *Cairns*, L. C., in *Goodman* v. *Mayor of Saltash*, (1882) 7 A. C. 642 (650) ; *Re Christ Church Inclosure Act*, (1888) 38 Ch. D. 520 (531) ; *Re St. Stephen's Coleman Street*, (1888) 39 Ch. D. 492 (501) ; per *Chitty*, J., in *Rymer* v. *Stanfield*, (1895) 1 Ch. 19 (25). See also Perry on Trusts, para 736.

5. *Hoare* v. *Osborne*, (1866) L. R., 1 Eq. 585; *In Re Vaughan—Vaughan* v. *Thomas*, (1886) 33 Ch. D. 187.

6. *Tyler* v. *Tyler*, (1891) 3 Ch. 252 ; *Christ's Hospital* v. *Grainger*, supra.

(2) As a consequence of the above, public charitable trusts may continue for an indefinite[1] period, but in the case of private charitable trusts, they can endure only for a life or lives in being and 21 years, *i. e.*, property cannot be so perpetually dedicated to a private charitable use as to be inalienable for ever[2]. **Period indefinite.**

(3) In the case of a private trust, the persons interested in the same have the power or authority to use the fund for any purpose and to divert the fund from the original object[3]. In the case of a public charitable trust this cannot be done[4]. **Diversion of fund.**

(4) As a consequence of the above, the beneficiaries in the case of a private charitable trust may condone maladministration by trustees[5]. But in the case of a public charitable trust the maladministration cannot be so condoned, for the wrong is done to the State and the trustees will still be liable[6]. **Condonation of maladministration.**

(5) In suits relating to private charities, the Attorney-General is not a necessary party[7]. But the Attorney-General will be a necessary party in the case of suits relating to public charitable trusts[8] and is entitled to interfere at any stage of the case[9]. **Attorney-General.**

(6) Where a general charitable intention is expressed absolutely but the mode in which it is to be carried into effect is left uncertain the Court will supply the mode in the case of a public charity[10]. So where the mode is expressed but such mode subsequently fails then the Court will still apply the fund *cypres* in **Cypres.**

---

1. Perry, para. 23 ; and cases cited in p. lxxxii note (2). See also *Stewart* v. *Green*, 5 L. R., (1) Eq. 470.
2. *Cadell* v. *Palmer*, (1833) 1 Cl. & Fin 372. : S. C. 36 R. R. 128. Perry on Trusts, paras 379 and 380.
3. Perry on Trusts, paras 384 and 849 to 853.
4. Perry on Trusts, paras 733 and 734.
5. Perry on Trusts, para 384.
6. Perry on Trusts, paras 379 and 380 ; *Swan* v. *Blair*, (1835) 3 Cl. & Fin. 610 (621) : S. C. 39 R. R. 78.
7. *Attorney-General* v. *Forster*, (1805) 10 Ves. 344 ; *Attorney-General* v. *Newcombe*, (1807) 14 Ves. 1 ; and *Fearon* v. *Webb*, (1807) 14 Ves. 19. See Perry on Trusts, para 732.
8. See Perry on Trusts, paras 732 and 744 ; *Attorney-General* v. *Aspinall*, (1837) 1 Keen 513 : S. C. 45 R. R., 142 (151) ; *Evan* v. *The Corporation of Avon*, (1860) 29 Beav. 144 (149) ; *Boyce* v. *Paddington Borough Council*, (1903) 1 Ch. 109 ; *Devonport Corporation* v. *Tozer*, [1903] 1 Ch. 759.
9. *The Advocate-General* v. *Vishvanath Atmaram*, (1855) 1 B. H. C. App. ix and the English cases cited therein ; and *The Advocate-General* v. *Muhammad Hussain*, (1867) 4 B. H. C. (O. C. J.) 208 and (P. C). 207 (note); *Ommaney* v. *Butcher*, (1823) T. & R. 260 : S. C. 24 R. R., 42 (47 and 48). See, however, the criticism upon this case in Perry on Trusts, para 712
10. *White* v. *White*, (1893) 2 Ch. 41, where charitable is used in the sense of public and not private, citing Lord *Eldon* in *Mills* v. *Farmer*, (1815) 19 Ves. 483 : S. C. 13 R. R. 247. See also *Morice* v. *Bishop of Durham*, (1805) 7 R. R. 232. In the latter case, however, it was held that a gift for objects of benevolence or liberality is a vague and indefinite gift which the Court cannot enforce. See also Perry on Trusts paras 723 and 727.

the case of public charity[1]; but in the case of private charity if the mode is left uncertain (as where the objects are indefinite) the Court will not supply the mode nor will it apply the fund *cypres* where the mode pointed out by the testator fails[2].

Applicability of distinctions in India—Cy-pres-Advocate-General.

The question that has to be considered is whether these distinctions are also applicable in India. The *last* point may be taken to be generally applicable here[3]. As regards the *fifth* point, it may be mentioned that though it may be true that the Advocate-General may maintain a suit on behalf of a public charity, the suit without the Advocate-General as party is nevertheless maintainable[4]. Where he maintains a suit with a relator as joint plaintiff he has the conduct of the suit and in cases under S. 539, Civil Procedure Code, it may be that he may interfere and take away the conduct of the suit from the plaintiff at any stage of the case[5].

Diversion of endowment by consensus of family.

As regards the *third* point the Privy Council have held, that in the case of a private religious endowment, the consensus of the family can give any turn to the endowment. Thus in *Konwar Doorganath Roy* v. *Ram Chunder Sen*[6] the Privy Council observed: "Where the temple is a public temple, the dedication may be such that the family itself could not put an end to it; but in the case of a family idol, the consensus of the whole family might give the estate another direction." But a public endowment cannot be so diverted[7]. This distinction is similar to the one between territorial or public and family customs. The latter can be discontinued and put an end to by persons interested in the same, but the same thing is not true of territorial or public customs. Thus in *Rajkishen Singh* v. *Ramjoy Surma*

1. *In re White's Trusts*, (1886) 33Ch. D. 449 (453); and *White* v. *White*, (1893) 2 Ch. 41. But where the gift is to a specific charitable institution and that institution ceases to exist in the testator's lifetime, then there is a lapse and the amount of the gift falls into the residue. The doctrine of *cy-pres* has no application in such a case. *Rymer* v. *Stanfield*, (1895) 1 Ch. 19 (where *Lord Herschell*, L. C. discusses all the cases on the point). Perry on Trusts, para 725.

2. *Ommaney* v. *Butcher*, (1823) 24 R. R., 42. This case decides that private charity is an object too indefinite to give the Crown jurisdiction or to enable the Court to execute the trust. This case is, however, severely criticised by Perry in his book on Trusts, paras 732 and 744. See also *Waldo* v. *Caley*, (1808) 16 Ves. 206; S. C. 10 R.R., 165; and *Horde* v. *Earl of Suffolk*, (1833) 2 My &K. 59: S. C. 39 R. R., 136. The last two cases are treated as overruled by *Lord Cottenham* in *Ellis* v. *Selby*, (1836) 1 My. & Cr. 286: S. C. 43 R. R., 188 (192).

3. *The Mayor of Lyons* v. *East India Company*, (1837) 1 M. I. A. 175; *The Mayor of Lyons* v. The *Advocate-General of Bengal*, (1876) I. L. R., 1 C. 303 (P. C.)

4. *Srinivasa Chariar* v. *Raghava Chariar*, (1897) I. L. R., 23 M. 28.

5. *The Advocate-General* v. *Muhammed Hussain*, (1867) 4 B. H. C. (O. C. J.) 203 and 206.

6. (1876) 4 I. A. 52 (58): S. C I. L R 2 C 341 See also W & B. Dig of H. L. 160.

7. W. & B. Dig. of H. L. 160.

Mozoomdar[1], the Privy Council observed: "Their Lordships cannot find any principle or authority for holding that in point of law a manner of descent of an ordinary estate, depending solely on family usage, may not be discontinued, so as to let in the ordinary law of succession. Such family usages are in their nature different from a territorial custom which is the *lex loci* binding all persons within the local limits in which it prevails. It is of the essence of family usages that they should be certain, invariable and continuous, and well-established discontinuance must be held to destroy them. This would be so when the discontinuance has arisen from accidental causes; and the effect cannot be less, when it has been intentionally brought about by the concurrent will of the family." It is also said that in the case of a private endowment an alienation of the shebait's office made with the concurrence of the whole family is valid and binding on the succeeding shebaits[2], though in the case of a public endowment the alienation of office of manager is illegal[3].

Alienation of Shebait's office.

The *fourth* follows from the *third* and must be equally applicable in India. Thus *Scott*, J., observed in *Thackersey Dewraj* v. *Hurbhum Nursey*[4]: "It is not enough for this present case to show that the gifts made to this temple were irrevocably made for charitable or religious purposes. It must also be shown that the charitable purposes were public in character; that the gifts were not made merely in the interest of the Dossa Oswall caste who, if they rank as sole beneficiaries of this as a private charity may condone any mal-administration. If the gifts were contributions to a public charity, or to a religious endowment, there would be no doubt of the incapacity of the caste to interfere by way of condonation. Mismanagement of any public trust is a distinct contravention of the law and is a case for the intervention of the state: 'The consent or private agreement of individuals is ineffectual in rendering validany contravention of the law, and it will altogether fail to make just or sufficient that which is unjust or deficient in respect to any matter which the law declares to be indispensable'[5]. This rule is embodied in the maxim *pacta privata juri publico derogare non possunt*."

Condonation of breach of trust.

1. (1872) I. L. R., 1 C. 186 (195 and 196).
2. *Khetter Chunder Ghose* v. *Haridas Bandopadhya*, (1890) I. L. R., 17 C. 557.
3. *Rajah Vurma* v. *Ravi Vurma*, (1876) L.R. 4 I. A. 76: S. C. I. L. R., 1 M. 235. See further as to alienation and partibility Chapters XII and XIII.
4. (1884) I. L. R., 8 B. 432 (454). But tolerating irregularities does not amount to a condonation. *Jugalkishore* v. *Lakshmidas*, (1899) I. L. R., 23 B. 659.
5. *Swan* v. *Blair*, (1835) 3 Cl. & Fin. 610 (621). See also *Ranga Pai* v. *Baba*, (1897) I. L. R., 20 M. 398.

Applicability of rule as to perpetuities and indefiniteness in India.

As regards the first two distinctions noted above, we have to observe that the rule as to perpetuities does not apply to a Hindu religious endowment, whether public or private[1]. Property can be so dedicated to an idol as to be inalienable for ever[2]. In the cases of both public and private religious endowments, inalienability is said not to be absolute, so that the property may be alienated if there is a sufficient necessity for the same. The alienation, however, is allowed for the purpose of and for the benefit of the idol or institution[3]. In Bombay it will appear that the inalienability is absolute[3].

Extent of rule in India.

It is said in a Calcutta case[4] that the law of perpetuities is not applicable in India. This is rather a broad proposition of law. The English Law of Perpetuities is no doubt not applicable[5]. As the PrivyCouncil observed in the *Tagore case*[5] the character of theHindu Lawof gifts renders the introduction of such law unnecessary. Agift in perpetuity for the private benefit of individuals and restraining the donees to alienate the property in any way or beyond the lives of the donees is equally void in India[5]. Where a grantor creates a secular estate with a religious motive, the grant does not stand on the same footing with a religious endowment (or a charitable gift) and is not exempt from the rule as to perpetuities[6]. It is a general rule of jurisprudence that where an estate in fee is given, a condition in restraint of alienation is a condition repugnant to the nature of the grant and as such inoperative[6]. The introduction of the English Law of perpetuties may, therefore, not be necessary in the case of Hindu and Mahomedan Laws. As *Markby*, J., observed in *Kumara Asima Krishna Deb* v. *Kumara Kumara Krishna Deb*[5]: "It being assumed to be a principle of Hindu Law that a gift can be made to an *idol* which is a *caput mortuum*, and incapable of alienating, you cannot break in upon that principle by engrafting upon it the English Law of perpetuities." So also Mr. Justice *West*

1. *Kumara Asima Krishna Deb* v. *Kumara Kumara Krishna Deb*, (1868) 2 B. L. R., (O. C. J.) 11; *Fatma Bibi* v. *The Advocate-General of Bombay*, (1881) I. L. R., 6 B. 42; *Ananthathirtha Achariar* v. *Nagamuthu Ambalagaran* (1881) I. L. R., 4 M. 200; *Colgan* v. *Administrator-General of Madras* (1892) I. L. R., 15 M. 424; *Bhuggobutty Prosonno Sen* v. *Gooroo Prosonno Sen*, (1897) I. L. R., 25 C. 112.

2. *Shri Ganesh Dharnidar* v. *Krishna Rao Govind Kulgavkar*, (1890), I. L. R., 15 B. 625; *Lalit Mohun Singh* v. *Chukkun Lal Roy*, (1897) L. R. 24 I. A. 76 (89): S. C. I. L. R, 24 C. 834.

3. See Ch. II, p. xvii and Ch. VIII, pp. xcix and c.

4. *Kherodemoney Dossee* v. *Doorgamoney Dossee*, (1878) I. L R., 4 C. 455 (464).

5. *Kumara Asima Krishna Deb* v. *Kumara Kumara Krishna Deb*, (1868) 2 B. L. R, (O. C. J.) 11. *The Tagore Case*, (1869) 4 B. L. R. (O. C. J.) 103; (1872), L. R., I. A., Supp., 47; and *Anandakrishna Bose* v. *Kumara Rajendra Narayan Deb* (1869), 3 B. L R., (O. C. J.) 23; *Lalit Mohun Singh* v. *ChukkunLal* supra.

6. *Ananthathirtha Achariar* v. *Nagamuthu Ambalagaran*, (1881) I. L. R., 4 M. 200.

observed in *Fatma Bibi* v. *The Advocate-General of Bombay*[1]: "The rule against perpetuities extends to a colony in which the English Law is in force only so far as it is adapted to the circumstances of the community. * * * That rule is subject to exceptions in the case of charities liberally construed as objects useful and beneficial to the community." He then observed that the rule had no application to cases of Hindu and Mahomedan religious endowments.

Applicability of rule to persons having no personal laws.

But this law has been applied to persons who are neither Hindus nor Mahomedans and who have no personal laws of their own. Thus the Madras High Court observed in *Colgan* v. *Administrator-General of Madras*[2]: "It is not a correct statement of the law applicable to India to say that because certain dispositions of property in perpetuity not allowed by English Law are allowed to Hindus and Mahomedans, the rule of perpetuities has no application to India. The rule being founded on public policy must be a part of the territorial law of England in all her colonies and dependencies. But Hindus and Mahomedans have had their respective personal laws preserved to them by the Charters of the High Court and by the Regulations. The personal law of the Hindus is intimately connected with their religion, and therefore allows of gifts in perpetuities to religious objects to a much greater extent than the English Law. Thus absolute gifts of land or money in perpetuity to an idol and for other religious purposes have been recognised by many decisions[3]. In his judgment in *Alami* v. *Konnu*[4] Mr. Justice *Muthusami Ayyar* observes: 'Neither the English Law which forbids bequests for supertitious uses, nor the rule which prohibits the creation of perpetuities is applicable to gifts to idols in this country'. So the Mahomedan Law of *wakf* or appropriation founded on theMahomedan religion allows of the appropriation of property in perpetuity for the performance of religious services, the maintenance and repair of tombs and other purposes not held to be charitable by the English Law." The Court then pointed out that the rule applied to those who had no such personal laws such as the Armenians and Parsis, and that this distinction between Her Majesty's subjects was undesirable.

---

1. (1888) I. L. R., 6 B. 42.
2. (1892) I. L. R., 15 M. 424.
3. Their Lordships cite the follownig:—*Mullick* v. *Mullick*, (1829) 1 Knapp. 245; *Juggut Mohini Dossee* v. *Mussumat Sokheemoney Dossee*, (1871) 14 M. I. A. 289.
4. R. A. Nos. 80 and 105 of 1886.

Rule applies to both kinds of property.

The rule against perpetuities, when it applies, applies to moveables as well as immoveables. It cannot be said that because the gift is only of moveables, therefore the rule does not apply[1].

Rule and exception founded on considerations of public policy.

The rule as to perpetuities is of general application[2] being one founded on considerations of public policy from which an exception, also on grounds of public policy, is allowed in favor of gifts for purposes useful and beneficial to the public and which in a wide sense are called charitable uses.[3] As observed by *Jardine*, J., in *Limji Nowroji* v. *Banaji Bapuji Ruttonji Limbuwalla*,[4] "The object of the rule against perpetuities is, to prevent the mischief of making property inalienable, unless for objects in some way beneficial or useful to the community. An exception is made also on grounds of public policy in favor of gifts for purposes useful and beneficial to the public, and which in a wide sense of the word are called 'charitable uses.'" It was, therefore, held that a gift by a Parsi testator which has for its object the consolation of the dead and the propitiation of the *forhars* (*i. e.*, guardian spirits of the dead) was not a gift for a general public use.

Distinction in England between a superstitious and a charitable use.

Here we have to observe that a distinction is drawn in English Law between a *superstitious* use and a *charitable* use. Superstitious uses are uses condemned by the English Law at or after the Reformation as maintaining superstition. These will include the providing of masses for the dead, &c. A superstitious use, according to Boyle, is "one which has for its object the propagation of the rights of a religion not tolerated by the law." Gradually, statutes were passed declaring that the disabilities as to Dissenters and Roman Catholics should be removed. The law relating to these uses depends partly upon common law and partly upon statute.

Law of superstitious uses not applicable in India.

But in India the English Law of superstitious uses has no application[5]. For instance, in English Law a gift for the performance of the masses would be void as being a gift for superstitious

1. Act IV of 1882, S. 14; Act X of 1865, S. 101; *Hoare* v. *Osborne*, (1866) L. R., 1 Eq., 585; *Cooper* v. *Laroche*, (1881) 17 Ch. D. 368 (372); and *Cowasji Nowroji Pochkanawalla* v. *Rustomji Dossabhoy Setna*, (1895) I. L. R., 20 B. 511.

2. *Fatma Bibi* v. *The Advocate-General of Bombay*, (1881) I. L. R., 6 B. 42 (50).

3. *Colgan* v. *Administrator-General of Madras*, (1892) I. L. R., 15 M. 424.

4. (1887) I. L. R., 11 B. 441. See also *Yeap Cheah Neo* v. *Ong Cheng Neo*, (1875) L. R., 6 P. C. 381.

5. *The Advocate-General* v. *Vishwanath Atmaram*, (1855) 1 B. H. C. App. 9; *Das Merces* v. *Cones*, (1864) 2 Hyde 65; *Andrews* v. *Joakim*, (1869) 2 B. L. R. (O. C. J.) 148; *Joseph Ezekiel Judah* v. *Aaron Hye Nusseem Ezekiel Judah*, (1870) 5 B. L. R. (O. C. J.) 433; *Khusalchand v. Mahdevgiri* (1875) 12 B. H. C. 214; and *Colgan* v. *Administrator-General of Madras*, supra, See also W. & B. Dig of H. L. 215 note (d).

uses[1], though *Lord Romily*, M. R., follows this principle reluctantly in the case of Roman Catholics, in *In re Blundell's Trusts*[1]. So gifts for the repair and upkeep of tombs or monuments only benefit the donor or other private individual and not the public and are, therefore, void[2]. But in India gifts to idols are not void as being gifts for superstitious uses[3]. It is said in one case that there is no State policy in introducing in India the restriction imposed by the Statute of Superstitious Uses, and it has been there held that a bequest for the performance of the masses in Calcutta is valid[4]. But this will not justify a perpetuity.

Objects allowed by Hindu and Mahomedan Laws.

Objects which the English Law will regard as "superstitious uses" are allowable and commendable according to the Hindu and Mahomedan laws[5]. A trust for the maintenance of an idol is a valid charitable (or rather religious) purpose according to Hindu Law and trusts for the benefit of the poor, for aiding pilgrimages and marriages and for the support of wells and mosques are charities among the Mahomedans and valid under the Mahomedan Law[5]. Although a gift for an idol has been held to be valid[6], yet it has been held that a gift by a Mahomedan for the purpose of the upkeep and the performance of the daily, monthly and annual expenses of his tomb is not a valid wakf and is void as not being a gift for charitable purposes[7]. This decision cannot but be regarded as a death-blow to most Mahomedan private endowments. The decision does not affect the validity of gifts for the support of tombs of saints which are said to be public and not private religious endowments[7]. This decision is said to be opposed to the usage of Mahomedans[8], and is also opposed to several cases which have apparently recognised such gifts[9].

1. *West* v. *Shuttleworth*, (1835; 2 My. & K. 684: S. C. 39 R. R. 327; *Heath* v. *Chapman*, (1854) 2 Drew 417: S. C. 23 L. J. Ch. N. S. 947; *In re Blundell's Trusts*, (1861) 30 Beav. 360 (362); *Yeap Cheah Neo* v. *Ong Cheng Neo*, (1875) L. R. 6 P. C. 381; and *Colgan* v. *Administrator-General of Madras*, (1892) I. L. R., 15 M. 424.

2. *Rickard* v. *Robson*, (1862) 31 Beav. 244; *Fowler* v. *Fowler*, (1864) 33 Beav. 616; *Fisk* v. *Attorney-General*, (1867) L. R. 4 Eq. 521. But see *Dawson* v. *Small*, (1874) L.R. 18 Eq. 114 where the Court held that the obligation to keep up the tombstone was merely honorary; *Colgan* v. *Administrator-General of Madras*, supra.

3. *Mullick* v. *Mullick*, (1829) 1 Knapp. 245: S. C. 12 Eng. Rep. P. C. 312; and *Colgan* v. *Administrator-General of Madras*, supra.

4. *Andrews* v. *Joakim*, (1869) 2 B. L. R., (O. C. J.) 148.

5. *Fatma Bibi* v. *The Advocate-General of Bombay*, (1881) I. L. R., 6 B. 42. *See* Amir Ali, Vol. I, pp 315 to 317.

6. *Rajessuree* v. *Jogendro* (1875) 23 W. R. C. R. 278; *Rupa Jagshet* v. *Krishnaji* (1884) I. L. R. 9 B. 169.

7. *Kaleloola Sahib* v. *Nuseerudeen Sahib*, (1894) I. L. R., 18 M. 201.

8. Per *Davies*, J. in *Kaleloola* v. *Nuseerudeen*, Supra. But see Baillie, Vol. I, 576.

9. *Huseni Begam* v. *The Collector of Moradabad*, (1897) I. L R. 20 A 46; *Nizamuddin* v. *Abdul Gafur*, (1888) I. L. R., 13 B. 264, where the High Court holding that a gift of property to one's own descendants in perpetuity was not a wakf held that a gift for the purpose of building the settlor's own tomb was a good wakf and this was not questioned by the Privy Council on appeal. *Abdul Gafar* v. *Nizamudin*, (1892) L. R. 19 I. A. 170: S. C. I. L. R., 17 B. 1.

In the case of *Nawab Umjad Ally Khan* v. *Mohumdee*[1], even a gift of money for the benefit of the donor's soul was recognized as valid The purposes for which this fund was to be utilised were the establishment of an imambara and cemetery and the payment of mohurrum expenses. It was a family private endowment and a scheme was settled and no objection on the score of superstitious uses was raised. The Madras case goes too far in holding that the gift is void and contravenes to this extent the decision of the Privy Council in the *Mayor of Lyons* v. *The East India Company*[2]. A private trust is recognised even by English law provided it does not offend the rule against perpetuties.

Bequest by Armenians for masses.

A bequest by an Armenian of a sum of money for the purpose of appfying the income for perpetual masses of his soul and of the souls in purgatory has, however, been held to be void[3]. This decision, however, proceeds not on the ground that the gift is one for superstitious uses, and is therefore void as being of the nature of superstitious uses but on the ground that it offends the rule of perpetuities Even this reasoning, however, does not reconcile the decision with that in *Andrews* v. *Joakim*[4], where a bequest of a sum of money for the performances of masses in Calcutta has been upheld. Consistently, however, with the later cases this latter decision must be treated as erroneous. The observations of *Jardine* J. in *Limji Nowroji Banoji* v. *Bapuji Ruttonji Limbuwalla*[5] are well worth perusal :—" A gift by a Roman Catholic for performing masses for the dead or by a Christian of any Church to maintain tombs of deceased relatives will be invalid, and these objects are analogous to a gift which has for its object the consolation of the dead among Parsis." In the above case a devise by a Parsi testator of a share in a bungalow in Bombay in order that the income accruing from the same should be devoted in perpetuity to the "performance of the *buj rozgar* ceremonies and the consecration of the *nirangain* and the recitation of the *Yazushin* and the annual *ghambar* and *dosla* ceremonies[6]" was held to be void[7].

1. (1867) 11 M. I. A. 517.
2. (1837) 1 M I. A. 175, where a direction for the testator's tomb being deposited in a certain house and for experses in connection therewith was upheld. But a gift for the testator's spiritual benefit is not charitable. *Joseph Ezekiel* v. *Aaron Hye* (1870) 5 B. L. R. (O. C. J.) 433.
3. *Colgan* v. *Administrator-General of Madras*, (1892) I. L. R., 15 M. 424.
4. (1869) 2 B. L. R. (O. C. J.) 148.
5. (1887) I. L. R., 11 B. 441.
6. See for the meaning of these ceremonies the remarks of *Jardine* J. in the above case and Dr. Haug's essays.
7. See also *Cowasji Nowroji* v. *Rustomji*, (1895) I. L. R., 20 B. 511, where a gift by a Parsi of certain Government pro-notes for the expenses of the anniversary day of the donor's deceased parents, brothers and sisters was held to be void. See *Ardeshir* v. *Sirinbai*, (1899) 1 Bom. L. R. 721.

Religious corporations were looked upon with jealousy in early times when there were disputes between the civil and ecclesiastical powers. Hence the old English statutes created a certain amount of incapacity in corporations to hold lands. The oldest statutes beginning with Magna Charta only dealt with religious bodies but later on lay corporations were included. And now, certain restrictions are imposed by the Mortmain and Charitable Uses Act, 1888 and 1891 with reference to conveyance of the freehold in real estate to charitable (including religious) purposes. But there are no statutes of Mortmain in India and, therefore, the principle of these statutes will not apply to a gift of immoveable property made in India for religious or charitable purpo[1]. **Statutes of Mortmain.**

Before concluding we have to advert to only one matter. This is in connection with the so-called principle o. Hindu Law that a gift to an unborn person or a person not in existence at the time of the gift is invalid. The Calcutta Court holds that this principle is equally applicable to gifts to idols. The principle has been first applied to gifts to private persons and for this the *Tagore case*[2] is the leading authority. But the *Tagore case* was one arising under the Dayabhaga Law and the Judicial Committee expressly stated in that case that their decision was according to the Dayabhaga system of law Mr. Justice *Willes* delivering the judgment of the Judicial Committee in that case observed[3] : "The questions presented by this case must be dealt with according to the Hindu Law prevailing in Bengal to which alone the property in question is subject." In fact he deduced the principle from a text in the Dayabhaga[4] which referred to a "relinquishment in favor of the donee who is a sentient person." This text of the Dayabhaga is not to be found in the Mitakshara. But even assuming that this principle is applicable to all the schools of Hindu Law, there is no warrant for its application to gifts for religious purposes. The earliest case which applied the principle to religious endowments is that of *Upendra Lal Boral* v. *Hem Chundra Boral*[5]. In **Gifts to idol-applicability of principle that the donee mustbe in existence.**

1. *Mayor of Lyons* v. *East India Company*, (1837) 1 M. I. A. 175 (296); *Das Merces* v. *Cones* (1864) 2 Hyde 70; *Sarkies* v. *Prosonomoyee Dossee*, (1881) I. L. R., 6 C. 794. But see now Indian Succession Act, S. 105.

2. *Juttendromohun Tagore* v. *Ganendromohun Tagore*, (1872) L. R. I. A. Supp. 47. The Privy Council express no opinion upon the question whether the rule is applicable to family or marriage settlements. Ibid at p. 70.

3. Ibid at p. 64. 4. Ch. I. v 21. 5. (1897) I. L. R. 25 C. 405.

that case the testator directed his wife to build a temple to establish the service of idol and perform the Sheba and manage his properties by making a will in its favor. The Court held that there was no devise of the property either to the widow or to the idol. If the learned judges had stopped with this, there might be some justification for the decision by reason of the ambiguity of the will. But they proceeded further and said that if there was a gift to the idol it was bad as there was no idol in existence at the time of his death. They observed: "We are unable to agree with the learned vakil for the appellant that the idol was in existence in contemplation of law. The deity, no doubt, is always in existence, but there could be no gift to the deity as such, and there was no personification of the deity, to whom the gift could have been made or who was capable of taking it." If it be a correct proposition to say that the deity is a juridical person[1] and that the deity is always in existence it is difficult to see why there can be no gift to the deity as such. A gift for the furtherance of Hindu religion must be held to be good on the analogy of the English cases[2]. So a gift for the worship of Shiva or Vishnu must also be good[3]. A gift for building a choultry and maintaining it is a proper gift[4]. No reason can be assigned for applying a different principle to a gift for erecting a temple. But the decision in the Calcutta case[5] is to the effect that even a gift for constructing a temple is bad. This is striking a blow at the whole Hindu system of religious endowments. It is scarcely necessary to say that such a proposition is supported neither by principle nor by authority. It is directly contrary to the decision of the Privy Council in *Ramtonoo Mullick* v. *Ramgopal*

---

1. See Chapter II, pp. xxx and xvii and Chapter VIII pp. xcvi to xcviii.

2. *Attorney-General* v. *Cock*, (1751) 2 Ves. Sen. 273 : S. C. 28 Eng. Rep. 177; *Shrewsbury* v. *Hornby* (1846) 5 Hare 406 ; *Attorney-General* v. *Lawes*, (1849) 8 Hare 32 ; *Walsh* v. *Gladstone*, (1843) 1 Ph. 290 ; S. C. 65 R. R. 327. See also *Thornton* v. *Howe*, (1862) 31 Beav. 14 (19) where a bequest of money for extending the Christian religion or for the purpose of propagating the sacred writings of one Southcote was held to be good.

3. Ghose on Hindu Law 693.

4. *Purmanundass Jeevundass* v. *Venayekrao Wasoodeo*, (1882) L. R. 9 I. A. 86 ; S. C. I. L. R. 7 B. 19 ; *Jamnabai* v. *Khimji Vullubdass*, (1889) I. L. R., 14 B. 1.

5. *Upendra Lal Boral* v. *Hem Chundra Boral*, (1897) I. L. R., 25 C. 405.

Mullick[1]. It is also contrary to a decision of the same Court in an earlier case[2]. None of these cases is cited in the case we are considering nor in the cases which followed it.

Rojomoyee Dassee v. Troylukho.

The case of *Rojomoyee Dassee* v. *Troylukho Mohiney Dassee*[3] which followed *Upendra Lal Boral* v. *Hem Chundra Boral*[4] does not, however, go so far. According to the former case, a gift for establishing a Thakoor is valid but a supplemental gift providing for the worship of the Thakoor when established is invalid. This is a very curious decision. According to it the law only allows an idol to be brought into existence but on its so being brought into existence must, if we may be allowed to say so, be starved to death as no provision for its maintenance when established is valid. But in a later case[5] *Stephen*, J., held that a gift for establishing a Thakoor or constructing a temple is also bad. This decision has, at any rate, the merit of being consistent. No independent reasoning except in one particular to be presently mentioned is assigned in either of these two later decisions[6] and therefore the remarks we have made with reference to the case of *Upendra Lal Boral* v. *Hem Chundra Boral*[4] will *a fortiori* apply to these[7].

It is said by *Stanley*, J, in *Rojomoyee Dassee* v. *Troylukho Mohiney Dassee*[3] that an idol cannot be said to have juridical existence unless it has been consecrated by the appropriate ceremonies and so has become spiritualized and that before this the deity of which the idol is the visible image does not reside in the idol. This is,

---

1. (1829) 1 Knapp. 245: S. C. 12 Eng. Rep. P. C. 312; See also Ch. I pp. iii to iv.

2. *Gokool Nath Guha* v. *Issur Lochun Roy*, (1886) I. L. R., 14 C. 222. See also *Jairam Narronji* v. *Kuverbai*, (1885) I. L. R. 9 B. 491. In *Surbomungola Dabee* v. *Mohendronath Nath*, (1879) I. L. R., 4 C. 508, it was held that a trust for a bathing ghat and two temples for Shiva was void not upon any ground taken in *Upendra Lal's case* but upon the ground of uncertainty.

3. (1901) I. L. R. 29 C. 260.

4. (1897) I. L. R. 25 C. 405.

5. *Nogendra-Nandini Dassi* v. *Benoy Krishna Deb*, (1902) I. L. R. 30 C. 521.

6. *Rajomoyee Dassee* v. *Troylukho Mohiney Dassee*, (1901) I. L. R. 29 C. 260; *Nogendra-Nandini Dassi* v. *Benoy Krishna Deb*, (1902) I. L. R. 30 C. 521.

7. See the criticisms in the Madras Law Journal, Vol. XII, p. 186, and Vol. XIII, p. 201.

however, not the true principle. As shall be seen hereafter[1] it is not the image that is regarded in Hindu Law as a juridical person but the deity of which the image is the visible representation. The deity is ever existent and exists apart from the image and the mystification ceremonies only have the effect of invoking the deity to have its seat in the particular place. But this invocation does not amount to creating the deity or giving birth to it. It is absurd to speak of the deity as being born. No doubt the mystification ceremonies may be the relics of the anthropomorphic idea of a corporation. But at the same time the Hindu religion knows of the deity as having its seat anywhere and when an image is set up and consecrated there is nothing in the Hindu Law to say that the image so set up and consecrated is the juridical person and not the deity.

Doorga Proshad v. Sheo Proshad.

Mr. Justice *Stanley* relies for his position upon the case of *Doorga Proshad Dass* v. *Sheo Proshad Pandah*[2]. There the facts were that certain lands sought to be recovered by plaintiffs were *debuttur* and that the plaintiffs' father sold these lands to the first defendant (who purchased the same together with the idol) wrongfully. The plaintiffs brought the suit for the recovery of lands. It was found by both the courts that they sued in the character of shebaits, that the endowments were real and that the plaintiffs were entitled to recover the same. It appeared during the trial of the case after remand that the idol (apparently a family idol) was in possession of the alienee, and that the latter objected that he was doing the worship and that the plaintiffs were not entitled to maintain the suit for the recovery of the lands without suing for the recovery of the idol. The plaintiffs answered that the alienee was only setting up a spurious idol and that even assuming that the idol was with the first defendant they were entitled to treat the idol as lost, to replace the latter by a new one and to recover the properties. The High Court which was from the first against the plaintiffs' case (at one stage even doubting whether there was any real endowment) held that the effect of a decree in plaintiffs' favor would be to sever the land from the idol and that the plaintiffs were, therefore, not entitled to recover the

1. See Chapter VIII, pp. xcvi to xcviii. It is on this hypothesis we can explain the view taken by the courts that idols are property. See *Subbaraya Gurukal* v. *Chellappa Mudali*, (1881) I. L. R., 4 M. 315 (316).

2. (1880), 7 C. L. R., 278.

land in the present suit. Assuming the principle laid down by the Calcutta High Court in this case to be correct (viz., that the deity of which the idol is the visible image resides in the idol consecrated and not in any substituted image) it does not follow that the plaintiffs are not entitled to recover the land without suing to recover the idol. The plaintiffs were suing as shebaits to recover the land for the deity in the wrongful possession of the first defendant and it would be allowing the latter to take advantage of his own wrong to defeat that suit by pleading that he was in possession of the idol also. It might be that if the plaintiffs should bring a second suit for the recovery of the idol they would be barred under S. 43 C. P. C. But that would be no answer to their suit for recovery of land. Further, where a plaintiff is suing for the idol he is also suing to recover the same for the deity. This cannot be done if the idol itself is a juridical person. It is absurd to suppose that the plaintiffs may sue for the recovery of the consecrated image (the juridical person)[1]. But if the true view is that the deity is the juridical person then the shebait may sue for the recovery of the idol wrongfully carried away. Moreover supposing the wrong-doer should break the idol or should throw it away into the open seas far from the reach of any process of Court can he be allowed to set up the plea that the land cannot be recovered in the absence of the idol ? It does not appear in the above case whether the idol was set up in a temple. We presume it to be so from the fact of reference to consecration. If so, when the plaintiffs are suing for all the lands of the deity (including we suppose the site of the temple) they are also suing for the idol. Further, it would be just under the circumstances that the plaintiffs should be allowed to amend their plaint by including a claim for the idol. But that is a different matter.

---

1. Of course the law knows of a suit for the custody of a minor &c. A minor is for this purpose regarded as a chattel. But when we can conveniently adopt an explicable position it is unnecessary to resort to analogies.

CHAPTER VIII.

EXAMPLES OF HINDU RELIGIOUS ENDOWMENTS —: TEMPLES AND MUTTS.

We shall now proceed to consider some examples of religious endowments and first of such as are recognised by the Hindu Law. In this connection we shall also discuss their precise jural character.

Temples.

It is said that a Hindu religious endowment is either a *devasthan* or *sevasthan*[1]. A *devasthan* is that which is established for God while *Sevasthan* is that which is established for service. The latter word does not appear in Wilson's Glossary. It is meant, we suppose, to denote an endowment for services to be done in temples. This division does not exhaust the category. However this may be, we know that temples are familiar examples of religious endowments known to Hindu Law. These institutions have been established for the spiritual benefit of the Hindu community in general or for that of particular sects or sections thereof. The famous temples at Chidambaram, Udipi, Puri and other places mentioned in the lists given in the notes to Ss. 3 and 4 of the Pagoda Act[2] and others too numerous to mention are public temples and as such are examples of public religious endowments.

Deity a Juristic person.

In Chapter II it has been already stated that under the Hindu Law, an idol, *i. e.*, the deity is a juristic person capable of possessing rights and owning property. That this is the true juristic notion has been affirmed in many cases[3]. This conception is not peculiar

---

1. Ch. II, p. xv. See also *Narayanan* v. *Chintaman*, (1881) I. L. R., 5 B. 393.
2. pp. 22 to 25 and 29 to 30. See also J. Bhattacharya's Hindu Law 608.
3. *Tayubunnissa Bibi* v. *Sham Kishore Roy*, (1871) 7 B.L.R. 621 (628): S. C. 15 W. R.C.R. 228; *Syud Shah Alleh Ahmed* v. *Mussamut Bibee Nuscebun*, (1874) 21 W.R.C.R. 415; *Prosunno Kumari Debya* v. *Golab Chand Baboo*, (1875) L.R. 2 I.A. 145 (152); *Juggodumba Dossee* v *Puddomoney Dossee*, (1875) 15 B.L.R. 318 (330); *Doorga Proshad Dass* v. *Sheo Proshad Pandah*, (1880) 7 C. L. R. 278; *Thackersey Dewraj* v. *Hurbhum Nursey*, (1884) I.L.R., 8 B. 432; *Rupa Jagshet* v. *Krishnaji Govind*, (1884) I.L.R., 9 B. 169; *Manohar Ganesh* v. *Lakhmiram*, (1887) I. L. R., 12 B. 247; *Mulji Bhulabhai* v. *Manohar Ganesh*, (1887) I. L. R., 12 B. 322; *Shri Ganesh Dharnidhar* v. *Kulgavkar*, (1890) I. L. R., 15 B. 625; *Nilmony Singh* v. *Jagabandhu Roy*, (1896) I. L. R., 23 C. 536; *Girijanund Dattajha* v. *Sailajanund Dattajha*, (1896) I. L. R., 23 C. 645; *Muthusami Pillai* v. *Queen-Empress*, (1895) 6 M L. J. R. 14; S. C. I. L. R., 21 M. 170 (212): S. C. I. L. R., 26 M. 243 (note); *Bhuggobutty Prosonno Sen* v. *Gooroo Prosonno Sen*, (1897) I. L. R., 25 C. 112; *Seshadri Ayyangar* v. *Nataraja Ayyar*, (1898) I. L. R., 21 M. 179; *Tulsidas Mahanta* v. *Bejoy Kishore Shome*, (1901) 6 C.W.N. 178; *Vidyapurna Thirthaswami* v. *Vidyanidhi Thirthaswami*, (1904) 14 M. L. J. R. 105. See also *Kumara Asima Krishna Deb* v. *Kumara Kumara Krishna Deb*, (1868) 2 B. L. R. O C. J., 11 (47) where Mr. Justice *Markby* observed that an idol was a *Caput Mortuum*; *Maharanee Shibessouree Debia* v. *Mothooranath Acharjo*, (1869) 13 M. I. A. 270, where it was held that the Shebait had no legal property; and *Ranjit Singh* v. *Jagannath Prosad Gupta*, (1885) I. L. R., 12 C. 375 where it was observed that the idol was the *cestui que trust*. But see *Raghubar Dial* v. *Kesho Ramanuj Das*, (1888) I. L. R., 11 A. 18.

to the Roman Law or those derived from it[1]. Thus Mr. Justice *Scott* in *Thackersey Dewraj* v. *Hurbhum Nursey*[2] observed: "The deity of the temple is considered in Hindu Law as a sacred entity or ideal personality possessing proprietary rights." The same view has been taken by the English text-writers on Hindu Law. Thus West and Buhler in their Digest on Hindu Law observe[3]: "The idol, deity or religious object is looked on as a kind of human entity."

Effect of vivification ceremonies.

No doubt the Hindu sacred writings the *Agama* Shastras as they are called provide an elaborate procedure to be followed or observed in building temples, making, &c., images and consecrating the same. Many of these observances are stated in Saraswati on Endowments[4]. But many of such observances are intended mainly though not solely for what are called the *pratishta*, established or artificial idols as distinguished from the *Svayambhu* or self-revealed idols. These *pratishta* idols are classified according to the modes and materials of construction. These idols may take the form of moulded figures or of pictures[5]. If they take the form of moulded figures they may be made of clay, wood, stone, or metals such as gold, silver, brass, copper, &c. In all these cases provisions are made in minute detail for the quality of clay &c., to be employed and the ceremonies to be observed in collecting the materials and in the process of manufacture. Rules are also made for the size, shape and figure of these images. Defects in proportion are said to result in evil consequences on various persons including the maker and therefore the greatest care has to be taken in the manufacture of these images. But so far as we are aware no sacred text tells us that when an image is made in breach of some of these rules or has some of these defects the deity represented by the image is not a juridical person. Rules are also made for the consecration of these images. There is a ceremony of

---

1. *Manohar Ganesh Tambekar* v. *Lakhmiram Govindram*, (1887) I. L. R., 12 B. 247; *Vidyapurana Thirthaswami* v. *Vidyanidhi Thirthaswami*, (1904) 14 M. L. J. R., 105.

2. (1884) I. L. R., 8 B. 432. See *Babajirao* v. *Laxmandas*, (1903) I. L. R. 28 B. 215 (223).

3. 3rd Edn. (1884) pp. 185 (*b*) and 201.

4. Chapters III and IV, pp. 42 to 132. Some of these rules are also stated in Rao Saheb Vishwanath Narayan Mandlik's Hindu Law Books (Mayukha) App. II pp. 335 to 337, 339 and 343.

5. *Gossamee Sree Greedharreejee* v. *Rumanloljee Gossamee*, (1889) L. R., 16 I. A. 137: S. C. I. L. R., 17 C. 3 where the dispute was as to a portrait for which worship was founded.

vivification or as it is called the *Prana Pratishta* and it is said that by the process of vivification the image from its previous status as an inanimate object (a simple piece of clay, stone or metal) acquires the status of a juridical personage capable of holding property[1]. The same view is endorsed by the Calcutta High Court in *Doorga Proshad Dass* v. *Sheo Proshad Pandah*[2]. It is there observed : "According to Hindu notions when an idol has once been, so to say, consecrated by the appropriate ceremony performed and mantra pronounced, the deity of which the idol is the visible image resides in it, and not in any substituted image and the idol, so spiritualised, becomes what has been termed a juridical person." The view above taken is, however, not quite accurate. It is not correct to say that the image which is mystified by the vivication ceremony is the juridical person. The juridical person is the deity who is invoked by the mantras used in the vivication ceremony to reside in the image and it is that deity and not that image[3] that is in law the juridical person. We do not think that by quoting the above passage in the *recent mutt case*[4] *Sir S. Subramania Iyer* Offg. C. J. meant to lay down anything contrary to what we have stated to be the correct principle. This view will avoid the absurdity to which the Calcutta High Court has been driven in more cases than one[5] where it has been held that a gift to an idol which is to be consecrated must be treated as a gift to an unborn person and therefore such gift is invalid and illegal. We can never understand a religion which takes a view that a deity is to be born hereafter and at any rate the Hindu religion is not such a one. The deity is always existent and it is idle and absurd to apply the principle that a gift to an unborn person is invalid (even assuming that the Mitakshara School of Hindu Law ever knows of such principle) to such a case.

---

1. Saraswati on Endowments p. 116.
2. (1880) 7 C. L. R., 278 (280).
3. In fact in the Hindu religion the deity may reside anywhere. It is not necessary that it should reside in the image made of clay or other substance. The deity may reside in a tree which is therefore, regarded as sacred. See *Baijulal Parbatia* v. *Bolaklal Pathuk*, (1897) I. L. R., 24 C. 385; *Dinonath Chuckerbutty* v. *Pratapchandra Goswami*, (1899) I. L. R., 27 C. 30. Worship performed for such image is regarded as worship performed for the *deity*.
4. *Vidyapurna Thirtha Swami* v. *Vidyanidhi Thirtha Swami*, (1904) 14 M. L. J., R. 105.
5. *Upendra Lal Boral* v. *Hem Chundra Boral*, (1897) I. L. R., 25 C. 405; *Rojomoyee Dassee* v. *Troylukho Mohiney Dassee*, (1901) I. L. R., 29 C. 260; *Nogendra-Nandini Dassi* v. *Benoy Krishna Deb*, (1902) I. L. R., 30 C. 521. See the criticism of these cases in Ch. VII pp. xcii to xcv and in Ghose on Hindu Law, 693. See also the criticism in the Madras Law Journal Vols. XII and XIII at pp. 186 and 201 respectively.

Ownership of endowed properties.

The idol, *i. e.*, the deity being the juridical person the property vests in such idol or deity and the image itself is not owned by any natural person. Property in such image and in the temple vests in the idol or deity of which the image is the visible representation. Property endowed for religious purposes is *res sacra*[1] and is said to be absolutely *extra commercium*[2] An idol is said to be *caput mortuum* and incapable of alienating[3] but it may not follow from this that the manager may not alienate for any proved necessity. If the principle is that property is ever tied up in the Almighty and the law of perpetuities has no application, it seems but reasonable to hold that endowed property—the *corpus* as distinguished from the *income*—cannot be pledged or mortgaged even for temple necessity. In fact this seems to be the view prevailing in Bombay[4]. The authority of the Bombay decisions is strengthened by S. 8 cl. (3) of Bombay Act II of 1863 which enacts[5] as follows:—"It is, however, hereby declared that lands held on behalf of religious or charitable institutions, wholly or partially exempt from the payment of land-revenue, shall not be transferable from such institutions either by assignment, sale (whether such sale be judicial, public or private), gift, devise or otherwise howsoever, and no nazarna shall be leviable on account of such lands". On this provision it may be observed at the outset that it applies only to lands held on behalf of religious or charitable institutions *wholly or partially exempt* from payment of land-revenue. If such lands be not exempt from payment of land-revenue the clause has no application. But it has been observed by *Westropp*, C. J. and *Birdwood*, J. in *Narayan* v. *Chintaman*[5] that the above section contained no new law but merely declared the pre-existing common law of this country. If this were so even lands not exempt from payment of land-revenue could not be alienated *i. e.*, the *corpus* as distinguished from the *income*. It may *next* be observed that although there is a prohibition against alienation by S. 8 cl. (3) of Act II of 1863 there is no absolute

---

1. *Thackersey Dewraj* v. *Hurbhum Nursey*, (1884) I. L. R., 8 B. 432.

2. *Thackersey Dewraj* v. *Hurbhum Nursey* supra. See also *Rajah Rajah Varma Valiya* v. *Kottayath Kiyaki Kovilagath Revi Varma*, (1873) 7 M. H. C. 210 where Mr. Justice *Holloway* says that the jewels devoted to the service of an idol as distinguished from other property are *res extra commercium*.

3. *Kumara Asima Krishna Deb* v. *Kumara Kumara Krishna Deb*, (1868) 2 B. L. R. (O. C. J.) 11 at p. 47.

4. *Narayan* v. *Chintaman*, (1881) I. L. R., 5 B. 393; *Collector of Thana* v. *Hari Sitaram*, (1882) I. L. R., 6 B. 546; *Shri Ganesh Dharnidhar Maharajdev* v. *Keshavrav Govind Kulgavkar*, (1890) I. L. R., 15 B. 625.

5. (1881) I. L. R., 5 B. 393. See also *Krishnarav* v. *Rangrav*, (1867) 4 B. H. C. A. C. J. 1.

prohibition against alienation of such lands so that on the wording of the clause it is still open whether it is intended to prohibit an alienation for a necessary purpose. It may be that this contention may not ultimately prevail. It seems only reasonable that the Government should make a special provision in respect of lands which are exempt from land-revenue and which are so exempted because of their being owned by a religious institution. The words "shall not be transferrable" may, therefore, be construed to mean *shall not be transferrable for any purpose or shall in no way be transferrable.* That may be a reasonable construction to be placed upon the clause.

Be this as it may, the rule enacted in that clause must be regarded as too wide in other parts of India in the light of the decided cases. Without referring to these in detail we may take it that the following observations of *Stanley* C. J. and *Banerji* J. in the recent case of *Parsotam Gir v. Dat Gir*[1] represent the correct law as understood in places not governed by Bombay Act II of 1863 :—" The result to be gleaned from the cases is that, with the exception of cases which come under the operation of Bombay Act II of 1863, there is no absolute prohibition against the alienation of the endowed property by the manager for the time being, but that, on the contrary, for the necessary purposes of preserving or

1. (1903) I. L. R., 25 A. 296 (311). See also *Rumonee Debia* v. *Baluck Doss* (1870) 14 W. R. 101 : S. C 11 B. L. R. 336 (note); *Tayub-un-nissa Bibi* v. *Sham Kishore Roy*, (1871) 7 B. L. R., 621; *Prosunno Kumari Debya* v. *Golab Chand Baboo*, (1875) L. R., 2 I. A. 145 (151) : S. C. 14 B. L. R., 450 (469); *Konwur Doorganath Roy* v. *Ram Chunder Sen*, (1876) L. R. 4 I. A. 52 (64): S. C. I. L. R., 2 C. 341. But see *Maharanee Shibessouree Debia* v. *Mothooranath Acharjo*, (1869) 13 M. I. A., 270 : S. C. 13 W. R. (P. C.) 18; *Durga Bibi* v. *Chanchal Ram*, (1881) I. L. R., 4 A. 81; and Per Justice *Sir V. BhashyamAiyangar* in *Vidyapurna Thirtha Swami* v. *Vidyanidhi Thirtha Swami*, (1904) 14 M. L. J R., 105 (120). See also Ghose on H. L 698. Even mutt property has been held to be alienable for mutt purposes. See *Ram Churn Pooree* v *Nunhoo Mundul*, (1870) 14 W. R C. R., 147; *Mohunt Burm Suroop Doss* v. *Khashee Jha*, (1873) 20 W. R. C. R., 471; *Sammantha Pandara* v. *Sellappa Chetti*, (1879) I. L. R., 2 M. 175 (179); *Giyana Sambandha Pandara Sannadhi* v. *Kandasami Tambiran*, (1887) I. L. R., 10 M. 375 (474); *Saminatha* v *Purushottama*, (1892) I. L. R., 16 M, 67; *Kasim Saiba* v. *Sudhindra Thirtha Swami*, (1895) I. L. R , 18 M. 359; *Sheo Shankar Gir* v. *Ram Shewak Chowdhri*, (1896) I. L. R. 24 C. 77; *Vidyapurna Thirtha Swami* v. *Vidyanidhi Thirtha Swami*, (1904) 14 M. L. J. R., 105 (109, 124 and 125). But such purposes must be limited. The cases of *Khusalchand* v. *Mahadevgiri*, (1875) 12 B. H. C., 214 and *Shankar Bharati Swami* v. *Venkapa Naik*, (1885) I. L. R., 9 B 422 may be explained as not being inconsistent with the Bombay view. See also cases cited in li note (2) and lii note (1).

maintaining the endowment, alienation of the endowed property by the manager is lawful."

Another instance of endowments familiar to Hindus is to be found in the case of *mutts*. In its original and narrow sense the term "mutt" signified the residence of an ascetic or sannyasi or paradesi. A Hindu mutt somewhat resembles a catholic monastery. It is primarily a building or set of buildings in which Hindu religious mendicants reside under a superior (mahant). Though a place of worship is not a necessary part of a mutt one is always found which is primarily intended for the inmates but in which the public may be admitted. From this circumstance it is said that the term mutt has acquired a secondary signification as a small temple[1]. The typical mutt, therefore, consists of an endowed temple or shrine with a dwelling place for the superior or head of the mutt (called Mohant) and his disciples (or chelas). The Mohant by devoting himself to a religious life severed himself from all worldly possessions and he thenceforward became theoretically dead to the world[2]. Even if he irregularly continues in the enjoyment of worldly property, it will, it is said, go on his actual death to his personal heirs, while the property belonging to the mutt will go to his successors in office[3]. But if the theory is that a person by renouncing the worldly pleasurers and by becoming a Sanyasi and a disciple of another ascetic is affiliated to the spiritual family of his preceptor[4] then it must, on the analogy of adoption, go to his disciple or preceptor. Mutts.

In most of the many sects into which the Hindus are divided, there apparently exists a clerical class which is commonly separated into two orders, *viz.*, (in European phraseology) the monastic (or ascetic) and the secular. The first of these is celibate and in a great degree erratic and mendicant but has anchorage places and head-quarters in the mutts. The class of ascetics or hermits has existed as a part of the social system obtaining among the Hindus from a very early period. They profess to have renounced all family ties and all desires for wealth and women and devoted themselves to religious Ascetics or hermits.

1. *Subraya* v. *Arundel*, (1883) I. L. R., 6 M. 287.

2. *Gossain Dowlut Geer* v. *Bissessur Geer* (1873), 19 W. R. (C. R.) 215.

3. *Gossain Dowlut Geer* v. *Bissessur Geer* supra; (1853), B. S. D. A. p. 1089; and see *Dharmapuram Pandara Sannadhi* v. *Virapandiyam Pillai* (1898), I. L. R., 22 M. 302, as regards Sudra parndesis.

4. *Giyana Sambandha Pandara Sannadhi* v. *Kandasami Tambiran*, (1887) I.L.R., 10 M. 375 at pp. 384, 385, 420, 493 and 501.

study, contemplation and service in the view of securing immunity from future births (to which according to their faith they believe they are liable) and spiritual happiness. Yajnavalkya in his Smriti has recognised this class and has propounded a special rule which, in the absence of special usage, governs the succession to his property[1].

Terms explained.

If an ascetic or hermit is a Brahmin, he is called a *yati* or *sannyasi*; if a Sudra, he is called a *paradesi*, and if a Sudra is attached to an Adhinam, he is called a *Tambiran*, and if the latter is at the head of the Adhinam, he is called a *Pandara Sannadhi*. The term "Adhinam" signifies the seat of the chief ascetic at the head of a religious institution or brotherhood or a holy crowd and takes its name from the village in which it is situated[2].

Origin of mutts.

The origin of mutts is generally as follows[3]. A preceptor of religious doctrines gathers around him a number of disciples whom he initiates into the particular mysteries of the order and instructs them in its religious tenets. Such of these disciples as intend to become religious teachers renounce their connection with the family and all claims to their family wealth and, as it were, affiliate themselves to the spiritual teacher whose school they enter. Originally, the ascetic who renounced the world and devoted himself to religion, confined his attention to the study of theology, to imparting religious instruction to his disciples and to complying with the ordinances prescribed for the guidance of his order. He then owned no property, except his cloths, sandals, religious books, the idols which he kept for his personal worship and a few other articles of trifling value which were absolutely necessary for him. He had no fixed residence and moved from village to village, accepting such lodgings and food as were provided for him by pious laymen who were in their turn enjoined by the *shastras* to honor and support him. As Justice *Sir T. Muthusawmy Iyer* observed in the *Tiruppanundal case*[2]: "This is the mode in which Brahman sannyasis live even at the present time." These mutts were, therefore, founded in the first instance in several villages by

1. *Sammantha Pandara* v. *Sellappa Chetti* (1879), I. L. R., 2 M. 175.

2. *Giyana Sambandha Pandara Sannadhi* v. *Kandasami Tambiran* (1887), I.L.R., 10 M. 375 (385).

3. *Sammantha Pandara* v. *Sellappa Chetti*, (1879) I. L. R., 2 M. 175 (179) cited with approval by *Sir V. Bhashyam Aiyangar*, J., in *Vidyapurna Thirtha Swami* v. *Vidyanidhi Thirtha Swami*, (1904) 14 M. L. J. R., 105 (123).

pious laymen who erected buildings for the residence of hermits when they visited their villages. When, however, the Buddhists assailed the Brahminical religion and when Sankaracharya, the founder of the *Advaita* or non-dualistic school of philosophy, ultimately prevailed against them, he established some mutts[1] in order to maintain and strengthen the doctrine and the system of religious philosophy he taught, sannyasis being placed at the head of these institutions. After him, the founder of the Vaishnava, the Madhva and other schools of religious philosophy in Southern India established mutts for a similar purpose.

History and growth of mutts—Their objects.

It would seem that Buddha was "the first teacher in history who founded regular establishments for monks and nuns"[2]. Ascetic life was the natural growth of the teaching of Buddhisms. The Sanghramas (glimpses of which are seen from the dramas of Kalidasa and Bhavabhuti) were the models for the future Brahministic mutts. Buddhism received a rude shock at the hands of the great Sankaracharya, the founder of the Advaita or non-dualistic school of philosophy. By his gigantic efforts Hinduism was re-established as the dominant religion of India. He established some mutts in order to maintain and strengthen the doctrine and system of religious philosopy he taught *sannyasis* being placed at the head of these institutions[3]. *Sir S. Subramania Aiyar* in his judgment in the recent *mutt case*[4] observed: "There can be no doubt that institutions of the class under consideration were established as centres of theological learning, and in order to provide a line of competent teachers with reference to the establised Hindu creeds of the country. If any proof of this statement were necessary, that is furnished by the unquestionable connection which exists between some of the more important of this class of institutions and the leading exponents of the tenets of those creeds. As pointed out in Mr. Ghose's Hindu Law p. 680, no less than seven mutts[5], being among the

1. *Giyana Sambandha Pandura* v. *Kandasami* (1887) I. L. R. 10 M. 375.
2. Ghose on Hindu Law 678.
3. The Sringeri mutt in Mysore was the one founded by him. Gradually it was divided into 5 or 6 mutts. He was the founder of the Smartava Sect and flourished more than 1,000 years ago. The Swamis of these mutts claim to be regarded as successors of Sri Sankaracharya. *Sri Sunkur Bharti Swami* v. *Sidha Lingayath Charanti*, (1843) 3 M. I. A. 198: S. C. 6 W. R. (P. C.) 39.
4. *Vidyapurna Thirtha Swami* v. *Vidyanidhi Thirtha Swami*, (1904) 14 M.L.J.R. 105 (107).
5. This is a little inaccurate. What he says is that Sankara established 4 mutts in four places Badrinath, Dwarka, Puri and Sringeri and that these 4 mutts are called the Sarada, the Joshi, the Goberdhan and Sree mutts.

most celebrated, owe their origin to Sankaracharya. Other mutts not less numerous or important following the tenets of the Vishishtadwaita system of Ramanujacharya are traceable to that teacher. The well-known eight mutts at Udipi, the centre of the dwaita system of thought, are on all hands admitted to have been founded by Madhwachariya, the great expounder of that system. The Sudra mutts of this Presidency of which those at Dharmapuram and Tiruvaduthorai are the chief, represent what is known as the Saiva Siddhantam." As regards Southern India, *Sir T. Muthusawmy Iyer*, in his learned judgment in the *Tiruppanandal case*[1], observed : "The origin of these institutions, their constitution and development form part of the history of the establishment and spread of Brahminical systems of religious doctrine among the Sudra communities in Southern India." Pious and learned ascetics among them actuated by a desire to disseminate religious knowledge and promote religious charity, established mutts in Tinnevelly, Madura, Trichinopoly, Tanjore and elsewhere.

Position and influence of mutts.

In former times these institutions exercised considerable influence over the laymen in their neighbourhood and were centres of classical and religious learning and materially aided in promoting religious knowledge and in encouraging religious and other charities. The ascetics who presided over them were, owing to their position as religious preceptors and often also in consequence of their own learning and piety, held in great reverence by Hindu princes and noblemen who from time to time made large presents to them and endowed the mutts under their control with grants of land[1]. In some cases the mutts were offshoots of an already existing wealthy mutt, and the endowment was made by such latter mutt[2]. Thus, a class of endowed mutts came into existence, in the nature of monastic institutions presided over by ascetics or sannyasis who had renounced the world, and it came to pass that the ascetic, who originally owned little or no property, came to own the mattam under his charge and its endowment in trust for the maintenance of the mutt, for his own support, for that of

---

1. *Giyana Sambandha Pandara Sannadhi* v. *Kandasami Tambiran* (1887), I. L. R., 10 M. 375. See also *Gossain Doulut Geer* v. *Bissessur Geer*, (1873) 19 W. R. C. R. 215 ; *Sammantha Pandara* v. *Sellappa Chetti* (1879), I. L. R., 2 M. 175.

2. *Gossain Doulut Geer* v. *Bissessur Geer*, supra.

his disciples, and for the performance of religious and other charities in connection with it. A home for the school is erected and a mutt is constituted[1].

Adhinam and Mutt distinguished.

There are two distinctions between an *Adhinam* and a *mutt* as an endowed institution. (1) A *mutt* is chiefly an isolated institution, whilst an *Adhinam* is chiefly a central institution from which the chief ascetic exercises control and supervision over a group of endowed institutions and religious trusts committed to his management and subject to his jurisdiction as the responsible trustee. (2) The general rule is that an ascetic is prevented by usage of his order from owning or managing property for personal enjoyment. In the case of a *mutt* there is only one exception to this general rule, *viz.*, that the head of a mutt is allowed to administer mutt endowments and the reason is that such administration is in furtherance of the cause of religion. In the case of *Adhinams,* however, an additional exception is allowed. For, among Sudras, "the administration of temple endowments, of endowments instituted for special services in Hindu temples, and of endowments founded for the support of religious and other charities either in particular places or on particular occasions," is also considered to fall under the exception[1].

Heads of mutts not confined to old pursuits.

There can be no doubt, however, that in many cases, the heads of mutts (or the mohunts), by deviation from the strict path of sanctity originally marked out for them, have made the acquirement of wealth by trade their great object. Now-a-days it is hard to find the heads of these institutions prosecuting with the rigour adhered to in old times the objects for which such institutions have been founded. In many cases the heads of these mutts have become worldly or are not even versed in the first principles of the Hindu religion, not to speak of the fact that they rarely attempt to propagate or promote religious knowledge, and that these mutts are only in name the centres of classical and religious learning.

Gosami mutts.

Gosami mutts are of a character different from the ordinary mutt. A *gosami* or a *gosavi* is not a religious ascetic like a Sanyasi or Tambiran who abjures the world and its pleasures and lives a life of celibacy, but a married man who is considered to live a pious life affording "religious instructions" to those who seek it from him, performing religious charities and delivering lectures on

1. *Giyana Sambandha Pandara* v. *Kandasami Tambiran,* (1887) I. L. R., 10 M. 375.

religious subjects and on the duty of man to God and his fellow creatures. The Gosavis as well as the Bairagis receive among their number Sudras and women. Concubinage is allowed by their custom and some marry. They cannot, therefore, claim to be Sanyasis[1]. But the property given to Gosavis who are heads of these mutts is not private but endowed property. Where, therefore, a grant was made to the head of a *Gosami* mutt to be enjoyed from generation to generation and the grant provided that the grantee was to improve the mutt and maintain the charity and be happy, it was held by the Madras High Court in *Sathianama Bharati* v. *Saravana Bagi Ammal*[2] that the grant was an endowment in trust for the mutt and the charities connected therewith (though what might remain after the due execution of the trust was intended to be applied for the maintenance of the grantee or his descendants) and not merely a grant of private property to the original grantee, on which certain trusts were engrafted so as to impose on him an obligation to apply a portion of the income of the village to those trusts and that the office of the head of this mutt was hereditary in the grantee's family. Among the Gosains of the Dekkhan and other places marriage does not work a forfeiture of the office of mahant and the rights and property appendant to such office[3].

Public or private mutts.

These mutts may be public or private. An instance of a private mutt is to be found in the case of *Sathappayyar* v. *Periasami*[4] decided by the Madras High Court. We shall have to advert later on about the rules governing the succession to mutts and the rights and duties of the heads of mutts.

Ideal person in the case of mutts.

We have next to consider the jural character of these mutts and their heads. We have seen that in the case of temples the ideal or the juristic person is the deity who is capable of possessing rights and holding property. In the *Ranchhod temple case*[5], *West*, J., observed : "The Hindu law recognises . . . . . . the juridical subjects or persons called foundations." We have to see whether the same or different principles apply in the case of *mutts*.

1. W. and B. Dig. of H. L., pp. 552, 553 and 572.

2. (1894) I. L. R., 18 M. 266. See also *Khusalchand* v. *Mahadevgiri*, (1875) 12 B. H. C. 214; *Shankar Bharati* v. *Venkapa Naik*, (1885) I. L. R., 9 B. 422.

3. *Gosain Rambharti* v. *Suraj Bharti*, (1880) I. L. R., 5 B. 682.

4. (1890) I. L. R., 14 M. 1.

5. (1887) I. L. R., 12 B. 247 (264).

In a recent case upon the subject[1] it is said that in the case of mutts the ideal person is the office of the spiritual teacher or Acharya which, as it were, is incarnate in the person of each successive Swami. The object of these mutts is, as already stated, to facilitate spiritual instruction and the acquisition of religious knowledge, to promote the Hindu religion and to represent to the laity the true nature of God according to the Hindu religion. The original founders of these mutts are generally regarded with great veneration and in fact the great Sankaracharya, the mutts founded by whom still retain a great part of their original pre-eminence, is regarded as a great saint[2] having miraculous or supernatural powers. So also Ramanujacharya and Madhwacharya, the founders respectively of the Visishtadwaita and Dwaita systems of philosophy, are regarded with great veneration and as great saints. But all these were simply mouth-pieces of the Deity and purported to teach the people the nature of the Deity according to their respective ideas of the Hindu religion. The heads of these mutts also worship the image of a deity purported to have been given to them or worshipped by the original founder or spiritual ancestor. It will be, therefore, more correct to say that in the case of these mutts the ideal person is also the Deity and that the property of these mutts vests in such Deity. According to strict Hindu notions, sanyasis (who are heads of these mutts generally) cannot hold or acquire any property, and as mutts are endowed with properties it is more in consonance with such notions to regard the *Deity* as being the owner of such properties. Thus Mr. G. Sarkar Sastri in his work on Hindu Law says[3]: "The property belonging to these *mutts* is regarded as *Debutter* belonging to the deity established by the founder." In support of this we may also point out that the property belonging to these mutts (at any rate those existing in Southern India) and the mutt accounts stand in the names of the deity worshipped by the heads of these mutts[4]. In the Ahobilam Mutt, the property stands and the accounts run in the name of Alagasingar. In the Sringeri Mutt the name of Chandramouleeswara

Office of spiritual teacher or deity.

1. *Vidyapurna Thirtha Swami* v. *Vidyanidhi Thirtha Swami*, (1904) 14 M L. J. R. 105.

2. In fact he is regarded as an incarnation of the Deity. *Sri Sunkur Bharati Swami* v. *Sidha Lingayah Charanti*, (1843) 3 M. I. A., 198; S. C. 6 W. R. P. C. 39.

3. Page 333. But it may be pointed out that the theory propounded in the recent mutt case receives some support from the fact that Mr. Mandlik says that the dedication in the case of a mutt is to a Brahmin or other person. Mandlik's H. L., Books (Mayukha), App. II, p. 336.

4. The Udipi mutts are also an instance. See Blue Books 1849 (Idolatry) 162.

Swami appears. This may be said to be benami and consistent with the view laid down in the *mutt case*. But the question of benami has to be proved by the person setting it up and must not be assumed.

Nature of interest possessed by heads of mutts.

But whatever may be the correct view (whether the ideal person is the office of the spiritual teacher or the deity as in the analogous case of temples or the mutt itself[1]) the view taken in the recent case on some false English analogy of the office of a Bishop that the head of a mutt for the time being is a real owner and has a beneficial interest in the usufruct or an estate for life[2] in its permanent endowments and an absolute property in the income derived from the offerings of his followers is, with all respect to the learned Judges who took part in that case, not in consonance with Hindu notions and not supported by authority. It is submitted that it is wrong to draw conclusions from supposed English analogies or to apply principles obtaining in English Law to a country wholly different in its circumstances and surroundings. Indeed under the common law the whole estate was vested in the Bishop who was only restrained from alienating by statutes.[3] The analogy of the Sajjadanushin of the Mahomedan Law though not complete may be more in point. Even there the property is regarded as that of the deity. That there are restrictions imposed on the head of a mutt in dealing with the income seems to have been admitted, but the learned judges try to get over the same by saying that such restrictions are not enforceable legal obligations[4]. No reasons are assigned for treating such restrictions as mere moral obligations. No doubt it will fit in with the theory propounded in the judgments in that case that a mutt resembles a bishopric and the office of the head of a mutt resembles that of a Bishop. As regards offerings made to the head of a mutt on principle there is no justification for supposing that he can utilise the same for his own benefit and at his pleasure. Where the head of a mutt is a *Sannyasi* there may, in the generality of cases[1] be practically no question of a dual capacity (one his own right and the other as representing the mutt)[5]. Therefore the principle that it is a question of intention whether a grant made to a person[6] enures

1. *Babajirao* v *Laxmandas*, (1903) I. L. R., 28 B. 215 (223).

2. See *Mohunt Rumun Doss* v. *Mohunt Ashbull Doss*, (1864) 1 W. R. C. R.. 160; and *Mohunt Burm Suroop Doss* v. *Khasheejha*, (1873) 20 W. R. C. R. 471 (472).

3. Coke upon Littleton Vol. I, 44*a*, Vol. II, 300*b* and 325*b*. See *The Mayor of Colchester* v. *Lowten*, (1813) 1 V. & B. 226 (244): S. C. 12 R. R. 216.

4. *Vidyapurna* v. *Vidyanidhi*, (1904) 14 M. L. J R., at pp. 111 and 124.

5. Strictly this may not be correct. The Madras High Court has even held that he can acquire property for his own use. *Sree Mahant Kishore Dossjee* v. *The Coimbatore Spinning and Weaving Company*, (1902) I. L. R., 26 M. 79.

6. Chapter IV, p. xliv.

to him in his private capacity or in his capacity as head may not apply to the extent it does in other cases. Be this as it may, the offerings are *prima facie* made for the *mutt* and it is rather a startling proposition to say that such offerings especially when they consist of land or of money are at the absolute disposal of the then presiding swami. It is no doubt a fact that some of these *Swamis* or *Sannyasis* misappropriate the endowments under their control. But their wrong will not give them any legal right. It may be good policy to hold that the head has an absolute right in the income and may deal with the properties for his life in any way he pleases. The present inflexible law of limitation is thus defeated. The successor will not be barred if he wishes to recover the property for the mutt. But good policy is not always law.

One of the learned Judges in the case under discussion[1] is at great pains in establishing that a series of life-estates[2] is not unknown to Hindu Law, but whether he is right or wrong in this respect[3], the office of head of a mutt is not one. It is absurd to suppose that he has any *estate* in the property of the mutt which is *vested* by law in the juristic person (*i. e.*, the God or the saint or the office[4] of head of the mutt) and not in any natural person. The position of the head of a mutt is explicable without bringing in aid the doctrine of a perpetual life-estate.

The office of mohunt is a corporation sole.

The head of a mutt may be a good example of a corporation sole[5] and may resemble a bishop, but it is submitted that the analogy between these two begins and ends with the concept of an ideal personality (*i. e.*, the office of Acharya or Bishop as the case may be) and to go further and say that the rights and duties of the head of a mutt and his estate are substantially similar to those of a Bishop is hardly warranted by the Hindu Law. For, in the Hindu mutt the founder is the original spiritual ancestor who is the Acharya or Preceptor and all his successors represent the line of Acharya or Preceptor. This may be no new conception peculiar to

1. *Vidyapurna Thirthaswami* v. *Vidyanidhi Thirthaswami*, (1904) 14 M. L. J. R., at pp 111 and 124.

2. *Kuriabin Hanmia* v. *Gururav*, (1872) 9 B. H. C., A. C. J. 282; and see *Jamal Saheb* v. *Murgaya Swami*, (1885) I. L. R., 10 B. 34.

3. The office of a Bishop &c., relied upon by the learned Judge as an example of a series of life-estates recognised in English Law is really an anamolous estate and is so dealt with. He has a qualified fee-simple. See Adler on Corporations, pp. 82, 83, and *Mulliner* v. *Midland Railway Company*, (1879) 11 Ch. D. 611 (622, 623). A series of inalienable life-estates is equally unknown to the English Law.

4. Salmond's Jurisprudence, p. 439.

5. Even the office of a manager of a temple is regarded as a corporation. See *Rajah Vurmah* v. *Ravi Vurmah*, (1876) L. R., 4 I. A. 76, S. C. I. L. R. 1 M. 235.

the Hindu Law. In the case of the Sajjadanashin the Mahomedan Law, as we shall see later on, expressly recognises that the actual incumbent is not only a mutwalli but also a spiritual preceptor who is supposed to continue the spiritual line of the original dervish who is regarded as a Saint.[1] But no such theory is recognised in the case of an English Bishop.

Head of Mutt mere manager.

If the juridical person is the Deity or Saint, ownership of the mutt properties vests in the Deity or Saint and the superior or head of the mutt is a mere manager. By adopting this view we do not militate against the theory that the office of the superior is a corporation sole. But if, as has been held in the *recent mutt case,*[2] the ideal person is the office of the spiritual teacher (Acharya), either the property of the mutt is vested in the preceptor for the time being[3] so that the latter will have an estate for life in the permanent endowments of the mutt and will, therefore, have a real and beneficial interest in the usufruct, or the property is vested in the ideal person, *i. e.*, the office of the spiritual teacher, so that the actual incumbent for the time being (*i. e.*, the person of flesh and blood) will be merely the agent and representative of the ideal person having, however, a real and beneficial interest in the usufruct. Anyhow, the corpus of the property is absolutely inalienable according to the law as applied in the Bombay Presidency and is inalienable in a qualified way in other parts of India, *i. e.*, in such other parts, the corpus will be inalienable except for a purpose necessary for the maintenance of the institution as a mutt. If the actual incumbent for the time being has a life-estate he has an absolute control over the income. But is he entitled to appropriate the same for his own purposes leaving the mutt to shift for itself with reference to expenses necessary for its maintenance and is he entitled to pledge the *corpus* for such purposes while he keeps in his own hands the income accruing from such property? Surely, the income accruing from such property should *first* be utilised for such purposes and it is only with reference to the surplus that any question should arise as to the disposing power of the head. Out of the surplus income, the head of the

---

1. *Mohiuddin* v. *Sayiduddin*, (1893) I. L. R., 20C. 810.
2. *Vidyapurna Thirtha Swami* v. *Vidyanidhi Thirtha Swami*, (1904) 14 M. L. J. R., 105.
3. The property is attached to the office. It does not descend to the disciples (or the elders in common). See *Sammantha Pandara* v. *Sellappa Chetti*, (1879) I. L. R., 2 M. 175 (179).

mutt has to maintain himself, but beyond this we do not see how he can have a property in the surplus[1]. If it is a question of policy we should be disposed to say that it is more expedient in the present state of these institutions and of the law to adopt the view laid down by the Madras High Court in the *recent mutt case*[2] as being best calculated to preserve at any rate the *corpus* of the property for the mutt as the same will not be affected by any disposition by the actual incumbent for other than mutt purposes and the successor will be entitled on the death of the Swami who has alienated to recover the corpus for the mutt[3] without fear of the statutory bar of limitation. In the case of mutts the necessary purposes are limited[4] and guided by usage and the "necessity can arise but rarely, at any rate not to the extent to which it may in the case of temples." A debt incurred by the mutt is not for a necessary purpose merely because it is incurred for general religious and charitable purposes appropriate to an ascetic or head of the mutt[5].

Mutts are classified according to the different ways in which their heads are appointed[6]:—(1) Mutts in which the mohantship (headship) goes to the last mohant's personal heir. (2) Mutts in which the succession goes by nomination by the previous mohant[7]. (3) Mutts in which the mohantship is by election. The mutts of the same sect in a district or mutts having a common origin are assembled together (the mohants of these acknowledging

Classification of mutts.

1. The case of *Sammantha Pandara* v. *Sellappa Chetty*, (1879) I. L. R., 2 M. 175 (179) shows that the head has no absolute right over the income. He can only apply it to a purpose which may fairly be regarded as being in furtherance of the objects of the institution. Cf. *Kolandai Mudali* v. *Sankara Bharadhi*, (1882) I. L. R., 5 M. 302.

2. *Vidyapurna Thirtha Swami* v. *Vidyanidhi Thirtha Swami*, (1904) 14 M. L. J. R. 105.

3. *Mohunt Burm Suroop Doss* v. *Khashee Jha*, (1873) 20 W. R. C. R. 471 (472).

4. *Vidyapurna Thirtha Swami* v. *Vidyanidhi Thirtha Swami*, (1904) 14 M. L. J. R., 105 (125).

5. *Vidyapurna Thirtha Swami* v. *Vidyanidhi Thirtha Swami*, (1904) 14 M. L. J. R., 105 (109 and 125). If the Judgment in *Sammantha Pandara* v. *Sellappa Chetty*, supra, had stated "for purposes necessary for his mattam" instead of "purposes connected with his mattam," then it would represent a strictly correct proposition of law. See also *Saminatha* v. *Purushottama*, (1892) I. L. R., 16 M. 67.

6. *Gossain Dowlut Geer* v. *Bissessur Geer*, (1873) 19 W. R. (C. R.) 215. See *Sitaperahad* v. *Thakur Dass*, (1879) 5 C. L. R., 73 and *Dhuncooverbai* v. *The Advocate-General*, (1899) 1 Bom. L. R. 743 (748), where mutts or the Mohunts are divided into *Hakimi*, *Punchaiti* and *Maurasi*. In the last case the successor comes in by the appointment of the old Mohant or failing that by the election of the neighbouring Mohants; in the *Punchaiti* the office is elective; and in the *Hakimi* the appointment is vested in the ruling power or in the endower. See also *Mohant Ramanooj Doss* v. *Mohunt Debraj Doss*, (1839) 6 B. S. D. 262.

7. *Greedharee Doss* v. *Nandkishore Dutt*, (1863) Marsh 573; *Trimbakpuri Guri Sitalpuri* v. *Gangabai*, (1887) I. L. R., 11 B. 514; *Bhagavan Ramanuj Das* v. *Ramprapanna*, (1895) L. R. 22 I. A. 94; S. C. I. L. R., 22 C. 843.

one of their number as a head) on the death of one of the mohants and the other mohants assemble to elect a successor out of the *chelas* or disciples of the deceased if possible, or if there be none of them qualified, then from the chelas of another mohant, and after the election, the chosen disciple is installed in the *gaddi* of his predecessor with much ceremony[1].

Parent and dependent mutts.

There are mutts which are offshoots of another parent mutt. The mutt at Benares affords an instance. It would seem that when one Masilamoni Desigar was the Pandara Sannadhi at Dharmapuram, a Tambiran of his Adhinam established the mutt at Benares. Benares being regarded as a holy city by the Hindus, the mutt at Benares naturally rose into pre-eminence and it came to own several subordinate mutts both in northern and southern India, such as the mutts at *Morangi* in Nepaul, at Ahiram in Travancore and at Chidambaram, Rameswaram, Kumbakonam and Trichinopoly. The mutt at Tiruppanandal in its origin the offshoot of the mutt at Benares soon, however, came to be the ultimate centre of control and the Benares mutt was relegated into a subordinate position and was constituted into a subordinate centre of control[2]. But the Tambiran of Tiruppanandal is not subordinate to the Pandara Sannadhi of the Dharmapuram mutt. In the same way the mutt at Pandharpur is an offshoot from the mutt of Shri Jairam Swami at Vadgaon in the Satara district[3].

Kattalai.

Another term which requires some explanation is 'Kattalai.' Counsel in *Subramanian Chettiar* v. *Arunachalam Chettiar*[4] were almost blundering about the meaning of this word. It has two meanings :—(1) Special endowment for certain specific service or religious charity in a temple. (2) The sources of income of a temple classified into distinct endowments placed under a separate manager. The term has been explained by *Sir T. Muthusawmy Iyer* in *Vythilinga Pandara Sannadhi* v. *Somasundara Mudaliar*[5]. He there observes : "In ordinary parlance the term 'Kattalai' as applied to temple endowments signifies a special endowment for certain specific service or religious charity in the temple. *Ardajama Kattalai*

1. *Madho Das* v. *Kanta Das*, (1878) I. L. R., 1 A. 539.

2. *Giyana Sambandha Pandara Sannadhi* v. *Kandasami Tambiran*, (1887) I. L. R., 10 M. 375 (391, 418 and 419). But see *Kashi Bashi Ramling Swamee* v. *Chitumbernath Koomar Swamee*, (1873) 20 W. R. 217 (P.C).

3. *Vithalbowa* v. *Narayan Daji Thite*, (1893) I. L. R., 18 B. 507. Same is the case with the Kapleshur and Hurlakhee mutts. *Mohant Muhader* v. *Bullubh*, (1846) B. S. D. A. 376.

4. (1902) I. L. R., 25 M. 603. S. C. L. R. 29 I. A. 138. 5. (1893). 5. I. L. R., 17 M. 199.

or endowment for midnight service is an instance of the former, and *Annadana Kattalai* or an endowment for distributing food to the poor gratis is an example of the latter. In this sense the word kattalai is used in contradistinction to the endowment designed generally for the upkeep and maintenance of the temple. In the case of some important temples, the sources of their income are classified into distinct endowments according to their importance, each endowment is placed under a separate manager and specific items of expenditure are assigned to it as legitimate charges to be paid therefrom. Each of such endowments is called also a kattalai and the manager who administers it is called theKattalaikar or the stanik of the particular kattalai."

The staniks of the kattalai (or the ulthurai kattalai) are not mere temple servants subordinate to the temple Dharmakartas or punchayatdars. They are managers themselves, and as such can only spend the income of the endowed property upon the particular trusts attached to the katlai of which they are managers.

Family idol—Samadhies of private persons.

An example of a private religious endowment allowed and recognized by the Hindu Law is that of an endowment made in favor of family idols so common in Bengal and other parts of Northern India. The characteristics of these endowments have been already dealt with. We have already referred to private mutts as another example. Whether beyond these endowments in favor of family idols and private mutts there can be found any example of private religious endowment allowed by the Hindu Law is a more difficult and doubtful question. Endowments made for the upkeep, &c., of tombs of saints[1] will be examples of public religious endowments. Whether endowments made for the upkeep of the tombs of persons who have led a religious and austere life, such as Samadhis of ascetics and paradesis, are valid in India, and whether if they are valid, they are exempt from the rule of perpetuities, are points which have not come for decision before the British Indian Courts. But the case of *Sathappayyar* v. *Periasami*[2], decided by the Madras High Court, upholds the validity of private mutts. We are not going very far from the above view, if we say that endowments for the purposes mentioned above are also valid.

1. *Trimbak* v. *Lakshman*, (1895) I. L. R., 20 B. 495.
2. (1890) I. L. R., 14 M. 1.

CHAPTER IX.

EXAMPLES OF MAHOMEDAN RELIGIOUS ENDOWMENTS:—DURGAS, KHANKAS, MOSQUES, &c.

We shall now proceed to consider some familiar instances of Mahomedan public and private religious endowments. We shall see how closely allied to the Hindu endowments some of these instances are as regards their origin, growth and the juristic notions involved[1].

Takkias, Dargas and Khankahs.

We shall first of all refer to Takkias, Dargas and Khankahs. A *takkia* is a place where a dervish resides before he attains sufficient public importance and before disciples gather round him and a lodgment is provided for such disciples[1]. A *darga* is the tomb of a dervish regarded in his life-time as a saint[2]. A khankah is a monastery or place where religious mendicants of the Mahomedan religion temporarily reside[3]. Khankah expenses are such as are incurred in feeding and supporting indigent students, beggars and travellers[4]. These institutions are similar to Hindu mutts.

Origin of Khankahs.

In fact the origin and history of these khankahs are similar to the origin and history of mutts. A dervish or sufi of particular sanctity settled in some locality. Till he attained sufficient importance his place of abode was called a *takkia*. When he should become a man of light and leading in the public estimation this place of abode was called *asthana*. Should his pious life or teaching attract public notice, disciples would gather round him and a place would be constructed for their lodgment and the humble *takkia* would then rise into a khankah. After his death, his grave would become a shrine and an object of pilgrimage not only for his disciples but for people of distant parts whether Hindus or Mahomedans[5].

---

1. *Mohiuddin* v. *Sayiduddin*, (1893) I. L. R., 20 C. 810. See also *Zafaryab Ali* v. *Bakhtawar Singh*, (1883) I. L. R., 5 A. 497. The famous *darga* at *Nagore* in the Tanjore District is a familiar instance of this class of Mahomedan public religious endowments. *Fakurudin Sahib* v. *Ackeni Sahib*, (1880) I. L. R., 2 M. 197. See also *Mija Vali Ulla* v. *Syed Bava Santi Miya*, (1896) I. L. R., 22 B. 496 and Amir Ali, Vol. I, p. 304.

2. *Piran* v. *Abdool Karim*, (1891) I. L. R., 19 C. 203.

3. *Jewun Doss Sahoo* v. *Shah Kubeer-Ood-Deen*, (1841) 2 M. I. A. 390; *Bibee Kuneez Fatima* v. *Bibee Saheba Jan*, (1867) 8 W. R. C. R. 313; and *Mohiuddin* v. *Sayiuddin*, supra.

4. *Bibee Kuneez Fatima* v. *Bibee Saheba Jan*, supra.

5. *Mohiuddin* v. *Sayiduddin*, (1893) I. L. R., 20 C. 810.

These dervishes professed esoteric doctrines and distinct systems of initiation. They were either sufis or the disciples of Mian Roushan Bayezid who flourished about the time of Akbar, and who had founded an independent esoteric brotherhood in which the chief occupied a peculiarly distinctive position. They called themselves *fakirs* on the hypothesis that they had abjured the world and were the humble servitors of God. They were honoured by their followers with the title of *Shah* or *King*. Dervishes.

The preceptor in these different brotherhoods is called the *pir*, and the disciple, the *murid*. On the death of the *pir* his successor assumes the privilege of initiating the disciples into the mysteries of dervishism or sufism. This privilege of initiation, of making *murids*, or of imparting to them spiritual knowledge, is one of the functions which the *Sajjadanashin* (superior) performs or is supposed to perform[1]. The *Sajjadanashin*, *i. e.*, the superior of these monasteries or khankahs, has, therefore, to perform certain spiritual functions. He is not only a mutawalli, but also a spiritual preceptor. He is the curator of the durga where his ancestor is buried and in him is supposed to continue the spiritual line (silsille)[1]. A *Sajjadanashin* literally means one seated on the prayer mat[2], *i. e.*, the chief or superior. So long as the original dervish who came to be regarded as a saint lived, he was the *Sajjadanashin* of the khankah. After his death, some one amongst his heirs indicated by him as qualified to initiate the murids into the mysteries of the tarikat or holy path succeeds him in his office, and then he is, as already observed, not only a mutawalli, but also a spiritual preceptor and is supposed to continue the spiritual line[3]. A *Sajjadanashin* will be justified in appropriating the surplus for the maintenance of himself and his family[3] just as in the case of certain mutts, paradesis are entitled to take some of the income for their *dehapuja*[4]. He is not a mere officer receiving remuneration for service but is an integral part of the institution whose existence depends on his personality[5]. The maintenance of the *Sajjadanashin* is a part of the purpose for which the khanka is established[5]. Pir and murid-Sajjadanashin.

1. *Piran* v. *Abdool Karim*, (1891) I. L. R., 19 C. 203.
2. Macnaghten's Mahomedan Law (Edn. 1890) Prec. End. Case IX, note p. 343
3. *Mohiuddin* v *Sayiduddin*, (1893) I. L. R., 20 C. 810.
4. *Sathappayyar* v. *Periasami*, (1890) I. L. R., 14 M. 1.
5. *The Secretary of State for India* v. *Mohiuddin Ahmad*, (1900) I.L.R., 27 C. 674.

Offices of Sajjadanashin and Mutwaili compared. Rights of woman.

The office of *Sajjadanashin* must not be confounded with the office of *Mutwalli.* The two offices are quite distinct[1]. The Sajjadanashin has charge of the spiritual affairs of the endowment. But the mutwalli has charge of its temporal affairs[1]. One consequence of this is that a woman may be a mutwalli but cannot be a Sajjadanashin. According to the Mahomedan Law, the duties of Mutwalli who has not to perform religious duties or spiritual functions may be discharged by proxy[2]. But the office of Sajjadanashin requires peculiar personal qualifications and the duties attached to that office cannot be discharged by proxy. A woman, therefore, cannot be appointed to such office[3]. Just as in the case of mutts, the appointment of a Sajjada must also be regulated by the practice followed in the particular dargah or khankah or neighbouring dargahs or khankahs. It may happen that in some cases the offices of Mutwalli and Sajjada are combined in the same person. Then also a woman cannot be appointed. The appointment of a child of tender years seems opposed to the constitution of the office[4]. It appears, however, that the appointment of a minor as mutwalli is also illegal unless the office should devolve upon a minor by virtue of a provision in the deed of wakf or unless a minor should be appointed by the endower himself[5].

Mosque.

Another example of a public religious endowment allowed by the Mahomedan Law is that of a mosque. We had to advert to the nature of a mosque on a former occasion. We there said that, in the absence of any reservation, a mosque is a place where all Mahomedans are entitled to go and perform their devotions as of right according to their conscience, and that no one sect or portion of the Mahomedan community can restrain any other from the exercise of this right[6]. In the absence of any reservation the mosque is a public one.

1. Macnaghten's Mahomedan Law (Edn. 1890), Prec. End. Case IX, note p. 343; Ibid. Case viii, p. 340 (note 1); Dig. No. 28, p. 469.

2. Macnaghten's Mahomedan Law (Edn. 1890) Prec. End. Case IX, note p. 343; Ibid. case viii, p. 340 (note 1); Ibid, Dig (No. 28) p. 469; *Hussain Beebee* v. *Hussain Sherif*, (1868) 4 M. H. C. 23. But the office of Mutwalli cannot be transferred. *Wahid Ali* v. *Ashruff Hossain* (1882) I. L. R., 8 C. 732.

3. Amir Ali Lectures on Mahomedan Law, Vol. I, p. 348. See also Macnaghten's Mahomedan Law, Prec. End. Case iv at pp. 332 and 333. See also *Ibid.* Dig. (No. 31) p. 470; Wilson's Digest, para 331, page 288; *Hussain Beebee* v. *Hussain Sherif*, (1868) 4 M. H. C. 23, and *Mujavar Ibrambibi* v. *Mujavar Hussain Sheriff*, (1880) I. L. R., 3 M. 95.

4. Amir Ali, Vol. I, p. 349.

5. Amir Ali, Vol. I, pp. 349 and 350.

6. Pp. xix and xx.

The question naturally arises whether there can be any reservation validly made, and if so, whether in such a case the mosque ceases to be public. Upon this point there seems to be a paucity of authority. If the deed of wakf expressly says that the mosque is dedicated to one sect of Mahomedans, two questions arise:—First whether the reservation is valid, and Secondly, if so whether the mosque is still public. On principle there seems to be no warrant for holding that the reservation in favour of a sect is not valid. Sir Roland Wilson in his Digest of Anglo-Mahomedan Law says that the reservation is valid in the Shafei School. He states the rule in Chapter XIII: "If the founder of a mosque directs that it shall be devoted to worship according to the ritual prescribed by a particular school (that of Shafei for instance) the limitation must be respected, and the followers of that school will be entitled to use the mosque, to the exclusion of all other believers." The same is recognized by Mr. Amir Ali in his book on Mahomedan Law (Vol. I, pp. 436 and 437): "The other conditions that may be added must be executed faithfully, as, for example, the condition .... that a mosque founded be specially dedicated to a certain rite such as the Shafei. In this latter case the members of this sect alone shall be entitled to share in the benefit of the *wakf*." Reservation in a Mosque.

The question still remains to be considered whether the reservation holds good in other schools. Sir Roland Wilson says that the ancient authorities upon this point do not appear to be conclusive. But it must be observed that the Shafei law is express and no notice of any difference upon the point is pointed out by the Hanafi writers. The Hedaya does not say that there is any difference upon this point in the Hanafi Law. It may also be observed that among the conditions pointed out by the ancient writers as being invalid this is not one. For instance, a condition in a wakfnama that the mutwalli is irremovable by the ruling authority, or that the wakf lands shall not be let or farmed out for more than a year, &c., is said to be invalid (Macnaghten's Principles of Mahomedan Law, Chapter X, para 8). This class of cases must be distinguished from another class of cases in which it has been declared by the ancient authorities that a wakf depending upon a remote contingency is invalid. There is no contingency whatever contemplated in the case of a mosque which is dedicated with a reservation that only mem- Validity of reservation according to Hanafi law.

bers of a particular sect may take part in the worship that may be conducted there. Syed Amir Ali is apparently of opinion that such reservations are valid in all the schools. For he says in his book on Mahomedan Law (Vol. I, page 451) that "a Mussulman mosque (unless it is a Masjid-i-Jamna), a private imambara, wakf created for the disbursement of private charity or for the benefit of a more or less restricted body of people, is not regarded by the Mahomedan lawyers to be vested in the public or that the public have any interest in them." In this, however, we cannot concur. The fact that a reservation is made does not show that the mosque is not a public one. As a ground for his opinion Amir Ali says that the Mahomedan Law makes a broad distinction between wakfs which are public in their nature and which are private. This, however, is no distinction peculiar to the Mahomedan Law. It is a distinction obtaining in all systems of rational jurisprudence.

If a mosque is dedicated for some sect of Mahomedans, it is a trust for some considerable portion of the public and is therefore a public trust. We have seen on a former occasion that a charity is not deprived of its public character merely because its objects are confined to a particular class[1]. Hence if a reservation in favor of a particular sect is valid, a mosque dedicated with such reservation, if otherwise public, does not cease to be public and we have seen that a mosque dedicated without any reservation is a public one.

Public and quasi-public.

Mr. Amir Ali suggests further that if such mosques are not private, they are *quasi-public* and do not fall within Act XX of 1863 and S. 539 of the Civil Procedure Code. We need hardly state that the law only knows of two kinds of trusts, public and private, and no rational system of jurisprudence distinguishes between public and *quasi*-public. Apparently Mr. Amir Ali is inspired by the distinction which is said to obtain in the English Law of Evidence as regards admissibility of evidence of reputation in matters of public as opposed to matters of general interest. But this distinction is hardly applicable to the Law of Trusts which only draws a distinction between trusts public and private.

---

1. Ch. VI pp. lxvii and lxx.

Distinction in appointment of Mutwalli.

In the appointment of a Mutwalli there is a distinction known to the Mahomedan Law, but the same is not inconsistent with the above view. The distinction in the words of Mr. Amir Ali (Vol. I, p. 365) is this: "The appointment of a Mutwalli by the congregation" is prohibited in the case of "endowments of a public nature like a Musjid-i-Jamaa and similar institutions in which the public at large, or the Mussulman public generally, are interested. But when an institution is dedicated to the inhabitants of a particular locality or to a particular sect or fraternity, the number of which is ascertainable, the modern Moslem Jurists have recognised the validity of an appointment by the congregation." We do not understand the force of the language "the number of which is ascertainable." In these days of civilization and census reports the number of Moslems in India is ascertainable in a sense, but probably Mr. Amir Ali does not use the expression in this sense. The members of a particular sect of Mussulmans can equally not be said to be ascertainable. The distinction, however, relates to the right of certain persons to appoint a trustee. Even in those cases where Mr. Amir Ali will say there is an undoubted public trust, the right of appointing a trustee may vest in certain persons. If the endower of a mosque intended for the public worship of all Moslems should, at the time of appropriation, reserve to himself the right of appointing a trustee, then such right will be recognised (Macnaghten's Principles, Ch. X, para. 5). It is a principle familiar to Mahomedan Law that he who makes an appropriation has the right of appointing a superintendent.

This distinction as stated by Mr. Amir Ali[1] does not, however, warrant the distinction of trusts into public and *quasi*-public. The test of a public trust is not whether a given or ascertained number of persons has or has not the right to appoint a trustee, but whether such persons have or have not the right to divert the trust. If they have no right to divert the trust, then the trust is public although the purposes of the trust may have been intended for the members of a particular class. But there may be no quarrel with the use of this expression (*quasi-public*) provided we understand that even in a *quasi-public* trust it is not possible to divert the trust even with the consent of the persons interested.

1. A different principle is, however, stated by Macnaghten in his Principles of Mahomedan Law, Ch. X, para. 10.

Cases upon reservation in a mosque.

The decided cases are not inconsistent with the view that a reservation, such as the one under discussion, is not invalid. The observations in *Jawahra* v. *Akbar Husain*[1] referred to on a former occasion[2] with reference to the nature of a mosque, are applicable with reference to a mosque which is dedicated to the public without any reservation, and the same holds good with reference to the observations of *Mahmood*, J., in *Queen-Empress* v. *Ramzan*[3] to the effect that "it is a fundamental principle of the Mahomedan Law of *wakf*, too well known to require the citation of authorities, that when a mosque is built and consecrated by public worship, it ceases to be the property of the builder and vests in God (to use the language of Hedaya) 'in such a manner as subjects it to the rules of Divine property whence the appropriator's right in it is extinguished and it becomes a property of God by the advantage of it resulting to his creatures. A mosque once consecrated cannot in any case revert to the founder, and every Mahommedan has the legal right to enter it and perform devotions'."

The observations of *Edge*, C. J., in *Ataullah* v. *Azimullah*[4] are, however, more pertinent though wide. He says: "No authority has been brought to our notice to show that a mosque which has been dedicated to God can be appropriated exclusively to or by any particular sect or denomination of Sunni Mahomedans; and without very strong authority for such a proposition, I, for one, could not as a matter of law say that there could be any such exclusive appropriation. As I understand, a mosque to be a mosque at all, must be a building dedicated to God, and not a building dedicated to God with a reservation that it should be used only by particular persons holding particular views of ritual." These were not necessary for the decision, there being no question in the case that any reservation was made by the deed of endowment. The observations of the other judges[5] are not so express and may be explicable on the footing that they have been considering the case of a mosque dedicated without any reservation. It was contended that if the mosque had been exclusively used by the Hanafis, it ought to be inferred as a matter of law that the other sects were excluded from the benefits of the worship in such mosque. But this contention was overruled. But their Lordships of the Privy Coun-

1. (1884) I. L. R., 7 A. 178.
2. p. xviii.
3. (1885) I. L. R., 7 A. 461 (473).
4. (1889) I. L. R., 12 A. 494 (501).
5. *Mahmood*, J. was the only other Judge who referred to this point.

cil[1] treat this *dictum* of *Edge*, C. J., as an actual ruling of the High Court of Allahabad, though they decline to express any opinion of their own upon the point.

The result of this discussion is that the authorities do not militate against the principle that a reservation clause, such as the one mentioned, is valid and ought to be given effect to.

Eedgah. An Eedgah is a place where prayers are performed at certain festivals (Bakrid and Ramzan). In Fallon's Dictionary it is said to be a platform sometimes enclosed by a wall where Mahomedans assemble for occasional devotions (at *Id* or other religious festivals).

Nature of endowed property. With regard to the nature of endowed property we find the same principles applying in Mahomedan Law as in Hindu Law. Indeed we find the Mahomedan lawyers discussing the matter in a clearer light and stating in *greater* detail the duties of manager or superintendent. According to the Mahomedan Law an endowment signifies the appropriation of property to the service of God[2]. Wakf property belongs virtually to Almighty God[3]. According to the two disciples "wakf" signifies[4] "the appropriation of a particular article in such a manner as subjects it to the rules of *divine* property, whence the appropriator's right in it is extinguished and it becomes a *property of God*, by the advantage of it resulting to his creatures." No claims of inheritance are admissible with reference to such property[5]. Indeed the nature of the property is clearly brought out in the cases dealing with mosques which we had to refer in a former chapter[6]. The property becomes on appropriation tied up in the ownership of the Almighty and, therefore, ownership is vested in the Almighty[7]. The Mutwalli is only a manager and as he is a mere manager[8], we find the Mahomedan

1. *Fuzul Karim* v. *Mowla Buksh*, (1891) L. R., 18 I. A. 59, (69): S. C. I. L. R., 18 C. 448 458 and 459.
2. Macnaghten's Mahomedan Law, (Edn. 1890), Prin. 1, p. 69.
3. Amir Ali's Lectures on Mahomedan Law, Vol. I, p. 433.
4. *Jewun Doss Sahoo* v. *Shah Kubeer-ood-deen*, (1841) 2 M. I. A., p. 390.
5. See Amir Ali, Vol. I, p. 388; and Macnaghten's Mahomedan Law (Edn. 1890) Prec. Case iii, p. 329; *Mahomed Kasim* v. *Mahomed Alum*, (1831) 5 B. S. D. A. 136; *Shah Imam Bukhsh* v. *Moosummat Beebee Shahee*, (1835) 6 B. S. D. A. 22. See also *Jewun Doss Sahoo* v. *Shah Kubeer-ood-deen*, (1841) 2 M. I. A. p. 390; *Amrutlal Kalidas* v. *Shaik Hussein*, (1887) I. L. R., 11 B. 492. See further Chapter XIII.
6. Chapter II, pp. xviii and xix.
7. Amir Ali's Mahomedan Law, Vol. I, p. 383.
8. See Macnaghten's Mahomedan Law, Prec. Case viii, p. 341, where it is said that the possession of the superintendent is not in virtue of any proprietary right, but merely for the purpose of securing the attainment of the objects contemplated by the founder of the appropriation; and *Shah Imam* v. *Beebee Shahee*, (1835) 6 B. S. D. A. 22, where it said that a Sujjadanashin is merely appointed to administer the affairs of wakf property and has no power of alienating any portion of it.

Law dealing in detail with his duties. The property is inalienable. It is not a fit subject of sale, gift, or inheritance[1]. As a general rule, therefore, private alienation, whether temporary or absolute by mortgage or otherwise of *wakf* property is illegal although such alienation may be for the repair or other benefit of the endowment[2]. It will, therefore, appear that as regards *wakf* property the rule applied by the Bombay Courts in respect of Hindu religious endowments is universal, *viz.*, that the corpus of the property is inalienable[3], though the income may be pledged for the necessary expense of the endowment. It appears, however, that by the custom of several places wakf property is alienable[4], but if the custom be that the same is alienable even for no necessity it is doubtful whether such a custom can be upheld as valid[5]. If the endower should provide in the deed about the alienation of the endowed land for any necessary purpose, such a provision may be enforced[6]. Even without such a provision wakf property "may be sold by judicial authority when the sale may be absolutely necessary to defray the expense of repairing its edifices or other indispensable purpose and where the object cannot be attained by farming or other temporary expedient[7]." It is even said that the specific property appropriated cannot be exchanged for other property unless it is otherwise expressly stipulated in the deed of endowment or unless circumstances render it impracticable to retain possession of the same or unless manifest advantage be derivable from the exchange[8].

---

1. Macnaghten's Mahomedan Law, Prin. 2, p. 69; Ibid, App. Dig. Nos. 4 and 36, pp. 466 and 471. See also *Kulb Ali Hossein* v. *Syf Ali*, (1814) 2 B. S. D. A. 110; *Mussummat Quadira* v. *Shah Kubeer Ooddeen*, (1824) 3 B. S. D. A. 407; *Shoojat Ali* v. *Zumeeroodeen*, (1866) 5 W. R. C. R. 158. See also Amir Ali, Vol. I, p. 388.

2. See *Moulvee Abdoolla* v. *Rajessi Dossea*, (1846) 7 B. S. D. A. 268; and *Shoojat Ali* v. *Zumeeroodeen*, supra. See also Amir Ali, Vol. I, p. 383. But see Macnaghten's Mahomedan Law, Prec. Case ii, p. 329 and 8, S. D. A. (N. W. P.) p. 483, where a sale of wakf property for necessary expenses of repairs has been upheld.

3. *Narayan* v. *Chintaman*, (1881) I. L. R., 5 B. 393. See Chapter VIII p. xcix.

4. See Macnaghten's Mahomedan Law, App. Dig. No. 20, pp. 468 and 469; and *Krishnarav Ganesh* v. *Rangrav*, (1867) 4 B. H. C. a. c. j. 1. (9).

5. *Rajah Vurmah* v. *Ravi Vurmah*, (1876) L. R., 4 I. A., 76. See *Sarkum Abu Torab Abdul Waheb* v. *Rahaman Buksh*, (1896) I. L. R., 24 C. 83 (93).

6. Cf. *Moonshe Golam Ali* v. *Sowlutoonissa*, (1864) W. R. (Sp). C. R. 241; and *Shoojat Ali* v. *Zumeeroodeen*, supra.

7. Macnaghten's Mahomedan Law, Princ. 3, p. 69, and Amir Ali's Lectures on Mahomedan Law, Vol. I, pp. 373 and 386. The Mutwalli cannot incur debts for the wakf or charge the estate for the same. But it appears this principle does not hold good in the case of such debts as, owing to the exigencies of the society, must necessarily be contracted from day to day for the due discharge of the office of Mutwalli and the performance of the necessary worship &c. See Amir Ali, Vol. I, p. 374, and Wilson's Digest of Anglo-Mahomedan Law, para 387, pp. 291 and 292.

8. Macnaghten's Mahomedan Law, Princ. No. 7, p. 70. But see Amir Ali, Vol. I, p. 433.

Validity of private religious endowments.

The next question that has to be considered is whether a private religious endowment is known to the Mahomedan Law. It is no answer to say that a private trust is recognised by the Mahomedan Law. For a private trust will be subject to the rule of perpetuties, and what we have to see is whether a religious endowment can be private and yet not subject to the rule of perpetuties. Upon this point it is useful to turn to Mr. Amir Ali. He says, "If a man were to build a mosque inside his house, it will not become a public mosque, subject to the rules governing a *public* religious institution, unless permission has been once granted to outsiders to come and pray. It is not necessary that such permission should be given in express terms, but without an actual or constructive permission, a mosque created within a private building will not become a public mosque so as to entitle the public, or any section of the public, to claim the use of it. At the same time though the public may have no right in a private mosque, it may constitute a good wakf so as to exclude the rights of the heirs over it." He gives a private Imambara as an example of this class.

Imambara a valid wakf.

The above observations of Amir Ali ought to be conclusive, but Sir Roland Wilson throws some doubt upon this. In his Digest of Anglo-Mahomedan Law he says[2]: "The practice of dedicating such private *imambaras* may perhaps be peculiar to Shiahs, but whether Shiah or Sunni the validity of such endowments must stand or fall with that of family settlements" It is not easy to see why the validity of private religious endowments of Mahomedans should depend upon the validity of wakfs in favour of the wakf's family. The Privy Council have no doubt held that wakfs in favour of the wakif's family are invalid and that there must be a substantial dedication to pious or charitable uses. But when a private imambara is dedicated and endowments are made for the support thereof, we do not see why there should not be a substantial dedication within the meaning of the Privy Council Rulings and why such endowments should not be valid. We are fortified in the above view by the observations of the Calcutta High Court in *Delroos Banoo Begum* v. *Ashgar Ally Khan*[3].

1. Vol. I, p. 305.

2. See p. 309.

3. (1875) 15 B. L. R., 167: S. C. 23 W. R. C. R. 453. In *Nawab Umjad Ally Khan* v. *Mohumdee Begum*, (1867) 11 M. I. A. 517 and *Zafaryab Ali* v. *Bakhtawar Singh*, (1883) I. L. R., 5 A. 497, an imambara is recognised as a valid wakf. See also *Wajid Ali* v. *Dianat-ul-lah*, (1885) I. L. R., 8 A. 31.

Glover, J., observed in that case: "An imambara is not a place of public worship as is a mosque or temple, but an apartment in a private house set apart no doubt for the performance of certain Mohurrum ceremonies, but no more open to the general public than a private oratory in England would be. As a matter of fact strangers are ordinarily excluded from these celebrations." In this case a lady purported to dedicate the whole of her property to an imambara in her house for the purpose of perpetuating various Shiah ceremonies. The High Court held that this would be a good wakf, that it was a private trust not coming under Act XX of 1863, but that no effect could be given to it as the deed was not explained to the lady who was a purdanashin. The Privy Council, in confirming the High Court's decision upon the latter ground, concurred with the view of the High Court that it was a private trust not coming under Act XX of 1863. If the wakf was invalid, as Sir Roland Wilson would seem to think, there was no necessity to say that it was a private trust not coming under Act XX, or that the deed could not be given effect to for some other reason.

Meaning of Imambara.

According to Amir Ali[1] the literal meaning of imambara is "the house of the Imam." It is a building consecrated to "services held in honour of the martyrdom of Hussain and is generally a Shiah institution, though many Sunnis also erect and maintain Imambaras." In order that a private imambara may be upheld as a valid endowment, there must be an appropriation, *i.e.*, the private owner's right of ownership in the property dedicated for the imambara must be extinguished; otherwise it is subject to rules of private property.

Hidaya on private endowments.

There are some observations in the Hedaya which may at first sight seem inconsistent with the above view[2]: "If a person convert the centre hall of his house into a mosque, giving general admission into it, it still does not stand as a mosque, but remains saleable and inheritable; because a mosque is a place in which no person possesses any right of obstruction; and wherever a man has such a right with respect to the surrounding parts, the same must necessarily affect the place inclosed in them. This place, therefore,

1. Lectures on Mahomedan Law, Vol. I, p. 303.

2. Vol. I, Book XV, p. 239.

cannot be a mosque; besides it is necessarily a thoroughfare for the family and consequently does not appertain solely to God." In the first place it has to be remarked that these observations have reference to the case of a public mosque. In the second place, even granting that they have reference to a private mosque, it has to be remarked that the above passage proceeds on the assumption that the appropriator reserves a right in the property dedicated by the mere fact that he reserves for his family or others a right of passage. But this assumption is not always correct. A wakf is valid even where a right of residence is given to the Mutwalli and his family[1], and it is competent to the appropriator to constitute himself as Mutwalli. Hence the mere fact that a right of passage is reserved by the appropriator is not inconsistent with the view that the appropriator's right in the property dedicated is extinguished. It may be different if the appropriator's right is not extinguished. The subsequent passages in the Hedaya confirm our view. For instance, it is said in the Hedaya[2]: "It is reported from Mahomed that the centre hall of a house thus constituted a mosque, cannot afterwards be given away, sold or inherited. He consequently considers it to stand as a mosque; and Aboo Yoosaf is of the same opinion, because, as the person in question was desirous that this place should become a mosque, and as it cannot become so without a road, or entrance into it, the road is included without specification, in the same manner as in the case of a hire." We must, therefore, hold that there is nothing inconsistent in the Hedaya with the view that a private religious endowment may be valid under the Mahomedan law, and that property endowed for a private religious purpose ceases to be private property and may be perpetually dedicated for the said purpose.

---

1. See cases cited in notes (5) and (6), p. xlix. See also *Rajender Dutt* v. *Shamchund Mitter*, (1880) I. L. R., 6 C. 106; *Ranjit Singh* v. *Jagannath Prosad Gupta*, (1885) I. L. R., 12 C. 375.

2. Vol. I, Book XV, p. 239.

CHAPTER X.

PROPERTY CAPABLE OF BEING ENDOWED WITH SPECIAL REFERENCE TO THE LAW OF WAKFS.

In this chapter we shall consider what property may be the subject of endowment with special reference to the Mahomedan Law of *Wakfs*. It is said that there are three essentials of a *wakf* according to Mahomedan Law:—(1) Existence of property which is a fit subject of wakf (2) Existence of proper or lawful objects and (3) Existence of a valid dedication. The *first* essential forms the subject of consideration in this chapter.

It may at first sight appear whether there is any thing in this subject which requires any detailed consideration. Indeed under the Hindu Law any property may be the subject of an endowment provided the endower has capacity to make the same. Even where ancestral property or other joint property is made the subject of an endowment by the father or other managing member a subsequent ratification by all the members will render the endowment valid[1].

Property that may be subject of wakf.

But there is a considerable discussion among the Mahomedan lawyers with reference to the property which may legally be appropriated as *wakf*. It is agreed on all hands that lands or immoveable property may be the proper subject of a *wakf*. The only question is with reference to moveables and with reference to the Sunni Law. The Hedaya states[2] as the opinion of Hanifa that "the appropriation of moveable property is altogether unlawful, whether purposely or as a dependant." But Abu Yusuf maintains that it cannot be unlawful if moveable property is appropriated as a dependant, *i. e.*, as being attached to land. For instance, he says, " if a person appropriate lands, together with the cattle and slaves attached to them, it is lawful, and the same of all instruments of husbandry; because these are all dependants of the soil in the fulfilment of the design." The opinion of Mahomed is also in accordance with this view. Mahomed further says, and in this it is said Abu Yusuf concurs, that the appropriation of horses, camels or arms to carry on war against the infidels is lawful.

Appropriation of slaves.

As regards the appropriation of slaves the same is not possible in British India. Slavery has been abolished[3] and trafficking in slavery is made an offence by the Penal Code[4]. The appropriation

---

1. *Purmanundass Jeevundass* v. *Venayekrao Wassoodeo*, (1882) L. R. 9 I. A. 86: S. C. I. L. R., 7 B. 19.

2. Bk. XV, p. 234. 3. Act V of 1843. 4. Ss. 370, 371 and 374.

of horses, camels or arms for the purpose of carrying on war against the infidel is likewise not permissible. The purpose is not lawful. Probably if the appropriation be for the purpose of providing the existing Government with horses, camels and arms for carrying on war with the country or people at war with the Government, then it may be permissible.

Articles of utility.

Mahomed further says that the appropriation of articles of utility is lawful by analogy. So that, according to him, "the appropriation is lawful of all moveables, the appropriation of which is commonly practised, such as spades, shovels, axes, saws, planks, coffins (and their appendages), stone or brazen vessels, and books." According to Abu Yusuf such appropriation is unlawful as analogy ought not to be abandoned except on the express authority of the sacred writings and express authority is not to be found for the above. Notwithstanding this, it seems to be agreed by all Mahomedan lawyers that the Koran and other books are fit subjects of appropriation, as they are useful for the purpose of reading and instruction.

Moveable property.

There is a greater conflict of authority as to the fitness in general of moveable property for the purpose of appropriation. It is said that "it is not lawful to appropriate moveables, the appropriation of which is unusual or uncommon," and some of the Mahomedan doctors argue that, as "appropriation requires perpetuity, and this cannot exist in moveables since these are not of a lasting nature," the appropriation of moveables in general is unlawful. This doctrine is controverted by Shafei. According to the latter "the appropriation is lawful of everything which admits of the use without a destruction of the subject, or of everything lawfully saleable, because such articles as admit usufruct resemble land, horses or arms." As civilization advances the value of moveables comes into prominence, and the doctrine that land only admits of usufruct speaks well only of a crude state of society. Nowadays it may be safely said that there are many moveables which are prized more than land, are even more permanent and yield a better usufruct than land. We, therefore, find Mr. Amir Ali controverting this crude doctrine and citing numerous passages from untranslated Arabic authorities for the position that even *money* can be a lawful subject of appropriation[1]. It must now

1. (See Amir Ali, Tagore Lectures, Vol. I, pp. 202—207).

be taken as settled (consistently with the rapid rise and progress of modern civilization) that every kind of moveable property which has a saleable value admits of being the subject of appropriation and the authorities are consistent with this view.

Fatima Bibee v. Ariff Ismailjee.

The case of *Fatima Bibee* v. *Ariff Ismailjee Bham*[1] is no doubt against this view. It was there held that shares in limited companies could not be the subject of *wakf*. *Wilson*, J., observed at p. 75: "Land according to all the authorities may be appropriated. And the power has been, it is universally agreed, extended to certain other kinds of property, though the exact degree of the extension is a matter in difference among the authorities. But it is agreed that it does not apply to such things as perish in the using, under which head money appears to be included. And if money cannot be appropriated, it seems to me clear that the possibility of money hereafter in the form of dividends cannot be."

The judgment proceeds on the ground of analogy. But we cannot see how it can be said that shares in companies are "such things as perish in the using." The shares can by no stretch of imagination be said to perish in the using. Of course the documents evidencing the right to the shares will be subject to wear and tear, for if they pass through various hands they may suffer from the use. Even if the papers were lost, the right to receive dividends is not gone. Moreover, as Mr. Amir Ali says in his Tagore Law Lectures, it is not true to say that money cannot be appropriated. The argument from analogy, therefore fails, and is rather in favor of the view that these modern forms of investments neither known nor even thought of by the old lawyers are fit subjects of appropriation. It is, therefore, satisfactory to find the Allahabad High Court upholding appropriation of moveable property in the recent case of *Abu Sayid Khan* v. *Bakar Ali*[2]. Mr. Justice *Banerji* and Mr. Justice *Aikman* held in that case, after a consideration of all the authorities, that a wakf of moveable property might be validly constituted, and that such a view was in

---

1. (1881), 9 C. L. R. 66. See per *Davies*, J., in *Kaleloola Sahib* v. *Nuseerudeen Sahib*, (1894) I. L. R., 18 M. 201 (209) where he says that the rule is that moveable, and therefore perishable properties are ordinarily not fit subjects for endowment but that there is an exception to this rule when the moveables are appurtenant to immoveable property.

2. (1901), I. L. R., 24 A., 190.

no way inconsistent with the principle that perpetuity was a necessary condition of a valid *wakf*. This was the opinion of Mr. Justice *Kemp* so long ago as 1869 in the Calcutta case of *Khajah Hossein Ali* v. *Shahzadee Hazara Begum*[1].

If money is appropriated it is said by some of the ancient doctors that such money should be invested in some partnership business and its profit applied to the purposes of *wakf*. This again shows how limited was the range of investments known to ancient society. It cannot be regarded as prohibiting other forms of investments known to recent civilization. Government Securities are of recent origin, and an investment in the same will be valid.

When a *wakf* is made of goods which are capable of being weighed or measured like corn or cloth, it will be valid and such goods will be sold and the proceeds invested. A *wakf* of clothing for the poor to be worn at particular seasons and then returned will be lawful.

Divergence view among ancient doctors—Validity of appropriation of moveables.

With reference to the divergence of view among the ancient doctors, Mr. Amir Ali says[2]: "The doubt, which one or two of the ancient Hanafi doctors had expressed as to the validity of the *wakf* of certain kinds of moveable property in contradistinction to certain other things, was the outcome of primitive and archaic conditions of society, and was founded on the notion that as perpetuity was essential to the validity of *wakfs*, it could hardly be secured by the dedication of moveable things generally. But as the Mussulman communities progressed in material civilisation and commerce developed, it came to be recognised universally that 'the *wakf* of everything which forms the subject of business transactions or which it is customary in any particular locality to make a *wakf* of is valid.' The observant reader will not fail to see that 'custom' or 'usage' is an important factor in Mahomedan Law[3].........It enables communities to progress and develop in spite of the strict letter of the law......According to the present usage 'wherever it has become customary to make *wakf* of any kind of moveable property, it will be held valid notwithstanding that, in the time of the companions, the custom may not have existed.' From this it is evident that the appropriation of

1. (1869) 12 W. R. C. R. 314 (346).
2. Vol. I, pp. 208 and 209.
3. See *Muhammad Yussub* v. *Sayad Ahmed*, (1861) 1 B. H. C. app. xviii.

moveables depends purely upon the circumstances of the age and the conditions of society and the usages of the people. According to this principle, the appropriation of mere rights and *profits a prendre* would appear to be valid." If it be objected to the above that history places the zenith of Mahomedan material civilisation before rather than after the date of the Hedaya[1] where you find this conflict stated, it may be observed that the Hedaya does contain passages admitting of the appropriation of gold and silver though these passages do not appear in the translation of Hamilton as edited by Grady[2].

Shiah school.

There is no such difficulty under the *Shiah* School. There a *wakf* may be made of any kind of property and there can be no objection on the score of property being moveable. As Sir Roland Wilson says in his Digest of Anglo-Mahomedan Law: "The Shiahs allow *wakf* of any specific thing, moveable or immoveable, from which any benefit can be lawfully derived consistently with the preservation of the thing itself."

Mortgaged property—Validity of appropriation

Then a question arises whether property which is subject to a mortgage may be validly appropriated as a *wakf.* There seems to be nothing in the Mahomedan Law books to invalidate such *wakfs.* Mr. Justice *Markby,* however, stated in one case (*Khajah Hossein Ali* v. *Shahzadee Hazara Begum*[3]) that in order that there might be a valid *wakf* there must be a complete appropriation, and that where there was a mortgage of property which was proposed to be constituted as *wakf,* there was no complete appropriation. He stated that though "if we carried out the doctrines of Aboo Yusoof, as stated in the Hedaya to their logical conclusion, * * * we should arrive at the result that even if there was not a complete appropriation by Khajah Syed Hossein, there was a binding obligation to make a complete appropriation by clearing off the mortgage," yet "if we should carry out the doctrines of Imam Mahomed, we should arrive at an opposite conclusion". The reason given by the learned judge was that an appropriation of a thing under mortgage would be void according to Mahomed,

---

1. Wilson's Digest of Anglo-Mahomedan Law, p. 269.

2. Some of the passages are given in Syed Amir Ali's book on Mahamedan Law, Vol. I, pp. 206 and 207, note (2).

3. (1869), 12 W. R. C. R. 344 at pp. 348 and 349.

as in that case there could be no absolute transfer to the Mutwallee of a thing defined (the thing appropriated being liable to be sold and an indefinite part abstracted from the appropriation[1]). In the above conflict of the two disciples, Mr. Justice *Markby* states, that he must have recourse to the only other work of Mahomedan law to which he had access, *viz.*, the work of Khalil Ibu Ishak translated into French by M. Perron. Quoting some passages from this translated work he states the effect of those passages to be that "the appropriation" is "obligatory on the *appropriator* even when the property is under pledge, but the appropriation is *evidently incomplete* and the obligation is upon the *appropriator* to complete it. If *he does not do so during his life-time,* the *appropriation is null* as the obligation does not pass to his heirs." (The italics are ours). But although the effect of the passages from Khalil Ibu Ishak is to make the appropriation null, the obligation not passing upon the heirs, Mr. Justice *Markby* says that this view ought not to be accepted as according to the Futwa Alumgeree the obligation passes to the heirs, and the latter are bound to render the appropriation effectual. It was, therefore, held by Mr. Justice *Markby* in that case as the result of all the authorities that there was no complete endowment of mortgaged property until the property was released, that it was the duty of the heirs to release it, that if they could not release it the appropriation was null, and that if the release was effected by a sale of the thing mortgaged, the surplus proceeds would have to be invested by the heirs for the purchase of immoveable property for the purpose of appropriation but that until the appropriation was complete the title of the heirs was not divested.

Mr. Justice *Kemp,* however, differed from this Judgment. He held that the mere fact of the subsistence of the mortgage at the time the endowment was made would not render such endowment invalid and that the equity of redemption was sufficiently definite to be made the subject of endowment. The question whether if

---

1. 12 W. R. at p. 348. *Cf. Mohinudin* v. *Manchershah,* (1882) I. L. R., 6 B. 650 in which it was held that a gift of property in possession of a mortgagee was invalid (the case was of a gift by a father to his daughter) but this case must be treated to have been overruled by the decision of the Judicial Committee in *Mahomed Buksh Khan* v. *Hosseini Bibi* (1888) L. R. 15 I. A. 81.

the endower had known, at the time of appropriation, that there were no other assets to pay off the mortgage and that there could be no surplus (after sale of the mortgaged property and discharge of the mortgage debt) though it afterwards should turn out that there was a surplus, was left open.

Upon appeal under the Letters Patent the Appellate Court consisting of *Peacock*, C. J., *Jackson* and *Macpherson*, JJ., upheld the judgment of Mr. Justice *Kemp* and held that the existence of a mortgage at the time of the endowment did not render the appropriation invalid under the Mahomedan law[1].

As regards the authority relied upon by Mr. Justice *Markby*, *Peacock*, C. J., observed in that case: "The authority quoted[2]**, does not appear to be binding in this country. Mr. Justice *Markby* himself remarks that 'the author belongs to a sect of Sunnis said not to be known in India.' But even if the authority of that work is to be admitted as binding in India, it does not appear to support the position for which it was cited, *viz.*, that if there be a mortgage prior to endowment, and no assets are left by the endower to pay off that mortgage, the endowment is absolutely void as against every one. I am of opinion, therefore, that the endowment was valid as against the heirs of the endower, and consequently that, by virtue of the endowment, the Mutwalli is entitled to the surplus proceeds of the sale, the mortgage having been satisfied."

Upon principle also the distinction taken by Mr. Justice *Markby* is not tenable. He says that there is an obligation which is imposed not merely upon the appropriator but also upon his heirs to discharge the mortgage. There is nothing inconsistent in the existence of this obligation with the validity of the endowment. The mere fact that the obligation is not discharged by the persons who are bound to discharge the same cannot annul the endowment.

The statement of Mr. Amir Ali in his book on Mahomedan Law (Vol. I, p. 210) that "the *wakf* of land which is on lease or which is subject to a mortgage is valid" is, therefore, absolutely correct and supported by principle and authority.

---

1. (1869) 12 W. R. C. R. 498: S. C. 4 B. L. R. A. C. J. 86.
2. M. Perron's translation of Khalil Ibu Ishak's work.

Musha doctrine.

The next question that has to be considered is whether the appropriation of an undefined part or portion of a thing is valid. In the Hedaya it is stated that an undefined part of a thing may be appropriated. Reference is then made to the conflicting doctrine of the two disciples. According to Aboo Yoosaf the appropriation of an undefined part or portion of anything (such as the half, or the fourth of a field, house, &c.) is lawful. According to Aboo Yoosaf the taking possession of the endowed property is not essential, and separation being only essential for taking possession the appropriation of an indefinite part is lawful. From this rule he excepts two cases, *viz.*, (1) a mosque and (2) a burial-ground. The appropriation of an undefined portion for the use of a mosque or burial-ground is stated by him to be unlawful although it be of an indivisible nature. According to Mahomed, the appropriation of an undefined part is unlawful. According to his doctrine, possession is essential to a valid appropriation and where this does not take place because there is no division, there is no valid appropriation. Even according to him, however, if a thing is incapable of division, the appropriation of an indefinite part of it is legal as the thing may be leased or let out on hire and the parties may divide the rent.

Reasons for the doctrine.

The reasons which led the Muhammadan Doctors to maintain the doctrine of *Musha* were two:—(1) Complete seisin which was necessary to validate a gift, would be impracticable with respect to an indefinite part of divisible things as it would be impossible to make seisin of the thing given without its conjunction with something that was not given as gift. (2) If it should be held that a gift of part of a divisible thing was lawful without separation it would be incumbent upon the giver to make a division which he did not engage for and which might possibly be injurious to him.

The reasons given do not appear to be satisfactory. As regards the first, it is not stated why it is impossible to give seisin of a part without giving seisin of the rest. If the donor has possession of the part, it is not impossible to give the donee such possession as the donor may have. It cannot be said that cosharers have no possession; each of them has possession and why should not such possession be transferred to another? If the donor is out of possession, why should it not be sufficient if he clothe the donee with the right to recover possession? The other reason is equally unsatisfactory. In cases where the part is divisible, how is it injurious to the donor to divide and enjoy the separated share? If he has already parted with the whole of his interest, what is the injury he will sustain which the law has to regard? The law has no concern with any injury the donor who has parted with his interest may sustain. If he has only transferred a part of his share, *primâ facie*, the donee must have the right to divide unless the donor expressly covenants that the donee should not exercise the right.

Decisions upon the doctrine of Musha.

The decisions upon this point are not altogether uniform and consistent. First of all the question has been considered whether the British Indian Courts are bound to administer the Mahomedan law of gifts as a rule of Mahomedan law.

Mahomedan law of gifts applied as a rule of justice, equity, &c.

The Civil Courts Acts, *i. e.*, III of 1873 (for Madras[1]) and XII of 1887 (for Bengal, North-Western Provinces and Assam[2]) provide that Mahomedan law is to be applied where the parties are Mahomedans in cases in which the question to be decided is one regarding succession, inheritance, marriage, or caste or any religious usage or institution. No specific reference is made to gifts though it is otherwise in the Punjab Laws Act IV of 1872 (as amended by Act XII of 78), S. 5. In cases not provided for as above, the Courts are asked to administer the rule of justice, equity and good conscience. It will be strange if the Mahomedan law of gifts is not to be administered as a rule of justice, equity and good conscience for otherwise the Mahomedans may create estates unknown to the Mahomedan Law of gifts. But this cannot be and the Mahomedan Law of gifts has been applied by Courts as a rule of justice, equity and good conscience.

In *Mussumat Shumsh-ool-nissa* v. *Mussumat Zohra Beebee*[3] a Full Bench of the Allahabad High Court held by a majority of Judges that under S. 4 of Act VI of 1871, questions of "gift" are not included under the term "succession" and that the law to be administered is not the Mahomedan Law of gifts but the rule of justice, equity and good conscience. As Mr. Justice *Pearson* observed in that case: "The Courts are not absolutely bound to apply the

1. See S. 16. 2. See S. 37. 3. [1873] 6 N. W. P. 2.

Hindu or the Mahomedan Law strictly to questions regarding gift or to any questions save those specifically mentioned in S. 24 of Act VI of 1871. It is urged that in practice the Courts have been used to administer the Hindu and the Mahomedan laws without any restriction; and there is ground for believing that some portions of that law relating to questions other than those specified in S. 24 have been frequently applied. These portions may continue to have a virtual operation in so far as they coincide with and express the principles of justice, equity and good conscience, but their application as parts of the Hindu and Mahomedan law is not binding."

In a later case before the same Court, *Nizam-ud-din* v. *Zabeda Bibi*[1] where the question was as to the validity of a gift of undivided property to two donees without making any division betwen them at the time, the Court held that the same was invalid under the Mahomedan Law and that justice, equity and good conscience did not require them to hold otherwise: though we fail to see the reasons upon which the actual decision in the case rests.

A similar principle has been affirmed by the same Court with regard to questions of pre-emption[2].

The Calcutta High Court has adopted the same view in an early case[3]. The Madras High Court has in a recent case[4] taken the same view of the question. It has been held by Mr. Justice *Benson* in that case[5] that the doctrine of *Musha* has not been applied in the Madras Presidency and that under S. 16 of the Madras Civil Courts Act it is not obligatory upon the Courts to apply the doctrine of Musha as obtaining in the Mahomedan Law.

---

1. (1874) 6 N. W. P. 338. The case of *Sahibunnissa* v. *Hafiza*, (1887) I.L. R., 9 A. 213 does not apply the rule, if any, of Mahomedan Law that a gift of more than a person's interest is void altogether on the ground of justice, equity and good conscience.

2. *Mussumat Chundo* v. *Hakeem Alim-ood-Deen*, (1873) 6 N. W. P. (F. B.) 28; *Gobind Dayal* v. *Inayatullah*, (1885) I. L R., 7 A. 775.

3. *Zohoroodden Sirdar* v. *Baharoollah*, (1864) W. R. Sp. C. R. 185.

4. *Alabi Koya* v. *Mussa Koya*, (1901) I. L. R., 24 M. 513. See also *Ibrahim Saib* v. *Muni Mirudin Saib*, (1870) 6 M. H. C. R. 26 where the Mahomedan doctrine of pre-emption has been held to be inapplicable to the Madras Presidency.

5. *Alabi Koya* v. *Mussa Koya*, supra. The other judge Mr. Justice *Shephard* did not express any opinion upon the point.

Mahomedan Law in questions of religious usage or institution.

But all this reasoning will not apply to the case we are considering. Courts are bound, under the sections of the Civil Courts Acts already referred to, to apply the Mahomedan Law in questions regarding any religious usage or institution. If the Mahomedan Law invalidates a gift of undivided property as wakf, it is difficult to see how the Courts can say that it is not a question affecting religious usage and institution, and that, therefore, they are not bound to apply the Mahomedan Law. Whatever answer may be given in cases where the gifts are to private persons, it seems to us that gifts of property in *wakf* (at any rate so far as religious purposes are concerned) are governed by the rules of Mahomedan Law and that Courts are bound to apply and administer such law.

Doctrine of Musha a refined one.

We have, therefore, to see what the Mahomedan Law is as regards gifts of undivided property. It is said that such gifts are invalid because of the doctrine of Musha. This doctrine as stated by the Judicial Committee in *Mahomed Buksh Khan* v. *Hosseini Bibi*[1] is: "That a gift of an undivided share in a subject capable of division is not good because it would lead to confusion." This doctrine is said to be a refined one and to extend it further will be in the language of their Lordships "a refinement on a refinement amounting almost to a *reductio ad absurdum*."

As regards the rule that a gift is invalid if possession is not given (and the rule as to Musha is said to be based partly upon this) the Privy Council observe that "the principle upon which the rule rests has nothing to do with feudal rules and that the European analogy is rather to be found in the cases relating to voluntary contracts or transfers; where if the donor has not done all he could to perfect his contemplated gift, he cannot be compelled to do more". We might further observe that the necessity for delivery of possession would seem to have been insisted on by the old writers more as a rule of evidence than as a rule of law, for non-delivery of possession was according to all ancient writers strong evidence of a benami transaction or of an intention upon the part of the donor not to transfer the property[2]. Publicity was required by the ancients of any transaction, and the only way they knew of

1. (1888) L. R., 15 I. A. 81 (95): S. C. I. L. R., 15 C. 684, (701).
2. It is only one test according to the modern view.

giving publicity to transfers of property was delivery of possession. We moderns also insist on publicity, and the way in which this is effected by us is registration. To clothe a rule of evidence or presumption suited to ancient civilization with the authority of a rule of substantive law is to disregard modern progress and unnecessarily to retard the development of individual property. As observed by the Privy Council in *Sheikh Muhummad Mumtaz Ahmad* v. *Zubaida Jan*[1]: "the doctrine relating to the invalidity of gifts of musha is wholly unadapted to a progressive state of society and ought to be confined within the strictest rules."

Exceptions to the doctrine.

There are several exceptions to this rule. The *first* exception is that which is recognised and acted on by the Privy Council in *Ameeroonissa Khatoon* v. *Abedoonissa Khatoon*[2]. Their Lordships held in that case that the rule had no application where the subject of the gift was a definite share in a Zamindari in which the nature of the right was defined and regulated by the public Acts of the British Government. According to these Acts, shares in Zamindaris were, in themselves and before any partition, definite estates capable of distinct enjoyment by perception of separate and defined rents. Similarly it has been held in *Ebrahimbhai* v. *Fulbai*[3] that there may be a gift of a person's share in a certain fund in court or of a person's definite share of the moneys in the hands of the Accountant-General[4].

1st exception:—gift of definite shares in Zamindaries.

2nd Exception:—gift by a co-sharer to another sharer.

A *second* exception to the rule is where the gift of an undivided property is made by one sharer to another sharer[5]. If there are only two sharers and there is no confusion when one gives his share over to the other, what difference does it make when there are more than two and one gives his share to any of the others? As observed by the judicial committee to extend the rule to such a case will be a refinement upon refinement amounting to an absurdity which ought not to be allowed to prevail[6].

1. (1889) I. L. R., 16 I. A. 205 (215): S. C. I. L. R., at 11 A. 460 (475). See also *Mullick Abdool Guffoor* v. *Muleka*, (1884) I. L. R., 10 C. 1112 at p. 1123.
2. (1875) L. R., 2 I. A. 87 at p. 105: S. C. 15 B. L. R. 67 (79). This case was followed in *Jiwan Bakhsh* v. *Imtiaz Begam*, (1878) I. L. R., 2 A. 93; and *Kasim Husain* v. *Sharif-un-nissa* (1883), I. L. R., 5 A. 285.
3. (1902) I. L. R., 26 B. 577.
4. See also *Alabi Koya* v. *Mussa Koya*, (1901) I. L. R., 24 M. 513 where *Shephard*, J., held that the rule had no application to the case of money to be paid as compensation by the Collector under the Land Acquisition Act.
5. *Ameena Bibee* v. *Zeifa Bibee*, (1865) 3 W. R. C. R. 37 approved by the Judicial Committee in *Mahomed Buksh Khan* v. *Hosseini Bibi* (1888), L. R., 15 I. A. 81: S. C. I. L. R., 15 C. 684.
6. (1888), L. R., 15 I. A. 81 at p. 95: S. C. I. L. R., 15 C. 684 (701).

3rd Exception:—gift to persons in *locoparentis*.

A *third* exception[1] is in a case where the gift is by a father to his child[2] or by a guardian to his ward[3].

4th Exception:—Possession given of undivided property.

A *fourth* exception also allowed by the judicial committee is that possession given and taken under a gift of undivided property transferred the property to the donee without reference to any question whether such a gift is invalid or otherwise[4].

5th Exception:—property incapable of division.

A *fifth* exception (which, however, is not a real one) is that the rule does not apply to property which is not capable of division. Reversionary interests, or *Malikana* or other *choses in action* are not capable of division and so may be validly gifted[5].

6th Exception-Donor out of possession.

If the rule as to Musha is founded upon the principle that a gift must be followed by possession, we may say that a *sixth* exception will hold good *i. e.*, a case where the donor is out of possession. In such a case if the donee is given the right to take possession, that must satisfy the requirements of the law. A person who is out of possession cannot of course transfer his *possessory right* and if a document recites that this has been done no effect as such can be given to the same. But when a trespasser is in possession what objection can there be where the true owner transfers the property by way of gift to a third person and clothes the latter with the right to take possession? This was the principle adopted by the Privy Council in *Kali Das* v. *Kanhya Lal*[6] which was a case decided under the Hindu Law, and this principle was approved by them in a case

---

1. A gift by a husband to his wife is not within the exception. Hence a gift of undivided property by a husband to his wife is bad under Mahomedan Law. Whether it is void or only invalid and whether in the latter case a subsequent partition makes it good has not been decided. *Emnabai* v. *Hajirabai*, (1888) I. L. R., 13 B. 352. But the husband living with the wife in the property conveyed is not inconsistent with possession being given over to the wife. *Amina Bibi* v. *Khatija Bibi*, (1864) 1 B. H. C. 157; *Azim-un-nissa Begum* v. *Dale*, (1868) 6 M. H. C. 455; *Esuph Ravutan* v. *Pattamsa* (1899), I. L. R., 23 M. 70. Macnaghten's Precedents, Case 22 pp. 231, 232. Same principles hold good in the case of a gift by a wife to her husband. See also *Kamar-un-nissa* v. *Hussaini*, (1880) I. L. R., 3 A. 266 (P. C.).

2. *Wajeed Ali* v. *Abdool Ali*, (1864) W. R., Spl. C. R. 121; *Fatima Bibee* v. *Ahmad Baksh*, (1903) I. L. R., 31 C. 319 (330). See also *Nawab Umjad Ally Khan* v. *Mohumdee Begum*, (1867) 11 M. I. A. 517, where a reservation by the donor of some interest has been held valid. Macnaghten's Precedents, Cases 9 and 13 pp. 206 and 212.

3. *Wajeed Ali* v. *Abdool Ali*, supra. In the case of a gift by a stranger to an infant seisin to the guardian is enough; or if the infant has attained years of discretion, seisin in the infant is enough. Macnaghten's Precedents, Case 19 at pp. 224, 225. Wilson's Digest of Anglo-Mahomedan Law, Sec. 304.

4. *Sheikh Muhummad Mumtaz Khan* v. *Zubaida Jan* (1889), L. R., 16 I. A. 205: S. C. I. L. R., 11 A. 460. A right to receive pension is not capable of partition. *Sahib-un-nissa* v. *Hafiza Bibi*, (1887) I. L. R., 9 A. 213.

5. *Mullick Abdool Guffoor* v. *Muleka*, (1884) I. L. R., 10 C. 1112.

6. (1884), L. R., 11 I. A. 218: S. C. I. L. R., 11 C. 121.

arising under the Mahomedan Law[1]. In the case of Government pro-notes it will be sufficient if authority to receive interest is given[2].

The case of property mortgaged with possession to the mortgagee already dealt with will conclusively show that the necessity as to possession is neither an invariable nor an inflexible rule. It has been already shown that a gift of mortgaged property as wakf is valid. It is upon this principle *Kemp*, J. has decided in *Khajah Hossein Ali* v. *Shahzadee Hazara Begum*[3] that a gift of undivided property as *wakf* is valid. But the judgment of the judges who decided the case in an appeal under the Letters Patent makes no reference to this point as probably being unnecessary for the decision.

Amir Ali's view on Musha doctrine.

The subject is fully discussed by Mr. Amir Ali in his book on Mahomedan Law, and he shows that the rule had its origin in a primitive condition of society and applied to small plots of lands or houses. He also gives some passages from later writers which bear the stamp of being written in a progressive age and show, therefore, due regard for progress. The gift of crops in a land will be valid if the donee had authority to reap the crops. This is consistent with the rule laid down in *Kali Das* v. *Kanhya Lal*[4].

Shiah Law on the doctrine of Musha.

The Shiah Law is different. The refined doctrine of *Musha* is not applicable to cases governed by that School. Hence a gift of undivided property is valid whether such property is or is not capable of partition. In a case of *wakf* of undivided property if the same is not capable of division, it is the doctrine of even Abu Yusuf, as already mentioned, that an appropriation of such property for building a mosque or for a burrial ground is invalid. The reason is obvious. No mosque can be built, and if it is so done it will affect other people's rights. But an appropriation of the same property for the expenses in connection with a mosque is valid. The same must hold good of the Shiah law.

---

1. *Mahomed Buksh Khan* v. *Hosseini Bibi* (1888) L. R., 15 I. A. 81 at p. 95. See also *Mullick Abdool Guffoor* v. *Muleka* (1884) I. L. R., 10 C. 1112 at pp. 1124 and 1125 and *Amir Ali*, Vol. I p. 75. See also the case of *Rahim Bakhsh* v. *Muhammad Hasan* (1888), I. L. R., 11 A. 1 (at p. 10) which recognises this distinction though the decision is that the gift is invalid for want of possession. The case of *Meherali* v. *Tajudin* (1888), I. L. R., 13 B. 156, which holds that the ruling of the Judicial Committee in *Kalidas* v. *Kanhya Lal* is inapplicable to Mahomedan Law must be treated to have been overruled. See *Totiram* v. *Ramkrishna* (1902), I. L. R., 27 B. 31 at p. 39.

2. *Nawab Umjad Ally Khan* v. *Mohumdee Begum*, (1867) 11 M. I. A. 517.

3. (1869) 12 W. R. C. R. 344. See also *Mussumat Hyatee Khanum* v. *Mussumat Koolsoom*, (1807) 1 B. S. D. A. 214.

4. (1884) L. R., 11 I. A. 218; S. C. I. L. R., 11 C. 121.

CHAPTER XI.

THE OBJECTS OF AN ENDOWMENT AND THE MODE OF CREATING IT WITH REFERENCE TO LAW OF WAKFS.

Having seen that there is much learning displayed by the Mahomedan lawyers about the property to be endowed, we shall next consider the objects of an endowment and the mode of creating it. These are the other two requisites mentioned in the previous chapter.

Hindu Law as regards the purposes of an endowment.

Here again we shall see that there is not much to be said in the Hindu Law. A Hindu Religious Endowment is, as we have already observed, a gift to an idol. It is said to be either a *devasthan* or *sevasthan*[1]. But these terms are apparently used indifferently to denote the same idea in many cases. *Sevasthan* used generally in Bombay seems to imply strictly a place where God is supposed to be actually present and incarnate[2]. It is apparently the *garbha griha* or the *sanctum sanctorum* of a temple. All gifts or bequests to temples as for the worship, &c., of idols in such temples are equally religious endowments[3]. Mattams are chiefly religious institutions, but as there are always some charities to be administered as part of the purposes of such institutions, (one of them being free board and education in Sanskrit) they may be called religious and charitable institutions.[4] Of course the Hindu Law also recognises charitable purposes as distinguished from religious purposes.

Charitable purposes.

Gifts or bequests for constructing a well[5], tank[6], avada[7], or porter's rest[8] for establishing and maintaining a choultry[9], dhar-

1. Chapter II, p. xv.

2. *Chintaman Bajaji Dev* v. *Dhondo Ganesh Dev*, (1888) I. L. R., 15 B. 612 at p. 620.

3. *Karuppa* v. *Arumuga*, (1882) I. L. R., 5 M. 383; *Thackersey Dewraj* v. *Hurbhum Nursey*, (1884) I. L. R., 8 B. 432; *Narasimha* v. *Ayyan Chetti*, (1888) I.L.R., 12 M. 157; *Raghubar Dial* v. *Kesho Ramanuj Das*, (1888) I. L. R., 11 A. 18; *In re Lakshmibai*, (1888) I. L. R., 12 B. 638 (640); *Jugalkishore* v. *Lakshmandas*, (1899) I. L. R., 23 B. 659. See *Rajessuree Debia* v. *Jogendro Nath Roy*, (1875) 23 W. R. C. R. 278, which upheld a bequest for the worship of a family thakoor.

4. *Thambu Chetti Subraya Chetti* v. *Arundel*, (1883) I. L. R., 6 M. 287, where it was held that feeding of Brahmins did not amount to public worship; *Krishnasami Chetti* v. *Virasami Chetti*, (1886) I. L. R., 10 M. 133; *Sathianama Bharati* v. *Sarvana Bagi Ammal*, (1894) I. L. R., 18 M. 266.

5. *Karuppa* v. *Arumuga*, supra. *Jamnabai* v. *Khimji Vallubdass*, (1899) I.L.R., 14 B. 1; *Tricamdass Mulji* v. *Khimji Vallubdass*, (1892) I. L. R., 16 B. 626.

6. *Tricamdass Mulji* v. *Khimji Vallubdass*, (1892) I. L. R., 16 B. 626.

7. *i. e.*, a cistern for animals to drink water from. *Jamnabai* v. *Khimji Vallubdass*, (1889) I. L. R., 14 B. 1.

8. *Karuppa* v. *Arumuga*, (1882) I. L. R., 5 M. 383.

9. *Narasimha* v. *Ayyan Chetti*, (1888) I. L. R., 12 M. 157; *Alagappa Mudaliar* v. *Sivaramasundara Mudaliar*, (1895) I. L. R., 19 M. 211.

masala[1], school[2] or dispensary[3], for advancement of education[4], for distributing food to poor[5], for feeding travellers[6], sadhus[7], or persons who are lame, diseased or otherwise deserving of charity[8] for giving presents to Brahmans[9] or pandits holding tolls for diffusion of Sanskrit learning[10], and for sadavart[11], are gifts or bequests for charitable purposes which have been upheld by the Courts. But a consideration of what are charitable as opposed to religious purposes is beyond the scope of the present work.

Ceremony of Utsarga.

With regard to the mode of constituting an endowment under the Hindu Law, we had occasion to deal with in a previous chapter[12]. We were there referring to the mode in which property might be set apart for religious uses. We shall here refer to the ceremony of *utsarga* observed or enjoined by the writers on ritual in building and consecrating a temple and the idol to be established there. Upon this Mr. Prannath Saraswati observes[13]: "The books of ritual contain a direction that before removing the image into the temple, the building itself should be formally given away to the god for whom it is intended. The *Sankalpa* or formula of resolve, makes the deity himself the recipient of the gift which, as in the case of other gifts, has to be made by the donor taking in his hands water, sesamum, the sacred *kusa* grass, and the like. It is

---

1. *Purmanundass Jeevundass* v. *Venayekrao Wassoodeo*, (1882) L. R. 9. I. A. 86; S. C. I. L. R., 7 B. 19; *In re Lakshmibai*; (1888) I. L. R., 12 B. 638; *Tricamdas Mulji* v. *Khimji Vallubdass*, (1892) I. L. R., 16 B. 626; *Jugalkishore* v. *Lakshmandas*, (1899) I. L. R., 23 B. 659.

2. *Hori Dasi Dabi* v. *The Secretary of State for India*, (1879) I. L. R., 5 C. 228; *Girdhari Lal* v. *Ram Lal*, (1899) I. L. R., 21 A. 200.

3. *Rajessuree Debia* v. *Jogendro Nath Roy*, (1875) 23 W. R. C. R. 278; *Hori Dasi Dabi* v. *The Secretary of State for India*, (1879) I. L. R., 5 C. 228.

4. *University of Bombay* v. *The Municipal Commissioners for the City of Bombay*, (1891) I. L. R., 16 B. 217.

5. *Tricamdass Mulji* v. *Khimji Vallubdass*, (1892) I. L. R., 16 B. 626.

6. *Sheo Shanker* v. *Ram Shewak*, (1896) I. L. R., 24 C. 77 (80); *Jugalkishore* v. *Lakshmandas* supra.

7. *Thackersey Dewraj* v. *Hurbhum Nursey*, (1884) I. L. R., 8 B. 432.

8. *Rajessuree Debia* v. *Jogendro Nath Roy*, (1875) 23 W. R. C. R. 278.

9. *Thambu Chetti Subraya Chetti* v. *Arundel*, (1883) I. L. R., 6 M. 287.

10. *Dwarkanath Bysack* v. *Burroda Persaud Bysack*, (1878) I. L. R., 4 C. 443.

11. *Jamnabai* v. *Khimji Vallubdass*, (1889) I. L. R., 14 B. 1; *Tricumdass Mulji* v. *Khimji Vallubdass*, (1892) I. L. R., 16 B. 626; *Morarji Cullianji* v. *Nenbai*, (1892) I. L. R., 17 B. 351; *Jugalkishore* v. *Lakshmandas*, (1899) I. L. R., 23 B. 659.

12. Chapter III, pp. xxxiv to xxxvi.

13. See Saraswati on Endowments, p. 127. There is also a ceremony of renunciation for tanks, wells &c., dealt with by Mr. Saraswati in Chapter VIII (Lecture X) of his book, but with this we have no concern.

this ceremony which divests the proprietorship of the temple from the builder and vests it in the image. The *utsarga* is the relinquishment of the donor's right and the gift is completed by the acceptance corporeally made by the donee—the image—which is made to take bodily possession of the premises." The question whether a dedication may take place otherwise than by means of this ritual has neither been raised nor decided in any case. If the Transfer of Property Act has no application[1] then it may be contended that the Hindu Law must be applied in matters of religious usage or institution according to the Civil Courts Acts for the several Presidencies, and that as the question raised in the particular case is one regarding religious usage or institution, the books of ritual must be followed. But we are not aware of any provision in the said books about the transaction being entirely null or void in case the observances about the ritual are not actually observed but some other formality is gone through, which indicates that the party intending to dedicate relinquished his own rights in favor of the deity or the institution. The question can rarely arise as in all such cases the letter of the text is in fact scrupulously adhered to.

Wakf—Religious and charitable purposes.

Now, as regards the Mahomedan Law, it may be observed that all religious and charitable purposes are the proper objects of a *wakf*. Professor Wilson accordingly says: "All works of religion, charity or public utility not condemned by the Mahomedan religion are proper objects of a *wakf*." Where a *wakf* is directly for the worship of God it is for the affluent and the indigent alike. Where it is not directly for the worship of God it may be for the affluent and the indigent alike or for the poor exclusively.

Muzhurool Huq v. Puhraj Ditarey.

In *Muzhurool Huq* v. *Puhraj Ditarey Mohapattur*[2] the High Court (*Kemp* and *Jackson*, JJ.) holding that the terms of the deed in question in that case had all the characteristics of a valid endowment under the Mahomedan Law observed: "The primary objects for which the lands are endowed and which are the objects which all Mahomedans have in view in endowing lands, are to support a mosque and to defray the expenses of the worship conducted in that mosque." Mr. Wilson in his Digest of Anglo-Mahomedan Law[3] has objection to this language and says that these remarks must have been made through sheer inadvertence. The language might not be felicitous, but we should feel no doubt that the

1. As to which see Chapter III, pp. xxxv and xxxvi.
2. (1870), 13 W. R. C. R. 235.
3. Page 272.

learned judges never meant to say that the objects mentioned by them exhausted the objects for which a valid *wakf* could be made. The support of a mosque and the expenses in connection therewith are the primary objects of the deed in question and these are the objects which all Mahomedans have in view. This does not negative the existence of other objects. There is nothing incorrect in saying that the above are the objects which any pious Mahomedan will have in view in endowing lands. Anyhow the mention of two objects in the case does not exclude other objects for which a *wakf* can be made.

Abdul Ganne v. Hussen Miya.

Then it is said by Mr. Amir Ali[1] that the judges in *Abdul Ganne Kasam* v. *Hussen Miya Rahimtula*[2] enunciate a rather startling proposition that a *wakf* in order to be valid must 'be solely to the worship of God.' No such proposition can be deduced from the judgment. The learned judges first proceed to consider the meaning of *wakf*. They then consider whether the term includes settlements on a person's self and children. The conclusion they come to and state at p. 12 of the report is that "the balance of authority is strongly in favour of the conclusion that, to constitute a valid *wakf*, there must be a dedication of the property solely to the worship of God, or to religious or charitable purposes." There is nothing startling in this. The judges do not intend to confine the objects of *wakf* as appertaining only to the *worship* of God. Consistently with the definition of *wakf* given by them already, they cannot have so intended. If Mr. Amir Ali should limit his observation to the view taken by the judges of family settlements, there might be some ground for his criticism. He apparently does not intend more than that. But the following passage in his book shows that according to him the judges in the Bombay case exclude other objects from the category of *wakf*. "It is difficult to understand the meaning of this comprehensive *dictum*. If that view were correct, a *wakf* to an *Imambara*, to a *Khankah*, to a *Dargah* &c., would be invalidated." It is needless to state that the passage already cited from the judgment of their Lordships shows that they never for a moment doubted the validity of *wakfs* for Imambaras, &c.

---

1. Tagore Law lectures, 1884, Vol. I, pp. 217 and 218.
2. (1873), 10 B. H. C. 7 at p. 12; see also *Mahomed Hamidulla Khan* v. *Lotful Huq*, (1881) I. L. R., 6 C. 744.

Luchmiput Singh v. Amir Alum.

The case of *Luchmiput Singh* v. *Amir Alum*[1] rightly understands the decision in *Abdul Ganne Kasam* v. *Hussen Miya*[2]. In the Calcutta case the facts were that a settlor provided that the manager appointed by him in the deed should discharge the debts in the first place and that he should then apply the income arising out of remainder of the property towards certain religious uses (*i. e.*, expenses of the masjid, the tombs of the holy personages of the settlor's family, and the servants of the *Astana*, and the expenses for performing the *urs* and *fatiha* at the tombs) and the maintenance of the settlor's male descendants. The High Court (*Tottenham* and *Bose*, JJ.) held that there was a good deal of controversy as to what was a valid *wakf*, that one theory was that no *wakf* was valid unless it was solely and wholly for pious and charitable purposes enduring all times, while the other theory was that what was practically a perpetual provision for the dedicator's family, might be a valid *wakf* and that there was a valid *wakf* in this case at any rate as regards the direction that the income should be applied for the religious uses. The judges observed that "the Bombay High Court had by a Full Bench in the above case decided that to constitute a valid *wakf*, there must be a dedication of property solely to the worship of God or to religious or charitable purposes." They did not consider it necessary to decide whether the further direction in the settlement that the manager should maintain the future male descendants of the settlor could be legally carried out or was a valid *wakf*.

As already observed there is a good deal of controversy among the Mahomedan lawyers and in the earlier cases whether *wakfs* in favor of the settlor or his family are valid. The decisions of the highest tribunal have settled this contention and it must now be taken that such *wakfs* are invalid. We do not propose to discuss the question as it does not properly arise within the scope of our present enquiry.

Religious or charitable, meaning of.

In *Meer Mahomed Israil Khan* v. *Sashti Churn Ghose*[3] *O'Kinealy* J. observed: "In judging of what is really meant by the words 'religious' or 'charitable' by a Mahomedan, we must

1. (1882), I. L. R., 9 C. 176.
2. (1873), 10 B. H. C. 7.
3. (1892), I. L. R., 19 C. 412.

take the view which their law takes and not what is to be found in the English Dictionary." It was, therefore, held in this case that gifts in favor of the settlor's family were valid *wakfs*. Apart from the fact that the decisions of the highest tribunal have dissented from the view that such gifts can be *wakfs*, it is impossible to recognise the sweeping doctrine that the English Dictionary cannot be looked at for understanding the words themselves. A religious purpose with reference to Mahomedanism is a purpose connected with the Mahomedan religion and although such purposes may not and will not exactly cover all the purposes connected with Christianity, yet the idea denoted by the word 'religious' and conveyed to us by its meaning as given in the English Dictionary cannot be essentially different. Of course in order to see what religious purposes are recognised as valid objects of a *wakf*, we must look to the Mahomedan Law. But the idea conveyed by the words "charity" or "religion" cannot be very different in different countries.

Intention to be explained by custom.

But whatever this may be, in determining whether a disposition of property made by a Mahomedan is or is not a valid *wakf* the intention of the *wakif* may be interpreted by reference to custom prevailing at the time the *wakf* is made. Thus it was held in *Phul Chand* v. *Akbar*[1] that the expenses of *fatiha* included under a local custom the distribution of alms and food to the poor though not under the Mahomedan Law and that, therefore, under a *wakf* of property for the expenses of the *fathia*, the distribution of alms and food to the poor could be validly made. The case of *Kale-Loola Sahib* v. *Nusee-rudeen Sahib*[2] is, therefore, distinguishable. There, property was dedicated for the upkeep of the settlor's husband's tomb, for the daily, monthly and annual expenses of the said tomb, such as lighting, frankincense, flowers and salaries of Hafizes (*i. e.*, repeaters of the Koran) and Daroodies (*i. e.*, readers of benediction) and for the Fatiha ceremonies of the settlor and her husband. The Madras High Court decided that these were not charitable purposes, and, therefore, there was no valid *wakf* according to the Mahomedan Law. We have already discussed the soundness of the decision in this case when considering the extent of the applicability of the rules as to superstitious uses in India.

1. (1896), I. L. R., 19 A. 211. 2. (1894), I. L. R., 18 M. 201.

Mahomedan religious trusts.

Trusts of a religious character are mosques[1], musallas or prayer-grounds[2], Imambaras[3], Dargas[4], Khankahs[5], cemeteries or grave-yards[6]. Expenses in connection with the above[7], such as repairs[8], lighting[9], reading prayers[10], recitation of Koran[11], worship[12], &c., are also religious purposes and trusts for such

---

1. *Doyal Chund Mullick* v. *Syud Keramut Ali*, (1871) 16 W. R. C. R. 116; *The Advocate-General* v. *Sultani Begam*, (1872) 9 B.H. C. 19; *Rahumtulla Sahib* v. *Mahommed Akbur Sahib*, (1875) 8 M. H. C. 63; *Zafaryab Ali* v. *Bakhtawar Singh*, (1883) I. L. R., 5 A. 497; *Jawahra* v. *Akbar Husain*, (1884) I. L. R., 7 A. 178; *Queen-Empress* v. *Ramzan*, (1885) I. L. R., 7 A. 461; *Ataullah* v. *Azimullah*, (1889) I. L. R., 12 A. 494; *Jangu* v. *Ahmadullah*, (1889) I. L. R., 13 A. 419; *Huseni Begam* v. *The Collector of Moradabad*, (1897) I. L. R., 20 A. 46.

2. *Doyal Chund Mullick* v. *Syud Keramut Ali*, (1871) 16 W. R. C. R. 116.

3. *Nawab Umjad Ally Khan* v. *Mohumdee Begum*, (1867) 11 M. I. A, 517; *Delroos Banoo Begum* v. *Ashgar Ally Khan*, (1875) 15 B. L. R., 167; S. C. 23 W. R. 453; *Zafaryab Ali* v. *Bakhtawar Singh*, (1883) I. L. R., 5 A. 497; *Huseni Begam* v. *The Collector of Moradabad*, (1897) I. L. R., 20 A. 46.

4. *Futtoo Bibee* v. *Bhurrut Lall Bhukut*, (1868) 10 W. R. C. R. 299; *Reasut Ali* v. *J. C. Abbott*, (1869) 12 W. R. C. R. 132; *Khajah Ashruf Hossein* v. *Mussamut Hazara Begum*, (1872) 18 W. R. C. R. 369; *Fakurudin Sahib* v. *Ackeni Sahib* (1880), I. L. R., 2 M. 197; *Zafaryab Ali* v. *Bakhtawar Singh*, supra (*Takia*, known by the name of *Najaf Ali Shah*); *Lakshmandas Parashram* v. *Ganpat Rav Krishna*, (1884) I. L. R., 8 B. 365; *Piran* v. *Abdool Karim*, (1891) I. L. R., 19 C. 203; *Mohiuddin* v *Sayiduddin*, (1893) I. L. R., 20 C. 810 (takkia): *Miya Vali Ulla* v. *Sayed Bava Santi Miya*, (1896) I. L. R., 22 B. 496; *Mahomed Nathubhai* v. *Husen*, (1897) I L. R., 22 B. 729.

5. *Jewun Doss Sahoo* v. *Shah Kubeer-Ood-Deen*, (1841) 2 M. I. A. 390. In *Bibee Kuneez Fatima* v. *Bibee Saheba Jan* (1867), 8 W. R. C. R. 313, it was held that the grant to the descendant of a Pir for the expenses of a Khankah among others was not a *wakf*. But this was questioned in *Sayad Mahomed Ali* v. *Sayad Gobar Ali*, (1881) I. L. R., 6 B. 88 (95). The case in 2 Moore is not referred to in the former case. See also *Piran* v. *Abdool Karim*, (1891) I. L. R., 19 C. 203; and *Mohiuddin* v. *Sayiduddin* (1893), I. L. R., 20 C. 810.

6. *Nawab Umjad Ally Khan* v. *Mohumdee Begum* supra; *Zafaryab Ali* v. *Bakhtawar Singh* (1883), I. L. R., 5 A. 497; *Muhammad Abdulla Khan* v. *Kallu* (1899), I. L. R., 21 A. 187. See *Mahomed Kasim* v. *Mahomed Alum* (1831) 5 B. S D. A. 136.

7. See *Syud Asheerooddeen* v. *Sreemutty Drobo Moyee*, (1876) 25 W. R. C. R., 557 where a grant for the expenses of a Khanka and Musjeed was upheld: and *Huseni Begam* v. *The Collector of Moradabad*; (1897) I. L. R., 20 A. 46 where the grant also provided for the upkeep of a mosque and imambara.

8. *Muzhurool Huq* v. *Puhraj Ditarey Mohapattur*, (1870) 13 W. R. C. R. 235; *Sheik Abdool Khalek* v. *Poran Bibee*, (1876) 25 W. R. C. R., 542; and *Muhammad Munawar Ali* v. *Rasulan Bibi*, (1899) I. L. R., 21 A. 329 (336), where, however, it was held that there was only a charge and that even this charge was invalid as the object was only to tie up the property in the family in the guise of a *wakf*.

9. *Muzhurool Huq* v. *Puhraj Ditarey Mohaputtur* supra; *Sheik Abool Khalek* v. *Poran Bibee*, supra; *Lakshmandass Parashram* v. *Ganpat Row Kristna*, (1884) I. L. R., 8 B. 365; *Lutifunnissa Bibi* v. *Nazirun Bibi*, (1884) I. L. R., 11 C. 33; *Kazi Hassan* v. *Sagun Balkrishna* (1899), I. L. R., 24 B. 170 (174).

10. *Nizamudin Gulam* v. *Abdul Gafur*, (1888) I. L. R., 13 B. 264.

11. *Doyal Chund Mullick* v. *Syud Keramut Ali*, (1871) 16 W. R. C. R. 116; *Nizamuddin Gulam* v. *Abdul Gafar* supra; and *Muhammad Munawar Ali* v. *Rasulan Bibi* supra, for which see page cxlix, note (2). The judges also observed in the latter case that as the reciter of the Koran should transfer his spiritual benefit to the settlors, the same would be invalid in accordance with the decision in *Kaleloola Sahib* v. *Naseerudeen Sahib*, (1894) I. L. R., 18 M. 201.

12. *Muzhurool Huq* v. *Puhraj Ditarey Mohapattur*, (1870) 13 W. R. C. R. 235.

expenses will be trusts for a religious purpose. Appropriation for the expenses of an annual 'urs' or religious assembly[1] or for the expenses of the well-known Mahomedan festivals[2], such as Eed[3], Bakrid[4], Mohurrum[5], &c., will also be trusts for religious purposes. A grant of property to be used by Mahomedans as a place of meeting on the great festivals of religion[6] is also a trust for a religious purpose. Gift to God[7], Allah[8] or religion[9] amounts to a *wakf* and is a gift for religious purpose. In fact a *wakf* is a dedication of property to the Deity as already mentioned.

There are of course trusts of a secular character, *i. e.*, purely charitable trusts, and these are also *wakfs*. Chief among the charitable objects are appropriations for the benefit of the poor or indigent. The application must be to objects not liable to become extinct, and as the poor are always with us, a gift for the benefit of the poor is a valid *wakf*[10]. The distribution of alms or of food to way-fairers[11], fakirs[12], travellers[13], or indigent persons[14], is

---

1. *Lakshmandas Parashram* v. *Ganpat Rav Krishna*, (1884) I. L. R., 8 B. 365; *Huseni Begam* v. *The Collector of Moradabad*, (1897) I. L. R., 20 A. 46; and *Muhammad Munawar Ali* v. *Rasulan Bibi* (1899), I. L. R., 21, A 329, for which see page cxlix note (2).

2. Per *Kemp*, J., in *Khajah Hossein Ali* v. *Shahzadee Hazara Begum*, (1869) 12 W. R. C. R. 344; S. C. 4 B L. R. A. C. J. 86.

3. *Sheik Abdool Khalek* v. *Poran Bibee*, (1876) 25 W. R. C. R. 542; *Lutifunnissa Bibi* v. *Nazirun Bibi*, (1884) I. L. R., 11 C. 33.

4. *Lutifunnissa Bibi* v. *Nazirun Bibi*, supra.

5. *Nawab Umjad Ally Khan* v. *Mohumdee Begum*, (1867) 11 M. I. A. 517; *Muhammad Munawar Ali* v. *Rasulan Bibi*, supra, for which, however, see page cxlix note (2).

6. Per *Kemp* J., in *Khajah Hossein Ali* v. *Shahzadee Hazara Begum*, (1869) 12 W. R. C. R. 344: S. C. 4 B. L. R. A. C. J. 86; *Doyal Chund Mullick* v. *Syud Keramut Ali*, (1871) 16 W. R. C. R. 116.

7. *Doyal Chund Mullick* v. *Syud Keramut Ali* (1871), 16 W. R. C. R. 116.

8. *Bikani Mia* v. *Shuk Lal Poddar*, (1892) I. L. R., 20 C. 116, where, however, there was held to be only a charge.

9. *Shoojat Ali* v. *Zameeroodden*, (1866) 5 W. R. C. R. 158; *Phate Saheb Bibi* v. *Damodar Premji*, (1879) I. L. R., 3 B. 84; and *Bikani Mia* v. *Shuk Lal Poddar*, supra.

10. *Khajah Hossein Ali* v. *Shahzadee Hazara Begum*, (1869) 12 W. R. C. R. 344: S. C. 4 B. L. R. A. C. J. 86; *Muzhurool Huq* v. *Puhraj Ditarey Mohapattur*, (1870) 13 W. R. C. R. 235.

11. *Lutifunnissa Bibi* v. *Nazirun Bibi*, (1884) I. L. R., 11 C. 33.

12. *Sheik Abool Khalek* v. *Poran Bibee*, supra; *Amrutlal Kalidas* v. *Shaik Hussein* (1887), I. L. R., 11 B. 492.

13. *Khajah Hossein Ali* v. *Shahzadee Hazara Begum*, supra; *Muzhurool Huq* v. *Puhraj Ditarey Mohapattur*, supra; *Sheik Abdool Khalek* v. *Poran Bibee*, supra; *Syud Asheeroddeen* v. *Sreemutty Drobo Moyee*, supra; *Lutifunnissa Bibi* v. *Nazirun Bibi*, supra.

14. *Khajah Hossein Ali* v. *Shahzadec Hazara Begum*, supra; *Muzhurool Huq* v. *Puhraj Ditarey Mohapattur*, supra; *Amrutlal Kalidas* v. *Shaik Hussein*, supra; and *Huseni Begum* v. *The Collector of Moradabad*, (1897) I. L. R., 20 A. 46.

a charitable object, and a gift of property for such purposes will be a valid *wakf*. Caravensarais, choultries[1], colleges, hospitals, wells, acqueducts, roads, bridges, inns, &c., are other instances of trusts of a secular character. A gift for charitable objects in Mecca is a charitable trust and is a valid *wakf*[2]. A gift of property so that the income might be utilized for educating poor scholars[3] or for scholarships in a college is a valid *wakf*. As already stated we are not concerned directly with the law as to trusts of a secular character except in so far as it may throw light on the law relating to trusts of a religious character.

Mode of constituting wakf.

We shall now consider how a *wakf* can be validly and legally constituted ? It has been settled by the decisions of the highest tribunal that there must be a dedication of property to religious or charitable purposes[4], that such dedication must be substantial[5] and not illusory and that it will be illusory where the time when the gift of property in *wakf* is to take effect is uncertain and remote (as the extinction of the descendants of the settlor)[6].

Provision for maintenance.

But where the primary object of the settlor is the permanent application of the property to serve an unfailing purpose, the mere fact that provision is made for the maintenance of the settlor or of the members of his family will not vitiate the validity of the *wakf*. As observed by *Kemp, J.*, in *Muzhurool Huq* v. *Puhraj Ditarey Mohapattur*[7]: "The mere charge upon the profits of the estate of certain items, which *must in the course of time necessarily cease* (the italics are ours) being confined to one family and for particular purposes and which, after they lapse, will leave the whole profits

---

1. *Gulam Hussain Saib* v. *Aji Ajam Tadallah Saib*, (1868) 4 M. H. C. 44 (where it was held that there was a gift subject to a trust); *Doyal Chund Mullick* v. *Syud Keramut Ali*, (1871) 16 W. R. C. R. 116 (where the direction was that charitable doles should be given at the time of the great festivals of the Mahomedan religion).

2. *Fatima Bibi* v. *Ariff Ismailjee Bham*, (1881) 9 C. L. R. 66.

3. *Muzhurool Huq* v. *Puhraj Ditarey Mohapattur*, (1870) 13 W. R. C. R. 235; *Bikani Mia* v. *Shuk Lal Poddar* (1892), I. L. R., 20 C. 116 (where it was held to be a charge only).

4. *Mahomed Ahsanulla Chowdhry* v. *Amarchand Kundu*, (1889) L. R. 17 I. A. 28; S. C .I. L. R., 17 C. 498.

5. *Mahomed Ahsanulla Chowdhry* v. *Amarchand Kundu* supra; *Abdul Gafur* v. *Nizamudin*, (1892) L. R., 19 I. A. 170: S. C. I. L. R., 17 B. 1.

6. *Abul Fata Mahomed* v. *Russomoy Dhur Chowdhry*, (1894) L. R., 22 I. A., 76; S. C. I. L. R., 22 C. 619 affirming *Rasamaya Dhur Chowdhuri* v. *Abul Fata Mahomed*, (1891) I. L. R. 18 C. 399.

7. (1870), 13 W. R. C. R. 235.

intact for the original purposes for which the endowment was made, does not render the endowment invalid under the Mahomedan Law." Mr. Wilson doubts, and very rightly too, whether the learned Judge was right in the particular case in stating that the charges would necessarily lapse in course of time, but whatever doubts may be entertained as to the correct application of the doctrine in the particular case, there can be no doubt about the correctness of the principle laid down by the learned Judge. These remarks of the learned Judge are quoted with approval by the Judicial Committee in *Mahomed Ahsanulla Chowdhry* v. *Amarchand Kundu*[1]. It is, however, not necessary that the charges should necessarily cease, for it has been held by the Judicial Committee in *Abul Fata Mahomed Ishak* v. *Russomoy Dhur Chowdhry*[2] that in order to establish a valid *wakf* there must be a substantial dedication of the property to charitable or religious purposes, and where that is the case a provision for the dedicator's family out of the income of the appropriated property may be consistent with a *wakf*.

Temporary intermediate application of profits.

But although there must be a dedication in favor of religious or charitable uses, there may be a *temporary intermediate* application of the whole of the benefits thereof to the family of the appropriator. If the intermediate application of the benefits to the appropriator's family is not merely temporary, but is to be permanent so long as that family should continue, then there is no real dedication of the property to religious or charitable uses and, therefore, no valid *wakf*[2]. Of course where there is no such interposition, but the gift is immediately to religious or charitable uses, there may be a direction that the surplus after the expenditure incurred for religious or charitable uses should go over for the maintenance of the Mutwalli and his family or the settlor and his family. These principles have been adverted and given effect to when we had to discuss the different kinds of dedication[3].

---

1. (1889), L. R. 17 I. A. 28; S. C. I. L. R., 17 C. 498. See also *Murtazai Bibi* v. *Jumna Bibi*, (1890) I. L. R., 13 A. 261; and *Deoki Prasad* v. *Inayit-Ullah*, (1892) I. L. R., 14 A. 375.

2. (1894), L. R. 22 I. A. 76: S. C.I. L. R., 22 C. 619. The case of *Muhammad Munawar Ali* v. *Rasulan Bibi*, (1899) I. L. R., 21 A. 329 should be explained upon the ground that even the charge was negatived in that case as there was no substantial dedication and there was no enforceable direction that the income should be utilised for charitable uses.

3. Chapter IV, pp. xlvii to lii.

Dedication not to depend on a contingency.

But although there may be such interposition, yet the gift of property for *wakf* must not be made to depend on a *contingency* *i. e.*, the dedication should not depend on a contingency, but the appropriation must be at once complete and not suspended on anything[1]. Thus, the interposition of an intermediate estate limited in duration will not invalidate the *wakf*, provided there is an out-and-out appropriation at the time of the deed[2]. The interposition of a life-estate may not be such a remote contingency within the meaning of the above rule, but as life-estates are unknown to Mahomedan Law[3], a gift of property to A for life with remainder to religious or charitable uses will not be valid. The prior estate according to the Mahomedan Law is a gift with a condition and the donee takes the estate absolutely irrespective of the condition[4] and the subsequent estate will have no operation and is void. Where the gift for life is by way of devise and the devisee for life is one of the heirs of the testator, the bequest for life is void altogether by want of the consent of the heirs and is not even good for one-third of the net assets of the testator, and the subsequent estate in favor of religious or charitable purposes is not accelerated but is void altogether[5]. Where by an instrument the settlor states that he has dedicated the property in *wakf*, but that the same is to take effect after his death there is in effect a testamentary disposi-

1. *Pathukutti* v. *Avathalakutti*, (1889) I. L. R., 13 M. 66 followed in *Rasamaya Dhur Chowdhuri* v. *Abul Fata Mahomed Ishak*, (1891) I. L. R., 18 C. 399. The case of *Syeda Bibi* v. *Mughal Jan* (1902), I. L. R., 24 A. 231 which holds that in the Shiah Law a *wakf* should not be made contingent upon a future event which may, however, be certain (such as one month or the time of registration) being based upon *Agha Ali Khan* v. *Altaf Hasan Khan* (1892), I. L. R., 14 A. 429 must be treated to have been overruled by the decision of the Privy Council in *Baker Ali Khan* v. *Anjuman Ara Begum*, (1903)L.R.30 I. A.94: S. C. I.L.R., 25 A. 236. But see Baillie Vol. II, p. 218.

2. *Massamut Humeeda* v. *Mussamut Budlun* (1872) 17 W. R. C. R. 525; *Chekkonekutti* v. *Ahmed*, (1887) I. L. R., 10 M. 196; *Abdul Gafur* v. *Nizamudin*, (1892) L. R. 19 I. A. 170 : S. C. I. L. R., 17 B. 1.

3. *Mussamut Humeeda* v. *Mussamut Budlun*, supra; *Suleman Kadr* v. *Dorab Ali Khan*, (1881) L. R. 8 I. A. 117 (122) : S. C. I. L. R., 8 C. 1 (7); *Nizamudin Gulam* v. *Abdul Gafur*, (1888) I.L.R., 13B. 264 at p.275 approved by the Privy Council in *Abdul Gafur* v. *Nizamudin* supra; *Sagun Balakrishna* v. *Kaji Hussen* (1903) I. L. R. 27 B. 500 (514).

4. *Ameeroonissa* v. *Abedoonissa*, (1875) L. R., 2 I. A. 87; *Ranee Khujooroonissa* v. *Roushun Jehan*, (1876) L. R., 3 I. A. 291 : S. C. I. L. R., 2 C. 184.

5. Per *Wilson*, J., in *Fatima Bibi* v. *Ariff Ismailjee Bham*, (1881) 9 C. L. R., 66 at p. 74. The contrary opinion of *West*, J., in *Fatmabibi* v. *The Advocate-General of Bombay*, (1881) I. L. R., 6 B. 42 (the decision itself having been disapproved by the Privy Council on other points) would only be explicable upon the ground that the primary objects of the settlor were the trusts for charity and that the application for the intermediate purposes was not the testator's immediate object and that this would make a difference in principle.

tion and operation may be given to it as such[1]. Where, however, the settlor after dedicating the property to pious and charitable uses *in presenti* provides that a part of the income is to be spent for his own maintenance, effect may be given to both provisions.

Wakf with option to revoke.

Upon a similar principle a provision in a deed that the settlor is at liberty or has the option to revoke the *wakf* at any time he pleases[2], or that the settlor may sell the *wakf* property and utilise the sale proceeds to his own personal use[3] invalidates or negatives the *wakf*.

Use of word wakf—Will.

In order that there may be a valid appropriation it is not necessary to use the term *wakf*[4]. The appropriation may be made orally[5] or by deed *inter vivos* or by will. In the case of bequests and death-bed gifts the *wakf* is not valid beyond a third of the net assets unless the heirs consent[6]. It was held by a Full Bench of the Allahabad High Court[7] that in the case of Shiah Law a *wakf* could not be constituted by a will as it was said that according to Shiah Law an appropriation was not a unilateral disposition of property as in the Sunni Law but a contract. *Mahmood*, J., delivered a lengthy judgment in this case referring to various texts as establishing the above position and further held that in the Shiah Law technical expressions and change of possession were necessary to constitute a valid *wakf*. This ruling of the Allahabad High Court has been, hewever, overruled by the recent decision of the Privy Council in the case of *Baker Ali Khan* v. *Anjuman Ara Begam*[8]. After this authoritative pronouncement it is of purely academical interest which view is more in accordance with the ancient writers on Mahomedan Law, and it is no use discussing the point further. We may, however, observe that the effect of this

---

1. Baillie Vol. I, p. 595. See the conflicting doctrines stated in the Hedaya Vol. II, Book XV, p. 237. cf. *Muzhurool Huq* v. *Puhraj Ditarey Mohapattur*, (1870) 13 W. R. C. R. 235 (where it is, however, not so stated in express language). See also *Fatma Bibi* v. *The Advocate-General of Bombay*, (1881) I. L. R., 6 B. 42.

2. *Fatma Bibi* v. *The Advocate-General of Bombay* supra ; *Puthukutti* v. *Avathalakutti*, (1889) I. L. R., 13 M. 66.

3. *Fatma Bibi* v. *The Advocate-General of Bombay*, supra.

4. See Chapter II p. xx notes (2) and (3). See also *Kulb Ali Hoosein* v. *Syf Ali*, (1814) 2 B. S. D. A. 110.

5. *Abul Hasan* v. *Haji Mohammad*, (1831) 5 B. S. D. A. 87.

6. *Baboo Jan* v. *Mahomed Noorool Huq*, (1868) 10 W. R. C. R., 375 ; *Fatima Bibi* v. *Arif Ismailjee Bham*, (1881) 9 C. L. R., 66.

7. *Agha Ali Khan* v. *Altaf Hasan Khan*, (1892) I. L. R., 14 A. 429. In *Murtazai Bibi* v. *Jumna Bibi*, (1890) I. L. R., 13 A. 261 (268) the question was raised but not decided.

8. (1903), L. R. 30 I. A. 94 : S. C. I. L. R., 25 A. 236.

decision of the Judicial Committee is not to take away any power which the Mahomedans may have possessed before but to confer a power which the Mahomedans may exercise at their pleasure.

No set form of words.

The appropriation becomes complete when there is a dedication. In order that there should be a dedication, it is not necessary that any set form of words should be used. There must, however, be words declaratory of the appropriation or something from which the same may be inferred[1]. It is sufficient if it appears, that the appropriator has stated verbally or in writing that he has made the property *wakf* to Almighty God. We have already considered the question whether possession is necessary to complete an appropriation otherwise valid[2] We may here observe that so far as wills are concerned the doctrine of *Mahmood*, J., that in the Shiah Law a bequest of property in *wakf* is not valid unless there is a transfer of possession having now been exploded by the Privy Council[3] it must now be taken to be settled that a bequest of property in *wakf* is complete and will take effect on the death of the testator although there is no change of possession during the testator's life-time. It has been held by the Allahabad High Court, that in the case of Sunni Law it is essential to the validity of *wakf* created by deed *inter vivos* that the *wakif* should actually divest himself of the possession of property[4]. The better view seems, however, to be that where there is a registered deed and a real dedication there is a transfer of property and that change of possession has only an evidentiary value as regards the *factum* of real dedication[5]. The Shiah Law is also stated to be similar to the Sunni Law in this respect[6]. But the Shafei Law is more reasonable. It is stated in the Hedaya[7] that according to the Shafei school an appropriation is complete from the moment

1. *Doyal Chund Mullick* v. *Syud Keramut Ali*, (1871) 16 W. R. C. R., 116.
2. See pp. cxxxvi, cxxxvii.
3. *Baker Ali Khan* v. *Anjuman Ara Begam*, (1903) L. R. 30 I. A. 94: S. C. I. L. R., 25 A. 236.
4. *Muhammad Aziz-ud-din* v. *The Legal Remembrancer to Government*, (1893) I. L. R., 15 A. 321. See also *Mogulsha* v. *Mahamad Saheb*, (1887) I. L. R., 11 B. 517 (which, however, states the rule only as regards ordinary gifts); *Murtazai Bibi* v. *Jumna Bibi*, (1890) I. L. R., 13 A. 261 (268).
5. See per *Mahmood*, J., in *Jawahra* v. *Akbar Husain*, (1884) I. L. R., 7 A. 178, where he says that the intention must be declared by some specific act.
6. Baillie Vol. II, pp. 218 and 219 and *Murtazai Bibi* v. *Jumna Bibi*, (1890) I. L. R., 13 A. 261.
7. Vol. II, Book XV, p. 232.

of the declaration by the appropriator and that it is not necessary that there should be an actual change of possession from the appropriator.

Time when appropriation becomes complete.

Much discussion is to be found in the books as to the time when the appropriation is complete in particular cases. In the Hedaya[1] it is stated that, according to Haneefa and Mahomed, the proprietary right of the builder in the case of a mosque is not extinguished until the people in general or a single person say their or his prayers in it when all proprietary rights are extinguished and the property becomes divine property. According to these, performance of the prayer is an essential requisite. But according to Aboo Yoosaf[2] the founder's right of property is destroyed immediately on his saying "I constitute this a mosque." The case of *Adam Sheik* v. *Isha Sheik*[3] shows that a mosque becomes consecrated for public worship either by delivery to a mutwalli or on the declaration of the wakif that he has constituted it into a musjid or on the performance of the prayers therein. In case of reservoirs for public use, caravanserais for travellers, or burial grounds there is a greater difference of opinion. According to Haneefa the appropriation in these cases is complete when there is a magisterial decree or when the appropriation is by a testamentary disposition. According to Mahomed the proprietor's right is extinguished as soon as people drink water out of the reservoir, or enter the caravenserai or as soon as interment takes place in the burial ground. According to Aboo Yoosaf the extinguishment takes place with the declaration in favour of the appropriation[4].

---

1. Vol. II, Book XV, p 239, impliedly followed in *Jangu* v. *Ahmad-ullah*, (1889) I. L. R., 13 A. 419 (429). See per *Mahmood*, J., in *Jawahra* v. *Akbar Husain*, (1884) I. L. R., 7 A. 178 (182). See Baillie, Vol. I, p. 615.

2. Impliedly followed in *Doyal Chund Mullick* v. *Synd Keramut Ali*, (1871) 16 W. R. C. R. 116 (118).

3. (1894) 1 C. W. N. 76.

4. Hedaya Vol. II, Book XV, p. 240. See also Baillie, Vol. I, p. 620.

CHAPTER XII.

WHO ARE TRUSTEES OR MANAGERS ACCORDING TO HINDU LAW?

We shall now consider about the persons who are in charge of these religious endowments and the position assigned to such persons by the Hindu law.

Idol is a juristic person- Manager no legal property.

We have seen in a previous chapter that the true theory is that an idol is regarded as a juristic person and as such can hold lands and that property can vest in such idol[1]. But from the very necessity of things property of the idol or deity has to be managed by its human attendant or some other person; the temporal concerns have to be looked after by some human being[2] and this person is rightly called the *manager.* The legal property does not vest in such manager[3] for the simple reason that the idol or deity being a juridical person is capable of acquiring rights and possessing property, and we have already said that the property vests in such idol or deity[1]. It is a misnomer to call such manager a trustee. If he is a trustee property must vest in him, but this is not the case[3]: That he is a mere manager and that the legal property does not vest in him has been affirmed by the decisions though courts have not always been uniform in the use of the word. The Indian Legislature in the Religious Endowments Act (XX of 1863) has not accurately defined his position but speaks of him indifferently as the *manager, trustee* or *superintendent.*

Manager is office-holder- Corporation.

But although he is a mere manager he holds an office and such office has been itself regarded by the Privy Council as a

1. Chapters II, pp. xv to xvii and VIII pp. xcvi and Note (3) to that page and xcix. See also *Babajirao* v. *Laxmandas*, (1903) I. L. R., 28 B. 215 (223); and *Maharaja Jagadindra Nath* v. *Rani Hemanta Kumari*, (1904) 8 C. W. N. 809 (820). The profits or income of such land also belongs to the deity. See *Ram Sundar Ray* v. *Heirs of Raja Udwant Singh*, (1832) 5 B. S. D. A. 210; and *Maharanee Shibessouree Debia* v. *Mothooranath Acharjo*, (1869) 13 M. I. A. 270.

2. *Prosunno Kumari Debya* v. *Golab Chand Baboo*, (1875) L.R. 2 I. A. 145 (152); *Nilmony Singh* v *Jagabundhu Roy*, (1896) I. L.R., 23 C. 536. See also *Ranjit Singh* v. *Jagannath Prosad Gupta*, (1885) I. L R., 12 C. 375 (379). See Salmond's jurisprudence p. 351.

3. We are here speaking of the first two kinds of dedication referred to in Ch. IV, pp. l, li. *Maharanee Shibessouree Debia* v. *Mothooranath Acharjo*, (1869) 13 M. I. A. 270: S. C. 13 W. R. (P. C.) 18; *Tayubunnissa Bibi* v. *Kuwar Sham Kishore Roy*, (1871) 7 B. L. R 621 (628); S. C. 15 W. R. C. R. 228; *Syud Shah Alleh Ahmed* v. *Mussamut Bibee Nuseebun*, (1874) 21 W. R. C. R. 415 (416); *Juggudumba Dossee* v. *Puddomoney Dossee*, (1875) 15 B. L. R. 318; *Konwur Doorganath Roy* v. *Ram Chunder Sen* (1876) L. R. 4 I. A. 52 (63); *Girijanund Datta Jha* v. *Sailajanund Datta Jha*, (1896) I. L R., 23 C. 645; *Vidyapurna Thirthasvami* v. *Vidyanidhi Thirtha Swami*, (1904) I. L. R., 27 M. 435 (441, 442, 451, 451). But see *Raghubar Dial* v. *Kesho Ramanuj Das*, (1888) I. L. R., 11 A 18; *Kunjunneri Nambiar* v. *Nilakunden*, (1880) I. L. R., 2 M. 167.

corporation[1]. The office may be held, by a single member or by a family or by a number of families. The manager will be liable as a trustee[2] and this liability is not inconsistent with his position as manager or does not raise him to the position of a trustee. In fact he is a mere agent[3] of the idol or deity having a limited authority to deal with its temporal concerns. The trustee (as he is termed) appointed by a Committee in respect of an institution falling under S. 3 of Act XX of 1863 can be in no higher position. Property does not therefore vest in the manager appointed by the Committee. It may be admitted as a correct proposition that he is not a servant of the Committee in the sense that he can be dismissed without sufficient cause. Subject to the control of the Committee he also holds an office, though he is appointed to such office by the Committee. But there may be no question of a freehold in the office. There is nothing in the Act which precludes the Committee from appointing a trustee for a definite term. In the absence of any express provision as to the term in the order of appointment, it may be that the trustee is entitled to hold the office for the period of his natural life[4]. In the notes to Ss. 7, 11 and 12 of the Act we have observed[5] that Committees are not precluded from managing at any rate the properties transferred to them by the Board of Revenue. The provision in S. 11 of the Act that "no member of a Committee appointed under this Act shall be capable of being or shall act also as a trustee &c" only means that a Committee shall not appoint one of themselves to be a trustee or manager either permanently or temporarily. S. 12 of Act XX of 1863 in fact expressly contemplates that the Committee is appointed for the *superintendence* of a mosque, temple, or religious establishment and for the *management* of its affairs[6]. The Privy Council having held in *Mayandi Chettiar* v. *Chokkalingam Pillai*[7], that the powers of a manager to alienate endowed property were taken away by the Regulations and vested in the Board, after

Trustee appointed by Committee is manager.

Committee not precluded from managing.

1. *Rajah Vurmah Valia* v. *Ravi Vurmah Mutha*, (1876) L. R. 4 I. A. 76 (81): S. C. I. L. R., 1 M. 235 (247). In this case their Lordships observed: "The unknown founder may be supposed to have established this species of corporation." See also West and Buhler 3rd Edition, p. 201. See Salmond's jurisprudence 349.
2. *Manohar Ganesh Tambekar* v. *Lakhmiram Govindram*, (1887) I. L. R., 12 B. 247 (265). See also *Thackersey Dewraj* v. *Hurbhum Nursey*, (1884) I. L. R., 8 B. 432 (461, 464).
3. *Muthusamy Pillai* v *Queen Empress*, (1895) I. L. R. 26 M. 243 (note).
4. See Bacon's Abridgment. Tit, "Office and Officers" Vol. V, pp. 199, 200. *Attorney-General* v. *Pearson*, (1817) 3 Mer. 352 at pp. 402, 403. See Tudor on Charitable Trusts, pp. 212, 221, 223. Stephen's commentaries Vol. II, pp. 630, 631. See Encyclopædia of the Laws of England Vol. 9, Tit "Office: Public Officer" p. 277. But the rules of the foundation, if any, must be adhered to. Tudor, p. 220.
5. Pp. 45, 46, 70 to 73 and 75 to 77.
6. *Jusagheri Gosamiar* v. *The Collector of Tanjore*, (1870) 5 M. H. C. 334 (341).
7. (1904) L. R., 31 I. A. 83 (88): S. C. I. L. R., 27 M. 291 (295).

Act XX of 1863 the Committee to whom the superintendence was transferred must have these powers. Indeed it seems to us that the Committee is also a sort of agent for the principal (*i. e.*, the idol), and has authority within certain limits to bind such idol.

Manager-Different names.

In different parts of India different nomenclatures are adopted for conveying the idea of the term manager of a temple. In the Madras Presidency in the Tamil and Telugu districts he goes by the name of *Dharmakarta*. In some districts such as Tanjore &c., he is also called *Panchayatdar*. In Malabar he is termed an *Urallen*. In South Canara he is called *Moktessor*. In Bengal or Northern India he is styled a *Shebait*. There are several temples in Bengal and Bombay which are administered by Hindustani Byragis and these are called Mahants. They are both ministrants (*pujaris*) and managers of temple funds or properties appointing *pujaris* when necessary[1]. In the Madras Presidency also there is a notable instance of a *byragi* (mohant) being the manager of a temple, *i. e*, the Mahant of Tirupati in the North Arcot District[2], and there are several instances of *sanyasis* or ascetics (not being *byragis*) being heads or managers of religious institutions, such as temples. The *Ahobilam Jeer* is the manager of Sri Veeraragavaswami temple in Trivellore in the Chingleput District[3]. The *Pandara Sannadis* or heads of Sudra Mutts are also in some instances heads or managers of temples[4]. In the Udipi Sri Krishna temple, the eight Swamis do the puja in turns and the Swami having the turn or the Paryaya Swami as he is called exercises an absolute control over the servants of the institution dismissing the old and appointing the new. It is also said that he has authority to reduce the expenses in one department and to increase them in another[5].

1. W. and B. on Hindu Law (3rd Edition) 572. See also per *Candy*, J. in *Dhuncooverbai* v. *The Advocate-General*, (1899) 1 Bom. L.R. 743 (751). See also *Khuggender Narain Chowdhry* v. *Sharupgir Oghorenath*, (1878) I. L. R., 4 C. 543.

2. See *Sri Sudagopa Pedda Jiyangarlu* v. *Sri Mahant Rama Kirore Dossjee* (1898) I. L. R., 22 M. 189. The Mahant is the *Vicharanakarta* of the *Tirumalai* and *Tirupati* temples and dharmakarta of some minor temples attached thereto. The *Pedda Jiyangar* is the dharmakarta of the Tirumalai and Tirupati temples, but it is said that the latter's rights and duties are of a limited character. We suppose he will resemble a manager appointed by the committee.

3. The Sunkara Charia Swami is the manager of Kamakshi Amman Pagoda in Conjeevaram in the Chingleput District. See Parliamentary Return 1849, Idolatry (India) p. 154.

4. *Giyana Sambandha Pandara Sannadhi* v. *Kandasawmy Tambiran*, (1887) I. L. R., 10 M. 375 (391); *RamalingamPillai* v. *Vythilingam Pillai*, (1893) L. R., 20 I. A. 150; S. C., I. L. R., 16 M. 490.

5. Statement No. 5 attached to the letter from the Principal Collector South Canara to the Secretary, Board of Revenue. Parliamentary Return 1849, Idolatry (India) p. 162. See also ibid p. 155.

An *archaka* of a temple or *pujari* or a *sherak* may be the manager but is not necessarily so. When the Archaka or the officiating priest of a temple has been managing its affairs with the knowledge and privity of the worshippers, the presumption is that he is the manager as well as the Archaka[1]. But the shebait need not necessarily be the pujari or Archaka[2]. Where the offices of Archaka and manager are different the Archaka holds a subordinate position. He is then a servant of the temple holding office under the manager[3]. In the famous Chidambaram temple in the South Arcot District the Archakas are also managers.[4] In Udipi in the South Canara District the heads of the eight mutts as already observed perform in turns the worship of Krishna in the celebrated temple at that place[5] and the Pariyaya Swami has the management. In the case of private endowments the shebait is also the pujari and performs the worship, though a priest is called in aid for reciting the necessary mantras.

Archaka may be a dharmakarta.

Sudras may be shebaits or managers and in fact it is more common for sudras being managers of temples in Southern India. In *Radha Mohun Mundul* v. *Jadoomonee Dossee*[6] a sudra was recognised as a shebait, but it does not appear clearly from the report whether the endowment was a public or a private one. We have already seen that Sudra paradesis or tambirans are managers of many temples.

Sudras may be managers.

The question next arises whether a female can be a manager. The case of *Radha Mohun Mundul* v. *Jadoomonee Dossee*[6] is equally an authority upon this point. There a widow was recognised as a joint shebait. But the authority of this case is much discounted by the fact that it is not clear whether the temple in question is a public or a private one. The rather unintelligible

Capacity of females to be Managers.

1. *Ramasami* v *Ramasami*, (1892) 2 M. L. J. R. 251. When the Government withdrew their connection with religious endowments they handed over the management to the village priest in the case of small village temples under their management.

2. The case of *Dubo Misser* v. *Srinivasa Misser* (1870) 5. B. L. R., 617 which holds that the shebait of a Hindu idol has to perform the worship of the idol. &c., must be taken as applicable either to a case where the offices of pujari and shebait are combined or to a case of a private idol owned by a family or, it means simply that the shebait has to provide for the worship.

3. *Ranee Parvata Varddhani Nachiar* v. *Mungaleswara Goorookul*, (1856) M. S. D. A. 165. See also *Manohar Ganesh Tambekar* v *Lakhmiram Govindram*, (1887) I. L. R., 12 B 247; *Mulji Bhulabhai* v. *Manohar Ganesh*, (1887) I.L.R., 12 B. 322 (324).

4. *Natesa* v. *Ganapati*, (1890) I. L. R., 14 M. 103 (104, 118).

5. *Visvapreya Teertaswami* v. *Vydyapati Teertaswami* (1851) M. S. D. A. 105. See also *Kasim Sahiba* v. *Sudindra Thirthaswami*, (1895) I. L. R., 18 M. 359.

6. (1875) 23 W. R., 369 (P. C.)

discussion in Colebrooke's Digest about the capacity of females[1] does not relate to the case of a manager of an endowment but to the case of hereditary officiating priests. He there considers the question whether wives and others have a title to the succession to this priestly office. As usual with the discussions of Jagannatha it is difficult to say what his final opinion is. But we should certainly think that Jagannatha's opinion is that women can inherit doing the duties through a substitute[2] but enjoying the emoluments attached to that office. Even assuming that according to Jagannatha women are not entitled to succeed to the office of an officiating priest it does not negative the right of a female to be a manager in a case where the offices of pujari and manager are not confined in the same person. In the case of private endowments the office of shebait which involves the duty of puja and worship may be held by females[3]. The decided cases bear out the view that a female may be a manager. Females can be heirs under the ordinary Hindu Law and if succession to the office of a manager is proved to be according to the ordinary Hindu Law it is a truism to say that females can be managers. The question rather is whether the ordinary law applies to the succession to the office of manager of the particular temple or religious establishment in question[4]. The decided cases cannot carry us further. There are, however, some decisions of the Madras Sadr.

---

1. Book II, Ch. III, S. ii § 43, pages 375 to 381.

2. Jagannatha's inclination is that such substitute must be the nearest male reversioner.

3. *Radha Mohun Mundul* v. *Jadoomonee Dossee*, (1875) 23 W. R. (P. C.) 369. In *Maharanee Shibessouree Debia* v. *Mothooranath Acharjo*, (1869) 13 M. I. A. 270 (272, 273) it would seem that the female styled as shebait was only guardian of a male ward who was the shebait, although in the following passage at p. 273 their Lordships clearly contemplate the office of shebait being held by a female: "The shebait had not the legal property but only the title of manager of a religious endowment. In the exercise of that office, she could not alienate the property though she might create proper derivative tenures". In *Konwur Dooryanath Roy* v. *Ram Chunder Sen*, (1876) L. R. 4 I. A. 52 (56) it was not questioned that a female could not hold the office of shebait. In *Hori Dasi Dabi* v. *The Secretary of State*, (1879) I. L. R. 5 C. 228 (245) a female was appointed as trustee but the endowment was only charitable although there was some charge in favor of religious uses for a family Thakoor. See the case at p. clx note (2).

4. The following passage from Colebrooke's Digest p. 380 will show that ordinances will not help us much and that ordinary rules of law do not apply at all:—"The usage in regard to Agraharicas (priests who attend at funerals) and others has been briefly discussed. No more express ordinance is found to determine consistently with usage, the suits which arise on these subjects. If ordinances alone be received, there is no authority for establishing the right of their heirs: and many excellent persons do not admit the rules of inheritance in these cases". Then at p. 381 he says that "the known customs at holy places, such as Gaya and the like and in other countries should be maintained in Judicial procedure".

Court to the effect that females may be Dharmakartas[1] and may even hold Architta, Poorohita and Lelay Mirassis though she cannot hold the office of Acharia Pooroosbah[2] and no valid reasons can be assigned against the soundness of this position. In *Jay Deb Surmah* v. *Huroputty Surmah*[3] the question whether a woman could succeed to a priestly office was raised but not decided. The case was sent back to the Lower Court for decision with the remark that Colebrooke's Digest Book II, Ch. II, S. 3 and S. 43 already cited[4] showed that a priestly office could not be performed by a woman. Case of actual priesthood are distinguished in this case from cases dealing with certain rights which give profits to a shebait. Very curiously this case is cited by some text-writers as authority for the view that females are not disqualified from being managers. But from what we have stated before it will be clear that the case does not decide anything of the sort. In *Janokee Debea* v. *Gopaul*[5] a female plaintiff claimed the shebaitship of certain dewutter properties and the question was raised whether a female could be a shebait at all. The High Court although they did not accept the view that females would by reason of their sex be excluded from the succession, held that the plaintiff had still to prove whether the ordinary laws of succession applied and that as she failed to prove it, the plaintiff's suit was dismissed. The Privy Council affirmed this decree and held that it was not correct that, in the absence of prescribed rules or usage, the ordinary law of inheritance would apply to a religious endowment. The true rule according to them is that when owing to the absence of documentary or other direct evidence, it does not appear what rule of

---

1. *Soondararaja Chanar* v. *Poonamungar*, (1850) M. S. D. A. 43 where the case was remanded to the lower court for consideration of that question; *Sashummal* v. *Parker* (1853) M. S. D. A. 237 ; *Parker* v. *Sashummal*, (1854) M. S. D. A. 182 ; *Sadagopah Charry* v. *Sadagopah Charry*, (1854) M. S. D. A. 55 ; *Clarke* v. *Sashummal*, (1856) M. S. D. A. 55.

2. *Sashummal* v. *Soondarrajiengar*, (1853) M. S. D. A 261.

3. (1871) 16 W. R. C. R. 282. In *Keshavbhat* v. *Bhagirathibai*, (1866) 3 B. H. C. A. C. J. 75 the Bombay High Court was inclined to hold that a Hindu female might be competent to minister in a temple either in person or vicariously when no usage was shown that she was incompetent. In *Sitarambhat* v. *Sitaram Ganesh*, (1869) 6 B. H. C. A. C. J. 250 (253) the Bombay High Court held that the descendants claiming through females (daughter's sons) could claim to succeed to a hereditary priestly office.

4. Col. Dig, p. 375.

5. (1877) I. L. R., 2. C. 365 affirmed in appeal to P. C. See *Srimati Janoki Debi* v. *Sri Gopal Acharyia*, (1882) L. R. 10 I. A. 32 : S. C. I. L. R., 9. C. 766. See also *Elder widow of Raja Chutter Sein* v. *Younger widow of Raja Chutter Sein*, (1807) 1. B. S. D. A. 180. Cf. *Mussumat Joymunnee Dibia* v. *Fakeer Chunder Chuckerbutty*, (1829) 4 B. S. D. A. 243.

succession has been laid down by the endower of a religious institution, it must be proved by evidence what is the usage[1].

Surendrakeshav Roy v. Doorgasundari Dassee.

The case of *Surendrakeshav Roy* v. *Doorgasundari Dassee*[2] was apparently a case of private endowment. There a testator after leaving all his property to his family Thakoor stated that out of the surplus after payment of the expenses of the *sheba*, a certain fixed allowance should be paid to two persons whom he described as his adopted sons. The Privy Council held that there was a mere charge in favor of the idol, that the testator contemplated double adoptions which were invalid under Hindu Law, that the gift to the two persons failed on the invalidity of the adoptions as the gift was not to the two persons as *persona designata* and that the testator's widows as his heirs would take the shebaitship. They thought it unnecessary to consider the broader question whether women could act as shebaits at all as in that particular case the testator directed his two widows to perform the duties of shebait during the minority of the adopted sons and that, therefore, no incapacity could attach. But when it is shewn that the ordinary rules of Hindu Law succession prevail, and they generally prevail where the endowment is a private one or the founder is the hereditary manager, the office of manager devolves on the demise of the last holder or holders upon the heirs of such holder or holders.

Dhuncoover v. The Advocate General.

In *Dhuncooverbai* v. *The Advocate-General*[3] it has been held by the Bombay High Court that even where mahants are managers of temples, females may be mahants and as such they may be managers especially when they belong to a sect of Byragees among whom marriages will be permissible.

Conclusion.

When females can be archakas and can hold other religious offices, it is difficult to see on what principle they are disqualified

1. The P. C. cite for this position the cases of *Greedharee Doss* v. *Nundokissore Doss*, (1867) 11 M. I. A. 405 (428); *Rameswaram Pagoda case* (1874) L. R. 1 I. A. 209 (228); and *Rajah Vurmah Valia* v. *Ravi Vurmah Mutha*, (1876) L. R. 4 I. A. 76 (83, 84); S. C. I. L. R., 1 M. 235 (250, 251).

2. (1892) L. R. 19 I. A. 108: S. C. I. L. R., 19 C. 513.

3. (1899) 1 Bom. L. R., 743. See the judgment of *Jenkins*, C.J., at p. 750 approving the decision of *Tyabji*, J. In this case the mohant belonged to the sect of *Sungojee Byragees*. In *Sitaram Bhat* v. *Sitaram Ganesh*, (1869) 6 B. H. C. A. C. J. 250 the head-note contains a semble that a priestly office (mule joshi) may descend through females. There the sale of a priestly office to the daughter's sons was upheld as the latter were the next in succession.

from being dharmakartas, the office of dharmakarta or manager not involving the performance of any religious duties[1]. In fact where a Zamindar makes endowments out of his estate and the management vests in him, the right of management follows the succession to the Zamindary and when the Zamindary is held by a widow of the last holder the latter will be entitled to manage the endowments also[2]. Where a widow holds the office as heir of her husband it has been held that she continues to hold it notwithstanding she may have adopted a son under her husband's authority[2].

Office of shebait—Founder's intention—Usage.

The office of manager may vest in a single person or in a number of persons[3] or in a single family[4] or in a number of familes[5]. It depends upon the will of the person who establishes the endowment and who is termed the founder. The rule of law is that in cases of religious endowments and in all cases of a known founder, the latter has the right to nominate a shebait and to direct the mode of succession to the office of shebait[6]. He may direct a single person or family[4] to hold the office of shebait or a number of persons[3] or families[5]

---

1. See *Kalee Churn* v. *Golabi*, (1878) 2 C. L. R., 128 (131).

2. *Srimant Rajah Yarlagadda* v. *Makerla Sridevamma*, (1897) L. R. 24 I. A. 73 (74): S. C., I. L. R., 20 M. 162 (166).

3. *Juggodumba Dossee* v. *Puddomoney Dossee*, (1875) 15 B. L. R. 318; *Velu Pandaram* v. *Gnanasambanda*, (1895) I. L. R, 19 M. 243: S. C. on appeal to P. C. in *Gnanasambanda* v. *Velu Pandaram*, (1899) L. R., 27 I. A. 69: S. C. I. L. R., 23 M. 271 (case of two brothers); *Sri Raman Lalji Maharaj* v. *Sri Gopal Lalji Maharaj*, (1897) I. L. R., 19 A. 428 (two brothers). Cf. *The Advocate General of Bombay* v. *David Haim Devaker*, (1886) I. L. R., 11 B. 185.

4. *Sreenath Bose* v. *Radha Nath Bose*, (1883) 12 C. L. R. 370; *Thackersey Dewraj* v. *Hurbhum Nursey*, (1884) I. L. R., 8 B. 432; *Alagappa* v. *Sivaramasundara*, (1895) I. L. R., 19 M. 211. It is more common to find the management in a single family unless the original family should by separation become divided into a number of small families. West and Buhler on Hindu Law, p. 202.

5. *Kesharbhat* v. *Bhagirathi Bai*, (1866) 3 B. H. C. A. C. J. 75 (four Hindu joint families); *Ukanda Varriyar* v. *Raman Nambudiri*, (1863) 1 M. H. C. 262 (two tarwads); *Paramathan Somayajipad* v. *Sankara Menon*, (1899) I. L. R., 23 M. 82 (3 Sabayogams). Where the families are tarwads in which no division of property is allowed, the question may arise whether the right of management vests in such tarwads as represented by their Karnavans or in all the members of the tarwads. The *prima facie*, presumption is that the right vests in the tarwads as represented by the Karnavan (the right of management going with the right to hold tarwad property). This will be important in considering the mode in which acts have to be done for the institution by the managers. See *Rajah Varma Valia* v. *Ravi Varmah Mutha*, (1876) L. R. 4 I. A. 76 (80, 81): S. C. I. L. R., 1 M. 235 (247, 248). See also *Ukanda Varriyar* v. *Raman Nambudiri*, supra.

6. *Lutchmee Ammal* v. *Rookmanee Ammal*, (1857) M. S. D. A. 152; *Greedharee Doss* v. *Nundkishore Dutt Mohunt*, (1863) 1 Marsh. 573 affd. on appeal to P. C. in (1867) 11 M. I. A. 405; *Gossain Dowlut Geer* v. *Bissessur Geer*, (1873) 19 W. R. C. R. 215 (216); *Rahamtulla Sahib* v. *Mahommed Akbar Sahib*, (1875) 8 M. H. C. 63; *Rajah Vurmah Valia* v. *Ravi Vurma Mutha* (1876) L. R., 4 I. A 76 (80, 81); *Sitapershad* v. *Thakur Dass*, (1879) 5 C. L. R. 73 (79); *Srimati Janoki Debi* v. *Sri Gopal Acharjia*, (1882) L R., 10 I. A. 32 (37): S. C. I. L. R., 9 C. 766 (771); *Gossamee Sree Greedhareejee* v. *Rumanlolljee Gossamee*, (1889) L. R., 16 I. A. 137: S. C. I. L. R., 17 C. 3; *Narayana* v. *Ranga*, (1891) I. L. R., 15 M. 183; *Alagappa* v. *Sivaramasundara*, (1895) I. L. R, 19 M. 211. See other cases cited in note (1) p. lxiv and West and Buhler on H. L., pp. 200, 201. See also F. Macnaghten's Hindu Law, Vol. II, p. 103 and Shamacharn Sircar's Vyavastha Darpana, p. 327.

to be shebaits and effect will be given to such direction. He may nominate himself as a shebait or he may reserve the right of nominating a shebait in himself and his heirs. It is said that, in default of any nomination by him[1], or in default of any nomination by the last shebait[2], the office vests in the founder and his heirs. The latter principle, however, can only apply in the absence of any usage to the contrary. For, in cases of religious endowments in the absence of the founder's intention as appearing from the deed of endowment, if any, usage is the governing test[3]. Usage, however, is given effect to only as a guide in finding out the intention of the founder, but not as over-riding such intention[4].

Nature of estate of manager.

The question as to the nature of the estate of the trustee or manager cannot be answered without considering the question as to the succession to his office. It is said that the estate of a trustee is governed by the Hindu Law[5]. We have shown that the correct view rather is that the shebait or dharmakarta is a manager rather than a trustee[6]. It may be that in the case of what in Indian Law

1. *Maharaja Jogadindra Nath* v. *Rani Hemanta Kumari Debi*, (1904) 8 C. W. N. 809 (818, 819); *Gossamee Sree Greedhareejee* v. *Rumanlolljee Gossamee*, (1889) L. R. 16 I. A. 137 : S. C. I. L. R., 17 C. 3.

2. *Mussumat Jai Bansi Kunwar alias Peet Koonwar* v. *Chattar Dhari Singh*, (1870) 5 B. L. R., 181 : S. C. 13 W. R. C. R. 396; *Ranjit Singh* v. *Jagannath Prosad Gupta* (1885) I. L. R., 12 C. 375; *Gossamee Sree Greedhareejee* v. *Rumanlolljee Gossamee*, (1889) L. R., 16 I. A. 137 : S. C. I. L. R., 17 C. 3; *Jagannath Prasad Gupta* v. *Runjit Singh*, (1897) I. L. R., 25 C. 354 (369). See also *Gopal Chunder Bose* v. *Kartick Chunder Dey*, (1902) I. L. R. 29 C. 716 at pp. 722, 723 (P. C.) where there was a failure of heirs indicated by the founder. The Allahabad High Court relying upon the P. C. decision in 16 I. A. 137 above referred to holds in *Sheoratan Kunwari* v. *Ram Pargash*, (1896) I. L. R., 18 A. 227 (232) that the founder will have the right to nominate under such circumstances. But this is clearly not warranted by the P. C. decision.

3. *Greedharee Doss* v. *Nundokissore Doss Mohunt*, (1867) 11 M.I.A. 405 (428); *Goosaeen Sree Choundawalee Bahoojee* v. *Girdhareeji*, (1868) 3 Agra. H. C. 226; *Gossain Dowlut Geer* v. *Bissessur Geer*, (1873) 19 W. R. C. R. 215; *Rajah Muthu Ramalinga Setupati* v. *Periyanayagum Pillai*, (1874) L. R., 1 I. A. 209; *Rahumtulla Sahib* v. *Mahommed Akbar Sahib*, (1875) 8 M. H. C. 63; *Rajah Vurma Valia* v. *Ravi Vurmah Mutha*, (1876) L. R., 4 I. A. 76 (83, 84); *Sitapershad* v. *Thakur Dass*, (1879) 5 C. L. R. 73 (80); *Anandrav Bhikaji Phadke* v. *Shankar Daji Charya*, (1883) I. L. R., 7 B. 323 (329); *Srimati Janoki Debi* v. *Sri Gopal Acharjia*, (1882) L.R., 10 I A. 32 (37); S. C. I. L. R., 9 C. 766 (771); *Genda Puri* v. *Chhatar Puri*, (1886) L.R., 13 I.A. 100; S.C. I.L.R., 9 A. 1; *Giyana Sambandha Pandara Sannadhi* v. *Kandasami Tambiran*, (1887) I. L. R., 10 M. 375 (488); *Venkatachalapati* v. *Subbarayadu*, (1890) I. L. R., 13 M. 293 (299); *Narayana* v. *Ranga*, (1891) I. L. R., 15 M. 183; *Ramalingam Pillai* v. *Vythilingam Pillai*, (1893) L. R., 20 I. A. 150 : S. C. I. L. R., 16 M. 490; *Dhuncooverbai* v. *The Advocate General*, (1899) 1 Bom. L. R. 743 (746, 747 and 758); *Mahanth Ramji Dass* v. *Lachhu Dass*, (1902) 7 C. W. N. 145 (147). See also W. & B. on Hindu Law 201.

4. *Venkatachalapati* v. *Subbarayadu*, (1890) I. L. R., 13 M. 287 (298); *Narayana* v. *Ranga*, (1891) I. L. R. 15 M. 183 (185). Usage is the best exponent of the right. See *Cherukunneth Manakel Neelakandhen Namboodiripad* v. *Vengunat Swaroopathil Padmanabha Revi Varma Valia Nambidi*, (1894) L. R. 22 I. A. 128 : S. C. I. L. R., 18 M. 1.

5. *In Re Kahandas Narrandas*, (1880) I. L. R., 5 B. 154 (174).

6. See p. cliv, supra.

must be called charitable trusts[1], the estate of a trustee is governed by the Hindu Law. But this is beside the question. We are on the subject of religious trusts where the position of shebait or dharmakarta is that of a mere manager who has no interest or ownership in the endowed property[2]. Further, ordinary Hindu Law cannot govern his estate unless the right to the succession to his office is also governed by Hindu Law. It cannot be predicated as a general proposition that in the absence of prescribed rules or usage, the ordinary law of inheritance will govern the succession to such office. Any such proposition is negatived by the judgment of the Judicial Committee in *Srimati Janaki Debi* v. *Sri Gopal Acharjia*[3]. Their Lordships there observed: "When, owing to the absence of documentary or other direct evidence, it does not appear what rule of succession has been laid down by the endower of a religious institution, it must be proved by evidence what is the usage." Therefore, first of all we must look to the deed of endowment, if any, and see whether the founder has laid down any rule of succession to the office of manager. Then we have to see to other direct evidence of the intentions of the founder. In the absence of these two, we have to look to usage. The person who relies upon succession by the law of inheritance must prove that the ordinary law applies or in cases where the contest is as between rival claimants to the office, the person who is the plaintiff must prove and succeed upon the strength of his case[4]. In most cases no decision need be arrived at as to the actual usage except negatively. The court may and often does state that a claim or usage set up by the plaintiff has

1. The beneficial owners are the objects of the trust and the legal owners the trustees. See *Purmanundass Jeevundass* v. *Venayekrao Wassoodeo*, (1882) L. R. 9 I. A. 86 (95): S. C. I. L. R. 7 B. 19. Whether this is a correct proposition even as regards charitable trusts may require further research.

2. See pp. cliv, clv, supra.

3. (1882) L. R., 10 I. A. 32 (37): S. C. I. L. R., 9 C. 766 (771).

4. *Greedharee Doss* v. *Nundokissore Doss*, (1867) 11 M. I. A. 405 (430, 431); *Joy Lall Tewaree* v. *Gossain Bhoobun Geer*, (1874) 21 W. R.C.R. 334; *Rahumtulla Sahib* v. *Mahomed Akbar Sahib*, (1875) 8 M. H. C. 63; *Srimati Janoki Debi* v. *Sri Gopal Acharjia*, (1882) L. R. 10 I. A. 32 (38): S. C. I. L. R., 9 C. 766; *Genda Puri* v. *Chhatar Puri*, (1886) L. R. 13 I. A 100: S. C. I. L. R., 9 A. 1; *Basdeo* v. *Gharib Das*, (1890) I. L. R., 13 A. 256; *Maina* v. *Brij Mohan*, (1890) I. L. R., 17 I. A. 187: S. C. I. L R., 12 A. 587; *Rangachariar* v. *Yegna Dikshatur*, (1890) I. L. R., 13 M. 524 (536); *Mahant Gajraj Puri* v. *Achaibar Puri*, (1893) L R. 21 I. A. 17: S. C. I. L. R, 16 A. 191. See also *Sitapershad* v. *Thakur Dass*, (1879) 5 C. L. R., 73 (80). All these were cases of ejectment and related to contests between rival claimants. Where the question is as to the removal of a manager and appointment of a new person and the plaintiff asserts a particular usage as regards appointment the failure on the part of the plaintiff to prove the usage set up by him will not relieve the Court from the necessity of finding out the correct usage.

not been proved. This is sufficient to dispose of the case although this by no means disposes of the litigation.

Rules of succession by founder not inconsistent with ordinary Hindu Law.

In cases where there is a deed of endowment, the question is whether the founder can prescribe rules as to succession not consistent with the ordinary Hindu Law. If the Judicial Committee in the recent case of *Gnanasambanda Pandara Sannadhi* v. *Velu Pandaram*[1] be taken to have decided this question in the negative, we should, with all deference to that august tribunal, have said that the same is utterly unwarranted and opposed to the current of authority prevailing hithertofore and to long established usage. But we do not think that the Privy Council intended to lay down anything of the sort. In the case under discussion it was admitted that the office was hereditary and governed by the Hindu Law. This would be clear from the following passage in their Lordship's judgment.[2] :—"It would appear... that the endowment had been held by the brothers as a joint family and that Kuppa had succeeded as heir to his father's interest in it." The question was whether a suit to establish a right to management and to recover endowed properties was within time. The argument on behalf of the plaintiff was that he had a fresh cause of action from the date of his father's death and that the office was held upon a succession of life-estates or upon an estate-tail. The Privy Council had no difficulty in saying that such estates were unknown to the Hindu Law as was established in the *Tagore case* and that the principle equally applied to an hereditary office and endowment. Where the contention is that the office of shebait is governed by ordinary Hindu Law and such contention is upheld, it is difficult to recognise and uphold a further contention that the estate of the shebait is held under a tenure of successive life-estates or under a tenure known in English Law as estate-tail and this is all the principle that has been recognised by the Judicial Committee in the above case.

But it cannot be laid down as a broad proposition that although the endower or founder has a right to lay down the rule of succession, yet he "cannot create a new form of estate or alter

1. (1899) L. R. 27 I. A. 69 : S. C. I. L. R., 23 M. 271.

2. (1899) L. R. 27 I. A. at p 75 ; S. C. I. L. R. 23 Mad. at p. 278.

the line of succession allowed by law, for the purpose of carrying out his own wishes or views of policy.[1]" The ordinary rule is that "a private individual, who attempts by gift or will to make property inheritable otherwise than the law directs, is assuming to legislate, and that the gift must fail, and the inheritance takes place as the law directs.[2]" Whether in this passage the expression "law" means *law* governing the particular person or law of the different schools of Hindu Law or even usage upheld by the Courts we need not pause to consider. But it is clear that in the case of a religious institution, the endower may frame rules of succession which though not recognised by the ordinary Hindu Law, are yet recognised as being in accordance with local and family usages[3]. For instance, the founder may say that the office of shebait may devolve in a family by right of primogeniture[4] or in the eldest male member of the family *i, e.*, in the member who is most senior in age[5] and this mode of devolution has even been recognised by the Judicial Committee[5]. So also a founder may direct the actual incumbent to appoint his successor during his life-time and this is in fact a common mode of devolution in most cases of religious endowments (such as mutts[6]). So also the founder may direct that upon the death of a manager certain persons will have the right to elect the manager. But it cannot be said that the latter two are modes of devolution altogether unknown to Hindu Law. They are analogous to powers of appointment which are known to Hindu

---

1. *Sreemutty Soorjeemoney Dossee* v. *Denobundoo Mullick*, (1857) 6 M. I. A. 526 at p. 555 cited by the Privy Council in *the Tagore Case*, (1872) L. R. I. A. Supp. Vol. 47 (65). The passage, however, is not to be found in the case itself nor in the case reported in 9 M. I. A. 123.

2. *Ganendromohun Tagore* v. *Juttendromohun Tagore*, (1872) L. R. I. A. Sup. Vol. 47 (65).

3. See *Goosaeen Sree Choundawalee Buhoojee* v. *Girdhareeji*, (1868) 3 Agra. H. C. 226 where the Allahabad High Court observed: "If the property is endowed, the right to interfere with the defendant's management and to claim the control must be brought in a properly framed suit. In such suit the plaintiff should not assert his right to succeed upon the ordinary Hindu Law but must base it upon the rules of the endowment as may be established by custom or otherwise."

4. *Chenna Kesavaraya* v. *Vaidelinga*, (1877) I. L. R., 1 M. 343 (346). *Nanabhai* v. *Shriman Goswami Girdhariji*, (1888) I. L. R., 12 B. 331. Generally the senior member is entitled to take Rajseva and keep it with the property belonging thereto. See *Damodardas Maneklal* v. *Uttamram Maneklal*, (1892) I. L. R., 17 B. 271.

5. *Srimati Kamini Debi* v. *Asutosh Mookerjee*, (1888) L. R, 15 I. A. 159 (166): S. C. I. L. R., 16 C. 103 (116). Cf. *Timmappa Heggade* v. *Mahalinga Heggade*, (1868) 4 M. H. C. 28.

6. See cases cited in pp. clxxiv to clxxviii.

Law[1]. Of course in such cases the nominee or appointee must be a person in existence[2]. Therefore, it cannot be said that in such cases the Hindu Law is not to any extent contravened. According to the ordinary Hindu Law the person upon whom a power of appointment is given must be a person in existence. But where the power is given in the incumbent for the time being or a body of electors this rule is not necessarily observed. In a case where the right to nominate vests in the holder of an office for the time being it may be said that the right is attached to the office which is a legal person and as such is a person in existence[3]. The founder while giving the actual incumbent the right to appoint his successor may point out a particular line, family or class of persons as a limitation for his choice[4] and the person appointing must nominate a person from such line, family or class of persons. In default of an appointment by the actual incumbent, or where there is a failure in the mode of succession pointed out by the founder[5] the office of shebait reverts to the founder and his heirs[6] and the devolution then is according to the ordinary Hindu Law. It is the usual custom in most cases for the founder to be the manager and the office is then hereditary in his family[7]. As most of the religious establishments of the Hindus and at their great temples, the various offices attached to them are considered as hereditary together with the perquisites belonging to them[8].

1. *Bai Motivahoo* v. *Bai Mamoobai*, (1897) L. R. 24 I. A. 93: S. C. I. L. R., 21 B. 709; *Upendra Lal Boral* v. *Hem Chundra Boral*, (1897) I. L. R., 25 C. 405 (408). But see *Javerbai* v. *Kablibai*, (1890) I. L. R., 15 B. 326 (330).

2. *Bai Motivahoo* v. *Bai Mamoobai*, (1897) L. R. 24 I. A. 93: S. C. I.L.R., 21 B. 709. See *Upendra Lal Boral* v. *Hem Chundra Boral*, supra where curiously the High Court applied this principle to gifts to idols. See remarks upon this case at pp. xci to xcvi.

3. The right will pass with the office. *Sathappayyar* v. *Periasami*, (1890) I. L.R., 14 M. 1 (12). See also *Eastick* v. *Smith*, (1904) 1 Ch. 139 and the cases cited therein.

4. *Giyana Sambandha Pandara Sannadhi* v. *Kandasami Tambiran*, (1887) I. L. R., 10 M. 375 (where the appointee had to be a *Dharmapuram Tambiran*); *Ramalingam Pillai* v. *Vythilingam Pillai*, (1893) L. R., 20 I. A. 150: S. C. I. L. R., 16 M. 490 where the appointee had to be a Vellala Pandaram; *Khuggender Narain Chowdhry* v. *Sharupgir*, (1878) I. L. R., 4 C. 543 where the manager had to be an ascetic. See also West and Buhler, p. 201.

5. *Gopal Chunder Bose* v, *Kartick Chunder Dey*, (1902) I. L. R., 29 C. 716 (P. C.)

6. *Mussumat Jai Bansi Kunwar* v. *Chattar Dhari Singh*, (1870) 5 B. L. R. 181: S. C. 13 W. R. C. R. 396; *Ranjit Singh* v. *Jagannath Prosad Gupta*, (1885) I. L. R., 12 C. 375 (380, 382); *Gossamee Sree Greedharceejee* v *Rumanlolljee Gossamee*, (1889) L. R. 16 I. A. 137: S. C. I. L. R., 17 C. 3; *Jagannath Prasad Gupta* v. *Runjit Singh*, (1897) I. L. R., 25 C. 354 (369). See also *Maharaja Jagadindra Nath* v. *Rani Hemanta Kumari Debi*, (1904) 8 C. W. N. 809 (818, 819) and the case cited in note (5). But see *Sheoratan Kunwari* v. *Ram Pargash*, (1896) I. L. R., 18 A. 227 (232).

7 Or follows the mode of devolution customary in such family. *Gossamee Sree Greedhareejee* v *Rumanlolljee Gossamee*, (1889) L. R. 16 I. A. 137: S. C. I. L. R., 17 C. 3; *Maharaja Jagadindra Nath* v. *Rani Hemanta Kumari Debi*, (1904) 8 C. W. N. 809 (819). See also Macnaghten's H. L. Vol. II p. 102 and West and Buhler p. 202.

8. 2 Strange's H. L. (Precedents) 302.

A direction by the founder that the office of shebait should be held by his wife, after her death by his son and after the son's death by his daughter, her husband and their male children successively, is however, not a direction contrary to Hindu Law as it only creates life-estates in favor of all to be held one after another, the donees being all persons in existence . So also a direction by the founder appointing B as shebait for life and after B's. death, the eldest male issue of B, or if no issue the adopted son of B or if no adopted son such person as B should by will or deed appoint is a valid direction[2].

In *Maharaja Jagadindra Nath* v. *Rani Hemanta Kumari Debi*[3], the Judicial Committee after observing that there was no reliable evidence as to who founded the religious endowment there in question or as to the terms and conditions of the endowment observed[4] : "The legal inference, therefore, is that the title to the property or to the management and control of the property, as the case may be, follows the line of inheritance from the founder." It is not easy to understand how when the founder is unknown it is possible to say that the management must go to such founder's heirs. What is meant in that passage by their Lordships is we suppose, that the ancestor of the person holding the office of shebait must have been the founder in the absence of any evidence that the founder is any other and that the management has continued unbroken and has followed the line of inheritence from him. This certainly is not warranted by the earlier decision referred to by their Lordships[5]. But the principle so stated resolves itself into a question of fact. If it was shewn that the present shebait's ancestor could not have found the endowment or there was a deviation in this succession, the case would not apply although it might not be shown who the founder was.

Maharaja Jagadindra Nath v. Hemanta.

Where it is admitted that the founder is a private person, the presumption is said to be in the absence of any evidence as to the origin of the endowment that it must have been by a gift from the

No presumption, founder is a private individual.

1. *Gopal Chunder Bose* v. *Kartick Chunder Dey,* (1902) I. L. R., 29 C. 716 (P.C.)
2. *Manorama Dassi* v. *Kali Charan Banerjee*, (1903) I. L. R., 31 C. 166 (170).
3. (1904) 8 C. W. N. 809.
4. Ibid at pp. 818, 819.
5. *Gossamee Sree Greedharreejee* v. *Rumanlolljee Gossamee*, (1888) L. R. 16 I. A. 137 : S. C. I. L. R., 17 C. 3.

founder[1]. If so, the private individual who is the founder cannot lay down any mode of succession inconsistent with the ordinary Hindu Law subject to the limitations which we have before pointed out. But there is no presumption that a private individual is the founder[2]. In many cases endowments have been made by the former rulers of this country and surely a sovereign is not bound down by the fetters of the ordinary law. He may create an estate unknown to the Hindu Law and he may, therefore, create successive life estates in the office of shebait of any particular religious endowment[3]. So also there are temples of remote antiquity whose origin is unknown. In such cases usage must govern and there can be no objection upon the ground that the usage is not in conformity with the ordinary Hindu Law.

Tenure of shebait's office analogous to widow's estate

Subject to the remarks above made, the tenure of office is not an estate tail. Nor is it a series of life estates. These estates may be unknown to the Hindu Law. But a widow's estate is not unknown to the Hindu Law, and we think the position of a shebait approaches more nearly that of a Hindu widow than that of any other person known to the Hindu Law[4]. We have to look to the Hindu Law of inheritance to determine the person who is entitled to succeed in cases in which it is proved that succession to the office of shebait is governed by the Hindu Law. But this does not determine the quality of the estate taken by him. It is not an ordinary estate held by a male under the ordinary Hindu Law. We must look to the Hindu Law of endowments for it. The manager or shebait is not the owner of the endowed properties. It is the idol that is the owner. He cannot alienate the properties except for certain purposes. In the office itself it cannot be said that he has any absolute right in the sense that he can deal with the

---

1. *Gnanasambanda Pandara Sannadhi* v. *Velu Pandaram*, (1899) L. R., 27 I. A., 69 : S. C. I. L. R., 23 M. 271.

2. The observations of the Judicial Committee in *Maharaja Jagadindra Nath* v. *Rani Hemanta Kumari Debi*, (1904) 8 C. W. N. 809 at pp 818 and 819 already referred to besides being mere dicta and not supported by the *earlier* case referred to therein could not be taken to negative this view.

3. *The Government of Bombay* v. *Desai Kullianrai Hakoomutrai*, (1872) 14 M. I. A. 551 (564); *Nawab Sultan Mariam Begum* v. *Nawab Sahib Mirza*, (1889) L. R. 16 I. A. 175 (182) : S. C. I. L. R., 17 C. 284 (245).

4. *Juggessur Buttobyal* v. *Rajah Roodro Narain Roy*, (1869) 12 W. R. C. R. 299 (301). Some of the cases proceed upon the footing that it is a fee simple. See *Greedharee Doss* v. *Nundkishore Dutt Mohunt*, (1863) 1 Marsh 573 (584). If it were so it is not a fee simple which attaches to an ordinary estate. The analogy of a widow, it is submitted more correctly brings out the position of a shebait and the true nature of his estate.

same as he may please as we shall presently see. The right to manage continues only so long as he holds office, and during his lifetime it cannot be alienated away by him. We should, therefore, think that his position is more analagous to that of a widow. A widow has not got a mere life estate nor is she a tenant in tail. She represents the estate fully and may alienate the estate absolutely for some purposes. So here the actual occupant of the office is not the holder of a life-estate[1]. We should have thought that a series of life-estates is not even known to the English Law. He is not a tenant in tail according to the decision in *Gnanasambanda Pandara Sannadhi* v. *Velu Pandaram*[2]. He represents the idol for all purposes and can alienate its property for purposes necessary for its sustentation[3]. The only respect in which the analogy does not hold is that a widow has a beneficial interest in her husband's estate for the period of her natural life. A manager necessarily has no beneficial interest whatever in the endowed properties[4]. But this does not militate against the view that the tenure of his office resembles the tenure held by a widow in her husband's estate under the Hindu law.

The office of dharmakarta may, therefore, be hereditary in the family of the founder or of any other person and governed by the laws of inheritance[5] or it may devolve by appointment by the founder[6] or by the holder of the office for the time being or any other person or it may go by election by a particular class of persons. In some cases the appointment of a Dharmakarta rests with the village in which the pagoda is situate upon the obvious ground that the villagers must have founded and endowed the village temple[7]. In Tanjore we are told in an early case that there

Mode of succession to office of manager.

1. But some of the cases dealing with the office of Mohunt proceed upon the view that the actual occupant is only a life-tenant. See *Mohunt Rumun Doss* v. *Mohunt Ashbul Doss*, (1864) 1 W. R. C. R. 160; *Mohunt Burm Suroop Doss* v. *Khashee Jha*, (1873) 20 W.R.C.R. 471 (472); *Jamal Saheb* v. *Murgaya Swami*, (1885) I.L.R., 10 B. 34 (39); *Mahanth Ramji Dass* v. *Lachhu Dass*, (1902) 7C. W. N. 145 (148, 149). See other cases cited in note (3) p. clxxvi and see also *Vidyapurna Thirtha Swami* v. *Vidyanidhi Thirtha Swami*, (1904) I L. R., 27 M. 435. See further Chapter XIV.

2. (1899) L. R. 27 I. A. 69: S. C. I. L. R., 23 M 271.

3. Chapter VIII pp. xcix to ci and cx to cxi and Chapter XIV.

4. This is only in respect of the absolute dedications referred to in Chapter IV.

5. *Elder widow of Raja Chutter Sein* v. *Younger widow of Raja Chutter Sein*, (1807) 1 B. S. D. A. 180. See also *Subbarayudu* v. *Kotayya*, (1892) I. L. R., 15 M. 389 (391). West and Buhler 202.

6. *Lutchmee Ammal* v. *Rookmanee Ammal*, (1857) M. S. D. A. p. 152.

7. West and Buhler p. 203. See also *Raghavachariar* v. *Yavaluppa*, (1849) M. S. D. A. 37.

was no hereditary right to the office of Dharmakarta of a temple[1]. Sometimes, a caste by means of subscriptions raised among themselves found and establish a temple in which case ordinarily the caste will have the right of management or a voice in it[2]. This is upon the principle that all who have contributed to the endowment must be regarded as founders[3] who will have *prima facie* the right of management (in the absence of any provision made by them).

Evidence and proof.

As regards the nature of evidence that is required to prove an hereditary right[4] in the office, it may be observed that the mode in which the office has been held will be material evidence[5]. The devolution of the office for generations from son to grandson is *prima facie* evidence that the office devolves by succession according to the ordinary laws of inheritance. The succession of a son to his father in an hereditary office is primarily referred to a right arising from that relation subsisting between them just as would his succession to ordinary property[6]. It cannot be presumed that such a son takes his place by being nominated by the other branches. But there must be evidence of a descent in the family of the person claiming[7]. But where the question is whether the office devolves by primogeniture or by appointment, proof that the persons appointed were eldest sons of the holders will not be proof of succession by primogeniture[8]. In Southern India in cases where the trusteeship is hereditary the trustee is ordinarily

1. *Sashiengar* v. *Cotton*, (1849) M. S. D. A. 65.

2. *Thackersey Dewraj* v. *Hurbhum Nursey*, (1884) I. L. R., 8 B. 432 (461, 462); and the instance of Kandasami Coil the special temple of the Beri Chetti caste, for which see *Krishnasami Chetti* v. *Virasami Chetti*, (1886) I.L.R., 10 M. 133 (146). See also *Dhuncooverbai* v. *The Advocate General*, (1899) 1 Bom. L. R. 743 (746). Cf. *The Advocate General of Bombay* v. *David Haim Devaker*, (1886) I. L. R., 11 B. 185 (194).

3. Cf. *Venkatachellamiah* v. *Narrainappah*, (1854) M. S. D. A 100; and *Lutchmee Ammal* v. *Rookmanee Ammal*, (1857) M. S. D. A. 152. See more upon this subject Chapter XV.

4. I am limiting the meaning of this term here to cases of succession by the ordinary law of inheritance. I shall show later on that even where the devolution is by appointment the office is also called hereditary. See Chapter XVI.

5. *Nimaye Churn Pojaree* v. *Moorooleе Chowdhry*, (1864) 1 W. R. C. R. 108 (109).

6. *Giriapa* v. *Jakana*, (1875) 12 B.H. C. 172 (174). Cf. *Maharanee Indurjeet Kooer* v. *Chundemun Misser*, (1871) 16 W. R. C. R 99. The same principle has been held to apply to the case of a tenancy. The hereditary character of the tenure will be presumed from evidence of long and uninterrupted enjoyment and of the descent of the tenure from father to son. *Ismail Khan Mahomed* v. *Aghore Nath Mukerjee*, (1903) 7 C. W. N. 734 following *Baboo Gopal Lall* v. *Teluck Chunder* (1865) 10 M. I. A. 183 (191), and *Rajah Satoosurrun* v. *Moheshchunder*, (1868) 12 M. I. A. 263 (268): S.C. 2 B. L. R. (P. C.) 23 (28). Cf. also *Ganapati* v. *Sitharama*, (1887) I. L. R., 10 M. 292 (294).

7. *Bubun Wullad Raja* v. *Davood Wullad Nunnoo*, (1841) 2 M. I. A. 479 (485).

8. *Rahumtulla Sahib* v. *Mohommed Akbar Sahib*, (1875) 8 M. H. C. 63 (80).

described in public and other documents as *Ádhina* dharmakartha[1]. Where two persons or branches of a family are in joint management for a number of years the presumption is that they have a joint right of management[2]. So that where two brothers were jointly managing the temple and its properties and one brother should die the son of the deceased would be ordinarily entitled to be placed in the same position as his father and would be entitled to joint management along with this uncle[3]. The usage is the best exponent of the right claimed[4]. Usage at the time of each succession must be shewn[5]. Where there is long continued user and enjoyment in assertion of a right courts will ascribe a legal origin[6] to such right and will also presume if necessary that those acts were done and those circumstances existed which were necessary to the creation of a valid title[7]. Hence where *Melkoima* which implied Sovereign rights of superintendence was claimed by the defendant whose family represented the former rulers of Palghat, the Court had no hesitation in ascribing a legal origin notwithstanding the sovereign rights of the former Rulers were determined by the assumption of British Sovereignty. When the ancient theory upon which the right was claimed was not possible some other legal origin with reference to the facts of each case ought to be presumed. The Court accordingly held that the legal origin for the usage (from which joint management was inferred) should be found in the continuance of what was *Melkoima* in ancient times as a co-trusteeship subsequent to the British rule or

---

1. *Appasami* v. *Nagappa*, (1884) I. L. R., 7 M. 499 (509). At p. 510 the court observed: "The mere succession of son to father in a trusteeship does not create an hereditary right; it is doubtless some evidence of an hereditary right, but it is not conclusive evidence". See also *Virasami Nayudu* v. *Subba Rao*, (1882) I.L. R., 6 M. 54 (57).

2. *Nilakandan* v. *Padmanabha*, (1890) I. L. R. 14 M. 153 (162). The joint right must otherwise be proved *Maina* v. *Brij Mohun*, (1890) L. R. 17 I. A. 187 (193): S. C. I. L.R., 12 A. 587 (594).

3. *Purappavanalingam Chetti* v. *Nullasivan Chetti*, (1863) 1 M. H. C. 415 (417).

4. *Cherukunneth Manakel Neelakandhen Namboodiripad* v. *Vengunat Swaroohathil Padmanabha Revi Varma Valia Nambidi*, (1894) L. R. 21 I. A. 128 (131): S. C.I.L.R., 18 M. 1 (12).

5. *Sitapershad* v. *Thakur Dass*, (1879) 5 C. L. R., 73, (80). See also *Greedharee Doss* v. *Nundokissore Doss*, (1867) 11 M. I. A. 405 (428).

6. *Muhammad Yussub* v. *Sayad Ahmed* (1861) 1 B. H. C. App. xviii (xxii and xxxii); *Anandrav Bhikaji Phadke* v. *Shankar Daji Charya*, (1883) I.L.R., 7 B. 323 (328, 329); *Nilakandan* v. *Padmanabha*, (1890) I. L. R., 14 M. 153 (161, 162). See also cases cited in note (2) liv. A grant from the founder will be presumed, See *Nimaye Churn* v. *Mooroolee*, (1864) 1 W. R. C. R. 108 (109).

7. See cases cited in note (2) p. liv. See also *Sumbhoolall Girdhurlall* v. *The Collector of Surat*, (1869) 8 M. I. A. 1 (39, 40); *Dhuncooverbai* v. *The Advocate General*, (1899) 1 Bom. L. R. 743 (749). See also note (6) supra.

in the *status* of the defendant's family as *patrons* of the institution[1].

Exercise of right—Long enjoyment.

Of course where the deed of endowment contains specific directions as to the management no difficulty may arise. But where it is sought to infer a right or title from long enjoyment or usage that necessarily implies that the right claimed has been exercised during the period of enjoyment. In the absence of the exercise of the right no question of enjoyment comes in and the right cannot be said to be established[2]. Where an annual allowance was being paid to the manager of a temple[3] or was being enjoyed by plaintiff's ancestors[4] from generation to generation and for a long series of years and the Sannad was silent on the question as to the duration of the allowance it was held that it should continue hereditarily in the family of the grantee. So far as it was held in such cases that this long enjoyment created a prescriptive title they must be treated to have been overruled by the Privy Council[5]. But it must be remembered that in the case of money allowances to a temple the payments are *prima facie* regarded as voluntary[6] and this is the case specially where a private individual makes the payment[7]. But this principle will not apply where the allowance is claimed as incidental to an herediary office or is a charge upon the revenues of a village[8] or is supported by a grant from the former Governments[9]. In the latter case the Hindu Kings generally regarded grants made to temples as irrevocable[10] and the succeeding Governments generally did not

---

1. *Nilakandan* v. *Padmanabha*, (1890) I. L. R., 14 M. 153 at p. 162 affirmed by P. C. in L. R, 21 I. A. 128 : S. C. I. L. R., 18 M. 1.

2. See *Ramasawmy Aiyan*, v. *Venkata Achari*, (1863) 9 M. I. A. 348.

3. *Collector of Kheda* v. *Harishankar Tikam*, (1868) 5 B. H. C. A. C. J. 23.

4. As attached to the office of Desai. See *Desai Kalyanraya Hukamatraya* v. *The Government of Bombay*, (1867) 5 B. H. C. A. C. J. 1.

5. *The Government of Bombay* v. *Desai Kullianrai Hakoomutrai*, (1872) 14 M. I. A. 551. See also *The Government of Bombay* v. *Gosvami Shri Girdharlalji*, (1872) 9 B. H. C. 222.

6. Cf. *The Collector of Surat* v. *Daji Jogi*, (1871) 8 B. H. C. A. C. J. 166 (173, 174). See Chapter V p. lxvi.

7. *Ramasami* v. *Apparu*, (1887) I. L. R., 12 M. 9 (15, 17). Cf. *Maadan* v. *Erlandi*, (1870) 5 M. H. C. R. 147.

8. See *Maharana Futtehsangji Jaswatsangji* v. *Dessai Kullianraiji Hekoomutraiji*, (1873) L. R. 1 I. A. 34 ; S. C. 13 B. L. R. 254 where their Lordships held that the right was immoveable property.

9. *The Government of Bombay* v. *Gosvami Shri Girdharlalji*, (1872) 9 B. H. C. 222.

10. See Chapter II, p. xvii.

disturb the arrangements. Where there is such long payment and no Sannad is traceable courts may presume a Sannad from Government when of course the payment can be enforceable especially where such payment is made as fees attached to an office[1].

In the case of a private temple where a person looks after the worship of the idol such person will be regarded as having been appointed by the shebait and though such person's heirs continue to perform the worship there is no hereditary and prescriptive right acquired by that person or his heirs and the shebait is at liberty at any time to appoint another priest[2]. But it will be different in the case of a public temple. Either an hereditary right will be presumed to have been given by the founder or the right will be acquired by prescription[3]. So also where it is proved that a person has been appointed by the shebait to look after the management the arrangement may be put an end to at any time and ceases at any rate with the death of the person making it. But if he asserts a hostile title such title may be acquired by prescription when there is the requisite enjoyment[4].

The legal position of the head of a mutt has been already considered in another place[5] and we need not repeat the observations made therein. Mutts.

As to the law governing these mutts and the succession to the office of headship in such mutts the rule is thus stated by the Judicial Committee in the leading case of Rajgunge Akra in Burdwan[6]: "The only law as to these *mohunts* and their offices, functions, and duties is to be found in custom and practice which is to be proved by testimony". To be more correct it must be said that "the law to be laid down is what is the usage of each mohuntee." Even with this qualification the rule is not quite accurate. We think the law is more correctly laid down by *Peacock*, C. J., when the matter was in appeal in the High Succession to mohantship—Founder's rule or usage.

1. *Muhammad Yussub* v. *Sayad Ahmed*, (1861) 1 B. H. C. app. xviii (xxiii, xxxvi).
2. *Maharanee Indurjeet Kooer* v. *Chundemun Misser*, (1871) 16 W. R. C. R. 99.
3. Ibid at p. 100.
4. *Mariya Pillai* v. *Govinda Pillai*, (1860) M. S. D. A. 285.
5. Chapter VIII, pp. cviii to cxi.
6. *Greedharee Doss* v. *Nundokissore Doss Mohunt*, (1867) 11 M. I. A. 405 (428).

Court. "If a person endows a college or religious institution, the endower has a right to lay down the rule of succession. When no such rule has been laid down, it must be proved by evidence what is the usage in order to carry out the intention of the original endower. Each case must be governed by the usage of the particular mohuntee[1]."

Succession in Mutts.

There are two classes of mutts. These are (1) mutts in which the head is an ascetic or not a married person, and (2) mutts in which the head is a married person. In the former class of mutts succession may go (*a*) by nomination or appointment by the last mohant, or (*b*) by election by the neighbouring mohants or by the disciples, or (*c*) by nomination of the endower or founder[2]. Generally in default of appointment by the last mohunt the usage is to elect[3]. In cases where the head of the mutt may be a married man as in the case of *Gosavi* mutts in addition to the above three modes of succession, another is possible, *i. e.*, the mohantship may go by succession to the last mohant's personal heir[4]. In the case of these *Gosavi* mutts where heads are allowed to marry although the mohantship may not go by succession to the last mohant's personal heir, still marriage will not work as a forfeiture of the office[5].

Right of incumbent to annex conditions.

In cases where the last mohant has the rights of nomination a question arises whether the last mohant in appointing a particular

---

1. *Greedharee Doss* v. *Nundkishore Dutt Mohunt*, (1863) 1 Marsh 573 (581) affirmed on appeal in 11 M. I. A. 405. See also *Ramdass* v. *Gangadass*, (1863) 3 Agra. H. C. 295; *Gossain Dowlut Jeer* v. *Bissessur Jeer*, (1873) 19 W. R. C. R. 215 (216); *Sitapershad* v. *Thakur Dass*, (1879) 5 C. L. R. 73 (80, 84); *Genda Puri* v. *Chhatar Puri*, (1886) L. R., 13 I. A. 100 (105): S. C. I. L. R., 9. A. 1 (8); *Busdeo* v. *Gharib Das*, (1890) I. L R., 13 A. 256 (258, 259). See other cases in note (3) p. clxii.

2. See cases cited in notes (6) and (7) p. cxi and note (1) p. cxii. The following are cases in which the usage of nomination by last Mohunt has been recognised. See *Dhunsing Gir* v. *Mya Gir*, (1806) 1 B. S. D. A. 153; *Ramrutan Das* v. *Bunmala Das*, (1806) 1 B. S. D. A. 170; *Mohunt Ram Nooj Doss* v. *Mohunt Debraj Doss*, (1839) 6 B. S. D. A. 262; *Ram Churn Das* v. *Chuttur Bhoje*, (1845) 7 B. S. D. A. 205; *Local Agents of Zillah Hooghly* v. *Krishnanund Dundee*, (1848) 7 B. S. D. A. 476; *Mahant Ramji Dass* v. *Lachhu Dass*, (1902) 7 C. W. N. 145. See the other cases referred to below under para dealing with nomination at pp. clxxvi to clxxviii. In the following cases the usage of election has been upheld. See *Narain Das* v. *Bindrabun Das*, (1815) 2 B. S. D. A. 151; *Mohunt Gopal Dass* v. *Mohunt Kerparam Dass*, (1850) B. S. D. A. 250.

3. *Madho Das* v. *Kamta Das*, (1878) I. L. R., 1 A. 539 (541). Cf. *Narain Das* v. *Bindrabun Das*, (1815) 2 B. S. D. A. 151; *Mohunt Gopal Dass* v. *Mohunt Kerparam Dass*, (1850) B. S. D. A. 250. See also *Rangachariar* v. *Yejna Dikshatur*, (1890) I. L. R., 13 M. 524 (530). See West and Buhler on Hindu Law pp. 554, 556.

4. See *Gossain Dowlut Geer* v. *Bissessur Geer*, (1873) 19 W. R. C. R. 215 (216); and *Dhuncooverbai* v. *The Advocate General*, (1899) 1 Bom. L. R. 743 (748).

5. *Gosain Rambharti* v. *Mahant Surajbharti*, (1880) I. L. R., 5 B. 682. See also *Sathappayyar* v. *Periasami* (1890) I. L. R., 14 M. 1 (9, 10, 11 and 16).

person can annex any conditions to his appointment. For instance the question has arisen whether the last mohant in appointing a person to succeed him can direct that upon the latter's death another named by him should be nominated. Upon this point *Peacock*, C. J., observed in *Greedharee Doss* v. *Nundkishore Dutt*[1] already referred to: "A person having a fee simple in an estate, with the power of appointing to the succession has no right to annex to it conditions which the person who gave him the power of appointment never gave him the power to annex. Now the power (in this case) came under the endowment, but there is nothing to show that one mohant when he is appointing his successor has a right to say what particular individual his successor shall appoint to succeed him." In the case in which the above remarks were made the mohant of an Akra (Rajgunge) in Burdwan by his will appointed one Ladlu Doss and directed the latter to keep with him one Gopal Doss and if he should find the latter capable appoint the latter as his successor. It was contended that Gopal Doss under the terms of this will had a reversionary interest, but the High Court held that there was no such reversionary interest created by the will, and that even if there was any such interest created, the same was invalid. The Judicial Committee on appeal[2] confimed the finding of theHighCourt that the will created no reversionary interest and considered it unnecessary to decide the validity of such appointments in point of law. Of course where it is proved that there is an usage of appointment in the manner contended by the unsuccessful litigant in the above case such usage may and ought to be given effect to as being an index of the founder's intention Custom or rule of action has, as already been pointed out more than once, value only as evidence of the terms of the original dedication of the property and of the law of descent or succession dependent thereon[3]. In the absence of such a custom or usage an arrangement by which one of two litigating parties is confirmed in the mohantship and the other is declared to be the mohant after the former's decease will not vest

1. (1863) 1 Marsh 573 (584).

2. (1867) 11 M. I. A. 405.

3. *Joy Lall Tewaree v. Gossain Bhoobun Geer*, (1874) 21 W. R. C. R. 334 (336). See cases cited in notes (3 and 4) p. clxii.

any present reversionary right in such other and will be void[1] though it is said it may be good as between the actual parties t the arrangement[2]. It is not competent to the presiding mohant t change the course of succession prescribed by the founder[3]. Henc the last incumbent having a right of nomination cannot give u his right in favor of any other person or persons and clothe th latter with such right[4]. This is altering the course of successio which is not permissible[3]. Hence where the head of a mutt i and ought to be an ascetic he cannot by marrying and begettin issue prevent his chelas from succeeding[5]. The question whethe by marriage the head forfeits his office has not been considered[6] Any conditions imposed on the successor will not bind th successor[7].

Nomination.

There are various ways of succession by nomination as alread stated. The nomination by the last mohant may not require an confirmation at all either by the disciples or by the neighbourin mohant. In such cases, however, installation by the assembly o mohunts may by usage seem to be necessary[8]. In the Ahobilan

---

1. See *Greedharee Doss* v. *Nundokissore Doss* (1867) 11 M. I. A. 405 (430) ; *Joy Lal Tewari* v. *Gossain Bhoobun Geer*, (1874) 21 W. R.C. R. 334; and cf. *Shri Dhundira Ganesh Dev* v. *Ganesh*, (1898) I. L. R., 18 B. 721 (731).

2 *Joy Lall Tewaree* v *Gossain Bhoobun Geer*, (1874) 21 W. R. C. R. 334 (337) *Shri Dhundiraj* v. *Ganesh*, supra. But this, it is submitted, is unsustainable. I the usage be that the succession goes by appointment unless the person in whos favour a reversionary interest is created is actually appointed he cannot claim an rights. There can be no two swamis at the same time or two mohants holding offic jointly unless the founder created such office at the time of dedication. *Greedhare Doss* v. *Nundokishore Doss*, (1867) 11 M.I. A. 405 (429).

3. *Mohunt Rumun Doss* v. *Mohunt Ashbul Doss*, (1864) 1 W. R. C. R. 160 *Joy Lall Tewaree* v. *Gossain Bhoobun Geer*, (1874) 21 W. R. C. R. 334 (336) *Rup Narain Singh* v. *Junko Bye*, (1878) 3 C. L. R., 112 (115) ; *Mahanth Ramji Dass* v *Lachhu Dass*, (1902) 7 C. W. N. 145 (149). So where the usage is to elect, the las mohunt cannot, by nominating a successor, give the latter any rights. *Narain Das* v *Bindrabun Das*, (1815) 2 B. S. D. A. 151.

4. *Rup Narain Singh* v. *Junko Bye*, (1878) 3 C.L. R.,112 (115); *Mahanth Ramj Dass* v. *Lachhu Dass*, (1902) 7 C.W.N. 145. Cf. also *Sitapershad* v. *Thakur Dass*, (1879 5 C. L. R., 73 (82).

15. *Mohunt Rumun Dass* v. *Mohunt Ashbul Doss*, (1864) 1 W. R. C. R. 160.

6. This can only be in cases where the head ought to be an Yati or a Sanyasi. Cf *Sattappayyar* v. *Periasami*, (1890) I. L. R., 14 M. 1 (pp. 9, 10, 11 and 16).

7. *Mariya Pillai* v. *Govinda Pillai*, (1860) M. S. D. A. 285. Cf, *Shah Moheeooddeen Ahmed* v. *Elahee Buksh*, (1866) 6 W. R. C. R. 277. The question was raised but not decided in *Greedharee Doss* v. *Nundkishore Dutt*, (1863) 1 Marsh 573 (584). But the P. C. did not decide the question.

8. *Dhunsing Gir* v. *Mya Gir*, (1806) 1 B. S. D. A. 153 ; *Ramrutun Das* v. *Bunmala Dass*, (1806) 1 B. S. D. A. 170 ; *Ganes Gir* v. *Amrao Gir*, (1807) 1 B. S. D. A. 218; *Viswapreya Teertaswamy* v. *Vidyavaty Teertaswamy*, (1851) M. S. D. A. 105 where installation by the *Dwandwa Swamy* or in the latter's absence by the swami having the idol of the deceased swami was held to be the usage. But the assembly has no right to reject the nomination and appoint another. Cf. *Rajah Muttu Ramalinga* v. *Periyanayagum*, (1874) L. R. 1 I. A. 209 (228); and *Sitapershad* v. *Thakur Dass*, (1879) 5 C. L. R., 73 (88, 91).

mutt the usage is for the Jeer for the time being to nominate his successor, failing which the disciples assembled at the place where the Jeer died have the right to elect his successor[1]. The eight mutts at Udipi founded by Madhwachariya are administered according to certain rules framed by the founder. The principal idol *Krishna Devooroo* is worshipped by each of the eight swamies in rotation for a period of two years, the Swami entitled to perform the puja being called the Pariyaya Swami. It is said that the founder himself performed the puja of the idol during his lifetime. Each of the eight Swamies was provided by the founder with a minor idol in the name of which separate mutts were founded and endowed. These mutts are enjoyed by their respective Swamies independently. These mutts form a sort of religious brotherhood among themselves each one being united to another by what is called Dwandva right. Two among these eight mutts form the Dwandva (*i. e.*, couple). Each Swamy has the power of appointing his successor during his lifetime. In the event of any of them dying without having nominated a successor, the brother Swami (or the Swami in Dwandva) has the right to nominate the successor.[2] If the deceased Swami nominated a successor but failed to ordain him, the Dwandva Swami would be entitled to ordain the nominee but if he was absent from Udipi on tour the Swami having the idol of the deceased Swami or the Paryaya Swami may ordain the nominee.[3] In cases where the usage is to nominate[4] the nomination may be by word of mouth or by a will. But where the usage is that the nomination should be by a written declaration such usage will be given effect to[5]. But in many cases, the nomination has to be confirmed by the neighbouring Mohants[6]. In default of

---

1. *Rangachariar* v. *Yegna Dikshatur*, (1890) I. L. R., 13 M. 524 (530). See also *Srinivasa Swami* v. *Ramanuja Chariar*, (1898) I. L. R., 22 M. 117 (118).

2. This account is taken from the statement of Principal Collector Blair attached to his letter to the Secretary, Board of Revenue, reporting the substance of the arrangements made by him for withdrawing Government connection in South Canara. See Parliamentary Return Idolatory (India), 1849 p. 162.

3. *Viswapreya Teertaswamy* v. *Vidyapaty Teeratuswamy*, (1851) M. S. D. A. 105 where the Sheroor and the Soday mutts were held to have Dwandva rights.

4. The usage is for Pandarams to appoint their successors. *Rajah Muttu Ramalinga* v *Periyanayagam*, (1874) L. R., 1 I. A. 209 (228).

5. *Trimbakpuri* v. *Gangabai*, (1887) I. L. R., 11 B. 514.

6. *Madho Das* v. *Kamta Das*, (1878) I. L. R., 1 A. 539 (541). See also *Dhunsing Gir* v. *Mya Gir*, (1816) 1 B. S. D. A. 153; *Genda Puri* v. *Chhatar Puri*, (1886) L. R. 13 I. A. 100 (105, 106): S. C. I. L. R., 9 A. (18). See West and Buhler 554, 556.

such nomination, the neighbouring Mohants[1] or the disciples together with the other Mohants[2] or the disciples only[3] will have the right to elect a successor according to the usage of the particular institution. Where the founder is some one other than the spiritual ancestor of the head and where he so directs, he may have the right of nomination but such a right will not carry with it a power to dismiss the nominee for misconduct unless a power of dismissal is expressly or impliedly reserved at the time of the dedication[4].

Restriction as regards choice and appointment.

Of course there may be a restriction that the person should be selected from among certain classes of persons and where that is the case the person having the right to nominate must select his successor from such class. Thus in the case of the Tiruppanandal mutt, the head of such mutt and not the Pandara Sannadhi of the Dharmapuram Adinam has the right to nominate his junior who will be his successor, but the junior must be selected from among the Tambirans of the Dharmapuram Adhinam[5].

Relation of parent mutt over its offshoot.

The fact that one mutt is the parent of another does not necessarily affect the right to nominate. If the branch mutt is independent the head of the parent mutt cannot exercise any control unless such control has been reserved originally or is established by usage.[6] The head of the parent mutt will also not be entitled to nominate a successor to the branch mutt in the absence of any rule laid down at the time of establishing the branch mutt or in the absence of usage.[7] If the branch mutt has not become independent the head of the parent mutt will also be the head of its off-shoot.

Ascetic succession.

In the case of succession to an ascetic's property the rule laid down by the Mitakshara is that the disciple should succeed[8]. In

1. *Gossain Dowlut Geer* v. *Bissessur Geer*, (1873) 19 W. R. C. R. 215. See West and Buhler on Hindu Law, pp. 554, 556.

2. *Madho Das* v. *Kamta Das*, (1878) I. L. R , 1 A. 539, (541). See also *Dhunsing Geer* v. *Mya Geer*, (1806) 1 B. S. D. A. 153; *Ramrutun Das* v. *Bunmala Das*, (1806) 1 B. S. D. A. 170; *Gajapati* v. *Bhagavan Doss*, (1891) I. L R., 15 M. 44 (45). Cf. *Genda Puri* v. *Chhatar Puri*, (1886) L. R. 13 I. A. 100 (105, 106): S. C. I. L. R., 9 A. 1 (8).

3. *Rangachariar* v. *Yegna Dikshatar*, (1890) I. L. R., 13 M. 524.

4. *Gajapati* v. *Bhagavan Doss*, (1891) I. L. R., 15 M. 44.

5. *Giyana Sambandha Pandara Sannadhi* v. *Kandasamy Tambiran*, (1887) I. L. R., 10 M. 375.

6. *Mohunt Muhadeo Geer* v. *Bullubh Geer*, (1846) B. S. D. A. 376.

7. The case of Udipi mutts. See note (2) p. clxxvii and note (5), supra.

8. See cases cited in notes (1) (2) and (5) supra; and *Mohunt Sheoprakash Doss* v. *Mohunt Joyram Doss*, (1866) 5 W. R. Mis. 57.

the absence of the disciple, the spiritual guru of the deceased and in his absence the spiritual brother or fellow disciple. In the case of succession to mutt property this rule is also followed in some cases[1]. Where there are more disciples than one, the deceased will have the right to nominate from among them[2].

Nomination when not valid.

The head of a mutt having the right to nominate forfeits such right if he is removed for misconduct from the headship[3]. The question whether leprosy has the effect of defeating the right of the head to nominate will depend upon the usage of the mutt. But in order that leprosy may have this effect the leprosy must be of a virulent type so as to incapacitate the person having the right of nomination from performing the ceremonies[4]. Nomination implies the conscious exercise of a discretion. So where the head having the right to nominate is a lunatic and is incapable of understanding the nature of his act he cannot exercise this right[5].

Disqualification.

Before concluding, we shall have to consider the effect, if any, of disqualifying circumstances upon the office of the head of a mutt. Of course where a disqualification recognized by the usage of the particular institution exists at the time of the appointment then the person who is so disqualified cannot be appointed and even if he is appointed his appointment will be null and void. But where a person who may be proved to have been guilty of immoral conduct is appointed the question is whether the appointment is to be regarded as null and as having no legal effect. The question arose in the recent *Jeer case* but it was not necessary to decide it as the High Court held that the suit as laid was not maintainable[6]. The true rule appears to be that where a person having authority to exercise a right exercises it *bona fide* and no fraud in the nomination either on the part of the nominee or any other person appears, courts have no jurisdiction to go into the question

---

1. *Mohunt Bhagaban Ramanuj Dass*, v. *Mohunt Roghunundun Ramanuj Dass*. (1895) L. R. 22 I. A. 94 (98) : S. C. I. L. R., 22 C. 843 (851). See also *Gossain Dowlut Geer* v. *Bissessur Geer*, (1873) 19 W. R. C. R. 215 (216).
2. The eldest may succeed in the absence of nomination. See *Mohunt Bhagbhan* v. *Mohunt Roghunundun*, (1895) L. R. 22 I. A. at p. 98.
3. *Sathappayyar* v. *Periasami*, (1890) I. L. R., 14 M. 1 (12); *Ramalingam Pillai* v. *Vythilingam Pillai*, (1893) L. R. 20 I. A. 150 : S. C. I. L. R., 16 M. 490.
4. *Mohunt Bhagaban Ramanuj Das* v. *Mohunt Roghunundun Ramanuj Dass*. (1895) L. R. 22 I. A. 94 (105, 106) : S. C. I. L. R., 22 C. 843 (858).
5. Cf. *Sayad Muhammad* v. *Fatteh Muhammad* (1894) L. R. 22 I. A. 4 : S. C. I. L. R., 22 C. 324.
6. *Srinivasa Swami* v *Ramanuja Chariar*, (1898) I. L. R., 22 M. 117.

of prior immorality and say whether a better man ought not to be appointed. It may be that the person having the right may appoint the person knowing him to have been once a rake but with the full belief that his nominee is the only fit person for the appointment and will make ample amends for his past conduct. It may also be that the person having the right has nominated a person after coming to the conclusion that the charge of immorality against the person of his selection has no foundation[1]. The question whether disqualification which will prevent a person from inheriting property will amount to a disqualification for the appointment has not so far as we are aware been the subject of any decision. It will appear that the appointment of a lunatic to the office will be bad[2]. But the sounder rule is to say that the invalidity of such appointment will depend on the usage of each institution[3]. Where the succession is shewn to be according to the ordinary laws of inheritance then these disqualifications may hold good. Misappropriation will be no disqualification. Conviction of house trespass is also not a disqualification[4].

Disqualifying circumstances after vesting of office.

But as regards matters subsequent to the appointment the question is whether such matters are a legal disqualification for the office and if so, whether the person is divested of his office by reason of such disqualification. There can be no doubt that a charge of immoral conduct subsequent to the appointment will be a valid ground for dismissing the head of a mutt who is required to be an ascetic[5]. So it was held in one case that the Swamis of the mutts at Udipi with their disciples had the right to inquire into the immorality of one of the eight Swamis and on proof of the same to outcaste him when he ceases to be the head[6]. Even where the head of a mutt is not required to be an ascetic but is permitted to marry the leading of an immoral and a vicious course of life

1. In *Sitapershad v. Thakur Dass* (1879) 5 C. L. R., 73 (82) the Court thought that the appointment of a person proved to be guilty of immoral conduct was invalid and that the question of the nominee's immoral conduct was one for decision by theCourts.

2. *Gureeb Doss v. Mungul Doss*, (1870) 14 W. R. C. R. 383 (384). When the Regulations (XIX of 1810 and VII of 1817) were in force as regards religious endowments misappropriation of endowed property operated as a disqualification although it was not so under the Hindu Law. *Ram Churn Das v. Chuttur Bhoje*, (1845) 7 B. S. D. A. 205.

3. *Sitapershad v. Thakur Dass*, (1879) 5 C. L. R. 73.

4. *Local Agents of Zillah Hoogly v. Krishnaund Dundee*, (1848) 7 B. S. D. A. 476.

5. *In the matter of the petition of Mohun Dass v. Lutchuman Dass*, (1880) I. L. R., 6 C. 11 (14) But see the remarks of *Holloway J.* in *Jusagheri Goramiar v. The Collector of Tanjore*, (1870) 5 M. H. C. 334 (344). See *Sathapayyar v. Periasomi*, (1890) I. L. R., 14 M. 1 and note (3) supra.

6. *Sudindrathirtha Swami v. Vijoyendrathirtha Swami*, R. A. 66 of 1881, dated 20th October 1883, an unreported judgment of the Madras High Court.

ught to be a sufficient ground for dismissal[1] as the duty of the ead is to impart spiritual instruction and to propagate the Hindu ligion and he is expected to lead a chaste and an austere life.

Effect of subsequent lunacy.

The question whether subsequent lunacy operates as vacating e office of the head of a mutt has been discussed and decided in recent case[2]. The answer to this will depend upon the custom usage of the particular institution. The ordinary Hindu Law inheritance applicable to private property[3] will not hold good ecause in the case of mutts except in certain cases of gosavi mutts where the headship goes to the personal heirs of the incumbent) the rdinary law of inheritance applicable to private individuals does ot apply. The plaintiff in the case alleged that the custom in e particular case was that subsequent lunacy created a vacancy at the Sub-judge who tried the case held that not merely no such istom was established but that the contrary was established as the le of the particular mutt. The High Court also upheld this finding. After this one would have thought that nothing remained to e said. But the learned judges proceeded to consider the matter on rst or general principles They held that the office of head of a mutt esembled that of a Bishop, that according to English Law lunacy id not vacate the office of Bishop and that, applying this principle, he head of a mutt did not vacate his office by reason of his lunacy. 'pon this, we must *first* observe that the statement of the English aw by the learned judges in this case was only according to the tatute[4] and without knowing what the law applicable was prior o the statute[5], it would be wrong to apply the law enacted in the tatute to the case in question. Again we may observe that even f the law enacted in the statute be not different from the prior law e do not think it ought to be applied to the case on hand. It

1. *Sathappayyar* v *Periasami*, (1890) I. L. R., 14 M. 1. (16). See also note (5) lxxx.

2. *Vidyapurna Thirtha Swami* v. *Vydyanidhi Thirtha Swami*, (1904) I. L. R., 27 M. 435.

3. The ordinary law seems to be that insanity will be a bar but will not divest a vested estate. See Mayne para 594 and Ghose page 183.

4. 6 & 7 Vict, Ch. 62. The learned judges cite Pope on Lunacy p 370. This statute has itself been repealed by the Bishops Resignation Act 1869 (32 & 33 Vict. C 111) which is made perpetual by 38 and 39 Vict. C. 19. There is substantially no difference as regards the principle involved between the two statutes and deduced by the High Court from the first; only under such circumstances provision is also made for resignation by the later statute.

5. We could not find this from any text book It is not given in Pope on lunacy nor in Wood-Renton on lunacy. But there is a note by the latter referring to Shelf. Lun p. 617 as to the old practice and authorities. Blackstone says a vacancy may be caused by resignation, deprivation for nonfeasance or neglect &c. Vol. I, pp. 382, 393.

must be remembered that according to the statute, a bishop has to be elected for looking after the spiritualities and that another person has to be appointed for the temporalities. But in the case of a mutt unless there is a provision for appointing a person to afford spiritual instruction in case of the head becoming a lunatic the analogy from the English statute will not hold good. But apart from this, we think it is wrong to apply principles applicable in one country to another where the conditions and circumstances are wholly different. According to the English law, the living of an incumbent is liable to sequestration by the creditors of the incumbent[1]. Even if he resigns, he is entitled to an allowance out of the income as a sort of pension. But as we have already had occasion to point out, the head of a mutt in India is a mere manager. His position is analogous to that of a manager for infant heir. There is no estate vested in him. He holds an office which from its nature is only personal. A lunatic cannot be a guardian or next friend of another and a guardian who becomes a lunatic will, therefore, cease to be the guardian. This seems to be the principle of the English Law in the case of other persons holding offices involving personal qualifications[2]. We have submitted that the true rule even in cases of income accruing from the mutt property is that the head has no absolute estate. He is entitled to spend the income for certain purposes recognised by the law but this does not give him any estate. If first principles have any application in a matter of this sort, one thing has to be remembered that the head of a mutt has at least in theory to impart religious instruction and to minister to the spiritual wants of the people[3]. Can he delegate his functions to another? Sombody may be appointed to look after the estate[4] but there is no provision so far as we are aware for appointing another in his stead to look after his spiritual duties. But as against this it must be stated that in the case of private trusts to which Act II of 1882 is applicable, lunacy operates only as a ground for removal. The grounds mentioned in S. 73 of the said Act do not operate as an *ipso facto* vacation of the office

1. *Ex Parte Hastings*, (1807) 14 Ves. 182 : S. C. 9 R. R. 272.

2. Pope on Lunacy p. 372.

3. It is an open question whether the present heads of the mutts observe this duty but the fact that in practice the head of a mutt may swerve from his duties should not alter the principle.

4. *Sitarama Charya* v. *Kesava Charya*, (1897) I. L. R., 21 M. 402.

but the Court must discharge him and appoint a new trustee in his place. Until he is discharged he is a trustee (See Ss. 70 and 71). The provisions of the Trusts Act do not apply to the religious endowments but certainly they are not favourable to view put forward by the appellant in that case that lunacy operated as an immediate forfeiture. This is the principle adopted in S. 8 of Regulation IV of 1892[1]. If the analogy of the ordinary Hindu Law is to be applied it is against the contention that subsequent lunacy operates as a vacation of the office. Lastly, the actual incumbent is supposed to represent the original ancestor or founder who is regarded as an incarnation of the Deity. When a successor is appointed to the office he is regarded in the same veneration as the original founder and in fact the founder is supposed to be living in the body of his successor. This theory will not readily be reconciled with the theory that the office is divested by the lunacy of the incumbent. Notwithstanding the lunacy how can it be said that the original founder is not living in the successor? These considerations strongly tend in favor of the view that there can be no *ipso facto* vacation of the office and the conclusion in the Udipi mutt case seems, therefore, to be right. But as we have alrady said there is no question of general principles involved in such cases and that the correct rule is to see what the rule laid down by the founder is or in its absence what the usage of the particular institution is[2].

A question may arise whether a person who is the head of a mutt and becomes a convert to the Christian or other religion ceases to hold office. To a Hindu mind there can only be one answer to this question and that is that such a head ceases to hold office. His duty is to teach the tenets of the Hindu religion and he must hold a particular status and these he cannot do when he becomes a convert. If he is excommunicated from caste there is authority for the view that he ceases to hold the office[3]. The Freedom of Religion Act (XXI of 1850) will have no application to such a case[4]. Another principle is that if an institution is intended for the benefit of persons holding a particular faith, others not holding that faith are not entitled to claim benefits under it.

Office-holder becoming a convert.

---

1. The Coorg Temple Funds Management Regulation, Appendix II at p. 189.
2. See pp. clxxiii, clxxiv.
3. *Sudindrathirtha Swami* v. *Vijayendrathirtha Swami*, App. No. 66 of 1881 unreported. *Quære*, whether a Sannyasi has any caste.
4. *Venkatachalapati* v. *Subbarayadu*, (1890) I. L. R., 13 M. 293.

CHAPTER XIII.

WHO ARE TRUSTEES UNDER THE MAHOMEDAN LAW?

We shall now proceed to consider the position of trustees and the nature of their office under the Mahomedan Law. We shall find that the same principles apply as in Hindu Law.

Wakf property—Ownership in Almighty.

The Mahomedan Law distinguishes between a Mutwalli and a Sajjadanashin. But whether a person is a Mutwalli or a Sajjadanashin his legal position is the same. According to Mahomedan Law where property is constituted as wakf the proprietary right of the *wakif* is extinguished[1] and the property is assigned over to God. The right of the person dedicating "drops" absolutely and the dedicated property is thenceforth "tied up" in the ownership of the Almighty[2]. This principle is recognised in the cases in which the nature of mosques has been discussed. We had occasion to refer to these cases in a former Chapter[3]. In *Jangu* v. *Ahmad Ullah*[4] Mr. Justice *Mahmood* observed: "It is a fundamental principle of Mahomedan Law that when a mosque is built and consecrated by public worship, it ceases to be the property of the builder and vests in God, to use the language of the Hedaya, in such manner as subjects it to the rules of divine property."

Mutwalli only a manager.

Endowed property under the Mahomedan Law as under the Hindu Law is not the subject of human ownership[5] and no right of inheritance attaches to such property[6]. The Mutwalli is, there-

1. *Abul Hasan* v. *Haji Mohammad*, (1831) 5 B. S. D. A. 87; *Doyal Chund Mullick* v. *Syud Keramut Ali*, (1871) 16 W. R. C. R. 116 (118). It cannot be alienated or resumed. See *Mussumat Qadira* v. *Shah Kubeer-Ooddeen*, (1824) 3 B. S. D. A. 407 *Abul Hasan* v. *Haji Mohammad*, (1831) 5 B. S. D. A. 87. See also Chapter II, pp. xviii and xix and Chapter IX, p. cxxi.

2. *Phate Saheb Bibi* v. *Damodar Premji*, (1879) I. L. R., 3 B. 84 (88). See other cases cited in pp. xviii to xx of Chapter II and notes (2) to (7) p. cxxi of Chapter IX.

3. Chapter II, pp. xviii to xx.

4. (1889) I. L. R., 13 A. 419 (429). See also *Jawahra* v. *Akbar Husain*, (1884) I. L. R., 7 A. 178 (182); and *Ata-ullah* v. *Azim-ullah*, (1889) I. L. R., 12 A. 494. See also per *Mahmood*, J. in *Queen-Empress* v. *Ramzan*, (1885) I.L.R., 7 A. 461 (473, 474).

5. Amir Ali Vol. I, p. 383. See *Amrutlal Kalidas* v. *Shaik Hussein*, (1887) I. L. R., 11 B. 492 (505). See note (4) above and Chapter II, pp. xviii to xx.

6. *Jaafar Mohi-u-din Sahib* v. *Aji Mohi-u-din*, (1864) 2 M. H. C. 19; *Syad Abdula Edrus* v. *Sayad Zain Sayad Hasan*, (1888) I. L. R., 13 B. 555 (561). See also cases cited in note (5) p. cxxi.

fore, a mere manager or superintendent appointed to administer the affairs of the endowment and holding the endowed property not by virtue of any proprietary right but only "for the purpose of securing the attainment of the objects contemplated by the founder." He is only a procurator[1] and has no beneficial interest[2]. This theory of manager has been worked out in the Mahomedan Law so well that the manager is prevented from making any temporary or absolute alienation of the wakf property even for necessity except under leave of the Kazi whose duties in this respect are undertaken in British India by courts of justice or except when expressly authorised by the deed of endowment[3]. Where there is no abso lute wakf and some beneficial interest is given under the deed of appropriation to a person, the latter is only a trustee so far as the wakf is concerned. In such a case it may be that a permanent lease of the property is permissible though of course the s.me must be subject to the trust[4].

Office of Mutwalli.

The mutwalli is a person who has charge of the secular affairs of the endowment. He administers the temporal affairs of the endowment and is bound to see that the intentions of the founder are properly carried out and the income duly appropriated according to such intentions.

Right to appoint Mutwalli. Rules by appropriator.

As under the Hindu Law the devolution of the office of mutwalli depends upon the rules, if any, framed by the founder or appropriator. The latter has primarily a right to appoint a mutwalli. He may lawfully appoint himself as the mutwalli, *i. e.*, reserve to himself the right of superintendence or he may appoint any other during his lifetime[5]. In the absence of any rules prescribed by the founder as evidenced by the deed of endowment

1. *Shah Imam Bukhsh* v. *Moosummat Beebee*, (1835) 6 B. S. D. A. 22. See Macnaghten's Precedents (Endowments) case VIII, pp. 340 and 341.

2. *Syud Asheerooddeen* v. *Sremutty Drobo Moyee*, (1876) 25 W. R. C. R., 557 (558). See also Macnaghten's Precedents (Endowments) case VIII, pp. 340 and 341.

3. See Chapter IX, p. cxxii and Chapter XIV.

4. *Dalrymple* v. *Khoondkar Azeezul*, (1858) B. S. D. A. 586. See also *Futtoo Bibee* v. *Bhurrut Lall*, (1868) 10 W. R. C. R. 299. See also *Ghulam Hussain Saib* v. *Aji Ajam Tadallah Saib*, (1868) 4 M. H. C. 44, where it was held that he was not liable to be removed. If these decisions hold that property which is dedicated as wakf but subject to a charge in favor of the mutwalli may be alienated they must be treated to have been overruled by the decision in *Bishen Chand Basawut* v. *Syed Nadir Hossein*, (1887) L. R. 15 I. A. 1; S. C. I. L. R., 15 C. 329.

5. *The Advocate General* v. *Fatima Sultani Begam*, (1872) 9 B. H. C. 19 (24). See also *Sheik Abdool Khalek* v. *Poran Bibee*, (1876) 25 W. R. C. R. 542 (544).

or as may be inferred from the usage of the institution, the right of appointing a successor upon the first vacancy will vest in the founder or appropriator[1]. If the latter dies without making any appointment, this right vests in his executor[2]. If the appropriator dies leaving no executor, then the right is said to vest in the Kazi or King and such right is exercised in British India by the Court[3]. Apparently in the absence of the executor the right to nominate does not vest in the appropriator's heirs. The Kazi or the Court has the right to nominate. If there are two or more executors, all must act jointly and therefore the nomination must proceed from all. If some one or more of them should die or become incapacitated, according to the Shiah Law the survivor or survivors among them may nominate[4], but it would seem that the doctrine of Hanifites is against this view. According to Hanifa and Mahammad the Kazi must appoint another in the place of the deceased executor. If the deceased executor should have appointed his executor, then the judge would have no authority to appoint another. So also where the deceased executor should appoint the surviving executor or executors as his executor or executors no appointment by the judge should be made[5]. According to Abu Yusaf the surviving executor or executors may act alone[6].

1. *Moohummud Sadik* v. *Moohummud Ali*, (1798) 1 B. S. D. A. 17. The question whether the appropriator has a right to appoint for a second vacancy has not been discussed. But the statement of Baillie, at pp. 603 and 604 (of Vol.I) is general.

2. *The Advocate General* v. *Fatima Sultani Begum*, (1872) 9 B. H. C. 19; *Sayad Abdula Edrus* v. *Sayad Zain Sayad Hasan Edrus*, (1888) I. L. R., 13 B. 555 (which, however, speaks of the appropriator's successor or executor). See Amir Ali, Vol. I, p. 352. Wilson's Digest of Anglo-Mahomedan Law, p 328. The right of a single executor to nominate when the other is incapable of acting is said to be not subject to the Court's sanction. See *The Advocate General* v. *Fatima Sultani Begum*, (1872) 9 B. H. C. 19 (26) (a case under the Shiah Law).

3. *Muhammad Kasim* v. *Muhammad Alum*, (1831) 5 B. S. D. A. 133; *The Advocate General* v. *Fatima*, supra; *Sheik Abdool Khalek* v. *Poran Bibee*, (876) 25 W. R. C. R. 542 (544); *Phate Saheb Bibi* v. *Damodar Premji*, (1879) I. L. R., 3 B. 84 (87); *Sayad Abdulla Edrus* v. *Sayad Zain Sayad Hasan Edrus*, (1888) I. L. R., 13 B 555 (561). Cf. *Moohummad Sadik* v. *Moohummad Ali*, supra. See Macnaghten's Principles (End.) No. 6, p. 70. Amir Ali, Vol. I. pp. 352 and 353. But see this rule discussed later on at p. clxxxix.

4. *The Advocate General* v. *Fatima Sultani Begam*, (1872) 9 B. H. C. 19 (26). If probate is taken of the will, the Probate Act says, that the powers of all may be exercised by any one who has proved or if all have proved and some have died then by the survivors. See Act V of 1881, Ss. 92 and 93 See also *Shaik Moosa* v. *Shaik Esa*, (1884) I. L. R., 8 B 241 (256). Whether this view can be taken as applicable to the case of an appointment of a Mutwalli and whether these sections override the Mahomedan law are difficult questions not yet solved.

5. Hedaya, Vol. IV, Book Lii, Ch. VII, p. 700.

6. Ibid, p. 698. But even according to him the Judge should appoint a substitute but until then he may apparently act solely. See ibid, p. 700.

Exercise of power by executor.

Whether an appropriator or his executor having the right to nominate can appoint some one other than himself has not so far as we are aware been discussed in any case. Of course if the founder has prescribed a class from which mutwallis must be selected the selection must be within that class and the appropriator himself will be bound by that rule unless he has expressly excepted himself at the time of the appropriation from the operation of the rule[1]. This of course does not solve the difficulty. In the case of trusts for sale the donee of the power cannot exercise it in his own favor under the English Law so that the donee cannot sell the property to himself[2]. If this principle is applied then the appropriator may not appoint himself[3]. But even in England the donee of a power to appoint new trustees may appoint himself as one of the trustees[4] and this principle may be applied to the case on hand[5]. It must be remembered that under the Mahomedan Law the right that is vested in the appropriator is the right of nomination but not the right of management as under the Hindu Law. In the latter case no question of appointment arises.

Mode of appointment.

The appropriator may make the appointment immediately after the vacancy. He may make it while in health but apparently if he makes it by will it appears that he must appoint by will made while on death-bed[6]. Apparently the latter rule applies to the case of mutwallis appointing their successors and it is difficult to see why this principle should be extended to the case of an appropriator. It will also seem that ordinarily the person selected ought not to be a stranger and that a relation of the wakif ought to be appointed in preference to a stranger. In the absence of any rule laid down in the deed of endowment we doubt whether the violation of this injunction will invalidate the appointment[7].

Right of Mutwalli to appoint.

When the first vacancy is filled or after the death of the appropriator or his executor it will appear that in the absence of any

1. *The Advocate General* v. *Fatima Sultani Begam*, (1872) 9 B. H. C. 19. See also *Aga Mahomed* v. *Abool Hossein*, (1857) B. S. D. A. 640.

2. *Boyce* v. *Edbrooke*, (1903) 1 Ch. 836.

3. But the case of *The Advocate General* v. *Fatima Sultani Begam*, (1872) 9 B. H. C. 19 at p. 26 apparently does not apply this principle.

4. *Montefiore* v. *Guedalla*, (1904) 2 Ch. 723.

5. *The Advocate General* v. *Fatima*, supra.

6. *Moohammed Sadik* v. *Moohammed Ali*, (1798) 1 B. S. D. A. 17.

7. *Mirza Daud Ali* v. *Syed Nadir Hossein*, (1869) 3 B. L. R. A. C. J. 46 : S. C. 11 W. R. C. R. 388. *Aga Mahomed* v. *Abool Hossein*, (1857) B. S. D. A. 640 was a case where the appointment of a stranger was prohibited by the deed of endowment. See also *Sayad Muhammad* v. *Fatteh Muhammad*, (1894) L. R., 22 I. A. 4 : S. C. I. L. R., 22 C. 324 (where the usage was for an agnate and worshipper to be appointed).

rule laid down by the appropriator the mutwalli newly appointed will have the right to appoint his successor. The statement of the rule in Baillie is more general[1]. But as it is stated at the same time that the court has the right to appoint if there should be no appropriator nor executor the rule is stated with the qualification pointed out above. It is a general principle of the Mahomedan Law that, in the absence of any rules laid down by the founder or appropriator, the mutwalli for the time being has the right to appoint his successor[2]. If this be so, the right of the Court to appoint will only be in default of nomination by the mutwalli for the time being and this has been in fact affirmed to be the right principle in a Bombay case. In *Sayad Abdula Edrus* v. *Sayad Zain Sayad Hasan Edrus*[3] the Bombay High Court observed: "It is by appointment that one officer succeeds to another, appointment either by the general appropriator, or by his successor or executor, or by the superintendent for the time being, or, *failing all these* by the ruling power." This is in fact the principle laid down by Macnaghten in his principles (No. 6) and must be accepted as correct. The mutwalli will also have the right to appoint where the founder lays down such rule. Where there are two mutwallis both must appoint. One cannot act solely nor can he appoint a sole successor[4].

Rules by founder—Appointment.

The rules laid down by the founder must of course be observed. If according to such rules the appropriator should reserve the right to nominate among his children or descendants the latter will have the right to appoint. If among them some should be minors the judge may empower the adults to exercise the power on behalf of the minors or may appoint another to represent the minors. If the appropriator appoints a minor that will not be invalid. But upon application the judge may associate with the minor an adult for managing the wakf affairs. If the appropriator has prescribed any class from which the mutwalli has to be selected the person

1. Baillie, Vol. I, p. 604, where it is said that where the superintendent has died and the appropriator is still alive, the appointment of another belongs to him and not to the judge; and if the appropriator is dead, his executor is preferred. But if he has died without naming an executor, the appointment of an administrator is with the judge.

2. *Aga Mahomed* v. *Abool Hossein*, (1857) B. S. D. A. 640. No specific provision in the deed of appropriation is necessary for this. *Piran* v. *Abdool Karim*, (1891) I. L. R., 19 C. 203 (219).

3. (1888) I. L. R., 13 B. 555 (561).

4. *Wasiq Ali Khan* v. *Government*, (1836) 6 B. S. D. A. 112 (131).

nominated should fall within that class as already stated[1] and an appointment outside that class will be invalid[2].

The Ruling power, *i. e.*, the Court will have the right to nominate in default of an appointment by the appropriator, or his executor or by the last mutwalli or any other person authorized to appoint. And generally on a vacancy unprovided for occurring the appointment rests with the Ruling power or Court[3] whereas under the Hindu Law we have seen that on such a vacancy the *right of management* itself vests in the founder's heirs[4]. The Court has the right to remove a mutwalli for misconduct[5]. When the latter is so removed he will not be qualified to appoint a successor[6] and the judge will have to appoint one[7]. The judge will ordinarily appoint from relatives of the wakif and will be bound by the rules laid down by the founder.

Appointment by court.

In the absence of any qualifications prescribed by the appropriator, the office of mutwalli may be held alike by males and females[8]. Sectarian and religious differences are said to constitute no disqualification so that a Shiah may be appointed as mutwalli although the appropriator may be a Sunni[9]. It is even said that freedom and Islam are not necessary conditions[10]. So that according to theory there is nothing bad in appointing a Hindu as a mutwalli[11] though this can rarely if at all happen. Where the wakf relates to an institution where services special to one sect or creed are held, a member of another sect or creed

Qualifications for office of Mutwalli.

---

1. *The Advocate General* v. *Fatima Sultani Begam*, (1872) 9 B. H. C. 19.

2. *Agu Mahomed* v. *Abool Hossein*, (1857) B. S. D. A. 640.

3. *Wasiq Ali Khan* v. *Government*, (1836) 6 B. S. D. A. 110 (131). Cf. *Advocate General of Bombay* v. *Moulvi Abdul Kadir Jitaker*, (1894) I. L. R., 18 B. 401.

4. See Chapter XII, p. clxii.

5. *Moohummad Sadik* v. *Moohummad Ali*, (1798) 1 B. S. D. A. 17; *Doyal Chund Mullick* v. *Syud Keramut Ali*, (1871) 16 W. R. C. R. 1.6. See also Baillie, Vol. I. pp. 608 and 609.

6. *Cf. Ramalingam Pillai* v. *Vythilingam Pillai*, (1893) L. R. 20 I. A. 150 : S. C. I. L. R., 16 M. 490.

7. *Doyal Chund Mullick* v. *Syud Keramut Ali*, (1871) 16 W. R. C. R. 116.

8. *Hussain Beebee* v. *Hussain Sherif*, (1868) 4 M. H. C. 23 (25); *Wahid Ali* v. *Ashruff Hossain*, (1882) I. L. R., 8 C. 732 (734); *Shekh Karimodin* v. *Nawab Mir Sayad Alamkhan*, (1885) I. L. R., 10 B. 119.

9. *Doyal Chund Mullick* v. *Syud Keramut Ali*, (1871) 16 W. R. C. R. 116.

10. Amir Ali, Vol. I, p. 351.

11. But see *Bishen Chand Basawat* v. *Syed Nadir Hossein*, (1887) L. R. 15 I. A. 1; S. C. I. L. R. 15 C. 329.

will not ordinarily be appointed. So that in the absence of any express rule bythe appropriator it might be inferred from the character of an institution and the services conducted in it that it could not have been intended by the founder that a person of a different creed be appointed as mutwalli[1]. Of course where the appropriator himself in creating the wakf appoints a person of a different creed to be a *mutwalli* such appointment may not be illegal according to the rule already stated. But where after the wakf is created, the person having the right to nominate (whether he be the appropriator, his descendant or a stranger) will not be properly exercising his power if he nominates a non-moslem as a mutwalli. So also a minor may not ordinarily be appointed as mutwalli by the person entitled to nominate[2]. But if the office descends according to the rules laid down by the founder or usage to the male descendants of a certain family and it happens that at some time a person on whom the office devolves is a minor the Kazi or the Judge may appoint a deputy[2].

Conditions for the valid exercise of the right of nomination.

A person having the right to nominate must exercise it when he is of sound mind and capable of understanding the nature and consequences of his act[3]. So also the appointment must be the result of his free will. Coercion, fraud and undue influence on the part of the appointee or of some other person will vitiate the appointment[4]. Ordinarily a relation should be preferred to a stranger but the appointment of a stranger in the absence of any rule or usage as to the qualification or otherwise of the person to be selected will not be invalid as already stated. The last incumbent entitled to nominate is only entitled to appoint on death-bed[5]. The appointment by will made in health is invalid unless otherwise directed in the deed of endowment[6]. A *fortiori* he is not entitled

1. *Bishen Chand Basawat* v. *Syed Nadir Hossein*, (1887) L. R. 15 I. A. 1 : S. C. I. L. R., 15 C. 329.

2. *Piran* v. *Abdool Karim*, (1891) I. L. R., 19 C. 203. See also *Shah Gulam Rahumtulla Sahib* v. *Muhammed Akbar Sahib*, (1875) 8 M. H. C. 63 (80).

3. *Sayad Muhammed* v. *Fatteh Muhammad*, (1894) L. R. 22 I. A. 4 : S. C I. L. R., 22 C. 324.

4. *Sayad Abdula Edrus* v. *Sayad Zain Sayad Hasan Edrus*, (1888) I. L. R., 13 B. 555 (561).

5. *Moohummad Sadik* v. *Moohummad Ali*, (1798) 1 B. S. D. A. 17.

6. *Aga Mahomed* v. *Abool Hossein*, (1857) B. S. D. A. 640. See Amir Ali, Vol. I, pp. 360 and 361.

to appoint by deed *inter vivos* as that will operate in *presenti* and a transfer of the mutwalliship is bad[1].

Office hereditary—Primogeniture—Custom.

The wakif may prescribe that the management be vested in several hands[2]. When under rules framed by the founders the management vested in a Kazi and ten mushavars and the office of Kazi ceased to exist the others will not be entitled to act unless new rules are framed under a revised scheme[3]. The office of mutwalli may again be hereditary in the holder's family. This may be so either because there is an express rule laid down by the founder to that effect or there is usage which in the absence of any express rule is the index of the founder's intention[4]. Where the question is whether the office is hereditary, usage must be strictly proved (in the absence of any rule laid down by the founder). Such usage must be the usage governing the particular institution. The general presumption, however, is that the last holder has the right to nominate a successor[5]. Where the usage set up is that the office devolves by right of primogeniture in the eldest son such a custom must be supported by strict proof[6]. Proof that of the actual holders some were eldest sons, some were sons and some were *only sons* would not be sufficient[6]. If it is proved that even these sons got the office by appointment the rule or usage of appointment is directly proved and the usage of primogeniture is negatived[6]. Even the fact that the person appointed was usually the eldest son of the incumbent would not prove the custom of primogeniture[7]. Where the founder directed that the office should vest in his son and his lineal descendants and the son had no issue he could not appoint a successor by will and such a contingency not being provided for, the Court[8] would

1. Amir Ali, Vol. I, pp. 360 and 361.

2. *The Advocate General of Bombay* v. *David Haim Devaker*, (1886) I. L. R., 11 B. 185 (case of a Jewish Synagogue); *Advocate General of Bombay* v. *Moulvi Abdul Kadir Jitaker*, (1894) I. L. R., 18 B. 401.

3. *Advocate General of Bombay* v. *Moulvi Abdul Kadir Jitaker*, (1894) I. L. R., 18 B. 401 (415, 416, 418).

4. See Chapter XII, pp. clxii.

5. See notes (2) and (3), p. clxxxviii.

6. *Sayad Abdula Edrus* v. *Sayad Zain Sayad Hasan Edrus*, (1888) I. L. R, 13 B. 556 (562).

7. *Rahumtulla Sahib* v. *Mahommed Akbar Sahib*, (1875) 8 M. H. C. 63.

8. Baillie, p. 604. The case of *Sheik Abdool Khalek* v. *Poran Bibee*, (1876) 25 W.R.C. R. 542 (544), however, seems to hold that the son may have the right of appointment.

have the right to appoint. When hereditary succession is provided for the right of nomination under the general law is impliedly negatived and if the mutwalli makes an appointment he is in effect altering the course of succession prescribed by the founder[1].

Where the office is directed to devolve upon a person and his "*awlad dar aulad*" the descendants claiming through females will not be entitled. The expression "aulad" is equivalent to "farzandan" and means according to the Mahomedan law lineal descendants in the male line[2] so that the expression applies exclusively to persons claiming through males. In order that descendants claiming through females may be entitled to hold the office the grant should have been to a person and his "*aulad va ahfad.*" "Ahvad" is a term of the largest and most general signification and in popular speech it is said to be equivalent to "descendants" and to include the descendants of females[3]. It is also said that daughter's children will not be included under the term "Ayal" (family) or "Atful" (children). Where participation in the profits of the endowment is allowed, no distinction is made between males and females[4] in awarding shares to persons entitled.

Appointment of Mutwalli by congregation-Mosques.

A special rule is to be found in the case of mosques. Where a mosque is a public one the congregation has not the right of appointing a mutwalli but where the mosque is dedicated only to the inhabitants of a particular locality, or to a particular sect, the congregation may have the right to appoint[5]. Where, however, a mosque of the latter kind is built by raising subscriptions all the persons who have subscribed will be appropriators and will have the right of patronage[6]. If the latter should prescribe any rules,

1. See Amir Ali, Vol. I, p. 354.
2. See Wilson's Glossary, pp.44, 157,. See also *Abdul Ganne Kasam* v. *Hussen Miya Rahimtula*, (1873) 10 B. H. C. 7 (14). In Macnaghten's Precedents Case IV, p.332, it is said that the expression "farzundan" when applied relatively to a person means his lineal descendants, or his descendants in the male line for three generations and even lower but not the grandson in the female line. See also *Mirazamalli* v. *Hidayatbi*, (1890) 3 Bom. L. R. 772 (777).
3. *Shekh Karimodin* v. *Nawab Mir Sayad Alamkhan*, (1885) I. L. R., 10 B. 119 (122, 123).
4. *Badi Bibi Sahibal* v. *Sami Pillai*, (1892) I. L. R., 18 M. 257 (263) following case No. III given in Macnaghten's Precedents (Endowments), p.329.
5. *Piran* v. *Abdool Kareem*, (1891) I. L. R., 19 C. 203 (222).
6. Case VI Macnaghten's Mah. Law. Prec. End. pp. 331 to 337. See also Chapter IX, p. cxix.

the same will be given effect to. When no rules are prescribed and all the appropriators should die, the right of patronage will we suppose vest in their executors. On the decease of the latter it will not vest in the heirs of the appropriators as such but in the congregation (which may partly consist of the heirs).

Sajjada.

A Sajjada must be distinguished from a mutwalli. The latter, as has been already pointed out, has charge only of the secular affairs of an endowment. But a Sajjada has spiritual duties to perform. He is the superior of the endowment. He is not only a mutwalli but also a spiritual preceptor. He is the curator of the *durga* where his ancestor is buried and in him is supposed to continue the spiritual line[1]. The nature of his office has been already described[2]. He has also no proprietary interest but has only a right to administer the affairs of the endowment[3] and endowed property cannot be alienated[4].

Qualifications for office of Sajjada.

As the office involves personal qualifications a female cannot be a Sajjada[5]. For the same reason a minor cannot hold this office[6] except we suppose in a case where succession to the office goes not by nomination but bypure hereditary right. Succession to this office does not depend on ordinary law of property and no right of inheritance can attach to this office as in the case of mutwalliship[7]. Succession depends on the rules, if any, made by the founder. Where the rules are not expressed in the deed of endowment they may be deduced from usage[8]. The usage that must be looked to is the usage that governs the particular institution[9]. The office involving

1. *Piran* v. *Abdool Karim*, (1891) I.L.R., 19 C. 203(220); *Mohiuddin* v. *Sayidud-din*, (1893) I. L. R., 20 C 810 (822).
2. See Ch. IX pp. cxv. and cxvi.
3. *Shah Imam Bukhsh* v. *Moosummat Beebee Shahee*, (1835) 6 B. S. D. A. 22.
4. *Musummant Qadira* v. *Shah Kubeer-Ooddeen*, (1824) 3 B. S. D. A. 407.
5. Mac. Prec. End. case IV p. 332 and note to case V at p. 343. See also *Shah Imam Bukhsh* v. *Moosummat Beebee Shahee*, (1835) 6 B. S. D. A. 22; *Shekh Karimodin* v. *Nawab Mir Sayad Alamkhan*, (1885) I.L.R., 10 B. 119 at p. 123 (where, however, the original founder contemplated the descendants in the female line also to hold office). See also *Hussain Beebee* v. *Hussain Sherif*, (1868) 4 M. H. C. 23 (25); *Mujavar Imbrambibi* v. *Mujavar Hussain Sheriff*, (1880) I. L. R., 3 M. 95.
6. *Rahumtulla Sahib* v. *Akbar Sahib*, (1875) 8 M. H. C. 63 (80); *Piran* v. *Abdool Karim*, (1891) I. L. R., 19 C. 203 (219).
7. *Shah Gulam Rahumtulla Sahib* v. *Mahommed Akbar Sahib*, (1875) 8 M. H. C. 63 (79); *Sayad Abdula Edrus* v. *Sayad Zain Sayad Hasan Edrus*, (1888) I.L.R., 13 B. 555 (561). See also *Shah Imam Bukhsh* v. *Moosummat Bebee Shahec*, (1835) 6 B. S. D. A. 22.
8. *Shah Gulam Rahumtulla* v. *Akbar Sahib*, supra.
9. *Piran* v. *Abdool Karim*, (1891) L. R. 19 C. 203 (222).

personal qualifications, hereditary succession or succession by primogeniture is out of place[1]. The succession, therefore, generally goes by appointment[2]. The custom generally in the case of *dargas* is for the fakirs and murids of the deceased man assembled on the third day of death and assisted by the Sajjadas of neighbouring dargas to elect a person and instal him as the successor of the deceased[3]. Where the succession is by appointment it has still to be proved who is entitled to appoint. The appointment may be either by the appropriator or his successor, or executor, or any person pointed out by the founder, or the ruling power[4]. But ordinarily the general usage is for the last incumbent to nominate[5]. But in whomsoever the right may vest he must when exercising his right be of sound mind and capable of understanding the nature of his act[6].

Hereditary succession-Evidence.

Where the eldest son of each holder in office is being appointed the fact of the eldest son so taking will not be proof that the rule of primogeniture governs the succession[7]. The person claiming title by the rule of primogeniture must prove it[8]. He must, if he is a plaintiff, prove and succeed on the strength of his own title and not upon the weakness of his adversary[9]. Where by custom or rule of the founder the succession is hereditary, only descendants in the male line (*aulad dar aulad*) will be entitled[10]. Descendants in the female line are regarded as strangers and will not be entitled[10] unless expressly mentioned (the expression which will include such descendants being *aulad va ahfad*[11]). Where succession goes in a

1. *Bebee Syedun* v. *Syud Allah Ahmed*, (1864) W. R. Sp. C. R. 327 (329).

2. *Shah Gulam Rahumtulla Sahib* v. *Mahommed Akbar Sahib*, (1875) 8 M. H. C. 63; *Sayad Abdula Edrus* v. *Sayad Zain Sayad Hasan Edrus*, (1888) I. L. R. 13 B. 555 (561, 562); *Piran* v. *Abdool Karim* (1891) I, L. R. 19 C. 203 (219, 222).

3. *Piran* v. *Abdool Karim*, (1891) I. L. R., 19 C. 203 (222).

4. *Sayad Abdula Edrus* v. *Sayad Zain Sayad Hasan Edrus*,(1888) I. L.R., 13 B. 555 (561, 562). See Macnaghten's Endowments,Case (Precedents) Case V p. 335 (336).

5. Ibid; and *Sayad Muhammad* v. *Fatteh Muhammad*, (1894) L. R. 22I. A. 4 (5): S. C. I. L. R., 22 C. 324 (332).

6. *Sayad Muhammad* v. *Fatteh Muhammad*, (1894) L. R. 22 I. A. 4: S. C. I. L. R., 22 C. 324.

7. *Shah Gulam Rahumtulla Sahib* v. *Mahommed Akbar Sahib*, (1875) 8 M. H. C. 63; *Sayad Abdula Edrus* v. *Sayad Zain Sayad Hasan Edrus*, (1888) I. L. R., 13 B. 555.

8. *Shah Gulam Rahumtulla* v. *Akbar Sahib*, supra; *Sayad Abdula Edrus* v. *Sayad Zain Sayad Hasan Edrus*, (1888) I. L. R., 13 B. 555.

9. *Shah Gulam Rahumtulla Sahib* v. *Akbar Sahib*,(1875) 8 M.H C. 63 (77, 79).

10. *Shah Ahmud Hossein* v *Shah Mohiooddeen*, (1871) 16 W. R. C. R. 198(195).

11. *Shekh Karimodin* v. *Nawab Mir Sayad Alamkhan*, (1885) I. L. R., 10 B. 119 (122).

particular line and a person in that line fails to take and is barred from taking, succession is diverted from his line altogethor and it cannot revert to that line[1]. Where the custom is for the last incumbent to appoint from among the congregation a person who is an agnate of the appointor as his successor an appointment of a stranger will be invalid[2].

Rights of Sajjada.

A Sajjada is entitled to manage the affairs and property of the endowment. He is entitled to the custody of the properties or as it is commonly said to the possession of such properties[3]. There are many subordinate officers under him as under the mutwalli and he as well as the mutwalli will be entitled to dismiss the holders of such offices for disobedience[4].

Right to surplus income.

There is one rule as to the disposal of the surplus income which must be noted here. Where the deed of endowment itself provides for the remuneration of the mutwalli &c., there is no difficulty and the mutwalli will be entitled to take such remuneration. But where there is no provision made in the deed of endowment then it is said the court will be entitled to fix an allowance to the mutwalli not exceeding one-tenth of the income[5]. So that even if the wakif provides a lesser sum the court is entitled to increase it provided the amount does not exceed one tenth of the income. Of course, if the wakif provides for an allowance which exceeds one-tenth of the income such provision is not invalid. In the case of a Sajjadanashin the rule of one-tenth is not applicable. He may take the whole surplus income[6]. It is allowed for his maintenance and this is not income for which he is liable to be assessed under the Income Tax Act[7].

Subordinate offices in Muhomedan religious establishment.

There are several subordinate offices in a Mahomedan relgious establishment. Ordinarily the mutwalli or superior of the endow-

1. *Shah Ahmud Hossein* v, *Shah Mohiooddeen*, (1871) 16 W. R. C. R., 193 (195).
2. *Sayad Muhammad* v. *Fatteh Muhammad*, (1894) L.R. 22 I.A. 4; S. C. I. L. R., 22 C. 324.
3. *Behari Lal* v. *Muhammad Muttaki*, (1898) I. L. R. 20 A. 482 (487). See also Chapter XIV, pp. cxcviii, cxcix.
4. *Meher Ali* v. *Golam Nuzuff*, (1869) 11 W. R. C. R. 333. See more upon this subject Chapter XIV, pp. ccliii to cclv.
5. *Mohiuddin* v. *Sayiduddin*, (1893) I. L. R., 20 C. 810 (821).
6. *Mohiuddin* v. *Sayiduddin*, (1893) I. L. R., 20 C. 810 (821, 823, 824).
7. *The Secretary of State for India in Council* v. *Mohiuddin Ahmad*, (1900) I. L. R., 27 C. 674.

ment is entitled to appoint persons to these subordinate officers. But these offices may be hereditary. In such a case the mutwalli will not be entitled to appoint to vacancies in such hereditary offices[1] except we suppose in cases where there are no heirs to the last incumbent. In the absence of a mutwalli and when not hereditary it is said[2] that "the power of nomination and appointment" of such officers as "*imam* and *muezin* to a mosque is given to the wakif's descendants and the members of his family." A religious office as in Hindu Law is not saleable[3]. The office of *Khadim* involves the reading of *namas* and the Koran and is held under the superior[4]. The hereditary and permanent nature of the tenure cannot be assumed but must be proved[5]. If any property is attached to such office the last holder's heirs will have no right to manage the same unless the office is also hereditary. Even then their rights will have to be inquired into and proved in each case[6]. But ordinarliy if an endowment is attached to such office the actual holder of the office is entitled to be in charge of such endowed property and is liable as a trustee[7]. He can have no higher rights than a mutwalli as his position is only inferior to that of a Mutwalli[7]. Whether a female can hold such offices has not been decided in Calcutta[8] but apparently from the nature of the duties a female cannot hold these offices ordinarily and this is the view taken in a Bombay case[9]. The office of *Khatib* is another subordinate office. It is the office of preacher and when an endowment is attached to such office the right to the income of the endowed propertyis like other similar offices

---

1. *Cf. Alagirisami Naickar* v. *Sundareswara Ayyar*, (1898) I. L. R., 21 M. 278 (284).

2. Amir Ali. Vol. I p. 369.

3. *Sarkum Abu Torab Abdul Waheb* v. *Rahaman Baksh*, (1896) I. L. R., 24 C. 83.

4. *Chand Mean* v. *Khondker Ashrutoollah*, (1866) 6 W. R. C. R., 89.

5. Ibid. See also *Sujawat Ali* v. *Busheerooddeen*, (1865) 2 W. R. C. R., 189.

6. *Sujawut Ali* v. *Busheerooddeen*, (1865) 2 W. R. C. R., 189.

7. *Shoojat Ali* v. *Zumeer-Ooddeen*, (1866) 5 W. R. C. R., 158. His position is perhaps similar to that of a shevak noticed in *Moolji Gulabhai* v. *Manohar Ganesh*, (1887) I. L. R., 12 B. 322.

8. *Sarkum Abu Torab Abdul Waheb* v. *Rahaman Baksh*, (1896) I. L. R., 24 C. 83.

9. *Mirasam Alli* v. *Hidayatbi*, (1901) 3 Bom. L. R.

inseparable from the office[1]. No claims of inheritance can attach to such property[1]. The office of *Mujavar* is also a similar subordinate office. The holder of such office is bound to make puja, to read koran, to distribute rice to fakirs and to perform certain festivals[2]. Such office entails on the holder the performance of religious duties and cannot, therefore, be held by a female[2]. The *muezzin* or *mojaj* is the caller to prayers[3] and the *imam* is the preacher and these offices as they involve the performance of religious duties cannot be held by females[4].

---

1. *Jaafar Mohi-u-Din Sahib* v. *Aji Mohi-u-Din Sahib*, (1864) 2 M. H. C. 19.

2. *Hussain Beebee* v. *Hussain Sherif*, (1868) 4 M. H. C. 23; *Mujavar Ibram Bibi* v. *Mujavar Hussain Sheriff*, (1880) I. L. 3 M. 95.

3. *Mushurool Huq* v. *Puhraj Ditarey Mohapattur*, (1870) 13 W. R. C. R., 235.

4. *Mirazam Alli* v. *Hidayatbi*, (1901) 3 Bom. L. R., 772.

CHAPTER XIV.

RIGHTS AND DUTIES OF MANAGERS OF ENDOWMENTS.

We have seen in a former chapter that it is a misnomer to style the Dharmakarta as a trustee in the sense that any estate in the endowed property is vested in him and that his real position in law is only that of a manager.

Manager's right of custody or possession of endowed property.

With reference to the endowed property he has a right of management. He is entitled to the custody of the endowed property. If his custody is disturbed he is entitled to sue for such disturbance. What ought to be strictly a custody is said to be possession. It is, therefore, loosely said that he is entitled to the possession of the endowed property. But whether he is entitled to possession or custody there can be no doubt that it is a right enforceable by the manager. It is both a right and a duty. It is both a right personal to the shebait as well as a right of the Thakoor that the rightful shebait should remain in custody or possession of the Thakur and the endowed properties[1]. He is entitled to collect the debts due to the endowment[2] and to see that the income is applied to its proper religious objects[3]. Of course where a person endows property for an idol and directs that the same should be in the possession of a trustee or manager appointed by him and that such trustee or manager should pay over the income to the dharmakarta of the temple for the sevices of the idol then the latter will not be entitled to the possession or custody of such endowed property[4]. Such is the nature of the several kattlais attached to a temple and referred to

---

1. *Brajanath Baisakh* v. *Matilal Baisakh*, (1869) 3 B.L. R.O. C. J. 92(94); *Nallathambi Battar* v. *Nellakumara Pillai*, (1873) 7 M. H. C. 3 6 (309, 311), *Koonwur Doorganath Roy* v. *Ram Chunder Sen*, (1876) L.R.4 I. A.52 (61, 62): S. C. I.L.R., 2. C. 341 (35); *Phate Saheb Bibi* v. *Damodar Premji*, (1879)I.L R., 3B. 84 at p. 88(case of wakf); *Durga Bibi* v. *Chanchal Ram*, (1881) I. L. R., 4. A. 81 (83); *Mulji Bhulabhai* v. *Manohar Ganesh*, (1887) I. L. R., 12 B. 322 ; *Nanabhai* v. *Sriman Goswami Girdhariji*, (1888) I. L. R., 12B 331 (332); *Gossamee Sree Greedhareejee* v. *Romunloljee Gossamee*, (1889) L, R., 16 I. A. 137: S. C. I. L.R., 17 C. 3; *Maharaja Jagadindra Nath* v. *Rani Hemanta Kumari Debi*, (1904) 8 C, W. N. 809. See also *Muddun Lal* v. *Komul Bibee*, (1867) 8 W. R. C. R. 42 (44).

2. *Mirza Daud Ali* v. *Syed Nadir Hossein*, (1869) 3 B. L. R., A. C. J. 46: S. C. 11 W. R. C. R., 388

3. *Brajanath Baisakh* v. *Matilal Baisakh*, (1869) 3 B. L. R., O. C. J.92 (94).

4. *Brajanath Baisakh* v. *Matilal Baisakh*, (1869) 3 B. L. R., O. C. J. 92 (94). So also where only a charge is created,

in a previous chapter[1]. The kattalaikars are themselves managers with reference to the endowments in their charge[2]. But with reference to other endowed properties no person other than the manager will be entitled to the possession or custody. Even the fact that the manager has committed a breach of trust will not disentitle him to hold such possession or custody or to sue in respect thereof[3]. Until removed he is entitled to be in possession or custody[4], and such possession or custody cannot be taken away from him so long as he is manager[5]. Such possession or custody cannot devolve on the personal heirs of the manager unless they are heirs to the office[6]. As trustee or manager he is a different *person*[7] although his right to custody of endowed properties may be personal[8].

Misappropriation by manager. Theft or breach of trust.

Possession or custody being rightfully that of the manager a question arises whether he will be guilty of theft under S. 378 of the Penal Code. He will certainly be guilty of breach of trust if he misappropriates temple moneys or other moveable properties[9]. Under the Code property in the possession of a person's wife, clerk or servant is in that person's possession within the meaning of the

---

1, Chapter VIII, pp. cxii and cxiii.

2. Chapter VIII, p. cxiii.

3. *Juggut Mohini Dossee* v. *Mussumat Sokheemoney Dossee*, (1871) 14 M. I. A. 289 (366, 367); *Biddia Soonduree Dossee* v. *Doorgunund Chatterjee*, (1874) 22 W. R., C. R., 97; S A. 1281 of 1900 dated 6th April 1903. M. H. Ct. Jud. Ind. for 1903 p. 68. See *Syud Asheeroodldeen* v. *Sreemutty Drobo Moyee*, (1876) 25 W. R., C. R. 557.

4. *Nanabhai* v. *Sriman Goswami Giridhariji*, (1888) I. L. R., 12 B. 322; *Goswami Shri Giridharji* v. *Madhowdas Premji*, (1893) I. L. R. 17B. 600 (613, 614); *Shriman Goswami* v. *Goswami Shri Girdharlalji*, (1890) I. L. R, 17 B. 620 (note).

5. Or from the idol. *Muddun Lal* v. *Sreemutty Komul Bibee*, (1867) 8 W. R. C. R. 42 (44).

6. *Radha Jeebun Moostofee* v, *Tara Monee Dossee*, (1865) 3 W. R. (Mis) 25; *Mirza Daud Ali* v. *Syed Nadir Hossein*, (1869) 3 B. L R. A. C. J, 46 : S. C. 11 W. R. C. R. 388. (case of Mutwalli).

7. So that his claim will fall under S. 246 of the Civil Procedure Code of 1859 (now 278C.P.C.) and he will be entitled to bring a suit. *Kali Charan Gir Gossain* v. *Bangshi Mohan Das*, (1871) 6 B L. R., 727; S C. 15 W. R. C. R. 339; *Nimaye Churn Putteetundee* v. *Jogendro Nath Banerjee*, (1874) 21 W.R., C. R., 365; *Roop Lall Dass* v. *Bekani Mech*, (1888) I. L. R., 15C. 437; *Murigeya* v. *Hayat Saheb*, (1898) I. L. R. 23 B. 237 (241, 242); *Ramanathan Chettiar* v. *Levvai Marakayar*, (1899) I. L.R., 23 M. 195; *Ram Krishna Mahapatra* v. *Mohunt Pudma Charan Deb*, (1902) 6 C. W. N. 663. He is also not bound by the rule of one year under Art.12. *Rupa Jagshet* v. *Krishnaji Govind*, (1884) I. L. R., 9 B. 169.

8. *Gossamee Sree Greedhareejee* v. *Romanloljee Gossamee*, (1889) I. L. R., 16 I. A. 137 : S. C. I. L. R., 17 C. 3; *Maharaja Jagadindra Nath* v. *Rani Hemanta Kumari Debi*, (1904) 8 C. W. N. 809.

9. See S. 405 of the Penal Code. See also *Buddhu* v. *Babu Lal*, (1895) I. L. R., 18 A. 116.

Code[1] and, therefore, of S. 378. The possession of an agent may or may not be that of the principal within the meaning of the Code according to the circumstances[2]. Where the agent is authorised to deal with the property placed in his possession his possession is not the possession of the principal within the meaning of the Code (though it may be otherwise under the civil law). A manager though an agent of the Deity is not a clerk or servant within the meaning of S. 378. He is authorised to deal with and dispose of endowed property under certain circumstances[3]. He may not, therefore, be guilty of theft. Where by usage certain articles are in the custody of certain hereditary officers who are accountable for the same a dishonest removing from such person's custody or possession by the general manager may be theft. In the case of a dharmakarta appointed by the temple committee there may be theft by the manager if the view be correct that the committee is entitled to possession or custody of the temple properties. A joint owner may be guilty of theft under the code and where the committee vested with the management of temple properties under Ss.7 and12[1] appoint the manager to look after the same taking the most favorable view of his position he may be regarded as in the position of a person who is jointly entitled with the committee. But as such person he may be guilty of theft. If his appointment does not authorise the disposal of the properties for the necessities of the temple[3], he may be simply a bare collector of rents and custodian and though he may hold the same in his right as manager he is in law holding it also for the committee[5].

Manager's right to sue. The right to the custody or possession being the manager's right he is the only person that is entitled to sue for such custody

1. S. 27 and Explanation.

2. See Ss. 378, 381 and 408 of the Penal Code. There may be a theft without S. 381 applying but in order that S. 381 may apply there must be a theft.

3. A manager appointed for an institution under S. 3 is not entitled to deal with or alienate endowed property. See *Mayandi Chettiar* v. *Chokkalingam Pillai,* (1904) L. R. 31 I. A. 83 (88) : S. C. I. L. R., 27 M. 291 (295), and notes to Ss. 7, 11 and 12 of Act XX of 1863 pp. 45, 46, 70 to 74, and 75 to 77. See also Ch. XII, p. clv.

4. *Jusagheri Gosamiar* v. *The Collector of Tanjore,* (1870) 5 M. H. C. 334 (341).

5. The case of *Muthusamy* v *Queen-Empress,* (1896) I. L. R., 26 M. 243 (note) S. C. 6. M. L. J. R. 14 was decided with reference to the view that committee would be incapable of holding property. This view we tried to shew elsewhere would be erroneous. At any rate it has to be reconsidered after the decision of the P. C. in the recent case of *Seena, Pena, Reena, Seena Mayandi Chettiar* v. *Chokkalingam Pillai,* (1904) L. R. 31 I. A. 83 (88) : S. C. I. L. R., 27 M. 291 (295).

or possession from outsiders and this is the general rule[1]. But exceptions must be recognised when special circumstances should exist. When the dharmakarta, mutwalli, or the general manager has alienated endowed property in breach of trust and he does not sue for the recovery of the same, the rule can be said to have no application and other persons interested in the endowment must be given and have the right to sue[2].

Joint managers. All must sue.

When there are more managers than one all are entitled to act and to be consulted with reference to the management of the affairs of the endowment[3]. So that all must ordinarily be joined in any suit with reference to the endowed property[4]. If all are not joined the suit is bad for non-joinder and is liable to be dismissed if upon objection being taken the plaintiffs nevertheless join issue upon the question as the objection is said to be one of substance[5]. The plaintiff may ask them to be made parties under S. 32, C. P. C. (S. 73 of Act VIII of 1859) and his suit is then not liable to be dismissed[6].

First exception:—others not joining even after notice.

But if he shows reason for not joining the others as plaintiffs then there is no force in the objection. Where the plaintiff being one of several joint shebaits, gives notice prior to institution of the suit and asks the others to join with him as plaintiffs and the others send no answer or refuse to join him[7], then one of several joint shebaits may maintain a suit without joining the others

---

1 *Huseni Begam* v. *The Collector of Moradabad*, (1897) I. L R., 20 A. 46 (50); *Sivayya* v. *Rami Reddi*, (1898) I. L. R., 22 M. 223 (228; *Kamaraju* v. *Asanali Sheriff*, (1899) I. L. R., 23 M. 99; *Subbarayudu* v. *Asanali*, (1899) I. L. R., 23 M. 100 (note).

2. See more on this subject, Chapter XV.

3. *Paramesicaran* v. *Shangaran*, (1891) I. L. R, 14 M. 489; *Puramathan Somayajipad* v. *Sankara Menon*, (1899) I. L. R., 23 M. 82. See *Wasiq Ali Khan* v. *Government*, (1836) 6 B. S. D. A 110 (131) a case of joint mutwallis.

4. *Rajendronath Dutt* v. *Shaik Mahomed Lal*, (1881) L. R. 8 I.A. 135 (139 to 141): S. C. I. L. R., 8 C. 42 (47 to 49); *Beehulal Oliullah*, (1885) I. L. R, 11 C. 338 (case of mutwallis); *Kali Kanta Surma* v. *Gouri Prosad Surma Bardeuri*, (1890) I. L. R., 17 C. 903 (910); *Paramesicaran* v. *Shangaran*, (1891) I. L. R., 14 M. 489; *Purumathan Somayajipad* v. *Sankara Menon*, (1899) I. L. R, 23 M. 82.

5. *Rajendronath Dutt* v. *Shaik Mohomed Lal*, (1881) L R, 8 I. A. 135 (141, 142): S. C I. L. R., 8 C. 42 (49); *Puramathan Somayajipad* v. *Sankara Menon*, (1899) I. L. R., 23 M. 82.

6. *Rajendronath Dutt* v. *Shaik Mohomed Lal*, (1881) L. R. 8 I. A 135 (141). There the objection was given effect to and when the High Court gave effect to the objection the plaintiff did not ask for the joi der of the omitted persons. In a case where the plaintiffs asked for such joinder the suit ought not to be dismissed. See *Angamuthu Pillai* v. *Kolandavelu Pillai*, (1899) I. L. R., 23 M. 190.

7. The practice is to take the plaint for the signature of the others along with the notice.

Second exception :—suit to set aside alienation made by one shebait.

as plaintiffs but may make the others defendants[1]. The nature of the suit may also furnish us with an exception. Where one shebait makes an alienation not binding on the endowment without consulting the others either because he denies the other's title to manage or otherwise, the latter will have a right to bring a suit for setting aside the alienation; but in such suit the person alienating need not be plaintiff and he has no right to be consulted. No notice need be given asking him to join[2].

Third exception :—suit for redemption.

Under the special provisions of the Transfer of Property Act, one of several managers (being one of several mortgagors) is entitled to redeem endowed property from the mortgagee and the others need not be joined as plaintiffs[3].

Fourth exception :—suit to enforce rights under contract entered into in the name of one.

Then again if a contract is made with one manager although the others may be interested in such contract, the person in whose name the contract is entered into may enforce it specifically and sue for rights under it[4]. Even where two or more persons are parties to a contract the Calcutta High Court holds[5] that if the person not joined as plaintiff is actually on the record as defendant, the suit should not be dismissed merely because it is not proved that the person joined as defendant has refused to be a plaintiff but

---

1. *Rajendronath Dutt* v. *Shaik Mahomed Lal*, (1881) L. R., 8 I. A. 135 (139); *Bechulal* v. *Oliullah*, (1885) I. L. R., 11 C. 338. If the plaintiffs should sue on behalf of all is it sufficient? In *Rajendronath Dutt* v. *Shaik Mahomed Lal*, supra, the point was taken at p. 140, but the P. C. only state that that was not the suit in that case. Such suit could only be brought under S. 30, C. P. C., which only applies to numerous parties. Cf *Puramathan Somayajipad* v. *Sankara Menon*, (1899) I. L. R., 23 M. 82. In *Biri Sing* v. *Nawal Singh*, (1898) I. L. R., 24 A. 226, it was held that it was enough if all the persons interested are made parties to the record and that it was not necessary to allege refusal on the part of those added as defendants to join as plaintiffs. But this is certainly against the *dicta* of the P. C. in the above case. But the case itself may be distinguished from the P. C. case on the ground that the defendants who were joined disclaimed all interest.

2. *Mariyil Raman Nair* v. *Narayanan Nambudiripad*, (1902) I. L. R., 26 M. 461. In *Rajendronath Dutt's* case the shebait not made party had also alienated and the suit was to recover the property so alienated. If the decision in the Madras case is to be correct it must be distinguished from the P. C. case on the ground that in the latter case the alienor was not even made a party defendant. But the P. C. case is not referred to at all.

3 But they must be joined as defendants. *Karattole Edamana* v. *Unni Kannan* (1903) I. L. R., 26 M. 649 (F. B.) doubting and overruling *Savitri Antarjanam* v. *Raman Nambudri*, (1900) I. L. R., 24 M. 296.

4. *Adaikkalam Chetti* v. *Marimuthu*, (1899) I. L. R., 22 M 326; *Ramanujachariar* v. *Srinivasachariar*, (1899) 9 M. L. J. R. 103. See also *Bungsee Singh* v. *Soodist Lall*, (1881) I. L. R., 7 C. 739 (745, 746); *Dayabhai Lallubhai* v. *Gopalji Dayabhai*, (1893) I. L. R., 18 B. 141; *Hari Vasudev Kamat* v. *Mahadu Dad Garda*, (1895) I. L. R., 20 B. 435. See *Subrahmania Pattar* v. *Narayanan Nayar*, (1900) I. L. R., 24 M. 130 (135). A benamidar is a trustee who can validly represent all parties under S. 437, C. P. C.

5. *Pyari Mohun Bose* v. *Kedarnath Roy*, (1899) I. L. R., 26 C. 409 (412).

that the Court has ample powers under S. 32, C.P.C., on application by the plaintiff[1]. If management by turns of these public offices is allowable and the right of the owner of the turn is interfered with, then he must sue himself for the enforcement of such right[2].

Fifth exception:—suit by owner of turn.

The manager or mutwalli is bound to see that the income of the endowed property is applied for its proper purposes[3]. He must see that the services are properly performed[4], and if he is himself the Archaka he must perform the same himself[5] and it may be where there is no cook recognised as a servant in the institution he must prepare food for the idol[6]. The shebait of a Hindu family idol has to perform similar duties. Ordinarily, he has to perform the services for the idol, *i. e.*, he has to perform the worship of the idol and to prepare food for it[6] but he may appoint a priest for doing these services[7]. The general manager of a temple is also bound to see that proper accounts are rendered by the outgoing manager and to recover any sums misappropriated or otherwise due by such ex-manager by suit against the latter or his legal representatives[8]. It is also his duty that the temple endowments in the hands of special managers, are duly appropriated[9]. It is also his duty to see that the emoluments attached to the several

Manager's duty (*a*) with reference to endowments,

and (*b*) with reference to special endowments.

---

1. It will then depend upon the circumstances of each case whether a suit should be dismissed upon the ground that the person was added as plaintiff after the period of limitation. See *Guruvayya* v. *Dattaraya*, (1903) I. L. R., 28 B. 11 (17, 18, 20).

2. See pp. ccxxvii to ccxxx.

3. *Brajanath Baisakh* v. *Matilal Baisakh*, (1869) 3 B. L. R. O. C. J. 92 (94); *Mulji Bhulabhai* v. *Manohar Ganesh*, (1887) I. L. R., 12 B. 322; *Nallayappa Pillian* v. *Ambalavana Pandara Sannadhi*, (1903) I. L. R., 27 M. 465 (473, 474). See also *Prosunno Kumari Debya* v. *Golab Chand Baboo*, (1875) L. R. 2 I. A. 145 (151); *Konwar Doorganath Roy* v. *Ram Chunder Sen*, (1876) L. R. 4 I. A. 52 (56).

4. *Reasut Ali* v. *J. C. Abbott*, (1869) 12 W. R. C. R. 132 (133) where the Court observed that the mutwalli (or superior of a saint's tomb) would be obliged to show that he kept up the tomb for which the grant was made and performed whatever other matters usually accompany the keeping up of a saint's tomb.

5. *Mohesh Chunder Chuckerbutty* v. *Koylash Chunder Chuckerbutty*, (1869) 11 W. R. C. R. 443 (444).

6. *Dubo Misser* v. *Srinibas Misser*, (1870) 5 B. L. R. 617 a case of a private endowment.

7. *Maharanee Indurjeet Kooer* v. *Chundemun Misser*, (1871) 16 W. R. C. R. 99.

8. *Jeyangarulavaru* v. *Durma Dossji*, (1868) 4 M. H. C. 2 (4); *Virasami Nayudu* v. *Subba Rau*, (1882) I. L. R., 6 M. 54.

9. *Nellaiyappa Pillai* v. *Thangama Nachiyar*, (1897) I. L. R., 21 M. 406 (408). See also *Vythilinga Pandara Sannadhi* v. *Somasundara Mudaliar*, (1893) I. L. R., 17 M. 199 (202). In *Narayana Ayyar* v. *Kumarasami Mudaliar*, (1899) I. L. R., 23 M. 537 (539) the question was raised but not decided.

subordinate offices in a temple are not improperly severed from such offices[1], or that the interests of the temple in the same are not prejudiced by any wrongful alienations made by the holders of such offices[2]. We have already seen that it is the duty of the committee to see that endowments are appropriated to their legitimate purposes and are not wasted[3].

Right of suit in the manager—suit in his name.

The dharmakarta or shebait being merely a manager and the deity, idol or mutt[4] being the juridical person capable of holding and acquiring property there may be no difficulty in holding that any suit brought for the purposes of the religious institution must be in the name of such idol, deity, &c. But the practice in such cases is for the manager to sue in his own name. As *Markby*, J., observed in *Juggodumba Dossee* v. *Puddomoney Dossee*[5]: "The ownership of the debutter property is vested in the idols, the shebaits strictly speaking being not trustees for the idols but managers though there is this peculiarity that all transactions, including even litigation, are carried on by the managers in their own names." Here the reason is stated to be the practice. If it is only a question of practice, a suit brought in the name of the deity or juridical person by the manager must not be legally unobjectionable and in fact there are instances in the reports of some such suits having been brought[6]. But the Allahabad High Court in *Thakur Raghunathji Maharaj* v. *Shah Lal Chand*[7] has held that such a suit is not maintainable though the plaint may be allowed to be amended by substituting the name of the manager. Although no reasons are given in the above case the decision may

1. *Chidambaram Chetti* v. *Minammal*, (1898) I. L. R., 23 M. 439 (440). See also *Mulji Bhulabhai* v. *Manohar Ganesh*, (1887) I. L. R., 12 B. 322.

2. Ibid. See also *Lotlikar* v. *Wagle*, (1882) I. L. R., 6 B. 596 which seems to hold that such an alienation may be valid so long as the service is not determined. See further, *Sagun Balkrishna* v. *Kaji Hussen*, (1903) I. L. R., 27 B. 500 (509).

3. *Tiruvengadath Ayyangar* v. *Srinivasa Thathachariar*, (1899) I. L. R., 22 M. 361 (363). See notes to S. 7 of Act XX of 1863, p. 44.

4. See Chapter VIII, p. xcvi, xcix, cvi, cvii, cviii.

5. (1875) 15 B. L. R. 318 (330) followed in *Babajirao* v. *Laxmandas*, (1903) I. L. R., 28 B. 215 (223).

6. *Shri Bhavani Devi of Fort Pratabgad* v. *Devrao Madhavrao*, (1887) I. L. R., 11 B. 485. See also *Rambabu Purbu Mirasi* v. *Members of the Committee of Management of Sevasthan of Shri Dev Rameshwar of Achare*, (1899) 1 Bom. L. R. 667. In the latter case, however, the members were named and the suit was really brought in the name of the committee.

7. (1897) I. L. R., 19 A. 330.

be supported upon the ground that the right to sue for recovery of possession, &c., is not simply that of the Thakur but is also that of the manager[1], and such right is a personal right[2]. The recent decision of the Privy Council in *Maharaja Jagadindra Nath* v. *Hemanta Kumari*[2] which holds that a manager suing for the recovery of endowed properties is entitled to claim exemption under S. 7 of the Limitation Act also supports this view[2]. We must therefore, treat it as settled that a manager must sue in his own name although he seeks to recover for the endowment. The description in the plaint will of course show that he is suing as manager.

Manager's powers of alienation over endowed property.

With reference to his powers of alienation over endowed property it need scarcely be said that he is not entitled to alienate it for his own purpose[3]. He has no proprietary interest over the same[4] and endowed property, therefore, cannot be attached and sold in execution of a decree against him personally[5], *i. e.*, in his individual right. If the decree itself directs the sale of endowed property that must be given effect to[6] unless in a case where the decree should be construed as a personal one against the manager when he can set up his claim as manager[7]. If he alienates either by way of mortgage or sale for satisfaction of his debts or for no necessary purpose of the institution, he may himself in his capa-

---

1. *Gossamee Sree Greedhareejee* v. *Romanloljee Gossamee*, (1889) L. R. 16 I. A. 137 : S. C. I. L. R., 17 C. 3.

2. *Maharaja Jagadindra Nath* v. *Rani Hemanta Kumari Debi*, (1904) 8 C. W. N. 809. See also case cited in note (1).

3. *Khusalchand* v. *Mahadevgiri*, (1875) 12 B. H. C. 214; *Parsotam Gir* v. *Dat Gir*, (1903) I. L. R., 25 A. 296 and other cases referred to in note (5).

4. See pp. cliv, clxxxiv, clxxxv. We are only speaking throughout of the first two kinds of dedication referred to in Chapter IV, pp. l and li. If the shebait has a beneficial interest and there is only a charge in favor of the endowment, an alienation subject to the charge will be good. *Soshikishore* v. *Putto Mohadubee*, (1864) W. R. Sp. C. R. 107; *Basoo Dhul* v. *Kishen Chunder*, (1870) 13 W. R. C. R. 200; *Ashutosh Dutt* v. *Doorgachurn*, (1879) L. R. 6 I. A. 182.

5. *Ranee Shibeshuree Debia* v. *Mothooranath Acharjee*, (1866) 5 W. R. C. R. 202; *Narayan* v. *Chintaman*, (1881) I. L. R., 5 B. 393; *Rupa Jagshet* v. *Krishnaji Govind*, (1884) I. L. R., 9 B. 169; *Girijanund Datta Jha* v. *Sailajanund Datta Jha*, (1896) I. L. R., 23 C. 645; *Murigeya* v. *Hayat Saheb*, (1898) I. L. R., 23 B. 237; *Ram Krishna Mahapatra* v. *Mohunt Padma Charan Deb Goswami*, (1902) 6 C. W. N. 663; *Parsotam Gir* v. *Dat Gir*, supra; *Venkatasami* v. *Kuppayee Ammal*, (1904) 14 M. L. J. R. 377 (378). See *Fegredo* v. *Mahomed Mudessur*, (1871) 15 W. R. C. R., 75 at p. 79 (apparently a case of wakf).

6. *Prannath Paurey* v. *Sree Mongula Debia*, (1866) 5 W. R. C. R. 176.

7. See pp. ccxxxi to ccxxxv and cases cited in note (5). But as there is no attachment in a mortgage decree no claim under S. 278, C. P. C., can be preferred. S. 244, C.P.C., does not apply as the manager must be regarded as a different person altogether. Of course a suit may be brought. *Ramkrishna Mahapatra* v. *Mohunt Padma Charan Deb Goswami*, (1902) 6 C. W. N. 663.

city as manager sue to set aside the mortgage and he will not be estopped from doing so[1]. There can be no question that his successors in office are not bound by any act of his prejudicial to the institution and can sue to recover alienated property if not barred[2]. The manager can have no rights of disposition except such as the law allows him[3]. We have already referred to this matter in a previous chapter[4]. We there said that such powers of disposition are necessarily limited and may be exercised only in case of necessity. His position has been in a former chapter[5] compared to that of a widow[6] and his authority to incur debts or to charge the estate is analogous to that of a manager for an infant heir[7]. It is, therefore, competent for the manager or shebait in his capacity as such manager or shebait to incur debts and borrow money for the proper expenses of keeping up the

---

1. *Shri Ganesh Dharnidhar Maharajdev* v. *Keshavrav Govind Kulgavkar*, (1890) I. L. R., 15 B. 625 (635, 636) dissenting from *Maniklal* v. *Manchershi*, (1876) I. L. R., 1 B. 269 (277, 278); *Mahomed* v. *Ganapati*, (1889) I. L. R., 13 M. 277 (279, 280). See also *Behari Lal* v. *Muhammad Muttaki*, (1898) I. L. R., 20 A. 482; *Dattagiri* v. *Dattaraya*, (1902) I. L. R., 27 B. 363; *Narayan* v. *Shri Ramchandra*, (1903) I. L. R., 27 B 373. Cf. *Veerabadra Varaprasada Row* v. *Vellanki Venkatadri*, (1899) 10 M. L. J. R. 114, (115). Cf. *Srimati Mallika Dasi* v. *Ratanmani Chakervati*, (1897) 1 C. W. N. 493. But see *Maniklal* v. *Manchershi*, (1876) I. L. R., 1 B. 269 (277, 278); and *Gulzar Ali* v. *Fida Ali*, (1883) I. L. R., 6 A. 24.

2. *Goluck Chunder* v. *Rughoonath*, (1870) 11 B. L. R. 336 (note: S. C. 17 W. R. C. R. 444; *Rupa Jagshet* v. *Krishnaji Govind*, (1884) I. L. R., 9 B. 169; *Vedapuratti* v. *Vallabha*, (1890) I. L. R., 13 M. 402; *Vithalbowa* v. *Narayan Daji Thite*, (1893) I. L. R., 18 B. 507; *Shri Dhundiraj Ganesh Dev* v. *Ganesh*, (1893) I. L. R., 18 B. 721; *Girijanund* v. *Sailajanund*, (1896) I. L. R., 23 C. 645 (662). See also the cases cited in note (1).

3. The general rule is that endowed property cannot be alienated. *Bhowanee Purshad* v. *Ranee Jagudumbha*, (1829) 4 B. S. D. A. 343; *Ram Sundur Ray* v. *Heirs of Raja Udwant Singh*, (1832) 5 B. S D. A. 210; *Ram Churn Das* v. *Chuttur Bhoje*, (1845) 7 B. S. D. A. 205; *Mohunt Kumulperkash Dass* v. *Mohunt Jugmohun Dass*, (1850) B. S. D. A. 532; *Basoo Dhul* v. *Kishen Chunder Geer Gossain*, (1870) 13 W. R. C. R. 200; *Rumonee Debia* v. *Baluck Doss*, (1870) 11 B. L. R. 336 (note): S. C. 14 W.R.C.R. 101; *Goluck Chunder Bose* v. *Rughoonath Sree Chunder Roy*, (1872) 11 B. L. R. 337 (note): S. C. 17 W. R. C. R. 444; *Rajah of Cherakal Korilagom* v. *Mootha Rajah*, (1873) 7 M. H. C. 210 where it was held that an alienation of office and endowed property subject to trust was bad; *Lotlikar* v. *Wagle*, (1882) I. L. R., 6 B 596; *Radhabai* v. *Anantrav Bhagvant*, (1885) I. L. R., 9 B. 198 (221); *In re Lakshmibai*, (1888) I. L. R., 12 B. 638; *Vedapuratti* v. *Vallabha*, (1890) I. L. R., 13 M. 402 (404); *Dattagiri* v. *Dattaraya*, (1902) I. L. R., 27 B. 363 (368). See also cases cited in Chapter VIII, pp. xcix and c. But see *Mohunt Gopal Dass* v. *Kerparan Dass*, (1850) B. S. D. A. 250; *Rane Shibeshuree* v. *Mothooranath*, (1866) 5 W. R. C. R. 202 (where it was held that only income may be attached); *Maharanee Shibessourie* v. *Mothooranath*, (1869) 13 M. I. A. 270; *Nallayappa Pillian* v. *Amblavana Pandara Sannadhi*, (1903) I. L R., 27 M. 465 (472, 473). Cf. *Muddun Lal* v. *Komul Bibee*, (1867) 8 W. R. C. R. 42 at p. 44 where it was said that endowed land could not be taken away from idol or shebait.

4. Chapter VIII, pp. xcix, c, cx, and cxi.

5. Chapter XII, pp. clxviii, clxix.

6. See *Juggessur Buttobyal* v. *Rajah Roodro Narain Roy*, (1869) 12 W. R. C. R. 299 (301).

7. *Prosunno Kumari Debya* v. *Golab Chand Baboo*, (1875) L. R. 2 I. A. 145 (151): S. C. 14 B. L R. 450; *Konwur Doorganath Roy* v. *Ram Chunder Sen*, (1876) L. R. 4 I. A. 52 (63); *Sheo Shankar Gir* v. *Ram Shewak Chowdhri*, (1896) I. L. R., 24 C. 77 (82); *Parsotam Gir* v. *Dut Gir*, (1903) I. L. R., 25 A. 296 (304, 311).

religious worship, repairing the temples or other possessions of the idol, defending hostile litigious attacks and other like objects[1]. We should very much wish that the law was otherwise but notwithstanding the recent Madras decision[2] such view would hardly be sustainable. What are necessary purposes must depend in a great measure upon the usage of each institution[3]. In Southern India these purposes are recorded[4] in what is called the "dittam" and when the income falls off the services are generally regulated with reference to the diminished income[5]. Payment of Government Revenue due upon the endowed lands will be a necessary purpose[6]. Whether costs incurred in defending a person's title as manager must be considered a necessary purpose and if so to what extent has not been fully discussed in any case. Of course where a person fails to establish his title as manager he must be regarded as a trespasser and debts incurred by him for meeting the costs of his defence are not binding on the institution[7]. But where a person is successful in establishing his claim and defending his title the question of his power to incur debts for meeting such defence will depend upon the question whether the manager or trustee is entitled to have his costs paid out of the trust funds and as will appear later on the general rule is that trustee is entitled to have his costs paid out of trust funds taxed as between party and party[8]. The power to incur debts is a limited and qualified one. It can only be exercised rightly in a case of need or for the benefit of the estate. The principles laid down in *Hanooman Pershad's case*[9] will, therefore, apply according to which the power to incur debts must be measured by the existing

---

1. *Prosunno Kumari Debya* v. *Golab Chand Baboo*, (1875) L. R. 2 I. A. 145 (151) ; *In re Lakshmibai*, (1888) I. L. R., 12 B. 638 (646). See also *Vythilinga Pandara Sannadhi* v. *Somasundara*, (1893) I. L. R., 17 M. 199 (202) where it was observed that Dharmakartas were bound to see that the temple was kept in proper repair by those who were bound to do so according to usage.

2 *Nallayappa Pillian* v. *Ambalavana Pandara Sannadhi*, (1903) I. L. R., 27 M. 465 (472, 473).

3. *Shankar Bharati Svami* v. *Venkapa Naik*, (1885) I. L. R., 9 B. 422 (426); *Vidyapurna Thirtha Swami* v. *Vidyanidhi Thirtha Swami* (1904) I. L. R., 27 M. 435 at p 455.

4. *Vidyapurna Thirtha Swami* v. *Vidyanidhi Thirtha Swami*, (1904) I. L. R., 27 M. 435 at p. 455.

5. *Nallayappa Pillian* v. *Ambalavana Pandara Sannadhi*, (1903) I. L. R., 27 M. 465 (473).

6. *Kasim Saiba* v. *Sudhindra Thirtha Swami*, (1895) I. L. R., 18 M. 359 (363). See also *Prosunno Kumari Debya* v. *Golab Chand Baboo*, supra

7. *Saminatha* v. *Purushottama*, (1892) I L. R., 16 M. 67 (69, 70).

8. See pp. cclxi and cclxii.

9. (1856) 6 M. I. A. 393.

necessity for incurring them. The shebait or manager will, therefore, be entitled to incumber the property for such debts. He is empowered to do whatever may be required for the service of the idol and for the benefit and preservation of its property[1] and to this extent and for this purpose he is authorized to deal with the endowed property. We have already seen in a former chapter that when the necessity exists he is authorized to deal with the corpus itself and not merely with the income[2]. He may mortgage or sell the property for such purposes according to the extent of the necessity and if he acts *bona fide*, and his act is one which a prudent manager will do, under the circumstances his discretion will not be interfered with and at any rate the creditor will not be affected. But the decision in *Nallayappa Pillian* v. *Ambalavana Pandara Sannadhi*[3] seems to throw doubt upon this view. The decision in this case no doubt correctly interprets the general feelings of the Hindu community and we wish that the Legislature will intervene to declare the law as laid down in this decision. But for the reasons already given we do not think that this case lays down the correct principle as now administered by the courts. It is unfortunate that the case of *Parsotum Gir* v. *Dat Gir*[4] was not cited before their Lordships who were a party to the decision in the Madras case[3]. If the founder had prohibited the alienation of the *corpus*, the same must be given effect to[5]. So also where property is endowed specially for some particular service or worship of the idol it cannot be utilised for other purposes such as repairs or alienated for the same[6] (though such other purposes may be necessary or beneficial for keeping up the worship &c of the idol).

Rights and position of creditor or alienee.

This leads us to the question of the creditor's position in such cases. The lender is not affected by the precedent mismanagement

1. *Prosunno Kumari Debya* v. *Golab Chand Baboo*, (1875) L. R. 2 I. A. 145 (152); *Khetter Chunder Ghose* v. *Haridas Bundopadhya*, (1890) I. L. R., 17 C. 557.

2. See Chapter VIII, pp. xcix and c and note (1) to p. c. But see *Ranee Shibeshuree Debia* v. *Moothooranath Acharjee*, (1866) 5 W. R. C. R. 202 and cases cited in notes (4) and (5), p. xcix. See also *Nallayappa Pillian* v. *Ambalavana Pandara Sannadhi*, (1903) I. L. R., 27 M. 465 (472, 473).

3. (1903) I. L. R., 27 M. 465 (472, 473).

4. (1903) I. L. R., 25 A. 296.

5. Cf. *Prosunno Moyee Dossee* v. *Koonjoo Beharee Chowdhree*, (1864) W. R. Sp. C. R., 157. But see *Kristna Mudali* v. *Shanmuga Mudaliar*, (1871) 6 M. H. C. 248.

6. *Nallayappa* v. *Ambalavana*, (1903) I. L. R., 27 M. 465 at p. 478. See also *Vythilinga Pandara* v. *Somasundara*, (1893) I. L. R., 17 M. 199 (202).

of the estate provided he acts *bona fide* and the charge is one that a prudent owner in the position of the manager will make in order to benefit the estate. The creditor has to look to the actual pressure on the estate, the danger to be averted or the benefit to be conferred upon the estate. If the danger has arisen from any misconduct to which the lender or alienee is a party he cannot take advantage of his own wrong to support a charge or alienation in his favour grounded on a necessity which has been brought about or at any rate furthered by his own wrong. But if he acts *bona fide* and fairly and if, after making proper inquiries, he is reasonably satisfied of the existence of a necessity he cannot be deprived of his rights by the fact that it is shewn that he has been deceived by the manager and that no necessity in fact exists. As observed by their Lordships in the leading case of *Hanoomanpersaud Panday* v. *Mussumat Koonweree*[1]: "The lender is bound to enquire into necessities for the loan and to satisfy himself as well as he can, with reference to the parties with whom he is dealing, that the manager is acting in the particular instance for the benefit of the estate. But if he does so enquire, and acts honestly, the real existence of an alleged sufficient and reasonably credited necessity is not a condition precedent to the validity of his charge and under such circumstances he is not bound to see to the application of the money." These observations, of course, related to the case of a manager for an infant heir, but they are equally applicable to the case on hand as the power of a manager of an endowment is, as we have already said, analogous to that of a manager for an infant heir. It may seem hard that endowed property can be incumbered even without the actual existence of a necessity. But it is equally hard upon the purchaser who has acted *bona fide* and made all proper inquiries if the rule be the other way. If there is an actual necessity, then the absence of inquiry will not defeat the lender's title[2] and is in fact immaterial. But if there is no necessity in fact, then the question of enquiry becomes material. Such is the position of persons advancing money to a Hindu widow and to a manager of a joint Hindu family for alleged necessities of the estate. The position of a person advancing money to a manager of endowed property for ostensible purposes of the trust must be similar. No doubt the

1. (1856) 6 M. I. A. 393 at p. 424.
2. *Hambro* v. *Burnand*, (1904) 2 K. B. 10 (23 and 24).

particular observations above quoted are not cited in the case of *Prosunno Kumari Debya* v. *Golab Chand Baboo*[1] which holds that the position of a shebait is similar to that of a guardian for an infant heir although some other observations made in the same case[2] are cited, but we do not think that this makes any difference and in fact those very observations are cited with approval in a later case before the Privy Council[3].

Personal liability of a manager.

Where a manager incurs a debt on behalf of the institution he is not personally liable upon the debt unless he so agrees. He must be assumed to be pledging only the credit of the institution so that he is not personally liable for the debt[4]. Even if it turns out that the debt is not binding on the institution as not being for a necessary purpose, the manager will not be personally liable[5]. The institution will not be liable if the lender fails to discharge the *onus* imposed on him by law, *i. e.*, fails to prove that he lent the loan after making due inquiries, &c. The fact that the creditor cannot hold the institution liable by reason of the invalidity of the debt will not make the manager contracting the loan for the institution personally liable[5]. If there is any misrepresentation made by the manager he will be liable to pay damages for such misrepresentation[6] but in the absence of any such special ground he will not be personally liable. In English Law it will appear that the trustee of a charitable institution contracting a loan will be personally liable[7] in the same way as an executor who contracts a loan[8] but creditors cannot proceed against the estate which a

1. (1875) L. R. 2 I. A. 145 : S. C. 14 B. L. R., 450.

2. (1856) 6 M. I. A. 393 at p. 423.

3. *Konwur Doorganath Roy* v. *Ram Chunder Sen*, (1876) L. R. 4 I. A. 52 (64) : S. C. I. L. R., 2 C. 341 (352).

4. *Shankar Bharati Svami* v. *Venkapa Naik*, (1885) I. L. R., 9 B. 422, a case of the Swami of a mutt but the same principle must apply to a manager who may no doubt have properties in his own individual right but is a different person with reference to such right. Cf. *Venkatasami* v. *Kuppayee*, (1904) 14 M. L. J. R. 377 (378).

5. *Shri Ganesh Dharnidhar Maharajdev* v. *Keshavrav Govind Kulgavkar*, (1890) I. L. R., 15 B. 625 (637). *Venkatasami* v. *Kuppayee*, supra.

6. *Krishnan* v. *Sankara Varma*, (1886) I. L. R., 9 M. 441 (444) is only explicable on the supposition that some such special ground existed.

7. *Strickland* v. *Symons*, (1884) 26 Ch. D. 245 (248).

8. *Farhall* v. *Farhall*, (1871) L. R. 7 Ch. App. 123 (126). See also Williams on Executors, Vol. II, pp. 1681 to 1687. But a promise by a person as an executor is not unknown to English Law: See ibid, Vol. II, pp. 1661 to 1666.

trustee or an executor respectively represents if such estate is not specifically charged by the trustee or executor for such debt.

Alienation of office.

A manager of a public religious endowment cannot transfer his rights to a stranger. It is a principle of law that a trustee cannot alienate his office[1]. Upon the same principle where the management is vested hereditarily in a certain person or family, such person or family will not be entitled to alienate the office. Even where a person holds the office for life he cannot transfer his rights. This does not prevent a manager from nominating his heir when such right of nomination is vested in him. The common law of India as it is said does not allow the alienation of a religious office in public religious institutions whether by way of sale, mortgage, or gift[2]. This is true of the office of a manager[3] as of all religious offices subordinate to the manager[4]. This question of inalienability must be taken as settled by the decision of the Judicial Committee in a case arising from Malabar. The right of management (uraima right) in the Tracharamana Pagoda was vested in that case in the karnavans of four tarwads. These urallers transferred their uraima right to a certain Raja (Cherakel) who brought an action for detinue against the defendants for keeping the jewels of the deity.

---

1. *Delegatus non potest delegare.* See S. 47 of the Trusts Act.

2. *Ukanda Varriyar* v. *Ramen Nambudiri,* (1863) 1 M. H. C. 262; *Ukoor Doss v. Chunder Sekhur Doss,* (1865) 3 W. R. C. R. 152; *Kiyake-Ilata Kotel Kanni* v. *Yadattil Vellayangot Achuda Pisharodi,* (1868) 3 M. H. C. 380; *Dubo Misser v. Srinibas Misser,* (187?) 5 B. L. R. 617; *Venkatrayar* v. *Srinivasa Ayyangar,* (1872) 7 M. H. C. 32 (case of Archaka. Here the question of the absolute inalienability was not decided but it was held that an alienation made with the object of altering the form of worship or in contemplation of such alteration was bad); *Narayanasami Mudali* v. *Kumarasami Gurukkal,* (1873) 7 M. H. C 267 (271); *Rajah Rajah Varma Valiya Rajah* v. *Kottayath Kiyaki Kovilagath Revi Varma Mootha Rajah,* (1873) 7 M. H. C. 210 affirmed by P. C. in *Rajah Vurmah Valia* v. *Ravi Vurmah Mutha,* (1876) L. R. 4 I. A. 76: S. C. I. L. R., 1 M 235; *Rup Narain Singh* v. *Junko Bye,* (1878) 3 C L. R. 112 (115); *Narasimma Thatha Acharya* v. *Anantha Bhatta,* (1881) I. L. R., 4 M. 391 (Archaka office); *Mancharam* v. *Pranshankar,* (1882) I. L. R., 6 B. 298 at p. 300 (priestly office of pujari apparently); *Trimbak Bawa* v. *Narayan Bawa,* (1882) I. L. R., 7 B. 188 (190); *Kuppa Gurukal* v. *Dorasami,* (1882) I. L. R., 6 M. 76 (Gurukkal or Archaka office); *Kannan* v. *Nilakandan,* (1884) I. L. R, 7 M. 337; *Khetter Chunder Ghose v. Hari Das Bundopadhya,* (1890) I. L. R., 17 C. 557 (561, 562); *Narayana* v. *Ranga,* (1891) I. L. R., 15 M. 183 (Pujari office); *Subbarayudu* v. *Kotayya,* (1892) I. L. R., 15 M. 389 (391); *Rangasami* v. *Ranga,* (1892) I. L. R., 16 M. 146 (office of Tiruvallakku Nayakam); *Alagappa Mudaliar* v. *Sivaramasundara Mudaliar,* (1895) I. L. R., 19 M. 211; *Srimati Mallika Dasi* v. *Ratanmani Chakervarti,* (1897) 1 C. W. N. 493; *Rajaram* v. *Ganesh,* (1898) I. L. R., 23 B. 131 (135); *Gnana Sambanda Pandara Sannidhi* v. *Velu Pandaram,* (1899) L. R. 27 I. A. 69: S. C. I. L. R., 23 M. 271. The case of *Kristna Mudali* v. *Shanmuga Mudaliar,* (1871) 6 M. H. C. 242 which held that an alienation subject to the performance of a charity was good must be treated as overruled. See other cases cited in note (1), p. ccxiii.

3. The cases cited in note (2) in which no mention is made of the nature of the office relate to the case of an alienation of the office of manager.

4. See the cases relating to Archaka, Gurukkal, Pujari referred to in note (2).

The Judicial Committee in holding that the transfer relied upon by the plaintiff was invalid observed[1]: "It was presumably the intention of the founder that the uraima right should be exercised by four persons representing four distinct families. The first question is whether, independently of custom, persons holding such a trust are capable of transferring it at their own will. No authority has been laid before their Lordships to establish this proposition; principle and reason seem to be strongly opposed to such a power, and particularly to such an exercise of it as has taken place in this instance. The unknown founder may be supposed to have established this species of corporation with the distinct object of securing the due performance of the worship and the due administration of the property by the instrumentality and at the discretion of four persons capable of deliberating and bound to deliberate together; he may also have considered it essential that those four persons should be the heads of particular families resident in a particular district, open to the public opinion of that district, and having that sort of family interest in the maintenance of this religious worship which would ensure its due performance. It seems very unreasonable to suppose that the founder of such a corporation ever intended to empower the four trustees of his creation at their mere will to transfer their office and its duties, with all the property of the trust, to a single individual who might act according to his sole discretion, and might have no connection with the families from which the trustees were to be taken. * * * This being the state of authorities their Lordships are of opinion * * * that the urallers had no power under what may be termed the common law of India to transfer their uraima right to the plaintiff, the Cherekel Rajah."

Transfer in execution of a decree.

The same principles must apply to the sale of an office in execution of a decree. In a sale in Court auction anybody may bid whether he be a Hindu, Christian or Mahomedan. It seems absurd to suppose that a right to such office is capable of being held by a Mahomedan or Christian. Courts have, therefore, held that such a right is not transferable in execution of a decree

1. *Rajah Vurmah Valia* v. *Ravi Vurmah Mutha*, (1876) L. R., 4 I. A 76 (81, 82, 83): S. C. I. L. R., 1 M. 235 (247, 248, 250).

against the trustee[1]. Even where a decree directs the sale of a religious office it has been held in a Madras case[2] that the manager may in execution set up the claim that a religious office cannot be sold and that therefore the decree which directs a sale of such office is illegal and cannot be executed[3]. In the Madras case the decree was based upon a compromise and as the compromise was illegal the court held following an earlier case[5] that such a compromise though merged in a decree was not enforceable. It is very doubtful whether the principle laid down in these two Madras cases can be accepted as correct. If a compromise is objected to as illegal and notwithstanding such objection, the court passes a decree in accordance with the compromise, it is an absurdity to allow the judgment-debtor to raise the question of illegality over again in execution proceedings. His remedy is only by way of appeal from the decree (or by suit where the decree is impeached for fraud) and the Code clearly allows an appeal where the legality of the compromise is in question[4]. Where no objection is raised and the court passes a decree or both parties join in getting the decree the question of illegality must be taken as overruled nd it is clearly not open to any of the parties thereto to set up the question of the illegality of the compromise in execution. Anyhow where after objection being taken and overruled, an adverse decree directing the sale of endowed property is passed it seems against all principle to hold that the party can again take the objection and defeat the execution[5]. It may be that the purchaser can acquire no rights[6], but the decree must

---

1. *Juggurnath Roy Chowdhry* v. *Kishen Pershad Surma*, (1866) 7 W. R.C.R. 266; *Dubo Misser* v. *Srinibas Misser*, (1870) 5 B. L. R., 617; *Kali Charan Gir Gosain* v. *Bangshi Mohan Das*, (1871) 6 B. L R., 727: S. C. 15 W. R. C. R. 33); *Jhummun Pandey* v. *Dinoonath Pandey*, (1871) 16 W. R. C. R. 171 (right to officiate at funeral ceremonies); *Durga Bibi* v. *Chanchal Ram*, (1881) I. L. R., 4 A. 81 (83); *Mancharam* v. *Pranshankar*, (1882) I. L. R., 6 B. 298 (300); *Trimbak Bawa* v. *Narayan Bawa*, (1882) I. L. R. 7 B. 188 (190): *Ganesh Ramchandra Date* v. *Shankar Ramchandra*, (1886) I. L. R, 10 B, 395 (398) (*Upadhikpana Vritti*); *Govind Lakshman Joshi* v. *Ramkrishna Hari Joshi*, (1887) I. L. R, 12 B. 366 (367, 368) (*Jotishi Vritti*); *Girijanund Datta Jha* v. *Sailajanund Dutta Jha*, (1896) I. L. R., 23 C. 645; *Rajaram* v. *Ganesh* (1898) I. L. R., 23 B. 131 (135). Cf. *James Fegredo* v. *Mahomed Mudessur*, (1871) 15 W. R. C. R. 75 at p. 79; and *Bishen Chand Basawat* v. *Syed Nadir Hossein*, (1887) L. R., 15 I. A 1: S. C. I. L. R., 15 C. 329 (case of wakf).

2 *Lakshmanaswami Naidu* v. *Rangamma*, (1902) I. L. R., 26 M. 31.

3. *Nagappa* v. *Venkat Rao*, (1900) I. L. R., 24 M. 265.

4. *Muthu Vijaya* v. *Thandavaraya*, (18 8) I. L. R., 22 M. 214. But see *Rakhal Moni Dassi* v. *Adwyta Prosad*, (1903) I. L. R., 30 C. 613 (615, 616). Cf. *Ponnusami* v. *Mandi Sundara*, (1903) I. L. R., 27 M. 255.

5. *Prannath Panrey* v. *Mongula Debia*, (1866) 5 W. R. C. R. 176; *Sadashiv Lalit* v. *Jayantibai*, (1883) I. L. R., 8 B. 185.

6. Whether it is open to the next heir to dispute the validity and claim the office as upon a vacancy has not been considered.

be given effect to as against the trustee[1]. Probably the hardship of the individual case might have been a factor in arriving at the actual decision in some cases. It must, however, be observed that the decided cases so far as Madras is concerned is in favor of the view that a transfer or relinquishment of a religious office by a razinama decree is void[2]. Where a partition was held and at the partition the haq right (to manage a public charity) was put up for auction and purchased by one of the members it was held that this was illegal and effect could not be given to such a transaction[3].

Custom permitting transfer of religious office.

A custom allowing an alienation for consideration is also invalid. In *Rajah Vurmah* v. *Ravi Vurmah*[4] their Lordships while holding that such custom was not proved in the particular case observed that a custom permitting the transfer for consideration of a religious office would be bad as unreasonable. "Their lordships desire to add that if the custom set up was one to sanction not merely the transfer of a trusteeship, but as in this case the sale of a trusteeship for the pecuniary advantage of the trustee, they would be disposed to hold that that circumstance alone would justify a decision that the custom was bad in law[4]". The same principles must apply to the case of a custom allowing the compulsory sale of such an office in execution of a decree. Stronger reasons may be urged against the validity of such a custom. In a court sale any person of whatever faith may be a purchaser and the purchaser may be a person not having the qualifications of the office. Even where a custom to allow a private alienation may be proved and is held valid it does not necessarily follow that a religious office may be transferable in execution of a decree. It may be that a custom permitting a voluntary relinquishment to the next heir or a person in the line of succession may be valid[5].

Transfer of office to a person in the line of heirs —Bombay view.

There is a conflict of decisions upon the question whether a transfer will be valid if the same be to a person who is next in succes-

---

1. *Prannath Panrey* v. *Sree Mongula Debia*, (1866) 5 W. R. C. R. 176.

2. See case cited in note (2), p. ccxiii. See also *Subbarayudu* v. *Kotayya*, (1892) I. L. R., 15 M. 389 (391).

3. *Alagappa Mudaliar* v. *Sivaramasundara*, (1896) I. L. R., 19 M. 211.

4. (1876) L. R. 4 I. A. 76 at p. 85 : S. C. I. L. R., 1 M. 235 at p. 252. The case of *Rangasami* v. *Ranga*, (1892) I. L. R., 16 M. 146 can scarcely be regarded as good law.

5. *Rajaram* v. *Ganesh*, (1898) I. L. R., 23 B. 131 (137).

sion or in the line of heirs. The question necessarily implies that the management is vested hereditarily in a family or person. The Bombay High Court has throughout consistently held that the transfer will be valid in such a case[1]. This is said to be consistent with the grounds upon which the transfer of a religious office is declared to be bad, *viz.*, (1) that it will be contrary to the intention of the founder if it should go outside the family and (2) that it is incompatible with the due performance of the duties involved in the office if it should be held by a person of a different religion or creed. Where succession to the office is hereditary a transfer of the office to the next heir may be taken as the least objectionable of transfers. If the actual incumbent relinquishes his rights in favor of the next heir, he may take but even there one is met with the difficulty that allowing such a relinquishment is allowing the delegation of the trustee's duties, and it is a principle of law that a trustee cannot delegate his duties to another[2]. The fact that such a relinquishment is allowed in the case of private endowments[3] does not necessarily help us in arriving at a similar principle with reference to public trusts. In the case of private endowments the persons interested can put an end to the endowment altogether as we have already seen[4]. The actual holder and his immediate successor or successors are the only persons interested in a private endowment, and an arrangement entered into with the persons so interested must be binding. Then again different principles ought to apply when the alienation is made by gift and when the alienation is made for consideration. There may be greater reason for upholding a gift of an office to the next heir which in effect is a relinquishment in favor of the next heir than for upholding an alienation for consideration. The sale of a public office is against public policy and we think the same principle must be applied to the case of religious offices connected with public trusts. Then again the same

---

1. *Sitarambhat* v. *Sitaram Ganesh*, (1869) 6 B. H. C. A. C. J. 250 (253); *Mancharam* v. *Pranshankar*, (1882) I. L. R., 6 B. 298 (300, 301); *Rajaram* v. *Ganesh*, (1898) I. L. R., 23 B. 131 (135).

2. *Rajah Varmah* v. *Ravi Varmah*, (1876) L. R. 4 I. A. 76: S. C. I. L. R., 1 M. 235.

3. *Goluck Chunder Bose* v. *Rughoonath Sree Chunder Roy*, (1872) 11 B. L. R. 337 (note): S. C. 17 W. R. C. R. 414.

4. See Chapter VII, pp. lxxxiii to lxxxv.

considerations which may apply to gifts in favor of the next heir will not apply to gifts in favor of a person who though a member of the family is not the next or immediate heir. In the latter case the gift in effect contravenes the intentions of the founder. If the office is hereditary, the founder whose right it is to make rules has prescribed a course of succession, and it is contravening the course of succession pointed out by the founder if we uphold a gift to a member of the family who may be remotely connected as a Samanodaka or a Bandhu.

Madras view.

In Madras it has been as consistently held that a transfer of a religious office will, under no circumstance, be valid. In *Kuppa Gurukal* v. *Dorasami*[1], the High Court while affirming the general principle that an alienation of a religious office would be illegal left open the question whether an alienation to a person standing in the line of heirs could be upheld. The High Court held that an alienation to a person not in the line of heirs though otherwise qualified for the performance of the office would constitute no exception to the general rule and would, therefore, be illegal. In *Narayana* v. *Ranga*[2] the sale was of the religious office of Pujari to a person who was only in the line of descent but who was not the sole immediate heir and the High Court held dissenting from the Bombay view[3] that such a sale was invalid. In *Alagappa* v. *Sivaramasundara*[4] the *Haq* right of a public charity was agreed to be sold to the highest bidder among the members of a family at a partition taking place among them. At such sale, it was purchased by one of the members for a considerable sum which was of course to be divided among the members. The High Court held that such a transaction amounted to an out and out alienation by which the other members and their line were entirely divested altogether from their management and that the same was, therefore, illegal.

The ground of decision in the Madras cases seems to be that the succession to a religious office is governed in the first instance by the will of the founder and if that cannot be ascertained by

1. (1882) I. L. R., 6 M. 76.
2. (1891) I. L. R., 15 M. 183.
3. *Mancharam* v. *Pranshankar*, (1882), I. L. R , 6 B. 298.
4. (1895), I. L. R., 19 M. 211.

usage of the particular institution from which the founder's will is to be inferred. Where the management of an institution is vested in a particular person hereditarily it will be defeating this rule of succession if the actual incumbent be allowed to transfer his right to the office to a stranger, and even if he be in the line of succession, the rule of succession is defeated if the transferee is not the next heir. Where, however, the transfer is to the next heir no rule of succession prescribed by the founder or obtaining by usage of the institution is defeated but as already said it may contravene the settled principle of law that a trustee must not be allowed to delegate his duties or office. But so far as we are able to discover there is no case in Madras which deals with this question[1].

Joint right of management—alienation.

Where the management is vested in a family a similar reasoning has been adopted. The founder's intention must be taken to be that the office should be held among all the members of the family in common. If one member renounces or waives his right in the matter that is going against the founder's intention and therefore such a renunciation must not be upheld. The founder's intention must not be contravened by any voluntary act of party. Of course it is a different thing where a right to the office is lost by the operation of the law of limitation. Upon this point their Lordships Justice *Sir T. Muthuswamy Iyer* and Mr. Justice *Shephard* observed[2]: "It is true that there is an apparent inconsistency in holding that by operation of law an alienation may be effected which cannot be effected by act of the party. The explanation lies in the fact that the law of limitation is a law of general and positive character, and no exemption from it is allowed in the case of charitable or religious offices."

Just as a manager cannot alienate his office he cannot alter the line of succession pointed out by the founder. If he has the right of nominating his successor, he cannot give up this right to any other person and such latter person cannot, by any arrangement made with the actual incumbent or other person having the right to nominate, acquire the right of nomination[3].

---

1. *Ramanathan Chetty* v. *Murugappa Chetty*, (1903) I. L. R., 27 M. 192 (199).
2. *Alagappa Mudaliar* v. *Sivaramasundara Mudaliar*, (1896) I. L. R, 19 M. 211 at p. 214.
3. *Mohunt Rumun Dass* v. *Mohunt Ashbul Dass*, (1864) 1 W. R. C. R. 160; *Rup Narain Singh* v. *Junko Bye*, (1878) 3 C.L R. 112 (115); *Mahanth Ramji Dass* v *Lachhu Dass*, (1902) 7 C. W. N. 145 (148, 149). See also per *Peacock*, C. J., in *Greedharee Doss* v. *Nundkishore Dutt*, (1863) 1 Marsh 573 (584) affirmed in 11 M. I. A. 405 (428, 429, 430).

Appointment of agent—No shifting of manager's responsibility

Although an alienation out and out is invalid and the manager must not delegate his duties, there may be no objection to a transaction which only amounts to the creation of agency. A manager may appoint an agent to look after the secular affairs of the endowment. Here the principal is the primary person that is responsible and does not by appointing an agent renounce his liability[1]. This can only apply to cases where the duties may be discharged by an agent. Where personal qualification is required and the discharge of a duty by an agent is incompatible with the nature of the office[2], then it may be that the duties attached to such an office must be performed by the office-holder and not by a deputy. It may be said that ordinarily the manager or dharmakarta of a temple may appoint an agent to look after the management of the endowed properties and other temporal concerns of the institution[3]. In Malabar it is usual for the Urallens to appoint an agent. The Karaima Samudayam is only an agent accountable to the Urallers and subject to be dismissed by the latter for misconduct[4]. The agent or Samudayam may be a creditor of the institution[5].

Divisibility of right to office.

Where the right of management of a public religious endowment is vested in a family consisting of several members, the question remains as to the mode of exercising this right. The answer depends more or less upon the mode of succession. If the usage of the institution is for the office to devolve on the most senior member of the family then the office must be held by such senior member[6]. Even where the usage is for the office to devolve by succession in the eldest line, then the succession is by

---

1. The principle is that a trustee must not shift his duty to other persons. *Krishnamacharlu* v. *Rangacharlu*, (1892) I. L. R., 16 M 73 (74, 75). See also *Turner* v. *Corney*, (1841) 5 Beav. 517. S. C. 59 R. R. 564 (565). *In re Speight-Speight* v. *Gaunt*, (1883) 22 Ch. D. 727 where it was held that a trustee using due diligence in the selection of an agent in cases where he must necessarily employ an agent or where he should employ one in the ordinary course of business will not be liable. See also *Speight* v. *Gaunt*, (1883) L. R. 9 A. C. 1 (5). See Evans on Agency, pp. 49, 50. See also S. 47 of the Trusts Act.

2. The office of head of a mutt is such an office so far as it relates to the *spiritualities*. The temporal concerns may be looked after by an agent.

3. *Narayanasami Mudali* v. *Kumarasami Gurukkal*, (1873) 7 M. H. C. 267 (271); *Krishnamacharlu* v. *Rangacharlu*, (1892) I. L. R., 16 M. 73.

4. *Kunjunneri Nambiar* v. *Nilakunden*, (1880) I. L. R., 2 M. 167. See also *Krishnan* v. *Veloo*, (1891) I. L. R., 14 M. 301; *Raman* v. *Shathanathan*, (1890) I. L. R., 14 M. 312.

5. *Krishnan* v. *Veloo*, supra.

6. *Sreenath Bose* v. *Radha Nath*, (1883) 12 C. L. R. 370; *Srimati Kamini Debi* v. *Asutosh Mookerjee*, (1888) L. R. 15 I. A. 159 (166): S. C. I. L. R., 16 C. 103 (116). See also *Damodardas* v. *Uttamram*, (1892) I. L R, 17 B. 271 (278). Cf. *Timmappa Heggade* v. *Mahalinga Heggade*, (1868) 4 M. H. C. 28 (office of Pattam or dignity).

primogeniture and only a single member will be entitled to hold the office[1]. But if the succession should devolve as under the ordinary Hindu Law, then all are entitled to the rights of management[2]. This right is indivisible and impartible[3]. The hitherto accepted opinion has been that the right as joint hereditary manager of a public temple cannot be partitioned and that all the members must manage jointly and not by turns or rotations[4]. One of several joint managers will not be entitled to hold endowed property exclusively[5], and it is said that when members are allowed to enjoy the right only by rotations there is in effect an exclusion within the meaning of this rule. But the principle of disallowing management by turns need not rest upon the above ground. When persons agree to hold an office by turns, there may be no question of any hostile exclusion. Trustees are entitled to manage jointly and any person excluding him from management will be answerable to the trustee excluded[6]. But the principle upon which the impartibility of the office rests is that the founder has prescribed a rule that all should manage jointly or at the same time[7]. The Hindu Law and usage regards such offices as indivisible, but in a recent case before the Madras High Court a different view seems to have been taken.

It cannot be said that the recent case in Madras[8] decides anything absolutely inconsistent with this view although some

---

1. *Manally Chenna Kesavaraya* v. *Mangadu Vaidelinga*, (1877) I. L. R., 1 M. 343 (346). Cf. *Purappavanalingam Chetti* v. *Nullasivan Chetti*, (1863) 1 M. H. C. 415.

2. *Juggodumba Dossee* v. *Puddomoney Dossee*, (1875) 15 B. L. R., 318 (324, 330); *Rajah Varmah* v. *Ravi Varmah*, (1876) L. R. 4 I. A. 76 (81) : S. C. I. L. R., 1 M. 235 (247); *Alagappa* v. *Sivaramasundara*, (1896) I. L. R., 19 M. 211 (214). Cf. *Purappavanalingam Chetti* v. *Nullasivan Chetti*, (1863) 1 M. H. C. 415. All must be consulted. See *Ukanda Varriyar* v. *Ramen Nambudiri*, (1863) 1 M. H. C. 262. See other cases cited at pp. cclv, cclvi.

3. *Vinayak* v. *Gopal*, (1903) L. R. 30 I. A. 77 (80) ; S S. C. I. L. R., 27 B. 353 (356).

4. *Purappavanalingam Chetti* v. *Nullasivan Chetti*, (1863) 1 M. H. C. 415; *Trimbak* v. *Lakshman*, (1895) I L.R., 20 B. 495 (501); *Sri Raman Lalji Maharaj* v. *Sri Gopal Lalji Maharaj*, (1897) I. L. R. 19 A. 428. The case of *Mancharam* v. *Pranshankar*, (1882) I. L.R., 6 B. 298 was distinguished as relating to a case of private endowment. Even in the case of private endowments where there is an absolute dedication and there is no beneficial interest in the surplus income joint management has been ordered and management by turns refused. *Juggodumba Dossee* v. *Puddomoney Dossee*, (1875) 15 B. L. R., 318 (324, 330).

5. *Tricumdass Mulji* v. *Khimji Vallabhdass*, (1892) I. L. R. 16 B. 626.

6. *Athavulla* v. *Gouse*, (1888) I. L. R., 11 M 283 ; *Tricumdass Mulji* v. *Kimji Vallabhdass*, (1892) I. L. R., 16 B. 626.

7. *Sri Raman Lalji Maharaj* v. *Sri Gopal Lalji Mahara*, (1897) I. L. R., 19 A. 428.

8. *Ramanadhan Chetty* v. *Murugappa Chetty*, (1903) I. L. R., 27 M. 192.

of the observations may not be easily reconcileable with it. In the first place, no partition was asked in that case. The suit was for the enforcement of the plaintiffs' turn of management. The learned judges only discussed the nature and validity of an arrangement entered into by the managers that each one of them should manage in rotation. The court proceeded upon the basis that an arrangement was made and considered a question raised whether such an arrangement could be put an end to at any time. We shall consider the latter question hereafter. But so far as the learned judges in this case say that such an arrangement has to be supported by reason of the existence of a general usage that the duties relating to such offices are generally discharged by rotation, we must with all deference to the learned judges who decided it say that the statement is absolutely unwarranted. There was no such usage asserted or proved in the case. Nor is there any such general usage in the country as can be taken judicial notice of by the Courts. In fact, the contrary has been asserted in the decisions[1]. No doubt in *Mancharam* v. *Pranshankar*, *Melville*, J. observed[2]: "No doubt, hereditary offices, whether religious or secular, are treated by the Hindu text-writers as naturally indivisible, but modern custom, whether or not it be strictly in accordance with ancient law, has sanctioned such partition as can be had of such property, by means of a performance of the duties of the office and the enjoyment of the emoluments, by the different co-parceners in rotation." In the *first* place these observations are only applicable to the case of an office to which emoluments are attached. In such cases it may be that enjoyment by turns of the emoluments is the only possible or at any rate convenient mode. In the *second* place these observations have been, in a later case before the same Court, held applicable only to the case of a private endowment. In this later case[3] which by the way is neither referred to nor cited in the Madras case[4] the Bombay High Court consisting of *Candy* and

1. *Trimbak* v. *Lakshman*, (1895) I. L. R., 20 B. 495 (501). See *Sri Raman Lalji Maharaj* v. *Sri Gopal Lalji Maharaj*, (1897) I. L. R., 19 A. 428.

2. (1882) I. L R., 6 B. 298.

3. *Trimbak* v. *Lakshman*, (1895) I. L. R, 20 B. 49. See also *Sri Raman Lalji Maharaj* v. *Sri Gopal Lalji Maharaj*, (1897) I. L. R., 19 A. 428. Cf. *Rajaram* v. *Ganesh* (1898) I. L. R., 23 B. 131 (136, 137).

4. *Ramanathan Chetty* v. *Murugappa Chetty*, (1903) I. L. R., 27 M. 192.

Ranade, JJ., observed[1]: "*Melville*, J., in deciding *Mancharam* v. *Pranshankar*[2] held that these offices were in general inalienable, and that according to the Hindu text-writers, religious offices are naturally indivisible, though modern custom has sanctioned a departure in respect of allowing the parties entitled to share to officiate by turns, and of allowing alienation within certain restrictions. The rulings in *Ram Coomar Paul* v. *Jogender Nath Paul*[3] and *Radha Mohun Mundul* v. *Jadoomonee Dossee*[4] and the remarks made by Mr. Mayne in paragraphs 307 and 308[5] must be understood in regard to *this growth of customary law* regulating *private* endowments. In the present case, however, the endowment is a public endowment." These remarks are no doubt, mere *obiter dicta*, but they are of great weight when the question is as to the existence of any such general usage.

Even as regards private endowments we cannot say that there is a well established custom that offices relating to these endowments are enjoyed by turns. Where the shebaits of an idol are entitled to a beneficial interest in the surplus income it may be admitted that there is a custom to enjoy the office with emoluments by turns. But as regards absolute dedications in which the shebait has no beneficial interest of any sort it cannot be said that there is an unbroken current of authority establishing a custom. In *Juggodumba Dossee* v. *Puddomoney Dossee*[6] the Calcutta High Court expressly held that in the case of an absolute dedication the office of shebait was not enjoyable by turns and that *no pallas* ought to be directed. The court directed that the joint shebaits should manage jointly and that the difficulty of a joint management should not deter the court from passing such a decree[7]. No doubt it must be admitted that there are several other cases

Discussion as to the existence of custom stated in the Madras case.

---

1. (1895) I. L. R., 20 B. 495 at 501.
2. (1882) I. L. R., 6 B. 298.
3. (1878) I. L. R., 4 C. 56.
4. (1875) 23 W. R. (P. C.) 369.
5. These must be paras. 397 and 398 of the 5th Edition. The last para corresponds to para 439 of the present Edition.
6. (1875) 15 B. L. R. 318.
7. See also *Purappavanalingam Chetti* v. *Nullasivan Chetti*, (1868) 1 M. H. C. 415 where *Holloway*, J., quoted the answer given by Lord *Brougham* to such a contention (i. e., "The Court will try"). See *Docker* v. *Somes*, (1834) My. & K. 655 (674): S. C. 39 R. R. 317 (324).

in which *pallas* have been directed, but as will be shown later on many of them are cases in which the shebaits had a beneficial interest in the surplus. In the case of *Anund Moyee Chowdhrain* v. *Boykantnath Roy*[1] there would seem to be not even a private endowment. The Court only said that places of worship and sacrifice were not divisible but that the parties unless they agreed to a *joint* worship might enjoy their turn of worship. There was no question about the office of shebait, and no general principle could be evolved out of the decision[2]. In *Ram Soondur Thakoor* v. *Taruck Chunder Turkoruttun*[3] the only question was with reference to the removal of an idol. It does not appear whether there was any endowment, or if there was any whether the dedication was absolute or conveyed a beneficial interest in the members. In *Ram Coomar Paul* v. *Jogender Nath Paul*[4] which was also a case of a private idol all that was stated was that there was no dedication or if there was any dedication only one subject to the trusts of idol and that in such a case a partition of the property might be made. No doubt the case of *Nobokissen Mitter* v. *Hurrischunder Mitter*[5] would seem to be one of absolute dedication and it was directed that the management should be by turns. But this was not the decision of the Court and the report expressly stated that the Court had doubts as to the correctness of the decision but that as the parties had acquiesced in it, the matter was dropped. It may be that the learned judges when stating the existence of such a custom in the Madras case had in mind the usage obtaining in some of the great temples in Southern India such as Chidambaram. But in Chidambaram the Dikshatars are both Archakas and Dharmakartas and *emoluments* are attached to their office as Archakas[6]. This is consistent with the statement by Mr. Strange that the

1. (1867) 8 W. R. C. R. 193.

2. The court could apparently have directed a partition of such places according to the later cases. See *Rajcoomaree Dassee* v. *Gopal Chunder*, (1878) I. L. R., 3 C. 514 and case cited in note (4).

3. (1872) 19 W. R. C. R. 28.

4. (1878) I. L R., 4 C. 56.

5. (1818) 2 Mor. Dig. 146.

6. *Natesa* v *Ganapati*, (1890) I. L. R., 14 M. 103. The same is the case with the famous Krishna temple at Udipi. See pp. clvi, clvii. In *Narayana* v. *Ranga*, (1891) I. L. R., 15 M.183, the question was as to the office of *pujari* to which emoluments were attached. The plaintiff alleged that the office was enjoyable by turns. This fact appears from the report of the same case in the Madras Law Journal, 2 M. L. J.R. 19 (20).

offices of Thirtham, &c., are enjoyable by turns and that the hereditary privileges of the family with the income arising from them are divisible like other patrimony[1]. But be this as it may, there is no single case[2] prior to the recent decision in Madras holding that there is any such custom with reference to a public endowment.

Amicable arrangement among managers—Enjoyment by turns.

An arrangement by the managers that they should manage by turns may be valid or may not be valid according to the circumstances. If by such an arrangement the right of the others to interfere even if they should think the management to be improper is curtailed such an arrangement must be taken as void as being against the rules laid down by the founder and as being against the interests of the institution. If by reason of such arrangement the person enjoying the turn is given an exclusive right to manage and deal with and incumber the endowed property it may be for the necessary purposes of the institution without any let or hindrance by the others and without any necessity to consult the others then also we think such an arrangement is equally void. This seems also to have been the view taken in the case of *Ramanathan Chetty* v. *Murugappa Chetty*[3]. It was there said[4]: "In fact, as a general rule, even during the turn of each co-trustee, all the co-trustees are entitled, and, in fact, are bound to *act jointly* in matters other than the ordinary routine duties." That is why it is said later on in the same case that "an arrangement by which the several co-trustees are to discharge their duties in rotation, each for a certain period, is not even during the period of management by each in rotation, a management and possession of the trust property (by such co-trustee) to the exclusion of and adversely to the other co-trustees[5]." It is impossible to give

1. 2 Strange, p. 302. A later passage at page 303 (*viz.*, "At most of the religious establishment of the Hindus and at their great temples the various offices attached to them are considered as hereditary together with the perquisites belonging to them") does not support the view that the offices are enjoyable by turns.

2. The statement by Mr. Mayne of the existence of a customary law has been judicially declared to relate if at all only to the case of a private endowment. See *Trimbak* v. *Lakshman*, (1895) I. L. R., 20 B. 495 (501).

3. (1903) I. L. R., 27 M. 192. See also *Alagappa Mudaliar* v. *Sivaramasundara Mudaliar*, (1895) I. L. R., 19 M. 211 at p 214 (511).

4. Ibid at p. 197.

5. *Ramanathan Chetty* v. *Murugappa Chetty*, (1903) I. L. R., 27 M 192 at p. 201.

greater effect to such an arrangement. It is said that this arrangement must be strictly adhered to upon the ground that it is in accordance with the usage which we have shewn does not exist and that such usage cannot be put an end to which has, according to their Lordships in the Madras case, a juristic basis (the juristic basis being the right of trustees to settle a scheme which must be adhered to unless it is prejudicial to the institution). We know that a founder has authority to settle a scheme for the administration of the trust he creates. We also know that, in the absence of such a direction by the founder, Courts have authority to frame a scheme. It is the first time that we find a case which recognises that such a power is exerciseable by the co-trustees[1]. The administration of the trust is one thing. If the trustee makes due provision for the carrying on of the trust he in effect frames a scheme but surely this does not mean that he is not at liberty afterwards to make provision for the carrying on of the trust in other ways. The settlement of the rights of co-trustees with reference to their management is quite a different thing. If it be proved that the management has been by turns for a long time, an usage may be established from which we may infer that the founder has so directed. We should rather think that in all such cases (in the absence of any rule by the founder) the arrangement has its origin more in purposes of convenience than in anything else. Such arrangements for convenience have been held by the Courts to be capable of being put an end to by the parties themselves and as not binding on the successor in more cases than one[2]. When one person withdraws from such an arrangement, we think the same is in furtherance of the interests of the institution as, according to the founder, in the absence of any direction joint trustees must manage jointly at the same time. If the arrangement be treated as creating a sort of agency in one of the co-trustees for a time,

1. The statement in Perry on Trusts, para 417, that trustees may apportion their duties may be unobjectionable, but his statement that when such duties are apportioned the others are not answerable for the defaults of one seems hardly to be correct or at any rate must be taken with great qualifications.

2. *Bunwaree Chand Thakoor* v. *Mudden Mohun Chuttaraj*, (1873) 21 W. R. C. R. 41; *Sivasankara* v. *Vadagiri*, (1889) I. L. R., 13 M. 6 (7); *Alagappa Mudaliar* v. *Sivaramasundara Mudaliar*, (1895) I. L. R., 19 M. 211 at p. 214. But see *Dado Ravji* v. *Dinanath Ravji*, (1865) 2 B. H. C. A. C. J. 72; and *Ramanathan Chetty* v. *Murugappa Chetty*, (1903) I. L. R., 27 M. 192 (201, 202).

such agency may be clearly revoked by all the co-trustees[1]. Whether it is open to one to revoke is a more difficult question. Even there we do not see why effect should not be given to such a revocation so far as the person revoking is concerned[2]. Surely effect must be given to it when it is shewn that the interests of the trusts are not otherwise prejudiced.

Private religious endowments.

As regards private religious endowments the position of the shebait is similar. Where the dedication is absolute, endowed property cannot be partitioned[3] or otherwise alienated[4]. The office of shebait cannot be alienated by private sale or in execution of a decree[5]. No stranger can intrude into the management[6]. The essence of a family endowment is that the members of the family alone are entitled to worship and to manage the affairs of the endowment[6] Where *palla* is directed such a right (*i. e.*, the right of management by turns) cannot also be alienated by private sale or in execution of a decree[7]. It may seem from the language of some early cases that the shebait may retain the surplus after providing for the services &c., of the idol even in cases of absolute dedication[8] although the right to such surplus

---

1. *Narayanasami Mudali* v. *Kumarasami Gurukkal*, (1873) 7 M. H. C. 267 (270).

2. See Evans on Agency p. 33. See also Bowstead on Agency Art. 142 p. 433.

3. *Mussumat Joymunee Debia* v. *Fakeer Chunder Chukurbutty*, (1829) 4 B S. D. A. 337; *Juggut Mohini Dossee* v. *Mussumat Sokheemoney Dossee*, (1871) 14 M. I. A. 289 (299); *Rughoonath Panjah* v. *Luckhun Chunder*, (1872) 18 W. R. C. R, 23 (24); *Kowwur Dooryanath Roy* v. *Ram Chunder Sen*, (1876) L. R. 4 I. A. 52 (62): S. C. I. L. R., 2 C. 341 (350); *Ram Coomar Paul* v. *Jogender Nath Paul*, (1878) I. L. R., 4. C. 56 (58); *Rajender Dutt* v. *Sham Chund Mitter*, (1880) I. L. R, 6 C. 106 (118). But see *Radha Mohun Mundul* v. *Jadoomonee Dossee*, (1875) 23 W. R. 369 (P. C.) For other cases see note (3) p. li.

4. *Bhowanee Purshad* v. *Ranee Jugudumbha*, (1829) 4 B. S. D. A. 343; *Ram Sundar Ray* v. *Heirs of Raja Udwant Singh*, (1832) 5 B. S.D.A. 210; *Ranee Shibeshuree Debia* v. *Mothooranath Acharjee*, (1866) 5 W. R. C. R. 202; *Maharanee Shibessouree Debia* v. *Mothooranath Acharjo*, (1869) 13 M. I. A. 270; *Dubo Missor* v. *Srinibas Misser*, (1870) 5 B.L.R. 617; *Busoo Dhul* v. *Kishen Chunder*, (1876) 13 W. R. C. R. 200; *Kali Charan* v. *Mohan Das*, (1871) 6 B. L. R. 727; *The Collector of Moorshedabad* v. *Ranee Shibessuree*, (1872) 11 B. L. R. 86 (112); *Goluck Chunder Bose* v. *Raghoonath Sree Chunder Roy*, (1872) 11 B. L. R. 337 (note): S. C. 17 W. R. C. R. 444; *Prosunno Kumari Debya* v. *Golab Chand Baboo*, (1875) L. R. 2 I. A. 145 (151): S. C. 14 B. L. R. 450. For other cases see note (2) p. li.

5. *Ranee Shibeshuree* v. *Moothooranath*, (1866) 5. W. R. C. R. 202; *Juggurnath Roy Chowdhry* v. *Kishen Pershad Surmah*, (1867) 7 W. R.C.R. 266; *Dubo Misser* v. *Srinibas Misser*, supra *Kali Charan Gir Gossain* v. *Bangshi Mohan Das*, (1871) 6 B. L. R. 727: S. C. 15 W. R. C. R. 339.

6. *Ukoor Doss* v. *Chunder Sekhur Doss*, (1865) 3 W. R. C. R. 152.

7. *Kalee Churn Gir Gossain* v. *Bungshee Mohun Doss*, supra.

8. *Kowwur Doorganath Roy* v. *Ram Chunder Sen*, (1876) L. R. 4 I.A. 52 (62): S C. I. L. R., 2 C. 341 (350).

being vague and uncertain may not be attacheable[1]. But this opinion cannot be maintained at the present day as regards such absolute dedications. Where a beneficial interest is created in the surplus the same may be alienable and attacheable[2]. The stranger can acquire no rights in the former class of dedications while he may acquire rights in the surplus in the latter class[3]. Even in the former class if a decree directs the sale of an office[4] or partition of property[5] such decree must be given effect to as between the parties. In the case of absolute dedications in which, as we have already said, no alienation is allowed, the incapacity on the part of the shebait to alienate (as in the similar case of public endowments) cannot be said to be absolute[6] but only relative. The shebait has, therefore, power to alienate endowed property for the necessary purposes of the endowment[7]. Even as regards the alienation of a religious office it has been held by the Calcutta High Court that an alienation by way of gift by the actual shebait of his right to the office together with the idol and the emoluments appertaining thereto to a member of the family will be valid provided it be for the benefit of the idol[8]. But in this case the gift of the idol together with its endowments was made with the concurrence of the whole family so that the ruling came within the principle stated in an earlier chapter[9] that in the case of private endowments the consensus of the whole family might give any turn to the endowment[10]. Where the father relinquishes his right to his son, such a relinquishment may be valid as the succession being here-

---

1. *Juggurnath Roy* v. *Kishen Pershad Surmah*, (1867) 7 W. R. C. R. 266.

2. *Soshikishore Bundopadhya* v. *Ranee Chooramoney Putto Mohadubee*, (1861) W. R. Sp. C. R. 107. See Chapter IV p. lii.

3. The case of *Rughoonath Panjah* v. *Luckhun Chunder Dullal Chowdhry*, (1872) 18 W. R. C. R. 23 cannot be taken as laying down anything inconsistent with this view.

4. *Prannath Panrey* v. *Sree Mongula Debia*, (1866) 5 W. R. C. R. 176.

5. Per *White, J.* in *Rajcoomaree Dassee* v. *Gopal Chunder Bose*, (1878) I. L. R., 3 C. 514. Conversely a decree that property should be joint must be given effect to. *Rughoonath Panjah* v. *Luckhun Chunder*, (1872) 18 W. R. C. R. 23.

6. *Maharanee Shibessouree Debia* v. *Mothooranath Acharjo*, (1869) 13 M. I. A. 270.

7. *Prosunno Kumari Debya* v. *Golab Chand Baboo*, (1875) L. R. 2 I. A. 145 (151, 152); *Konwur Doorganath Roy* v. *Ram Chunder Sen*, (1876) L.R. 4 I.A. 52 (56, 63, 64).

8. *Khetter Chunder Ghose* v. *Hari Das Bundopadhya*, (1890) I. L. R., 17 C. 557.

9. Chapter VII, pp. lxxxiv, lxxxv.

10. *Konwur Doorganath Roy* v. *Ram Chunder Sen*, (1876) L. R. 4 I. A. 52 (58). See also *Radhabai* v. *Anantrao*, (1885) I. L. R., 9 B. 195 (212) and West and Buhler H. L. 185 note (*b*) and 785.

ditary, the son is the only person affected or interested in this matter and he is a consenting party to the transaction[1].

Private endowments—joint shebaits—turns.

Where there are more shebaits than one, a question arises whether all are entitled to a joint management or whether the management can be made by turns. Religious offices are as a general rule indivisible, but it is said that modern custom has permitted the enjoyment of the office by rotations[2]. Mr. Mayne in para 439 of his book on Hindu Law[3] after stating that endowed property and its management are not divisible among the members of the family, states that where no other arrangement or usage exists, the management may be held in turns by the several heirs. No reference being made to custom, this can only be by agreement of the parties and the arrangement that he refers to previously must be the arrangement, if any, of the founder. No distinction is made by him in thus stating the law between absolute dedications and dedications in which a beneficial interest is also created in the surplus. Of the cases cited by him (and they all relate to private endowments) that of *Nubokissen* v. *Hurrischunder*[4] is the only case of an absolute dedication. The decision was based upon the Pundit's opinion, but as already mentioned it would appear from page 148 of the report that the Court expressed doubts as to the correctness of the Pundit's opinion. This case can hardly be taken as a decision binding in subsequent cases. In the cases of *Anund Moyee* v. *Boykantnath Roy*[5], as observed elsewhere[6], there was no question of endowment at all. The same is the case with *Ram Soondur Thakoor* v. *Taruck Chunder Turkoruttun*[7]. The question there was for removal of the idol for purposes of worship which implied that the idol was property at the disposal of the members. As against these, there is the case of *Juggodumba*

---

1. *Goluck Chunder Bose* v. *Raghoonath Sree Chunder Roy*, (1872) 11 B. L. R. 337 (note): S. C. 17 W. R. C. R. 444.

2. *Mancharam* v. *Pranshankar*, (1882) I. L. R., 6 B. 298; *Trimbak* v. *Lakshman* (1895) I. L. R., 20 B. 495 (501); *Sri Raman Lalji Maharaj* v. *Sri Gopal Lalji Maharaj* (1897) I. L. R., 19 A. 428. See Mayne Paras 397 and 398 of the 5th Edn.

3. 6th Edn., p. 568.

4. (1818) 2 Mor. Dig. p. 146.

5. (1867) 8 W. R. C. R. 193.

6. Pp. ccxxi, ccxxii.

7. (1872) 19 W. R. C. R. 28.

Dossee v. *Puddomoney Dossee*[1], in which it has been expressly decided that no pallas can be directed in cases of absolute dedications and that there must be joint management.

There are some cases[2] in the Weekly Reporter not referred to by Mr. Mayne, in which it has been held or assumed that the members of a family being joint shebaits are entitled to their turn of worship and manage the affairs of the endowment in turns. These are, in many instances, cases in which the shebaits have a beneficial interest in the surplus. In such cases the shebaits are either entitled to divide the property itself where there is only a charge in favor of the idol[3] or to divide the income by their shares[4] and manage by turns where the surplus is directed to be given to the shebaits. Then again, as already pointed out, there are instances in which there is no dedication but the property being indivisible by Hindu law, its enjoyment by turns has been directed[5]. A right to worship an idol which is regarded as property of the members may be enjoyed by turns. If all do not agree to a joint worship *pallas* may be directed. Such a right of worship (or palla) may not be sold in execution of a decree[6]. A person whose right to a turn of worship may be obstructed may have

---

1. (1875) 15 B L.R. 318 (324, 330). See also *Juggut Mohini Dossee* v. *Mussumat Sokheemoney Dossee*, (1871) 14 M. I. A. 289 (299) where it was held that shebaits were not entitled to possession of a fractional share. A decree that the idol and lands should be joint must of course be binding. See *Rugoonath Panjah* v. *Luckhun Chunder Dullal Chowdhry*, (1872) 18 W. R. C. R. 23 (24).

2. *Ukoor Doss* v. *Chunder Sekhur Doss*, (1865) 3 W. R. C. R. 152; *Dwarkanath Roy* v. *Jannobee Chowdhrain*, (1865) 4 W. R. C. R. 79 (80). The case of *Mitta Kunth Audhicarry* v. *Neerunjun Audhicarry*, (1874) 14 B. L. R. 166 (16.), relates to the office of priest. It does not appear whether the idol was a private or public one.

3 *Ram Coomar Paul* v. *Jogender Nath Paul*, (1878) I. L. R., 4 C. 56.

4. But see *Gunga Gobind Singh* v. *Joy Gopal Panda*, (1868) 10 W. R. C. R. 105 where it is said that a co-shebait suing for a declaration may be given a decree that he is entitled to a fourth share of the debutter land; and *Radha Mohun Mundul* v. *Jadoomonee Dossee*, (1875) 23 W. R. P. C. 369, (373) where the P. C. held that plaintiff as shebait was entitled to a fifth share in certain Government pronotes and to keep in her possession such share after giving security and to hold the same subject to trusts. But see *Bunwaree Chund Thakoor* v. *Muddun Mohen Chuttoraj*, (1873) 21 W. R. C. R. 41, (42) where a decree for joint possession was given, and *Juggut Mohini Dossee* v. *Mussumat Sokheemoney Dossee*, (1871) 14 M. I. A 289.

5. *Anund Moyee* v. *Boykuntnath Roy*, (1867) 8 W. R. C. R 193 (194). See also *Ram Soondur Thakoor* v. *Taruck Chunder Turkorutun*, (1872) 19 W. R. C. R. 28.

6. *Dubo Misser* v. *Srinibas Misser*, (1870) 5 B. L.R. 617; *Kali Charan Gir Gossain* v. *Bangshi Mohan Das*, (1871) 6 B. L. R. 727 ; S. C. 15 W. R. C. R. 339.

a cause of action to sue in the civil courts for such obstruction[1]. Such a right is property[2] which, if interfered with, will entitle the party to seek redress in a court of law. There is a conflict of decisions upon the question whether such right is a recurring one[3].

Nature of right to turn.

Where the shebaits are also priests doing services to the idol[4], such a right to do service as distinct from the right to management may and must necessarily be performed in turns[5], and that seems to be the real foundation of the several cases in which *pallas* have been directed. It appears that in the case of private or family idols which have no local habitation such as a temple, such idols may be removed to the house person entitled to the turn[6]. But if there is a temple and the idol is placed and consecrated there, it does not seem how the turn owner will be entitled to remove the idol to his house In cases of absolute dedication where the management takes place by turns by agreement of parties, such agreement may be given effect to upon the ground peculiar to private endowments that the consensus of the family may give any turn to such an endowment. Such an agreement is enforceable and may not be put an end to unless with the consent of all parties. If one person is obstructed in his right, he may and must sue as sole plaintiff to prevent such obstruction[7]. If third parties obstruct they may also be sued. But if an usurper takes possession of the endowed property, the question may arise whether all the shebaits ought to sue or only the turn owner. *Prima facie*, all may have to sue. In the case of suits against

---

1. *Dwarkanath Roy* v. *Jannobee Chowdhrain*, (1865) 4 W. R C. R 79 (80); *Ramessur Mookerjee* v *Ishan Chunder*, (1868) 10 W. R. C. R. 457 (458); *Debendronath Mullick* v. *Odit Churn Mullick*, (1878) I. L. R., 3 C. 390.

2. *Mitta Kunth Audhicarry* v. *Neerunjun Audhicarry*, (1874) 14 B L. R. 166 (169): S. C. 22 W. R. C R. 437 (438).

3. In *Gaur Mohun Chowdhry* v. *Madan Mohan Chowdhry*, (1871) 6 B. L. R. 352 (355): S. C. 15 W. R. C. R. 29 (30), a distinction is drawn between a right to a share in the idol and a right to worship. But see *Eshan Chunder Roy* v. *Monmohini Dassi*, (1878) I. L. R., 4 C. 683 (685); *Gopi Kishen Gossami* v. *Thakoordass Gossami*, (1882) I. L. R., 8 C. 807. See also Chapter XVI.

4. *Dubo Misser* v. *Srinibas Misser*, (1870) 5 B. L. R. 617 (618).

5. See *Mitta Kanth Audhicarry* v. *Neerunjun Audhicarry*, (1874) 14 B. L. R., 166.

6. *Dwarkanath Roy* v. *Jannobee Chowdhrain*, (1865) 4 W. R. C. R. 79 (80); *Ram Soondur Thakoor* v. *Taruck Chunder Turkoruttun*, (1872) 19 W. R. C. R. 28, 29, 30). See also *Debendronath Mullick* v. *Odit Churn Mullick*, (1878) I. L. R., 3 C. 390. But he must return it at his own expense to the next turn owner.

7. *Ramessur Mookerjee* v. *Ishan Chunder Mookerjee*, (1868) 10 W. R. C. R. 457 (458); *Gaur Mohan Chowdhry* v. *Madan Mohan Chowdhry*, (1871) 6 B. L. R. 352 (355): S. C. 15 W. R. C. R. 29 (30).

tenants for rent it may be that the turn owner may sue as sole plaintiff[1], and where he is the person that has settled the tenancy and let the tenant into possession there can be no question as to his right to sue.

Right of mutwalli under the Mahomedan Law.

Under the Mahomedan Law we have already seen that the position of a mutwalli is only that of a manager He is not entitled to alienate endowed property even for necessity[2]. Wakf property cannot be sold in satisfaction of a claim against the mutwalli[3]. The fact that the office is hereditary will not make such property alienable[4] The court (Kazi of the Mahomedan Law) may, however, sanction the alienation of the same for necessity[5]. Where an express power is conferred upon the mutwalli by the deed of appropriation for alienating endowed property for necessity, such power may be given effect to and no consent of the court is necessary[6]. In some places it is said that by custom wakf property may be sold[7]. But if the custom be that the same may be sold even for no necessary purposes of the endowment and for the private benefit of the mutwalli, such a custom will be invalid as unreasonable provided of course the property is absolute wakf and no beneficial interest is possessed by the mutwalli[8]. Where there is a beneficial interest created in favor of the mutwalli such interest may be sold[9]. An unauthorized alienation is void and not merely voidable[5]. An

1. *Dado Ravji* v. *Dinanath Ravji*, (1865) 2 B. H. C. A. C. J. 72 (74).

2. *Kulb Ali Hossein* v. *Syf Ali*, (1814) 2 B. S. D. A. 110; *Mussummat Qadira* v. *Shah Kubeer-Ooddeen* (1824), 3 B. S. D. A. 407 ; *Jewun Dass Sahoo* v. *Shah Kubeer-Ooddeen*, (1841) 2 M. I. A. 390 (421); *Moulvee Abdoolla* v. *Mussummat Rajesri Dossea*, (1846) 7 B. S. D. A. 268 ; *Shoojat Ali* v. *Zumeerooddeen*, (1866) 5 W. R., C. R., 158 (159) ; *Futtoo Bibee* v. *Bhurrut Lall Bhukut* (1868) 10 W. R. C R., 299 ; *Muzhurool Huq* v. *Puhraj Ditarey Mohapattur*, (1870) 13 W. R. C. R., 235 (237) ; *Sheik Abdool Khaleck* v. *Poran Bibee*, (1876) 25 W. R., C. R. 542 (549) ; *Kazi Hassan* v. *Sagun Balakrishna*, (1899) I. L. R, 24 B. 170 (175).

3. *James Fegredo* v. *Mahomed Mudessur*, (1871) 15 W. R. C. R., 75 (79).

4. *Shoojat Ali* v. *Zumeerooddeen*, (1866) 5 W. R. C. R., 158 dissenting from *Dalrympyle* v. *Khoondkar*, (1858) B. S. D. A. 586.

5. *Shama Churn Roy* v. *Abdul Kabeer*, (1898) 3 C. W. N. 158. As to the exercise of power by court, see *Dinshaw Nowroji Bode* v. *Nowroji Nasarwanji*, (1895) I. L. R., 20 B. 46. See Macnaghten's Principles (Endowments) 3.

6. *Moonshe Golam Ali* v. *Mussamut Sowlutoonnissa Bibee*, (1864) W. R. Sp. C. R., 241.

7. *Abas Ali* v. *Ghulam Muhammed*, (1863) 1 B. H. C. A. C. J. 36.

8. Cf. *Sarkum Abu Torab Abdul Waheb* v. *Rahaman Baksh*, (1896) I. L. R., 24 C. 83.

9. *Dalrympyle* v. *Khoondkar Azeezul*, (1858) B.S.D. A. 586. See also *Futtoo Bibee* v. *Bhurrut Lall*, (1868) 10 W. R. C. R , 299; *Syud Nadir Hossein* v. *Baboo Pearoo Thovildarinee*, (1873) 19 W. R. C. R., 255 (262) ; *Kazi Hassan* v. *Sagun Balkrishna*, (1899) I. L. R., 24 B. 170 (179).

alienation of the office of mutwalli or any other religious office is equally illegal[1]. Even a custom allowing the sale of a religious office will be bad[2]. But the mutwalli may appoint an agent to look after the secular affairs of an endowment[3]. A deputy may be appointed to look after the temporal concerns provided the principal does not thereby shift his responsibility[3]. The appointment of the deputy will not release the liability of the office-holder[3]. The principal may revoke the authority of the delegate at any time. But duties involving personal qualifications cannot be performed by deputy. The office of Sajjadanashin and many other religious offices referred to in a previous chapter[4] cannot be performed by deputy[5] as they involve personal qualifications. Where there are joint mutwallis all of them must act[6] so that in a suit to recover wakf property from third parties all mutwallis must be joined as plaintiffs and if any of them refuse they should be made defendants[7]. As mutwalli he must keep up the wakf and if it be a saint's tomb he must maintain the same properly and perform other matters which usually accompany the keeping up of the saint's tomb[8].

Effect of decree obtained by or against manager.

Although Dharmakartas or mutwallis may not be entitled to alienate endowed property and will not be entitled to divert the line of succession pointed out by the founder, they represent the institution completely so that a decree hostilely passed against them as representing the institution will be binding on their successors[9] in

---

1. *Wahid Ali* v. *Ashruff Hossain*, (1882) I. L. R., 8 C. 732 (734, 735); *Sarkum Abu Torab Abdul Waheb* v. *Rahaman Buksh*, (1896) I. L. R., 24 C. 83 (91 to 94).

2. *Sarkum Abu Torab* v. *Rahaman Buksh*, (1896) I. L. R., 24 C. 83 (93).

3. *Hussain Beebee* v. *Hussain Sherif*, (1868) 4 M. H. C. 23; *Wahid Ali* v. *Ashruff Hossain*, (1832) I, L. R., 8 C. 732.

4. Chapter XIII.

5. *Hussain Beebee* v. *Hussain Sherif*, (1868) 4 M. H. C. 23.

6. *Wasiq Ali Khan* v. *Government*, (1836) 6 B. S. D. A 110.

7. *Bichu Lal* v. *Olieullah*, (1885) I. L.R., 11 C. 338 (340).

8. *Reasut Ali* v. *Abbott*, (1869) 12 W. R. C. R., 132 (133).

9. *Golab Chand Baboo* v. *Prosunno Coomary Debee*, (1873) 11 B. L. R., 332: S. C. 20 W. R., C. R., 86 affd. on appeal to P. C., in *Prosunno Kumari Debya* v. *Golab Chand Baboo*, (1875) L. R. 2 I. A. 145; S. C. 14 B. L. R. 450; *Ardesir Jehangir Framji* v. *Hirabai*, (1884) I. L. R., 8 B. 471; *Sudindra* v. *Budan*, (1885) I. L. R. 9 M. 80; *Kelu* v. *Paidel*, (1886) I. L. R., 9 M. 473; *Madhavon* v. *Keshavan*, (1887) I. L. R. 11 M. 191 (where a decree against four out of five uralers was held to be binding on all); *Tulsidas Mahanta* v. *Bejoy Kishore Shome*, (1901) 6 C. W. N. 178 Cf. *Radhabai* v. *Anantrav Bhagavant*, (1885) I. L. R., 9 B. 198 (221) and *Nilmony Singh* v. *Jagabandhu Roy*, (1898) I. L. R. 23 C. 536 at p. 545 (where it is said that the succeeding shebaits only form a continuing representation of the idol's property).

the absence of fraud or collusion[1]. A money decree against the institution can be executed against the endowed property or its income but the right of the Deity to the votive offerings to be made by worshippers being an uncertain right is not attacheable[2]. If the decree is binding on the mutt, it must be executed and no question can be raised in execution proceedings whether the debt forming the basis of the decree has been contracted for the benefit of the institution or otherwise[3]. But the question whether the decree is really obtained against the institution can be raised in execution for, if the decree is obtained against the manager personally, such decree will not affect the endowed property or the institution[4]. A claim that the property attached is endowed property in possession of the debtor as a trustee and therefore not attacheable in execution of a personal decree against him is a claim falling under S. 278 C. P. C.[5]. The principle is that the judgment-debtor as a trustee is a different person[6] and the decree against him in his personal capacity will not bind him in his capacity as manager of the institution[7]. A party against whom an order is passed under Ss. 280 and 281 can, by the express language of S. 283 C.P.C. bring a suit and S. 244, C.P.C. will be no bar[8]. A decree obtained by the manager in favor of the institution such as a decree for possession can only be executed by his successor

---

1. *Prosunno Kumari Debya* v. *Golab Chand Baboo*, (1875) L. R. 2 I. A. 145 : S. C. 14 B. L. R. 450 ; *Sudindra* v. *Budan*, (1885) I. L. R., 9 M. 80.

2. *Shoilojanund Ojha* v. *Peary Charan Dey*, (1902) I. L. R., 29 C. 470.

3. *Sudindra* v. *Budan*, (1885) I. L. R . 9 M. 80.

4. *Ranee Shibeshuree Debia* v. *Mothooranath Acharjee*, (1866) 5 W.R.. C.R. 202; *Juggurnath Roy Chowdhry* v. *Kishen Pershad Surmah*, (1867) 7 W. R., C. R., 266; *James Fegredo* v. *Mahomed* v. *Mudessur*, (1871) 15 W.R.,C.R., 75 (79) ; *Narayan* v. *Chintaman*, (1881) I. L. R , 5 B. 393 (399) ; *RupaJagshet* v. *Krishnaji Govind*, (1884) I. L. R , 9 B. 169 ; *Murigeyav. Hayat Saheb*, (1898) I, L. R., 23 B. 237; *Ram Krishna Mahapatra* v. *Padma Charan Deb*. (1902) 6 C. W. N. 663.

5. Per *Ranade J* in *Murigeya* v. *Hayat Saheb*. (1898) I. L. R., 23 B. 237 *Ramanathan Chettiar* v. *Levvai Marakayer*, (1899) I. L. R., 23 M, 195. See also; *Roop Lall* v. *Bekani Meah* (1888) I. L. R., 15 C. 437.

6. *Mirza Daud Ali* v. *Nadir Hossein*, (1869) 3 B. L. R., A. C. J. 46; *Radha Kishen* v. *Shah Ameeroodddeen*, (186.) 11 W. R. C. R. 204 (205); *Nimaye Churn* v. *Jogendro Nath*, (1874) 21 W. R. C, R. 365 (366) ; *Rupa Jagshet* v. *Krishnaji Govind*, (1884) I. L. R., 9 B. 169 ; *Ramanathan Chettiar* v *Levvai Marakayar*, (1899) I. L. R., 23 M. 195; or the right is different, see *Babuji Rao* v. *Laxmandas*, (1903) I. L. R., 28 B. 215.

7. *Tulsidas Mahanta* v. *Bejoy Kishore Shome*, (1901) 6 C. W.N. 178 ; *Babaji Rao* v. *Laxmandas*, (1903) I. L. R., 28 B. 215 (223); *Venkatasami* v. *Kuppayee*, (1904) 14 M. L. J R. 377 (378).

8. *Kali Charan* v. *Bangshi Mohan*, (1871) 6 B. L. R. 727 ; *Ram Krishna* v. *Padma Charan*, supra. See also cases cited in notes (5) and (6).

in office and not by his personal heir[1]. Even where the manager dies before decree the same principles will apply. The suit has to be revived by or as against the successor in office. But in a suit as between rival claimants where one of the claimants dies the person entitled to come in as legal representative must be some person who claims under a similar title to the deceased not a person who claims hostilely to him[2]. Thus in a case where a suit is brought after the death of the last Mohunt by the Chela of his predecessor for establishing his right to the office of Mohunt as against the last Mohunt's Chela and the plaintiff dies the suit cannot be revived by one who is not the Chela of the plaintiff but who is the Chela of the last Mohunt's predecessor and who is thus in the position of a rival claimant to the plaintiff[2]. In such suits no set-off personal as against the manager can be set up[3]. A decree for costs obtained by the late manager in a suit brought on behalf of the institution or a decree for costs obtained by him as a defendant and as representing the institution must be executed only by his successor in office even though he might have incurred the costs out of his own pocket and not out of the funds of the institution[4]. A decree obtained against the defendant as manager of one institution (idol) cannot be executed against the funds of another idol in his hands[5]. So also a decree against him as manager ceases to be executable as against him when he ceases to be manager[6]. He has only a right to represent the institution until removed. This right ceases on his removal. If any appeal is to be preferred the ex-manager

---

1. *Radha Jeebun Moostofee* v *Tara Monee Dossee*, (1865) 3 W. R., Mis. 25. Cf. also *Daud Ali* v. *Nadir Hossein*, (1869) 3 B. L. R., A. C. J. 46 : S. C 11 W. R. C. R., 388. No probate or succession certificate will be necessary for getting decrees for debts due to an institution. *Bhyrub Bharuttee Mohunt*, (1874) 21 W.R.C. R. 340 ; *Jogendronath Bharati* v. *Ram Chunder Bharati*, (1891) I. L. R., 20 C. 103 ; *Srimant Rajah Yarlagadda* v. *Makerla Sridevamma*, (1897) L R. 24 I. A. 73 : S. C. I. L. R., 20 M. 162 (166). But see *Mohunt Susman Gossain* v. *Ramchurn Bhukut*, (1866) 5 W. R., Mis. 48 ; *Daud Ali* v, *Nadir Hossein*, supra ; *Dukharam Bharti* v. *Luchman Bharti*, (1879) I. L. R., 4 C. 954. But the last three cases can no longer be regarded as law after the decision of the P. C. So also no letters of administration are necessary to enforce claims against trustees for breaches of trust. *Treepoorasoondery Dossee* v. *Debendronath Tagore*, (1876) I. L. R., 2 C. 45 (54).

2. *Sham Chand Giri* v. *Bhayaram Panday*, (1894) I. L. R., 22 C. 92 (99).

3. *Sri Dhundiraj Ganesh Dev* v. *Ganesh*, (1893) I. L. R., 18 B. 721. See also *Ram Sundar Ray* v. *Heirs of Raja Udwant Singh*, (1832) 5 B. S. D. A. 210.

4. *Jogendronath Bharati* v. *Ram Chunder Bharati*, (1891) I. L. R., 20 C. 103. See 13 M. L. J. (Rec-cas) p. 58. Cf. *Radha Jeebun Moostoffee* v. *Tara Monee Dosse*, (1865) 3 W. R. Mis. 25 (26).

5. *Moonshee Mahomed Akbar* v. *Kalee Churn Geeree Gossamee Mohunt*, (1876) 25 W. R. C. R. 401.

6. *Monna Tamberan* v. *Vadamaly Oodian*, (1854) M. S. D. A. 113.

is not the proper person to appeal[1]. The next holder must appeal. For a similar reason such a decree can only be executed against a person who is his successor in office[2]. If the decree is for the possession or recovery of specific property and the ex-manager is not in possession, the decree may be executed against the manager in office and it cannot be executed against the ex-manager. But if the old manager is still in possession he must surrender the property. A decree for damages obtained against the manager as representing the institution is not a personal decree against him and cannot be executed against his private property or against him when he ceases to be manager[3]. But where the damage is brought about by a wrong of his and the party aggrieved proceeded for this wrong both as against him personally and as representing the institution then he cannot escape liability by being removed from office. The question in all such cases is whether the decree is against the institution exclusively and is not also against him personally. In the case of loans by a manager for the purposes of the institution we have already seen that the manager is not personally liable and that the institution only is liable[4]. In such cases a decree, obtained by the creditor ceases to be enforceable against the manager when he ceases to hold office and must be executed only as against the property of the institution (whether in the hands of the successor or in the hands of the ex-manager)[5]. But the private property of the manager or his person is not liable for the debt or the decree based thereon[5]. Where a decree expressly directs execution against the manager personally then of course his person and private property are liable. The same principles apply to a decree for costs obtained against him under similar circumstances. But where the defence is vexatious the court may direct the unsuccessful defendant to pay costs personally in suits brought against him as representing the institution. It cannot be said that

---

1. *Dwarka Nath Biswas* v. *Debendra Nath Tagore*, (1899) 4 C. W. N. 58.

2. *i. e.*, against the estate represented by him See notes 1, 4 and 6 to p. ccxxxiii.

3. *Monna Tambiran* v. *Vadamaly Oodian*, (1854) M. S. D. A. 113; *Venkatasami Pillai* v. *Kuppayee Ammall*, (1904) 14 M. L J. R., 376 (377). See also *Sudindra* v. *Budan*, (1885) I. L. R., 9 M. 80

4. See pp. ccx and ccxi. The trustee is not personally liable and the responsibility attaches to the office. See *Monna Tambiran* v. *Vadamaly Oodian*, (1854) M. S. D. A 113.

5. *Monna Tambiran* v. *Vadamaly Oodian*, (1854) M. S. D. A. 113; *Venkatasami* v. *Kuppayee*, supra.

there is no power in the court to award costs against the manager personally when the suit is brought against the institution. But apparently unless the decree is expressly stated to be also against the manager personally the proper construction or the *prima facie* inference is that the decree is only against the institution when the suit is against such institution[1]. When the suit is against the manager personally the decree is also *prima facie* against him personally. Where a suit is brought by the creditor against the manager personally and the defence is that he is not so liable as the debt is only for the institution the suit may be amended so as to claim relief in the alternative against the defendant as representing the institution or if he has ceased to hold office as against the persons who represent it[2].

The powers of the manager being necessarily limited, he cannot grant a permanent lease of the endowed property with a fixed and invariable rent. The granting of such permanent leases will be void unless there is some necessity or benefit shewn[3]. But *prima facie* it is void and the onus will be on the lessee to shew that there existed circumstances justifying the grant of such a lease[4]. This principle is applicable equally to public and private endowments under the Hindu Law. The leading case on the subject is that of ***Maharanee Shibessouree Debia* v. *Mothooranath Acharjo*[4]** decided

Power to create derivative tenures.

1. *Monna Tamberan* v. *Vadamaly Oodian*, (1854) M. S. D. A. 113.

2. *Gopal Chunder Sircar* v. *Adhiraj Aftab Chand Mahatab*, (1884) I.L.R., 10 C. 743; *Saminatha* v. *Muthayya*, (1892) I. L. R., 15 M. 417. So in a suit by a person for possession of property as his private property he may be given a decree for possession as shebait, if the trust is proved and the other side has opportunity to meet this case. See *Radha Mohun Mundul* v *Jadoomonee Dossee*, (1875) 23 W. R. C. R. 369 (P. C.). In *Krishnan* v. *Sankara Varma*, (1886) I. L. R., 9 M. 441 the creditor prayed for the recovery of the debt due to him out of the funds of the institution and out of the urallens personally and a decree was given that the tarwad of which the urallens were the Karnavans was liable as the debt was utilised for tarwad purposes.

3. *Radha Bulubh Chand* v. *Juggut Chunder*, (1829) 4 B. S. D. A. 151; *Motee Dosse* v. *Mudhoo Soodun Chowdhry*, (1864) 1 W R. C. R. 4 (where specific performance was refused); *Juggessur Buttobyal* v. *Rajah Roodro Narain Roy*, (1869) 12 W. R C. R. 299 (301); *Maharanee Shibessourie Debia* v. *Mothooranath Acharjo*, (1869) 13 M. I. A. 270; *Tayubunnissa* v. *Sham Kishore*, (1871) 7 B. L. R., 621: S. C. 15 W. R. C. R., 228; *Ramchandra Shankarbava Dravid* v. *Kashinath Narayan Dravid*, (1894) I. L. R., 19 B. 271; *Prosunno Kumar Adhikari* v. *Saroda Prosunno Adhikari*, (1895) I.L.R., 22 C. 989; *Chockalinga Pillai* v. *Mayandi Chettiar*, (1896) I. L. R., 19 M. 485 where, however, it was held that a permanent lease of waste land for the purpose of bringing it under cultivation was beneficial and that a necessity ought to be presumed after some lapse of time but this was reversed by the P. C. in *Mayandi Chettiyar* v. *Chokkalingam Pillay*, (1904) L. R. 31 I. A. 83 (88): S. C. I. L. R., 27 M. 291 (295); *Nallayappa Pillian* v. *Amblarana Pandara Sannadhi*, (1903) I. L. R., 27 M. 465 (472).

4. *Maharanee Shibessource Debia* v. *Mothooranath Acharjo*, (1869) 13 M. I. A. 270.

by the P. C. as early as 1869. Their Lordships there observed[1]: "In the exercise of that office, she could not alienate the property, though she might create proper derivative tenures and estates conformable to usage." Again at p 275 their Lordships observed: "There is no satisfactory proof in the cause that these jummas were ever held at a fixed and invariable rent. One important element in this inquiry has been wholly lost sight of viz., the nature of the *Shebait* title and its legal inability to be the source of such a derivative title. To create a new and fixed rent for all time, though adequate at the time, in lieu of giving the endowment the benefit of an augmentation of a variable rent from time to time would be a breach of duty in a Shebait, and is not, therefore, presumable. Where variableness of jumma is the normal condition, the mere naming a sum certain in connection with the grant of a descendible tenure does not impart of itself fixity to that sum in the absence of positive words, or of other evidence to show that such was the original design." The alienee *i. e.*, (the lessee) must show that he satisfied himeslf as far as he could that there was a fair and a sufficient ground of necessity for the alienation. The creation of a derivative tenure at a fixed and invariable rent although adequate at the time without giving the endowment the benefit of an augmentation at a variable rent would be a breach of trust on the part of the manager who was a party to the transaction[1]. Such an alienation is void and cannot be said to be binding during the lifetime of the grantor[2]. If an absolute alienation such as a sale[3] or a temporary alienation such as a mortgage[4] is void

1. (1869) 13 M. I. A. 270 at p. 273. See also *Mayandi Chettiyar* v. *Chokkalingam Pillay*, (1904) L. R. 31 I. A. 83 (88): S. C. I. L. R., 27 M. 291 (295). For the English law on the powers of lease by a trustee, see *Attorney-General* v. *Cross*, (1817) 3 Meriv. 524 (539 to 541): S. C. 17 R. R. 121 (122, 123).

2. *The Advocate General of Bombay* v. *Bai Punjabai*, (1894) I.L.R., 18 B. 551 (562); *Prosunno Kumar Adhikari* v *Sarodu Prosunno Adhikari*, (1895) I L R., 22 C. 989. But see *contra*, *Radha Bulubh Chund* v. *Juggut Chunder*, (1829) 4 B. S. D A. 151; *Prosunno Moyee Dossee* v. *Koonjo Beharee Chowdhree*, (1864) W. R. Sp. C. R. 157; *Arruth Misser* v. *Juggurnath Indraswamee*, (1872) 18 W. R. C. R. 439 (where, however, the lease was held to be proper and binding only during the life-time of the shebait or during the time he holds the office); *Ramchandra Shankarbava Dravid* v. *Kashinath Narayan Dravid*, (1894) I.L.R, 19 B. 271. In *Narayan* v. *Shri Ramchandra*, (1903) I. L. R., 27 B. 373 (378) the question was not decided. The English cases clearly shew that such a lease would be invalid from the date of the lease. See *Attorney General* v. *Magdalen College*, (1857) 6 H. L. C. 189 216: S. C. 10 Eng. Rep. 1267 (1278); *Attorney-General* v. *Payne*, (1859) 27 Beav. 168 (174); *Attorney-General* v. *Davey*, (1859) 4 De. G. & J. 136 (140). In *Vithalbowa* v. *Narayan Daji Thite*, (1893) I. L. R., 18 B. 507 the court held that possession would be adverse from the date of the tenant setting up permanent tenancy.

3. *Dattagiri* v. *Dattatraya*, (1902) I. L. R., 27 B. 363.

4. *Rumonee Debia* v. *Baluck Doss*, (1870) 11 B L. R. 336 (note) S. C. 14 W. R. C. R. 101; *Shri Ganesh Dharnidhar Maharajdev* v. *Keshavrav Govind Kulgavkar*, (1890) I. L. R., 15 B. 625.

from the beginning in the absence of necessity and if the principle be that the manager making the aliention is himself entitled to question the same[1] it is difficult to lay down a different rule as regards leases[2]. So that acceptance of rent either by the manager creating the lease or by his successor will not create an estoppel so as to disentitle such persons to sue to set aside the lease[3]. There is no beneficial interest in the shebait with reference to absolutely endowed property. In the case of mutts if the correct view be that the head has a beneficial interest in the income[4] an alienation may be binding during the lifetime of the head or during the time he holds his office and therefore such alienation may not be void from the beginning[5]. In such a case acceptance of rent may estop the person so receiving the rent[3] and the latter may be treated to have made the lease and so on *ad infinitum* when there will be no bar of limitation for a successor if he chooses to set aside the lease and recover the mutt property. Even in the case of mutts where the alienation is not made subject to the trusts of the endowment, it may be that the alienation is void from the beginning[6]. We have tried to show elsewhere that such is not really the position of the head of a mutt and no distinction can be made between the position of the head of a mutt and that of a shebait or manager of a temple. Where an alienation is expressly prohibited by the deed of endowment[7] or is permitted under certain circumstances effect may be given to the same. But a condition that the manager should sell endowed property for his own necessity would be a condition repugnant to the prior gift to the trust and would be void. Under Madras Act VIII of 1865, S. 11 cl. (5) even though a lease at a fixed and invariable rent be created, the successor of the manager creating the lease may not be bound under certain circumstances by the rent fixed by his predecessor but will be entitled to increase the

---

1. See cases cited in note (1) p. ccvi. See also pp. ccx, ccxi.

2. *The Advocate-General of Bombay* v. *Punjabi*, (1894) I. L. R., 18 B. 551 (562) and other cases cited in note (2) p. ccxxxvi. But see *Arruth Misser* v. *Juggurnath*, (1872) 18 W. R. C. R., 439; *Ramchandra* v. *Kashinath*, (1894) I. L. R., 19 B. 271.

3. The case of *Jugessur Buttobyalv. Rajah Roodro Narain Roy*, (1869) 12 W.R.C. R. 299 (301) must in this view be taken to have been wrongly decided unless it be held that in the case of mutts the head has an estate in the corpus of the estate and an absolute interest in the income.

4. *Vidyapurna Thirtha Swami* v. *Vidyanidhi Thirtha Swami*, (1904) I. L. R. 27 M. 435, (455).

5. *Mohunt Burm Suroop Dass* v. *Khashee Jha*, (1873) 20 W. R C. R. 471 (472).

6. *Mohunt Muhadeo Geer* v. *Mohunt Raj Bullubh Geer*, (1846) B. S. D. A. 250.

7. *Prosunno Moyee Dossee* v. *Koonjo Beharee Chowdhree*, (1864) W. R. Sp. C. R. 157. In the case of *Krishna Mudali* v. *Shanmuga Mudaliar*, (1871) 6 M.H.C. 248 it was simply held that an alienation was not under the proper construction of the deed prohibited.

rent[1] but this right is very limited[2]. *First of all* according to the section, the rates fixed by the predecessor must be low even at the time when the grant was made. So that, if they were not low then, the mere fact that there was an increase subsequently in the rates of rent payable for lands would not entitle the successor to claim the enhanced rate (assuming that he was barred from setting aside the lease and assuming that under the lease the rent was fixed and invariable). Even where the rate should be low, the rent could not be increased where the patta should have been *bona-fide* granted for the erection of dwelling houses, factories or other permanent buildings or for the purpose of clearing and bringing waste land into cultivation or for the purpose of making any permanent improvement thereon and the tenant should have substantially performed the conditions on which such lower rates of assessment were allowed[3]. *Secondly*, the grantor or his successor would be entitled to increase the rent with the sanction of the Collector if additional value should be imparted to the land by works of irrigation or other improvements executed at the expense of such landlord or constructed at the expense of Government provided in the latter case additional revenue is levied from the landlord by the Government[4]. But the shebait or manager may create proper derivative tenures and estates conformable to usage[5]. Thus it has been held in Bombay that a lease for 99 years for building purposes at a rental beneficial to the trust with the usual covenants to build and repair may be granted[6]. So also a lease from year to year being the ordinary form of tenancy in the case of cultivable lands will be binding. The usage of the institution is also the guide. For instance, in *Satyanama Bharati* v. *Saravana Bhaji Ammal*[7] it was held by the Madras High Court that a grant of endowed property (belonging to a private mutt) for

1 *Obai Goundan* v. *Ramalinga Ayyar*, (1898) I. L. R., 22 M. 217.

2. Ibid, at p. 220 where it was observed that an agreement to pay for lands at a fixed rent whether cultivated or not might be binding.

3. S. 11 Cl. IV proviso (2).

4. S. 11 Cl. IV proviso (1).

5. *Maharanee Shibessouree Debia* v. *Mothooranath Acharjo*, (1869) 13 M.I A. 270 ; *Nallayappa Pillian* v. *Amblavana Pandara Sannadhi*, (1903) I. L. R., 27 M. 465 (472).

6. *In re Lakshmibai*, (1888) I. L. R., 12 B. 638.

7. (1894) I. L. R., 18 M. 266.

the maintenance of a member of the family of the original grantee was binding provided the grant should enure only during the life-time of such member.

Mahomedan Law—mutwalli power of lease.

Under the Mahomedan Law, a mutwalli is also not competent to make a permanent lease[1] and no distinction exists between a mutwalli whose office is hereditary and a mutwalli whose office is not so hereditary[2]. But he may grant a lease of house property for not more than a year or lands for agricultural purposes for not more than three years[3]. He is not competent in the absence of any directions[4] in the deed of appropriation to grant agricultural leases for more than a year or leases of house property for more than one year. He may, however, grant such leases on obtaining the sanction of the Court.

Exchange of endowed property.

If the test of the validity be the benefit of the institution, it may seem at first sight that a manager has the right to exchange property originally endowed for other property. But the question is whether an exchange is for the benefit of the institution. *Prima facie* it will not be for benefit of the institution. Generally, the motive of a Hindu grantor in making the endowment is that the property which he endows the institution with will endure perpetually for the institution, that the income of such property will contribute to the services of the idol and that, thereby, he will attain the greatest spritual bliss. Sometimes the motive is that by the perpetual existence of this property for the trust the donor will be perpetually remembered. These motives are frustrated by an exchange. Again, the property is generally known by repute to belong to the trust. By an exchange this reputation or tradition evidence is lost (because the original property with reference to which this reputation evidence has grown is alienated) and we have to wait for generations before a reputation is acqired for the exchanged property. This reputation or tradition is a great factor in checking the wrongful alienation of the trust property. In the Mahomedan

1. *Dhalrympyle* v. *Koondkar Azeezul*, (1858) B. S.D.A. 586 ; *Luteefun* v. *Bego Jan*, (1866) 5 W. R. C. R. 12 ; *Shoojat Ali* v, *Zumeeroddeen*, (1866) 5 W. R. C. R. 158.

2. *Shoojat Ali* v. *Zumeeroddeen*, (1866) 5 W. R.C. R. 158 dissenting from *Dhalrympyle's case*, supra.

3. *Shoojat Ali* v. *Zumeeroddeen*, (1866) 5 W. R. C. R. 158 following Baillie 596. See Amir Ali Vol. I pp. 378, 379.

4. In *Luteefun* v. *Bego Jan*, supra, the validity of such directions was recognised. See also *Shoojat Ali* v. *Zumeeroddeen*, (1866) 5 W. R. C. R. 158.

Law, therefore we find that wakf property cannot be exchanged by the mutwalli except with the sanction of the Court[1]. Of course if the deed of endowment contains provisions as to exchange that must be given effect to.

Manager's power of compromise.

The question of the manager's power of compromise is more difficult. In order that a compromise may be valid, it must be shewn that he acted honestly and in the interests of the institution[2]. Fraud on his part will vitiate. If the compromise derogates from the rules laid down by the founder it will not be valid. For instance, a compromise between rival claimants by which one is recognised as the head and the other is given a reversionary interest after the death of the person recognised for the time being will be invalid[3]. It will not take away the holder's right to appoint his successor. The principle seems to be that the act of the manager in buying off a rival claimant cannot be regarded as a proper and reasonable exercise of his office[4].

But where a person claims a joint right of management with others a compromise by the latter with the former admitting his right would be perfectly valid especially where such was the practice even before the compromise and the compromise had been acted upon for a long series of years. Under such circumstances the compromise could not be re-opened and must be given effect to[5]. Where a right of joint management is brought into controversy in a Court of Justice and is by way of compromise recognised as a subsisting right and as being in accordance with the prior usage of the institution the compromise must be given effect to and is binding upon the parties[6]. It is binding upon the other persons interested in the trust if it has been acted upon for a series of

---

1. Amir Ali Vol I. p. 332.

2. *Howley* v. *Blake*, (1904) 1 Ch. 622.

3. *Greedharee Doss* v. *Nundkissore Dutt*, (1863) 1 Marsh 573 affirmed on appeal to P. C. in *Greedharee Doss* v. *Nundokissore Doss*, (1867) 11 M. I. A. 405; *Joy Lall Tewaree* v. *Gossain Bhoobun Geer*, (1874) 21 W. R. C. R. 334 (336).

4. *Shri Dhundhiraj Ganesh Dev.* v. *Ganesh*, (1893) I. L. R., 18 B. 721; *Girijanund Datta Jha* v. *Sailajanund Datta Jha*, (1896) I. L. R., 23 C. 645 (662).

5. *Nilakandan* v. *Padmanabha* (1890), I. L. R., 14 M. 153 (158) affirmed by the Privy Council in *Cherukunneth Manakel Neelakandhen Namboodiripad* v. *Vengunat Swaroopathil Padmanabha Revi Varma Valia Nambidi*, (1894) L. R. 21 I. A. 128 : S.C. I. L. R., 18 M. 1.

6. Ibid.

years. It may be that the persons interested may bring a suit that this recognition is against the usage of the institution and that the persons recognised under the compromise must be treated as trespassers[1] provided the latter have not acquired a right by prescription. But where prescriptive title has been acquired and effect given to the compromise for a long series of years it is not open to the persons interested to question the compromise[2]. If, however, a decree relating to the rights of the endowment or the rights of worshippers is obtained by the manager as representing the institution and there is an appeal pending against such decree it is not open to the manager to give up the rights declared by the decree under appeal and to compromise with the appellants.[3] Such a compromise will not be binding[4] and at any rate the Court is not bound to pass a decree in accordance with the same but may make others interested in opposing the appeal as parties and proceed with the hearing on the merits[5].

De facto manager distinguished from trespasser—Rights of trespasser.

The rights of *de facto* manager remain to be considered. Apparently some distinction is drawn between a *trespasser* and a *defacto* manager. If a person is a trespasser it is difficult to conceive what rights he can have as against the trust or the rightful manager. A person who ousts the rightful manager from possession is deemed to be a trespasser. It was held by *Couch*, C. J., in *Ram Churn Pooree* v. *Nunhoo Mundal*[6] that such a trespasser could not be treated as a *de facto* manager entitled to create a charge upon the estate under certain circumstances. He could not, therefore, renew bonds executed by the lawful manager or

1. Cf *Gossamee Sree Greedharreejee* v. *Rumanlolljee Gossamee*, (1889) I. L. R., 16 I. A. 137 (146); S. C. I. L. R., 17 C. 3 (22) where the Privy Council say that it is also the right of the Thakoor to be in proper custody.

2. Cf. *Chinnasami Mudali* v. *Advocate General of Madras*, (1894) I.L R.,17 M. 406.

3. *Rajah M. Bhaskara Sethupathi* v. *Narayanasamy Gurukkal*, (1902) 12 M. L. J. R., 360, (361 and 365).

4. Ibid. Cf. *Gyanananda Asram* v. *Kristo Chandra Mukherji* (1901), 8 C. W. N. 404.

5. *Narayanasami Gurukkal* v. *Irulappa Nadan*, (1902) 12 M. L. J. R., 355; *Rajah M. Bhaskara Sethupathi* v. *Narayanasamy Gurukkal*, (1902) 12 M. L. J. R., 360; *Gyanananda Asram* v. *Kristo Chandra Mukherji*, (1901) 8. C. W. N. 404. In England the trustee's powers after suit and decree are suspended and he must afterwards get the directions of the Court See *Mitchelson* v. *Piper*, (1836) 8 Sim. 64, (66); S. C. 42 R. R. 104 (106); *Minors* v. *Battison*, (1876) L. R. 1 A-C 428 (438).

6. (1870) 14 W. R. C. R. 147 at p. 148. *Shri Ganesh Dharnidhar Maharajdev* v. *Keshavrav*, (1890) I. L. R., 15 B. 625 (637, 638).

31

create other charges upon the estate. This judgment was concurred in by Mr. Justice *Bayley* and Mr. Justice *Dwarkanath Mitter*. We do not think that the authority of this judgment is in any way shaken by the observations of the Judicial Committee in *Dakshina Mohun Roy* v. *Saroda Mohun Roy*[1]. It was not even cited before the Privy Council. In *Dakshina Mohun Roy* v. *Saroda Mohun*[1] the Privy Council held that a person in possession under a decree of Court was not during such time a person in wrongful possession so as to disentitle him to recover sums paid by him on account of Government revenue although that decree should ultimately be reversed by the Privy Council. Reference was made by the Judicial committee to a decision of the House of Lords in *Peruvian Guano Co.* v. *Dreyfus Brothers*.[2] But even this decision does not, in our opinion, touch the authority of the case of *Ram Churn* v. *Nunhoo*[3]. In the House of Lords case, the question was whether a person receiving cargo under a consent order was entitled to be recouped certain necessary expenses. The House of Lords held that under the terms of the consent order there was an agreement that such expenses should be recouped. Lord *Watson* thought[4] that the receipt was *neutral* and was not wrongful but did not consider whether under such circumstances *a claim for reimbursement* would be sustainable or otherwise. Lord *Macnaghten* indeed suggested that in equity such a claim might be sustainable by a trespasser although he left the question open. If his suggestion was that in an action of detinue the wrongdoer could claim reimbursement for the expenses of his wrongful acts such suggestion could hardly be regarded as sound law in the face of the decision in the recent case of *Glenwood Lumber Company* v. *Phillips*[5]. This is a decision of the Privy Council and at any rate is binding upon the Courts in India. In this case the action was one for detinue. The plaintiff (respondent) sued to recover timber which he alleged was wrongfully cut by the defendants (appellants). The latter claimed reimbursement of the

---

1. (1893) L. R. 20 I. A. 160; S. C. I. L. R., 21 C. 142. See also *Perumal Udayar* v. *Krishnama Chettiyar*. (1894) I. L. R., 17 M. 251 (252).

2. [1892] A. C. 166 (170 note et seq.)

3. (1870) 14 W. R. C. R. 147.

4. [1892] A. C. at p. 171.

5. [1904] A. C. 405.

expenses of cutting the timber and floating the logs down the river The cutting and floating were the wrongful acts complained of. These expenses were disallowed by the supreme court of Newfoundland and in affirming this judgment the Privy Council observed[1]: "Their Lordships think that the judgment is in the form usual in actions for detinue and it would not be right to impose on the respondent the obligation of paying the appellants the expenses of their wrongful acts as a condition of recovering what must be considered in this action as his property although such expenses might properly, but would not necessarily, be taken into account in estimating the alternative damages". Of course in assessing damages or mesne profits these expenses may properly be taken into account but that does not mean that a trespasser is entitled to sue for the expenses of his wrongful acts or to charge the estate for such expenses. The Madras case of *Kasim Saiba* v. *Sudhindra Thirtha Swami*[2] proceeds upon an imperfect understanding of the ruling in *Dakshina Mohun Roy* v. *Saroda Mohun Roy*[3]. The ruling of the House of Lords referred to in both these cases lays down nothing in contravention of the principle stated above and we have already stated that if in the House of Lords case it must be taken that Lord *Macnaghten* suggests that a trespasser is entitled to claim reimbursement of the expenses of his wrongful act that suggestion can hardly be maintainable after the recent decision of the Privy Council in *Glenwood Lumber Company* v. *Phillips*[4]. Probably all Lord *Macnaghten* meant was that a person though he might be held to have no title ultimately, might claim reimbursement for the expenses of an act which was not wrongful but which might be regarded as neutral. Indeed there is scarcely any authority for the proposition that although a person may claim reimbursement of the expenses actually incurred by him he may create charges upon the estate binding as against the rightful owner for such expenses.

Rights of *de facto* manager

A *de facto* manager is however, not a trespasser. He is one actually holding and doing the duties of the office not having obtained possession of the same without fraud or force. Such a

1. (1904) A. C. 405 at p. 412.
2. (1895) I. L. R., 18 M. 359 (362).
3. (1893) L. R. 20 I. A. 160: S. C. I. L. R., 21 C. 142.
4. (1904) A. C. 405.

de facto manager is in the position of the manager for an infant heir who is entitled, as has been held by the Privy Council in the leading case known as *Hanoomanpersaud's case*, to create binding charges upon the estate under certain circumstances. "It is to be observed that under the Hindoo Law, the right of a *bona-fide* incumbrancer[1] who has taken from a *de facto* manager a charge on lands created honestly for the purpose of saving the estate or for the benefit of the estate, is not (provided the circumstance would support the charge had it emanated form a *de facto* and *dejure* manager) affected by the want of union of the *de facto* with the *dejure* title[2]". To entitle a creditor to the security of the estate " proof of imminent pressure or danger of loss or of such close inquiries as to the position of the estate and the immediate circumstances of the pressure or apprehended danger as to satisfy a prudent and reasonable mind of the truth of the alleged pressure and impending danger should be given[3]". The observations of the Judicial Committee quoted above[2] were with reference to the powers of the *de facto* manager of an infant heir but they were equally held applicable to the *de facto* manager of a religious establishment in a Calcutta case[4].

A person who wrongly holds as trustee and pretends to act as such cannot be entitled to reprobate the right which he asserts and to contend that he holds adversely to his *cestui que trust*[5]. Such a person incurs a responsibility for the due application of the trust property and is answerable as trustee even though he may not have consciously accepted a trust and a remedy may be sought against him for maladministration by a suit[6].

Trustee's right to ask advice of court.

Under S. 43 of Act XXVIII of 1866 which is similar to S. 23 of 22 & 23 Vict. C. 35 it is open to a manager to take the

1. See also *Kasim Saiba v. Sudhindra Thirtha Swami* (1895) I. L. R., 18 M. 359 (364).

2. *Hunoomanpersaud Panday v. Munraj Koonweree*, (1856) 6 M. I. A. 393 (412).

3. *Kota Ramasami Chetti v. Bangari Seshama Nayanivaru*, (1881) I. L. R, 3 M. 145 at p. 151. See also *Ram Churn v. Nunhoo*, (1870) 14 W. R.C. R. 147 (148); *Kasim Saiba v. Sudhindra Thirtha Swami*, (1895) I. L. R., 18 M. 359 (362, 363).

4. *Sheo Shankar Gir v. Ram Shewak Chowdhri*, (1896) I. L. R., 24 C. 77 (82, 83).

5. Ibid at p. 81.

6. *Manohar Ganesh v. Lakhmiram*, (1887) I. L. R., 12 B. 247 (265); *Jugalkishore v. Lakshmandas*, (1899) I. L. R., 23 B. 659 (664).

advice of the Court on any question respecting the management or administration of the trust property. Though this Act like Act XXVII of 1866 states that it applies only in cases in which the English Law is applicable, applications have been made under S. 43 of Act XXVIII for advice in cases of Hindu religious endowments[1]. But under the section the Court can only lay down general principles and cannot deal with the particular subject-matter on hand[2]. Such petitions must relate only to the management and administration of trust property. Under the English statute it was held that the Court could neither construe an instrument nor make any order affecting the rights of parties[3]. The Bombay Court in *In re Lakshmibai*[4] appears to have adopted the cases dealing with the English statute as equally applicable to the Indian Act. So also the Bombay High Court has said that disputed points of law or of fact must be excluded under the section[4]. The questions dealt with in the English Courts under this section were questions of advancement, maintenance, change of investment, sale of trust property, compromises and taking proceedings. It is difficult to see why the English decisions should be adopted on the construction of Indian Act XXVIII of 1866. Questions of difficulty, detail, or importance excluded under S. 34 of the Trust Act are not excluded under S. 43 of Act XXVIII of 1866, so that these questions may be dealt with under the latter section. The reason for excluding adjudications on nice questions of law under S. 30 of Act 22 & 23 Vict. Ch. 35 was that the latter Act did not give any right of appeal[5]. But that reason will not apply to S. 43 of the Indian Act as by the section the juridiction is conferred upon a Judge of the High Court and there is an appeal under S. 15 of the Letters Patent from a Judgment

---

1. *In re Lakshmibai*, (1888) I. L. R., 12 B. 638, Cf. *In re Kahandas Narrandas*, (1881) I. L. R., 5 B. 154, a case under Act XXVII of 1866. S. 34 of the Trusts Act is also similar but there questions of detail, difficulty or importance are expressly excluded.

2. *In re Lakshmibai*, (1888) I. L. R. 12 B. 638. Cf. *In the matter of the Madras Doveton Trust Fund*, (1895) I. L. R., 18 M. 443 (a case under S. 34 of the Trusts Act II of 1882).

3. *Re Lorenz's Settlement*, (1861) 1 Dr. & Sm. 401 (404); *Re-Evans*, (1861) 30 Beav 282.

4. *In re Lakshmibai* (1888) I. L. R., 12 B. 638 (645).

5. *Re Mockett's Will*, (1860) 1 Johns 625. (630). But the petition might be converted into a bill. Ibid. See also Lewin on Trusts (8th) Edn. p. 310. See now for the present practice Edn. of 1898 pp. 404 to 408.

of a single Judge of the High Court not being a sentence or order passed in any criminal trial. In England the practice of obtaining advice under S 30 of 22 & 23 Vict. Ch. 35 is obsolete as upon a summons taken out under OrdorLV rule(3) juridiction is more complete and we think S. 43 covers the cases mentioned in that order. Anyhow S. 539, of the Civil Procedure Code is more effective and according to this section jurisdiction is conferred upon the High Courts as well as the District Courts.

Trustee's duty to take reasonable sare.

On taking up office he must acquaint himself with the nature and circumstances of the endowed property and take steps to get in endowed funds invested on insufficient and hazardous securities[1]. In managing and dealing with the trust estate he must take that reasonable care which a prudent person under similar circumstances will do with reference to his own property[2]. The duty to take reasonable care is similar to the duty imposed on the bailee under S. 151 of the Contract Act. He is not an insurer of trust property so that if he has exercised reasonable care he has discharged his duty and he is not liable for any loss[3]. If an agent is appointed to look after the collections but the managers fail to detect sums misappropriated by him and to get in the same they will be liable[4]. If property has been wrongfully alienated by a breach of trust on the part of his predecessor it is his duty to rocover the property for the trust; otherwise he may be liable for the loss[5]. If by his negligence property is lost for the trust he has to make good the same himself. So also when trust moneys are invested in bad securities it is his duty to realize them at once[6]. If by reason of his negligence in not realizing the same sooner the debt becomes irrecoverably lost either because of the subsequent insolvency of the debtor or of the debt becoming barred by limitation he will be liable to make good the same[7]. He

To repair predecessor's breach of trust.

To realize bad securities.

1. *Thackersey Dewraj* v. *Hurbhum Nursey*, (1884) I. L. R., 8 B. 432 (464 and 465.

2. *In re Speight—Speight* v. *Gaunt*, (1883) L. R. 9 A. C. 1. (10, 11, 19, 29).

3. See S. 152 of the Contract Act.

4. *Advocate General of Bombay* v. *Moulvi Abdul Kadir Jitaker*, (1894) I. L. R., 18 B. 401 (425).

5. *Thackersey Dewraj* v. *Hurbhum Nursey*, (1884) I. L. R., 8 B. 432 (465). But see Agnew on Trusts, p. 136.

6. *Thackersey Dewraj* v. *Hurbhum Nursey*, (1884) I. L. R., 8 B. 432 (465).

7. Ibid, at p. 465. See also *Jones* v. *Higgins*, (1866) L. R., 2 Eq. 538 (544); and *Desouza* v. *Desouza* (1875) 12 B. H. C. 184.

is bound not merely to press for the payment of the debt but also to institute legal proceedings if the debt is not paid within a reasonable time. He may compound with the debtor and remit a portion of the amount due if the arrangement is fair and *bona-fide* and is such as a prudent person will enter into with reference to his own estate[1]. If in the exercise of a reasonable discretion he considers it inexpendient to institute legal proceedings and considers it more advantageous to wait or give time and loss nevertheless ensues he will not be liable. He is not liable for mere errors of judgment[2]. It is also his duty to invest in proper securities trust funds in his hands as soon as they are got in or within a reasonable time[3]; otherwise he will be charged with interest[4]. The rules of English Courts as to the proper modes of investments are not bodily applicable in India[5]. They can only be applied with great qualifications. A trustee is not liable merely because he has not invested the funds in his hands in Government or other public securities. He may invest it in any securities provided they are of a permanent and not perishable or terminable nature[5]. But he should not advance on insufficient or no security or in a manner prohibited by the deed of endowment[6]. Where he makes such an unauthorized investment he will be liable[7]. He is of course entitled to remedy this breach of trust without instituting a suit[8].

Right to compound or remit.

Duty to invest in proper securities.

The trustee is bound to keep accounts of the trust[9] (*i.e.* of the income and expenditure). He must be ready with them at any time. He must not mix his own moneys with the trust funds[10]. If in con-

Duty to account—not to make any profit out of trust.

1. *Rajaram Devai* v. *Lakshmi Sankara*, (1901) 18 M. L. J. R. 206.

2. *Burton* v. *Burton*, (1835) 1 My & Cr. 80 (95): S. C. 40 Eng. Rep. 307 (313); *Paddon* v. *Richardson*, (1855) 7 D. M. & G. 563 (582, 583); *Annaji Raghunath* v. *Narayan Sitaram*, (1896) I. L. R., 21 B. 556 (559); *Tiruvengadath Ayyangar* v. *Srinivasa Thathachariar*, (1899) I. L. R., 22 M. 361 (364). Cf. *Jackson* v. *Dickinson*, [1903] 1 Ch. 947 (952).

3. *Thackersey Dewraj* v. *Hurbhum Nursey*, (1884) I L. R., 8 B. 432 (468); *Rajaram Devai* v. *Lakshmi Sankara*, supra.

4. Lewin on Trusts p. 380. See also *Shepherd* v. *Mouls*, (1845) 4 Hare 500 (503): S. C. 67 R. R. 138 (141, 142).

5. *Desouza* v. *Ignasio Francisco Desouza*, (1875) 12 B. H. C. 184; *Thackersey Dewraj* v. *Hurbhum Nursey*, (1884) I. L. R., 8 B. 432 (466). As to the powers of court to sanction such acts as would be breaches of trust if done by trustees without such sanction, see *In re New* [1901] 2 Ch. (534) and *In re Tollemache*, [1903] 1 Ch. 955.

6. *Thackersey Dewraj* v. *Hurbhum Nursey*, (1884) I. L. R. 8 B. 432 (466).

7. *In re Davis-Davis* v. *Davis*, [1902] 2 Ch. 314.

8. *In re Jenkins and H. E. Randall and Co's. contract*, [1903] 2 Ch 362.

9. *Thackersey Dewraj* v. *Hurbhum Nursey*, (1884) I. L. R, 8 B. 432 at p. 470. See also Lewin on Trusts p. 843.

10. Lewin on Trusts pp. 321, 1095 to 1097. See also *In the matter of the petition of D. Cowie*, (1880) I. L. R., 6 C. 70; *Chintaman Bajaji Dev* v. *Dhondo Ganesh Dev*, (1888) I. L. R., 15 B. 612 (623); *In re Oatway-Hertslet* v. *Oatway*, [1903] 2 Ch. 356.

sequence of it loss occurs to the trust he must make good such loss. If by reason of this mixing, difficulties arise in finding out the money due to the trust accounts will be ordered by debiting the manager with all sums that have been withdrawn and applied to his own use so as to be no longer recoverable and debiting the trust with any sums taken out and duly invested in the names of the managers[1]. If the mixture assumes a form in which it is impossible to ascertain the shares of the trust and the shares of the manager personally the trust will be entitled to the whole mixture[1]. The manager cannot make a profit out of the trust[2]. He is not entitled to any remuneration and he must not trade with the trust fund for his own private benefit and make a profit out of it. The trust will be entitled to the profit[3] or in cases there is a loss the manager will have to recoup the money with interest[4].

Trustees cannot set up hostile title.

Trustees cannot acquire by any act of their own an adverse interest. They cannot acquire trust property by adverse possession[5]. They cannot after accepting office set up the invalidity of the trust[6]. If he has taken possession under the trust he is estopped from setting up a title adverse to that of the trust. But this does not mean that trustees on being sued can never plead that the property belongs to them. If they have taken possession under the trust it is said that in the case of ordinary trust they must surrender it to the beneficiary and then claim the property as their own[7]. In the case of managers of endowments the question is one of more difficulty. Where the office devolves according to ordinary laws of inheritance it cannot be said that the successor has taken possession of trust property under the trust. The ancestor was in possession of both private and endowed properties and, therefore,

1. *In re Oatway-Hertslet* v. *Oatway* [1903] 2 Ch. 356.

2. Lewin on Trusts, pp. 296 to 304. See also *Webb* v. *Earl of Shaftesbury* (1802) 7 Ves 488: S. C. 6 R. R. 154; *Aberdeen Town Council* v. *Aberdeen University* (1877) L. R. 2 A. C. 544. Cf *In re Biss-Biss* v. *Biss*, [1903] 2 Ch. 40.

3. *Vyse* v. *Foster*, (1872) L. R. 8 Ch. 309 (329).

4. Lewin on Trusts, pp. 298, 299, 383 to 387. *In re Davis-Davis* v. *Davis* (1902) 2 Ch. 314.

5. Lewin on Trusts pp. 307, 308. S. 10 of the Limitation Act. See *Bitto Kunwar* v. *Kesho Pershad*, (1897) L. R. 24 I. A. 10 (21): S. C. I. L. R., 19 A 277 (291). Cf. Ss. 63, 64 of the Trusts Act.

6. This is especially so where the action is for the administration of the trust. *Wallis* v. *Solicitor General for New Zealand*, [1903] A. C. 173, (186).

7. *Pomfret* v. *Lord Windsor*, (1752) 2 Ves. Sen. 472: S. C. 28 Eng. Ref. 302 (308, 309); *Attorney General* v. *Munro*, (1848) 2 DeG. & Sm. 122 (141, 142, 162, 163

the only question would be as to the nature of the property[1]. But if it is shewn that managers have come into possession of trust property under the trust they will be answerable as trustees although they may not have consciously accepted a trust[2].

Manager's power to do acts reasonably necessary for the protection of the endowment.

These duties will give us some of the rights or powers of the managers. The latter will be entitled to do all that is reasonable for the proper realisation, protection or benefit of the endowment. If any repairs are necessary that may be done by him although it is said he ought not to borrow or charge the estate for the purpose of such repairs[3]. He is entitled to receive the debts and his receipt will discharge the debtor although he may be only one of several managers[4]. His right to compound with the creditors has already been stated. He must defend suits against the endowment and his powers of compromise so far as the management of the trust and the succession to the office are concerned have already been stated. If he is sued for any debt due by the endowment he may compound with the plaintiff provided he has acted fairly and honestly. He may spend money out of the trust estate for the purpose of defending hostile litigious attacks[5]. He may submit the dispute to arbitration[6].

Right of indemnity.

A manager is bound to perform the services and worship connected with the idol out of the income accruing from the endowed funds and is not bound to spend for these out of his pocket[7]. But if he meets the expenses out of pocket he will be entitled to an indemnity from the institution[8]. Even where he incurs costs out of pocket in defending hostile suits against the

1. *Chintaman Bajaji Dev* v. *Dhondo Ganesh Dev*, (1888) I. L. R., 15 B. 612; *Shri Ganesh Dharnidhar Maharajdev* v. *Keshavrav*, (1890) I. L. R., 15 B. 625.

2. *Manohar Ganesh* v. *Lakhmiram*, (1887) I. L R.. 12 B. 247 (265).

3. *Nallayappa Pillian* v. *Amblavana Pandara Sannadhi*, (1903) I. L. R., 27 M. 465 (473). For a discussion of this case, see p. ccviii.

4 *Rambabu Parbu Mirasi* v. *Members of the Committee of Management of Savasthan Shri Dev Rameshwar of Achare*,(1899) 1 Bom. L. R. 667. Cf. S.42 of the Trusts Act.

5. *Prosunno Kumari* v. *Golabchand*, L. R. 2 I. A. 145 (151); *Thackersey Dewraj* v. *Hurbhum Nursey*, (1884) I. L. R., 8 B. 432 (467).

6. *Davies* v. *Ridge*, (1800) 6 R. R., 817. See Lewin on Trusts, pp. 703, 704. See Trustee Act 1893 (56 & 57 Vict. Ch. 53) S.21 and Russel on Arbitration and Award p. 31. See also Tudor on Charitable Trusts 318.

7. *Tayubunnissa Bibi* v. *Kuwar Sham Kishore Roy*, (1871) 7 B. L. R., 621, (629): S. C. 15 W. R., C. R. 228.

8. *Radha Jeebun Moostofee* v. *Tara Monee Dossee*, (1865) 3 W. R. Mis. 25 (26). See Lewin on Trusts, pp. 755 to 757.

institution, he has this right of indemnity[1]. Where he has so incurred expenses, he is not entitled to claim contribution personally from the other co-managers or trustees unless there is an express or implied contract among them that one should incur expenses out of pocket and that others should contribute[2].

Duty to accept voluntary contributions and perform festivals.

A manager is under a duty to perform all festivals and to do all acts necessary for the worship and service of the idol out of the trust funds. In India it is customary to perform festivals out of voluntary contributions made by worshippers and in fact endowments of temples and mutts are frequently founded by such contributions[3]. The manager, therefore, cannot refuse to accept such contributions and to perform the festivals at his mere whim and pleasure[4]. But it cannot be said that the manager has no discretion in the matter[4]. If in the exercise of his discretion he acts with an absence of indirect motive, with honesty of intention and with a fair consideration of the subject he will not be guilty of any misconduct. But if, on the contrary, he should, from corrupt or improper motives or without any sufficient cause, refuse to accept voluntary contributions offered for purposes not inconsistent with the principles, rules, or usages of the institution or to allow such contributions to be applied for those purposes, then the manager will be liable[5]. If it is the custom for the manager so to receive contributions and perform the festivals, *a fortiori* he will be guilty of a breach of trust if he refuses without any sufficient cause to do the same in any particular year[6]. Courts will restrain a trustee or manager from injuring the interests of the

1. Lewin on Trusts pp. 755 to 758. See also *In re Ormsby*, (1809) 1 B. & B. 191: S. C. 12 R. R. 13; *Blackford* v. *Davis*, (1869) L. R. 4 Ch. 304; *Poole* v. *Pass*, (1839) 1 Beav. 600 (604, 605); *Feoffees of Heriot's Hospital* v. *Ross*, (1846) 12 Cl. & Fin. 506 at p. 515.

2. *Radha Jeebun Mosstuffy* v. *Taramonee Dossee*, (1869) 12 M. I. A. 380 (393, 394).

3. West and Buhler, (3rd Edn.) p. 201; See also *Sammantha Pandara* v. *Sellappa Chetti*, (1879) I. L. R., 2 M. 175 (179); *Thackersey Devraj* v. *Hurbhum Nursey*, (1884) I. L. R., 8 B. 432 (454,462); *Elayalwar Reddiar* v. *Namberumal Chettiar*, (1899) I. L. R., 23 M. 298 (303).

4 Per *Subramania Iyer*, J. in *Elayalwar Reddiar* v. *Namberumal Chettiar*, (1899) I. L. R., 23 M. 298 (303).

5. *Elayalwar Reddiar* v. *Namberumal Chettiar*, (1899) I. L. R., 23 M. 298 (303, 304).

6. See *Elayalwar Reddiar* v. *Namberumal Chettiar*, (1899) I. L. R., 23 M. 298 (304,306)

institution under his charge by corruptly, arbitrarily or wantonly departing from the ordinary course of procedure in regard to essential or important matters connected with the institution[1]. He will, therefore, be directed specifically to accept the offerings and to perform the festivals.

Power of manager to make rules as to admission.

The manager of a temple cannot make rules preventing free admission into the institution. It is the right of every worshipper to have free access into the institution for purposes of worship[2]. The manager cannot levy fees for admitting people into the institution for purposes of worship[3]. Of course the worshipper must be orderly and behave properly. If he does not observe this condition, he may be ejected by the manager[4]. The latter may, therefore, frame rules for preserving orderliness and decency of worship. It may also be that in particular parts of the institution, entrance may be regulated with the permission of the manager owing to the extraordinary value of the idol and its ornaments[5]. In some places, such as Chidambaram it has been the usage to levy fees for shewing particular parts of the institution more on account of their sanctity than on account of the extraordinary value of anything to be found there. Whether such a usage is legal and reasonable may be open to question. If the fee is to be regarded as remuneration for the service of the attendant in making an exhibition of the place then there may be some reason for upholding it. Even then, one does not see why a worshipper should not be allowed to do it himself. Anyhow the power to regulate admission must be exercised, not capriciously, but only in good faith on necessary occasions and for necessary and legal purposes[6].

Ritual.

Under the Hindu Law and usage there is a code of ritual. In fact the Agama Shastras provide for this in detail and the Agama of each institution has also to be consulted. The Archaka or Gurukkal is the person who has to conduct the worship and observe

---

1. Per *Subramania Iyer*, J. in *Elayalwar Reddiar* v. *Namberumal Chettiar*, (1899) I. L. R., 23 M. 298 at p. 304.

2. *Kalidas Jivram* v. *Gor Parjaram Hirji*, (1890) I. L. R., 15 B. 309 (316, 317, 318 and 321).

3. Ibid at pp. 318 and 321; or cannot close the temple for which see *Natesa* v. *Ganapati*, (1890) I. L. R., 14 M. 103. (110). Cf. *Marrian Pillai* v. *Bishop of Mylapore*, (1894) I. L. R., 17 M. 447.

4. *Kalidas Jivram Gor Parjaram Hirji*, (1890) I. L. R., 15 B. at pp. 317 and 318. See also *Thackersey Dewraj* v. *Hurbhum Nursey*, (1884) I. L. R., 8 B. 432 (459).

5. *Kalidas Jivram v. Gor Parjaram Hirji* (1890) I. L. R. 15 B. 309 (321).

6. *Kalidas Jivram* v. *Gor Parjaram Hirji*, (1890) I. L. R., 15 B. 309 at p. 322.

the ritual. He cannot change this ritual or the form of worship[1]. Nor has the manager of a temple any right to interfere in matters of ritual in the sense that he can change the ritual. He is, of course, entitled to see that the Archaka observes the usual ritual and to set the Archaka right when the latter departs from the established ritual. In some cases it may be that by usage the dharmakarta has the authority to regulate the ceremonies and processions in connection with idols[2]. But this authority can only be to act in accordance with usage and does not give him any power to change the ritual. When there is a breach of duty in respect of this either on the part of the Archakas or Managers they will be liable for the same in Civil Courts. In such a case if any question is raised as to the proper form of the ritual, Civil Courts are bound to determine and cannot refuse to try the same[3]. Such questions of ritual are determined incidentally with reference to the civil rights of the parties *viz.*, whether the Archaka or the Dharmakarta has been guilty of a breach of trust or neglect of duty[4]. There may be no State Church in India and there may be no Ecclesiastical Court[5] but this will not prevent Civil Courts from determining such questions when it is necessary to decide the rights of the parties. If the Archaka having an hereditary right in his office is dismissed for not observing a particular ritual he may in a suit for reinstatement claim that it is not the ritual observed according to usage. In such a case Civil Courts ought necessarily to try the question. So also where the manager is charged with misconduct on account of his having deviated from usage and a question arises as to the existence of the usage it seems unreasonable to be told

1. *Venkatarayar* v. *Srinivasa Ayyangar* (1872) 7 M, H. C. 32 (35, 36).
2. *Subbaraya Gurukal* v. *Chellappa Mudali*, (1881) I. L. R, 4 M, 315. See also *Nanjappa* v. *Pullapa* (1869) 5 Mad. Jur. 13.
3. Per *Subramania Iyer*, J. in *Elayalwar Reddiar* v *Namberumal Chettiar*, (1899) I. L. R., 23 M. 298 at p. 304. See also *Subbaraya Gurukal* v. *Chellappa Mudali*, supra.
4. Ibid. See also *Dasika Ayengar* v. *Guntavatara Iyengar*, (1858) M.S. D. A 256; *Narasimma Chariar* v. *Sri Kristna Tata Chariar*, (1871) 6 M. H. C. 449 (451); *Tiru Krishnama* v. *Krishnasawmi*, (1879) L.R. 6 I. A. 120: S. C. I.L.R., 2 M 62; *Krishnasami Tatacharyar* v. *Krishnamacharyar*, (1882) I. L. R.. 5 M. 312; *Srinivasa Thathachariar* v. *Srinivasa Aiyangar*, (1899) 9 M. L. J. R., 355 (357, 358); Per *Davies*, J. in *Nagiah Bathudu* v. *Muthacharry*, (1900) 11. M. L. J. R., 215 (226). The decision of the Privy Council in *Browne* v. *Cure de Montreal*, (1874) L. R. 6 P. C. 157 may also be usefully borne in mind in this connection.
5. *Vasudev* v. *Vamanaji*, (1880) I.L.R., 5B. 80; *Venkatachalapati* v. *Subbarayadu*, (1890) I. L. R, 13 M. 293 (305). If in the Bombay case the committee had a right to dismiss pujaris for breach of duty and if they had dismissed them the question whether they were properly dismissed would be one triable by civil courts. If, on the other hand, there was no such right and the pujaris were managers along with the committee a suit to compel trustees to do their duty or make them liable for breach of trust would be one triable in the civil courts. See *Fazul Karim* v. *Mowla Buksh*, (1891) L. R. 18 I. A. 59: S. C. I. L. R., 18 C. 448.

that such question cannot be tried by the Civil Courts. Under the Mahomedan Law there seems to be no code of ritual[1]. It is also said that the right of every Mahomedan to use the mosque for the purpose of prayer is not affected by his non-conformity in matters of ritual[2]. The Imam cannot, be said to vary the ritual if the variation or departure is only slight. The question in each case of dispute must be as to the magnitude or importance of the alleged departure[3]. If there be any dissentients they may pray in their own way. But they cannot set up another leader (Imam) at the same time when prayer is being conducted by the duly authorized Imams. If they behave improperly they may be ejected.

Rights and duties of managers with reference to subordinate office-holders.

This brings us to the question as to the authority of the manager to deal with the subordinate servants of the institution. There are many such persons holding hereditary offices in the Hindu temples. The Gurukkal or the Archaka for instance is very often an hereditary office-holder. In many cases endowments are attached to his office the income of which will represent the remuneration for his services. His duties consist in the performance of the rites of consecration, worship, festivals &c[4]. In Vishnu temples it is also the right of the worshippers to take from his hand sacred water (thirtha) and leaf and to have the God's Shadagopam placed on their head. In many cases he has also the custody of jewels. The dharmakarta or manager has the right to see that the Archaka or any subordinate office-holder performs his duty properly. We have already referred to the subordinate office-holders under the mutwalli. If the office-holder does not do his duty properly he may be fined or dismissed by the manager or mutwalli[5]. The dharmakartas or mutwallis have a right to dismiss the office-holders subordinate to them for sufficient cause[6] without

---

1. *Fazul Karim* v. *Mowla Buksh*, (1891) L. R. 18 I. A. 59: S. C. I. L. R., 18 C. 448.

2. Per *Mahomed*, J. in *Queen Empress* v. *Ramzan*, (1885) I. L. R., 7 A. 461; *Jangu* v. *Ahmad Ullah*, (1889) I. L. R., 13 A. 419; *Adam Sheik* v. *Isha Sheik*, (1894) 1 C. W. N. 76. Cf. *Maine Moilar* v. *Islam Amanath*, (1891) I. L. R., 15 M. 355.

3. *Fazul Karim* v. *Mowla Buksh*, (1891) L.R. 18 I. A. 59: S. C. I. L. R., 18 C. 448.

4. *Soobboo Goorookkul* v. *Tayoo Ummal*, (1857) M. S. D. A. 80. See *Kristnasami Tatacharry* v. *Gomatum Rangacharry*, (1868) 4 M. H. C. 63 (9th thirtham Arulappadu). For the *Stanik*, see *Venkatarayar* v. *Srinivasa Ayyangar*, (1872) 7 M. H. C. 32.

5. *Lotlikar* v. *Wagle* (1882) I. L. R., 6 B. 596.

6. *Raghavacharry* v. *Yavaluppa*, (1849) M. S. D. A. 37; *Subtursky Gooroolul* v. *Tumbia Pillai*, (1854) M. S. D. A. 81; *Vedachella Goorookul* v. *Sabupati Chetti*, (1855) M. S. D. A. 78; *Ranee Parvata Vardhany Nauchiar* v. *Mungalaswara Goorookul* (1856) M.S.D.A. 165; *Kristnasamy Tatacharry* v. *Gomatum Rangacharry*, (1868) 4 M.H.C. 63.

recourse to any suit. Misconduct[1], disobedience to the dharma karta or contempt of his authority[2] will be a sufficient cause. The sufficiency of the ground will be liable for revision in Civil Courts[3]. We have seen that similar principles hold good in the case of Committees appointed under Act XX of 1863 and Dharmakartas of institutions falling under S. 3 and the cases dealing with the questions of notice, of sufficient cause &c., may be usefully referred to in this connection[4]. No general rules can be laid down defining the degree and kind of misconduct which will justify the dismissal of such servants by the dharmakarta or mutwalli[5]. Each case must depend upon its own merits and the particular circumstances established in it. On dismissal and until a new person is appointed the dharmakarta may be entitled to the custody of the jewels[6]. But in cases of hereditary offices, Dharmakartas have no right to appoint to the office[7]. Upon a vacancy the office will vest in the next heir[8] or if the Dharmakartas have the right to appoint he must appoint the next heir provided he is competent[9]. Apparently if the next heir is a minor the dharmakarta may appoint a person temporarily to do the duties until the next heir attains age[10]. The manager is also bound to see that the emoluments attached to the office are not improperly severed from the office[11]. The emoluments must not be severed from the office and a sale of the lands will be illegal[12]. In

1. See cases cited in note (7) p. ccliii. See also *Chand Mean* v. *Khondker Ashrutoollah*, (1866) 6 W. R. C. R. 89 (Office of Khadim).

2. *Meher Ali* v. *Golam Nuzuff*, (1869) 11 W. R. C. R. 333 (334) (office of Takkiadar). See also *Dooteram Surmah* v. *Lukhee Kant*, (1869) 12 W. R. C. R. 425 (427) distinguishing *Ram Doss* v. *Mohesur Deb Misseree*, (1867) 7 W. R. C. R. 446. See also notes to S. 7 of Act XX of 1863 p. 50.

3. *Vadachella Goorokul* v. *Sabapathy Chetty*, (1855) M. S. D. A. 78; *Kristnasamy Tatacharry* v. *Gomatum Rangacharry*, (1868) 4 M. H. C. 63. Cf. *Ridgway* v. *The Hungerford Market Co.*, (1835) 3 Ad. & Ell. 171: S. C. 42 R. R. 352; *Horton* v *M'Murtry*, (1860) 29 L. J. Ex. 260 (264).

4. See notes to S. 7 pp. 48 to 50. Cf. *The Advocate General of Bombay* v. *David Haim Devaker*, (1886) I. L. R., 11 B. 185 (194, 195).

5. *Kristnasamy Tatacharry* v. *Gomatum Rangacharry*, (1868) 4 M. H. C. 63.

6. See *Sriranga Charlu* v. *Madhavagiri Aplachari*, (1860) M. S. D. A. 52.

7. *Alagirisami Naickar* v. *Sundareswara Ayyar*, (1898) I. L. R., 21 M. 278 (284).

8. *Gopinadha Panda* v. *Ramachandra*, (1896) 6 M. L. J. R., 255.

9. *Alagirisami* v. *Sundareswara Ayyar*, supra. As to the right of the Court to appoint managers on a vacancy when the office is hereditary, see p. ccxciii.

10. Cf. *Gopinadha Panda* v. *Ramachandra* (1896) 6 M. L. J. R., 255.

11. *Moolji Bhulabhai* v. *Manohar Ganesh*, (1887) I. L. R., 12 B. 322; *Chidambaram Chetti* v. *Minammal*, (1898) I. L. R., 23 M. 439 (440).

12. *Lakshmanaswami Naidu* v. *Rangamma*, (1902) I. L. R., 26 M. 31.

Bombay it seems that the objection is only against compulsory alienations or sales in *invitum* but that according to custom private alienations may be allowed in some cases[1]. The possession of the servant cannot become adverse to the deity or to the manager as representing the institution[2]. We have seen that the manager's right is only a right to custody. In the case of a servant the latter's right to hold the endowed properties must be still less. He has only a bare authority or license to deal with the thing in a certain way[3] and he need not, therefore, sue for possession but may sue to establish his right and to prevent others from interfering with such right[4]. A suit to establish such a hereditary office will lie in the Civil Courts[5]. Such servants cannot be entitled to hold the temple properties when the manager is not dismissed[6] although they may be interested in bringing suits for removal of managers and may be entitled to bring such suits[7]. But when the manager remains in office they cannot ordinarily be entitled to bring suits with reference to the properties of the institution[8] or be placed in possession of such properties[9].

Co-managers or mutwallis—Rights and duties.

We have already seen that joint managers or mutwallis must act jointly. Any act done by one without consulting the others will be

---

1. *Rajaram* v. *Ganesh* (1898) I.L.R., 23 B. 131 (135, 136). The view suggested here that only Madras takes the extreme view is obviously wrong See *Srimati Mallika Dasi* v. *Ratenmani Chakervati*, (1897) 1 C.W.N. 493. In *Lotlikar* v. *Wagle*, (1882) I. L.R., 6B. 596 however, it was held that a sale in execution of a decree of a Gurrao's interest in lands held by him as emoluments to his office was held to be legal and that the purchaser could hold the same until the removal of the office-holder for failure to perform the services or for other cause.

2. *Moolji Bhulabhai* v. *Manohar Ganesh*, (1897) I. L. R., 12 B. 322.

3. *Janardana Shetti Govindarajan* v. *Badara Shetti Giri*, (1899) I. L. R., 23 M. 385 (388).

4. Ibid at pp. 387 and 388; *Vengan Poosari* v. *Patchamuthu*, (1903) 14 M L. J R. 290.

5. *Pucha Counden* v. *Kotha Counden*, (1856) M. S. D. A. 198; *Narasimma Chariar* v. *Sri Kristna Tata Chariar*, (1871) 6 M. H. C. 449; *Tiru Krishnamachariar* v. *Krishnasawmi*, (1879) L. R. 6 I. A. 120: S C. I. L. R., 2 M. 62; *Krishnasami Tatacharyar* v *Kristnamacharyar*, (1882) I. L. R., 5 M. 313 (318, 319); *Mamat Ram Bayan* v. *Bapu Ram Atai Bura Bhakat*, (1887) I. L. R., 15 C. 159; *Srinivasa* v. *Tiruvengada*, (1888) I. L. R., 11 M. 45·; *Sayad Hashim Saheb* v. *Huseinsha*, (1888) I. L. R., 13 B. 429; *Krishnaswami Thatha Chariar* v. *Appanaiyangar*, (1896) 7 M. L. J. R. 23; *Srinivasa Thathachariar* v. *Srinivasa Aiyangar*, (1899) 9 M. L. J. R. 355.

6. *Ranee Parvata Vurdhany Nauchear* v. *Mungalaswara Goorookul*, (1856) M. S. D. A. 165 where it was said that if such a decree was passed it was placing the servant *above* the master (manager) and not *under* the latter.

7. Ibid. For other cases see Chapter XV.

8. *Kunjunneri Nambiar* v. *Nilakunden*, (1880) I. L. R., 2 M. 167.

9. *Ranee Parvata* v. *Mungaleswara*, supra.

void[1]. The acts of the majority will bind[2] the rest although they will not bind them or the trust if such acts amount to a breach of trust[3]. The usage in each institution must be followed. If, for instance, the usage is to appoint pattamalais in a meeting of the yogakars (*i. e.*, the general body of worshippers) and the adhikaris an appointment made in contravention of the usage will be invalid and a declaration will be made at the suit of a co-manager that the appointment is invalid[4]. There is no such thing in law as a passive trustee[5]. All must look after the management. If trustees delegate the execution of the trust to one of their own body and a loss ensues through the wrongful act of such delegate all will be liable[6]. But it is not necessary that all should join in the act. If so, a dissentient minority can upset the working of the trust. It is enough if the act is that of the majority provided all are given the opportunity to put forth their views and are consulted as aforesaid. The control of the trust funds must be with all. If one is allowed to have sole possession of the trust funds and loss ensues all will be responsible[7]. It is said that the personal right of trusteeship is not joint though the rights of trustees against strangers are joint[8]. It is not easy to understand the distinction that is sought to be made or the statement is a mere truism. On the death of one joint manager his place will be taken by his sons if the office goes according to the ordinary laws of succession and the sons will be entitled to be placed in his rights.

---

1. *Wasiq Ali Khan* v. *Government*, (1836) 6 B. S. D. A. 110 (mutwallis); *Errumbala Chundoo* v. *Coomery Chatoo*, (1849) M. S. D. A. 53; *Ukanda Varriyar* v. *Ramen Nambudiri*, (1863) 1 M. H. C. 262. See for other cases at p. cci.

2. *Charavur Teramuth* v. *Urath Lakshmi*, (1883) I. L. R., 6 M 270; *Natesa* v. *Ganapati*, (1890) I. L. R, 14 M. 103 (110). See cases under notes to S. 7 pp 52 to 57. See also *Wilkinson* v. *Malin*, (1832) 2 Tyr. 544 (562): S. C 37 R. R. 791 807); *Younger* v. *Welham*, (1711) 3 Swanst 180 n: S. C. 19 R. R. 196. Cf. Yajnawalkya Ch. II vv. 188, 192 (Mandlik 230).

3. See Tudor on Charitable Trusts pp. 233, 234 and Lewin on Trusts, pp. 279, 710. See also *Ward* v. *Hipwell*, (1862) 3 Giff. 547: S. C. 6 L. T. N. S. 238 (240).

4. *Janardana Shetti Govindarajan* v. *Badava Shetti Giri*, (1899) I. L. R., 23 M. 385 (387).

5. Lewin on Trusts pp. 278 to 281 and Agnew p. 240. See also *Thackersey Dewraj* v. *Hurbhum Nursey*, (1884) I. L. R., 8 B. 432 (471).

6. *Langford* v. *Gascoyne*, (1805) 11 Ves. 333: S. C. 8 R. R. 170 (172). *Eaves* v. *Hickson*: (1861) 30 Beav. 136 (where the trust funds were paid by the trustees on the faith of a document which turned out to be forged and the trustees were held liable to repay those funds for the trust); *Clough* v. *Bond*, (1861) 3 M. & Cr. 497: S. C. 45 R. R. 314 (317 and 318). See *Kannan* v. *Pazhaniandi*, (1901) I. L. R., 24 M. 438 where it was held that a Karnavan could not appoint another to take his place as manager.

7. *Lewis* v. *Nobbs*, (1878) 8 Ch. Div. 501.

8. *Velu Pandaram* v. *Ganasambanda Pandara Sannadhi*, (1895) I. L. R., 19 M. 243 at p. 248.

Being endowed property no one manager is entitled to claim a partition and a fractional share of the endowed property. But all managers must claim the whole and only in case any one refuses that the others can sue. An arrangement among them as to the management is not binding upon them absolutely[1]. Trust funds must not be lent to a co-trustee unless independent securities are taken[2]. A remission to a co-trustee will be a breach of trust[3]. If a trustee remains passive and takes no steps to see the trust carried into execution, he will be liable for losses caused by a breach of trust on the part of his co-trustee[4]. A suit by one trustee against his other co-trustees for breach of trust will not be maintainable when the plaintiff is also in default and is responsible for the breach of trust[5]. But if he is excluded at the time then an action will lie[6]. A trustee excluded by his co-trustees may bring a suit for an account[7]. It is said that this is his only remedy[7]. But we fail to see why when a person's title as joint manager is denied the proper suit is not a suit for the establishment of his title, and such suits have been recognised by the Courts[8]. It may be that the ruling in 16 Bombay applies where the title is recognised and there is only an exclusion from management of the trust property. The question what is a breach of trust is rather large. Any wrongful violation by the trustee of his duty will be a breach of trust. If all the trustees are equally guilty and no distinction is to be found in the guilt of the several trustees a person who has been compelled to pay the whole loss will be entitled to claim contribution from the others[9]. This claim cannot of course be enforced in a suit instituted against the trustees for breach of trust. If any party has acted fraudulently in the matter and his guilt is therefore greater it may be that he cannot maintain a claim for contribution[10].

Account.

Contribution.

1. See cases cited in note (2) ccxxiv. See also *Mariya Pillai* v. *Govinda Pillai* (1860) M. S. D. A. 285.
2. *Thackersey Dewraj* v. *Hurbhum Nursey*, (1884) I. L. R., 8 B. 432 (466). See Trusts Act S. 54. See Agnew pp. 265, 266.
3. *Ranga Pai* v. *Baba*, (1897) I. L. R., 20 M. 398 at p. 405.
4. *Bai Jadav* v. *Tribhuvandas Jagjivandas*, (1872) 9 B H. C. 333 followed in *Sayad Husseinmiyan* v *Collector of Kaira*, (1895) I. L. R., 21 B. 48 (52).
5. *John Boyle Barry* v. *Octavious Steel*, (1877) 1 C. L. R., 80; *Bahin* v. *Hughes*, (1886) 31 Ch. D. 390 followed in *Ranga Pai* v. *Baba*, (1897) I. L. R., 20 M. 398 (402, 403). See Trusts Act, S. 27.
6. *Ranga Pai* v. *Baba*, (1897) I. L R., 20 M. 398 at p. 403.
7. *Tricumdass Mulji* v. *Khimji Vullabhdas*, (1892) I. L. R., 16 B. 626.
8. *Purappavanalingam Chetti* v. *Nullasivan Chetti*, (1863) 1 M. H. C. 415; *Juggodumba Dossee* v. *Puddomoney Dossee*, 1875) 15 B. L. R., 318; *Athavulla* v. *Gouse*, (1888) I. L. R., 11 M. 288; *Ranga Pai* v. *Baba*, supra.
9. Cf. S. 27 of the Trusts Act. See also *Jackson* v. *Dickinson*, (1903) 1 Ch. 947.
10. Cf. S. 27 (last para) of the Trusts Act.

Removal of hereditary managers.

In case of maladministration by the managers, a suit by the persons interested for remedying the same will lie[1]. The circumstances under which hereditary managers may be removed from office are varied and no general rules can be laid down. The first thing, however, that has to be remembered at the outset is that this is not a question of criminal punishment. The jurisdiction to remove managers is purely a civil jurisdiction exercised by the Courts as ancillary to their duty to see that trusts are properly executed[2]. It is not necessary that any misconduct should be proved. A manager may, of course, be removed for any proved misconduct but dismissal need not necessarily follow[3]. It is no question of right between man and man[4]. The question always is whether the circumstances are such that in the interests of the institution the defendant should be removed. If it is incompatible with the interests of the institution to retain him in office he will be removed[5] and the fact that he belongs to a powerful faction and his removal will probably decrease the votive offerings of the worshippers will not deter a Court from removing him[6]. As Mr. Justice *Scott* observed[7]: "The Court cannot allow an evil precedent to be established and the maladministration of a public trust to go without redress, because the wrongdoers are men of influence, leaders of the caste, able to persuade a number of private persons members of the same caste to throw a cloak over the abuse." So also the difficulties in executing a decree will not deter a Court from passing the decree[8]. But language such as the following is too pessimistic and will certainly not be adopted at the present day. "To talk of the

---

1. *Manohar Ganesh* v. *Lakhmiram*, (1887) I. L. R., 12 B. 247 (265).

2. *Letterstedt* v. *Broers*, (1884) L. R. 9. A. C. 371 (386) followed in *Perumal Naik* v. *Saminatha Pillai*, (1896) I. L. R., 19 M. 498 (500).

3. *Letterstedt* v. *Broers*, (1884) L. R. 9 A. C. 371 at pp. 385, 386.

4. Ibid. See also *Chinna Jiyan Garula Varu* v. *Sri H. M. Mahant Durma Dossji*, (1870) 5 Mad. Jur. 214.

5. *Damodar Bhatji* v. *Bhat Bhogilal Kasandas*, (1896) I. L. R., 22 B. 493; *Tiruvengadath Ayyangar* v. *Srinivasa Thathachariar*, (1899) I. L. R., 22 M. 361 at p. 364. See *Chinna Jiyan Garula Varu* v. *Durma Dossji*, supra.

6. *Thackersey Dewraj* v. *Hurbhum Nursey*, (1884) I. L. R., 8 B. 432 (471).

7. Ibid at p. 471.

8. *Purappavanalingam Chetti* v. *Nullasivan Chetti*, (1863) 1 M. H. C. 415; *Juggodumba Dossee* v. *Puddomoney Dossee*, (1875) 15 B. L. R., 318 (324). See *Docker* v. *Somes*, (1834) My. & K. 655: S. C. 39 R. R. 317 (324).

preservation of the funds of any institution of this character (temple at Tripati) would be idle. They have always been funds for embezzlement and what embezzlement has left will speedily be swallowed up in litigation[1]." This surely ought not to prevent a court from doing its duty. It should try whether there cannot be a better management. In the case in which the above remarks were made what weighed with the Court most was the fact that the plaintiff who should have been appointed if the defendant was removed was no better than the latter and there was no likelihood that the management would be in any way better. Probably no other person could be found. Anyhow the question of removal as was said in that case was one of mixed law, fact and discretion[2]. Mere error of judgment on the manager's part will not entail dismissal[3]. There must be proof of such misconduct as to render his removal from office necessary in the interests of the institution of which he is manager[4]. Where the Court sees nothing but mistake while it gives directions for the better management in future it refuses to visit with punishment what has been transacted in times past[5]. If there is a *bona fide* mistake as to the defendant's true legal position even the assertion of a hostile title on the part of the manager and a contention that he is not a person accountable to anybody need not entail the consequence of removal provided the manager recognises his true position and gives an assurance that he will in future act in accordance with the trust[6]. Some degree of latitute is also allowed by the Courts who do not order accounts against managers where there is no fraud or dishonesty but only mere error of judgment[7] on the part of the latter especially when the taking of such accounts will be too

1. *Chinna Jiyan Garulu Varu* v. *Durma Dossji*, (1870) 5 Mad. Jur. 214 (215).

2. Ibid.

3. *Tiruvengadath Ayyangar* v. *Srinivasa Thathachariar*, (1899) I. L. R., 22 M. 361 at p. 364.

4. Ibid at p. 363. See also notes to S. 14 of Act XX, pp. 104, 105.

5. Lewin on Trusts p. 1149 followed in *Annaji* v. *Narayan*, (1896) I. L. R., 21 B. 556 at p 559.

6. *Annaji* v. *Narayan*, (1896) I. L. R., 21 B. 556 at p. 559; *Damodar Bhatji* v. *Bhat Bhogilal Kasandas*, (1896) I. L. R., 22 B. 493. See also *Muhammad Jafar* v. *Muhammad Ibrahim*, (1900) I. L. R., 24 M. 243.

7. *Advocate General of Bombay* v. *Moulvi Abdul Kadir Jitaker*, (1894) I. L. R., 18 B. 401; *The Advocate General of Bombay* v. *Punjabai*, (1894) I. L. R., 18 B. 551. See *Andrews* v. *M'Guffog*, (1886) L. R. 11 A. C. 313 (324). See also *Attorney General* v. *The Master, Wardens, &c. of the Wax Chandlers' Company*, (1873) L. R. 6 H. L. 1.(14).

costly and not commensurate with the benefit to be derived by the trust by opening the accounts[1]. Courts in England never refuse to stop the improper application of charity funds[2], however, long the misapplication may be but in India where there is no dishonesty or fraud, the Statute of Limitations will be a bar to an account being opened for more than six years[3]. The Courts have power to remove even hereditary managers[4]. Wilful acts of mismanagement and misappropriation (such as not carrying on services, alienating endowed property &c.,) will entail dismissal[5]. The failure to keep accounts together with the fact that the endowed property has been wrongfully alienated will entail dismissal[6]. The wrongful alienation and pledging of God's property, jewels and ornaments for the manager's own private purposes will entail dismissal[7]. In some cases it may be that the Court instead of dismissing the manager will put him on terms[8]. Obstruction to the carrying out of the resolutions of the majority of the managers and opposition to the repair of the temple are acts of misfeasance which may entail dismissal[9]. If the manager is old and infirm and cannot perform the duties of his office or if he becomes insolvent he may be discharged (or removed) from office[10]. If the managers are obdurate and obstruct the smooth management as in the case of joint managers the obdurate managers may be removed[11]. So also neglect to carry out the

---

1. *The Advocate General of Bombay* v. *Bai Punjabai*, (1894) I. L. R., 18 B. 551.

2. Ibid. See Tudor on Charitable trusts, pp.303 to 305.

3. See Chapter XVI, p. cccxxiii.

4. *Fakurudin Sahib* v. *Ackeni Sahib*, (1880) I.L.R., 2M.197(199); *Natesa* v. *Ganapati*, (1890) I. L. R., 14 M. 103 (110, 118); *Chintaman Bajaji Dev* v. *Dhondo Ganesh Dev*, (1888) I. L. R., 15 B. 612; *Annaji* v. *Narayan*, (1896) I. L. R., 21 B. 556 (558).

5. *Sathappayyar* v. *Periasami*, (1890) I. L. R., 14 M. 1 at pp. 11 and 12.

6. *Fakurudin Sahib* v. *Ackeni Sahib*, (1880) I.L.R., 2M. 197(199). Cf. *Anantanarayana Ayyar* v. *Kuttalam Pillai*, (1899) I. L. R., 22 M. 481 at p. 483.

7. *Sreenath Bose* v. *Radhanath Bose*, (1883) 12 C. L. R. 370; *Chintaman Bajaji Dev* v. *Dhondo Ganesh Dev*, I. L. R., 15 B. 612 (624).

8. *Sivasankara* v. *Vadagiri*, (1889) I. L. R., 13 M. 6; *Natesa* v. *Ganapati*, (1890) I. L. R., 14 M. 103 (118).

9. *Natesa* v. *Ganapati*, (1890) I. L. R., 14 M. 103 at p. 110.

10. *Thackersey Devraj* v. *Hurbhum Nursey*, (1884) I. L. R., 8 B 432 (470, 471). See also *Adam's Trust* (1879) 12 Ch. Div. 634 for insolvency; and Cf. S. 7 of the Trusts Act. A member of committee may be removed for unfitness under S. 10 of Act XX of 1863.

11. *Juggodumba Dossee* v. *Puddomoncy Dossee*, (1875) 15 B. L. R., 318 (324); *Natesa* v. *Ganapati*, (1890) I. L. R., 14 M. 103 (110).

trust and allowing the buildings of the instititution to fall into decay will entail dismissal[1].

Effect of dismissal in a foreign state.

In cases in which the institution is in foreign territory and it has got proporties both in foreign and British territories an order of removal made by a competent Court of such foreign territory must be given effect to. Where the foreign territory is a Hindu state and the ruler of that state dismissed a manager of an institution in his territory no effect has been given to such order of dismissal and the dismissed manager has been regarded as the rightful manager by the British Indian Courts[2]. It is doubtful whether the decisions laying down this principle are good law. The Hindu kings are possessed with the functions of the founder of an elymosynary institution in England and in the exercise of such functions they may rightly dismiss the managers for misconduct. This aspect of the matter has not been considered. Where a person has jurisdiction to dismiss a manager the only question is as to the sufficiency of the ground for such dismissal. But where the institution is not in such foreign territory the ruler may not be entitled to dismiss a manager although some endowments may be in his territory.

Costs.

As between strangers on the one hand and trustees on the other, the ordinarily rule as to costs will apply *i.e.*, the costs will follow the event. The trustee can be on no better footing than any ordinary plaintiff or defendant. If a stranger plaintiff who is unsuccessful is ordered to pay the trustee's costs the latter can only get from the former costs as between party and party and not as between attorney and client[3] although he will be entitled to get reimbursement out of the trust funds for any extra costs incurred[4]. In the case of administration suits the trustee will ordinarily be entitled to his costs. But if the suit was rendered necessary owing to the trustee's breach of trust he must pay the costs of a suit to repair it although he may be entitled to the subsequent costs relating to the ordinary taking of

1. *Ganapati Ayyan* v. *Savithri Ammal*, (1897) I. L. R., 21 M. 10 (11, 15).

2. *Nanabhai* v. *Shriman Goswami Girdharij*i, (1888) I. L. R., 12B. 331; *Shriman Goswami* v. *Goswami Shri Girdharlalji*, (1878) I. L. R., 17 B. 620 (note); *Goswami Shri Girdharji* v. *Madhowdas Premji*, (1893) I. L. R., 17 B. 600.

3. Lewin on Trusts, pp. 1200 to 1212. See *Mohun* v. *Mohun*, (1818) 1 Swan 201: S. C. 18 R. R. 58 (59) where it was held that the trust was void and that, therefore, no costs could be ordered out of trust funds (which did not exist).

4. *i. e.*, the difference between the two sets of costs. See Tudor, p. 347. If costs are not recoverable the whole must come out of charity funds. *Attorney General* v. *Lewis*, (1845) 8 Beav. 179. He is not necessarily entitled to get all that he has paid to the attorney. *The Advocate General of Bombay* v. *Jitaker*, (1895) I. L. R., 20 B. 301.

accounts[1]. If the suit be for removal of the trustee on account of his misconduct or dereliction of duty the manager on the charge being established will not be entitled to his costs although he is not removed but must pay the costs of the proceedings[2]. Even where he is successful it will appear that according to the English Practice he will not be entitled to recover costs out of the trust funds as that would be a purely personal action and not one against the estate[3]. Where he is decreed to pay costs personally he cannot afterwards deduct them from the trust funds in his hands[4]. Even where the immediate cause of the institution of the suit is the manager's mere caprice and obstinacy the above principles will apply[5]. But if misconduct is discovered in the course of the suit the trustee will not be directed to pay the whole costs of the suit but only of so much of it as is connected with his misconduct[6]. Where the breach of trust is trivial the Court may give the trustee his whole costs[7]. The Court never gives costs to a defaulting trustee while he continues in default[8]. The costs of the suit will be cast upon the trustee if the latter should set up a title of his own[9]. One co-trustee is entitled to have the bill of costs taxed notwithstanding others may have paid the bill without taxation[10]. Costs against a manager as representing one idol cannot be realized against the funds in his hands but belonging to another idol[11].

---

1. *Pride* v. *Fooks*, (1840) 2 Beav. 430 : S. C. 50 R. R. 217 (232) ; *Hewett* v. *Foster*, (1844) 7 Beav. 348 : S. C. 64 R. R. 98 ; *Bate* v. *Hooper*, (1855) 5 De. G. M. & G. 338 at p. 345 : S. C. 43. Eng. Rep. 901 (904).

2. *Thackersey Dewraj* v. *Hurbhum Nursey*, (1884) I. L. R., 8 B. 432 (473). For English cases, see *Cooper v Skinner*, [1904] 1 Ch. 289 (292, 293); *Brinklow* v. *Singleton* [1904] 1 Ch. 648. See also notes to S. 18 of Act XX pp. 138 to 140.

3. *Brinklow Singleton* [1904] Ch. 648 (657).

4. *Attorney General* v. *Daugars*, (1864) 33 Beav. 621 (623, 624). Tudor, p. 349.

5. Lewin on Trusts p. 1206. See *Penfold* v. *Bouch*, (1844) 4 Hare. 271, (272, 273) and other cases cited in Lewin 1206 note (h).

6. Lewin on Trusts, p. 1209. See *Pride* v. *Fooks*, supra.

7. *Bailey* v. *Gould*, (1840) 4 Y. & C. 221 : S. C. 54 R. R. 479 (483) ; *Knott* v. *Cottee*, (1852) 16 Beav. 77 (81). Cf. *Cotton* v. *Clark*, (1852) 16 Beav. 134.

8. *Birks* v. *Micklethwait*, (1864) 33 Beav. 409 (411).

9. *Willis* v. *Hiscox*, (1838) 4 My. & Cr. 179 : S. C. 48 R. R. 69 (73) ; *Attorney General* v. *The Draper's Company* (1841) 4 Beav. 67 : S. C. 55 R. R. 20 (23) ; *Attorney General* v. *Christ's Hospital*, (1841) 4 Beav. 73 : S. C. 55 R. R. 24 (25). See Lewin on Trusts, p. 1212.

10. *Jijibhoy Muncherji Jijibhoy* v. *Byramji Jijibhoy*, (1893) I. L. R., 18 B. 189.

11. *Attorney General* v. *Grainger*, (1859) 7 W. R. 684 ; *Moonshe Mahomed Akbar* v. *Kalee Churn*, (1876) 25 W. R. C. R. 401.

CHAPTER XV.

RIGHTS OF FOUNDERS AND WORSHIPPERS.

Founder according to the Hindu Law.

According to the Hindu Law, a person who founds a temple and establishes an idol there and endows it with lands &c., will be regarded as the founder[1] and we have seen he will be entitled to annex conditions to his grant. He is entitled to appoint a manager for it with rights of hereditary succession or otherwise and if he fails to do so he will be entitled to manage it and upon his death his heirs will step in his place. But it may not always be easy to say who the founders are. The site of the temple may be given by one, the temple maybe built by another who may establish an idol in it while a third person may endow it with property for carrying on the daily services of such idol. If a person relinquishes his right in a site and makes it over to another for building a temple he may not in law be regarded as a founder[2], unless he expressly or impliedly indicates at the time of relinquishment that he is joining the other in carrying out the object and that he has not given up his rights as a founder. Ordinarily, all persons who establish a worship are entitled to take part in the management as being the founders of the worship and persons who afterwards give endowments for the support of services connected with the idol and its worship are not entitled, only by reason of such endowments, to take part in the management of the worship[3]. In order that they may be entitled to such management they must stipulate to that effect with the founder of the worship[4]. They are not bound to make an endowment and if they make one they are at liberty to stipulate for and impose any conditions. So also the founder of the worship is not bound to accept such a gift with the conditions annexed (especially when they relate to the altering of the Shebaitship of the Thakur) but he is not entitled to treat the condition as null and to recover the endowment. Where, therefore, a person founded an idol and its worship and subse-

1. This must be so according to any system of law.

2. *Venkatachellamiah* v. *Narrainappah*, (1854) M. S. D. A. p.100.

3. *Gossamee Sree Greedhareejee* v. *Rumanlolljee Gossamee*, (1889) L. R. 16 I. A. 137 (144): S. C. I. L. R., 17 C. 3 (20).

4. Ibid. L. R. 16 I. A. at p. 147: S. C. I. L. R., 17 C. at p. 23.

quently a temple was built by another who imposed the condition that the temple and the idol should be managed by a third person and not by the founder of the idol and its worship the latter, if he should claim the idol, would not be entitled to recover the temple for the idol and the idol could not have that habitation but must find out some other or change its shebait and accept the conditions[1].

Founder of worship.

The founder of the worship is the general manager. He will be entitled ordinarily to the custody of all endowments. But where endowments are made and the endowers make provisions of their own for the management as where they appoint themselves as managers with hereditary rights or appoint others with such rights, the founder of the worship as general manager will not be entitled to the custody of such endowments. A person who builds a temple and establishes an idol is the founder of the worship and will be entitled to the management and the mere fact that he appoints a purohit to look after the worship will not disentitle him or his heirs after his death to manage[2]. The management is not by such act given up to the Purohit[3]. The latter is only in the position of an Archaka.

Sometimes the members of a caste subscribe for the building of a temple and for establishing an idol in it. In such a case the caste will, ordinarily, be entitled to appoint somebody for the management[4] and it often happens that the headman of the caste or other person who is entrusted from his position and influence to look after the collection of the subscriptions and the work of construction, &c., is appointed as the manager[5]. The founders *i. e.*, the caste have a voice in the management[6] but others not of the caste are not entitled to any voice in the management by

---

1. *Gossamee Sree Greedharreejee* v. *Rumanlolljee Gossamee*, (1889) L. R. 16 I. A. 137: S. C. I. L. R., 17 C. 3.

2. 2 Macnaughten's H. L. p. 102.

3. Ibid. See also *Maharanee Indurjeet Kooer* v. *Chundemun Misser*, (1871) 16 W. R. C. R. 99 (100).

4. *Thackersey Dewraj* v. *Hurbhum Nursey*, (1884. I. L. R., 8 B. 432 (461 and 462). The caste will have the right of management but it is usual for the caste to appoint one to conduct the management on its behalf.

5. *Thackersey Dewraj* v. *Hurbhum Nursey*, (1884) I. L. R., 8 B. 432 (462). But a person who builds a temple at his own cost on site given up to him will have the right of management. *Venkatachellamiah* v. *Narrainapah*, (1854) M. S. D. A 100.

6. *Thackersey Dewraj* v. *Hurbhum Nursey*, (1884) I. L. R., 8 B. 432 at p. 462.

the fact that they have subscribed for the maintenance and upkeep of the services relating to the worship of the Thakur[1]. But if they were original subscribers to the building itself then it might be different.

Where a charity is established by subscriptions, the original subscribers alone are the founders and any subsequent benefactions[2] are mere accretions or additions to the existing foundation[3]. So also where subscriptions are raised for the purpose of rebuilding a temple the person or persons who collect the subscriptions or who pay the subscriptions cannot be regarded as founders[4].

Founder's rights under Hindu Law.

The founder's rights depend on rules made by him at the time of the deed of foundation or must be gathered from usage[5]. Where there are numerous subscribers who can be regarded as founders and they are so numerous as to preclude the possibility of their all concurring in any instrument declaring the trust, a declaration of trust made by the person or persons in whom the property may have vested or who may have collected the subscriptions at or about the time of the subscriptions being raised may be taken as a *prima facie* true exposition of the intentions of the contributors[6]. In cases where there is no shebait appointed with hereditary rights of succession[7] or the provision made as to the office of shebait ceases to apply owing to the fact that the last holder does not carry out the conditions made in the deed[8] or is incapacit-

---

1. *Thackersey Dewraj* v. *Hurbhum Nursey*, (1884) I. L. R., 8 B. 432 (461).

2. *Lutchmee Ammal* v. *Rookmanee Ammal*, (1857) M S. D. A. 152; *In the matter of the Endowed Schools Act*, (1884) L. R. 10 A C. 304 (308, 309), See Tudor on Charitable Trusts, p. 97.

3. Tudor on Charitable Trusts, pp. 97, 614. See *In the matter of the Endowed Schools Act*, (1884) L. R. 10 A, C. 304 at pp. 308, 309.

4. *Annasami Pillai* v. *Ramakrishna Mudaliar*, (1900) I. L. R., 24 M., 219 at p. 229. Cf. *Appasami* v. *Nagappa* (1884) I. L. R., 7 M. 499 (502, 504); *Thackersey Dewraj* v. *Hurbhum Nursey*, (1884, I. L. R, 8 B. 432 (461).

5. Tudor on Charitable Trusts 117. See *Attorney General* v. *Pearson*, (1871) 3 Meriv. 353 (400): S. C. 17 R. R. 100 (101).

6. *Attorney General* v. *Clapham*, (1854) 4 DeG. M. & G. 591 (626): S. C. 43 Eng. Rep. 638 (652).

7. Cf. *Lutchmee Ammal* v. *Rookmanee Ammal*, (1857) M. S. D. A. p. 152.

8. *Mussamat Jai Bansi Kunwar* v. *Chattar Dhari Sing*,(1870) 5 B. L. R., 181 (184); *Ranjit Singh* v. *Jagannath Prosad Gupta*, (1885) I. L. R., 12 C. 375 (380); *Jagannath Prasad Gupta* v. *Runjit Singh*, (1897) I. L. R., 25 C. 354 (369). In both these cases each incumbent was empowered to appoint his successor but no appointment was made by the last incumbent and no other provision was made in the deed of endowment

ated from carrying out the same by reason of any disqualification such as insanity[1] or removal for misconduct[2] the management is said to vest in the founder and his heirs[3]. But this does not mean that the founder or his heirs have a right to nominate *i. e.*, a very different thing from saying that the office of management vests in the founder and his heirs[4]. If a right of nomination is claimed by the founder such right[5] must be reserved at the time of endowment or be established by usage[6]. Even if a right to nominate is established by usage that will not carry with it a right to dismiss the shebait or Dharmakarta for misconduct.[6] Such a right must be conferred at the time of endowment[7] or established by usage and cannot be inferred from the existence of a right to nominate a successor[8]. The principle is that in the *management* of religious or charitable foundations or institutions the founder and his heirs will have no right to intefere when another is entitled to manage unless any special rights of interference are reserved[9]. A right of supervision or control reserved to the founder without the necessity

---

1. *Syed Muhammad* v. *Fatteh Muhammad*, (1894) L.R. 22 I. A. 4 : S. C. I.L.R., 22C 324.

2. *Ramalingam Pillai* v. *Vythilingam Pillai*, (1890) L.R. 20 I A. 150: S.C. I.L.R., 16 M. 490 (where a Pandarum being head of a mutt and temple was removed for misconduct under S.14 of Act XX of 1863). Where it should appear from the deed of endowment or otherwise that a certain qualification was prescribed by the founder for the office, the same would not revert to the founder and his heirs unless perhaps in a case where the qualification should attach to the founder and his family. The Court would alone be entitled to appoint in such a case, or if the founder reserved the right to nominate he may nominate one. *Gajapati* v *Bhagavan Doss*, (1891) I. L. R., 15 M. 44. Cf. *Sathappayyar* v. *Periasami*, (1890) I. L. R, 14 M. 1 (12).

3. *Mussumat Jai Bansi Kunwar* v. *Chattar Dhari Sing*, (1870) 5 B. L. R., 181; S. C. 13 W.R.C.R. 396; *Ranjit Singh* v. *Jagannath Prosad Gupta*, (1885) I. L. R., 12 C. 375 (380); *Gossamee Sree Greedharreejee* v *Rumanlollji Gossamee*, (1889) L R., 16 I A. 137 ; S. C. I. L. R., 17 C. 3 ; *Jagannath Prasad Gupta* v. *Runjit Singh*, (1897) I.L.R., 25 C. 354 (369) ; *Maharaja Jagadindra Nath* v. *Rani Hemanta*, (1904) 8 C. W. N. 809 (818, 819). But see *Sheoratan Kunwari* v. *Ram Pargash*, (1896) I. L. R, 18 A. 227 which is discussed in p. clxii.

4. Where the right of management vests in the founder and his heirs the latter will have no right to nominate.

5. *Lutchmee Ammal* v. *Rookmanee Ammal*, (1857) M. S. D. A. 152.

6. *Gajapati* v. *Bhagavan Doss*, (1891) I. L. R., 15 M. 44.

7. In *Lutchmee Ammal* v. *Rookmanee Ammal*, (1857) M. S. D. A. p. 152 where a right to dismiss the trustee for misconduct was reserved by the founder at the same time that he reserved the right to nominate a trustee on a vacancy arising. See *Gulam Hussain Saib Saiyad* v. *Aji Ajam Tadallah Saib Kuraishi*, (1868) 4 M. H. C. 44 (48) a case under the Mahomedan Law.

8. *Gajapati* v. *Bhagavan Doss*, (1891) I. L. R., 15 M. 44.

9. *Teertarappa Moodelly* v. *Soonderarajien*, (1851) M. S. D. A. p. 57.

for seeking the aid of Court similar to the right of the founder under the English Law is a personal right and may be barred by the law of limitation[1]. It is said that such a suit is governed by Article 125 of the Limitation Act or where property is sought to be recovered by Article 144[1]. In the absence of a deed of endowment the obligations attaching to the relation of the founder and manager of an institution can only be deduced from the usages of the institution.

Founder's rights when manager misconducts.

Where the manager is guilty of misconduct and is not appropriating the endowments for the proper purpoes of the institution the founder is neither entitled to resume[2] nor to revoke his grant[3]. The property does not revert to the founder by reason of such misconduct[4] nor does the office of shebait or manager vest in such founder[5] so that he will not be entitled to recover possession of the endowed property for himself either in his own right or in his right as manager[6]. The existing manager is entitled to hold his office until he is duly removed and until he is removed none else has the right to represent him in the management[7].

---

1. *Balwant Rao Bishwant Chandra Chor* v. *Purun Mal Chaube*. (1883) L. R., 10 I. A. 90; S. C. I. L. R., 6 A. 1.

2. *Gulam Hussain Saib Saiyad* v. *Aji Ajam Tadallah Saib Kuraishi*, (1868) 4 M. H. C. 44 (47); *Nam Narain Singh* v. *Ramoon Paurey*, (1874) 23 W. R. C. R. 76 But see *Reasut Ali* v. *Abbott*, (1869) 12 W. R. C. R. 132 (133) where the observations are too wide.

3. *Gulam Hussain Saib Saiyad* v. *Aji Ajam Tadallah Saib*, (1868) 4 M. H. C. 44 (47); *Mohesh Chunder Chuckerbutty* v. *Koylash Chunder Chuckerbutty*, (1869) 11 W. R. C. R. 443; *Doyal Chund Mullick* v. *Syud Keramut Ali*, (1871) 16 W. R. C. R. 116 (118). See also *Hidait-Oon-Nissa* v. *Syud Afzul Hosssein*, (1870) 2 N. W. P. 420 (a case under the Mahomedan Law). Breach of trust will not negative the trust. See Chapter III, p. xxx note (4).

4. *Reasut Ali* v. *Abbott*, (1869) 12 W. R. C. R. 132. See *Syud Asheerooddeen* v. *Sremutty Drobo Moyee*, (1876) 25 W. R. C. R. 557 (559); *Jangu* v. *Ahmad-Ullah*, (1889) I. L. R, 13 A. 419 at p. 429 (a case under the Mahomedan Law).

5. *Biddia Soonduree Dossee* v. *Dooorganund Chatterjee*, (1874) 22 W. R. C. R. 97.

6. *Bhurruck Chunder Sahoo* v *Golam Shuruff*, (1868) 10 W. R. C. R. 458 (459); *Mohesh Chunder Chuckerbutty* v. *Koylash Chunder Chuckerbutty* (1869) 11 W. R. C. R. 443; *Biddia Soonduree Dossee* v. *Doorganund Chatterjee*, (1874) 22 W. R. C. R. 97 (98); *Nam Narain Singh* v. *Ramoon Paurey*, (1874) 23 W.R. C. R. 76. See also note(7).

7. *Gulam Hussain Saib Saiyad* v. *Aji Ajam Tadallah Saib Kuraishi*, (1868) 4 M. H. C. 44; *Biddia Soonduree Dossee* v. *Doorganund Chatterjee*, (1874) 22 W. R. C. R., 97 (98); *Phate Saheb Bibi* v. *Damodar Premji* (1879) I.L.R., 3 B. 84 (88). See also S.A. 1281 of 1900, dated 6th April 1903 M. H C. Jud. Ind. for 1903, p. 8. Cf. *Reasut Ali* v. *Abbott*, (1869) 12 W. R. C. R. 132 (133).

Founder's rights to sue for enforcement of trusts and for preventing maladministration.

But although the founder and his heirs may not resume or revoke the grant it is undoubted that they have a right in case the trusts are not carried out to sue for enforcement of the same and for the due preservation and proper administration of the endowments. In *Kassyvassy Krishna Putter* v. *Vangula Shangaranath*[1] a suggestion was made to this effect. In 1864 this right was recognised by the Calcutta High Court in *Prosunno Moyee Dossee* v. *Koonjo Beharee Chowdhree*[2]. But the Calcutta High Court thought in 1880 that it was not decided prior to that case that the founder's heirs had any right to sue for the enforcement of trusts created by the founder for religious and charitable purposes[3]. In that case, it was held that the founder's heirs would have a right to sue for the enforcement of the trusts founded by their ancestor for religious and charitable purposes. It was stated that as there was no public officer in India as the Attorney General in England endowed with the faculty of enforcing administration of public trusts, the founder and his heirs should at least be given the right to sue for enforcement of trusts even prior to S. 539, C. P. C.[4]. It is a question to be considered whether the Advocate-General did not stand in that position for India even prior to S. 539 C. P. C. But apart from this even in England the founder of an eleemosynary corporation is entitled as visitor to redress abuses and it is to be regretted that Courts in India have not clothed the founder[5] with the high powers which he certainly possesses according to the English Law[6]. But it must now be taken to be settled that the founder or settlor or the founder's

---

1. (1858) M. S. D. A., p. 39. It was also assumed in a case in the Bengal Sadr Diwani Adalat. See *Bejayee Gobind Burral* v. *Kallee Dass*, (1850) B. S. D. A. 447.

2. (1864) W. R. Sp. C. R., 157. See *Biddia Soonduree Dossee* v *Doorganund Chatterjee*, (1874 21 W. R C. R., 97 (where, however, the suit was not so brought and the Court refused an amendment of the plaint); *Nam Narain Singh* v. *Ramoon Paurey*, (1874) 23 W. R. C. R., 76. See also *Bhurruck Chunder Sahoo* v. *Golam Shuruff*, (1868) 10 W. R. C. R., 458 where it was remarked that a descendant of the founder (though he was not the latter's heir) was entitled to bring such a suit. Cf. *Mohesh Chunder Chuckerbutty* v. *Koylash Chunder Chuckerbutty*, (1869) 11 W. R. C. R., 443. But see *Phate Saheb Bibi* v. *Damodar Premji*, (1879) I. L. R., 3 B. 84(88).

3. *Brojomohun Doss* v. *Hurrololl Doss*, (1880) I. L. R , 5 C. 700 (705).

4. See Chapter XVI. See also *Shri Ganesh Dharnidhar Maharajdev* v. *Keshavrav Govind Kulgavkar*, (1890), I. L. R., 15 B. 625 (636) dissenting from *Manicklal Atmaram* v. *Manchershi Dinsha*, (1876) I. L. R., 1 B. 269, on another point.

5. *Teertaruppa Moodelly* v. *Soonderarajien*, (1851) M. S. D. A. 57.

6. Tudor pp. 77, 78 See *Bishop of Ely* v. *Bentley*, (1732) 2 Bro. P. C. 220: S. C.1 Eng. Rep. 898; *Attorney General* v. *Magdalen College* (1847) 10 Beav. 402 (408); *Thomson* v. *The University of London*, (1864,) 33 L. J. Ch. 625 (634, 635).

or settlor's heirs are entitled to enforce the due administration of the trusts under both the Hindu[1] and the Mahomedan laws[2].

Nature of suit.

The suit by the founder or his heirs must in substance allege a breach of trust[3] when it is brought against the manager or there must be an allegation that the trusts are not properly performed. In such suit the founder or his heirs may sue for the enforcement of the trust, for the removal of the old trustee, for appointment of a new one and for the properties being placed in the possession of such new trustee[4]. The founder or his heir is not incompetent to sue for such possession to be given over to the new trustee although without asking for the removal of the old trustee he will not be entitled to sue merely for possession[5]. He is also entitled to sue to set aside any alienations made by the trustee (manager or mutwalli) and to restore the endowed properties for the trust[6]. Where trust property is attached for the private debts of the manager he is entitled to sue for a declaration that the property is not liable to attachment for the private debts of

1. *Prosunno Moyee Dossee* v. *Koonjo Beharee Chowdhree*, (1864) W. R. Sp. C. R. 157; *Biddia Soonduree Dossee* v. *Doorganund Chatterjee*, (1874) 22 W. R. C R. 97; *Nam Narain Singh* v. *Ramoon Paurey*, (1874) 23 W. R. C. R., 76; *Brojomohun Doss* v. *Hurrololl* (1880) I. L. R. 5 C. 700; *Sathappayyar* v. *Periasami*, (1890) I. L. R., 14 M. 1 (at pp. 7, 14 and 15); *Sheoratan Kunwari* v. *Ram Pargash*, (1896) I. L. R., 18 A. 227. Cf. *Mohesh Chunder Chuckerbutty* v. *Koylash Chunder Chuckerbutty*, (1869) 11 W. R. C. R 443.

2. *Bhurruck Chunder Sahoo* v. *Golam Shuruff*, (1868) 10 W. R. C. R. 458; *Hidait-Oon-Nissa* v. *Syud Afzul Hossein*, (1870) 2 N. W. P. 420; *Futmabibi* v. *The Advocate General of Bombay*, (1881) I. L. R., 6 B. 42 (53, 54); *Lakshmandas Parashram* v. *Ganpatrav Krishna*, (1884) I. L. R., 8 B. 365 (case of a Hindu endowing property for celebrating '*urus*' in honor of a Mahomedan Saint); *Kazi Hassan* v. *Sagun Balkrishna*, (1899) I. L. R., 24 B. 170 (176, 180.) Cf. *Syud Asheeroddeen* v. *Sreemutty Drobo Moyee*, (1876) 25 W. R. C. R. 557. But see *Phate Saheb Bibi* v. *Damodar Premji*, (1879) I. L. R., 3 B. 84.

3. *Brojomohun Doss* v. *Hurrololl*, (1880) I. L. R., 5 C. 700.

4. *Bhurruck Chunder Sahoo* v. *Golam Shuruff*, (1868) 10 W. R. C.R. 458; *Mohesh Chunder Chuckerbutty* v. *Koylash Chunder Chuckerbutty*, (1869) 11 W. R. C. R. 443 (where it was said that a suit for the proper administration of the trust would lie); *Biddia Soonduree Dossee* v. *Doorganund Chatterjee*, (1874) 22 W. R C. R. 97; *Sheoratan Kunwari* v. *Ram Pargash*, (1896) I. L. R, 18 A. 227. See also *Giyana Sambandha Pandara Sannadhi* v. *Kandasami Tambiran*, (1887) I. L. R., 10 M. 375 (502); *Satthappayyar* v. *Periasami*, (1890) I. L. R, 14 M. 1 (13); and *Gajapati* v. *Bhagavan Doss*, (1891) I. L. R., 15 M. 44. See also *Ganapati Ayyan* v. *Savithri Ammal*, (1897) I. L. R., 21 M. 10 (11, 15).

5. See cases cited in note (6) p. cclxvii. But see *Lakshmandas Parashram* v. *Ganpatrav Krishna*, (1884) I. L. R., 8 B. 365.

6. *Prosunno Moyee Dossee* v. *Koonjo Beharee Chowdhree*, (1864) W.R. Sp. C R. 157; *Nam Narain Singh* v. *Ramoon Paurey*, (1874) 23 W. R. C R. 76; *Kazi Hassan* v. *Sagun Balkrishna*, (1899) I L. R., 24 B. 170 (176) where it was said that members of the mutwalli's family will be entitled to bring such suits. See also *Lakshmandas Parashram* v. *Ganpatrav Krishna*, (1884) I. L. R., 8 B. 365.

the manager or mutwalli[1]. If misconduct is proved a decree might be passed for removing the old manager or mutwalli from his office and from possession of the endowed properties, for appointment of a new one and for the properties being placed in the possession of such new manager or mutwalli[2]. In a case where the management would vest in the plaintiff as the founder's heir on a vacancy caused by the removal of the actual incumbent for mis conduct the decree should recognise the plaintiff's right and give him possession as such manager[3]. If the plaintiff as the founder's heir is entitled to nominate a successor on a vacancy arising the decree should direct that the plaintiff should nominate a successor within a certain time fixed by the Court and should report the matter to the Court at least in cases of public trusts[4].

Founder's right of suit not controlled by S. 539, C. P. C.

A suit by the founder or his heir for enforcement of the trusts is one which can be brought independent of S. 539, C. P. C., and the founder is not obliged to sue under that section[5]. But there is nothing to prevent him from suing under S. 539, C. P. C., after obtaining sanction[6]. Of course where he chooses to bring a suit under S. 539, C. P. C., he must bring such a suit as can be taken

---

1. *Kazi Hassan* v. *Sagun Balkrishna*, (1899) I. L. R., 24 B. 170 (181). See also Chapter XIV, pp. ccv, ccvi, ccxxxi, ccxxxii.

2. *Sheoratan Kunwari* v *Ram Pargash*, (1896) I. L. R., 18 A. 227. See *Giyana Sambandha Pandara Sannadhi* v. *Kandasami Tambiran*, (1887) I. L. R., 10 M. 375 (502). See also *Sathappayyar* v. *Periasami*, (1890) I. L. R., 14 M. 1 (a case relating to a private mutt). The case of *Bhurruck Chunder Sahoo* v. *Golam Shuruff*, (1868) 10 W. R. C. R. 458 must be taken as justifiable only upon the facts of the case. The plaintiff did not prove who the next manager would be and a decree for possession to the plaintiff for the rightful mutwalli was regarded as uncertain and vague. But it does not appear that there was anything preventing the High Court from holding that the Court should appoint in case nobody was entitled to succeed upon the vacancy. Such decrees have been actually passed under S. 539, C. P. C. See notes (2) to (7) p. cclxxxviii.

3. *Biddia Soonduree Dossee* v. *Doorganund Chatterjee*, (1874) 22 W. R. C. R. 97; *Kazi Hassan* v. *Sagun Balkrishna*, (1889) I. L. R., 24 B. 170 (176).

4 *Sathappayyar* v. *Periasami*, (1890) I. L. R., 14 M. 1 (13) (a case of private trust). In default, the Court should appoint. See *Giyana Sambandha Pandara Sannadhi* v. *Kandasami Tambiran*, (1887) I. L. R., 10 M. 375 (503, 505). In the case of private endowments the decree passed in *Sathappayyar* v. *Periasomi*, (1890) I. L. R., 14 M. 1 (13) was that the suit should stand dismissed in default of nomination. But the proper decree would seem to be that the other members interested in the private endowment should appoint.

5. *Sathappayyar* v. *Periasami*, (1890) I. L. R., 14 M. 1 (15); *Sheoratan Kunwari* v. *Ram Pargash*, (1896) I. L. R., 18 A. 227 (232). See also *Giyana Sambandha Pandara Sannadhi* v. *Kandasami Tambiran*, (1887) I. L. R., 10 M. 375 (506).

6. See *Chintaman Bajaji Dev* v. *Dhondo Ganesh Dev*, (1888) I. L. R., 15 B. 612. Cf. *Sheoratan Kunwari* v. *Ram Pargash*, (1896) I. L. R., 18 A. 227; and *Narayana Ayyar* v. *Kumarasami Mudaliar*, (1899) I. L. R., 23 M. 537.

cognizance of under that section so that a suit by him for recovery of property from outsiders cannot be brought under that section[1]. But there may be nothing to prevent him from joining such reliefs in a suit under that section The same principles will apply to S. 14 of the Religious Endowments Act[2].

It need hardly be stated that the other members of the founder's family[3] not being his heirs have at least an interest within the meaning of S. 539, C. P. C., but for the fact that it is denied by an unreported decision of the Madras High Court[4]. Apparently it has not been brought to the notice of the Judges in this case that it has been held in some cases that they have a right under the ordinary law[5] even apart from S. 539, C. P. C., to bring suits for maladministration or for the enforcement of trusts.

Founder or heir party to misconduct.

The suit by the founder or his heirs is not defeated by the fact that the plaintiff is also guilty of similar mismanagement or is a party or privy to the misconduct of the manager. The principle that a plaintiff must come with clean hands is hardly applicable to a case where it is sought to rectify the mismanagement of a public trust and to enforce its proper administration[6]. Even a manager who alienates the property wrongfully is entitled to recover the property so alienated for the trust[7] as the question is

---

1. *Lakshmandas Parashram* v. *Ganpatrav Krishna*, (1884) I. L. R., 8 B. 365 (367); *Kazi Hassan* v. *Sagun Balkrishna*,(1899) I.L.R.. 24B. 170 (181). Even where the party in possession belongs to a member of the founder's family if he is not entitled to be in possession he must be a wrongdoer and S. 539, C. P. C., will not apply. See *Sri Dhundiraj Ganesh Dev* v. *Ganesh*, (1893) I. L. R., 18 B. 721.

2. *Hidait-Oon-Nissa* v. *Syud Afzul Hossein*, (1870) 2 N. W. P. 420 (which was a suit by an endower to set aside a trust deed). In *Sheoratan Kunwari* v. *Ram Pargash*, (1896) I. L. R., 18 A. 227 the suit by the founder was brought under S. 14.

3. In *Sathappayyar* v. *Periasami*, (1890) I. L. R., 14 M. 1 (13) all the members in the case of a private endowment were held to be interested in the appointment of a proper manager.

4. App. 101 of 1901, dated 25th September 1902, M. H. Ct. Jud. Ind. for 1902, p 260.

5. *Bhurruck Chunder Sahoo* v. *Golam Shuruff*, (1868) 10 W. R. C. R 458. See also *Thackersey Dewraj* v. *Hurbhum Nursey*, (1884) I. L. R., 8 B. 432 (461 and 462); *Chintaman Bajaji Dev* v. *Dhondo Ganesh Dev*, (1888) I. L R., 15 B. 612 (a case under S. 539, C. P. C.) See further below pp. cclxxv, ccxci. But see *Lutifunnissa Bibi* v. *Nazirun Bibi*, (1884) I. L. R., 11 C. 33.

6. The case of *Bejayee Gobind Burral* v. *Kallee Dass* (1850) *B. S. D. A.* 447 which takes a contrary view is obviously erroneous. It is not like the action referred to in *Towers* v. *African Tug Company*, [1904] 1 Ch. 558 where the plaintiff had to succeed upon his own merits

7. *Shri Ganesh Dharnidhar Maharajdev* v. *Keshavarav Govind Kulgavkar*, (1890) I. L. R., 15 B. 625 (635 to 637) dissenting from *Maniklal Atmaram* v. *Manchershi Dinsha*,(1876) I. L.R., 1 B. 269. For other cases, see Chapter XIV pp. ccv, ccvi. It has also been held that a former abuse or breach of trust will not disentitle the trustee or manager from seeking to prevent maladministration or repetition of abuse. *Juggut Mohini Dossee* v. *Mussumat Sokheemoney Dossee*, (1871) 14 M. I. A. 289 at pp. 306 and 307; *Girijanund Datta Jha* v. *Sailajanund Datta Jha*, (1896) I.L.R. 23 C. 645 (663).

as to the right of the institution and not as to the right of any individual. The motives of the suitor are immaterial and irrelevant[1].

A suit involving a breach of trust must allege distinctly the acts charged as breach of trust. It cannot be left to be inferred for, where the allegations contained in a plaint are susceptible of two constructions, one being consistent with the defendant's innocence and the other implying a breach of trust on his part, the court will not put that construction on the plaint as will imply a breach of trust[2]. The principle is the same as in cases of fraud, and there it has been held that fraud must be specifically averred and details given[3].

Founder's rights under Mahomedan Law.

In finding out the persons who may be regarded as founders under the Mahomedan Law the same principles will apply. If a mosque is built by raising subscriptions all the subscribers will be regarded as founders If one gives his land for building a mosque and the mosque is built by raising subscriptions the person who has given the land and the subscribers will be regarded as founders[4]. The position of a founder under Mahomedan Law is similar to that of a founder under the Hindu Law. He has no right to alienate wakf property after the appropriation is complete[5]. He has the right to appoint a mutwalli[6]. He may reserve the superintendence to himself or appoint somebody else[7]. On the death of the first mutawalli he is ordinarily entitled to appoint to the vacancy thus created[8]. The circumstances under which he is entitled to nominate have been already mentioned in an earlier chapter[9]. Endowed property can never revert to the founder[10].

---

1. *Manohar Ganesh Tambekar* v. *Lakhmiram Govindram*, (1887) I. L. R., 12 B. 247 (259).
2. *Attorney General* v. *The Mayor of Norwich* 2 My & Cr. 406, (420 to 423): S. C. 44 RR. 143 (149 to 152) followed in *Brojomohun Doss* v. *Hurrololl Doss*, (1880) I. L. R., 5 C. 700 (706).
3. *Gunga Narain* v. *Tiluckram*, (1888) L. R. 15 I. A. 119: S.C. I. L. R. 15 C. 533.
4. Macnaghten's Precedents (Endowments) Case V pp. 335, 336.
5. *Abul Hussan* v. *Haji Mohammad*, (1831) 5 B. S. D. A. 87. See for other cases, Chapter XIII, pp. clxxxiv, clxxxv and Chapter XIV, p. ccxxx.
6. *Muhammad Kasim* v. *Muhammad Alum*, (1831) 5 B S. D. A. 133.
7. *The Advocate General* v. *Fatima Sultani Begam*, (1872) 9 B. H. C. 19.
8. *Mohummud Sadik* v. *Muhammad Ali*, (1798) 1 B. S D. A. 17.
9. Chapter XIII, pp. clxxxv to clxxxvii. See also Macnaghten's Mahomedan Law Precedents (Endowments) Case V, p.336.
10. *Reasut Ali* v. *J. C. Abbott*, (1869) 12 W. R. C. R. 132; *Jangu* v. *Ahmed-Ullah*, (1889) I. L. R., 13 A. 419.

He is only entitled to nominate on a vacancy but he or his heirs will not be entitled to assume management[1]. The misconduct of the mutwalli or breach of trust on his part will not entitle the donor to revoke the trust[2] and to resume the wakf property[3]. If the mutwalli misconducts or commits breach of trust, the settlor and his heirs will be entitled to bring suits for enforcement of the trusts[4] but they will not be entitled to remove the mutwalli unless such a power is reserved in the deed of appropriation[5]. The founder or his heir may sue for removal of the mutwalli for such misconduct and for the appointment of a new one[6]. He is entitled to bring a suit for setting aside any alienation made by the mutwalli, for restoring to the endowment the properties so alienated and for establishing the wakf after removal of the mutwalli[7]. But whether he can frame such a suit without asking for removal of the mutwalli seems to be a question in which the authorities are in conflict[8].

We shall now proceed to consider the rights of votaries or worshippers.

Devotees in what sense beneficiaries.

Sometimes they are loosely termed beneficiaries. But when they are spoken of as beneficiaries[9] it must not be supposed that they have any beneficial ownership in the endowed properties. The properties as already observed belong to the Deity under both the Hindu and Mahomedan laws and, therefore, worshippers can have no sort of ownership in such properties. But it is quite certain that as the worship or service is intended for the spiritual welfare of the different classes of the Hindu and Mahomedan communities, the

1. *Phate Saheb Bibi* v. *Damodar Premji*, (1879) I. L. R., 3 B. 84.

2. *Gulam Hussain Saib* v. *Aji Ajam Tadallah Saib Kuraishi*, (1868) 4 M. H. C. 44; *Doyal Chand Mullick* v. *Syud Keramut Ali*, (1871) 16 W. R. C. R. 116.

3. *Gulam Hussain* v. *Aji Ajam Tadallah*, supra.

4. *Doyal Chand Mullick* v. *Syud Keramut Ali*, (1871) 16 W. R. C. R., 116; *Fatmabibi* v. *The Advocate General of Bombay*, (1881) I. L. R., 6 B. 42 (53, 54).

5. *Gulam Hussain* v. *Aji Ajam Tadallah*, (1868) 4 M. H. C. 44; *Hidait-Oon-Nissa* v. *Syud Afzul Hossein*, (1870) 2 N. W. P. 420. See also Baillie 591.

6. *Bhurruck Chunder Sahoo* v. *Golam Shuruff*, (1868) 10 W. R. C. R. 458. Where he is entitled to nominate he may pray that such right may be declared and that the nominee appointed by him be declared entitled to take. *Giyana Sambandha* v. *Kandasami*, (1887) I. L. R., 10 M. 375 (502, 503).

7. *Kazi Hassan* v. *Sagun Balkrishna*, (1899) I. L. R., 24 B. 170. See also *Lakshmandas Parashram* v. *Ganpatrav Krishna*, (1884) I. L. R., 8 B. 365.

8. See note (7) supra. But see *Bhurruck Chunder Sahoo* v. *Golam Shuruff*, (1868) 10 W. R. C. R. 458; *Phate Saheb Bibi* v. *Damodar Premji*, (1879) I. L. R., 3 B. 84.

9. *Kazi Hassan* v. *Sagun Balkrishna*, (1899) I. L. R., 24 B. 170 (176, 181).

members belonging to such classes have a direct interest[1] in seeing that their respective worship or service is properly conducted or that their respective spiritual wants[2] are properly ministered to.

Right of condonation.

Although they have this interest yet they cannot by any consent of theirs condone any maladministration on the part of the manager or convert any act of the manager which may in itself amount to a wrong or breach of trust into something which is either legal or justifiable[3]. I am of course speaking of an endowment which is a public one[4]. This shews that although these institutions are intended for the public or a class of the public the latter will have no proprietary interest either in the institutions or the endowments attached to such institutions. No amount of consent on the part of the public will justify a breach of trust by the manager[5]. Maladministration in the case of a public trust cannot be condoned[6].

Rights of worshippers—*First*, free access for worship.

If a particular institution is intended for a class of the public such as Hindus[7] or Mahomedans or is intended for a portion of such class (as a sect of Hindus[8]) each member of that class or sect will certainly be entitled as of right to the free access of the institution for the purposes of worship[9]. So far there can be no doubt that this is a personal or individual right[10]. So also he will be entitled to present the usual offerings to the Deity and do other acts of worship[11]. If by reason of any act done by such person he ceases to belong to that sect or is so regarded by the usage of his sect[12] he will not be entitled to that right[13]. If the manager or any other person interferes with this right as by imposing a condition that he should take out a ticket of

---

1. Or a bare interest.

2. Which these institutions intend to supply. See *Vidyapurna Tirtha Swami* v. *Vidyanidhi Tirtha Swami*, (1904) I. L. R. 27 M. 435 at p. 451.

3. *Thackersey Dewraj* v. *Hurbhum Nursey*, (1884) I. L. R., 8 B. 432 (454); *Ranga Pai* v. *Baba*, (1897) I. L. R., 20 M. 398. See Chapter VII, lxxv.

4. I am not speaking in this Chapter of private endowments.

5. See note (3) supra.

6. See note (3) supra.

7. *Sajedur Raja* v. *Baidyanath Deb*, (1892) I. L. R., 20 C. 397. See Chapter VI, p. lxxviii.

8. See *Kanhaya Lal* v. *Salig Ram*, (1894) A. W. N. 159. Chapter VI, p. lxxix.

9. See Chapter VI, p. lxxiii.

10. *Jawahra* v. *Akbar Hussain*, (1884) I. L. R., 7 A. 178 (a Mahomedan case). See also *Anandrav Bhikaji Phadke* v. *Shankar Daji Charya*, (1883) I. L. R , 7 B. 323.

11. *Vengamuthu* v. *Pandaveswara*, (1882) I. L. R., 6 M. 151.

12. *Nathu Velji* v. *Keshawji*, (1901) I. L. R., 26 B. 174 (183).

13. *Venkatachalapati* v. *Subbarayadu*, (1890) I. L. R., 13 M. 293. See also *The Advocate-General ex relatione Daya Muhammad* v. *Muhammad Husen Huseni*, (1866) 12 B. H. C. 323.

admission for a fee that is an infringement of his right and he is entitled individually to assert this right and claim redress for its infringement in a Civil Court[1]. It is only an appplication of the above principle if we say that such a worshipper when he finds that the worship is not conducted in the accustomed manner and his spiritual wants not served in the usual way by reason of the maladministration of the trusts by the manager he is entitled as of right to see that the worship is conducted in the usual way and rectify this maladministration. That is why we see that this right is recognised very early by the Courts. In *Daseekamiengar v. Singamiengar*[2] the Madras Sadar Adalat held that the plaintiffs in that case as some members of the village community had such an interest in the village temple as would entitle them to sue the wardens for malversation although the Court in the particular case refused relief on the ground that Regulation VII of 1817 barred the plaintiff's suit. This latter reason was admitted to be erroneous as was afterwards held in later cases[3]. The principle that persons as members of the Hindu[4] or Mahomedan[5] communities respectively and as worshippers in a pagoda or mosque are entitled as of right to sue under the ordinary law has also been affirmed in later cases

Secondly, Right to sue for rectifying maladministration.

1. As by claiming an injunction against the manager from interfering with his right. Cf. *Kalidas Jivram* v. *Gor Parjaram Hirji*, (1890) I. L. R., 15 B 309. Or he may sue for damages. See *Vengamuthu* v. *Pandaveswara*, (1882) I. L. R., 6 M. 151.

2. (1857) M. S. D. A. 5. The same principle was affirmed in *Ranee Parvata Vurdhany Nauchiar* v. *Mungalaswara Goorookul*, (1856) M. S. D. A. 165 where the plaintiffs were also servants in the pagoda. In both the cases Regulation VII of 1817 was regarded as a bar to the suit. See *Kassyvassy Kristna Puttar* v. *Vangala Shangaranat Josser*, (1858) M. S. D. A. 39; and *Narasimha Charry* v. *Tundree Coomara Tata Charry*, (1858) M S. D. A. 141.

3. *Kassyvassy Kristna Puttar* v. *Vangala Shangaranat Josser*, (1858) M. S. D. A. 39; *Ponnambala Mudaliyar* v. *Varaguna Rama Pandia Chinnatambiar*, (1872) 7 M. H. C. 117.

4. *Radhabai* v. *Chimnaji Bin Ramji Sali*, (1878) I. L. R., 3 B. 27 followed in *Shri Ganesh Dharnidhar* v. *Keshavrav*, (1890) I. L. R., 15 B. 625 (636); *Thackersey Dewraj* v. *Hurbhum Nursey*, (1884) I. L. R., 8 B. 432 (450). See this latter case discussed in *Srinivasa Chariar* v. *Raghava Chariar*, (1897) I. L. R., 23 M. 28 (32). See *Nam Narain Singh* v. *Ramoon Paurey*, (1874) 23 W. R. C. R. 76. See also *Ponnambala Mudaliyar* v. *Varaguna Rama Pandia Chinnatambiar*, (1872) 7 M. H. C. 117; *Subbayya* v. *Krishna*, (1890) I. L. R., 14 M. 186 (197, 199, 220, 221). But see *contra*, *Jan Ali* v. *Ram Nath Mundul*, (1881) I.L.R., 8 C. 32; *Raghubar Dial* v. *Kesho Ramanuj Das*, (1888) I. L. R., 11 A. 18 (26) which relied upon *Wajid Ali* v. *Dianat-ul-lah*, (1885) I. L. R., 8 A. 31; and *Sajedur Raja* v. *Baidyanath Deb*, (1892) I. L. R., 20 C. 397.

5. *Bhurruck Chunder Sahoo* v. *Golam Shuruff*, (1868) 10 W. R. C. R. 458; *Abdul Rahman* v. *Yar Muhammad*, (1881) I. L. R., 3 A. 636 (640, 641) following *Radhabai* v. *Chimnaji*, supra; *Zafaryab Ali* v. *Bakhtawar Singh*, (1883) I. L. R., 5 A. 497 (500); *Jawahra* v. *Akbar Hussain*, (1884) I. L. R., 7 A. 178; *Mohiuddin* v. *Sayiduddin*, (1893) I. L. R., 20 C. 810 (816). See *Syud Asheerooddeen* v. *Sreemutty Drobo Moyee*, (1876) 25 W. R. C. R. 557. See *Parsons*, J. in *Kazi Hassan* v. *Sagun Balkrishna*, (1899) I. L. R., 24 B. 170 (176). But see *contra*, *Phate Saheb Bibi* v. *Damodar Premji*, (1879) I. L. R., 3 B. 84 (88); *Wajid Ali Shah* v. *Dianat-ul-lah Beg*, (1885) I. L. R., 8 A. 31; *Lutifunnissa Bibi* v. *Nuzirun Bibi*, (1884) I. L. R., 11 C. 33.

though it must be observed that it cannot be said that there are no decisions the other way[1]. If the plaintiff is a servant of the temple or mosque there is greater reason why he should be allowed to maintain such a suit for malversation[2]. There is no question of there being any difference in the Hindu and Mahomedan Laws in this respect. The cases holding that a Hindu has or has not the right in question follow cases decided with reference to Mahomedan Law and *vice versa*. Hence if the principle is affirmed in one case it must equally be affirmed in the other, and if it is denied in the one it must be denied in the other.

It is said by Mr. Amir Ali that "every Mahomedan who derives any benefit from an admitted wakf is entitled to maintain an action against the mutwalli to establish his right thereto or against a trespasser to recover any portion of the *wakf* property which has been misappropriated without joining any other persons who may participate with him in the benefit." Does this benefit include "the spiritual benefit" which a worshipper obtains in these institutions? It will certainly include "a pecuniary benefit" derivable from the income of the endowed properties given to a person under the deed of endowment but that is beside the question.

It must be admitted that until the code of 1882 when S. 539, C. P. C., was modified[3] by enacting that the section applied to both religious and charitable trusts there was a strong current of authority to the effect that a worshipper under both the Hindu and Mahomedan Laws was entitled to sue the manager or mutwalli for malversation. The only two cases against this current of authority were *Jan Ali* v. *Ram Nath Mundul*[4] and *Lutifunnissa Bibi* v.

---

1. See decisions noted *contra* in notes (4) and (5), p. cclxxv.

2. *Ranee Parvata Vurdhany Nanchear* v. *Mungalaswara Goorookul*, (1856) M. S. D. A. 165. But see *Dhadphale* v. *Gurrav*, (1881) I. L. R., 6 B. 122 which may, however, be explained on the footing that the suit was brought to establish the individual right of the servant. See also p. cclxxv, note (4).

3. *Manohar Ganesh Tambekar* v. *Keshavram*, (1878) I. L. R., 12 B. 267 (note). The case reported at p. 247 was thereupon brought under S. 539, C. P. C.

4. (1881), I. L. R., 8 C. 32. See also *Phate Saheb Bibi* v. *Damodar Premji*, (1879) I. L. R., 3B. 84 (88), but here the plaintiff claimed to be entitled to succeed on the vacancy of a manager when according to the case only the Court had the right to fill the vacancy. That was why it was said that the parties interested were not of themselves entitled to assume the office. No suit was brought by the plaintiff as a devotee.

Nazirun Bibi[1] both cases of *wakf*. In none of these cases the earlier cases were noticed. As regards the second case it might be observed that the Court having held that S. 539 applied[2] the remarks about the right of worshippers were mere *obiter*. The case of *Jan Ali* v. *Ram Nath Mundul*[3] holds that a person as the follower of the Moslem religion and as worshipper has not a "direct interest" within the meaning of S. 539, C. P. C.[2], and that as regards some of the prayers the plaintiff must have instituted the suit under S. 14 of Act XX of 1863 after obtaining sanction under that Act and that with regard to the prayers outside the scope of S. 14 he must sue under S. 30, C. P. C. The latter portion will be discussed later on. We may take it, therefore, that the above current of authority is not shaken by any decision prior to the Code of 1882 and I shall consider later on how far they have been shaken by the decisions under or after the code of 1882.

Nature and frame of suit.

According to the current of authority already referred to, a worshipper is entitled to sue the manager or mutwalli for malversation. The nature and frame of that suit are well pointed out in *Kalee Churn Giri* v. *Golabi*[4]. The Court there observed : "Assuming that this case does not come under the Act (XX of 1863) the only way in which the plaintiff can frame his suit is this, that he amongst other persons, is interested in the proper worship of the idol and in the religious trust being carried out in accordance with the terms—whatever they may be—of the endowment and that this person the defendant who is now in charge of the guddee has neglected the worship and abused the trust and then praying the Court to remove her from the *guddee* and appoint

1. (1884), I. L. R., 11 C. 33. The suit was instituted in 1879, see p. 35.
2. It was not brought to the notice of the Court that S. 539 of the Code of 1877 did not apply to trusts for religious and charitable purposes. The court in *Jan Ali* v. *Ram Nath Mundul*, (1881) I. L. R., 8 C. 32 also proceeded upon this mistaken view. At any rate the decisions proceeded upon the assumption that the section would apply to such cases.
3. (1881) I. L. R., 8 C. 32.
4. (1878) 2 C. L. R., 128. It was apparently a case of hereditary manager. See for reliefs to be asked *Bhurruck Chunder Sahoo* v. *Golam Shuruff*, (1868) 10 W. R. C. R. 458; *Doyal Chund Mullick* v. *Syud Keramut Ali*, (1871) 16 W. R. C. R. 116 (both cases of wakfs). See also *Ranee Parvata Vurdhany Nauchear* v. *Mungalaswara Goorookul*, (1856) M.S.D. A. 165; *Thackersey Dewraj* v. *Hurbhum Nursey*, (1884) I.L.R., 8 B. 432 at pp. 444, 471, 473 (where, however the plaintiffs may be regarded as being in the position of some of the founders); and *Mohiuddin* v. *Sayiduddin*, (1893) I. L. R., 20 C. 810 (825). The fact that the office of manager was hereditary could not make a prayer for the appointment of a new manager under the directions of the court if the old manager should be removed unsustainable in law. See S. 539, C. P. C., and cases under that section. See also pp. cclxxxvii, cclxxxviii, ccxciii.

some proper person, under any direction which the Court may think it right to give, to carry out the trusts, and also if reason there be to call upon the defendant to account." This case was followed in *Rup Narain Singh* v. *Junko Bye*[1] where, however, the judges observed that the plaintiff or plaintiffs should sue in his or their names on behalf of himself or themselves and all others interested in the due performance of the trust. Apparently no leave, according to this case, need be obtained[2]. Apparently such worshippers might also sue for removal of the manager from possession of endowed properties and for placing the trustee to be newly appointed in possession of such properties[3] or they might ask that they might be placed in possession on behalf of the endowment[4]. We shall now proceed to see whether there is any reason for taking a different view under the Code of 1882, C. P. C.

Right of worshippers to bring representative suits under S. 30, C. P. C.

Before we proceed to consider this matter we shall refer to a point frequently discussed in some of the cases, *viz.*, as to the right of worshippers to bring suits under S. 30, C. P. C., and as to the necessity of worshippers resorting to the procedure prescribed by that section in order to enforce their rights in cases not covered by S. 539, C. P. C., or S. 14 of Act XX of 1863, or in cases where the plaintiffs do not wish to proceed under those sections. It must, however, be observed that the section is only regulative and not constitutive[5]. It does not create a right. There must be a right to sue under the ordinary law before the section can be applied[6]. If there is no right to sue in a person the section

1. (1878) 3 C. L. R., 112.

2. This would seem to be also the view taken in *Panchcowrie Mull* v. *Chumroolall*, (1878) I. L. R., 3 C. 563 (571). But there it would seem that a *panch* had the right of management and that the plaintiffs were some members of that *panch*. See also the case of 1861 referred to in *Panchcowric Mull* v. *Chumroolall*, (1878) I. L. R., 3 C. 563 at pp. 571, 572. But there must be leave under S.30, C.P.C., if a suit is brought on behalf of all.

3. See cases under S. 539, C. P. C. But see *Dhurruck Chunder Sahoo* v. *Golam Shuruff*, (1868) 10 W. R. C. R. 458.

4. *Radhabai* v. *Chimnaji Bin Ramji Sali*, (1878) I. L. R., 3 B. 27; *Zufaryab Ali* v. *Bakhtawar Singh*, (1883) I. L. R., 5 A. 497. See other cases cited under S. 539, C. P. C., pp. cclxxxvii, cclxxxviii. But see *Kamaraju* v. *Asanali Sheriff*, (1899) I. L. R., 23 M. 99; *Subbarayadu* v. *Asanali Sheriff*, (1899), I. L. R., 23 M. 100 (note); and *Huseni Begam* v. *The Collector of Moradabad*, (1897) I. L. R., 20 A. 46 (50).

5. *Anandrav Bhikaji Phadke* v. *Shankar Daji Charya*, (1883) I. L. R., 7 B. 323 (328).

6. Ibid.

does not give such person a right by joining with other persons[1]. There was no similar provision under the Code of 1859 but that did not deprive those whose legal interests were affected as members of a class of the right to sue[2] and so it could not be said that representative (class) suits were not known prior to 1877. In fact instances of such suits are to be seen in the reports[3]. In *Srikhanti Narayanappa's* case[4] the Madras High Court observed: "Convenience, if not necessity, requires that in suits of this nature (boundary disputes between villages) where there is community of interest amongst a large number of persons, a few should be allowed to represent the whole, and if the whole body be represented in the suit then it is proper that the whole body should be bound by the decree, though some members of the body are not parties named on the record. In such a case there is that fictitious extension of parties which is referred to in the judgment of this Court in *Yarakalamma v. Ankala Naramma*[5]." But as it was only a question of convenience a person having an interest common with others was not obliged to sue on behalf of others and the only effect of not suing in such a way would be that the decree would not bind the others[6]. That was all the effect of not suing on behalf of others though if he had so sued the decree would bind all if there was an effectual representation[7].

S. 30, C. P. C., when introduced into the Code of 1877 did not lay down any new law. It regulated the procedure to be adopt-

---

1. The case of *Jan Ali v. Ram Nath Mundul*, (1881) I. L. R., 8 C. 32 (41) which seems to suggest a contrary view is rightly dissented from by Mr. Justice *Shephard* in *Srinivasa Chariar v. Raghava Chariar*, (1897) I. L. R., 23 M. 28 (32).

2. *Anandrav Bhikaji Phadke v. Shankar Daji Charya*, (1883) I. L. R., 7 B. 323 (328).

3. *Srikhanti Narayanappa v. Indupuram Ramalingam*, (1866) 3 M. H. C. 226 and the cases there referred to. See also the case of 1861 referred to in *Panchcowrie Mull v. Chumroolall*, (1878) I. L. R., 3 C. 563 (571, 572). In *Sadagopachariar v. Rama Rao*, (1902) I. L. R., 26 M. 376 (384) all that was held was that the plaintiffs in the old suit were not described as representing others. But such a description is at best mere evidence that the plaintiffs were as a matter of fact allowed to sue on behalf of others.

4. (1866) 3 M. H. C. 226, at p. 229.

5. (1864) 2 M. H. C. 276 (288).

6. *Venkataswami Nayakkan v. Subba Rau*, (1864) 2 M. H. C. 1. This is the same under S. 30, C. P. C. *Srinivasa Chariar v. Raghava Chariar*, (1897) I. L. R., 23 M. 28.

7. *Srikhanti Narayanappa v. Indupuram Ramalingam*, (1866) 3 M. H. C. 226 (230).

ed[1] in representative class suits. There was no change in this section by the code of 1882 nor by any of the subsequent amending Acts[2]. S. 30, C. P. C., is only permissive[3]. It does not compel a plaintiff to bring a suit on behalf of all and a plaintiff will not be non-suited if he does not frame his suit in such a way[4] and the only effect of his not joining others similarly interested is that the decree passed in his suit will not bind the others[5].

Interest of worshipper.

The interest of a worshipper is as we have already observed an individual right[6]. It may be a right enjoyed in common with others[7] but it cannot be said that it is a joint right vested in the whole body of worshippers and not vested in a single worshipper. When this individual right is infringed, Civil Courts must afford a remedy to the party aggrieved. If he has no interest in himself he cannot get an interest along with others who equally can have no interest taken individually. It may be that when the parties are definite all persons having similar interests may bring a joint action against the defendant for the alleged infringement[8]. It may also be that if the parties are indefinite some of the plaintiffs may be allowed to sue on

---

1. *i. e.*, notice and sanction of Court. See *The Oriental Bank Corporation* v. *Gobind Lal Seal*, (1883) I. L. R., 9 C. 604.

2. See *Baiju Lal Parbatia* v. *Bulak Lal Pathuk*, (1897) I. L. R., 24 C. 385 which must in effect be treated as explaining away the observations made apparently by an oversight in *Mohiuddin* v. *Sayiduddin*, (1893) I. L. R., 20 C. 810 (816).

3. *Thackersey Dewraj* v. *Hurbhum Nursey*, (1884) I. L. R., 8 B. 432 (450); *Baiju Lal Parbatia* v. *Bulak Lal Pathuk*, (1897) I. L. R., 24 C. 385, (389, 390); *Srinivasa Chariar* v. *Raghava Chariar*, (1897) I. L. R., 23 M. 28.

4. *Baiju Lal Parbatia* v. *Bulak Lal Pathuk*, (1897) I. L. R., 24 C. 385 (389, 390).

5. *Anandrav Bhikaji Phadke* v. *SankarDaji Charya*, (1883) I. L. R., 7 B. 323; *Srinivasa Chariar* v. *Raghava Chariar*, (1897) I.L.R., 23 M. 28; *Baiju Lal Parbatia* v. *Bulak Lal Pathuk*, (1897) I. L. R., 24 C. 385 (390). But curiously enough in some of the cases it is said that if objection be taken the plaint ought to be amended and the plaintiffs permitted to proceed under S. 30, C. P. C. See *Moidin Kutti* v *Krishnan*, (1887) I. L. R., 10 M. 322 (330,333); per *Best*, J., in *Subbayya* v. *Krishna*, (1890) I.L.R., 14 M. 186 (209); and per *Shephard*, J., in *Srinivasa Chariar* v. *Raghava Chariar*, (1897) I. L. R., 23 M. 28 (32). These are merely *dicta* and are besides hardly consistent with the view as to the effect of S.30, C. P. C.

6. See *Radhabai* v. *Chimnaji*, (1878) I. L. R., 3 B. 27; *Abdul Rahman* v. *Yar Muhammad*, (1881) I. L. R., 3 A. 636; *Zafaryab Ali* v. *Bakhtawar Singh*, (1883) I. L. R., 5 A. 497; *Thackersey Dewraj* v. *Hurbum Nursey*, (1884) I. L. R., 8 B. 432 (450); *Jawahra* v. *Akbar Husain*, (1884) I. L. R., 7 A. 178; per *Parsons*, J., in *Kazi Hassan* v. *Sagun Balkrishna*, (1899) I. L. R., 24 B. 170 (176). See also *Mohiuddin* v. *Sayiduddin*, (1893) I. L. R., 20 C. 810 (816). But an association not incorporated will have as such no interest. See *The Muhammadan Association of Meerut* v. *Bakshi Ram*, (1884) I. L. R., 6 A. 284. Cf. *Yusuf Beg* v. *The Board of Foreign Missions*, (1894) I. L. R., 16 A. 429. Even if incorporated it can have no interest as worshipper. But its members may have such interest.

7. *Baiju Lal Parbatia* v. *Bulak Lal Pathuk*, (1897) I. L. R., 24 C. 385 (390).

8. *Kalidas Jivram* v. *Gor Parjaram Hirji*, (1890) I. L. R., 15 B. 309 (where the hereditary gors or priests were held entitled under S. 26, C. P. C., to sue upon a common cause of action for the interference of their right by reason of a rule passed by the Shevaks).

behalf all under S. 30 C. P. C.[1] But this does not mean that such persons must only sue under S. 30 C. P. C., or be nonsuited on default.[2] We should, therefore, think that the cases which lay down a coutrary view *viz.*, that worshippers if they do not sue under S. 539 C. P. C., or S. 14 of the Religious Endowments Act must sue under S. 30 C. P. C.[3] do not lay down a sound proposition of law.

Cases holding worshippers cannot sue under S. 30, C. P. C., discussed.

If the view that worshippers have no individual right were correct it seems to be an astounding proposition to be told that no suit at all can be brought by worshippers under S. 30 C. P. C[1]. But this view has, at any rate, the merit of being consistent. A person having no interest cannot, by joining with others similarly situated as himself, get a right by reason of S. 30 C. P. C[5]. It is not proposed to discuss the classes of persons coming within the purview[6] of S 30 C. P. C., as being outside the scope of this work. But it is clear that no pecuniary or proprietary interest is required for the application of S. 30 C. P. C., and a worshipper has such a right or interest as will satisfy S. 30 C. P. C[7]. The case of *Raghubar Dial* v. *Kesho Ramanuj Das*[4] proceeds upon the view that a worshipper's right to sue for enforcement of the trusts of a religious institution is neither sanctioned nor prohibited by the

1. *Baiju Lal Parbatia* v. *Bulak Lal Pathuk*, (1897) I. L. R., 24 C. 385 (388, 389). See *Dhunput Singh* v. *Paresh Nath Singh*, (1893) I. L. R., 21 C. 180 ; *Fernandez* v. *Rodrigues*, (1897) I. L. R., 21 B. 784 (where the Churchwardens sued under S. 30 C. P. C., on behalf of themselves and all other parishioners against the vicar) ; *Ganapati Ayyan* v. *Savithri Ammal*, (1897) I. L. R., 21 M. 10.

2. Cf. *Hoole* v. *G. W. Railway Company*, (1867) L. R. 3Ch. App. 262 (272) which was an action by a member of corporation to restrain the corporation from doing an act which is *ultra vires*. See also *Pulbrook* v. *Richmond Consolidated Mining Company*, (1878) 6 Ch. D. 610.

3. *Jan Ali* v. *Ram Nath Mundul*, (1881) I. L. R., 8 C. 32 ; *Lutifunnissa Bibi* v. *Nazirun Bibi*, (1884) I. L. R., 11 C. 33 (37). See *Kamaraju* v *Asanali Sheriff*, (1899) I. L. R., 23 M. 99. No argument can be drawn from the analogy of English cases. See *Srikhanti Narayanappa* v. *Indupuram Ramalingam*, (1886) 3 M. H. C. 226 (230). The English cases show that there can be no such suit by some on behalf of an indefinite body of persons. Public rights are enforced in England by the Advocate General at the relation of some person interested.

4. *Raghubar Dial* v. *Kesho Ramanuj Das*, (1888) I. L. R., 11 A. 18 ; *Sajedur Raja* v. *Baidyanath Deb*, (1892) I. L. R., 20 C. 397. In *Wajid Ali Shah* v. *Dianat-ul-lah Beg*, (1885) I. L. R., 8 A. 31 which was followed in the first case no question of the applicability of S. 30 C. P. C., arose. All that was held in that case was that a Mahomedan who was not a resident of the village in which the mosque stood had no interest at all.

5. *Srinivasa Chariar* v. *Raghava Chariar*, (1897) I. L. R., 23 M. 28.

6. See *Srinivasa Chariar* v. *Raghava Chariar*, (1897) I. L. R., 23 M. 28. Daniell's Chancery Practice Vol.I, pp. 195 to 199.

7. *In the Oriental Bank Corporation* v. *Gobind Lall Seal*, (1883) I. L. R., 9 C. 604 Mr. Justice *Norris* thought that the right of a creditor to sue for himself and on behalf of other unsatisfied creditors for administration of his deceased debtor's estate was similar to the right of a worshipper to sue for himself and on behalf of others. See pp. 607 and 608.

Hindu Law and that, therefore, S. 30 has no application. If it is said that there is no particular text dealing with the matter the statement may be correct. But Courts have never thought themselves precluded from deducing principles of Hindu Law merely because there is no express text dealing with the matter. In the case of religious institutions the question is one of usage and if a person's right to worship is recognised it seems to follow that such a person has a right to enforce that right. The right to sue for malversation has, as already observed by us, long been enforced by the Courts. The case[1] relied upon by the Allahabad High Court[2] has no application to the case of a worshipper who is a near resident of the village in which the institution is located and does not notice any of the earlier cases before the same and other courts.

The case of *Sajedur Raja* v. *Baidyanath Deb*[3] tries to give some reason why such worshippers cannot sue under S. 30, C. P. C., According to it the section has application only to cases where the parties are capable of being ascertained and that the whole Hindu community is incapable of ascertainment. For this the Calcutta Court relies upon *Adamson* v. *Arumugam*[4]. In the latter case the suit was for removal of an obstruction to a highway and the plaintiffs brought the suit on behalf of all the villagers under S. 30, C. P. C. The Madras High Court held that the plaintiffs could not sue without special damage and that S. 30, C. P. C., did not allow persons to sue on behalf of the general public. Whether this decision be right or wrong the decision in the Calcutta case is not warranted by any principle laid down in the Madras case. On the other hand the observation of the Madras High Court[5] that the section (S. 30, C. P. C.,) "is rather designed to allow one or more persons to represent a class having special interests" seems to shew that the decision in the Calcutta case is incorrect even according to the Madras case. Certainly the whole Hindu community is not the general public[6] but is only a particular portion of the public which consists of various races in India. The Hindu community is divided into various castes which are again sub-divided into numberless

---

1. *Wajid Ali* v. *Dianat-ul-lah Beg*, (1885) I. L. R.. 8 A. 31.
2. *Raghubar Dial* v. *Kesho Ramanuj Das*, (1888) I. L. R., 11 A. 18.
3. (1892) I.L.R.,20 C 397. See *Ambalavana* v. *Bappu*, (1899) 9 M.L.J. R.,93(97).
4. (1886) I. L. R., 9 M. 463.
5. *Adamson* v. *Arumugam*, (1886) I. L. R., 9 M. 463 at p. 466.
6. Per *Petheram* C. J. in *Jawahra* v. *Akbar Husain*, (1884) I. L. R., 7 A. 178 at p. 182.

sub-castes or sub-sects and religious institutions are in many instances designed for one sect or another. It is, therefore, hardly correct to say that S. 30, C. P. C., has no application to a limited class of the public.

Of course in order to sue under S. 30, C. P. C., the procedure laid down in that section must be observed. First of all persons having the same interest only can come in under S. 30, C. P. C[1]. Then there must be an order under that section by which the plaintiffs should be permitted to sue on behalf of others. An order directing the issue of a proclamation inviting all persons interested to come in and be made parties is not an order directing such permission[2]. It seems now to be settled that such order need not be express, but may be inferred[3] and may be obtained even after the institution of the suit[4]. Where, upon notice issued under S. 30, C. P. C., some of the persons object to the suit they will be made defendants[5], but if they object to the particular plaintiffs conducting the suit on their behalf they may be allowed to appoint one to act for them and he may be made plaintiff along with the actual[6] plaintiffs. A judgment in that suit will bind all the members of the class who may have been represented by the plaintiffs.[7] But those not named on the record cannot apply for execution unless they apply to be made

Procedure under S. 30, C. P. C.

1. *Ragava* v. *Rajarathnam*, (1890) I. L. R., 14 M. 57 (61). See also *Dhunput Singh* v. *Paresh Nath Singh*, (1893) I. L. R., 21 C. 180 at p. 189.

2. *Ragava* v. *Rajaratnam*, (1890) I. L. R., 14 M. 57 (60).

3. *Dhunput Singh* v. *Paresh Nath*, (1893) I. L. R, 21 C. 180 dissenting from the *dictum* of *Stuart*, C.J. in *Hira Lal* v. *Bhairon*, (1883) I. L. R., 5 A. 602 at p. 604. See also *Kalu Khabir* v. *Jan Meah*, (1901) I. L. R., 29 C. 100.

4. *Hira Lal* v. *Bhairon*, (1883) I. L. R., 5 A. 602; *Geereeballa Dabee* v. *Chunder Kant Mookerjee*, (1885) I. L. R., 11 C. 213 (218,219) only inferentially; *Fernandez* v. *Rodrigues*, (1897) I. L. R., 21 B. 784; *Srinivasa Chariar* v. *Raghava Chariar*, (1897) I. L. R., 23 M. 28; *Baldeo Bharthi* v. *Bir Gir*, (1900) I. L. R., 22 A. 269; *Chennu Menon* v. *Krishnan* (1901) I. L. R. 25 M 399. But see *contra*, *Jan Ali* v. *Ram Nath Mundul*, (1881) I. L. R., 8 C. 32 (41); *The Oriental Bank Corporation* v. *Govind Lall Seal*, (1883) I. L. R., 9 C. 604 (608); *Puramathan Somayajipad* v. *Sankara Menon*, (1899) I. L. R, 23 M. 82.

5. *Fraser* v. *Cooper, Hall & Co.*, (1882) 21 Ch D. 718; *May* v. *Newton*, (1887) 34 Ch D. 347 (349). See also *Srinivasa Chariar* v. *Raghava Chariar*, supra. But see *Maharaj Bahadur Singh* v. *Paresh Nath Singh*, (1904) I. L. R., 31 C. 839 at p. 845 citing *Hira Lal* v. *Bhairon*, (1883) I. L. R., 5 A. 602.

6. The conduct of the case may be taken away altogether from the hands of the original plaintiffs. See *Watson* v. *Cave*, (1881) 17 Ch D. 19; and *Dhuncooverbai* v. *The Advocate General*, (1899) 1 Bom. L. R., 743 (745).

7. *May* v. *Newton*, (1887) 34 Ch D. 347; *Ragava* v. *Rajarathnam*, supra. But see *Sadagopachari* v. *Krishnamachari*, (1889) I. L. R., 12 M. 356.

parties to the record nor can they appeal from such judgment without applying to be made parties in the original Court[1]. But if there is an appeal from the decree either by the named plaintiffs or by the unsuccessful party against the named plaintiffs then if the named plaintiffs compromise or otherwise attempt to prejudice the interests which they purport to represent, on application made to the appellate court by the persons interested, those on the record to whom the conduct of the proceedings has been entrusted may be removed and the names of the applicants may be substituted or the applicants may be placed on the record along with the others[2].

S. 539, C. P.C. —Public trusts—Persons having interest.

We shall now consider how far this right of suit has been effected by the enactment in S. 539, C. P. C. This section was first introduced in the Code of 1877. As it then stood, the section had application to any express or constructive trusts created for public charitable purposes. As already said it was held under this Code that the section had no application to public religious trusts[3] though it could not be said that there was no conflict of decisions upon the point[4]. Then again the old section spoke of two or more

1. *Watson* v. *Cave*, (1881) 17 Ch. D. 19 which was, however, an appeal from the order permitting the plaintiffs to sue. In the English practice the notice to the parties contemplated by S. 30 C. P. C. is not absolutely necessary. Under the Code if notice is sent to a particular person he may appeal from the order giving permission if he is either made a plaintiff or defendant. (See S. 32 and S. 588 cl. (2) C. P. C.). But a party not named on the record may not appeal from an adverse decree passed in the suit although he may apply for leave to appeal. See *Dhuncooverbai* v. *The Advocate General*, (1899) 1 Bom. L. R. 743 (745). But parties who have no *locus standi* cannot apply. *Ragava* v. *Rajaratnam*, (1890) I. L. R., 14 M. 57 (61). Cf. *Dungarsi Dipchand* v. *Ujamsi Velsi*, (1897) I. L. R., 22 B. 727. Daniell's Chancery Practice Vol. I, pp. 171, 172.

2. *Gyanananda Asram* v. *Kristo Chandra Mukherji*, (1901) 8 C. W. N. 404. The same principles apply when the suit is brought by or against the manager. *Narayanasami Gurukkal* v. *Vellasami Tever*, (1902) 12 M. L. J. R. 355.

3. *Karuppa* v. *Arumuga*, (1882) I. L. R., 5 M. 383; *Thackersey Dewraj* v. *Hurbhum Nursey*, (1884) I. L. R., 8 B. 432 (450,451); *Giyana Sambandha Pandara Sannadhi* v. *Kandasami Tambiran*, (1887) I. L. R., 10 M. 375 (506). In *Radhabai* v. *Chimnaji*, (1878) I. L. R., 3 B 27 (28) a doubt was raised as to the applicability of the section to such trusts but the point was not decided. See *Kanhaya Lal* v. *Salig Ram*, (1894) A. W. N. 159 (160).

4. See *Lutifunnissa Bibi* v. *Nazirun Bibi*, (1884) I. L. R., 11 C. 33. In *Manohar* v. *Keshavram*, (1878) I. L. R, 12 B. 267 (note) a suit was brought under the ordinary law and the court dismissed it on the ground that S.539 C. P. C. applied. The suit in *Manohar Ganesh Tambekar* v. *Lakhmiram Govindram*, (1887) I. L. R., 12 B. 247 was instituted in 1880 under S.539 and the court held that the plaintiffs had an interest (259) and that accounts must be taken preparatory to a scheme. This decree was affirmed by the P. C. in *Chotalal* v. *Manohar*, (1899) L.R.26 I. A. 199: S. C. I. L. R., 24 B. 50. In all these cases the question was not raised but the applicability of the section was assumed. *Jan Ali* v *Ram Nath Mundul* (1881) I.L. R., 8 C. 32 (35) really said that the section had no application though on the ground that the plaintiffs had no interest.

persons having a "direct interest" as being entitled to apply and there was a conflict in the different High Courts upon the construction to be placed upon this expression (which was repeated in the Code of 1882). The Calcutta High Court held that a mere worshipper as such had not a "direct interest" within the meaning of the section and that, therefore, two or more worshippers could not bring a suit under S. 539 C. P. C., of the Code of 1877 and the Code of 1882 (before the Amendment Act VII of 1888)[1]. The Madras High Court went further and held that even a general manager of a temple had not a "direct" interest for enforcing the proper administration of the Kattalais attached to the temple in the hands of the Kattalaikars or special managers[2]. The Allahabad and Bombay High Courts held differently[3]. But by the Amendment Act VII of 1888 the word "direct" has been omitted and now there can be no doubt that such worshippers may apply under S. 539, C. P. C.[4].

S. 539, C. P.C. only permissive.

It has been held that the section is only permissive and enabling[5] like S. 14 of the Religious Endowments Act so that the section does not compel persons to bring their suits under the section. The word "may" confirms this interpretation. It has also been held that the section does not take away pre-existing rights or remedies[6]. So that it has been held that a general manager of a

1. *Jan Ali* v. *Ram Nath Mundul*, (1881) I. L. R., 8 C. 32 (35) ; *Latifunnissa Bibi* v. *Nazirun Bibi*, (1884) I. L. R., 11 C. 33 (35). Cf. *Chintaman Bajaji Dev* v. *Dhondo Ganesh Dev*, (1888) I. L. R.. 15 B. 612 (622).

2. *Narasimha* v. *Ayyan*, (1888) I. L. R., 12 M. 157 (160). But see *contra*, *Monohar Ganesh* v. *Lakhmiram*, (1887) I. L. R., 12 B. 247 (258, 259).

3. *Jawahra* v. *Akbar Husain*, (1884) I. L. R., 7 A. 178. So that they may sue apart from S 539 C.P.C. See *Zafaryab Ali* v. *Bakhtawar Singh*,(1883) I.L.R.. 5 A. 497. See also *Raghubar Dial* v. *Kesho Ramanuj Das*,(1888) I. L. R., 11 A. 18. For Bombay, see *Manohar* v. *Kesharram* (1878) I. L. R., 12 B. 267 (note) ; *Manohar Ganesh Tambekar* v. *Lakhmiram Govindram*, (1887) I. L. R., 12 B. 247 (259).

4. *Subbayya* v. *Krishna* (1890) I. L. R., 14 M. 183 (188, 189); *Sajedur Raja* v. *Baidyanath Deb*. (1892) I. L. R., 20 C. 397 (409) ; *Sajedur Raja Chowdhuri* v. *Gour Mohun Das Baishnav*, (1897) I. L. R., 24 C. 418 (427) ; *Jugalkishore* v. *Lakshmandas*, (1899) I. L. R., 23 B. 659 (663). Pujaris have brought suits, under S.539 as persons having interest. See *Lakshmandas* v. *Jugalkishore*, (1896) I. L. R., 22 B. 216 ; *Jugalkishore* v. *Lakshmandas*, (1899) I. L. R., 23 B. 659 (661, 663). See also *Sajedur Raja* v. *Gour Mohun* supra. They have no right to mortgage endowed property. *Sambanda* v. *Nana*, (1863) 1 M. H. C. 298.

5. Per *Best* J. in *Sathappayyar* v. *Periasami*, (1890) I. L. R., 14 M. 1 (15). See *Sajedur Raja Chowdhuri* v. *Gour Mohun Das Baishnav*, (1897) I. L. R., 24 C. 408 (425). See also *Thackersey Dewraj* v. *Hurbhum Nursey*, (1884) I. L. R., 8 B. 432 (451,452) ; and *Mohiuddin* v. *Sayiduddin*, (1893) I. L. R., 20 C. 810.

6. *Giyana Sambandha Pandara Sannadhi* v. *Kandasami Tambiran*, (1887) I. L. R., 10 M. 375 (506) ; *Subbayya* v. *Krishna*, (1890) I. L. R., 14 M. 186 (197,220,221) referring to *Ponnambala Mudaliyar* v. *Varaguna Rama Pandia Chinnatambiar*, (1872) 7 M. H. C. 117 ; *Nellaiyappa Pillai* v. *Thangama Nachiyar*, (1897) I. L. R., 21 M. 406.

temple is entitled to bring a suit with reference to the special endowments in charge of the special managers[1]. We have already seen that founders and their heirs may bring suits independent of S. 539, C. P. C.[2]. It has also been held that worshippers may sue in a suit under S. 30, C. P C.[3]. But if the section is only permissive or enabling it is difficult to conceive why the suits formerly allowed to worshippers individually cannot be brought. The section is not mandatory as to one class of suitors and permissive as to another class. If suits under the general law are allowed notwithstanding S. 539, C. P. C., in favour of managers they must be equally allowed in favour of worshippers[4]. No doubt it would have been good policy to adopt that in the case of a numerous body such as the worshippers the section should be mandatory and restrictive of their prior rights but the section has not been framed in that way.

But although the section may be enabling persons having special or other interests allowed by law may take advantage of the section by bringing suits under it[5] when a case is made out under that section and there is a compliance with the other fulfilments of the law. The recognition of this principle is important as it is doubtful whether under the ordinary law a suit merely for a scheme is maintainable without an allegation of a breach of trust. The ordinary law gave a remedy only in cases of malversation but when S. 539, C. P. C. was enacted a suit merely for a scheme could be brought under that section without any allegation of a breach of trust.

1. *Nellaiyappa* v. *Thungama*, (1897) I. L. R., 21 M 406. *Narasimha* v. *Ayyan*, (1887) I. L. R., 12 M. 157 so far as it decides that a general manager has no *direct* interest is obviously wrong. See also *Augustine* v. *Medlycott*, (1892) I. L. R., 15 M. 241.

2. See pp. cclxx, cclxxi.

3. *Sajedur Raja Chowdhuri* v. *Gour Mohun Das Baishnav* (1897) I. L. R., 24 C. 418 (425). In *Srinivasa Chariar* v. *Raghava Chariar*, (1899) I. L. R., 23 M. 28, Mr. Justice *Shephard* thought that worshippers could bring a suit without joining others but that if objection was taken that leave was not obtained under S. 30 C.P.C., permission might be given to amend the plaint and to obtain the leave. See also note (5) p. cclxxx. But see *Ambalavana* v. *Bappu*, (1899) 9 M. L. J. R., 93 (97).

4. This is the real effect of the decision in *Zafaryab Ali* v. *Bakhtawar Singh*, (1883) I. L. R., 5 A. 497. When it was said that the institution was a religious institution and that therefore Mahomedan law governed the same and not S. 539, C. P. C., all that was meant was that S. 539, C. P. C., did not enact a substantive law and that the Mahomedan substantive law which allowed an individual right of suit to a worshipper was not modified by S. 539, C. P. C.

5. Suits under the section have been brought by the general manager. See *Manohar Ganesh* v. *Lakhmiram*, (1887) I. L. R., 12 B. 247 (258; 259). See also *Narayana Ayyar* v. *Kumarasami Mudaliar*, (1899) I. L. R., 23 M, 537.

The Bombay High Court, however seems to hold in one case that the section is mandatory and not merely enabling [1]. According to it one trustee cannot sue for the removal of his co-trustee and for account without the sanction referred to in S. 539, C. P. C.[2]. If this principle is applied it will apply to all classes of persons having interest and it has at least the merit of being sensible. But it is clear that the wording of the section is against the construction adopted in this case.

Nature of suits under S. 539, C. P. C.

That this cannot be the effect of the section will be clear from the nature of suits which can be brought under S. 539, C. P. C. It has been held by the Madras High Court that a suit to remove a manager for misconduct does not lie under S. 539, C. P. C. as the English statute (52 Geo. III C. 101) from which it has been borrowed has been held inapplicable to cases in which the hostile removal of a trustee is required[3]. But the High Courts of Allahabad[4], Bombay[5] and Calcutta[6] hold differently. Of course the section mentions expressly that the prayers for the appointment of new managers, vesting the endowed properties in such new managers and for scheme &c. may be asked under the section. It has been held that an account may be asked under this section[7] and that this relief is included in the general language adopted after clause -

1. *Tricumdass Mulji* v. *Khimji Vullabhdass*, (1892) I. L. R., 16 B. 626 (628) followed in *Sayad Hussein Miyan* v. *Collector of Kaira*, (1895) I. L.R., 21 B. 257 (262). But see other cases cited in notes (5) and (6) p. cclxxxv.

2. *Tricumdass Mulji* v. *Khimji Vullabhdass*, supra.

3. *Rangasawmi Naickan* v. *Varadappah Naickan*, (1894) I. L. R., 17 M. 462 following the *dictum* in *Narasimha* v. *Ayyan*, (1888) I. L. R , 12 M. 157 and not following the majority in *Subbayya* v. *Krishna*, (1890) I. L. R., 14 M. 186.

4. *Huseni Begam* v. *The Collector of Moradabad*, (1897) I. L. R., 20 A 46; *Girdhari Lal* v. *Ram Lal*, (1899) I. L. R., 21 A. 200.

5. *Chintaman Bajaji Dev* v *Dhondo Ganesh Dev*, (1888) I. L. R., 15 B. 612; *Tricumdass Mulji* v. *Khimji Vullabhdass*, (1892) I. L. R., 16 B. 626 (629); *Sayad Husseinmian* v. *Collector of Kaira*, (1895) I. L. R., 21 B. 48. In the subsequent cases, therefore, no question is raised.

6. *Sajedur Raja* v. *Baidayanath Deb*, (1892) I. L. R., 20 C. 397 (408); *Mohiuddin* v. *Sayiduddin*, (1893) I. L. R., 20 C. 810 (816); *Sajedur Raja Chowdhuri* v. *Gour Mohun Das Baishnav*, (1897) I. L. R., 24 C. 418 (pp. 422 to 426).

7. *Tricumdass Mulji* v. *Khimji Vullabhdass*, (1892) I. L. R., 16 B. 626 (629). In *Manohar Ganesh* v. *Lakhmiram*, (1888) I. L. R., 12 B 247 (267) the High Court directed an account to be taken from the shevaks of the properties and the Privy Council held on appeal that the account was necessary before a scheme could be framed. *Chotalal* v. *Manohar*, (1899) L. R., 26 I. A. 199: S. C. I. L. R., 24 B. 50. See also *Sayad Husseinmian* v. *Collector of Kaira*, (1895) I. L. R., 21 B. 48 (51).

(*e*) (*i. e.*, granting such further or other reliefs). A question has been raised whether a suit for a declaration that the properties are endowed will lie under the section and in one case it has been held that such a suit will not lie[1]. But when the manager *bona fide* claims a particular property as his, it seems absurd to suppose that no suit can be brought without asking for his removal. When removal is claimed the declaration will certainlybe incidental to such relief. A declaration that particular property is endowed involves a declaration that its income is available for the objects of the trust and such a declaration may be asked for under clause (*c*) of S 539, C.P.C. Whether a suit for possession *i. e.*, for removal of the old manager frompossession and for the new manager to be placed in possession is maintainable has not been considered by the Courts although there are a number of cases in which such prayers have been asked[2]. When clause (*b*) enables the Court to vest property in the new managers, the further relief consequent upon such vesting *viz.*, placing such new managers in possession of such property may also be awarded under the powers given to the Court "to grant further relief as the nature of the case may require[3]". The question whether the plaintiffs can ask for possession until a new manager is appointed has been made to depend upon the question whether as worshippers they are entitled to possession[4]. But as S. 539, C. P. C., is a representative suit[5] the only question that ought to be considered is whetherS. 539,C.P.C., precludes such a relief from being asked[6] and we are of opinion as already remarked that the section does not preclude the asking of such relief for possession[7].

---

1. *Jamaluddin* v. *Mujtaba Husain*, (1903) I. L. R., 25 A. 631. But see *dictum* of *Ranade*, J. in *Kazi Hassan* v. *Sagun Balkrishna*, (1899) I. L. R., 24 B. 170 at p. 181 where, however, he only says that a suit for declaration against strangers is not barred by S. 539, C. P. C.

2. *Chintaman Bajaji Dev* v *Dhondo Ganesh Dev*, (1888) I. L. R., 15 B. 612; *Sajedur Raja* v. *Baidyanath Deb*, (1892) I. L. R., 20 C. 397 (403); *Lakshmandas* v. *Jugalkishore*, (1896) I. L. R., 22 B. 216 (219).

3. *Sajedur Raja Chowdhuri* v. *Gour Mohun Das Baishnav*, (1891) I. L. R., 24 C. 418 (423, 429). See *Strinivasa Ayyangar* v. *Strinivasa Swami*, (1892) I. L. R., 16 M. 31.

4. *Subbarayadu* v. *Asanali Sheriff*, (1899) I. L. R., 23 M. 100 (note); *Kamaraju* v. *Asanali Sheriff*, (1899) I. L. R., 23 M. 99. See *Huseni Begam* v. *The Collector of Moradabad*, (1897) I. L. R., 20 A. 46 (50). But see p. cclxxviii and notes to S. 14 of Act XX, pp. 113, 114.

5. *Lakshmandas* v. *Jugalkishore*, (1896) I. L. R., 22 B. 216 (220).

6. Such a relief was asked in *Lakshmandas* v. *Jugalkishore*, (1896) I.L.R., 22 B. 216 (220). See *Subbarayadu* v. *Asanali Sheriff*, (1899) I. L.R., 23 M. 100 (note).

7. *Sajedur Raja Chowdhuri* v. *Gour Mohun Das Baishnav*, (1897) I. L. R., 24 C. 418 (423, 429). For other cases, see note (2).

Persons against whom suits may be brought under S. 539, C. P. C.

With regard to the persons against whom a suit may be instituted under S. 539, C. P. C., it may be observed that the section does not contain the limitation introduced by S. 14 of the Religious Endowments Act which it may be remembered speaks of "the trustee, manager or superintendent". If the cases decided under Lord Romilly's Act from which S. 539, C. P. C., is borrowed be not applicable it must be consistently held that as the section contains no limitation of the persons against whom the suit is to be brought all persons interested in the subject-matter and against whom relief may be asked and ought to be asked in an ordinary suit are proper parties. So that if the trustee makes an alienation or the property is in the possession of a trespasser, a suit against the alienee or trespasser must be maintainable under the section and this seems to be the view of the Calcutta High Court[1]. But all the other Courts are agreed in holding that suits against trespassers[2], alienees[3], persons who have ceased to hold the office of manager[4] or the deceased manager's legal representatives[5] cannot be brought under the section. So that according to the view laid down in these High Courts no relief can be asked against strangers in possession of endowed properties and wrongful alienations of the same cannot be set aside as against the alienees and properties recovered for the trust in suits under S. 539, C. P. C.

Constructive trustees.

A claim may be made under the section against constructive or *de facto* trustees although they may deny their character as trustees[6]. The section expressly applies to constructive trusts and

---

1. *Sajedur Raja* v. *Gour Mohun Das*, (1897) I. L. R., 24 C. 418 (423, 429).

2. *Vishvanath Govind Deshmane* v. *Rambhat*, (1890) I. L. R., 15 B 148 (151); *Augustine* v. *Medlycott*, (1892) I. L. R., 15 M. 241; *Strinivasa Ayyangar* v. *Strinivasa Swami*, (1892) I. L. R., 16 M. 31 (33); *Sri Dhundiraj Ganesh Dev.* v. *Ganesh* (1893) I. L. R., 18 B 721; *Muhammad Abdullah Khan* v. *Kallu*, (1899) I. L. R., 21 A. 187; But see *Hashmat Bibi* v. *Muhammad Askari*, (1895) A. W. N. 2.

3. *Lakshmandas Parashram* v. *Ganpatrav Krishna*, (1884) I. L. R., 8 B. 365; *Sheoratan Kunwari* v. *Ram Pargash*, (1896) I. L. R., 18 A. 227 (232); *Huseni Begam* v. *The Collector of Moradabad*, (1897) I. L. R., 20 A. 46 (49); per *Ranade*, J. in *Kazi Hassan* v *Sagun Balkrishna* (1896) I. L. R., 24 B. 170, at p. 181. See also *Amblavana* v. *Bappu*, (1899) 9 M. L. J. R., 93 (97).

4. *Augustine*, v. *Medlycott*, (1892) I. L. R., 15 M. 241.

5. See notes (2) and (3). But see *Sayad Husseinmiyan* v. *Collector of Kaira* I. L. R., 21 B. 48.

6. *Manohar Ganesh* v. *Lakhmiram*, (1887) I. L. R., 12 B. 247 (265) affirmed in *Chotalal* v. *Manohar Ganesh*, (1899) L. R., 26 I. A. 199: S. C. I. L. R., 24 B. 50; *Lakshmandas* v. *Jugalkishore*, (1896) I. L. R., 22 B. 216; *Jugalkishore* v. *Lakshmandas*, (1899) I. L. R., 23 B. 659. See also *Raghubar Dial* v. *Kesho Ramanuj Das*, (1888) I. L. R., 11 A. 18 (26) where it was said that the defendants might be trespassers.

there can, therefore, be no question that suits against constructive trustees may be filed under the section. Where the claim is that the defendant's appointment is illegal *i. e.*, not in accordance with the custom, the plaintiff may apply for the appointment of a new manager as upon a vacancy[1]. But this does not mean that the section will apply to cases of contests for establishing the rival or preferential claims of parties[2]. A claim by a person alleging that he is the rightful manager and that the defendant is not lawfully entitled is outside the scope of S. 539, C. P. C. So also a claim by a manager to enforce his vested right as against his co-manager[3] or to restrain the manager from excluding him from management is not necessarily governed by S. 539, C. P. C.[4]

Sanction for instituting suits under S.539, C. P. C.

The section requires that sanction should be obtained from the Advocate General or the Collector or other officer appointed by the local Government[5] as the case may be and it has been held that the obtaining of this sanction is a pre-requisite for the *institution* of the suit[6] though the Madras High Court seems to hold the other way[7]. But it must be pointed out that the language of the section is very different from S. 14 of the Religious Endowments Act and in the absence of such clear language we have to read into the section language which is not contained in it if the Allahabad view should prevail[8]. But be this as it may, the

1. *Bishen Chand Basawat* v. *Nadir Hossein*, (1887) L. R. 15 I. A. 1 (10): S. C. I.L.R., 15 C. 329 (341). The remarks in this case that a new trustee might be appointed under the Code of 1877 would seem to have been made without reference to the language of that code and the decisions under it. It was doubtful whether S. 539 of the Code of 1877 was applicable to religious trusts. See also *Neti Rama Jogiah* v. *Venkatacharulu*, (1902) I. L. R., 26 M. 450.

2. *Vishvanath Govind Deshmane* v. *Rambhat*, (1890) I.L.R., 15 B. 148 (151, 152).

3. *Athavulla* v. *Gouse*, (1888) I, L. R., 11 M. 283 (286).

4. *Athavulla* v, *Gouse*, (1888) I.L. R., 11 M. 283 (286); *Miya Vali Ulla* v. *Sayed Bava Santi Miya*, (1896) I. L. R., 22 B. 496; *Navroji Manekji* v. *Dastur Kharsedji*, (1903) I. L. R., 28 B. 20 (54, 55).

5. The Legal Remembrancer has been appointed in Allahabad to exercise the powers of the Advocate General under this section. See the N. W. P. and Oudh Rules 1893 p. 114.

6. *Gopal Dei* v. *Kanno Dei*, (1903) I. L. R., 26 A. 162.

7. *Ramayyangar* v. *Krishnayyangar*, (1886) I. L. R., 10 M. 185 applied to cases under S. 30 C. P. C., by *Shephard*, J. in *Srinivasa Chariar* v. *Raghava Chariar*, (1897) I. L. R., 23 M. 28 (32).

8. The Allahabad High Court says that the words "two persons having obtained the consent in writing &c., ... may institute" are equivalent to "two persons with the previous consent of the Advocate General &c." The language of S. 17 of the Charitable Trusts Act referred to in the Allahabad case seems to be stronger. Stress has to be laid upon the words "no suit shall be *entertained*" as well as upon the word "continued" and yet in *Rendall* v. *Blair*, (1890) 45 Ch. D. 139 the Court held that sanction might be obtained before the hearing. Cf. Ss. 5 and 6 of Act 23 of 1871 (the Pensions Act). See *Nawab Muhammad Azmat Ali Khan* v. *Lalli Begum*, (1881) L. R. 9 I. A. 8: S. C. I. L. R., 8 C. 422; *Vyankaji* v. *Sarjarao*, (1891) I. L. R., 16 B. 537; *Miya Vali* v. *Santi Miya*, (1896) I. L. R., 22 B. 496.

sanction must shew that the Collector or other officer has exercised his discretion in granting the sanction[1] and the suit brought under the section must correspond with the sanction as no reliefs can be awarded which are not contained in the sanction[2]. But where sanction is obtained and persons have the interest mentioned in the section their motives are irrelevant and will not defeat their suit[3]. If a person should bring a suit claiming the office of manager and fail in such suit that would not disentitle him to bring a suit as worshipper under S. 539 C. P. C., or otherwise for removing the defendant on the ground of misconduct[4]. The former decision would not operate as *res judicata*[5].

From this *resume* of authorities it will appear that the suits allowed before S. 539, C. P. C., to worshippers are not in any way restricted by the enactment of that section and for reasons similar to those adopted with reference to managers and founders whose rights to sue independent of S. 539, C. P. C., have been held not to be taken away it ought to be held that the rights of worshippers are also not taken away. But it must be admitted that there are decisions both ways[6]. In some respects the reasons for holding that such suits are maintainable are also stronger. If it should be held Conclusion.

---

1. *Sajedur Raja Chowdhuri* v. *Gour Mohun Das Baishnav*, (1897) I. L. R., 24 C. 418 (428). But the fact that the order does not show that the Collector has exercised a discretion as to interest &c., is merely an irregularity which will be cured under S. 578, C. P. C. But see *Gopal Dei* v. *Kanno Dei*, (1903) I. L. R., 26 A. 162 (165).

2. *Sayad Hussein Miyan* v. *Collector of Kaira*, (1895) I. L. R., 21 B. 257 following *Srinivasa* v. *Venkata*, (1887) I. L. R., 11 M. 148.

3. *Manohar Ganesh* v. *Lakhmiram*, (1887) I. L. R., 12 B. 247 (259).

4. Suits in which the plaintiff asserts his title to manage cannot be converted into a suit for trying the question of the defendant's title. *Greedharee Doss* v. *Nundokissore Doss*, (1867) 11 M. I. A. 405 (431). The cases of *Gunga Dae* v. *Tiluk Dass*, (1810) 1B. S.D.A.309 and *Sarubanund* v. *Deosing*,(1810)1B.S. D.A. 296 so far as they maintaintain a contrary view can hardly be regarded as laying down any sound law.

5. *Lakshmandas* v. *Jugal Kishore*, (1896) I. L. R., 22 B. 216. Cf. *Sathappayyar* v. *Periasami*, (1896) I. L. R., 14 M. 1 (9, 15).

6. *Manohar* v. *Keshavram*, (1878) I. L. R., 12 B. 267 (note); *Lutifunnissa Bibi* v. *Nazirun Bibi*, (1884) I. L. R., 11 C. 33: *Raghubar Dial* v. *Kesho Ramanuj Das*, (1888) I. L. R., 11 A. 18; *Tricumdass Mulji* v. *Khimji Vullabhdass*, (1892) I. L. R., 16 B. 626 (case of trustee); *Sayad Hussein Mian* v. *Collector of Kaira*, (1895) I. L. R., 21 B. 257 (we suppose all that is meant is that the procedure laid down in S. 539 C. P. C., must be strictly followed); *Sajedur Raja* v. *Baidyanath Deb*, (1892) I. L. R., 20 C. 397; *Kanhaya Lal* v. *Salig Ram*, (1894) A. W. N. 159 (160); *Hashmat Bibi* v. *Muhammad Askari*, (1895) A. W. N. 2; *Nellaiyappa Pillai* v. *Thangamma Nachiyar*, (1897) I. L. R., 21 M. 406. But see *Zafaryab* v. *Ali Bakhtawar Singh*, (1883) I. L. R., 5 A. 497; *Jawahra* v. *Akbar Husain*, (1884) I. L. R., 7 A. 178; *Thackersey Dewraj* v. *Hurbhum Nursey*, (1884) I. L. R., 8 B. 432; *Mohiuddin* v. *Sayiduddin*, (1893) I. L. R., 20 C. 810. See also *Radhabai* v. *Chimnaji*, (1878) I. L. R., 3 B. 27(28); *Abdul Rahman* v. *Yar Muhammad*, (1881) I. L. R., 3 A. 636; and *Baiju Lal Parbatia* v. *Bulak Lal Pathuk*, (1897) I. L. R., 24 C. 385. For other cases, see notes (4) and (5) p. cclxxv.

that no suits for declaration or for possession against alienees, trespassers and strangers or for hostile removal of managers are maintainable by worshippers under S. 539, C. P. C., the result will be that worshippers will have no effectual remedy whatever and if the view of the Calcutta High Court in *Sajedur Raja* v. *Baidyanath Deb*[1] be upheld, the result will be disastrous. No doubt if new managers be appointed they may sue for possession but in the meantime property may be lost altogether by operation of the law of limitation. If it be should asked what might be the reason for enacting S. 539, C. P. C., when the law allowed suits without reference to that section it might be said that it was doubtful whether some of the reliefs such as scheme &c., were awardable in suits under the ordinary law. So also it was doubtful whether worshippers were entitled to ask for the appointment of new managers when there was a mere case of vacancy[2]. There must be malversation alleged[3] and that was why in 1863, S. 14 was enacted which only treated of suits for misfeasance. But under S. 539, C. P. C., jurisdiction may be exercised whenever the direction of the Court is necessary for the administration of the trust[4]. Then again under S. 35 of Act 7 of 1866 (corresponding to S. 32 of 13 & 14 Vict. Ch. 60) which was held applicable by the Bombay High Court even to Hindu trusts[5] an application for removal of trustees on the ground of misappropiation &c., and for the appointment of new trustees was held not to be sustainable if the trustees were willing to act as the matters were too grave to be disposed of in a petition and that a suit should be filed[6]. Such a suit was provided for under S. 539, C. P. C., although curiously enough the prayer for removal of the manager was omitted. So that some such enactment as S. 539, C. P. C., was necessary for parties to whom the English Law was applicable[7] and it might have

---

1. (1892) I. L. R., 20 C. 397 which held that S. 30 C.P.C., would be inapplicable to the case of an indefinite body such as the Hindu community.

2. Per *Muthusami Iyer*, J. in *Subbayya* v. *Krishna*, (1890) I. L. R., 14 M. 186 (199 to 201).

3. See *Kalee Churn Giree* v. *Golabi*, (1878) 2 C. L. R. 178 and other early cases already referred to as recognising the right of worshippers. But see *Panchcowrie Mull* v. *Chumroolall*, (1878) I. L. R., 3 C. 563.

4. S. 539 C. P. C., first para.; and *Raghubar Dial* v. *Kesho Ramanuj Das*, (1888) I. L. R., 11 A. 18 (22).

5. *In re Kahandas Narrandas*, (1880) I. L. R., 5 B. 154 although under S. 3 of the Act the powers conferred under the Act can only be exercised in cases to which the English Law is applicable.

6. *In the Goods of James Powell junior*, (1873) 6 N. W. P. 54.

7. See S. 3 of Act 27 of 1866.

been thought expedient not to exclude other classes of subjects from the advantages of that enactment. Lastly the *forum* constituted under S. 539, C. P. C., was different.

Worshippers no right to remove managers—only remedy suit.

Although a suit for the removal of the manager and for appointment of a new one may be brought either by worshippers individually or jointly under S. 30 C.P.C. or by two or more of them under S. 539, C. P.C., the whole body of worshippers have no right to remove the manager without recourse to a civil suit and the Advocate General as representing that body of worshippers will equally have no right[1]. In cases of hereditary managers reliefs may be asked not simply for removal but also for the appointment of new managers. The fact that the office is hereditary and will vest in the next heir[2] will not make a suit for removal of the old trustee and for appointment of a new trustee unsustainable either as regards the whole suit or with reference to the latter part of it. This is also the case under S. 539, C.P.C[3]. The old trustee is removed on the ground of expediency or for better administration of the trust. It is in the interest of the trust that he is either removed or retained when misconduct is proved. So also if the interest of the trust requires that a new person should be appointed the Court is at liberty to appoint one either jointly with the person who is entitled by succession to the office or in supercession of such person[4]. But a strong case of expediency or necessity must be made out before the rightful person is superseded[6]. A committee to supervise the manager may be appointed[5]. The Court has jurisdiction to appoint although persons entitled to

Removal of hereditary manager and appointment of new.

---

1. *Dhuncooverbai* v. *The Advocate General*, (1899) 1 Bom. L. R. 743 (746, 747) Even the founders would have no right to dismiss the manager unless a power to that effect was reserved at the time of the endowment.

2. *Gopinadha Panda* v. *Ramachandra Punigrahi*, (1896) 6 M. L. J. R., 255.

3. *Subbayya* v. *Krishna*, (1890) I.L. R., 14 M. 186 (195, 205); *Sajedur Raja* v. *Baidyanath Deb*, (1892) I. L. R., 20 C. 397; *Mohiuddin* v. *Sayiduddin*, (1893) I. L. R., 20 C. 810 (814) case of *Sajjadanashin*; *Annaji* v. *Narayan*, (1896) I. L. R., 21 B. 556; *Sajedur Raja Chowdhuri* v. *Gour Mohun Das Baishnav*, (1897) I. L. R., 24 C. 418.

4. S. 35 of Act 27 of 1866 applied to Hindu trusts in *In re Kahandas Narrandas*, (1880) I. L. R., 5 B. 154. See *Purmanundass Jeevundass* v. *Venayekrao Wassoodeo*, (1882) L. R. 9 I. A. 86 (97). See Lewin on Trusts, Ch. XXVI, pp.780 to 784.

5. *Annaji* v. *Narayan*, (1896) I. L. R., 21 B. 556 (560).

6. In the absence of any such special circumstance the Court will direct inquiry as to the person who is the heir. Tudor p. 186. See also *Attorney General* v. *Gaunt*, (1790) 19 R. R., 186 (187); *Ludlow (Corporation of)* v. *Greenhouse*, (1827) 1Bligh. N.S. 17(80): S.C. 4 Eng. Rep. 780 (802); *Attorney General* v. *Boucherett*, (1858) 25 Beav. 116, (119, 120).

appoint may exist[1]. Where the heir is a minor a person may be appointed to act until the minor comes of age[2].

Right to elect.

In many cases disciples or a class of worshippers have the right to elect to the vacant office of manager or headship of a mutt. Such a right must and ought to be protected by the Courts. The Court will control such persons in the exercise of their powers after decree[3]. But when a person intrudes himself and claims to have been appointed by the disciples and the latter or some of them object upon the ground that he has not been duly appointed it seems ridiculous to tell such persons that they have no right of suit under S. 539, C.P.C., and that their only right (if any) is to enforce their claim in a suit under S. 30, C.P.C., and then when such latter suit is brought to tell them that the same is not maintainable. This in fact happened in the *Jeer case*[4]. In *Srinivasa Swami* v. *Ramanuja Chariyar*[5] the Madras High Court held that a suit by some of the disciples of the Ahobilam mutt alleging that the custom of the institution was for the disciples to elect, that in the actual case the defendant was an intruder and was not legally appointed, that there being a vacancy they were entitled to elect and were entitled to a declaration to that effect, that an election should take place under the guidance of the Court, that the defendant should be ejected and that the person appointed by them should be placed in possession was not maintainable. Such a case clearly falls under S. 539, C. P. C., but yet the plaintiffs were told in *Strinivasa Ayyangar* v. *Strinivasa Swami*[4] that their suit under S. 539, C. P. C., was not maintainable and probably the Court in *Srinivasa Swami* v. *Ramanuja Chariar*[5]

1. Tudor p. 186. But an appointment made by such persons would not be void although suit might be pending. *The Attorney General* v. *Clack*, (1839) 1 Beav. 467: S. C. 49 R. R. 405; *Eastwood* v. *Clark*, (1883) 23 Ch. D. 134; *Thomas* v. *Williams*, 24 Ch. D. 558(568).

2. *In re Shelmerdine*, (1864) 33 L. J. Ch. 474. See *Gopinadha Panda* v. *Ramachandra Punigrahi*, (1896) 6 M. L. J. R., 255 a case of committee appointing a person to the hereditary office of Bhandari in place of the holder removed for misconduct. The appointment was to enure only until the rightful heir should attain majority. The question whether a committee had a right to appoint was not considered. According to the decisions under Act XX a committee has no such power. See p. 47.

3. *Webb* v. *The Earl of Shaftesbury*, (1802) 6 R. R. 154.

4. *Strinivasa Ayyangar* v. *Strinivasa Swami*, (1892) I. L. R., 16 M. 31.

5. (1898) I. L. R., 22 M. 117. The Court suggested in this case that the decree for the appointment of a new manager would be wrong as the validity of the new appointment could not be gone into. Apparently the court did not notice the decision of the Privy Council in *Ponnambala Tambiran* v. *Sivagnana Desika Gnana Sambanda*, (1894) L. R., 21 I. A. 71 : S. C. I. L. R., 17 M. 343 which held that the validity of such appointment could be gone into in execution. Such a decree was in fact given in *Sathappayyar* v. *Periasami*, (1890) I. L. R., 14 M. 1 (13). In *Ragava* v. *Rajarathnam*, (1890) I. L. R., 14 M. 57 the suit was for a declaration as to the oper mode of elect ion.

was right in holding that a suit such as the one already mentioned was not maintainable under the ordinary law when it was alleged that nobody interfered with their right to appoint a new jeer.

As regards costs, the rule observed in England which is equally applicable here is that the relator in a charity information where there is nothing to impeach the propriety of his suit and no special circumstances to justify a special order is, upon obtaining a decree for the charity, entitled to have his costs as between solicitor and client and to be paid the difference between the amount of costs which he may recover from the defendants out of the charity[1]. But if the information should fail as to part and no previous application was made to the trustees the relators were allowed in one case party and party costs[2]. Costs.

Then with reference to the rights of the Advocate General so far as these endowments are concerned he only represents the public[3]. He may maintain a suit in his own name[4] or some relators may with his sanction bring a suit. This can only be in the Presidency Towns. The objection that he cannot maintain a suit for a dissenting charity has been long ago overruled[5]. When the suit is brought by the relators the suit is brought in the names of the latter and it need not be brought in the name of the Advocate General. The Advocate General in India is a counterpart of the Attorney General in England but the English practice as to the necessity of the suit by the relators being brought in the name of the Attorney General has not prevailed in India[6]. When the Advocate General brings a suit in his name it is usual to have some relators with him and he is said to lay the information at the relation of some private individual but relators are required only for the purposes of costs.[7] There was no such officer in the mofussil as the Attorney General in England and the Advocate General, therefore, could not apparently have brought suits in the mofussil. There was no public officer Advocate General.

1. Tudor, p. 345. See also *Attorney General* v. *Kerr*, (1841) 4 Beav. 297 (303): S. C. 55 R. R. 85.

2. *Attorney General* v. *Fishmongers' Company*, (1837) 1 Keen 492 (501,502).

3. *The Advocate General of Bombay* v. *Bai Punjabai*, (1894) 18 B. 551 (561).

4. *Attorney General* v. *Brodie*, (1846) 4 M. I. A. 190. See also *Srinivasa Chariar* v. *Raghava Chariar*, (1897) I. L. R., 23 M. 28 (30) ; *Dhuncooverbai* v. *The Advocate General*, (1899) 1 Bom. L. R. 743.

5. See Chapter I, pp. iii to viii.

6. *Panchcowrie Mull* v. *Chumroolall*, (1878) I. L. R., 3 C. 563 (571) ; *Thackersey Dewraj* v. *Hurbhum Nursey*, (1884) I. L. R., 8 B. 432 (452) ; *Srinivasa Chariar* v. *Raghava Chariar*, (1897) I. L. R., 23 M. 28 (30).

7. *Edward Strettell* v. *John Palmer*, (1816) 2 Mor. Dig. 104.

answering the Advocate General in the mofussil[1] entitled to bring suits which the Advocate General could have bought[2] in the Presidency Towns. But where the Advocate General was made a party in a suit brought at the instance of a person and instituted in the mofussil and the Advocate General employed a counsel he would be entitled to gets the costs of such counsel and other expenses of suit[3]. But after the Code of 1877 it has been expressly enacted by S. 539, that the Advocate General may sue[4]. But even after that section it is not necessary that he should be made a party either as a plaintiff[5] or as a defendant although if he is made a party defendant and appears by counsel he will be entitled to costs[3]. The Advocate General is at liberty to intervene at any stage of the litigation instituted by the relators[6] and is entitled to be heard[7]. The old relators can be dismissed and new persons can be permitted to come in with the permission of the Court on terms as to security and otherwise[8]. A bill filed by one Advocate General does not abate by the fact that the latter leaves the country. The new Advocate General may proceed with the bill[9]. The Advocate General having no rights independent of the public he will be bound by all acts and omissions of the manager which are not in themselves fraudulent. Where the trustees brought a suit against the representatives of the last trustee but failed to ask for an account they would be barred by S. 43, C. P. C., from instituting a fresh suit for an account. The Advocate General will equally be barred[10].

---

1. *Brojomohun Dass* v. *Hurro Lall*, (1880) I. L. R., 5 C. 700; *Shri Ganesh Dharnidhar Maharajdev* v. *Keshavrav*, (1890) I. L. R., 15 B. 625 (636); *Rangasami Naickan* v. *Varadappa Naickan*, (1894) I. L. R., 17 M. 462 (465). It is doubtful whether this statement is correct so far as regards the charitable institutions which are governed by Regulations XIX of 1810 and VII of 1817. The Collector must be regarded as such official.
2. He still can bring such suits.
3. *Hori Dasi Deabi* v. *The Secretary of State*, (1879) I. L. R., 5 C. 228.
4. *Shri Ganesh Dharnidhar* v. *Keshavrav*, (1890) I. L. R., 15 B. 625 (636). See also *Horidasi Devi* v. *The Secretary of State*, supra a case after the Code of 1877.
5. *Lakshmandas Parashram* v. *Ganpatrav*, (1884) I. L. R., 8 B. 365 (367).
6. *The Advocate General* v. *Muhammad Huseni*, (1867) 4 B. H. C. O. C. J. 203 at p. 206 (note).
7. *Attorney General* v. *Brodie*, (1846) 4 M. I. A. 190 (200).
8. *The Advocate General* v. *Muhammed Huseni*, (1867) 4 B. H. C. O. C. J. 203. Where all or some of the old relators die no further proceeding can be taken until the name of a new relator is inserted. *Strettel* v. *John Palmer*, (1816) 2 Mor. Dig. 104.
9. *Edward Strettell* v. *John Palmer*, (1816) 2 Mor. Dig. 104.
10. *The Advocate General of Bombay* v. *Bai Punjabai*, (1894) I. L.R., 18 B. 551 (568). See *Magdalen College, Oxford* v. *The Attorney General*, (1857) 6 H. L. C. 189 (214); S. C. 10 Eng. Rep. 1267 (1277).

CHAPTER XVI.

SUITS RELATING TO ENDOWMENTS AND LIMITATION.

Suits by managers—Two classes.

We shall first of all refer to suits by managers. It is said by *Jenkins*, C.J. in *Babajirao* v. *Laxmandas*[1] that there are *two* distinct classes of suits in connection with endowed property :—(1) those in which the manager seeks to enforce his private and personal rights ; and (2) those in which he seeks to vindicate the rights of the institution of which he is the manager. But for the decisions of the Privy Council in *Gossamee Sree Greedhareejee* v. *Rumanlolljee Gossamee*[2] and *Maharaja Jagadindra Nath* v. *Rani Hemanta*[3] one may be disposed to accept this classification as substantially correct.The decision in the first case points out that when a person sues for establishing his right to the office of manager of a temple or to any other religious office, he sues for establishing his right which is *personal* in a sense and for establishing the right of the Thakoor as it is also the right of the Thakoor to be in proper custody. This personal right which is recognised as such by the decision of the Privy Council in the second case must in law be distinguished from the private individual right of the manager as such right is distinct from his right as manager. If a person claims property as belonging to him in his individual capacity, he is claiming a right inconsistent with the property being endowed and this right has nothing whatever to do with an endowment or with his right as manager. Such a purely personal claim must be distinguished from his claim to hold the property as manager of an institution. This *purely personal* claim is not apparently the claim referred to in the first class of suits mentioned by *Jenkins*, C. J. in *Babajirao* v. *Laxmandas*[1] as his Lordship gives the case of *Gnanasambanda Pandara* v. *Velu Pandaram*[5] as an illustration of his first class of suits. The case of *Velu Pandaram*[5] relates to a claim to establish an hereditary office. And yet the statement of *Jenkins*, C. J. that the rights of the "math cannot ordinarily be prejudiced by the result of a suit of that class" (that is to say, by one in which the private and personal rights of the manager alone are in question) may lead one to suppose that his Lordship is really dealing with the

1. (1903) I. L. R., 28 B. 215 at p. 223.
2. (1889) L. R. 16 I. A. 137: S. C. I. L. R., 17 C. 3.
3. (1904) 8 C. W. N. 809.
4. (1903) I. L. R., 28 B. 215 at p. 223.
5. (1899) L. R. 27 I. A. 69 : S. C. I. L. R., 23 M. 271.

case of a suit in which the claim is purely personal and has nothing whatever to do with the property being endowed. Anyhow this statement of the law must be taken with great qualifications as shall be shewn later on. For the present it may be stated that a decision in a claim by a person that the property sued on is his own (*i. e.*, is his ordinary property) will not bind the same person when he sues for the same property as endowed property which he has a right to hold as shebait or manager. That was in fact the decision in that case.

Suit to establish right as manager and to recover emoluments.

A person may sue to establish his right as manager of a religious institution whether emoluments are attached to it or not[1]. In fact in the generality of cases, the office of manager is only burdensome. Such a claim is cognizable by the Civil Courts[2] just as suits relating to other subordinate hereditary offices[3] in a temple are cognizable by the Civil Courts as mentioned in a previous chapter[3]. We need not pause to consider whether Courts ought to take cognizance of claims to any office though not attached to temples and though no emoluments are attached to the same and whether the decisions holding that no suits will lie in cases in which the office is not attached to any temple[4]

---

1. *Srinivasa* v. *Tiruvengada*, (1888) I. L. R., 11 M. 450 (451, 452).

2. *Pucha Counden* v. *Thotha Counden*, (1856) M. S. D. A. 198; *Shriman Sadagopa* v. *Kristna Tata Chariar*, (1863) 1 M. H. C. 301 (307); *Pranshankar* v. *Prannath Mahanand*, (1863) 1 B. H. C. A. C. J. 12 (13); *Archakam Srinivasa Dikshatulu* v. *Udayagiry Anantha Charlu*, (1869) 4 M. H. C. 349 (353); *Nanjappa* v. *Pullapa*, (1869) 5 Mad. Jur. 13 (a decision of the Judicial Commissioner Mr. Kindersley afterwards Mr. Justice *Kindersley* of the Madras High Court); *Narasimma Chariar* v. *Tata Chariar*, (1871) 6 M. H. C. 449; *Vasudev* v. *Vamanaji*, (1880) I. L. R, 5 B. 80 (82); *Chuni Pardey* v. *Birjo*, (1883) 13 C. L. R. 49 (50); *The Advocate General of Bombay* v. *Devaker*, (1886) I. L. R., 11 B. 185 (194); *Sayud Hashim Saheb* v. *Huseinsha*, (1888) I. L. R., 13 B. 429 (433); *Mamat Ram Bayan* v. *Bapu Ram*, (1878) I. L. R., 15 C. 159; *Srinivasa* v. *Tiruvengada*, supra; *Limba Bin Krishna* v. *Rama Bin Pimplu*, (1888) I. L. R., 13 B. 548 (550); *Gursangaya* v. *Tamana* (1891) I. L. R., 16 B. 281 (283); *Jagannath* v. *Akali Dassia*, (1893) I. L. R., 21 C. 463; *Krishnasawmi Thatha Chariar* v. *Appanaiyangar*, (1896) 7 M. L. J. R, 23; Per *Ranade*, J. in *Appaya* v. *Padappa*, (1898) I. L. R., 23 B. 122 at p. 127; *Dino Nath Chuckerbutty* v *Pratap Chandra Goswami*, (1899) I. L. R., 27 C. 30 (32, 33); *Srinivasa Thathachariar* v. *Srinivasa Ayyangar*, (1899) 9 M. L. J. R., 355. See also *Appanna* v. *Nagiah*, (1880) I. L. R., 6 B. 512. Cf. *Koondoo Nath* v. *Dheer Chunder*, (1873) 20 W. R. C. R. 345.

3. See Ch XIV p. ccliv. The right to break a curdpot on a certain day in a particular part of the temple is apparently regarded as a right attached to an office and a claim for the enforcement of the same is held maintainable in *Narayan Sadanand Bava* v. *Balkrishna Shidheshvar*, (1872) 9 B. H. C. 413 (414, 416). Apparently the point was not argued. See *Sangapa Bin Baslingapa* v. *Gangapa Bin Niranjappa*, (1878) I. L. R., 2 B. 476. Cf. *Rama* v. *Shivram*, (1882) I. L. R., 6 B. 116; and *Narayan* v. *Krishnaji*, (1885) I. L. R., 10 B. 233. Even claims to the office of temple dancing girls have been recognised. *Kamalam* v. *Sadagopa Sami*, (1878) I. L. R., 1. M. 356; *Tara Naiken* v. *Nana Lakshman*, (1889) I. L. R., 14 B. 90

4. *Mamat Ram* v. *Bapu Ram*, supra; *Srinivasa* v. *Tiruvengada*, supra; *Subbaraya* v. *Venkatanarasu*, (1891) 2 M. L. J. R. 83; *Venkatavaratha* v. *Anantha*, (1893) I. L. R., 16 M. 299: S. C. 3 M. L. J. R., 350; *Tholappala Charlu* v. *Venkata Charlu*, (1895) I. L. R., 19 M. 62.

are rightly decided. Nor need we consider whether claims to caste offices and caste questions are or are not cognizable by Civil Courts and whether the statement of the law as given by Mr. *Justice Ranade* in *Appaya* v. *Padappa*[1] is more correct than that of Mr. *Justice Chandavarkar* in *Nathu* v. *Keshawji*.[2] So far as our subject is concerned it is enough to accept the principle that suits relating to offices in a religious institution are maintainable in Civil Courts whether emoluments are attached to such offices or not. If emoluments are attached to the office then a suit for such emoluments against an intruder will lie[3]. Where no emoluments are attached to the office but the intruder receives voluntary offerings from the worshippers, the rightful holder on principle must be entitled to get such offerings[4]; otherwise it is allowing the trespasser to profit by his own wrong. The cases, however, seem not to recognise this right. But when carefully analyzed many of these are cases of claims for damages caused by loss of voluntary offerings which do not imply that as a matter of fact the intruder received the offerings by virtue of his holding the office although other cases cannot be so distinguished[5]. No doubt the holder of an office to which no fees are attached cannot ask from the intruder presents which were not made in fact but which would have been paid if he (the real holder) had been in the undisturbed enjoyment of his office. The claim for this is also one for damages, but these damages are too uncertain and remote.[6] They may or may not have been paid.[7] These cases can have no application where

Claim for voluntary offerings.

1. (1898) I. L. R., 23 B. 122 at pp. 127, 128, 129 and 130.

2. (1901) I. L. R., 26 B. 174 at pp. 181 to 189.

3. *Pranshankar* v. *Pranrath Mahanund*, (1863) 1 B. H. C. A. C. J. 12 (where the right to receive proceeds of mandir was affirmed); *Sitarambhat* v. *Sitaram Ganesh*, (1869) 6 B. H. C. A. C. J 250; *Kali Kanta Surma* v. *Gouri Prosad Surma Bardeuri*, (1890) I. L. R, 17 C. 906 (909,910); *Gurusangaya* v. *Tamana*, (1891) I. L. R., 16 B. 281.

4. *Sheo Suhaye Dhamee* v. *Bhooree Muhtoon*, (1865) 3. W. R. C. R. 33; *Krishnasami* v. *Krishnama*, (1882) I. L. R., 5 M. 313 (319).

5. *Muhammad Yusub* v. *Sayad Ahmed* (1861) 1 B. H. C. app. xvii (xxii, xxxvi, xxxvii); *Ramessur Mookerjee* v. *Isham Chunder*, (1868) 10 W. R. C. R. 457; *Sitarambhat* v. *Sitaram Ganesh*, (1869) 6 B. H. C. A. C J. 250 (253); *Shankara Bin Marabasapa* v. *Hanma Bin Bhima*, (1877) I. L. R., 2 B. 470 (471); *Srinivasa* v. *Tiruvengada*, (1888) I. L. R., 11 M. 450 (451); *Kali Kanta Sarma* v. *Gouri Prosad Surma Bardeuri*, (1890) I. L. R., 17 C. 906 (909); *Kashi Chandra* v. *Kailash Chandra*, (1899) I. L.R., 26 C 356. In many of these, the point did not arise.

6. *Narayan Sadanand Bava* v. *Balkrishna Shidheshwar*, (1872) 9 B. H. C. 413 (416, 417).

7. *Narayan Sadanand Bava* v. *Balkrishna Shidheshwar*, (1872) 9 B. H. C. 413 (417).

voluntary offerings are in fact paid for services done in the course of the office. If the intruder is not justly entitled to hold the office he is not equally entitled to hold the profits which but for his wrong he will not have made. The English case of *Boyter* v. *Dodsworth*[1] no doubt supports the view that gratuities received by an intruder cannot be recovered by the rightful holder of the office. Even there later decisions shew that the fee need not be a fixed one but may be of a reasonable amount.[2] We think the payments made to temple office-holders come within the latter rule. Anyhow it is not safe to follow the English decisions as they are not suited to the circumstances of this country. According to the decision of the Bombay High Court in *Vithal Krishna Joshi* v. *Anant Ramchandra*[3] "under the Hindu system though the amount of the priest's fee is left to the conscience and the means of the person for whom his functions are performed, yet the payment of some fee is regarded as essential to the efficacy of the ceremonies performed." A suit for partition and share of such offerings will lie so that where a member wrongfully refuses to give to the others their share, a suit will lie[4]. This is said to be on an agreement express or implied.

Nature of suit for establishing hereditary office of manager.

A suit for the recovery of such offerings may be a suit for establishing a purely personal right. But a suit for establishing an hereditary office of manager and to recover the endowed properties is not necessarily a suit for a purely personal right. If the manager establishes his claim, he holds the endowed properties as manager with the liability of a trustee, and if in that suit he has

---

1. (1796) 6 T. R. 681 : S. C. 3 R. R. 315.

2. *Bryant* v. *Foot*, (1868) L. R. 3 Q. B. 497 (508).

3. (1874) 11 B. H. C. 6 at p. 11. This has been adopted in Bombay ever since. See *Dinanath Abaji* v. *Sadashiv Hari Madhave*, (1878) I.L.R., 3 B. 9 (11); *Raja Valad Shivapa* v. *Krishnabhat*, (1879) I. L. R., 3 B. 232 ; *Ganesh Ramchandra Date* v. *Shankar Ramchandra*, (1886) I. L. R., 10 B 395 (398) ; *Waman Jagannath Joshi* v. *Balaji Kusaji Patil*, (1888) I. L. R., 14 B. 167. The case of *Mugjoo Pandaen* v. *Ram Dyal Tewaree*, (1871) 15 W. R.C. R. 531 held that there was no office. In *Dayaram Hargovan* v. *Jetha Bhat Lakhmiram*, (1895) I. L. R., 20 B. 784 the priest was dismissed. In *Jowahur Misser* v. *Bhagoo Misser*, (1857) B. S. D. A. 362 it was held that there was no office which the law could recognise. The same was held in the cases of *Behari Lal* v. *Babu*, (1867) 2 Ag. H. C. 80 and *Ramakrishna* v. *Ranga*, (1884) I. L. R., 7. M 84.

4. *Jugdanund Gossamee* v. *Kessul Nund Gossamee*, (1864) W. R. Sp. C. R. 146 ; *Khedroo Ojha* v. *Mussamut Deo Ranee Koomar*, (1866) 5 W. R. C. R. 222 ; *Oochi* v. *Ulfat* (1898) I. L. R., 20 A. 234 ; *Dino Nath Chuckerbutty* v. *Protap Chandra Goswami*, (1899) I. L. R., 27 C. 30. See also *Durga Pershad* v. *Budree*, (1874) 6. N. W.P. 189.

failed to ask for the recovery of any portion of the endowed properties from the intruder or is unsuccessful with reference to a portion of the same, he cannot afterwards ordinarily bring a second suit against the same person.[1] If an adverse decision is passed that the manager is not entitled to recover a portion of the properties on the ground that they do not belong to the institution, clearly no second suit is maintainable. If the decision affirms the right of the endowment but proceeds upon some point which may be regarded as personal to the plaintiff, then the decision only affects the rights of the parties. Where a person fails to prove his claim for an hereditary office or where such claim is held to be barred and the defendant contends that he is the manager, then the plaintiff does not represent the trust[2] and any decision in it does not purport to affect the rights of the trust. The same plaintiff as a person interested may bring a suit for any act of maladministration by the defendant recognising his title as manager, and the decision in the former suit will be no bar for the trial of this latter suit.[3] The question of res-judicata depends both upon the nature of the suit and upon the nature of the adjudication. Where, therefore, a person after suing for the recovery of certain property as his own *private* property and failing in such suit, brings another suit as manager for the recovery of the same property as being endowed property he can hardly be barred by the former decision. This was the decision in *Babajirao* v. *Laxmandas*[4].

Limitation for such suits—Article 124.

A suit for possession of an hereditary office is governed by Art. 124 of the present Limitation Act (XV of 1877). According to this article, such a suit would be barred if twelve years should expire from the time the defendant had taken possession of the office adversely to the plaintiff. According to the explanation, an hereditary office is possessed when the profits thereof are usually received or if there are no profits, when the duties thereof are usually performed. When no emoluments are attached to the

---

1. *The Advocate General of Bombay* v. *Bai Punjabai*, (1894) I.L.R., 18 B. 551 (568).
2. *Lakshmandas* v. *Jugalkishore*, (1896) I. L. R., 22 B. 216 (220).
3. Ibid.
4. (1903) I. L. R., 28 B. 215.

office, the latter part of the explanation will apply. Art. 124 will, therefore, govern a suit to establish the plaintiff's right to the hereditary office of manager and to recover endowed property[1]. The right to recover the idol as appurtenant to such office is not barred if the right to the office is not barred[2]. There is no distinction between the office and the property of the endowment. The one is attached to the other[3]. So that, if the right to the office is barred, the right to recover the property as attached to that office is also barred and the limitation for both is that provided by Art. 124 of the Indian Limitation Act. S. 10 of the Limitation Act does not govern such cases[4]. The plaintiff in such cases is suing only for his own personal right to manage or in some way to control the endowment[5]. In such cases there is no suit for recovering the property for the trusts in question. The expression "for the purpose of following in his or their hands such property" means "for the purpose of recovering the property for the trust[6]." So that, S. 10 only applies when property is used for some purposes other than the proper purposes of the trusts in question and it is sought to be recovered from the hands of the persons indicated in the section[6]. The right to control and interfere in the management may also become barred[6]. If one holder is barred his successors in office will equally be barred[7].

In all such cases *i.e.*, where twelve years have elapsed, the right of the person out of possession is said to be extinguished

---

1. *Gossamee Sree Greedharreejee* v. *Rumanlolljee Gossamee*, (1889) L. R. 16 I. A. 137 : S. C. I. L. R., 17 C. 3 ; *Sarkum Abu Torab* v. *Rahaman Buksh*, (1896) I. L. R., 24 C. 83; *Jagannath Prasad Gupta* v. *Ranjit Singh*, (1897) I. L. R., 25 C. 354; *Alagirisami Naickar* v. *Sundareswara Ayyar*, (1898) I. L. R., 21 M. 278 (287) ; *Gnanasambanda Pandara* v. *Velu Pandaram*, (1899) L. R. 27 I. A. 69 : S. C. I. L. R., 23 M. 271. Cf. *Balwant Rao Bishwant Chandra Chor* v. *Purun Mal Chaube*, (1882) L. R 10 I. A. 90 (97) ; and *Nilakandan* v. *Padmanabha*, (1890) I. L. R., 14 M. 153 (162).

2. *Gossamee Sree Greedharreejee* v. *Rumanlolljee Gossamee*, supra.

3. *Gnanasambanda Pandara* v. *Velu Pandaram*, (1899) L. R. 27 I. A. 69 (77) : S. C. I. L. R., 23 M. 271 at p. 279. See also *Tammirazu* v. *Narsiah*, (1871) 6 M. H. C. 301 (303) ; *Kidambi Ragava Chariar* v. *Tirumalai Asari Nallur Ragavachirar*, (1902) I. L. R., 26 M. 113.

4. *Balwant Chandra Chor* v. *Purun Mal Chaube*, (1882) L. R. 10 I. A. 90 (96) ; *Karimshah* v. *Nattan Bivi*, (1883) I. L. R., 7 M. 417; *Nilakandan* v. *Padmanabha*, (1890) I. L. R., 14 M. 153 (162) ; *Ranga Pai* v. *Baba*, (1897) I. L. R., 20 M. 398 (402, 403).

5. See cases cited in note (4).

6. *Balwant Chandra Chor* v. *Purun Mal Chaube*, (1882) L. R. 10 I. A. 90 (96).

7. *Gnanasambanda* v. *Velu Pandaram*, (1899) L. R. 27 I. A. 69 : S. C. I. L. R., 23 M. 271 ; *Veerabhadra* v. *Venkatadri*, (1899) 10 M. L. J. R., 114. See *Radhabai* v. *Anantrav*, (1885) I. L. R., 9 B. 198.

under Art. 28 of the Limitation Act.[1] and the person in possession acquires a prescriptive title.[2] Art. 28 of the Limitation Act refers to the "right to *any property*". The right to the hereditary office of manager or of priest of a temple was regarded as immoveable property[3] but after the definition of "immoveable property" in the General Clauses Act, such right is not immoveable property. So also a claim to joint management will be barred if the claimant is excluded from management for over twelve years.[4] But the mere fact that the claimant did not take any active part in the management would not bar his right. There must be a denial of his right coupled with his exclusion or his non-interference.[5] Where there is joint possession there can be no adverse possession.[6] So also, a claim to joint management may be acquired by prescription where a person having no right claims joint management[7] and is in joint management for over twelve years.

The question next arises as to the scope of Art. 124 of the Limitation Act. The article speaks of an hereditary office. If the succession to the office is governed by the ordinary laws of succession or if the office goes to a single member by right of primogeniture or to Scope of Article 124.

---

1. *Manally Chennakesavaraya* v. *Mangadu Vaidelinga*, (1877) I. L. R., 1 M. 343 ; *Alagirisami Naickar* v. *Sundareswara Ayyar*, (1898) I. L. R., 21 M. 278 (287) ; *Gnanasambanda Pandara* v. *Velu Pandaram*, (1899) L. R. 27 I. A. 69 (77) : S. C. I. L. R. 23 M. 271 (279).

2. *Manally Channakesavaraya* v. *Mangadu Vaidelinga*, (1877) I. L. R., 1 M. 343 ; *Nilakandan* v. *Padmanabha*, (1890) I. L. R., 14 M. 153 (162) ; *Alagirisami Naickar* v. *Sundareswara Ayyar*, (1898) I. L. R., 21 M. 278 (287).

3. *Krishnabhat Bin Hyragange*, (1869) 6 B. H. C. A. C. J. 137 ; *Appanna* v. *Nagiah*, (1880) I. L. R., 6 B. 512. Cf. *The Government of Bombay* v. *Desai Kullianrai Hakoomutrai*, (1872) 14 M. I. A. 551 ; *Balvantrao T. Bapaji* v. *Purshotam Sidheswar*, (1872) 9 B. H.C.R. 99 (village Joshi) ; *Maharana Fattehsangji Jaswant Sangji* v. *Dessai Kullianraiji Hekoomutraiji*, (1873) L. R. 1 I. A. 34 ; S. C. 21 W. R. (P. C.) 178 following *Sumbhoolall Girdhurlall* v. *The Collector of Surat*, (1859) 8 M. I. A. 1 ; *Kundoo Nath Surma Gossamee* v. *Dheer Chunder Surma Odhikar Gossamee*, (1873) 20 W. R. C. R. 345; *Raghoo Pandey* v. *Kassy Parey*, (1883) I. L. R., 10 C. 73 (right to officiate as priest at funeral ceremonies). These decisions may not hold good under the Limitation Acts of 1871 and 1877. The right to worship an idol is not immoveable property. See *Eshan Chunder Roy* v. *Monmohini Dassi*, (1878) I. L. R., 4 C. 683. An annuity to a temple is regarded by some judges as immoveable property and by some as otherwise. *The Government of Bombay* v. *Gossami Shri Girdhar Lalji*, (1872) 9 B. H. C. 222 (it is not immoveable property) ; per *Sarjent*, J. in *Collector of Thana* v. *Krishnanath Govind*, (1880) I. L. R., 5 B. 322 (it is immoveable property) affirmed in *The Collector of Thana* v. *Hari Sitaram*, (1883) I. L. R., 6 B. 546.

4. *Gnanasambanda Pandara* v. *Velu Pandaram*, (1899) L. R. 27 I. A. 69 : S. C. I. L. R., 23 M. 271.

5. *Ranga Pai* v. *Baba*, (1897) I. L. R., 20 M. 398 (401, 402).

6. *Athavulla* v. *Gouse*, (1888) I. L. R., 11 M. 283.

7. *Nilakandan* v. *Padmanabha*, (1890) I. L. R., 14 M. 153 (162) ; *Alagirisami Naickar* v. *Sundareswara Ayyar*, (1898) I. L. R., 21 M. 278 (287).

the eldest male member of the family, there can be no doubt that the office is hereditary within the meaning of Art. 124. So also the right of management vested in the founder and his heirs in default of appointment is a right to an hereditary office within the meaning of Art. 124[1]. If, however, the office goes by nomination either by the last incumbent or by the founder and his heirs or by any other person, then it has been held in a Calcutta case[2] that the office is not hereditary and that the rule of six years under Art. 120 but not that of twelve years under Art. 124 will apply. It seems to us that the decision in this case is, with all deference to the learned judges who decided it, erroneous. It was said in the Calcutta case that if succession to the office were by inheritance the case would have fallen under Art 124 but that as in that particular case the office went by nomination Art. 120 only would govern. It seems to us that it is the descendible quality of the office that is apparently pointed out by the expression " hereditary office ". If the office goes by descent then there is an hereditary office. The mode of descent is immaterial[3]. Where the office goes by nomination there is certainly a succession to the office. Is there not a succession by inheritance? *Inheritance* either means the act of inheriting in any sense of that word (Century Dictionary Vol. IV, p.3098 Title "Inheritance") or it means in law an estate cast upon the heir immediately on the death of the ancestor (Ibid, 2nd meaning)." Hereditary" according to the Century Dictionary (Vol. IV, p 2802) means descending by inheritance or passing to or held by an *heir* or *heirs*. An "heir" according to the same Dictionary (Vol. IV, p. 2773) means one who inherits or has a right of inheritance in the property of another or one who receives or is entitled to receive possession of property or a vested right on the death of the owner either as his natural or legal successor. In English Law an heir at law has acquired a special signification, but this is certainly not the sense in which the word is used here. In India no such special significance is known. The general meaning given above is wide enough to cover a case of nomination. There are heirs by custom even according to the English

1. *Jagannath Prasad Gupta* v. *Runjit Singh*, (1897) I. L. R., 25 C. 354 (364), distinguishing the first case cited in note (2) below.

2. *Jagan Nath Das* v. *Birbhadra Das*, (1892) I. L. R., 19 C. 776 (779). See also *Kidambi Ragava Chariar* v. *Tirumalai Asari Nallur Ragavachariar*, (1902) I. L. R., 26 M. 113 (115).

3. But see *Gopinadha* v. *Ramachandra*, (1896) 6 M. L. J. R., 255 which held that the descent must be in the direct line of heirs.

Law (Wharton's Law Lexicon, 9th Edn., p. 344), and we speak of the hereditary right to the Crown although the descent is subject to limitation by Parliament. The test is, therefore, simply the descendible quality of the office. Moreover, the nominee succeeds as heir of the last incumbent and the last incumbent having the right to appoint is said to *appoint his successor* to the office. The office *descends* to the nominee and we may add by the customary mode of succession. Then again, in early Bengal cases the succession in this way was regarded as hereditary. Mutts were said to be of *three* classes, according to these cases, (*a*) Mouroosi, (*b*) Punchaiti, (*c*) Hakmi[1]. In the *last* class, the appointment rested with the ruling power or founder; in the *second*, the appointment was elective; and in the *first*, the office was said to be hereditary. Hereditary succession as explained in these cases either meant devolution upon the chief disciple or nomination[2]. So that the Calcutta view at any rate as regards offices devolving by such nomination is not sustainable. Lastly, when a person is appointed to the office either by nomination by the last incumbent or by the founder or by any other person or by a class of persons an heir is appointed to the last incumbent by a power of appointment recognised by law or by custom. Such powers of appointment are similar to the powers of adoption known to the Hindu Law where by the act of adoption a person is appointed as an heir either to the adopter or to the adopter's husband. Moreover in the case of these mutts ordinarily the deceased's disciple is nominated and according to Yajnawalkya the disciple is the heir in such cases. If this view were not to prevail claims to the headship of mutts or to the offices of Mutwalli and Sujjadanashin should be treated as not dealt with specifically, and it could hardly be imagined that the Legislature meant that these should be caught in the universal Article 120 as held in the Calcutta case. In previous chapters we have shewn that the theory in the case of Mutts and Khankas is that the founder is the spiritual ancestor, and that his spiritual line is continued by his successors in office. Claims to such office must be dealt with

---

1. See Chapter VIII, pp. cxi, cxii and cases cited in note (6) to p. cxi.

2. *Mohant Ram Nooj Doss* v. *Mohant Debraj Doss*, (1839) 6 B. S. D. A. 262. See also *Ram Churn Das* v. *Chuttur Bhoje*, (1845) 7 B.S. D. A. 205 ; *Local Agents of Zillah Hooghly* v. *Krishnanund Dundee*, (1848) 7 B. S. D. A. 476.

under Art. 124. Again, the Calcutta decision hoids that Art. 144 will not apply to a suit by such an office-holder to establish his office and to recover the endowed property as appertaining to such office as the suit is not for the possession of immoveable property[1]. We have already seen that there is a large body of decisions in which it has been held that the right to such offices should of themselves be regarded as immoveable property[2] but these could not be regarded now as good law after the definition of immoveable property in the General Clauses Act. However this may be, we fail to see why a suit for establishing an office and for recovery of endowed immoveable property is not a suit for possession of immoveable property. No doubt the property is appurtenant to the office and must go with the office. If a special period is provided for the office, then such special period also covers the claim for endowed property. But if no such period is provided for, it is difficult to see why a suit for endowed property by the Manager does not fall under Art. 144 merely because the person seeking to recover has to prove his title to recover or merely because the defendant sets up a title to hold such property[3]. The fact that the title rests with the idol has no bearing upon the applicability of Art. 144[4] unless it is thought that possession in this Article is used in a limited sense and does not include the custody of a Manager.

Suit to establish turns—Limitation.

In cases of private endowments the management may, as we have already seen, be made by turns by agreement and according to the recent decision of the Madras High Court the management may also be by turns in cases of public endowments[5]. The right of a shebait to a pala or turn of worship is a periodically recurring right and is governed by Art. 131 of the Limitation Act[6]. A suit by a shebait for sole management or joint management will, if the office be hereditary, be governed by Art. 124 of the Limita-

1. See also *Tammirazu Ramazogi* v. *Pantina Narsiah*, (1871) 6 M. H. C. 301 (303). This was a case under Act XIV of 1859 relating to the office of *Karnam*, Under that Act the right to the office of manager was regarded as immoveable property. See also *Kidambi Ragava Chariar* v. *Ragava Chariar*, (1902) I. L. R., 26 M. 113 (115).

2. See note (3) to p. ccciii.

3. In *Kannan* v. *Nilakandan*, (1884) I. L. R., 7 M. 337 (338), Art. 144 was applied.

4. *Maharaja Jagadindra Nath Roy* v. *Rani Hemanta Kumari Debi*, (1904) 8 C. W. N. 809 (820). See also *Thakur* v. *Ram Charn*, 8 Cent. Prov. L. Rep. 49.

5. Chapter XIV, pp. ccxviii to ccxxviii.

6. *Eshan Chunder Roy* v. *Monmohini Dassi*, (1878) I. L. R., 4 C. 683; *Gopeekishen Gossumy* v. *Thakoordass Gossamy*, (1882) I. L. R., 8 C. 807.

tion Act[1]. So a suit by a person to establish his right to manage by turns is governed by Art. 131.[2] It is not a right to joint management which is governed by Art. 124 and which implies that the plaintiff has along with others a right to present management and that the others also have a right to present management along with the plaintiff. But to establish a claim to a right of management by turns the plaintiff must have a present sole right of management for the period of his turn while the others will not be entitled by reason of their turns not having arrived. Such a claim is not governed by Art. 124 but by Art. 131[3].

It is said that a suit to recover endowed property does not lie without suing to recover the idol[4]. We have already discussed this matter on a previous occasion. No valid reason can be assigned why such a suit will not lie. Where the right to the office is not barred a suit for recovery of the idol is not barred[5].

Prescriptive title. A claim to the office of shebait may be acquired by prescription[6]. We have seen that such a claim is only one to enforce a personal right of management to which S. 10 of the Limitation Act will not apply[7]. The person in wrongful possession acquires a correspond-

---

1. See pp. ccci to cccvi. But in *Eshan Chunder Roy* v. *Monmohini Dassi*, (1878) I.L.R., 4 C. 683, Art. 118 of Act IX of 1871 (corresponding to Art. 120 of the present Act) was applied. Art. 123 was apparently not cited. A right to recover an idol established in a temple for purposes of worship may be a right to recover an interest in immoveable property. Apparently the idol was not established in a temple in the above case.

2. *Sinde* v. *Sinde*, (1867) 4 B. H. C. A. C. J. 51 (54) a case under Act XIV of 1859 concerning the office of Potail. See also the cases cited in note (5), p. cccvi.

3. But see *Ramanathan Chetty* v. *Murugappa Chetty*, (1903) I. L. R., 27 M. 192 (196).

4. *Doorga Proshad Dass* v. *Sheo Proshad Pandah*, (1880) 7 C. L. R., 78. See Chapter VII, pp xciv, xcv and Chapter VIII, p. xcviii.

5. *Gossamee Sree Greedharreejee* v. *Rumanlolljee Gossamee*, (1889) L.R., 16 I. A. 137 (147): S. C. I. L. R., 17 C. 3.

6. *Chenna Kesavaraya* v. *Vaidelinga*, (1877) I. L. R., 1 M. 343; *Venkatasubbaramayya* v. *Surayya*, (1880) I. L. R., 2 M. 283 (karnam office); *Kannan* v. *Nilakandan*, (1884) I. L. R., 7 M. 337; *Jagan Nath Das* v. *Birbhadra Das*, (1892) I.L. R., 19 C. 776; *Alagappa Mudaliar* v. *Sivaramasundara*, (1895) I. L. R., 19 M. 211; *Alagirisami Naicker* v. *Sundareswara Ayyar*, (1898) I. L. R., 21 M. 278 (287); *Gnanasambanda Pandara Sannadhi* v. *Velu Pandaram*, (1899) L. R. 27 I. A. 69 (77): S. C. I. L. R., 23 M. 271 (279); *Kidambi Ragava Chariar* v. *Tirumalai Asari Nallur Ragavachariar*, (1902) I.L.R., 26 M. 113; *Ramanathan Chetty* v. *Murugappa Chetty*, (1903) I.L.R., 27 M. 192 (197). See also *Subbaramayyar* v. *Nigamadullah*, (1895) I.L.R., 18 M. 342 (346, 347).

7. *Balwant Rao Bishwant Chandra Chor* v. *Purun Mal Chaube*, (1880) L. R. 10 I. A. 90: S. C. I. L. R., 6 A. 1.; *Karimshah* v. *Nattan Bivi*, (1883) I. L. R., 7 M. 417; *Sheik Karimudin* v. *Nawab Mir Sayad Alam Khan*, (1885) I. L. R., 10 B. 119; *Giyana Sambandha Pandara Sannadhi* v. *Kandasami Tambiran*, (1887) I. L. R., 10 M. 375 (477); *Nilakandan* v. *Padmanabha*, (1890) I. L. R., 14 M. 153 (162). Cf. *Suppammal* v. *The Collector of Tanjore*, (1889) I. L. R., 12 M. 387 as explained in *Vedapuratti* v. *Vallabha*, (1890) I. L. R., 13 M. 402 (404, 405). See also *Sankaran* v. *Krishna*, (1893) I. L. R., 16 M. 456 (459); *Ranga Pai* v. *Baba*, (1897) I. L. R., 20 M. 398 (402, 403); *Alagirisami Naicker* v. *Sundareswara Ayyar*, (1898) I. L. R., 21 M. 278 (287).

ing title[1]. Where the office is held by a single person hereditarily the right of the holder will be barred under Art. 124 of the Limitation Act[2] and the person in wrongful possession acquires a corresponding right by prescription. So an office held by one person may become by prescription a joint office. Where the office is held by two persons jointly with rights of hereditary succession the right of one will be extinguished under Art. 124 where the other excludes him from management[3]. The case can hardly be governed by Art. 127 of the Limitation Act although the person excluding is not a stranger and is the only other joint manager[4]. The claim to enforce joint management can hardly be regarded as one to enforce a right to share[4]. But even if the right to the joint office be "joint family property" and the claim to enforce the same be one "to enforce a right to share therein[5]" (*i.e.*, in such joint family property) time runs from the date when the exclusion becomes known to the plaintiff (*i.e.*, the person excluded) and on the expiry of twelve years from such date his right will be barred. Where the office is held by turns by agreement of parties[6] a claim to such office is governed by Art. 131 of the Limitation Act which gives a period of twelve years from the time when the plaintiff is *first* refused the enjoyment of the right. This can only be when he is refused "the enjoyment" during his turn. A refusal before his turn has accrued will be of no avail. Apparently the same line of reasoning was adopted in a case where according to the view of the court Art. 124 or 127

---

1. *Gunga Gobind Mundul* v. *The Collector of the 24-Pergunnahs*, (1867) 11 M. I.A. 345; *Gossain Dass Chunder* v. *Isser Chunder Nath*, (1877) I. L R., 3 B. 224 (226); *Radhabai* v. *Anantrav*, (1885) I. L. R., 9 B 198 (228); *Sambasiva* v. *Ragava*, (1890) I. L. R., 13 M. 512 (516); *Nilakandan* v. *Padmanabha*, (1890) I. L. R., 14 M. 153 (162); *Jugan Nath Das* v. *Birbhadra Das*, (1892) I. L. R, 19 C. 776; *Alagirisami Naickar* v. *Sundareswara Ayyar*, (1898) I. L. R., 21 M. 278 (287); *Ramanathan Chetty* v. *Murugappa Chetty*, (1903) I. L. R., 27 M. 192 (197). Cf. *Giriapa* v. *Jakana*, (1875) 12 B. H. C. 172. A mortgage of endowed property by a person whose title is extinguished is invalid. *Subbaramayyar* v. *Niyamadullah*. (1895) I.L. R, 18 M. 342.

2. Of course where he claims to be a joint manager along with others such a right may be acquired. *Nilakandan* v. *Padmanabha*, (1890) I. L. R., 14 M. 153 (162); *Alagirisami Naicker* v. *Sundareswara Ayyar*, (1898) I. L. R., 21 M. 278 (287).

3. Cf. *Kannan* v. *Nilakandan*, (1883) I. L. R., 7 M. 417; *Radhabai* v. *Anantrav*, (1885) I. L. R., 9 B. 198 (211, 212, 224, 225, 231); *Ranga Pai* v. *Babu*, (1897) I. L. R., 20 M. 398 (401, 402); and *Gnanasambandha Pandara Sannadhi* v. *Velu Pandaram*, (1899) L. R. 27 I. A. 69: S. C. I. L. R., 23 M. 271.

4. Cf. *Gour Mohun Chowdhry* v. *Muddun Mohun Chowdhry*, (1871) 6 B. L. R. 352: S. C. 15 W. R. C. R. 29.

5. *Ramananathan Chetty* v. *Murugappa Chetty*, (1903) I. L. R., 27 M. 192 (196). But see *Gour Mohun Chowdhry* v. *Muddun Mohun*, supra.

6. See pp. ccvi supra.

applied[1]. In that case the office of manager was held by turns but the court thought strangely enough that notwithstanding such arrangement the others who had no right to the turn could interfere in other than routine matters and were, therefore, entitled to immediate management. But under Art. 124 the question that has to be considered is whether the defendant's possession is adverse. If such possession is adverse for a period of twelve years then there is a prescriptive title acquired. But where a right to turn is recognised in however limited a form it seems more reasonable to hold that Art. 131 applies[2]. The right that is acquired by prescription must be a right substantially corresponding to the one that is extinguished. So that we have already observed that if the office is held by hereditary succession the prescriptive title that can be acquired is a right to such office (to be also held by hereditary succession). If the office is held by nomination then the wrongdoer also acquires a prescriptive title to the same office so that he will be entitled to appoint a successor. Where the succession is hereditary a wrongdoer cannot by prescription as against the rightful holder claim a right by prescription not consonant with the right under which the rightful holder held the office and cannot claim to hold an office in which succession goes by appointment. Otherwise the rules laid down by the founder are diverted. If the founder has laid down that the office should be held by hereditary succession it would be acting contrary to his rule if it should be held that the holder has the right to nominate a successor. The law of Limitation, no doubt, gives a prescriptive title to the person in wrongful possession[3]. If even the rightful holder cannot divert the rule of succession laid down by the founder[4] we can hardly see the reason or justice of the rule that a wrong-doer who has perfected his title by prescription and who thus stands in the position of the rightful holder can divert the rule of succession laid down by the founder. It is not a case in which a person claims to hold property adverse to the trust. It is the case of a person who admits the trust who is therefore

---

1. *Ramanathan Chetty* v. *Murugappa Chetty*, (1903) I. L. R., 27 M. 192.

2. See pp. cccvi, cccvii, supra.

3. *Alagappa* v. *Sivaramasundara*, (1895) I. L. R., 19 M 211.

4. See Chapter XIV, p. ccxvii, note (3).

liable as trustee[1] and who must be a *fortiori*, bound by the rules laid down by the author of the trust. The law of limitation only affects the individuals concerned and to that extent the founder's rule is no doubt departed from[2]. But beyond that limitation does not affect the trust. This is no doubt inconsistent with the ruling in *Annasami Pillai* v. *Ramakrishna Mudaliar*[3]. There the Madras High Court held that a trusteeship with power to appoint a successor was an estate well known to and recognised by law and might be prescribed for. It may be admitted that such an estate is recognised by law but is the right to appoint a successor when the succession pointed out by the founder is hereditary acquired by prescription against the trust ?. We think that when once such a person admits the trust he is subject to the rules laid down by the founder and he cannot acquire by prescription a right to divert the rules of succession laid down by the founder. Such a diversion is a breach of trust and a trustee (even thought he mayhave only acquired a title by prescription) and any persons claiming under him cannot by any length of possession legalize a breach of trust. S. 539 C.P. C., expressly says that whenever the *direction of the Court is necessary* application may be made for all or any of the matters mentioned in the section and no limitation can apply when it is sought against the trustee to enforce the trust.It has been held by the Privy Council that the owner of a life estate cannotby any amount of declaration inconsistent with such life-estate claim to hold the same absolutely notwithstanding long possession coupled with such declaration[4]. The case *Padapa* v. *Swamirao*[5] relied upon by the learned Judges in the Madras case is not an authority either way. There a watan was acquired by prescription and it was held that the adverse holder acquired such estate with the incidents attaching to that tenure.If anything the case is really in favour of

---

1. *Lyell* v. *Kennedy*, (1889) L.R. 14 A.C. 437 (459,460,463); *Manohar Ganesh Tambekar* v. *Lakhmiram Govindram*, (1887) I. L. R., 12 B. 247; *Moolji Bhulabhai* v. *Manohar Ganesh*, (1887) I. L. R., 12 B. 322 ; *Sheo Shankar Gir* v. *Ram Shevak Chowdhri*, (1896) I. L. R., 24 C. 77 ; *Jugalkishore* v. *Lakshmandas Ragunathdas*, (1899) I. L. R , 23 B. 659.

2. *Alagappa* v. *Sivaramasundara*, (1895) I. L. R., 19 M. 211.

3. (1900) I. L. R., 24 M. 219.

4. *The Government of Bombay* v. *Desai Kullaianarai Hakoomutrai*, (1872) 14 M. I. A. 551 (564).

5. (1899) I. L. R., 27 I. A. 86 : S. C. I. L. R., 24 B. 556.

the view which we have been contending for *viz.*,that when a person contends to be a trustee he acquires the right of trusteeship with the incidents attached to such right bythe founder(or by law in cases where no incidents have been attached by the founder).If in that case the adverse-holder claimed to hold the watan coupled with a declaration that the incidents attaching to such tenure by law or custom (*viz*, inalienability beyond life) did not attach and if the Privy Council should have given effect to the declaration then the case wouldbe exactly in point and support the principlelaid down bythe learned Judges. We think also the very illustration given by the learned Judges supports the principle we are contending for. The learned Judges say[1]: "Suppose a person holds for the statutory period possession of property under *mortgage*,purporting to confer on the mortgagee *a power to sell* granted by a person who had no title to the property but who, *under the law*, was competent to make a mortgage with such power". If *under the law*, he is incompetent to make a mortgage with power of sale although the mortgage right may be acquired by prescription he can acquire no right by prescription of a power of sale notwithstanding his declaration. So here in a case where the author of the trust prescribes hereditary succession as the rule to be observed, a person who claims to be a trustee by prescription cannot prescribe for a contrary rule of devolution. The person against whom the prescription is claimed is not "under the law" competent to make such a devolution.In the illustration ofthe mortgage if the right prescribedfor is an absolute transfer or sale then a power of sale being incident to ownership is necessarily acquired. So also,if the person claimed to hold inconsistently with the trust, it may be different.

Hereditary office—Alienation by widow—Limitation for reversioners.

A transfer of a religious office is void *ab initio* and the transferor himself may recover the same[2]. He can only recover before he is barred by limitation and his right is extinguished. A suit to recover an office so alienated will also be governed by Art. 124 of the Limitation Act if the office is hereditary. Where the actual holder is a widow and the office has devolved upon her in right of her husband, a question may arise whether the same rule will

1. *Annasami* v. *Ramakrishna*, (1900) I. L. R., 24 M. 219 at p. 231.
2. Chapter XIV, pp ccxi to ccxvii. See also *Kannan* v. *Pashniandi*, (1901) I. L. R., 24 M.438. Successor may sue. *Sathianama* v. *Sarvanabagi Ammal*, (1894) I. L. R.,18 M. 266 (273); *Gulam Nabi* v. *Nagaminal*, (1897) 6 M L.J. R., 270. See also pp. ccxi to ccxvii.

apply if she has alienated the office. So far as she is concerned there can be no doubt the same rule will apply. But the question is whether possession which becomes adverse against her will be adverse also against the reversioners. Where the female shebait actually endows the property and the office of shebait vests in her either because she reserves such right or because no other provision is made by her there can be no difficulty[1]. She is herself the root of title and after her death it is only her heirs who will be entitled to the office So that possession which is adverse to her will *prima facie* be adverse to the heirs claiming through her unless the law is that, in all such cases, a successor does not claim through his predecessor and the latter has only a life-estate but this of course cannot be the law after the decision of the Privy Council in *Gnanasambanda Pandara* v. *Velu Pandaram*[2]. Even if the law were otherwise possession adverse to the life-tenant may also be adverse to the successor. But where, upon the demise of a male shebait, the office devolves on his widow succession after her death is to be traced to her husband, so that the heirs of the husband will be entitled to take the office. In such a case the question that has to be considered is what is the proper article of the Limitation Act to be applied. If it is the case of an ordinary estate, Art. 141 will apply. Under that Article, the reversioner has twelve years from the date of the widow's death to recover possession of immoveable property to which he becomes entitled on the death of a Hindu or Mahomedan female. But as we have already observed after the definition of immoveable property in the General Clauses Act it cannot be said that an hereditary office is immoveable property and as a suit for the recovery of an hereditary office is separately provided for by the Limitation Act far from their being any repugnancy, the latter Act in effect recognises that an hereditary office is not "immoveable property." Art. 124 is the next article that may be thought applicable. According to that article the period is twelve years when the defendant takes possession of the office adversely to the *plaintiff*. Where a transfer of religious office is made by the widow it is not even

1. *Rajah Chundernath Roy* v. *Koonr Gobindnath Roy*, (1872) 11 B. L. R., 86 (111).

2. (1899) L. R. 27 I. A. 69: S. C. I. L. R., 23 M. 271.

good for her lifetime. It is so even where a male transfers the office. It is, therefore, adverse to the widow. It is also adverse to the reversioner. If the reversioner can be said to be a person deriving his right to sue from or through the widow possession adverse to the widow will be adverse to the reversioner. The reversioner does not derive his right to sue from or through the widow but S. 3 of the Limitation Act does not purport to contain any real definition of a "plaintiff". All that it says is that it includes a "person from or through whom a plaintiff derives his right to sue." The use of the term "includes" shows that the definition, if any, is not exhaustive[1]. This view receives strong support from the remarks we have made in a previous chapter as to the nature of the estate of a manager under the Hindu Law. We have seen that although succession to the office of manager may devolve by ordinary Hindu Law, his position is similar to that of a widow. Even where a male holds the office there can be no absolute estate in such office and the properties appurtenant to such office. It is so in the case of a female holding the office as heir to her husband. Art. 124 may, therefore, apply if the suit is for possession. But during the lifetime of the widow a reversioner is not entitled to sue for possession. If the widow alienates the office with the endowments he may be entitled to sue for removal of the widow as manager, but to such a suit Art. 124 will have no application. Art. 120 seems to be the proper article applicable as the matter at present stands under the Limitation Act. But there can be no doubt that it is a pure case of *casus omissus* by the Legislature. It can never have been intended by the Legislature that this shorter period should govern such a case. It is to be hoped that the Legislature will give a similar period as that mentioned in Art. 141 to the reversioners claiming hereditary offices alienated by widows. Either Art. 141 may be extended to cover such a case or an additional article may be inserted after Art. 125.

Suits for recovery of endowed properties—Limitation Act, S. 10.

So far with regard to a suit for the recovery of the office together with the endowed properties. A suit for the recovery of the profits of an office will be governed by Art. 120.[2] But a suit by the manager may be simply to recover endowed properties without suing

1. *The Empress* v. *Ramanjiyya*, (1878) I. L. R., 2 M. 5(7); *Balvantrav* v. *Purushotam*, (1872) 9 B. H. C. 99; *Rodger* v. *Harrison*, [1893] 1 Q. B. 161 (167, 171).
2. *Subbier* v. *Ranga Aiyangar*, (1899) 9 M. L. J. R. 163.

to recover or establish his right to the office. The predecessor of the manager may have wrongfully alienated the endowed property or the actual incumbent may have so wrongfully alienated. The alienation by the trustee or manager may be by way of sale, mortgage, lease or gift. In all such cases the property so alienated is sought to be recovered for the endowment or trust. The question, therefore, arises whether S. 10 of the Limitation Act will apply to such a case. S. 10 of Act XV of 1877 corresponds substantially to S. 10 of Act IX of 1871. It must not be supposed that it was a new provision in the Act of 1871. S. 2 of Act XIV of 1859 gave a more complete protection for trusts. Under the latter Act, no length of time could bar a suit for the recovery of specific trust property from a trustee or his representative. So that under the Act of 1859 even a purchaser could not acquire title by prescription with reference to trust property unless the purchase was *bona fide* and for valuable consideration when S. 5 applied[1]. Only a trespasser who did not claim under any alienation from the former or present manager and who claimed to hold endowed property as his own did not come within the section. The section also applied to constructive trusts[2]. So that no limitation could have run as between trustee and a *cestui que* trust and as between a beneficiary and an alienee from the trustee. Moreover in the case of public rights or claims the Act of 1859 did not apply and the rule of limitation applicable prior to the Act would apply (see S. 17). Therefore, the statement in the recent case of *Jagamba Goswamini* v. *Ram Chandra Goswami*[3] that "neither in the two statutes previously in force, which deal with the subject of limitation, viz., Regulation III of 1793 and Act XIV of 1859 is there any provision similar to S. 10 of Acts IX of 1871 and XV of 1877" is, so far as regards Act XIV of 1859, made out of pure inadvertence. If in the recent Calcutta case[4] the trust was a public one Ss. 2 and 5 of the Act of 1859 would not apply, but at the same time

---

1. *Luteefun* v. *Bego Jan*, (1866) 5 W. R. C. R. 120.

2. *Maniklal* v. *Manchershi*, (1876) I. L. R., 1 B. 269; *Dayal* v. *Jivraj*, (1875) I.L.R., 1 B. 237; *Greender* v. *Mackintosh*, (1879) I. L. R., 4 C. 897. The Acts of 1871 and 1877 did not apply to implied trusts. *Greender* v. *Mackintosh*, supra; *Kherodemoney* v. *Doorgamoney*, (1878) I. L. R., 4 C. 455.

3. (1903) I. L. R., 31 C. 314 at p. 317.

4. *Jagamba Goswamini* v. *Ram Chandra Goswami*, (1903) I. L. R., 31 C. 314. If it was a private trust, S. 2 of Act XIV of 1859 applied.

the old rule of limitation would be applicable. (See S. 17 of Act XIV of 1859. According to Bengal Regulations III of 1793 and II of 1805, suits for enforcement of public rights might be brought within sixty years[1]. In the Calcutta case the gift was in 1820 so that before 1st of April 1873 the title was not extinguished and on that date when Act IX of 1871 applied, S. 10 of the latter Act said that no limitation would run at all[2]. We do not here forget the fact that Act XX of 1863 repealed the Regulations (XIX of 1810, Bengal and VII of 1817, Madras) so far as religious endowments were concerned. We are also conscious of the fact that after Act XX of 1863 it was held that a manager could not sue as procurator of Government[3]. But although this was the effect of Act XX of 1863 S. 17 of Act XIV of 1859 still applied, so that the old rules of limitation would still apply notwithstanding the repeal of Bengal Regulation II of 1805 by Act VIII of 1868. If S. 17 of Act XIV of 1859 did not apply, then S. 2 would cover such a case and prevent any limitation from running at all in favor of a mere volunteer[4].

Turning to the applicability of S. 10 of the Acts of 1871 and 1877, three requisites are laid down in the section: (1) property must be vested in a person in trust for a specific purpose, (2) the suit must have for its object the recovery of specific property for the trust, and (3) the suit must be either (*a*) against the person in whom property is vested in trust for a specific purpose, or (*b*) against the latter's representative. The explanation to S. 10 of the Act of 1871 expressly declared that a purchaser in good faith and for value was not a representative within the meaning of the section. In the Act of 1877 there is no reference to "good faith." Suits against legal representatives or assigns other than assigns for valuable consideration will not be barred. So that an assignee for valuable consideration may acquire a title by prescription and limitation will run in his favor. It is unfortunate that the limitation in respect of suits for enforcing the trust as against assigns for valuable consideration has been unduly and unnecessarily curtailed by the Legislature. **Requisites of S. 10.**

---

1. *Jewun Doss Sahoo* v. *Shah Kubeer-Ood-Deen*, (1840) 2 M. I. A. 390.
2. See *Abdul Karim* v. *Manji Hunsraj*, (1876) I. L. R., 1 B 295 (303, 304).
3. *Shaikh Laul Mahomed* v. *Lalla Brij Kishore*, (1872) 17 W. R. C. R. 430 (431); *Behari Lal* v. *Muhammad*, (1898) I. L. R., 20 A. 482.
4. *Sathianama* v. *Saravanabagi Ammal*, (1894) I. L. R., 18 M. 266 (272 ,273).

Suits against alienees of endowed property.

A suit by a manager or trustee to recover endowed property alienated by himself or his predecessor is a suit to recover property for the trust, but S. 10 will not apply to suits against alienees for valuable consideration[1]. For some time it was thought that the successor had twelve years from the date of his appointment to recover the property wrongfully alienated from the alienee and that limitation which barred the predecessor did not necesarily bar the successor. In fact the Privy Council held[2] that this was the law under the Bengal Regulation II of 1805 S. 2, although strictly speaking even under that Regulation, the successor would not have a fresh starting point from the date of his appointment[3]. As already observed by us according to that Regulation, suits for enforcement of public rights were governed by sixty years' limitation. But after Act XX of 1863 repealed the Regulations (XIX of 1810 and VII of 1817) so far as religious endowments were concerned this special period of sixty years was no longer applicable[4]. Notwithstanding this it was still thought that the successor had twelve years from the date of his appointment and this view was maintained in many cases[5]. The ground upon which these cases proceeded was that the successor in such cases was not claiming through his predecessor and that as the acts of the latter prejudicial to the trust or to the interest of his successor would not bind the latter limitation running against the predecessor did not also run against the successor. But this view could not long prevail[6]. Even in the case of life-estates if possession had been adverse to the estate represented by the life-tenant such possession would be adverse not merely to the

1. Under the Act of 1871 the alienee should have purchased the property in *good faith.*

2. *Jewun Doss Sahoo* v. *Shah Kubeer-Ood-Deen*, (1840) 2 M. I. A. 390.

3. The observations of the Judicial Committee in 2 M. I. A. 390 at p. 421 lend color to the view that the successor might sue within 12 years from the date of his appointment.

4. *Sheikh Laul Mahomed* v. *Lalla Brij Kishore*, (1872) 17 W. R. C. R. 430; *Behari Lal* v. *Muhammad*, (1898) I. L. R., 20 A. 482 dissenting from *Piran* v. *Abdool Karim*, (1891) I. L. R., 19 C. 203.

5. *Kuria Bin Hammia* v. *Gururar*, (1872) 9 B. H. C. A. C. J. 282 (vatan); *Mohunt Burm Suroop Dass* v. *Khashee Jha*, (1873) 20 W. R. C. R. 471 (472) (case of mohunt); *Trimbak Bawa* v. *Narayan Bawa*, (1882) I. L. R., 7 B. 188 (right to management of temple); *Modho Kooery* v. *Tekait Ram Chunder Singh*, (1882) I. L. R., 9 C. 411; *Jamal Saheb* v. *Murguya Swami*, (1885) I. L. R., 10 B. 34; *Mahomed* v. *Ganapati*, (1889) I. L. R., 13 M. 277; *Vedapuratti* v. *Vallabha*, (1890) I. L. R., 13 M. 403; *Piran* v. *Abdool Karim*, (1891) I. L. R., 19 C. 203; *Syed Gulam Nabi* v. *Nagammal*, (1896) 6 M. L. J. R. 270.

6. *Maniklal* v. *Manchershi*, (1876) I. L. R., 1 B. 269; *Babaji* v. *Nana*, (1876) I. L. R., 1 B. 535; *Gnanasambanda* v. *Velu*, (1899) L. R. 27 I. A. 69: S. C. I. L. R., 23 M. 271.

life-tenant but also to his successors[1] though the possession would not be adverse to the estate if the person in possession only claimed under an alienation made by the life-tenant[2]. After the decision of the Privy Council in *Gnanasambanda Pandara* v. *Velu Pandaram*[3] it is no longer open to a manager to say that he claims independently of his predecessor in such a way as not to be affected by the Statute of Limitation. This case may not apply to a case where the office is held by a succession of life-estates and where such succession is allowed by law or custom. But the case will apply to other cases. It may now be taken to be settled that a person claiming under an alienation made by the manager (which is wrongful to the trust) will acquire a prescriptive title on the lapse of the prescribed time and that a suit for the recovery of the endowed property from the alienee will be barred under Art. 134 on the lapse of twelve years from the date of the alienation[4]. The last column of Art. 134, speaks of "purchase" but this word is apparently used in a generic sense and has been held to include not merely a "sale" but also a "mortgage[5]" and a "lease[6]." But this article will not apply where the alienee

Limitation Act, Art. 134.

---

1. *Radhabai* v. *Anantrav*, (1885) I. L. R., 9 B. 198 followed in *Veerabhadra* v. *Venkatadri*, (1899) 10 M. L. J. R. 114.

2. See cases cited by Mr. Mitra in the analogous case of widows alienating property inherited from their husbands (at pp. 155, 156, 827, 828).

3. (1899) L. R. 27 I. A. 69; S. C. I. L. R., 23 M. 271.

4. *Doyal Chund Mullick* v. *Syud Keramut Ali*, (1871) 16 W. R. C. R. 116; *Maniklal Atmaram* v. *Manchershi Dinsha Coachman*, (1876) I.L.R., 1 B. 269 (277, 282); *Vithalbowa* v. *Narayan Daji Thite*, (1893) I L.R., 18 B. 507 at p. 511 (no article was referred to but the learned judges spoke of twelve years from the date of alienation. As a matter of fact twelve years had also expired from the date of the predecessor's death); *Nilmony* v. *Jagobandhu*, (1896) I. L. R., 23 C. 536; *Sojedur Raja* v. *Gour Mohan Das*, (1897) I. L. R, 24 C. 418; *Behari Lal* v. *Muhammad Muttaki*, (1898) I. L. R., 20 A. 482; *Chidambaram Chetti* v. *Minammal*, (1898) I. L. R., 23 M. 439 (no article was referred to but the case would seem to be one of bare trespass); *Ramchandra* v. *Sheikh Mohidin*, (1899) I. L. R., 23 B. 614 (619); *Duttagiri* v. *Dattatraya*, (1902) I. L. R., 27 B. 363; *Narayan* v. *Shri Ramchandra*, (1903) I. L. R., 27 B. 373; *Sagun Balkrishna* v. *Kaji Hussen*, (1903) I. L. R, 27 B. 500 (case of alienation of wakf property). The decisions for the opposite view are clearly erroneous and have been passed without adverting to several earlier cases some of which are Privy Council cases. See *Maharanee Brojosoondery Debia* v. *Ranee Luchmee Koonwaree*, (1873) 15 B. L. R. 176 (note): S. C. 20 W. R. 95 (P. C.); *Mohunt Nursingh Dass* v. *Moosharoo Bhandaree*, (1876) 25 W. R. C. R. 282. See also *Mussumut Chundrabullee Debia* v. *Luckea Debia*, (1865) 10 M. I. A. 214. Cf. *Bejoy Chunder Banerjee* v. *Kally Prosonno Mukerjee*, (1878) I L. R., 4 C. 327; and *Chintamani Mahapatro* v. *Sarup Se*, (1888) I. L. R., 15 C. 703, (705, 706). Limitation will not stop although there may be no manager. *Vithalbowa* v. *Narayan*, supra.

5. *Yesu Ramji* v. *Balkrishna*, (1891) I. L R., 15 B. 583; *Behari Lal* v. *Muhammad Muttaki*, (1898) I. L. R., 20 A. 482; *Ramchandra* v. *Sheikh Mohidin*, (1899) I. L. R., 23 B. 614 (619).

6. *Narayan* v. *Shri Ramchandra*, (1903) I. L. R., 27 B. 373, (377): See also *Nilmony* v. *Jagabandhu*, (1896) I. L. R., 23 C. 536.

acquires no possession under his alienation and where notwithstanding such alienation the manager remains in possession[1]. If a person enters posssion of the endowed land as a permanent tenant the assertion of such right coupled with the possession for over twelve years will give him a prescriptive title[2]. But if he should not enter as a permanent tenant at the time of his entering into possession, his subsequent assertion of a right of permanent occupancy coupled with possession will not give him a prescriptive title[3]. It is to be regretted that in cases of public rights the longer period of limitation (sixty years) allowed by the old Regulations should not have been uniformly adopted. Even in England where rights are more quickly asserted than in India twenty years is the ordinary period for recovering immoveable property. A Hindu is not so assertive of his rights as in other countries. He will submit himself as much as possible to a wrong and see whether he cannot get a remedy by peaceful means even where his own individual interest is affected. There is not the tendency as in England or other countries to assert a right for the sake of its mere assertion or to seek remedy for a wrong merely for the wrong done though no actual damage may have accrued. So also there is greater public spirit in England which asserts itself more often when a public right is violated and people are ready in England to seek remedy for the violation. In India there is no such public spirit and a Hindu taught by nature, religion, or other circumstance to be meek is accustomed to look on calmly while maladministration of public property is going on. His individual interest is not affected in such cases and he does not, therefore, concern himself with anything that does not affect his individual interest. Under the circumstances prevailing in India, therefore, a longer period must be allowed. The same policy which induced the Legislature to allow a period of sixty years for suits by Government must

---

1. *Ramchandra* v. *Sheikh Mohidin*, (1899) I. L. R., 23 B. 614, (619). But absence of knowledge is immaterial. *Baiva* v. *Bhiku*, (1885) I. L R., 9 B. 475. But see *Ambalavana* v. *Bappu Row*, (1899) 9 M. L. J. R., 93 (96). The decision in this case under Art. 144 is clearly erroneous after *Velu Pandaram's* case.

2. *Narayan* v. *Shri Ramchandra*, (1903) I. L. R., 27 B. 378.

3. *Srinivasa Ayyar* v. *Muthusami Pillai*, (1900) I. L. R, 24 M. 246; *Seshamma Shettati* v. *Chickaya Hegade*, (1902) I. L. R., 25 M. 507; *Ramasami Naik* v. *Thayammal*, (1902) I. L. R., 26 M. 488. The case of *Thakore Fatesingji* v. *Bamanji A. Dalal*, (1903) I. L. R., 27 B. 515 is not really inconsistent with the above. In such a case under Article 139 of the Limitation Act no bar can arise until the determination of the tenancy.

induce the Legislature to allow the same period for suits for endowed property. If Government with its numerous executive ever vigilant in guarding the Government interest wants a period of sixty years, institutions which have no such executive and which have no responsible officers as in England[1] to keep watch over their affairs and prevent maladministration must have at any rate the same period allowed to them for enforcing their rights. This is in fact the hope of every sincere well-wisher of these institutions or of every person who does not wish to see them die out or disintegrate and we hope that the Legislature will see fit to give effect to the observations of Mr. Justice *Bhashyam Aiyangar* at the end of his learned judgment in the *recent mutt case*[2] where he says :"I sincerely trust that in the interests of the moral well being of the people of this country and of its 'peace and good Government' the notion will not die out in the case at any rate of ecclesiastical and eleemosynary institutions * * * and that their corporate character will be preserved and their disintegration arrested by extending to them the beneficient provision of Madras Regulation X of 1831 * * * by prescribing in lieu of the existing period of twelve years from the date of alienation or adverse possession * * a period of limitation of sixty years for suits to recover possession of immoveable property forming the endowment of a public charitable or religious institution which has been improperly alienated or held adversely to the institution." In the case of Municipalities and other public bodies this policy has been to a certain extent adopted as such public bodies are now allowed under Article 146 A[3] a period of thirty years to bring a suit for the recovery of possession of immoveable property.

Suits against managers may be of three classes :—(*a*) suits by managers against co-managers, (*b*) suits by founders or worshippers against managers and (*c*) suits by strangers against the trust. We do not propose to consider the latter class of suits or the period of limitation affecting such suits. There is nothing special in such a case. **Suits against managers.**

1. The charity Commissioners perform many useful functions in England.

2. *Vidyapurna Thirtha Swami* v. *Vidyanidhi Thirtha Swami*, (1904) I. L. R., 27 M. 435, (462).

3. See Act XI of 1900.

Suits by managers against co-managers.

With regard to suits by managers against co-managers some are personal and some relate to the endowment. In the latter case such suits do not differ much from suits by worshippers. But suits to enforce personal rights are not upon the same footing. If one manager excludes the others from management we have already said that the person so excluded may not merely sue for account but also for enforcing his joint right of management[1]. Such a suit does not fall under S. 10, of the Limitation Act. The manager so excluded may sue for a declaration of his right and for an injunction restraining the other from interfering with his right of management[2] or if he is also ousted from possession he must sue for joint possession.

Suits against managers for breach of trust.

Suits by worshippers or other persons interested in the endowment against the managers for breach of trust or for enforcing the trust form the remaining class of suits[3]. If in such suit the alienee is made a party and it is sought to recover property from the alienee for the trust the rules of limitation applicable in the case of suits brought by trustees for a similar purpose and already referred to will apply[4]. We shall, therefore, consider a suit brought only against the trustee or manager. Although no property vests in the manager and no proprietary interest is vested in him the property may vest in the manager for the purposes of S. 10 of the Limitation Act. As Mr. Justice *Markby* observed in *Kherodemoney Dossee* v. *Doorgamoney Dosse*[5]: "Ordinarily persons who are called trustees do not, under Hindu law become the owners of the property which is placed in their charge. Possibly, however, as this is an Act which contains the law of limitation for all classes of persons, the word '*vest*' may be used when speaking of a

1. Chapter XIV, p. cclvii.

2. *Juggodumba Dossee* v. *Puddomoney Dossee*, (1875) 15 B. L. R. 318; *Athavulla* v. *Gouse*, (1888) I. L. R., 11 M 263.

3. Suits for compelling manager to take idol through certain streets may be maintainable. *Mahomed Abdul* v. *Latif*, (1897) I. L. R., 24 C. 524; per *Davies*, J. in *Nagiah* v. *Muthacharry*, (1900) 11 M. L. J. R. 215. But see *Kazi Sujaudin* v. *Madhavdas*, (1893) I. L. R., 18 B. 693; per *Arnold White*, C. J. in *Nagiah* v. *Muthacharry*, supra.

4. *Sajedur Raja* v. *Gour Mohan Das*, (1897) I. L. R., 24 C. 418; *Behari Lal* v. *Muhammad Muttaki*, (1898) I. L. R., 20 A. 482. Even where a *de facto* manager alienates, the same limitation will apply. *Sheo Shankar Gir* v. *Ram Shevak Chowdhri*, (1896) I. L. R., 24 C. 77. Suits by the founder will also be subject to the same principles. The case of *Prosunno Moyee Dossee* v. *Koonjo Beharee Chowdhree*, (1864) W. R. Sp. C. R. 157 which decides that limitation running against the manager does not run against the founder even if right under the old law (which is more than doubtful) can hardly be taken as correct at the present day.

5. (1878) I. L. R., 4 C. 455, (468).

person standing in a fiduciary relation not in the sense of '*owned,*' but in the sense of 'held in possession."

A trustee holding property for the trust cannot acquire a title by prescription[1]. S. 10 of the Limitation Act will exactly cover such a case. This principle will apply even where the manager or trustee is not the *de jure* but only the *defacto* trustee or manager[2]. A person who wrongfully holds as trustee and pretends to act as such cannot be allowed to reprobate the right which he asserts and to contend that he holds adversely to the trust or his *cestui que trust*[3]. We have already seen that in cases of breach of trust or malversation by the manager a suit for the latter's removal will lie[4] A suit for removal charging the trustee or manager with breach of trust is never barred by limitation[5]. With every breach of trust there is a fresh cause of action[6]. Where a suit for removal is brought and it is compromised a suit to set aside such compromise for fraud will be governed by Art. 95 of the Limitation Act[7]. But there seems to be no necessity for setting aside such decree. Other worshippers may bring a suit for removal upon the same grounds and the compromise decree will be no bar to such suit. It will appear that a breach of trust committed by the manager and not rectified by him will give rise to a continuing cause of action. But apart from this a suit may lie under S. 539, C.P. C. against the trustee or manager whenever the direction of the court is necessary and a manager may be removed whenever it is necessary for the administration of the trust or in the interests of the institution. Apart from authority one will find it difficult to see how a suit for removal of the manager is

---

1. *Busl Rahim* v. *Moonshee Lutaful Hossein*, (1864) W. R. Sp. C. R. 171; *Hurro Coomari Dossee* v. *Tharini Churn Bysack*, (1882) I. L R., 8 C. 766; *Hemangini Dasi* v. *Nobinchund Ghose*, (1882) I. L. R., 8 C. 788; *Sreenath Bose* v. *Radha Nath Bose*, (1883) 12 C. L. R. 370; *Bitto Kunwar* v. *Kesho Pershad*, (1897) L. R., 24 I. A. 10 (21): S. C. I. L. R., 19 A. 277 (291). Cf. *Virasami* v. *Subba*, (1882) I. L. R., 6 M 54 (59).

2. *Sheo Shankar Gir* v. *Ram Shevak Chowdhri*, (1896) I. L. R., 24 C. 77; *Jagannath Prasad Gupta* v. *Runjit Singh*, (1897) I. L. R., 25 C. 354, (370); *Jugalkishore* v. *Lakshmandas*, (1899) I. L. R., 23 B. 659.

3. *Sheo Shankar Gir* v. *Ram Shewak Chowdhri*, (1896) I. L. R., 24 C. 77.

4. Such a claim is cognizable by the Civil Courts. See pp. vii to x, ccxxxv.

5. *Sreenath Bose* v. *Radhanath Bose*, (1883) 12 C. L. R., 370; *Sathapayyar* v. *Periasami*, (1890) I. L. R., 14 M. 1. (8); *Sajedur Raja* v. *Gour Mohun Das*, (1897) I. L. R., 24 C. 418.

6. *Jugalkishore* v. *Lakshmandas*, (1899) I. L. R., 23 B. 659.

7. *Muhammad Baksh* v. *Muhammad Ali*, (1888) I. L. R., 5 A. 294.

a suit for recovery of property specifically for the trust. Of course upon removal of the old manager the property must be recovered from the latter but if recovery is not asked for in the suit does S. 10, still apply? One feels that S. 10, does not correspond to S. 539, C. P. C., and after the enactment of the latter section in the Civil Procedure Code, S. 10, should have been modified so as to correspond with the principles laid down or assumed in S. 539, C.P.C.

Suits to declare manager disqualified or to set aside appointment.

A worshipper or founder may bring a suit for removing the manager on account of a subsequent disqualification. If the disqualification operates to divest the holder of his office the suit will be for a declaration that the old manager is disqualified from holding the office, for appointment of a new manager &c. What the circumstances are which will constitute such a disqualification is properly determinable in Civil Courts[1]. Such suits are also not subject to any rules of limitation.[2] But a suit to declare that an appointment is illegal[3] and that a vacancy exists will be subject to limitation. So also a suit to set aside as illegal an appointment made by a District Judge of a committee member is not a suit for declaration governed by Article 120 but is one governed by Art. 13 of the Limitation Act[4]. Such a suit to set aside an appointment or for a declaration of the invalidity of the appointment may be brought independently of S. 42 of the Specific Relief Act[5]. If a person claims to hold the office of manager and holds possession of the same for over the statutory period no suit will lie to declare that he is a trespasser and that a vacancy exists and to get a new manager appointed. The worshippers have to recognise, after the lapse of the statutory period, that the person actually holding the office is the rightful manager and the latter can only be removed for breach of trust or mismanagement. The rightful manager after failing to recover possession of his office by reason of the fact that his suit is barred by the statute of limitations may bring a suit

---

1. *Sitapershad* v. *Thakur Dass*, (1879) 5 C. L. R. 73. A suit for a declaration that a person is qualified for the office is also maintainable. *Ningangavda* v. *Satyangavda*, (1874) 11 B. H. C. 232.

2. *Sathapayyar* v, *Periasami*, (1890) I. L. R., 14 M. 1.

3. Art. 120 will govern such suits. *Lakshminaruyanappa* v. *Venkataratnam*, (1893) I. L. R., 17 M. 395. See also *Giyana Sambandha* v. *Kandasami*, (1886) I. L. R, 10 M. 375 (405), where, however, no article is mentioned; *Jagganath* v. *Birbhadra* (1892) I. L. R., 19 C. 776.

4. *Subramania Sastri* v. *Minakshi Naidu*, (1892) 8 M. L. J. R. 128.

5. *Janardana Shetti* v. *Badara Shetti*, (1899) I, L. R., 23 M. 385.

for removal of the manager who is in possession of the office for breach of trust. Where two persons claim to be the rightful office-holders and it is held that the right of one is not proved the latter, although he may bring a fresh suit as a person interested that the other person is not the rightful holder, cannot seek to establish that such other person is a trespasser in a suit to establish his own title[1].

Suits for account.

A suit against the trustee or manager simply for an account is held to be governed by Art. 120 of the Limitation Act[2]. It has also been held that S. 10 of the Limitation Act will not apply to such a suit[3] unless it is alleged that some specific property or sum has been misappropriated and it is sought to charge the trustee or manager with reference to such sum[4]. A suit for account is not a suit for following trust property. If the suit be not governed by any limitation then staleness of demand may be a valid defence[5]. A suit for damages for loss occasioned by the trustee's neglience is equally not governed by S. 10 of the Limitation Act[6] although a suit for return of trust money lost by the trustee's negligence may fall under the section[7].

---

1. *Greedharee Doss v. Nundokissore Doss*, (1867) 11 M. I. A., 405 (430, 431). See also *Rahumtulla Sahib v. Mahommed Akbar Sahib*, (1875) 8 M H. C. 63 (77).

2. *Saroda Pershad Chattopadhya v. Brojo Nauth Bhuttacharjee*, (1880) I. L. R., 5 C. 910; *Mahammad Habibullah Khan v. Safdar Hussain Khan*, (1884) I. L R., 7 A. 25 (27,29); *Shapurji Nowroji Pochaji v. Bhikaiji*, (1886) I. L. R., 10 B. 242; *Sethu v. Subramanya*, (1887) I. L. R., 11 M. 274 (278, 279); *Advocate General of Bombay v. Moulvi Abdul Kadir Jitaker*, (1894) I. L. R., 18 B. 401 (423, 424); *The Advocate General of Bombay v. Punjabai*, (1894) I. L. R., 18 B. 551 (566). See also *Ranga Pai v. Baba*, (1897) I. L. R., 20 M. 398 (403); *Sri Raman Lalji Maharaj v. Gopal Lalji Maharaj*, (1897) I. L. R., 19 A. 244. In *Treepoorasoondery Dossee v. Debendro Nath Tagore*, (1876) I. L. R., 2 C. 45 (55, 56) an unlimited account was ordered against an express trustee. See also *Syud Shah Alleh Ahmed v. Mussamut Bibee Nuseebun*, (1874) 21 W. R. C. R. 415. The question whether S. 10 applies to a suit charging the trustee with breach of trust and claiming an account has been left open in *Ranga Bai v. Baba*, (1867) I. L. R., 20 M. 398 (402). A suit for recovery of trust funds improperly used by the trustee in trade &c. or mixed up by the trustee with his own funds or wrongfully converted by the trustee with other property falls under S 10. See *Sethu v. Subramanya*, (1887) I. L. R., 11 M. 274 (279). See also *Thackersey Dewraj v. Hurbhum Nursey*, (1884) I. L. R., 8 B. 432 (468, 469).

3. See cases cited in last note.

4. *Hurroo Coomaree Dossee v. Tarini Churn Bysack*, (1882) I. L. R., 8 C. 766 (768). See also *Virasami v. Subba*, (1882) I.L.R., 6 M. 54 (58, 59); *Shapurji Nowroji Pochaji v. Bhikaiji*, (1886) I. L R., 10 B. 242 (247); and *Sethu v. Subramanya*, (1887) I. L. R., 11 M. 274 (279).

5. *Buzl Ruhim v. Munshee Lutafut Hossein*, (1864) W. R. Sp. C. R. 171 a case under the old law. If a suit for account is governed by the rule of six years it is difficult to maintain the view that staleness of demand of itself will be a valid defence Cf. *Nanu v. Komu*, (1897) I. L. R., 21 M. 42 (44).

6. *Sayad Hussein Miyan Dada Miyan v. The Collector of Kaira*, (1895) I. L. R., 21 B. 257 (264. 267). Such a suit is governed by Article 98 of the Limitation Act. A suit for charging the trustee with interest upon trust moneys not invested is governed by Art 120 of the Limitation Act. See *Advocate General of Bombay v. Moulvi Abdul Kadir Jitaker*, (1894) I. L. R., 18 B. 401 (424).

7. *Thackersey Dewraj v. Hurbhum Nursey*, (1884) I. L. R. 8 B. 432 (468, 469).

Suit for administration. A suit for the administration of the trust or charity established in British India is maintainable and the Courts in British India have jurisdiction to frame a scheme with respect to such charity[1]. In such suit, funds may be lodged with the Accountant General[2]. But without such suit there is no jurisdiction to pay over the funds of a charity to the court or to the Accountant General and the court is no bank for charitable funds[3]. A suit for the administratration of a foreign charity is not ordinarily maintainable[4]. But where the charity is to be established in states subject to the feudatory Princes of India a suit for the administration of such charity muy be maintainable[5]. Even in other cases it is not the law that a court will not assist a foreign charity where the trustees and the fund are within its jurisdiction[6]. A suit for compelling manager to administer according to original trusts is not merely a suit for rectification and falls under S. 10 of the Limitation Act[7].

Suits for scheme. Suits for scheme are maintainable under S. 539, C. P. C. If a scheme is framed and approved by a Court acting under S.539,C.P. C.and the scheme does not provide for a certain contingency there can be no doubt that the court can amend the scheme so as to cover the contingency that has arisen[8] but the question has been mooted whether the amendment can be affected by an application to amend or by a suit. If liberty to apply for fresh directions is given by the decree as it is generally the case according to the English practice and according to the practice of the High Courts of India when exercising original civil jurisdiction then the scheme may be amended by an application in the suit in which the

---

1. *Panchcowrie Mull* v. *Chumroolall*, (1878) I. L. R., 3 C, 563 (571): S. C. 2 C. L. R., 121; *Bhuggobutty Prosonno Sen* v. *Gooroo Prosonno Sen*, (1897) I. L. R., 25 C 112. See Tudor on Charitable Trusts pp. 123 to 125. The court may construe a will declaring certain trusts even without a suit for administration of the estate. See also *Jagannath Prasad Gupta* v. *Runjit Singh*, (1897) I. L. R., 25 C. 354; *Bhuggobutty* v. *Gooroo Prosonno*, (1897) I. L. R., 25 C. 112 (120).

2. *Purmanundass Jeevundass* v. *Venayekrao Wussoodeo*, (1882) L. R. 9 I. A. 86: S. C. I. L. R., 7 B. 19.

3. *Satoor* v. *Satoor*, (1865) 2 M. H. C. 8 (11).

4. Tudor pp. 127 to 128.

5. *Mayor of Lyons* v. *East India Company*, (1836) 1 M. I. A. 175 (293, 296). The Court before parting with the fund must be satisfied that the charity can be carried into effect. It cannot part with the funds to persons who are not amenable to its jurisdiction (291, 292).

6. *The Advocate General of Bombay* v. *Bai Punjabai*, (1894) I. L. R., 18 B. 551, (561).

7. Ibid, at pp. 561, 562.

8. Per *Jenkins*, C. J.in *Kandas Dayaram* v. *Talukdari Settlement Officer*, (1901) 3 Bom. L. R. 258.

decree is made[1]. We do not see why this practice should not be adopted by the courts exercising jurisdiction under S. 539, C.P.C.[2] There can be no doubt, however, that the amendment may be effected by a suit framed for the purpose[3]. But the proposed alteration in order to be successful must be necessary in the interests of the institution and in harmony with its objects[4]. If it was in a matter of detail upon which opinions may differ the court will be slow to act[1].

As regards the question of Court Fees, we have more or less referred to this matter in the notes to S. 14[5]. If a suit is brought by a manager for ousting a trespasser from possession of endowed properties the suit is one for recovery of possession and S. 7 Clauses (1) and (3) of the Court Fees Act, if the properties are moveable, or S. 7 Clause (5), if the properties are immoveable, will govern the question of Court Fees. If a suit is brought for removal of the manager from office and from possession and for placing the plaintiff (a worshipper) in possession on behalf of the manager to be newly appointed (assuming such latter prayer is maintainable) the suit is one for possession and an *advalorem* court-fee has to be paid with reference to the properties claimed in the suit as in the case of a manager suing for possession[6]. But if a worshipper brings a suit for removal of the old manager and for appointment of a new one and for vesting the properties in the new manager the suit is one incapable of valuation and court-fee has to be paid under Schedule II, Article 17 Clause VI[7]. But if the plaintiff (a worshipper) asks that possession be given over to the manager to be newly appointed, the suit is one for possession virtually and different considerations will apply. Art. 17, Clause VI of Sch. II of the Court Fees Act will also apply to a suit for scheme and to a suit for removal of manager[8] and for scheme. Court fee.

---

1. *Advocate General of Bombay* v. *Jitaker*, (1894) I. L. R., 18 B. 401 (427).
2. Cf. *Fischer* v. *Secretary of State*, (1898) L. R. 26 I. A. 16 (29): S. C. I. L. R., 22 M. 270 (283).
3. The question was left open in *Kandas Dayaram* v. *Talukdari Settlement Officer*, (1901) 3 Bom. L.R. 258. See Tudor on Charitable trusts, pp. 130, 1..1.
4. *Kandas Dayaram* v. *Settlement Officer*, supra.
5. See pp. 121 to 125.
6. *Sonachala* v. *Manika*, (1885) I. L. R., 8 M. 516.
7. *Thakuri* v. *Bramha Narain*, (1896) I. L. R., 19 A. 60; *Muhammad Sirajul-Haq* v. *Imam-Ud-Din*, (1896) I. L. R., 19 A. 104; *Girdhari Lal* v. *Ram Lal*, (1899) I. L. R., 21 A. 200. For other cases see notes to S. 14 of Act XX, pp. 121 to 124.
8. *Veerasami* v. *Chokappa*, I. L. R., 11 M. 149 (note); *Srinivasa* v. *Venkata*, (1887) I. L. R., 11 M. 148 (149, 150). For other cases see notes to S. 14 of Act XX, pp. 121 to 124.

A suit for account is governed by S. 7, Clause 3 (*f*). A suit by a committee to establish their right of control or that the institution falls under S. 3 of Act XX or 1863 is a suit for declaration and court-fee has to be paid under Schedule II, Article 17, Clause (3). We have seen that a committee may be entitled to possession and when a suit is brought by the committee for recovery of possession, court-fee has to be paid under S. 7 Clauses (1) and (3) or S. 7 Clause (5). A suit by two managers or by several joint subordinate office-holders for a declaration that their dismissal by the committee or manager as the case may be is wrongful and for reinstatement in office[1] is not a suit for possession of moveable or immoveable property but is only a suit for a declaration and court-fees paid under Schedule II, Article 17, Clause 3 will be proper[2]. But if such plaintiffs should have asked for an injunction with reference to the property of the religious establishment (as when the plaintiffs ask that they should not be interfered with by the defendant in the management of the endowed property in exercise of their office) then S. 7, Clause iv, (d) will apply[3]. But a more difficult question is whether one suit by several managers or office-holders for wrongful dismissal and reinstatement will lie. If they all have a common cause of action or the same cause of action a single suit will lie. This will be so in a case where they are dismissed for purporting to do the same (but not similar) wrongful act. But if their dismissal proceeds upon different grounds (though such grounds may be similar) they cannot unite in one suit but must bring separate suits[1]. So also a suit for possession of immoveable property may be combined with one for possession of moveable property if the cause of action is the same[4]; otherwise such joinder will be opposed to S. 44, Rule A, C. P. C.

---

1. *Ramanuja* v. *Devanayaka*, (1885) I. L. R.. 8 M. 361; S. C. 9 Ind. Jur. 264.

2. See *Thandavaraya Pillai* v. *Subbayyar*, (1899) I. L. R., 23 M. 483; and cf. *Thakuri* v. *Brahma Narain*, (1896) I. L. R., 19 A. 60.

3. *Gulabsingji* v. *Lakshmansingji*, (1893) I. L. R., 18 B. 100 In *Thakuri* v. *Bramha Narain*, (1896) I. L. R., 19 A. 60 (61) it was thought that such a relief would fall under Art. 17 clause VI but apparently the court was only regarding the suit as one for removal of the manager.

4. *Giyana Sambandha* v. *Kandasami*, (1887) I. L. R, 10 M. 375 (506); *Mazhar Ali Khan* v. *Sajjad Husain Khan*, (1902) I. L. R., 24 A. 358 (360); *Chowdhry Ganesh Dutt* v. *Jewach Thakoorain*, (1903) L. R. 31 I. A. 10(16): S. C. I.L.R., 31 C. 262 (272).

CHAPTER XVII.

SOME OBSERVATIONS ON ACT XX OF 1863.

In this chapter, we shall proceed to make a few remarks upon what is commonly known as the Pagoda Act, but before we proceed to do so we shall briefly advert to some of the circumstances relating to the connection of the Government with the native religious establishments and the withdrawal of such connection.

Government connection prior to Regulations and the history of the subsequent connection.

Long prior to the passing of the Regulations XIX of 1810 and VII of 1817 in Bengal and Madras (and it may be said XVII of 1827 in Bombay) the British Government or the East India Company in virtue of their Sovereign rights claimed the right to visit public endowments and to prevent and redress abuses in management. This was similar to the right to interfere which a visitor would have under the English Law to prevent abuses by corporations of their powers. The king in the case of ecclesiastical corporation is the visitor of Archbishops. He is also the visitor of eleemosynary corporations in the absence of the founder and his heirs.[1] But it is not in virtue of this power that the British Government claimed to exercise a right of superintendence over the native religious and other establishments. The agitation which led to the absolute withdrawal of Government connection would have it that this right was exercised not from any disinterested motives but to secure by love what was obtained by fear[2]. But whether political motives were the origin of the early government connection or otherwise we must observe that the native rulers whom the East India Company gradually replaced were exercising this superintending authority. When the country passed into the hands of the East India Company, these rights or duties also devolved upon the latter and this superintending authority was, therefore, exercised in right of the native rulers through the executive officers of government. It must also be observed that the duty of protecting all public property or rights primarily lay with the government. Even countries little advanced in civilization and in the concept of a 'law' as we now understand it recognise this duty. It was only in recognition of this duty that the English

1. Tudor on Charitable Trusts, pp. 79, 73.
2. See Calcutta Review Vol. XVII, (1852) p. 116,

Government exercised this right of superintendence. The manner of exercising this right was defined by the Regulations (XIX of 1810 and VII of 1817) which expressly recognised in the preamble the duty already adverted to. There could be no two opinions upon the question whether this Government superintendence had any beneficial effect upon the institutions concerned. Indeed the fact that benefits had been conferred upon the institutions was considered by some of the persons connected with the agitation already referred to as a cogent argument why a Christian Government whose duty, it was said, was to see that the so-called false religions productive of evils did not thrive should have no connection with these establishments. It was said[1]: "Idolatry received new strength and its service, rendered efficient and attractive. The income of temples and pagodas was carefully spent; the buildings were kept in good repair; the tanks were cleaned and rendered serviceable; vacancies were filled amongst the officers; the festivals were celebrated with zeal; the daily ceremonies were duly performed. Formerly the whole system was in a state of decay, but, under English superintendence, it everywhere revived. Formerly, the endowment lands were ill-managed and proved unprofitable: on this account such large estates were brought under the Collector's charge; but, under Government, private peculation was prevented, the cultivators were well treated, the income was improved and rendered sure." Would these be at least plausible arguments for not taking up estates of disqualified proprietors by the Court of Wards? It was said that conscientious scruples apparently fanned by the missionary agitation began to possess some of the executive officers of Government and afterwards the British public and the Government began to withdraw their connection with native religious endowments. In 1833, Lord Glenleg's despatch was issued pointing out the desirability of withdrawing the Government superintendence over these endowments. But nothing would seem to have been done for some time. The missionary agitation became loud. The temple of Jagannath was the first institution to which their attention was drawn. The temple is said to have been built in 1128 A. D., by Raja Anund Bhirur Deo, one of the most illustrious of the Gajapati Rajas of Orissa. It is specially sacred to the Hindus.

1. The Calcutta Review for 1852 Vol. XVII, p. 149.

The Government interference was complete in that institution. A large sum of money was given by Government. A pilgrim tax was raised either to meet the demand upon the Government or partly for that and partly for purposes of sanitation and police so that proper arrangements might be made for the large crowd which used to assemble in Puri for the great festivals. Those who thought that they could easily convert the great mass of the Hindu population to the Christian faith saw in this connection of the British Government a great obstacle. The English press and public were called to their aid. The Court of Directors and the Government of India had to bow. The pilgrim tax was abolished and the superintendence of the temple made over to the Raja of Koordah by Act X of 1840. This Act has been printed in some of the Civil Court Manuals[1]. But curiously enough, it is not noticed that the whole of this Act has been repealed by Act XII of 1891. The *first* section repealed the pilgrim taxes at Jagannath, Gya and other places. It also repealed certain old regulations relating to these taxes. As the force of this provision was spent, Act VIII of 1868 repealed this section. The *second* section dealt with the superintendence of the temple and stated that the management should continue vested in the Raja of Khoorda but he and all persons connected with the temple must be guided by the recorded rules and institutions or the ancient usage. This was repealed by S. 539 of Act XIV of 1882. The *third* section prohibited the levying of any fees by the said Raja from the pilgrims but the Raja was to be at liberty to receive voluntary offerings, if made. The *fourth* and *last* section declared the liability of the Raja and the other officers of the temple to be sued in Civil Courts for misfeasance, &c. This section was also repealed by Act VIII of 1868 (The Repealing Act). So that this temple is in the same position as other temples. That at the present day will also be the effect of the Act even if it should not have been repealed. But turning back to our subject, despatches were frequently sent by the Court of Directors pointing out the desirability of withdrawing the Government connection. Definite instructions were also given to carry out this object. One consequence of this was that the endowments belonging to the temple of Jagannath *viz.*, Satais Hazaree Mehal &c., were made over to the Raja in November 1843 and an

Jagannath Act X of 1840.

---

1. See Kuppusami Naicker's edition, Vol. III, p. 1145.

annual sum of Rs. 23,821 for the expenses was given to the Raja in supersession of all former grants.

Government connection in Bombay—History.

In Bombay, Government connection was said to be the least. There was no Regulation in Bombay[1] corresponding to Regulations VII of 1817 and XIX of 1810. Of course, the Bombay Government was exercising visitatorial jurisdiction over these endowments just as the other Governments did before the Regulations referred to above. These rights and duties were not defined in Bombay as in the other Presidencies. Bombay Regulation XVII of 1827 gave powers to the Collectors to resume inams in certain cases. In the case of inams granted for religious purposes, duty was imposed on the Collector to give notice to the trustee and to give a chance to the persons interested to secure the due performance of the services. The Collector was, therefore, bound or entitled to see whether the objects of the grant were being properly fulfilled. In this sense Bombay Regulation XVII of 1827, S. 38, Cls. 2, 3 and 4 could be said to impose a duty on the Collector of a Zilla to see that endowments were honestly appropriated or that the duties to the native communities with which their enjoyment was meant to be accompanied were properly performed.[2] On June 2nd, 1840, the Court of Directors sent a despatch explaining their views upon the matter.The year 1841 was a memorable year in the history of these religious endowments. The Bombay Government on February 27th, 1841 made a report[3] to the Government of India explaining the degree of interference, which the Government officers were exercising hitherto in each district and how it was proposed to be withdrawn. This was approved by the Government of India[4] on April 5th, 1841 and the proceedings transmitted to the Court of Directors. On 19th September 1842, the Revenue Commissioner made a report[5] of the measures adopted subsequent to February 27th, 1841 in connection

1. Parliamentary Return, 1849, India (Idolatry) Paper No. 1 (Paper from the Government of India to the Court of Directors, dated 7th January 1846, para. 24 at p. 3). See also Ibid. Paper No. 142, Minute by Mr. Millett, dated 15th September 1845, p. 447 at p.453; and Paper No. 139 (Note by Secretary Mr. Bushby, dated 20th May 1845), p. 426 at p. 429.

2. *Mathura Naikin v. Esu Naikin*, (1880) I. L. R., 4 B. 545 (at pp. 553, 554).

3. Parliamentary Return, 1845, Paper Nos. 10 to 11, pp. 10 to 14, dated 27th February 1841.

4. Parliamentary Return, 1845, Paper No. 12, dated 5th April 1841, p. 14.

5. Parliamentary Return, 1849, Paper No. 129 at pp. 313 to 320.

with the withdrawal of Government interference in the affairs of religious establishments. So that it may be stated that the withdrawal of Government interference was more or less complete in Bombay in 1843 when the Government approved the above proceedings. Committees of management were appointed and transfer was made to such committees. In some places the village communities were required to elect four or five of the principal persons professing the religion of the temple and these formed the committee. In some others, the Collector appointed a committee of such persons.

History of Government connection in Bengal.

In the other Presidencies where the Regulations defined the rights and duties of the Government, the withdrawal was not so simple. In Bengal it would seem that there was no direct interference in the internal affairs of the religious inistitutions. In 1838 returns were called for as to the repeal of Regulation XIX of 1810, the withdrawal of Government interference and the transfer of superintendence to native trustees. Apparently there was direct interference in the internal management only in two cases *viz.*, Jagannath temple and the Syedpore Endowment (attached to the Hooghly Imambara) and after the withdrawal of Government interference from the temple of Jagannath there was only the Syodpore endowment and even here the superintendence extended to the endowed lands which were in charge of the Local agents. But be this as it may, the Local agents must have exercised control over many of the religious endowments although the Regulation would seem not to have been fully enforced in all the districts of Bengal[1]. In 1844 the Government of Bengal recommended the absolute repeal of the Regulation but only with prospective effect so that the suggestion was that with regard to endowments which were then in charge of the Local agents, the old system might be continued. In a statement of allowances for the native religious institutions called for by the House of Commons on the 5th February 1858 and furnished by the Government of Bengal[2] for the year 1857 we find instances of endowments in charge of Local Agents. There was of course no direct interference. The native managers were liable to render accounts and were giving accounts.

---

1. See Parliamentary Return, 1849, Abstract of Return to Circular Order No. 70, dated 23rd October 1838 pp. 333 to 339.

2. Parliamentary Return, 1859, pp. 3 to 13.

Government connection in North-West Provinces.

In the North-Western Provinces the interference was varied. According to the reports, it would seem that in Meerat, Rohilcund and Kumaon Divisions there were no endowments in charge of the local agents. In the latter division, however, it would seem to have been the practice of the rouwals of Badrinath, Kedarnath and Gopesir to refer disputes arising among the officers of these establishments to the Commissioner and to receive a sunnad of investment from the Government. In Delhi division the local agents were in charge of the mosques of the Delhi City but beyond this there was no interference. In the Allahabad Division the interference of the local agents extended only to the Allahabad District but not to the other districts. In Agra there was direct interference so far as the endowments at Futtehpore Sickree was concerned. In the Benares division the district of Mirzapore would seem to have been the only one in which the local agents interfered with the native religious endowments. The local agents appointed successors in vacancies arising in the case of the mosque at Chunar[1]. In some cases an immediate transfer was directed to Native agents to be appointed by the parties interested in the institutions and in some others, the existing persons were left in uncontrolled management. The return of sums paid to native shrines called for by the House of Commons in 1858 and submitted by the N. W. Provinces Government for 1857 would show that in some cases the local agents scrutinized the accounts of the native committees and that in a few cases the lands constituting the endowments were also in charge of the local agents[2]. This was due to the fact that it was found there was peculation among the servants or the trustees or there were some other extraordinary causes demanding the interference of the local agents.

Government connection in Madras.

In Madras, the interference was greater and more complete than in the other Presidencies and the withdrawal more difficult and necessarily slow. There were no less than 7,600 institutions under the superintendence of the local agents who were Government officers and Europeans[3] and in almost all the districts in the Madras Presidency there were religious institutions under the charge

1. See Parliamentary Return, 1849, Paper No. 136 together with enclosures pp. 363 to 408.
2. Parliamentary Return, 1859, East India (Hindu Shrines) pp. 14 to 32.
3. It was only in Bengal that natives were appointed as local agents.

of the local agents. Reports were called for by the Board in 1841 as to the measures taken by the Collectors for withdrawing the Government connection in pursuance of the despatches of the Court of Directors. In Guntoor[1] and Ganjam, the interference was very limited. Only the pagodas of two villages in Guntur District were under the cognizance of the local agents and these were transferred to the officiating Brahmins *i. e*, the pujaris. In Rajahmundry only one pagoda was superintended by the Collector and this was transferred to a Zamindar in the district. In Vizianagaram there was also only one (the Nuckapally pagoda) under the charge of the Government officers and the superintendence over this was transferred to the proprietor of the Nuckapally estate. There were some pagodas in the Vizianagaram Samasthanum which were under the charge of the Agent to the Governor in the absence of the Maharaja at Benares. But these might be left out of account. Some forty-nine pagodas were merely receiving small sums from the Government Treasury. In Masulipatam there were two under Government control and these were made over to Zamindars. In Nellore, there were twelve pagodas managed by the Collector and the superintendence over these was transferred to committees composed of priests (which we suppose would refer to Archakas) and the head inhabitants of the village *i. e.* the village Reddi or Karnam. Vacancies in the committees were also provided for. In the case of priests or pagoda servants, it was provided that the office should devolve by inheritance while other offices should go by election of committees. In Chingleput there were twenty-four pagodas and one mosque under the charge of the Collector and these were transferred to managers. The former dharmakartas or their heirs were selected. For the Trivellore temple the Ahobilam Jheer was selected and the dharmakartaship vested in the office of Jheer and for the Kamakshee Amman Pagoda the Sankaracharyaswami at Kumbaconum was selected. In Bellary there were twenty-six pagodas and these were transferred to panchayets. In Malabar there were twenty-six pagodas, and two chattrams and twenty pagodas were made over to the Raja of Palghat, and six pagodas and two chattrams were made over to the Zamorin of Calicut. One mosque was

---

1. This was formerly a separate District. It became part of Kistna District and now it is a separate district.

receiving allowance from Government. In Madura, there were thirty-four and these were transferred to dharmakartas selected by the Collector. Where the temples were situated in Zamindaries, the superintendence was made over to the Zamindars. In South Arcot great difficulty was felt. There were one hundred and seven tasdik temples, and much difficulty was felt in finding out dharmakartas. There were no rich proprietors. The difficulties were sooner or later overcome and with the exception of the Tiruvannamalai pagoda, arrangements were made. The Collector, it was said, had to go a-begging to induce people to accept the dharmakartaship of the Tiruvannamalai pagoda, and at last four persons who were all inhabitants of Madras were selected[1]. The Chidambaram temple would seem not to have been under the control of the local agents[2]. In North Arcot it would seem that the lands attached to the pagodas were never under the management of the Collector. There were one hundred and eighty-six tasdik institutions, and excluding one hundred and fourteen as petty devasthanams, the interference had extended according to the Collector's letter[3] to every detail of management over seventy-two of the above institutions. With the exception of the temple at Tripati the management was provided for. A statement of these particulars was attached to the above letter[4]. The Board of Revenue insisted upon the trustees signing a trust-deed[5]. As regards Tripati various proposals were made and at last it was resolved to assign the superintendence to one individual though the people would seem to have strenuously objected to this course. The mahant of Tripati was selected as dharmakarta. There was one mattam called *Poonji Mattam* the head of which would seem to have been dismissed in 1842 by the Collector on account of his gross mismanagement and other misconduct[6]. In Salem there were one hundred and ninety-three institutions and these were trans-

---

1. Parliamentary Return, 1845, East India Appendix 10 to Part I, pp. 32 to 62.

2. See Parliamentary Return, 1849, letter, dated 6th October 1842, from Secretary to Board of Revenue to Collector of South Arcot, p. 214.

3. Letter, dated 29th September 1841, para 12, Parliamentary Return, 1849, p. 197 at p. 199.

4. Parliamentary Return, 1849, at pp. 200 to 207.

5. Ibid p. 208. The taking of trust deeds were in all cases not approved by Government. Ibid p. 416.

6. Parliamentary Return, 1849, Papers Nos. 109 and 110, pp. 194 to 196.

ferred to the superintendence of panchayets. In Coimbatore there were one hundred and thirty-two institutions, and these were transferred to native dharmakartas. There were about three thousand ninety-four village temples supported by small inams of land but these were not interfered with by the Government officers. There were two hundred and eighty-five institutions under the Government superintendence. They were made over to the superintendence of influential men in the district. A trust deed was taken from each. In Kurnool there were about two thousand three hundred and thirty-eight institutions large and small which were receiving money allowances, sader-ward allowances &c., or which had inam lands[1].

In Trichinopoly one hundred and sixteen pagodas were managed by the Collector. The degree of interference, however, varied much. Dharmakartas were selected to whom the superintendence was transferred. In Tinnevelly there were three hundred and fifty institutions which were transferred to the superintendence of trustees selected from the chief men of the village. In Tanjore there were about two thousand eight hundred and seventy-four under the superintendence of the Collectors. In some, panchayats were appointed and the superintendence transferred to them. In a few cases, the superintendence was left to heads of mutts. In others it was left to dharmakarthas selected from among the influential natives of the district. Trust deeds were taken from all these persons. In Canara the number was the largest. It was said to be three thousand six hundred and sixty-eight. Of these, three thousand three hundred and seventy-two were pagodas, and one hundred and thirty-six were mosques. The remainder (one hundred and sixty) were mattams[2]. But although mattams were said to be under the management of the Collector, yet the truth would seem to have been that the mutts and mosques were always under the sole management of the presiding priests or hereditary superintendents who never gave an account of their administration to the Government officers[3]. Some of the servants of the pagoda

1. See Parliamentary Returns, 1849, Paper No. 127 and enclosures, pp. 287 to 309 and Paper No. 128 and enclosures, pp. 310 to 312. See also pp. 278 to 286.

2. Parliamentary Return, 1849, at p. 443. See also Ibid Paper No. 115 at p. 248.

3 Letter from the Collector of Mercara to the Board of Revenue, dated 10th December 1843, para 12. Parliamentary Return. 1849, p. 227 at p. 229.

conjointly with the potails and other influential ryots were appointed trustees to whom the superintendence was transferred[1]. In cases where the tasdik did not exceed Rupees thirty, the pujaris were appointed trustees. The number of trustees appointed for an institution varied from three to five.

In Madras there were fifteen pagodas under the supervision of the Collector. As many of these pagodas were supported by contributions from Government, the Government officers were in the habit of receiving and auditing the accounts. Some muchilikas were apparently taken in December 1796 by which the supervision became vested in the Collector. The Government approved this superintendence in 1822. No direct interference in the internal affairs was, however, exercised. But the Triplicane Pagoda was an exception. In connection with the withdrawal, the Collector reported that in the case of the Mylapore Pagoda, the appointment of dharmakartas was allowed to rest with the general suffrages of the community interested therein (*i.e.*, the Poonamallee Moodelliars). For the Triplicane pagoda, three dharmakarthas were appointed by the Collector and any vacancy among these was to be filled up by the suffrages of the Tengalai sect. The report is imperfect in not containing information about the other pagodas. But the jurisdiction of the Supreme Court was in no way interfered with at any time.

Withdrawal of connection in Madras—Summary.

In the Madras Presidency, therefore, the withdrawal was effected by the Government ceasing to interfere in the internal affairs of the institutions and in the expenditure of the revenues and by the Government providing for the appointment[2] of dharmakartas and ceasing to make appointments on vacancies arising. But the Government of Madras was strongly against giving up the management of endowed lands but in this the Government was overruled by the Court of Directors. The reason for this unwillingness was that injustice would be caused to the ryots. The Government of India in September 1845 requested the Madras Government to consider the propriety of transferring the lands after giving the

1. Parliamentary Return, 1849, pp. 217 to 234.

2. In the case of village temples Poojaris were appointed hereditary dharmakartas In the case of large temple committees or panchayats were appointed. In some cases a single person or two or more were appointed. In some others heads of mutts or influential ryots were appointed.

ryot pattas specifying the terms and conditions of his holding. The Board in pursuance of an order from Government issued circular letters, dated 1846, June 15 to the Collectors to make over the management of the Devastanam lands and the arrangements made in each district were reported to Government on 1854, February 27. The Government of Madras also insisted upon an Act which would take the place of the Regulations as a measure of justice to the institutions themselves. Difference of view prevailed as to the exact scope of this measure, and it was only in 1863 that an Act was passed. As this necessarily took some length of time, the Madras Government which always took a cooler and more sensiable view of the matter authorised the local agents to interfere under the Madras Regulation in urgent and pressing cases of complaint[1] although at the same time the Government pointed out that cases involving disputes of a religious nature should be left to be decided by Courts of Law and a suggestion was made to the Court of Sadr Adalut regarding the propriety of giving precedence to such cases to ensure a speedy adjudication[2].

Passing of Act for legalising withdrawal of Government connection—Act XX of 1863.

It is not proposed to go into the propriety of the reasons adduced for the withdrawal of Government interference as the question has been finally settled and is, therefore, outside the pale of practical discussion. The withdrawal of Government connection was legalized for all India by Act XX of 1863. Act XX of 1863 repealed Regulations XIX of 1810 and VII of 1817. As regards Bombay, West J. observed[3]: "The connection of the Government in its executive capacity with Hindu and Mahomedan foundations was brought to an end for Bombay by Bombay Act VII of 1863." But Act VII of 1863 S. 1 only repealed Chapters IX and X of Regulation XVII of 1827. The only section in this Regulation having any bearing upon the matter on hand would be S. 38 Cl. (2) but this only provided in an indirect way for these institutions[4]. Moreover Act VII of 1863 applies only to such parts of Bombay as Act XI of 1852 does not govern.

1. See Maskell, pp. 465 to 467.

2. Maskell, p. 467, Note (a) 1, 35.

3. *Manohar Ganesh Tambekar* v. *Lakhmiram Govindram*, (1887) I. L. R., 12 B. 247 (260). But a more correct view is taken in West and Buhler's Dig. of H. L. 175 and note (c) to that page.

4. See also West and Buhler's Dig. of H. L. 175 and note (b) to that page.

Act XI of 1852 applies only to the Dekhan, Khandesh, Southern Maratha Country and other districts which were more recently annexed to the Presidency of Bombay. Rule 7, Schedule B of that Act provides that inams held for the support of mosques, temples or similar institutions should be permanently continued. But Act XX of 1863 S. 22 is general and applies to the whole of India. Ever since the withdrawal of Government, there has been a scandalous mismanagement of these institutions against which Act XX of 1863 affords little or no remedy. West J observed in *Mathura Naikin* v. *Esu Naikin*[1]: "The general impression is, these measures have led to a great deal of fraud, against which the law for many years afforded no effectual protection." He refers to S. 539 of the Civil Procedure Code (Act X of 1877) as affording a protection. Whether this section really affords all the necessary protection may be doubtful. But apparently it has been construed and worked in a liberal spirit by the High Court of Bombay. The same liberal construction has been adopted in Calcutta and Allahabad. But the scope of the section is confined to a very limited class of cases according to the construction placed by the Madras High Court. So that S. 539 is not of much use in Madras. But the question is as to the protection afforded by Act XX of 1863. This is what is to be found in the standing information regarding the Official Administration of the Madras Presidency prepared under the orders of the Government by Mr. C. D. Maclean the then Acting Sub-Secretary to the Board of Revenue[2]: "So far as endowments for religious purposes were concerned this control was transferred by Act XX of 1863 from the Board to District Committees appointed by Government. These have proved a failure and the mismanagement and malversation of public funds have been so great that a revision of the law is again under contemplation." We shall not advert to the opinions of others after this official opinion. The revision of the law is yet to come and for this the Government of India is chiefly to blame. Our present object is to show that there is a *case* for the interference of theLegislature and with this object we shall proceed to consider the sections of the Act.

---

1. (1880) I. L. R., 4 B. 545 at p. 554.

2. See Revised Edition of 1879 pp. 73 and 74. Similar language is to be found in the Madras Manual of Administration (Edn. of 1885) Vol. I. p. 61 note (1).

Sections considered—S. 5-Disputed succession.

The first section that one need consider is S. 5. This section makes provision for the appointment of a temporary manager in cases of disputed succession. The object is to make due provision for the proper administration of the trust when there is a scramble for office. If this is the object, we fail to see why the section should be limited in its application. It has been held that the section only applies when there is a vacancy arising in the office of a trustee &c., of an endowment transferred to a trustee &c., under S. 4 and a dispute arises as to the succession[1]. In the notes to S. 5 we have pointed out[2] that the words of S. 5 seem to suggest that the section is confined to the case of a vacancy caused by death &c. of the trustee &c., to whom property has been transferred under S. 4 although this is not the intention of the Legislature. It is satisfactory to note that the Calcutta High Court has in a recent case[3] placed a liberal construction by adopting the view suggested in the notes to S. 5. While there is a scramble for office provision ought to be made for the due protection of the endowments. This is effected by Act XIX of 1841 in cases of disputed succession to a private person's estate. It is doubtful whether this Act applies to a case of disputed succession to the office of manager and whether it enables a court to appoint a manager of endowed property. The dispute contemplated under the Act more or less relates to private property. Endowed property is not "the property of the deceased" trustee. Provisions analogous to this are to be found in Bombay Regulation VIII of 1827 and it is also a question whether that Regulation applies to endowed property. There may be a dispute as to succession but the question is whether endowed property is "the property of a person deceased" within the meaning of S. 9 of the Regulation. The same difficulty must be felt under Madras Regulation III of 1802, S. 16 Cl. (4). Is it the "estate of a person dying intestate"? The same is the case with S. 4 of Bengal Regulation V of 1799. This difficulty we think exists notwithstanding the recent decision of the Privy Council in *Maharaja Jagadindra Nath* v. *Rani Hemanta*[4]. But there are some

---

1. *Ittuni Panikkar* v. *Irani Nambudripad*, (1881) I. L. R., 3 M. 401 ; *Gyanananda Asram* v. *Kristo Chandra Mukherji*, (1901) 8 C. W. N. 404.

2. See notes p. 32 under heading [3].

3. Per *Banerjee* J. in *Gyanananda Asram* v. *Kristo Chandra Mukherji*,(1901) 8 C. W. N. 404 a case decided after the proofs of the notes to S. 5 were struck off.

4. (1904) 8 C. W. N. 809.

dicta in the cases that Act XIX of 1841 and, therefore, the corresponding provisions already referred to would apply to such cases. In *Mahant Dhanraj Giri Goswami* v. *Sripati Giri Goswami*[1] the Bengal High Court held that S. 318 of the old Code of Criminal Procedure (Act XXV of 1861) applied only to cases of disputed possession but not to those of disputed succession and that Act XIX of 1841 applied to the latter class of cases. This view is not inconsistent with the cases in *Mahomed Musaliar* v. *Kunji Chuk Musaliar*[2] and *In re Pandurang Govind*[3] which have held that a dispute regarding the right to perform religious service or worship in a public temple is a dispute within the meaning of S. 145 of the Codes of 1882 and 1898. The case of *Shri Vishwambhar Pandit* v. *Vasudev Pandit*[4] a case under Bombay Regulation VIII of 1827 related only to the private estate of a deceased person. Be this as it may, it passes one's comprehension why when provision is made for the appointment of a temporary manager in cases of disputed succession such provision should not extend to all classes of religious establishments falling under S 4. Indeed we should have thought that a similar provision would be useful even in cases of institutions falling under S. 3. Provision should also have been made for the duties of such temporary manager the second para of the section being vague[5] or nothing need be said about them at all.

S. 7—Committees.

Turning to S. 7 which provides for the appointment of District Committees for the different institutions falling under S. 4 there is a particular vagueness having regard to S. 8 of the Act about the mode of appointment. Was the appointment of the committee to be for each mosque, temple &c. or was it to be separately for all the Mahomedan institutions taken together and separately for the Hindu

1. (1869) 2 B. L. R. app. cr. j. 27. An order passed by the Deputy Magistrate under S. 144 of the Criminal Procedure Code of 1882 directing the managers newly appointed by a temple committee not to interfere with the management of the dismissed managers is not liable to revision. *Palaniappa Chetti* v. *Dorasami Ayyar*, (1895) I. L. R., 18 M. 402.

2. (1888) I. L. R., 11 M. 323 (326).

3. (1900) I. L. R., 24 B. 527.

4. (1888) I.L.R., 13 B. 37. In *Sayad Husseinmian* v. *Collector of Kaira*, (1895) I. L.R., 21 B. 48 an administrator was appointed under Regn. VIII of 1827 and the suit was to remove such administrator on the ground that his appointment was bad under S. 22 of Act XX of 1863. It does not appear whether the proceedings as to the appointment of administrator went to the High Court. Anyhow the case would have no application as the trusts were only declared by the will of the testatrix and the estate taken was clearly that of the testatrix.

5. Notes under heading [9] to S. 5 of Act XX p. 37.

establishments or was it to be one Committee for the whole district and for the all different religious establishments (irrespective of their being Hindu or Mohomedan)? In the first two cases what was to be the jurisdiction of the committees so appointed? Could they have jurisdiction over the whole district and could their jurisdiction be curtailed by the local Government? If committees appointed for the Mahomedan establishments could, notwithstanding the appointment, have jurisdiction over the whole district (because under S. 7 they have to be appointed for a district or a division) there would be the absurdity of Mahomedan Committees superintending the affairs of Hindu establishments. If that was the intention of the Legislature effect should be given to it. Was that the intention of the Legislature? If that was not the intention, did the Legislature express its intention correctly? The Legislature by using language more apt could have avoided all this discussion. In S. 7 the Legislature contemplated the appointment of one or more committees for a district so that where a district contained both Hindu and Mahomedan establishments, two committees might be appointed. But then S. 8 provided that the persons who were to constitute the committee should be selected from "among the persons professing the faith for which the mosque, temple &c. was founded" How was this provision to be given effect to? It ought to have said that when a Mahomedan committee was being appointed, the Hindus should be excluded. So should the Mahomedans when a Hindu committee was appointed. But the section would not say anything of that sort. Even if a liberal interpretation was to be given[1] what about the jurisdiction of these committees?

Then with respect to the tenure of office and the filling up of vacancies Ss. 9 and 10 are also vague. The language of the Coorg Temple Funds Regulation 1892 is very clear. As we have pointed out in the notes to Ss. 9 and 10 of Act XX, the question is whether they provide only for the members originally appointed by Local Government or for all members to come. Either of the two constructions is possible. If the former construction should prevail, the committees

Ss. 9 and 10—Tenure and vacancy.

1. The question has not directly arisen in any case. In *Gandavathara* v. *Devanayaga* (1883) I. L. R.. 7 M. 222 (224) the Madras High Court suggested that a Sivite and a Vaishnavite committee was contemplated. Members of either sect might be appointed. *Alwar Ayyangar* v. *Krishnamachariar*, (1899) 9 M. L. J. R. 173. But see *Subbramaniya Sastri* v. *Meenakshi Naidu*, (1882) 6 Ind. Jur. 128 aff'd on review 6 Ind. Jur. 632.

must die out if they had not already done so and provision must be made immediately by the Legislature. If the latter construction were to prevail, it would seem unreasonable to make membership in the committee a life appointment. Such a provision is not to be found in the case of Municipal Commissioners nor in the case of Legislative Councils. We had an instance in the case of the University Fellows but even this has now been altered by the Legislature (Act VIII of 1904). The term of 3 or 5 years must be the possible limit. The latter is the limit provided for by the Coorg Temple Funds Management Regulation[1] 1892, S. 6.

System of committees a failure—Reasons

There must have been many reasons which need not now be discussed why this system of committees should have proved a failure. It is no wonder that a system abounding in such defects as are to found in Act XX can ever have proved otherwise. *First* of all, the fixing of the tenure of office for a person's life does not tend to make the members exert themselves. The voters have no opportunity to show their sense of displeasure to persons who never cared to exert themselves and who must have comforted themselves in the idea that their appointment cannot be disturbed for life. There is a premium for laziness or mischief. *Secondly,* the qualifications for the persons to be elected are not laid down in the Act. It is doubtful whether the provision in S. 8, requiring the members to be selected from among the persons professing the religion for the purposes of which the mosque &c. is maintained applies at all to the case of a vacancy to be filled under S. 10. But even assuming that it does apply further provision should be made for the qualifications of the candidates for election. It should have been enough if the Local Governments were empowered to frame rules for the purpose as in the Coorg Temple Funds Management Regulation 1892, S. 5, Cl. (*c*). The rules framed by the Local Governments do not effectually provide for this. Again, although there is nothing in the Act which prohibits a person who may be employed under Government from being appointed as a member of committee in his individual capacity and not in virtue of his office yet provision should have been made expressly that the native uncovenanted Judicial and Revenue officers were eligible for election. The papers connected

1. See Appendix II pp. 186 to 192.

with the withdrawal would clearly show that this was a necessary provision. The reports called for by the several Boards would show that some Collectors were in favor of this while others were against it. In Bengal, Government was prepared to make its Native Judicial and Revenue officers eligible. In fact the Draft Act sent by the Bengal Government in 1844 made a provision that the native local agency should be extended and that Principal Sadr Amins, Sadr Amins and Munsifs should be considered eligible for nomination and appointment as local agents[1]. The Madras Board of Revenue thought that the appointment of Native officers of Government to any charge connected with the religious institutions was incompatible with the principles governing the withdrawal of Government connection. But although Mr. Elliott who was entrusted with the making of a report upon the arrangements made in the Presidency of Madras stated in his report that this opinion of the Madras Board of Revenne was not supported by the orders of the Court of Directors[2] yet it would have been better if express provision were made in the Act. *Thirdly,* the principle of election has introduced a new phase into the circumstances of the country. But it has brought at the same time some disadvantages. It has brought all the evils of election which we are told are also to be seen in England. The anxiety of the candidates in canvassing votes and the method of canvassing them are anything but desirable. In the case of Municipal elections especially one is rather staggered at the considerable sums of money expended by candidates in these elections. Much is not heard of this in the case of university elections. Even there, the question is regarded as one of promise irrevocable in favor of the party who has obtained it rather than a question as to the comparative merits or demerits of the competing candidates. Naturally some people about whose qualifications there can be no question are deterred from seeking election while others object on principle to offer themselves as candidates instead of being offered. But this may be no argument to do away with the principle of election if it should be still thought fit to continue the system of committees. In other cases we find the principle of nomination going hand in hand with the principle of election. While a certain number is to be elected certain others

1. See Parliamentary Return 1849 p. 331.
2. Parliamentary Return 1849 at p. 416.

are to be nominated and both the nominated and the elected members form one council or committee to do the duties imposed on them by law. This may also be usefully introduced into the Act. A certain proportion (say a third or fourth) may be nominated by the District Judge (who is already entitled under S. 10 to appoint members to the committee) and Government officers may be expressly declared entitled to be appointed[1]. *Lastly*, there is no duty imposed on the Committee to pass the accounts after an independent audit and to publish such accounts. It is the audit of the accounts by an *independent* person and the publication of the same to the outside world that is an effectual check upon peculation and misappropriation. That is how the Nidhis established under the Companies Act have hitherto thrived. Even there many companies in Madras which were formed immediately after the Act of 1882 were wound up by the mismanagement of the so-called founders of these Nidhis and the mismanagement was not brought into light because there was no independent audit. We should have thought that it would have been better if an official auditor or auditors were appointed with a regular staff for auditing regularly the accounts of these religious institutions and Nidhis just as it is done with reference to the accounts of the Municipalities. The expenses should certainly be contributed by these institutions and Nidhis and this would be an effective check upon bad management and peculation. At any rate, a provision similar to the one made by S. 17 of the Coorg Temple Funds Management Regulation should be introduced in Act XX of 1863 with reference to all religious institutions and the District Judge may be empowered to appoint an auditor to audit the accounts of each institution and to publish them in such manner as he may think fit.

Coorg Regulation more clear.

One is struck with the clearness and precision of the provisions containted in Ss.4to 9 of theCoorg Regulation.The Regulation goes into details which theAct for some reason or other avoids.Provision is made for the appointment of the first committee by the Chief Commissioner and for filling up of *all* vacancies. The term of

1. In the absence of the declaration referred to by us District Judges have regarded the holding of office under Government as a disqualification. *Meenakshi Naidu* v. *Subramaniya Sastri*, (1887) I. L. R., 11 M. 26 (28).

office is expressly limited and the District Judge is empowered to remove members for various reasons usually to be found in the case of Municipal commissionerships and other offices. If a member refuses or neglects without sufficient excuse to act or has become incapable of acting or absents himself from *three* consecutive meetings or has been declared an insolvent or has been convicted of an offence, he may be removed by the District Judge. Curiously enough no such provision is to be found in Act XX of 1863 although S. 9 says that a committee member may be removed for "unfitness." Then power is given to the Chief Commissioner to frame rules for elections and qualifications for the voters are stated. Two of these may be usefully introduced into the rules framed under the Act[1]. An insolvent and a person convicted of an offence are not entitled to vote under the Coorg Regulation but they are entitled to vote under the rules framed under the Pagoda Act. Upon a revision of this Act the provisions to be found in Ss. 4 to 9 may be usefully borne in mind.

Rights and duties of committees—No express provision.

Then no mention is made in the Act about the rights and duties of the committees *inter se*, and with reference to managers appointed by the Committees. Why should there be this vagueness? It is rather the business of the Legislature to define clearly the rights and duties of offices created by statute. This principle is altogether forgotten. It is left for adjudication by courts and thus the Act itself promotes litigation which it is the business of the Legislature and of the Act to prevent. No provision is made as to the mode in which business should be conducted whether at meetings or otherwise, as to the appointment of Chairmen and as to votes. All these are left to be supplied by the decisions of the courts[2]. No provision is also made as to the relation which should subsist between the Committee and the Manager appointed by the Committee. What are their respective rights and duties in relation to the institutions? Here instead of the courts construing the Act in a liberal spirit, we find them construing strictly. The principle which has hitherto guided the Courts seems to be that Committees must prove every right they assert and that it must be assumed that any such right exists not in the Committees but in the managers. In this

1. See Appendices VI to VIII, pp. 207 to 214.
2. Notes to S. 7, pp. 45 to 47.

they were no doubt guided by the fact that Committees were the creation of a statute so that their rights should be found in the statute itself while managers were not newly appointed by the statute but were known to the law already. Even this principle will not justify the decisions[1] adverted to in the notes to S. 7 and other sections[2]. The first matter that one ought to refer to is the decision of the courts that Committees have no right to possession of endowed properties and could not, therefore, sue for such possession. We have tried to show in pp.45 46 and 69 to 77 of the notes that this view is utterly erroneous and not justified by the language of the Act. Ss. 7 and 12 direct the transfer of endowed properties to the Committee and vest the management in such committee. It is a twisting of the language to say that possession or custody is not one of the incidents of management and that the committees have no right to sue for such possession or custody. How otherwise they can enforce management seems hardly comprehensible. Then the Act declares that the powers of the Board over the property transferred are determined by the Act. S. 7 says that the committee shall perform all the duties imposed on the Board and local agents except in respect of property retained by the Board under S 12. It is notorious that the Board and local agents had management of these lands in many cases. That is why they were directed to hand over or transfer the property. So that the committies would, *prima facie,* have the right to manage. No doubt S. 12 para. 2 does not declare that the powers of the Board determined by the transfer are to devolve on the committee and the last para. of that section only deals with the right to recover rent of land transferred. But this does not take away the effect of S. 7. Then it is said that S. 11 of the Act incapacitates committees from holding or possessing property. A similar provision is to be found in S. 10 of the Coorg Regulation and we have no doubt that the only effect of those sections is that a member of committee shall not hold the office of manager either permanently or temporarily. This is clear from the language of S. 10 of the Coorg Regulation[3] which says that "no member of committee shall be capable of being or acting as Manager."

Right of committees to possession of endowed properties and to enforce management.

1. Pages 45 to 47.
2. Notes to Ss. 11 and 12, pp. 69 to 77.
3. See Appendix II, p. 189.

This is the same as S. 11 of the Pagoda Act which runs thus :— "No member of a committee . . . . *shall be capable of being* or *shall act*, also as a trustee" &c. Under S. 3 of the Coorg Regulation the "*funds*[1]" are under the management of the committee and under S. 10 of the same Regulation the committee may prescribe the duties to be performed by the manager and under S. 18 the committe may institute legal proceedings in the name of its President. It is clear that under the Act as it is under the Coorg Regulation, committees may sue for possession and that there is nothing in S. 11 of the Act as in S. 10 of the Coorg Regulation which disqualifies committees from possessing endowed property or from suing to recover possession of *any* endowed property belonging to the institutions under their control. It is to be regretted that the Act is not more clear and it is a matter of greater regret that the Legislature has not intervened all these years to make the provisions of the Act more clear when the complaint is that the Act has not stated in detail the rights and duties of committees.

Right of committees to interfere in internal management.

Then as regards the rights of the committee members to interfere in the internal affairs of the institutions, there is a hopeless muddle. Two extreme views are suggested in the decisions. One that committees have no right to interfere with the managers in the internal affairs even though such managers may be appointed by committees and the other is that they have full right to interfere even in the internal affairs. We must take it that the trend of decisions of the Madras High Court is to accept the former view as sound[2]. There are no decisions of the other Courts (Bengal and Allahabad) and curiously enough there is a paucity of decisions upon these and other questions bearing upon the Act in the other courts. In favor of the latter view it must be observed that committees have taken the place of the Board and must therefore have all the rights exercised by such Board and local agents. The degree of interference exercised by the Board and local agents cannot be better stated than in the language of the Principal Collector of North Arcot in his report to the Board, dated 1841, Septr., 29. He there states[3]: "We

1. These are according to S. 2 (*a*) cash allowances paid by Government, (*b*) all bequests, gifts and offerings, (*c*) all funds invested or in hand to the credit of the institutions at the time of the Regulation and (*d*) income accruing from all lands.
2. *Seshadri Ayyangar* v. *Nataraja Ayyar*, (1898) I. L. R., 21 M. 179.
3. Parliamentary Return, 1849, p. 197.

have hitherto stood to these pagodas in the obligation of sovereigns and our interference has extended to every detail of management; we regulate their funds, superintend the repairs of their temples, keep in order their cars and images, appoint the servants of the pagodas, purchase and keep in store the various commodities required for their use, investigate and adjust all disputes, and at times even those of a religious nature; there is nothing appertaining to or connected with the temples that is not made a subject of report, except the religious worship carried on daily in them. In like manner, our superintendence of the celebrated pagoda on the hill of Tirupati, extends over its interior economy, the conduct and management of its affairs, the control over the parpotigars, Jyengars, archakas and of all the other priests and servants who are or may be attached to the pagoda[1]". Language similar to this will be found in the reports by the other Collectors. Naturally enough Mr. Justice *Davies* held in *Seshadri Ayyangar* v. *Nataraja Ayyar*[2] that this right to interfere in the internal management must have devolved upon the committee. The other judges held that the committee had no such right. *Collins*, C. J. thought that the interference by the Board could not be arbitrary[3]. If his attention had been drawn to S. 2 of the Regulations he would have observed that only the superintendence of *endowments* and not of *establishments* vested in the Board. But the Government or Board did not derive its rights only from the Regulations. As has been observed in the beginning of this chapter[4] and in the notes to the Regulations[5], the Government exercised rights of superintendence over these endowments and establishments even before the Regulations which, however, did not curtail those rights. So that the question is whether the exercise of these rights in right of former native sovereigns was illegal. *Collins*, C. J. thought that the Board had power only to prevent and redress abuses and could have no other powers[6]. But he did not consider whether the former sovereigns were not within their powers in exercising these rights. But the Act does no attempt to grapple with any question

1. Parliamentary Return 1849 at p. 199.
2. *Seshadri Ayyangar* v. *Nataraja Ayyar*, (1898) I. L. R., 21 M. 179 at pp. 197 to 199.
3. Ibid, at p. 219.
4. Pages cccxxvii to cccxxviii.
5. Pages 155 to 156, 163.
6. *Seshadri Ayyangar* v. *Nataraja*, supra at p. 220.

of this sort and omits as we have already said to define the rights and duties of committees either *inter se* or in relation to the managers.

One finds a great sense of relief when he turns to the provisions of the Coorg Regulation. It provides for business being conducted in meetings, for the quorum at such meetings, for questions being decided by a majority of votes and for the casting vote of the President in cases of equality of votes. It also provides that the "funds" should vest in the committees and that the latter have the right to prescribe the duties to be performed by the managers (S. 16) and no distinction is drawn between hereditary managers and other managers (S. 15). In case of hereditary managers, the committee is bound to appoint the lawful heir but beyond this the hereditary managers can claim no higher rights. The committee may fine or remove *any* manager for sufficient cause.

The next Section to which attention must be drawn is S. 13 of the Pagoda Act. It has been held by the Madras High Court that this section has no application to the case of hereditary managers so as to empower committees to call for accounts from such managers[1]. But a different construction has been placed by the Calcutta High Court[2]. There is no doubt about the good policy of the ruling of the Calcutta Court. It necessarily compels the hereditary manager to keep some accounts. This construction seems also to be the more correct one. Anyhow when two courts hold different views upon a section, it is but right that the Legislature should intervene and declare which is the correct one. Provision must also be made for the inspection of accounts by the persons interested. The section makes no such provision. As it is, the right to inspect the accounts can only be exercised after the expense of a suit under S. 14. Further as observed already, provision must be made for publishing and auditing the accounts without which there can be no effective check upon management. Accounts.

---

1. *Ramiengar* v. *Gnanasambanda* (1867) 5 M. H. C. 53; *K. Venkatabalakrishna Chettiyar* v. *Kaliyanaramaiyangar*,(1869) 5 M. H. C. 48; *Fakurudin Sahib* v. *Ackeni Sahib*, (1880) I. L. R., 2 M. 197.

2. *Jan Ali* v. *Ram Nath Mundul*, (1881) I.L.R., 8 C. 32. The cases in the Madras Court are not, however, noticed in this case.

Suits under Act—Reliefs claimable and awardable.

The last section that we may refer to is S. 14. The provisions of this section have given rise to much adverse criticism. Suits under this section are confined to breaches of trust, misfeasance or neglect of duty. A committee member may be removed for unfitness (*vide* S. 9) but apparently this cannot be effected in a suit under S. 14 although S. 9 declares that he cannot be removed without an order of the Civil Court as provided in S. 14. Apparently the Legislature forgot the enactment in S. 10 when enacting S. 14. The unnecessarily restricted scope of the section is, therefore, not calculated to be of any real use as a check upon maladministration. It is thought that the Act excepting S. 22 is not applicable to Bombay[1] although the wording of S. 14 itself is general so as to apply to all public religious institutions. Greater resort is made to S. 539, C. P. C. in Bombay and the liberal construction put upon this section by the Bombay Court is of greater benefit to the suitor or any person aggrieved in respect of these institutions. This could only be after the Act of 1882 as the corresponding section in the Act of 1877 had no application to public religious trusts[2]. S. 539, C. P. C. is not confined to the case of a breach of trust[3]. But no benefit can be derived by resort to this section in Madras as the Madras High Court has limited the application of the section to a friendly suit and not to a hostile suit so that, accord-according to the view of the Madras Court, a trustee cannot be remov-

1. It is clear that S. 3 cannot apply to Bombay as it refers only to the Regulations and therefore the provisions in Ss. 8, 7 and 12 of the Act and according to Madras view S. 13 will not apply to Bombay except so for as they have been extended by Bombay Act VII of 1865 (which extends Act XX of 1863 to Canara.) Ss. 4 to 6 may also not apply to Bombay. S. 4 beins with "such mosque &c." *i.e.* a mosque &c. to which the Regulations were applica'le. But S. 14 is general and the observations in *Protab Chandra Misser* v. *Brojonath Misser*, (1891) I. L. R., 19 C. 275 ought not to beheld as amounting to a decision that the Act would not apply to places not governed by Regulations XIX of 1810 (Bengal) and VII of 1817 (Madras). The decisions holding that S. 14 do not apply to private religious trusts ought not to be regarded as authorities on the question as to the extent (or place) of applicability of the Section. Nor does the fact that Act XVI of 1874 (The Laws Local Extent Act) does not mention Act XX of 1863 as applicable to the whole of British India negative the suggestion that S. 14 may apply to all public religious institutions in India (except the Scheduled Districts). Act XVI of 1874 (The Laws Local extent Act) does not equally mention S. 22 as applicable to Bombay and no question has been raised that that section is not applicable to Bombay. So also no adverse inference ought to be drawn from Bombay Act VII of 1865 which extends the whole of Act XX of 1863 to Canara. But Messrs. West & Buller in their Digest of Hindu Law at p. 175 draw an adverse inference, so that even S. 14 will not seem to apply to Bombay.

2. *Radhabai* v. *Chimnaji*, (1878) I.L.R., 3 B. 27 where, however, the point was doubtfully expressed; *Karuppa* v. *Arumuga*, (1882) I. L. R., 5 M. 383; *Thackersey Dewraj* v. *Hurbhum Nursey*, (1884) I. L. R., 8 B. 432 (450, 451); *Giyana Sambandha* v. *Kandasami*, (1887) I. L. R., 10 M. 375 (506). But see *Mathura Naikin* v. *Esu Naikin*, (1880) I. L. R., 4 B. 545 (554) See also p. cclxxxiv.

3. See Chapter XV, p. ccxcii.

ed hostilely[1]. This interpretation is of course not followed by the other Courts[2]. That is why we find that in Madras, resort must necessarily be had to the provisions of S. 14 of the Pagoda Act and there are a greater number of cases in the Madras High Court under that section than in the other High Courts. It is not easy to see why in 1863 it was thought prudent to confine suits under S. 14 to cases of breach of trust or neglect of trust. The section should have been made applicable whenever it was necessary to provide for the administration of the trust. Instead of amending this section the Legislature has provided for these cases only in S. 539 of the Code of 1882 which enacts that a suit may be brought whenever the direction of the Court is deemed necessary. We shall proceed to consider the defects in S. 14 of the Act under the following heads (*a*) parties against whom suits may be brought and (b) the reliefs that may be asked and awarded in suits under the section. We shall find that the same defects exist in a suit under S. 539, C. P. C. in respect of parties and that, therefore, so far as such defects are concerned both sections stand upon the same footing.

Strangers cannot be parties.

As pointed out by us in the notes to S. 14 it has been held by the Madras High Court that a suit under S. 14 can only be brought against the trustee, manager &c., and not against a person who has ceased to fill such office nor against the representatives of the old trustee &c., nor against persons claiming under wrongful alienations by the trustee &c., nor against strangers[3]. The Allahabad High Court, however, holds differently[4] but the Madras cases have not been brought to the notice of that court. There being this conflict the Legislature should have intervened at any rate to declare which construction was correct so that there may be uniformity in the administration of justice on the construction of a statute throughout

---

1. *Narasimha* v. *Ayyan*, (1888) I. L. R., 12 M. 157; *Rangasami Naickan* v. *Varudappa Naickan*, (1894) I. L. R., 17 M. 462 overruling majority in *Subbayya* v. *Krihsna*, (1880) I. L. R., 14 M. 186

2. *Sayad Husseinmian Dadumian* v. *The Collector of Kaira*, (1895) I. L. R., 21 B. 48; *Sajedur Raja* v. *Gour Mohundas Vishnav*, (1897) I. L. R., 24 C. 418; *Huseni Begam* v. *The Collector of Moradabad*, (1897) I. L. R., 20 A. 46. For other cases, see Chapter XV, p. cclxxxvii.

3. See S. 14 notes under heading [4] pp. 97 to 100.

4. *Sheoratan Kunwari* v *Ram Pargash*, (1896) I. L. R., 18 A. 227. The suit being by a founder the decision may be explained on the footing that the founder combined the suit under S. 14 with the suit which he was entitled to bring under the ordinary law.

India. Even if the construction placed by the High Court of Allahabad should be wrong we think the Legislature should adopt it as being in accordance with good policy S.539C.P.C. has also been construed as excluding a suit brought against persons whose term of office as trustee&c., has expired[1] or against alienees[2] from trustees &c., or against trespassers[3]. The Calcutta High Court, however, takes a different view and holds that the section has application to suits against trespassers[4]. Nor has this section any application to cases of contests as between rival claimants as to who are the lawful managers[5] and the same view has been held with regard to S. 14 of the Pagoda Act[6]. There can be no doubt about the sound policy of a provision which enables a plaintiff to get all the reliefs in one suit. The object of the processual law must be to enable a plaintiff to bring a suit in such a way that he may effectually get an adjudication upon the subject-matter in dispute in one suit. He must not be driven to another suit for the same subject-matter. For effecting this object all parties interested in the subject-matter must be made defendants according to the Civil Procedure Code. But these provisions of the Civil Procedure Code are frustrated by holding that in a suit under S. 539 C. P. C. or S. 14 of the Pagoda Act strangers though in possession of the trust property and though interested in the subject-matter in dispute are not proper parties in the sense that they cannot be made parties. When the question is whether an alienation is wrongful and whether a trustee is removable from his office for misconduct the question of the validity of the alienation is necessarily in issue and there is no use of an adjudication which does not bind the alienee. The same is the case with reference to persons in wrongful possession of trust property as trespassers but asserting a claim of right. There is no

---

1. *Augustine* v. *Medlycott*, (1892) I. L. R., 15 M. 241.

2. *Lakshmandas Parashram* v. *Ganpatrav Krishna*, (1884) I. L. R., 8 B. 365; *Shri Dhundiraj Ganesh Dev* v. *Ganesh*, (1893) I. L. R., 18 B. 721 ; *Sheoratan Kunwari* v. *Ram Pargash*, (1896) I. L. R., 18 A 227 (*quaere*, whether this point was really before the court) ; *Huseni Begam* v. *The Collector of Moradabad*, (1897) I. L. R., 20 A. 46 ; and per *Ranade*, J. in *Kazi Hassan* v. *Sagun Balkrishna*, (1899) I. L. R., 24 B. 170 (181).

3. *Vishvanath Govind Deshmane* v. *Rambhat*, (1890) I. L. R., 15 B. 148 ; *Augustine* v. *Medlycott*, (1892) I. L. R., 15 M. 241 ; *Strinivasa Ayyangar* v. *Strinivasa Swami*, (1892) I.L. R., 16 M. 31 ; *Shri Dhundiraj Ganesh Dev* v. *Ganesh*, (1893) I. L. R., 18 B. 721 ; *Muhammad Abdullah Khan* v. *Kallu*, (1899) I. L. R., 21 A. 187.

4. *Sajedur Raja Chowdhri* v. *Gour Mohundas Vishnav*, (1897) I. L. R., 24. C. 418.

5. *Vishvanath Govind Deshmane* v. *Rambhat*, (1890) I. L. R., 15 B. 148.

6. *Kishore Bon Mohunt* v. *Kalee Churn Giree*, (1874) 22 W. R. C. R. 364.

use of an adjudication against the trustee when it does not bind the trespasser. The adjudication does not bind the alienee or trespasser when he is not made a party and cannot be made a party in a suit under S. 539. So that S. 539 C. P. C., and S. 14 of the Pagoda Act are not of much use when it is essential to recover property for the trust from alienees or strangers. So far as S. 539 is concerned there can be no objection upon the score of the inquiry under the section being summary. All available evidence may be given and in fact the trial has been protracted in many cases.[1] No such objection can also be raised to the trial of a suit under S. 14. The objection that the Act contains a provision for compulsory reference if regarded as weighty may be easily removed by enacting that S. 16 so far as it provides for a compulsory reference will not apply to suits in which the alienees or persons in possession who may be strangers are parties. In *Sivayya* v. *Rami Reddi*[2] *Shephard*, J. while holding that the Section did not apply to stangers observed : " With the view to obviating further litigation it is clearly expedient that they (alienees) should be joined and that the property should be recovered from them in the same suit. "

Reliefs—Appointmen of new managers—Scheme.

Then with regard to the reliefs claimable and awardable under the Section the trend of decicions is to limit the reliefs claimable and awardable to the three matters mentioned in the section viz,(1) directing that any specific act should be done by the trustee, &c. (2) awarding damages and (3) directing removal of trustee, &c. But it is impossible to suppose that a suit under S. 14 should only be confined to the three matters specified above. Hence it has been held that a suit for a declaration is maintainable under the section and that a declaration that the properties are endowed may be granted under the section[3]. But courts have held that a prayer for appointment of new trustees or managers[4] or one for scheme[5] cannot be asked in a suit under S. 14 and that such reliefs cannot be awarded[6]. But the Allahabad High Court has held[7] that a prayer for appointment of new trustees, &c. may be asked under S. 14. Here,

1. *Manohar Ganesh Tambekar* v. *Lakhmiram Govindram*, (1887) I. L. R., 12 B. 247.
2. (1899) I. L. R., 22 M. 223 at p. 227.
3. Notes to S. 14, under heading (6) pp. 111 and 112.
4. Notes to S. 14, under heading (6) pp. 116 and 117.
5. Notes to S. 14, under heading (6) pp. 109 and 110.
6. I have tried to show that these reliefs are properly claimable under S. 14. See pp. 109 to 111, 116, 117. But if the courts hold differently they must be set right by the Legislature.
7. *Sheoratan Kunwari* v. *Ram Pargash*, (1896) I. L. R., 18 A. 227.

therefore, is an occasion for the interference of the Legislature. Even if the Allahabad High Court is wrong and may hereafter be induced to hold differently there is a case for such interference. It is doubtful whether a prayer for declaration merely is maintainable under S. 539, C. P. C.[1] But a prayer for the appointment of new trustees &c., and a prayer for scheme may be asked under S. 539, C. P. C. If the decisions of the courts are correct, there is no reason assigned by the Legislature why a suit under S. 14 should not comprise these reliefs when under the cognate Section (539, C. P. C.) they are expressly provided for. One consequence of this is that a party is driven to a second suit for obtaining reliefs not claimable under S. 14 of Act XX. No doubt if a party has obtained the sanction of the Collector under S. 539, C. P. C., he may bring *one* suit under S. 14 of the Pagoda Act and S. 539, C. P. C.[2] To bring such suit, a party must apply for sanction to the Civil Court under S. 18 of the Pagoda Act and to the Collector under S. 539, C. P. C. He cannot simply apply to the Collector for sanction for the appointment of new trustees because there are trustees already existing and without removing them there can be no appointment of new trustees. So that he must apply to the Collector for some of the very reliefs for which he has to apply for sanction under S. 18, together with the additional reliefs obtainable only under S. 539, C. P. C. According to the construction placed by the Madras High Court upon S. 539, C.P.C., it is not enough if he obtains sanction under that section He has necessarily to apply for sanction under S. 18 of the Act if he wants to remove the trustee in a hostile suit and certainly no trustee says that he is guilty of misconduct and, therefore, may be removed. It is rather difficult to comprehend why a party who is acting in the interests of the trust (which is necessarily unable to protect itself) should thus be compelled to take this circuitous method of attaining his object. Even then, the Collector may come in his way. The Collector is justly entitled to say that he is not justified in granting sanction if the trustee or manager objects as the Madras High Court has held that under such circumstances S. 539, C. P. C., has no application. So that there is not merely the possibility but also the probability of a plaintiff under S. 14 of the Act being necessarily compelled to bring

---

1. *Jamal-uddin* v. *Mujtaba Husain*, (1903) I. L. R., 25 A. 631.
2. *Narayana Ayyar* v. *Kumarasami Mudaliar*, (1897) I. L. R., 23 M. 537.

another suit for appointment of new trustees. If the object is to compel a plaintiff to be driven to two suits that object has been attained at considerable injury to the trust. But surely that is not the object of the Legislature and it is unfortunate that the Legislature has still not taken effective steps to to get the law amended in the interests of these institutions. A provision may be usefully introduced in Act XX that a person who is removed under S. 14, is not entitled to be appointed. Such a provision is to be found in Coorg Regulation S. 18 which otherwise follows S. 14 (as regards suits against committee and manager). This is very necessary where the rules framed by the Local Government enact nothing about the qualifications of the members to be elected or appointed. Provision may also be made that the Civil Judge should ordinarily direct that in cases where he removes a committee member the committee should hold an election for appointing a new member within a given period of time and that the name of the person elected should be reported to him and that in default he will on the application of the plaintiff appoint a member himself. In cases where the Civil judge removes a manager of an institution under S. 3, he may direct that the committee should appoint and report as aforesaid and that in default ho will appoint one on plaintiff's application. Where the manager of an institution under S. 4 is removed, the Civil Judge may be empowered to appoint the next heir or the next in succession or to direct that the person entitled should appoint and report as aforesaid failing which he may himself be empowered to appoint somebody.

I have not considered the question of the propriety of extending the provisions of the Act to private religious endowments as objections may exist to persons having the bare interest under S. 15 being allowed to bring suits and as we have got very few endowments of that nature in the Madras Presidency.[1] In Bengal where we meet with most endowments of this kind we do not think there is any agitation about the necessity of legislation of this kind for private endowments. In considering the question regard must be had to the fact that the consensus of the whole family interested in the endowment may put an end to the endowment and divert it altogether.

If any doubt should still exist as to the necessity for legislation the Government may take some important temples and mosques

---

1. There are some private endowments in Malabar. *Nilakandan* v. *Padmanabha*, 1890) I. L. R., 14 M. 158 (161).

such as the ones at Tripati &c., on hand and pass an Act with reference to some of them seperately. Any Act dealing with such institutions will provide for the framing of a scheme for the administration of the said institutions and endowments and if the experiment should meet with success it may be extended to other institutions. This is also one way of testing whether the proposed new provisions will have the desired effect of safe-guarding the interests of these institutions.

Court Fees. Before closing we have to consider two matters. The first relates to the subject of Court Fees. Suits against trustees prescribed by S. 14 of Act XX or S. 539, C. P. C being suits relating to public trusts ought not to be taxed in the same way as suits in which only private interests are involved and ought not to be treated in the same way as other suits by ordinary litigants. Mr. Eliott in his report to the Government of India, (1st March 1845) states that in England in suits instituted by the Attorney General or with his sanction the proceedings are exempted from stamp duty[1]. It is regrettable that this suggestion has not been adopted. It cannot be reasonably objected that the exemption will promote vexatious suits. The necessity for sanction (either of the Civil Court or of the Advocate General or the Collector) will be an effective check against such vexatious suits and so it has been regarded in England. Even if the necessity for a court fee is felt a uniform fee of Rs. 10 in all cases with an exemption as to all fees for processes in the suit will satisfy the purpose. No *advalorem* fee ought to be levied upon the property sought to be recovered.

Costs. The next matter is with reference to costs. The provision in S. 18 as to award of costs out of the trust funds must be extended to a greater class of cases so that the provision may accord with the ordinary rule on the subject. A person who is successful in a suit instituted under S. 14 must ordinarily get his costs out of the trust funds. No doubt the misconducting trustee or manager who is removed or who is retained on terms must be primarily liable. But if costs are irrecoverable from such trustee the person instrumental in getting him removed or in preventing maladministration must not be held disentitled to recover costs out of trust funds. Otherwise it will be punishing him with a vengeance for his instrumentality in putting the administration of the trust on a better footing.

1. Paliamentary Return 1849, p. 409 at p. 417. See also Tudor, pp. 359, 360.

COMMENTARIES

ON

ACT XX OF 1863.

THE RELIGIOUS ENDOWMENTS ACT.

ACT No. XX OF 1863.

PASSED BY THE GOVERNOR-GENERAL OF INDIA IN COUNCIL.

(Received the assent of the Governor-General on the 10th March 1863.)

An Act to enable the Government to divest itself of the management of Religious Endowments.

Preamble.

WHEREAS it is expedient to relieve the Boards of Revenue, and the Local Agents, in the Presidency of Fort William in Bengal, and the Presidency of Fort Saint George, from the duties imposed on them by Regulation XIX, 1810, of the Bengal Code *(for the due appropriation of the rents and produce of lands granted for the support of mosques, Hindoo temples, colleges and other purposes; for the maintenance and repair of bridges, serays, kuttras, and other public buildings; and for the custody and disposal of Nuzzal property or escheats)* and Regulation VII, 1817, of the Madras Code *(for the due appropriation of the rents and produce of lands granted for the support of mosques, Hindoo temples, and colleges or other public purposes; for the maintenance and repair of bridges, choultries, or chuttrums, and other public buildings; and for the custody and disposal of escheats)*, so far as those duties embrace the superintendence of lands granted for the support of mosques or Hindoo temples, and for other religious uses; the appropriation of endowments made for the maintenance of such religious establishments; the repair and preservation of buildings connected therewith, and the appointment of trustees or managers thereof; or involve any connexion with the management of such religious establishments :[and whereas it is expedient for that purpose to repeal so much of Regulation XIX, 1810, of the Bengal Code, and Regulation VII, 1817, of the Madras Code, as relate to endowments for the support of mosques, Hindoo temples, or other religious purposes,[a]] it is enacted as follows :—

NOTES.

Preamble: How far an aid in construction:—It is a rule of construction that where the words of a statute are plain and unambiguous, effect must be given to the same though such construction may run counter to the intention expressed in the preamble. The preamble ought not to be looked at to control the general language used in the section where the words are clear and capable of no ambiguity. But if the words are ambiguous, then the preamble may be looked at in order to arrive at a correct construction of the section[1]. "The function of the preamble is to explain what is ambiguous in the enactment and it may either restrain or extend it as best suits the intention[2]."

The preamble cannot either restrict or extend the enacting part, when the language, the object and scope of the Act are not open to doubt. Mr. Maxwell says: "The preamble is often no more than a recital of some of the inconveniences, and does not exclude any others for which a remedy is given by the Statute. The evil recited is but the motive for legislation; the remedy may both consistently and wisely be extended beyond the cure of that evil; and if on a review of the whole Act a wider intention than that expressed in the preamble appears to be the real one, effect is to be given to it notwithstanding the less extensive import of the preamble. So where the preamble is found more extensive than the enacting part, it is equally inefficacious to control the effect of the latter, when otherwise free from doubt."

---

1. *Vide* Maxwell on the Interpretation of Statutes, pages 59 to 71, and Dwarris on Statutes, p. 655. See also *Attorney-General* v. *Brodie* (1846), 4 M. I. A. 190; *Oolagappa Chetty* v. *Hon. D. Arbuthnot*, (1873-4) L. R. 1 I. A. 268 : S. C. 14 B. L. R. 268; *Omrao Begum* v. *Government of India*, (1882) L. R. 10 I. A. 39 : S. C. I. L. R. 9 C. 704; and *Vithu* v. *Govinda*, (1896) I. L. R., 22 B. 321 (F. B.).

2. Maxwell, p. 71.

a. **The words in closed brackets have been repealed by Act XVI of 1874.**

So it has been held under section 14 that though the words of that section are general and may apply alike to a trustee of a private and public trust, yet looking at the preamble and the whole scope of the Act, the section has no application to the case of a private trust but to a trust to which the old Regulations applied, *viz.*, a public trust[1].

Preamble given effect to: Cases.

In *Jan Ali* v. *Ram Nath Mundul*[2], the Calcutta High Court, in arriving at the conclusion that Ss. 3, 4, 5, 6, 13 and 14 of the Act only applied when the temple, mosque, or other religious establishment was one to which the provisions of the old Regulations applied, *viz.*, when the temple, &c., was one for the support of which endowments had been granted in land by the preceding Governments of this country and by individuals, referred among other matters to the preamble of the Act and to the preamble of the old Regulations as an aid in construing the said sections. The decision in this case as regards S. 13 is, however, it is submitted, erroneous. For the present it may be noted here that the Madras High Court in *Ramiengar* v. *Gnanasambanda Pandara Sannada*[3], arrived at a construction different from that of the Calcutta Court in the above case, and held that the same construction ought not to be placed upon S. 13 as upon S. 14 and that S. 13 did not apply to a trustee under S. 4. (See also notes on Ss. 13 and 14).

In *Jusagheri Gosamiar* v. *The Collector of Tanjore*[4], the Madras High Court held that, though the wording of S. 4 of the Act, by itself referred to the case of a trustee who had, at the time of the passing of the Act, the personal management of the temple, mosque, or other religious establishment, yet looking at the whole scope and purpose of the Act (as declared in the preamble) it applied to the case of all independent trustees and that, therefore, the Government could not refuse to transfer the land to a person who was lawfully entitled as a trustee, and whose nomination to such office was independent of Government and that the latter must surrender possession of the land to such trustee.

1. *Delroos Banoo Begum* v. *Nawab Syud Ashgur Ally Khan*, (1875) 15 B. L. R., 167: S. C. 23 W. R.. 453—aff'd. on appeal to P. C. in, (1877) I. L. R., 3 C. 324; *Dhurrum Singh* v. *Kissen Singh*, (1881) I. L. R, 7. C. 767; *Sathappayyar* v. *Periasami*, (1890) I. L. R., 14 M. 1. See also notes to S. 14.

2. (1881) I. L. R., 8 C. 32. 3. (1867) 5 M. H. C. 53. 4. (1870) 5 M. H. C. 334.

Section given effect to: Case.

In *Ittuni Panikkar* v. *Irani Nambudripad*[1], however, the Madras High Court gave effect only to the plain language of S. 5 and held that the section was inapplicable to a case where the Board of Revenue did not take up the management of a temple, mosque, or other religious establishment and did not transfer the land to any trustee of such temple, mosque, or religious establishment, though the intention of the legislature as disclosed by the preamble and other parts of the Act might have been otherwise.

The preamble mentions several duties from which it was intended that the Board and Local Agents should be divested[2]. But it could hardly be supposed that such description of duties was intended to be exhaustive. The duties mentioned are the following:—

(1) The *superintendence of lands* granted for the support of mosques, Hindu temples, and for other religious uses.

(2) The *appropriation* of endowments made for the maintenance of such religious establishments.

(3) The *repair and preservation of buildings* connected therewith.

(4) The *appointment of trustees* or managers thereof.

(5) Duties involving any *connection with the management* of such religious establishments.

'*Local Agents*' are the Collectors and other officers of Government who had the superintendence and management of religious endowments.

'*Mosques*' represent Mahomedan religious institutions.

'*Hindoo temples*'. The word 'Hindoo' is here used in a wider sense. It is not limited only to persons who are governed by Hindoo Law. (See Introduction, pp. 13, 14 and 15).

'*Religious use.*' 'Religious' must be distinguished from 'charitable.' In England a *charitable purpose* includes a *religious purpose*. But in India in many enactments a distinction is drawn between a *charitable purpose* and a *religious purpose*. So that, a

1. (1881) I. L. R., 3 M. 401.

2. Vide *Chinna Rangaiyangar* v. *Subbraya Mudali*, (1867) 3 M. H. C. 334.

charitable purpose does not include a *religious purpose*. In S. 539 of the Civil Procedure Code of 1877 (Act X of 77), the words used were "trusts created for public charitable purposes" and it was held that the section had no application to trusts for religious purposes nor to trusts for a charitable and religious purpose[1]. It was to remedy this defect that the legislature in the code of 1882 added the words "or religious purposes" in S. 539 so as to include "trusts created for public, charitable, or religious purposes."

In the Religious Endowments Act also, a distinction is drawn between trusts for a religious purpose and trusts for a charitable purpose. It was only with reference to the former, the Act was passed. The express object of the Act was to relieve the Board of Revenue from the duty of superintending over religious endowments[2]. But the duty of superintending over charitable endowments imposed on the Board of Revenue by the old Regulations is still retained and, in fact, express care is taken in the Act to declare that this duty over charitable endowments is not intended to be affected, or interfered with (see Ss. 21 and 23 of the Act).

'*Religious use*' is also to be distinguished in England from a 'superstitious use.' See Introduction, Ch. VI.

'*Endowments*.' See for them eaning of this term, Introduction, pp. 11 and 12.

'*Such religious establishments*,' *i. e.*, mosques, Hindu temples, &c. For the meaning of the term 'religious establishment,' see Indroduction, p. 12.

Government control :—The duties of superintendence and the proper appropriation of the endowments of Hindu and Mahomedan temples and religious establishments, of the preservation of the structures of such temples and establishments and of the management of their affairs, through trustees or managers, were, without doubt, exercised by the officers of the Local Government indis-

---

1. *Radhabai* v. *Chimnaji*, (1878) I. L. R., 3 B. 27; *Karuppa* v. *Arumuga*, (1882) I. L. R., 5 M. 383; and *Thackersey Dewraj* v. *Hurbhum Nursey*, (1884) I. L. R., 8 B. 432 at pp. 450 and 451.

2. See cases cited in the notes to S. 1, pp. 7 and 8 *post*.

criminately, and in 1817 the general management of all endowments of religious establishments in this Presidency, as also the duty of seeing that the trustees or managers of such establishments were properly qualified and duly appointed, were made, without exception, a legal obligation on the Board of Revenue and their local agents by Madras Regulation VII of 1817[1]. This obligation was previously created in Bengal by Regulation XIX of 1810. Prior to Act XX of 1863, the Government exercised control over both the classes of religious institutions referred to in Ss. 3 and 4 of the Act, and the recitals and enactments of the said Act would show that the two classes of temples and religious establishments described in Ss. 3 and 4 and the property belonging thereto were, at the time of its passing, alike subject to the control of the Board of Revenue and their local agents, in the performance of all the above duties[2]. It was the very purpose of the Act to provide differently for the future exercise of such duties, according as the nomination of the trustee, manager, or superintendent of each temple or religious establishment had or had not been ascertained to be a right possessed independently of the Government[3].

Reasons for the passing of the Act :—The Government, it appears, became, in 1841, strongly influenced by conscientious, moral, and religious scruples, and considering that they were at liberty in their executive capacity to divest themselves of the duties and responsibilities imposed by law in connexion with Hindu and Mahomedan religious establishments, they called for a report from the Collectors of all the Districts with a view of carrying out their determination that all duties and trusts excepting the management of the lands attached thereto should be left finally and completely in the hands of properly qualified individuals[1].

The report of the Collector of Tanjore "deals with the temples in the Tanjore District in classes and provides for the appointment of respectable panchayets to superintend the affairs of the temples in each class with the exception of the class in which the Kumba pagoda appears as one of the ten pagodas attached to

1. *Ramiengar* v. *Gnana Sambanda Pandara Sannada*, (1867) 5 M. H. C. 53.

2. *Ramiengar* v. *Gnana Sambanda*, supra; and *Seshadri Ayyangar* v. *Nataraja Ayyar*, (1898) I. L. R., 21 M. 179 (F. B.). For Bombay see Reg. XVIII of 1827, S. 38, and *Mathura Naikan* v. *Esu*, (1880) I. L. R., 5 B. 545 (553, 554).

3. *Ramiengar* v. *Gnana Sambanda*, supra; *Fakruddin Sahib* v. *Ackeni Sahib*, (1880) I. L. R., 2 M. 197; *Kalianasundaram Ayyar* v. *Umamba Bayi Saheb*, (1897) I. L. R., 20 M. 421; and *Seshadri Ayyangar* v. *Nataraja Ayyar*, supra.

Dharmapuram mutt. This class containing in all 17 pagodas is described, as distinguished from the rest, as 'authinam,' that is, the right of appointing the local managers of which belongs to certain muttams or colleges of Tambirans, and 'this right has been respected during their superintendence by the Government officers and its complete acknowledgment by abstaining from all interference is all that is required.' These provisions, it is agreed, were approved of by the Board of Revenue and had operation given to them in 1842"[1].

The Government of India became anxious[2] to divest itself and its officers of the charge of religious endowments and the lands under its management and was apparently better advised subsequently, and in order that the Government might legally carry out its object[3] enacted Act XX of 1863 by which all duties and trusts including the management of lands attached thereto were transferred from the Government to the Committee if the institution fell under S. 3 or to the trustee if the institution fell under S. 4 of Act XX of 1863[4].

Regulations repealed.

[I. *So much of Regulation XIX,* 1810 *of the Bengal Code, and so much of Regulation VII,* 1817 *of the Madras Code, as relates to endowments for the support of mosques, Hindu temples, or other religious purposes, are repealed*[a].]

NOTES.

Effect of Act :—The effect of this provision is to repeal Regulations XIX of 1810 and VII of 1817 in so far as they relate to *endowments* for the support of mosques, Hindu temples, or other

---

a. Repealed by the Repealing Act XIV of 1870.

1. *Ramiengar* v. *Gnana Sambanda Pandara Sannadu*, (1867) 5 M. H. C. 53.

2. *Kalianasundaram Ayyar* v. *Umamba Bayi Saheb*, (1897) I. L. R., 20 M. 421.

3. *Jan Ali* v. *Ram Nath Mundul*, (1881) I. L. R., 8 C. 32. See for Bombay, Act VII of 1863.

4. *Bibee Kuneez Fatima* v. *Bibee Saheba Jan*, (1867) 8 W. R. 313; *Shaikh Laul Mahomed* v. *Lalla Brij Kishore*, (1872) 17 W. R. 430; *Jusagheri Gosamiar* v. *The Collector of Tanjore*, (1870) 5 M. H. C. 334; *Khajah Ashruf Hossein* v. *Mussamut Hazara Begum*, (1872) 18 W. R. 396; *Fakurudin Sahib* v. *Ackeni Sahib*, (1880) I. L. R., 2 M. 197; *Jan Ali* v. *Ram Nath Mundul*, supra; *Dhurrum Singh* v. *Kissen Singh*, (1881) I. L. R., 7 C. 767; *Kalianasundaram Ayyar* v. *Umamba Bayi Saheb*, supra; and *Seshadri Ayyangar* v. *Nataraja Ayyar*, (1898) I. L. R., 21 M. 179 (F. B.).

religious purposes[1] and to relieve the Board of Revenue and local agents from the duties imposed on them by the Regulations[2] so that the Government has divested[3] itself of direct responsibility for the superintendence of religious institutions and all the powers relating to the superintendence and management of religious establishments vested by the Regulations in the Board of Revenue and the Collectors throughout the country have been completely determined[4]. But the Act provides otherwise for the management of religious endowments[5] and also provides a machinery by which the rights and powers of trustees in reference to religious endowments may be ascertained[6].

The duties imposed by the Regulations with reference to such endowments on Government not only do not exist now but S. 22 actually declares the exercise and undertaking of such duties on the part of Government or any of its officers in their official capacity as unlawful[7].

The connection of Government in its executive capacity with Hindu and Mahomedan foundations was brought to an end for Bombay by Act VII of 1863 and for Bengal and Madras by

1. *Shaikh Laul Mahomed* v. *Lalla Brij Kishore*, (1872) 17 W. R. 430; *Delroos Banoo Begum* v. *Nawab Synd Ashgur Ally Khan*, (1875) 15 B. L. R. 167 : S. C. 23 W. R. 453; and *Mahomed* v. *Ganapati*, (1889) I. L. R., 13 M. 277.

2. *Chinna Rangaiyangar* v. *Subbraya Mudali*, (1867) 3 M. H. C. 334; *Bibee Kuneez Fatima* v. *Bibee Saheba Jan*, (1867) 8 W. R. 313; *Delroos Banoo Begum* v. *Nawab Syud Ashgur Ally Khan*, supra; *Fakurudin Sahib* v. *Ackeni Sahib*, (1880) I. L. R., 2 M. 197; *Dhurrum Singh* v. *Kissen Singh*, (1881) I. L. R., 7 C. 767; *Behari Lal* v. *Muhammad Muttaki*, (1898) I. L. R., 20 A. 482 (F. B.).

3. *Shaikh Laul Mahomed* v. *Lalla Brij Kishore*, supra; *Jan Ali* v. *Ram Nath Mundul*, (1881) I. L. R., 8 C. 32; *Gnana Sambanda Pandara Sannadhi* v. *Velu Pandaram*, (1899) I. L. R., 23 M. 271 : S. C. L. R. 27 I. A. 69.

4. *Jusagheri Gosamiar* v. *The Collector of Tanjore*, (1870) 5 M. H. C. 334; *Bibee Kuneez Fatima* v. *Bibee Saheba Jan*, supra; and *Dhurrum Singh* v. *Kissen Singh*, supra.

5. *Shaikh Laul Mahomed* v. *Lalla Brij Kishore*, supra; *Sabapathi* v. *Subraya*, (1878) I. L. R., 2 M. 58; and *Wajid Ali Shah* v. *Dianat-ul-lah Beg*, (1885) I. L. R., 8 A. 31.

6. *Wajid Ali Shah* v. *Dianat-ul-lah Beg*, supra.

7. Vide *Jusagheri Gosamiar* v. *The Collector of Tanjore*, supra; and *Mahomed* v. *Ganapati*, (1889) I. L. R., 13 M. 277.

Act XX of 63[1]. Mere neglect of Government to appoint a committee under S. 7 is no ground for thinking that the Board may be deemed to be still invested with the powers and duties attached to it under the Regulation[2].

Applicability of the Act:—The Act relates to temple or religious endowments and is in force in all Presidencies except Bombay and even in the latter Presidency, it is in force in North Canara[3]. But the provisions of S. 22 of the Act are apparently applicable also to all parts of the Bombay Presidency[3].

Act XI of 1852 and Act II of 1863 apply to religious endowments in some parts of Bombay (Dekhan, Khandesh, Southern Mahratta country, &c.), while Act VII of 1863 applies to religious endowments in some other parts of Bombay (Broach and Surat)[4].

Operation of Criminal Law:—The ordinary Criminal Law is not excluded by the Act (or by the Regulations). Permission of the committee (or of the Board) is not required for prosecuting a trustee appointed by the committee for criminal breach of trust[5].

Operation of Act in the Presidency Towns:—A question arises whether the Act is applicable to the Presidency Towns. It was mooted but not decided in *Sabapathi* v. *Subraya*[6]. The question was decided in the affirmative by *Norman*, J., in *Ganes Singh* v. *Ram Gopal*[7] and his decision was followed by *Kennedy*, J., in the *Panch Cowrie Mull* case[8]; but on appeal from his decision, the Division Bench took a contrary view and held that the Act did not apply to the Presidency Towns[8]. The ground of decision in the Division Bench was that it was not in the contemplation of the legislature to interfere with the procedure of the Supreme Courts in reference to charitable and religious trusts, that the charity properties and religious endowments in the Presidency Towns could not

1. *Mathura* v. *Esu*, (1880) I. L. R., 5 B. at 554; *Manohar Ganesh Tambekar* v. *Lakhmiram*, (1887) I. L. R., 12 B. 247.
2. *Mahomed* v. *Ganapati*, (1889) I. L. R., 13 M. 277.
3. *Sayad Husseinmian Dadumian* v. *The Collector of Kaira*, (1895) I. L. R., 21 B. 48.
4. *Krishnarav Ganesh* v. *Rangrav*, (1867) 4 B. H. C. (A. C. J.) 1.
5. Proceedings of the High Court, dated 22nd February 1876, I. L. R., 1 M. 55.
6. (1878) I. L. R., 2 M. 58.
7. (1870) 5 B. L. R., App. 55.
8. *Panch Cowrie Mull* v. *Chumroo Lall*, (1878) I. L. R., 3 C. 563. See also *Kalee Churn Giri* v. *Golabi*, (1878) 2 C.L.R., 128 following the above case.

come under the direct control of Government and that this jurisdiction of the Supreme Courts was inherited by the High Courts. This ground, however, is not decisive for we know that the old Regulations relating to stamp laws were not applicable to the Supreme Courts and yet the Stamp Act which repealed the earlier Regulations applied and the present Stamp Act applies to the High Court. Act XX of 1863 is general in its terms, and the mere fact that the old Regulations did not apply would not be of itself decisive to show that the Act did not apply to the High Court. Notwithstanding this, the Madras High Court held in two recent cases that the Act did not apply to the Presidency Towns[1].

The Calcutta High Court has pointed out the desirability of extending the Act (or at least some sections of it) to the Presidency Towns[2].

Procurator of Government:—Since the passing of the Act, the manager of a religious endowment cannot be a procurator of Government[3] as he was held to be before the Act[4]. A suit by such manager cannot after the Act be regarded as a suit on behalf of Government and the rules of limitation applying to private persons will apply[5].

Repealing Act:—The effect of repealing the section is not to alter the law above laid down. As it was thought that the operation of the section was spent, Act XIV of 1870 was passed repealing it.

Applicability of Act to Private Religious Endowments:—If an institution or religious establishment is not public, but is the private property of an individual, or if the trust is a private trust, the Act has no application[6]. The question in such cases is whether any particular person or body has the right to control the worship and prevent the public from attending the worship. Such is the

---

1. *Srinivasa Appangar* v. *Raghavachariar*, (1896) 6 M. L. J., 239; *Annasami Pillai* v. *Ramakrishna Mudaliar*, (1900) I. L. R., 24 M. 219. See also notes to S. 14.

2. *Panch Cowrie Mull* v. *Chumroo Lall*, (1878) I. L. R., 3 C. 563 followed in *Kalee Churn Giri* v. *Golabi*, (1878) 2 C. L. R., 128.

3. Per *Banerji*, J., in *Behari Lal* v. *Muhammad Muttaki*, (1899) I. L. R., 20 A. 482 (F. B.)

4. *Jewun Doss Sahoo* v. *Shah-Kubeer-Ood-deen*, (1841) 2 M.I.A. 390; *Shaikh Laul Mahomed* v. *Lalla Brij Kishore*, (1872) 17 W. R. C. R. 430.

5. *Shaikh Laul Mahomed* v. *Lalla Brij Kishore*, supra; *Behari Lal* v. *Muhammad Muttaki*, supra, dissenting from *Piran* v. *Abdool Karim*, (1891) I. L. R., 19 C. 203.

6. *Bibee Kuneez Fatima* v. *Bibee Saheba Jan*, (1867) 8 W. R. C. R. 313; *Delroos Banoo Begum* v. *Ashgar Ally*, (1875) 15 B. L. R., 167 affirmed by P. C. in (1877), I. L. R., 3 C. 324; *Sathappayyar* v. *Periasami*, (1890) I. L. R., 14 M. 1.

case where a Hindu family endows property to the family god. On this principle it has been held by the Calcutta High Court that Act XX of 1863 is not applicable to endowments in favor of ancestral family idols which are endowments not for public but private purposes[1]. The Act only applied to endowments to which the provisions of the Regulations XIX of 1810 and VII of 1817 were applicable[2] and those Regulations, as would appear from the preamble and S. 16, had application only to endowments for public purposes[3].

For the difference between a public and a private religious endowment and the tests for distinguishing these, see Introduction, Chs. VI and VII.

Number.

II. In this Act words importing the singular number shall include the plural, and words importing the plural number shall include the singular.

Gender.

Words importing the masculine gender shall include females.

"Civil Court," and "Court."

The words "Civil Court" and "Court" shall mean the Principal Court of Original Civil Jurisdiction in the District in which the mosque, temple, or religious establishment is situate, relating to which, or to the endowment whereof, any suit shall be instituted or application made under the provisions of this Act.

NOTES.

This is the "Interpretation" clause. 'Civil Court' and 'Court' represent what now is the District Court.

Local Government to make special provision respecting Mosques, &c., in certain cases.

III. In the case of every mosque, temple, or other religious establishment to which the provisions of either of the Regulations specified in *the preamble to this Act*[a] are applicable, and the nomination of

---

a. Substituted for the words "sec. 1" by Act XII of 1891.

1. *Protapchandra Misser* v. *Brojonath Misser*, (1891) I. L. R., 19 C. 275. See also cases cited under S. 14.

2. *Jan Ali* v. *Ram Nath Mundul*, (1881) I. L. R., 8 C. 32.

3. *Sathappayyar* v. *Periasami*, (1890) I. L. R., 14 M. 1.

the trustee, manager, or superintendent whereof, at the time of the passing of this Act, is vested in, or may be exercised by, the Government, or any public officer, or in which the nomination of such trustee, manager, or superintendent shall be subject to the confirmation of the Government, or any public officer, the local Government shall, as soon as possible after the passing of this Act, make special provision as hereinafter provided[a].

NOTES.

Requisites of S. 3 :—The applicability of this section depends on two conditions or requisites[1] :—

(1) That the mosque, Hindu temple or other religious institution must be one to which the provisions of the Regulations were applicable, *i. e.*, it must be a public religious institution[2].

(2) The manager, trustee or superintendent of such institution must be one *(a)* whose nomination is, at the time of the passing of this Act, *vested in* or *may be* exercised by Government or any public officer, or (*b*) whose nomination is subject to the confirmation of Government or any public officer[3].

In such a case the Local Government has to make special provision as provided in Ss. 7 to 12[4], *i. e.*, the Local Government has to appoint District Committees, and the duties of the Board of

---

a. *i. e.*, Ss. 7 to 12. *See* note (4).

1. *Dhurrum Singh* v. *Kissen Singh*, (1881) I. L. R., 7 C. 767.; and *Jan Ali* v. *Ram Nath Mundul*, (1881) I. L. R., 8 C. 32.

2. *Bibee Kuneez Fatima* v. *Bibee Saheba Jan*, (1867) 8 W. R. C. R. 313; *Hajee Kalub Hossein* v. *Mussumut Mehrum Beebee*, (1872) 4 N. W. P. 155; *Sathappayyar* v. *Periasami*, (1890) I. L. R., 14 M. 1. See also cases cited in S. 14.

3. *Agri Sharma Embrandri* v. *Vistnu Embrandri*, (1866) 3 M. H. C. 198; *Ramiengar* v. *Gnana Sambanda Pandara Sunnada*, (1867) 5 M. H. C. 53; *Jusagheri Gosamiar* v. *The Collector of Tanjore*, (1870) 5 M. H. C. 334; *L. Venkatesa Nayudu* v. *Shrivan Shatagopa Shri Shatagopaswami*, (1870) 7 M. H. C. 77; *Hajee Kalub Hossein* v. *Mussumat Mehrum Beebee*, supra; *Khajah Ashruf Hossein* v. *Mussamut Hazara Begum*, (1872) 18 W. R. C. R. 396; *Fakurudin Sahib* v. *Ackeni Sahib*, (1880) I. L. R., 2 M. 197; *Jan Ali* v. *Ram Nath Mundul*, supra; *Appasami* v. *Nagappa*, (1884) I.L.R., 7 M. 499; and *Ponduranga* v. *Nagappa*, (1889) I. L. R., 12 M. 366.

4. *Jan Ali* v. *Ram Nath Mundul*, supra. The reference to S. 4 and Ss. 4 and 7 in *Khajah Ashruf Hossein* v. *Mussamut Hazara Begum* supra, and *Delroos Banoo* v. *Ashgar Ally*, (1875) 15 B. L. R. 167 is an obvious oversight.

Revenue are with certain reservations transferred to such committees[1]; so that the committees may in such cases be said to take the place of the Board of Revenue[1]. Should the mosque, Hindu temple or other religious institution be a public religious one, and the trustee, manager, or superintendent was not an independent one, *i. e.*, one whose nomination was vested in the Government or was under the control and approval of Government, then such trustee, &c., became after the Act, subject to the control and superintendence of the Temple District Committee, the members of which had the power to appoint or remove trustees of such institutions[2].

Second requisite explained.

The section says the nomination of the trustee, &c., should be vested at the time of the passing of this Act in the Government or any public officer, or the nomination might have been exercised by the Government or such officer, or the nomination should be subject to the confirmation of Government or such officer. Any one of the following conditions is therefore sufficient to comply with the terms of the section.

(1). The nomination must be vested in the Government or any public officer. Of course, as observed in *Ponduranga* v. *Nagappa*[3], it must be lawfully vested. The nomination would be lawfully vested :—

(*a*) where former Governments were vested with such power and this Government had been exercising it or might have exercised it;

(*b*) where the deed of endowment gave such power to Government[3];

(*c*) where the Government acquired such power by prescription notwithstanding it possessed no such power lawfully before. If the Government rightfully or wrongfully were to appoint trustees and exercise control over the nomination of trustees for over the statutory period, then the Government would lawfully have such rights vested in it; and

1. Vide *Chinna Rangaiyangar* v. *Subbraya Muduli*, (1867) 3 M. H. C. 334; *Jan Ali* v. *Ram Nath Mundul*, (1881) I. L. R., 8 C. 32.

2. *Dhurrum Singh* v. *Kissen Singh*, (1881) I. L. R., 7 C. 767.

3. (1889) I. L. R., 12 M. 366.

(*d*) where there was no provision about the appointment according to the original grant, and the trusteeship was not hereditary or by nomination by a private person, the Government under the Hindu Law and the Regulations would have the right to nominate.

With respect to (*a*), (*b*), and (*d*), the case of *Ponduranga* v. *Nagappa*[1], is authority. As regards (*c*), see *Balwant Rao* v. *Purun Mal*[2], *Gnana Sambanda Pandara Sannadhi* v. *Velu Pandaram*,[3] and *Annasami Pillai* v. *Ramakrishna Mudaliar*[4].

It is not necessary that the right should have been exercised where the Government had in fact such right, though the fact of non-exercise by the Government of the right of nomination might be some evidence that the Government did not possess such right[5] but would not be conclusive if the right could be established otherwise. In fact it must be admitted that in a large majority of instances, the Board of Revenue did not take charge of the land which had been granted by individuals for the support of mosques, &c.[6].

So that, under this section, though the Government may not have had the control under the Regulations if the trusteeship is not hereditary, and if the institution is one capable of coming under the Regulations[7] and the nomination is vested in the Government, then the control of such institution passes to the Temple Committee.

Can the Government divest itself of its right to nominate a trustee?

A question might arise whether the Government could legally divest itself of the right to nominate a trustee which it possessed under the Regulations, and of the duties of superintendence and management of religious establishments imposed on them by such Regulations. In *L. Venkatesa Nayudu* v. *Shrivan Shatagopa Shri Shatagopaswami*[8], *Holloway* and *Kindersley*, JJ., observed :

1. (1889) I. L. R., 12 M. 366. See also *Agri Sharma Embrandri* v. *Vistnu Embrandri*, (1866) 3 M. H. C. 198.
2. (1883) L. R., 10 I. A. 90 ; S. C. I. L. R., 6 A. 1.
3. (1899) I. L. R., 23 M. 271 ; S. C. L. R., 27 I. A. 69.
4. (1900) I. L. R., 24 M. 219.
5. *K. Venkatabalakrishna Chettyar* v. *Kaliyanaramaiyangar*, (1869) 5 M. H. C. 48 ; and *Delroos Banoo Begum* v. *Nawab Syud Ashgur Ally Khan*, (1875) 15 B. L. R., 167 ; S. C. 23 W. R., 453.
6. *Jan Ali* v. *Ram Nath Mundul*, (1881) I. L. R., 8 C. 32.
7. *Punch Cowrie Mull* v. *Chumroo Lall*, (1878) I. L. R., 3 C. 563.
8. (1872) 7 M. H. C. 77.

"We can see nothing in Regulation VII of 1817 to prevent them from renouncing that right if they chose." In support of this position the judges pointed out that "the scope of the Regulation is" only "the prevention of the misapplication of endowments and all its provisions are to be read with reference to that purpose." They then observed that S. 13 of the Regulation expressly supported their position for, according to their opinion, the section gave "the largest power of making any arrangement which the Board may consider best adapted to secure the purposes which the Regulation had in view, and in their letters the Board show that they conceived that this purpose would be best secured by vesting the management in the Jheer himself, instead of in persons elected from his disciples. They seem to have believed that his reputed piety and position would be the best security against embezzlement. It seems to us, that they had full power to act, and that the effect of their act was to vest in the Jheer for the time being the management of this institution." The above observations were made with reference to the report of the Collector of Chinglepat who recommended the transfer of certain temples in his district to various persons (and among them the Trivellore temple to the Jheer) and the withdrawal of all interference on the part of the Government officers upon such transfer, and the Board of Revenue accepted the report, and in 1842 did, so far as it could, divest itself of all right to interfere.

The above position was, however, doubted in a later case by the Madras High Court[1]. In that case their Lordships, *Turner*, C. J., and *Brandt*, J., observed: "With all deference to the opinion of the learned judges in *L. Venkatesa Nayudu* v. *Shri Shatagopaswami*[2], we doubt whether, so long as Regulation VII of 1817 subsisted, it was competent to the Government absolutely to divest itself of the obligations imposed on it by the Regulation. The Board might certainly have recognized, but it is doubtful whether they could have created, an hereditary trusteeship; the utmost that can be urged is, that it was competent to them to withdraw from the administration of the trust; they could not create an heritable title in others." A distinction was then pointed out between a case in which the Government, in assuming

1. *Appasami* v. *Nagappa*, (1884) I. L. R., 7 M. 499 (509).
2. (1872) 7 M. H. C. 77.

to make a permanent arrangement, respected rights they had already recognized and a case in which they purported to create a new right in derogation of the obligations imposed upon them by the Regulation. The position laid down in the above two cases must be taken with some qualification. In all cases of religious endowments, the intention of the founder as appearing from the deed of endowment or in its absence the usage of the institution as showing the index of the founder's intention is the governing principle. Where a certain rule should prevail, even the Government exercising sovereign rights of superintendence could not derogate from the rule. There could be no act of state in such a case. The Government might have the power to frame a scheme for the good management of the institution. But where persons had no vested rights, we do not think how the Government would violate any rule if they should create an hereditary trusteeship for the better management of the institution provided they did not give up their right (or duty) of superintendence under the Regulation. A grant of land burdened with a service but with a hereditary title in the donee (as for doing Archaka service) was the most common form of grant among the old Hindu Kings.

In the case of Fort Devastanams in Tanjore which were seized by an act of state from the Tanjore Raja it may be different. The Government being competent to deal with them in any way they pleased, chose to deal with them as if they belonged to the class of institutions governed by S. 4 and granted the management or trusteeship of the said Devastanams to Kamakshi Boyi Sahiba, the senior widow of the late Raja. There was no reservation of any reversionary right in the Government to make a new appointment[1]. Even here where any private rights had been recognized by Government, the latter could not by such grant affect those vested rights[2].

Or (2). The institution must be one whereof nomination of the trustee may be exercised by Government or any public officer, *i. e.*, may be exercised lawfully though not in fact[3].

Or (3). The nomination of the trustee should be subject to the confirmation of Government. This contemplates a case in which

1. *Kalianasundaram Ayyar v. Umamba Bayi Saheb*, (1897) I. L. R., 20 M. 421.
2. *Ramiengar v. Gnana Sambanda Pandara Sannada*, (1867) 5 M. H. C. 53.
3. *Ponduranga v. Nagappa*, (1889) I. L. R., 12 M. 366.

some other person may have the right to nominate a trustee, but the nomination does not become perfected or take effect unless the appointment or nomination is confirmed by Government.

Tests in considering whether an institution falls under S. 3 or 4 :—It is a question of fact whether a particular religious establishment falls within S. 3 or 4 of the Act. The test is to see whether the office of trustee, &c., is hereditary (or by nomination by a private person), or whether it is one subject to the nomination of the Board or Government or public officer or subject to their confirmation at the time of the passing of the Act[1].

If the latter be the case, the powers and responsibilities of the Board would have to be transferred to the committee to be appointed by Government under Ss. 7 and 12, and such committee would have, as already been observed, the control of such mosque, temple or other religious establishment, and could exercise all such powers as had been exercised by the Board of Revenue.

Acts of control referable to executive functions of Government.

The wrongful assumption of power by Government[2] or by a public officer in constituting a trustee which can as well be traced to the action of the officer concerned as an act of the executive[3] does not give any right to Government not previously existing and is not a test in ascertaining whether an institution falls within S. 3 or 4. The proper view is that Government can interfere in the appointment of a manager only when the appointment vested with Government[1]. In *Ponduranga* v. *Nagappa* [2] the respondent claimed to be the hereditary trustee and as such claimed the right to receive the tasdik payable to the temple of Kodandaramasami in Palamcottah in the District of Tinnevelly as against the appellants (plaintiffs), the members of the Devastanam Committee who claimed the management and control

---

1. *Ramiengar* v. *Gnana Sambanda Pandara Sannada*, (1867) 5 M. H. C. 53; *Khajah Ashruf Hossein* v. *Mussamut Hazara Begum*, (1872) 18 W. R. C. R. 396; *Fakurudin Sahib* v. *Ackeni Sahib*, (1880) I. L. R., 2 M. 197; *Jan Ali* v. *Ram Nath Mundul*, (1881) I. L. R., 8 C. 32; and *Kalianasundaram Ayyar* v. *Umamba Bayi Saheb*, (1897) I. L. R.. 20 M. 421.

2. *Ponduranga* v. *Nagappa*, (1889) I. L. R., 12 M. 366.

3. *Ramiengar* v. *Gnana Sambanda Pandara Sannada*, supra; and *L. Venkatesa Nayudu* v. *Shrivan Shatagopa Shri Shatagopaswami*, (1877) 7 M. H. C. 77.

4. *Agri Sharma Embrandri* v. *Vistnu Embrandri*, (1866) 3 M. H. C. 198.

of the said temple as falling under S. 3 of the Act and sued among others, for a declaration of their right. The first Court held that the institution did not fall under S. 3 but under S. 4, and that, therefore, the plaintiffs had no right of controlling the defendant (respondent). The High Court held that the trusteeship of the said temple was not hereditary and that the committee could, therefore, appoint a trustee on a vacancy arising. The High Court made several useful observations with regard to the tests to be considered in deciding whether an institution fell under S. 3 or 4 which would be well worth perusal. The High Court observed: "The main point to be kept in view in coming to a finding upon the evidence is whether at the time of the passing of Act XX of 1863 the nomination of the trustee of the temple was *vested* in, or was *exercised* by, the Government or any public officer, or whether such nomination was subject to the confirmation of the Government or of any public officer. As observed by the High Court in *Sami* v. *Rajagopala*[1] it was *certainly not intended* that the *wrongful assumption* of power either by Government or by a public officer to *constitute a trustee should place the temple in the category of institutions* which it was the intention of the Legislature to transfer to the committee appointed under the Act. The true construction of S. 3 is *that the power of nomination or confirmation must be lawfully vested in the Government* or a public officer or lawfully exercised by them; and it is therefore *necessary to see whether the actual exercise of such power is referable to a legal origin*, either to the exercise of a like power by the former Government, or to the terms of the deed of endowment or to the grant of endowment made by the Government or to the power to provide a competent trustee when a religious institution has no competent trustee. It must also be borne in mind that acts of public officers done in the exercise of general supervision and control over trustees under Regulation VII of 1817 should be distinguished from the right to nominate a trustee or to confirm such nomination which alone is constituted as the test of the committee's jurisdiction."

Again, in the leading case of *Ramiengar* v. *Gnana Sambanda Pandura Sannada*[2], in which it was held that the Kumba Areswara-

1. S. A. 644 of 1884 unreported. 2. (1867) 5 M. H. C. 53.

swami pagoda at Tribhuvanam in the Kumbaconum Taluq was an institution falling under S. 4, their Lordships (*Scotland*, C. J., and *Innes*, J.) observed: "Now all the Tanjore temples and their endowments appear to have been brought under the superintendence of the Collector in 1812, and a large portion of the evidence from that time relates to the possession and application of the property of the pagoda, and to acts of control exercised over panchayets or trustees in the appointment of the stanikam and other subordinate servants, and as respects the repairs of the pagoda, the expenditure of its income and the general conduct of its affairs. In those respects the evidence indisputably shows that the Government did exercise an authoritative superintendence and interference, even to the extent of using the pagoda funds for the construction of bridges and other public works, and in so subordinate a matter as the setting of hired watchers to detect thefts within the pagoda. But considering every such act to have been within the executive functions of the Government, it seems clear to us that no weight can be given to this portion of the evidence."

Government control indiscriminate.

The Government exercised rights of superintendence indiscriminately over religious institutions which had an hereditary trustee and over those which had a trustee subject to the nomination of Government[1]. Hence the mere exercise of acts of superintendence before Act XX of 1863, does not show that the trustee is not an independent trustee and is subject to the nomination of Government. Thus in the above case of *Ramienyar* v. *Gnana Sambanda Pandara Sannada*[1], the learned judges, after stating that the Local Government was controlling through its officers the two classes of religious establishments aforesaid long before the assumption of the Tanjore territory and temples by the British Government, observed: "It is obvious, therefore, that as acts of management and control of the kind proved by this portion of the evidence were exercised over religious establishments, whether the appointment or succession to the office of panchayet or trustee was

---

1. *Ramiengar* v. *Gnana Sambanda Pandara Sannada*, (1867) 5 M. H. C. 53; *Ittuni Panikkar* v. *Irani Nambudripad*, (1881) I. L. R., 3 M. 401; *Sheoratan Kunwari* v. *Ram Pargash*, (1896) I. L. R., 18 A. 227; and *Seshadri Ayyangar* v. *Nataraja Iyer*, (1898) I. L. R., 21 M. 179 F. B.

or was not independent of the Government, they can be of no aid in determining to which of the classes defined in Ss. 3 & 4 of the Act, the Kumba pagoda belongs. ....The exercise of duties which had before the Act been indiscriminately performed, and which it was the purpose of the Act to transfer, are of no weight in the decision of this question."

Again in *L. Venkatesa Nayudu* v. *Shri Shatagopa Swami*[1] where the right of the Jeer as trustee of the Trivellore temple was in question, *Holloway* and *Kindersley*, JJ., observed: "The fact of their (Government) interference and the assertion of their right to interfere are the only evidence of the existence of such right. That, for many years, they, most beneficially for the institution, perhaps irregularly, assumed such a right in every pagoda, this and many other cases distinctly show. It would, however, be impossible to treat the fact of interference as evidence of a strictly legal right to interfere. This has been several times noticed in previous cases."

Trustees submitting applications for expenditure.

The mere fact that the trustees were submitting to the local agents applications connected with the expenditure of temple funds would be no proof that the nomination of the trustee was subject to the approval of Government, as the Government officers continued on grounds of expediency to manage the pagoda lands and to hold the income for the use of the pagoda[2].

Muchilika by Government containing term as to trustee's dismissal.

The mere fact that the Government put in a term in the muchilikas taken by them from persons to whom they handed over charge after the famous report of 1842 and prior to Act XX of 1863 to the effect that the trustee should be liable for dismissal in case of misconduct, would also not be sufficient to show that an institution fell within S. 3, as the "Government on transferring their legal duties and responsibilities in the management of the lands would be as likely to require that provision if the Pandara Sannadhi was trustee by independent appointment as they would if the nomination to the office was subject to confirmation[3]."

1. (1872) 7 M. H. C. 77.

2. *Ramiengar* v. *Gnana Sambandu Pandara Sannada*, (1867) 5 M. H. C. 53.

3. *Appasami* v. *Nagappa*, (1884) I. L. R., 7. M. 499.

One test of seeing whether an institution falls under one or the other of the classes mentioned in Ss. 3 and 4 of the Act is to be found in *Appasami* v. *Nagappa*[1], but is apparently confined to the Madras Presidency. It is there observed that when the trusteeship is hereditary, it is ordinarily described in Southern India as *athinam*, and the trustee as *Athina Dharmakarta*. From the absence of the use of this word and for several other reasons, it was held in that case that the trusteeship was not hereditary.

Athinam.

Effect of seizure by Government of Tanjore Raj—Act of State :—The seizure by Government of the Tanjore territory in 1811 and the consequent assumption by the Government of the management of the temples and their endowments in that State was an act of State, but that act of State in itself did not alter existing private rights in connection with the temples or religious establishments within the ceded territory. The British Government never claimed greater rights and powers in regard to the property and management of these religious establishments than were considered to belong to the Rajas of Tanjore prior to the British assumption. The Tanjore temples and endowments would appear to have been brought under the superintendence of the Collector in 1812[2]. As regards the Tanjore Fort Devastanams and their endowments of which the late Raja of Tanjore was hereditary trustee, they were seized by an act of State together with the Raja's other private properties by the British Government after the Raja's death in 1855. A few days before Act XX of 1863 received the sanction of the Governor-General, the Government made over the management to the senior widow of the late Rajah. This was held to give no right of reservation to the Government to resume it after the death of the Rani. The transfer was absolute as against the Government though the grant to the senior widow only created a widow's interest[3].

Applicability of Section :—Ss. 3, 4 and 5 have application only to public religious institutions or endowments[4] to which the provisions of the Regulations would have been applicable[5].

1. (1884) I. L. R., 7 M. 499.
2. *Ramiengar* v. *Gnana Sambanda Pandara Sannada*, (1867) 5 M. H. C. 53.
3. *Kalianasundaram Ayyar* v. *Umamba Bayi Saheb*, (1897) I. L. R., 20 M. 421.
4. *Khajah Ashruf Hossein* v. *Mussamat Hazara Begum*, (1872) 18 W. R. 396. See also pp. 10 and 11 *ante*.
5. *Jan Ali* v. *Ram Nath Mundul*, (1881) I. L. R., 8 C. 32. See also notes to S. 14.

The following have been held to be institutions falling under S. 3.

(1) Temple of idol Gopinath[1] in Satiabadi Mutt in the district of Cuttack. In this case a question arose whether a Committee could sue independently of Act XX for restraining a trustee whom they had dismissed from interfering with the temple.

(2) Temple of Markandeswara Swami in Rajahmundry in the Godaveri District[2]. The question in this case was whether a Brahmin who married a widow was entitled to attend the temple for purposes of worship.

(3) Mosque of Kalavoi in the North Arcot District[3]. In this case a question arose whether a suit by an officer of a mosque to be reinstated in office was governed by the special provisions of Act XX.

(4) Devanadaswami (Vishnu) temple at Tiruvandipuram in the South Arcot District[4]. This was a temple which came under S. 3 though the point did not arise; Committee had the power to appoint trustees, and the question was whether they could appoint a person who was a Sivite and not a Vaishnavite as trustee.

(5) Pataliswaraswami temple in Tirupapuliyur in the South Arcot District.[5] The Dharmakartha of the said temple was found not to be hereditary, and the court finding that S. 3 applied held that the Committee had power to dismiss him for proper cause and the court upheld such dismissal.

(6) Nachiarkovil in the Tanjore District (Kumbakonum Taluq)[6]. The question arising in this case was whether the Committee could dismiss the trustees of

1. *Puddolabh Roy* v. *Ramgopal Chatterjee*, (1882) I. L. R., 9 C. 133.

2. *Venkatachalapati* v. *Subbarayadu*, (1890) I. L. R., 13 M. 293.

3. *Syed Amin Sahib* v. *Ibram Sahib*, (1868) 4 M. H. C. 112.

4. *Gandavathara Ayyangar* v. *Devanayaya Mudali*, (1883) I. L. R., 7 M. 222.

5. *Virasami Nayudu* v. *Subba Rau*, (1882) I. L. R., 6 M. 54. See also *Virasami Nayudu* v. *Arunachella Chetti*, (1880) I. L. R., 2 M. 230.

6. *Chinna Rangaiyangar* v. *Subbraya Mudali*, (1867) 3 M. H. C. 334.

the temple, and it was held that the Committee could do so *without recourse to suit*, provided of course there were sufficient grounds. As there were found to be no sufficient grounds, the trustees were reinstated by the court.

(7) Rajagopalasawmy temple at Mannargudy[1] in the Tanjore District. The question in this case was whether three out of six members of a Committee could validly dismiss the temple trustee.

(8) Musiri Devastanam in the Trichinopoly District[2]. The suit was by the Dharmakarta against the Committee members for reinstatement in office.

(9) Srirangam temple in Srirangam in the Trichinopoly District[3]. The question arose in the first cited case[3] as to the maintainability of a suit under S. 14 of the Act when not brought in accordance with the sanction of the court under S. 18. In the second case cited below[3] a question arose whether a Committee had the right to suspend the trustee of a temple pending a charge of misconduct against him.

(10) Supta Rishiswara Swami temple in Lalgudi, Trichinopoly District[4]. The question was whether a trustee who was wrongfully dismissed by the Committee was entitled to restitution.

(11) Bhagavathi Amman temple in Edayakottai village in the Madura District[5]. The question was as to the Collector's right to appoint a trustee for a religious institution after the Act.

(12) Goripalayam durga in Goripalayam in the Madura District[6]. The question in this case was whether the Committee could sue for rents of temple lands.

---

1. *Pandurungi Annachariyar* v. *Iyathory Mudaly*, (1869) 4 M. H. C. 443.
2. *Thandavaraya Pillai* v. *Subbayyer*, (1899) I. L. R., 23 M. 483.
3. *Srinivasa* v. *Venkata*, (1887) I.L.R., 11 M. 148 ; *Seshadri Ayyangar* v. *Nataraja Ayyar*, (1898) I. L. R., 21 M. 179.
4. *Dorasami Ayyar* v. *Annasami Ayyar*, (1899) I. L. R., 23 M 306.
5. *Mahomed* v. *Ganapati*, (1889) I. L. R., 13 M. 277.
6. *Kaliyana Ramayyar* v. *Mustak Shah Saheb*, (1896) I. L. R., 19 M. 395.

(13) Kalla Alagar Devastanam in the Madura District[1]. The suit was by the trustee against his predecessor for damages caused to the devastanam by the latter's negligence.

(14) Minakshi Sundaravasal Devastanam in Madura[2]. The question in this case was as to the right of the District Judge to appoint on a vacancy arising in the Committee and as to whether such right was controlled by any appellate authority.

(15) Palani Devastanam (The Palani temple being one) in the Madura District[3]. The question was whether S. 16 of the Act authorized reference of a suit under S. 14 when the point involved was that of removal of a Devastanam Committee member.

(16) Branthiswara Pagoda at Palamcottah in the Tinnevelly District[4]. It was found that the trusteeship was not hereditary and that the Committee could appoint one.

(17) Kodandaramasami temple in Palamcottah in the Tinnevelly District[5]. The question was whether the institution was under the control of the Committee and whether the latter could therefore dismiss the trustee.

(18) Sri Narambunadaswami temple at Tiruppudaimaruthur, Tinnevelly District[6]. The question in this case was as to the right of the Committee to dismiss the trustee for not furnishing accounts.

(19) Srivilliputtur temple in Srivilliputtur taluq in the Tinnevelly District[7]. The suit in this case was for removal of a member of the Vishnu Devastanam Committee for alleged misconduct.

---

1. *Krishnayyar* v. *Soundararaja Ayyangar*, (1897) I. L. R., 21 M. 245.
2. *Minakshi Naidu* v. *Subramanya Sastri*, (1887) I. L. R., 11 M. 26; S C. L. R. 14 I. A. 160.
3. *Perumal Naick* v. *Saminatha Pillai*, (1896) I. L. R., 19 M. 498.
4. *Appasami* v. *Nagappa*, (1884) I. L. R., 7 M. 499.
5. *Ponduranga* v. *Nagappa*, (1889) I. L. R., 12 M. 366.
6. *Anantanarayana Ayyar* v. *Kuttalam Pillai*, (1899) I. L. R., 22 M. 481.
7. *Tiruvengadath Ayyangar* v. *Srinivasa Thathachariar*, (1899) I. L. R., 22 M. 361.

(20) Subramania Sami Kovil in Trichendur, Tinnevelly District[1]. The suit was by the Dharmakarta for recovery of certain amounts alleged to have been embezzled by his predecessor in office.

(21) Thandanainar temple in the Tinnevelly District[2]. The suit was by the Dharmakarta to enforce a trust with reference to a special fund raised for the service of the idol and in the hands of a special trustee.

(22) Viswanathaswamy Covil in Sivakasi in Tinnevelly District.[3] In this case a question arose whether a suit for recovery of temple property could be brought by the Dharmakarta or by the Committee.

(23) Jumma Mosque or Musjid at Kundapur in South Canara[4]. The question that was considered in this case was as to the validity of appointment of additional trustees by the Committee.

(24) Venkataramana Temple at Mangalore in South Canara[5]. The question was whether certain trustees of the temple appointed by a Committee were entitled to a declaration of their right and to prevent a breach of trust by the other trustees also appointed by the Committee.

(25) Vishnu Mangala Devasthan in Ajanur village in South Canara[6]. The question was as to the right of the trustee to sue for recovery of properties belonging to the Devasthan. It is, however, not very clear whether the institution fell under S. 3. The District Judge referred the parties to the Committee, but the High Court merely held that this was wrong.

---

1. *Sethu v. Subramanya*, (1887) I. L. R., 11 M. 274.
2. *Nellaiyappa Pillai v. Thangama Nachiar*, (1897) I. L. R., 21 M. 406.
3. *Sankaramurti Mudaliar v. Chidambara Nadan*, (1893) I. L. R., 17 M. 143
4. *Sheik Davud Saiba v. Hussein Saiba*, (1893) I. L. R., 17 M. 212.
5. *Ranga Pai v. Baba*, (1897) I. L. R., 20 M. 398.
6. *Agrisharma Embrandri v. Vistnu Embrandri*, (1866) 3 M. H. C. 198.

IV. In the case of every such mosque, temple, or other religious establishment which, at the time of the passing of this Act, shall be under the management [1] of any trustee, manager, or superintendent,[2] whose nomination shall not vest in, nor be exercised [3] by, nor be subject to the confirmation of, the Government, or any Public Officer, the Local Government shall, as soon as possible after the passing of this Act, transfer to such trustee, manager, or superintendent, all the landed or other property which, at the time of the passing of this Act, shall be under the superintendence or in the possession of the Board of Revenue, or any Local Agent, and belonging to such mosque, temple, or other religious establishment, except such property as is hereinafter provided [4];

Transfer to independent Trustees, &c., of all Property belonging to their Trusts, &c., remaining in charge of Revenue Board or others.

and the powers and the responsibilities of the Board of Revenue, and the Local Agents, in respect to such mosque, temple, or other religious establishment, and to all land and other property so transferred except as regards acts done and liabilities incurred by the said Board of Revenue, or any Local Agent, previous to such transfer, shall cease and determine.

Cessation of Board's powers as to such property.

NOTES.

[1] "**Which at the time of the passing of this Act shall be under the management**", **&c.**—These words do not mean that the endowment should be under the personal management of such trustees at the time of the passing of the Act; so that even if the institutions were not personally managed by the trustees and the Government should manage them, still if the trusteeship were hereditary or the Government or any public officer had no right of nomination, the section would apply and the Board must transfer the land to the hereditary trustees. This duty they can be compelled to perform.

Personal management not necessary.

In the case of *Jusagheri Gosamiar* v. *The Collector of Tanjore*[1], the facts were that the Government took possession in 1856 of the

1. (1870) 5 M. H. C. 334.

Nadiem Mutt and its properties on account of the misconduct of the Madathipathy. The person dispossessed brought a suit against Government for possession. The Court held that he was entitled to recover though he was not managing actually, and that the fact of his misconduct was no defence to the suit, as the Government was bound to restore the property to him though steps might be taken to remove him from the management. *Scotland*, C. J., observed: "These words (*under the management of any trustee*, &c.) by themselves no doubt import personal management; but what follows in the section shows clearly that the words were not intended to be applicable in that sense to the property of religious establishment, for it is expressly provided that the property in the possession of the Board of Revenue at the time of the passing of the Act shall be transferred. Giving effect to the language of the whole section and reading it with Ss. 5 and 6, I think it must be construed as including the endowments of all religious establishments the management of which had belonged to independently appointed trustees. A different construction would leave in the hands of Government the landed property of some religious establishments which would be contrary to the plainly declared purpose and whole scope of the Act."

If the decision is correct and we suppose looking to the scope and object of the Act it must be so, the section is very badly conceived. Under the Regulations, the Government can take possession of lands in case the trustee, though hereditary, misconducts himself and misappropriates the trust funds. But apparently they had no right to remove him. However that might be, supposing the trustee should not be removed, the effect of the decision would be to compel the Government to transfer the lands (under S. 4) to the very person from whom possession was taken under the Regulations on account of misconduct. After the Act, such person sued for possession and it was held that the question of the plaintiff's misconduct and unfitness to remain in office was outside the scope of the suit and that the Government had no defence.

Surely the framers of the Act ought to have provided for such a case, but as it is, such cases can rarely now occur and so the matter is not of much importance at the present day. But at the time of the Act, the effect of this decision must have been disastrous. It may be said that a suit for removal of the trustee may next day be brought and the possession of the properties be taken over from such erring trustee. But law's delays are proverbial and the danger of losing the trust properties the moment the erring trustee takes possession is so great as to render the remedy worse than useless.

Even before the Act Government gave up the management but the fact that they gave up the management to the wrong person by mistake would not prevent the rightful trustee from recovering[1].

[2]. "**Any trustee.**" **&c.** :—The singular will include the plural. Hence if there were several joint hereditary trustees, the Board, it is supposed, must transfer the land to all of them. To fall within the scope of the section, the trusteeship need not be hereditary as it refers generally to trustees of endowments or of establishments, the management of which belongs to independently appointed trustees[2]. As to the distinction, if any, between trustee, manager &c., see Introduction.

[3]. "**Nor be exercised.**" :—This means, we submit, "nor be legally exercised." The construction is that S. 4 would not apply notwithstanding the Government might not have nominated in fact provided the right should be vested in the Government. But S. 4 would apply where the Government had not exercised the right and lost it by prescription and what was not originally an hereditary trusteeship became so by prescription.

[4]. "**Except such property as is hereinafter provided** :"—Reference is here made to S. 21, by which the Board of Revenue is enabled to transfer in case of endowments partly of a religious and partly of a secular character, such portion as it may determine, to the committee or trustee as the case may be and to retain the rest for appropriation to secular uses.

S. 4 imposes a *duty* on the Board of Revenue to transfer all property in its possession at the time of the passing of the Act to the hereditary trustee.

Tests :—The tests of seeing whether an institution falls under S. 3 or S. 4 have been considered in the notes to S. 3[3].

---

1. *Nallathambi Battar* v. *Nellakumara Pillai*, (1873) 7 M. H. C. 306.

2. *Jusagheri Gosamiar* v. *The Collector of Tanjore*, (1870) 5 M. H. C. 334.

3. *Ramienyar* v. *Gnanasambanda*, (1867) 5 M. H. C. 53; *K. Venkatabalakrishna Chettyar* v. *Kaliyanaramaiyangar*, (1869) 5 M. H. C. 48; *Jusagheri Gosamiar* v. *The Collector of Tanjore*, supra: and *L. Venkatesa Nayudu* v. *Shri Shatagopaswami*, (1872) 7 M. H. C. 77.

Applicability of section :—This section applies only to public religious institutions to which the provisions of the Regulations would have been applicable[1].

The following have been held to be institutions falling under S. 4.

(1). Temple of Guru Gobind Singh or Harmandir at Patna[2]. This temple is regarded as holy by the Sikhs. It is on the site of the Guru's birth-place and contains his cradle (Pandura) and several copies of Granth (or sacred law of the Sikhs)—one of the Granths being sent by Guru Gobind himself. The cradle and the book are objects of great veneration among the Sikhs. Mr. Justice *Mitter* held that, though the institution came under S. 4, the trustee was subject to the jurisdiction of the Civil Court under S. 14[2]. It is difficult to say what Mr. Justice *Macleau* said. He would say that Government exercised superintendence and that S. 14 was applicable[2]. It must be taken that he also held that the institution came under S. 4 as he made a reference to the appointment under S. 5.

(2). Tomb of Khaja Anwar Sahib in the town of Burdwan[3].

(3). Veeraragavaswamy Temple at Trivellore in the Chingleput District[4]. It was held that the institution came under S. 4, that the Jheer of the Agobalam (Ahobilam) Mutt was the *ex-officio* and hereditary trustee of the temple and that the committee had no power of control over him, much less could they dismiss him for misconduct[4].

(4). Chidambaram Temple in Chidambaram, South Arcot District[5]. The spiritual shrines in the temple are called (1) Chit Sabha, (2) Kanaka Sabha, (3) Deva Sabha, (4) Amman Covil, (5) Mulasthanam. It was held by the High Court that the institution was used as a place of public worship from time immemorial, that it was not the Dikshadars' private property, that the Dikshadars were hereditary trustees, and that they could be removed under S. 14[5].

(5). The Kumba Areswaraswami Pagoda at Tribhuvanam in the Kumbakonum Taluq, Tanjore District[6]. It was hold that the Pandara Sannadhi of the Dharmapuram Mutt was the *ex-officio* trustee or panchayatdar of the said temple and that a District Committee had no right to call for accounts from him or to dismiss him.[6]

---

1. See p. 21 notes (4) and (5).
2. *Dhurrum Singh* v. *Kissen Singh*, (1881) I. L. R., 7 C. 767.
3. *Khajah Ashruf Hossein* v. *Mussamat Hazara Begum*, (1872) 18 W. R. C. R. 396.
4. *L. Venkatesu Nayudu* v. *Shri Shatagopa Swami*, (1872) 7 M. H. C. 77.
5. *Natesa* v. *Ganopati*, (1890) I. L. R., 14 M. 103.
6. *Ramienyar* v. *Gnanasambanda Pandarasannada*, (1867) 5 M. H. C. 53.

(6). **Nadiem Mutt situated in Nadiem village, Tanjore District** in the road to Rameswaram[1]. Lands to meet the expenses of the mutt and of Aradana and other ceremonies in the temple situated in the mutt were endowed by the Raja of Tanjore in 1744. Some of these lands were afterwards taken away by the Raja of Tanjore and given to Setu Bava Choultry for the purpose of feeding travellers which was only a charitable purpose. It was held[1] that the Gosayi or Madathipathy of the Mutt was its hereditary trustee and was entitled to a transfer of land from Government under S. 4.

(7). **Durga at Nagore in Negapatam in the Tanjore District**[2]. It was held in *Fakurudin Sahib* v. *Ackeni Sahib*[2] that the trustees of this Durga were hereditary, but were nevertheless liable to be removed by the Civil Court under S. 14 of the Act.

(8). **The Devastanams in Tanjore Fort**[3]. It was held[3] that the committee had no right of appointment after the death of the Rani to whom the Government made over the management.

(9). **Sri Teyagaraja Swami Temple in Tiruvalur**[4], **Tanjore District**. The trustees of the *Kattalays* attached to this temple were held to be hereditary and to be under no duty to account to the Temple Committee, Negapatam Circle.

(10). **Rameswaram Devasthanam in Madura District**[5]. It was held in *Gopala Ayyar* v *Arunachellam Chetty*[5] that the District Judge had jurisdiction under S. 5 to appoint a temporary manager[5].

Procedure in case of dispute as to right of succession to vacated Trusteeship, &c.

V. Whenever, from any cause, a vacancy [1] shall occur in the office of any trustee, manager, or superintendent [2], to whom any property shall have been transferred under the last preceding section[3], and any dispute

---

1. *Junagheri Gosamiar* v. *The Collector of Tanjore*, (1870) 5 M. H. C. 334.

2. *Fakurudin Sahib* v. *Ackeni Sahib*, (1880) I. L. R., 2 M. 197; *Sultan Ackeni Sahib* v. *Shaik Bava Malimiyar*, (1879 I. L. R., 4 M. 295.

3. *Kalyanasundaram Iyer* v *Umamba Bayi Sahiba*, (1897) I.L.R., 20 M. 421.

4. *K. Venkatabalakrishna Chettiar* v. *Kaliyanaramaiyangar*, (1869) 5 M. H. C. 48. See also *Somasundara Mudaliar* v. *Vythilinga Mudaliar*, (1894) I.L.R., 19 M 285.

5. *Ramalingam Pillai* v *Vythilingam*, (1893) I. L. R., 16 M. 490 (P. C.); *Gopala Ayyar* v. *Arunachellam Chetty*, (1902) I. L. R., 26 M. 85.

shall arise respecting the right of succession to such office[4] it shall be lawful for any person interested[5] in the mosque, temple, or religious establishment, to which such property shall belong, or in the performance of the worship or of the service thereof, or the trusts relating thereto, to apply to the Civil Court [6] to appoint a manager [7] of such mosque, temple, or other religious establishment, and thereupon such Court may appoint such manager to act until some other person shall by suit have established his right of succession to such office.[8]

Powers of managers appointed by court.

The Manager so appointed by the Civil Court shall have, and shall exercise, all the powers[9] which, under this or any other Act, the former trustee, manager, or superintendent, in whose place such Manager is appointed by the Court, had or could exercise in relation to such mosque, temple, or religious establishment, or the property belonging thereto.

NOTES.

Requisites of Section :—For the applicability of this section three conditions must be satisfied[1] :—

(*a*). There must be a vacancy in the office of the hereditary trustee—though such vacancy may arise *from any cause*.

(*b*). The Trustee, Manager, or Superintendent must be one to whom or to whose predecessor property shall have been transferred by the Board[2] under S. 4, *i. e.*, there must be a *transfer in fact*; and

(*c*). A dispute, though it may be of *any* nature, should arise respecting the right of succession to such office.

If these conditions are satisfied, then jurisdiction is given to the District Court for appointing a temporary manager to act until the dispute as to the succession is finally settled by a suit.

1. *Gopala Ayyar* v. *Arunachallam Chetty*, (1902) I. L. R., 26 M. 85.

2. See *Khajah Ashruf Hossein* v. *Mussamat Hazara Begum*, (1872) 18 W. R. 396; and *Ittuni Panikkar* v. *Irani Nambudripad*, (1881) I. L. R., 3 M. 401.

[1]. "**Vacancy**" may arise in many ways, e. g. by (1) death, or (2) loss of caste, or (3) change of religion or (4) resignation or abdication. The last three amount to civil death under Hindu law.

[2]. "**In the office of any trustee" &c.** :—The singular number includes the plural. See also note [4] below. As to the distinction, if any, drawn between trustee, manager or superintendent see, Introduction.

[3]. "**To whom any property shall have been transferred under the last preceding section.**"—These words seem to suggest that S. 5 has application only where the original trustee to whom property has been transferred vacates. But that is not the intention. The conjunction of the word 'office' negatives any such suggestion. Where the Board of Revenue had not taken the control of a religious institution and no property could consequently be transferred, it was held that the Court would have no jurisdiction under S. 5 to appoint a manager pending settlement by suit of disputes as to succession[1]. This class must be considerable as the Government did not take up the management of many religious institutions[2].

Supposing the Board had taken the superintendence, but as a matter of fact did not transfer any land (as where a religious institution had only a bare charge over the profits and the land itself was given to secular trusts) the question arises whether there can be a transfer and whether the section has any application. S. 21 may seem not to cover such a case, but it may be said that where a religious institution is only entitled to a charge upon the profits and the Board should consent to give such profits, there is a transfer of the charge, (*i. e.* property) within the meaning of S. 5. It seems to us, however, that, under Ss. 5 and 21 the Legislature was contemplating the transfer of the whole or part of the land and other property under Government management.

If in a case under S. 21 a portion of the land is transferred, then the section has application. The section has also application to a case where the Government had taken charge under the Regulations and refused to hand over the land to the

1. See *Khajah Ashruf Hossein* v. *Mussamat Hazara Begum*, (1872) 18 W. R. 396; and *Ittuni Panikkar* v. *Irani-Nambudripad*, (1881) I. L. R., 3 M. 401.

2. See p. 14 notes (5) and (6).

trustee, but the trustee nevertheless got it by a decree of court[1]; for, all that the section requires is an actual transfer. It does not say it must be a voluntary transfer. Possession by an adverse decree of court is a transfer of land within the meaning of the section.

It must be stated that the mischiefs which the section intends to remedy are equally apparent in the cases already referred to and ought to have been provided for. The Act is peculiarly full of these and similar defects owing to the inartistic way in which it has been drawn. With respect to the particular matter on hand if the section had, instead of stating, "to whom any property, &c.," simply stated "whose nomination to the said office shall not vest in, nor be exercised, nor be subject to the confirmation of the Government or any public officer" as used in the first portion of S. 4, this would have completely covered all the cases.

It is unfortunate that the language employed should be thus defective and that greater attention was not bestowed upon the matter. It is a pity that the Legislature should not take the initiative and come forward to remedy these defects when the section might have been long ago amended to cover all cases. To amend the section no objection can be raised that the time that has elapsed since the passing of the Act is short. Surely a period of 40 years is long enough for the Indian Legislature to move in the matter. The only reason that may be possibly assigned for the Legislature staying its hand is the policy of non-interference in religious matters. But it is submitted that there is no question of religious interference as regards the provision in S. 5, and as regards the amendment thereof to remedy certain defects.

The observations of *Innes* and *Tarrant*, JJ., in the case of *Ittuni Panikkar* v. *Irani Nambudripad*[2], wherein it was held that S. 5 had no application if there should be no transfer of land under S.4, would be well worth perusal:—"It is contended that if the Board of Revenue did not, they ought to have exercised control over this and other religious institutions in Malabar, and that, though this institution was not transferred, we should regard it as having been transferred, as by so doing we should carry out the intention of

1. *Jusagheri Gosamiar* v. *The Collector of Tanjore* (1870) 5 M. H. C. 334.

2. (1881) I. L. R., 3 M. 401.

the Act. The Act, no doubt, was intended to *embrace all* religious institutions over which the Board of Revenue had formerly a power of control, and it was probably, therefore, the design of the framers of the Act to embrace in its provisions *this and other institutions similarly situated.* But in the particular question before us, we must hold that this institution is not within the language of S. 5 of the Act, and that if the legislature intended that the provisions of S. 5 should apply to institutions which had not been transferred in accordance with S. 4 as well as to those which had been so transferred, it has not expressed what it intended. We cannot give effect to the Act beyond the expressed intention which confines the operation of S. 5 to cases in which the property has not been transferred[1]."

But what strikes one at first sight by a perusal of the section is that some of the defects might be due to the fact that the legislature of the day was confining its attention only to the endowments which were then under the actual management of the Government and which were being withdrawn from Government management though this might be no justification for the other defects.

[4.] "**Any dispute shall arise respecting the right of succession to such office.**"—Where there are several offices and they are held by a single manager or several managers for the several offices, one for each, then there is no difficulty. But if there is a single office and it is held by a plurality of managers, the question arises as to the period when it can be said that there is a dispute as to the *succession to such office.* If *all the managers die*, there is a vacancy in the office, and any dispute as to the succession among the persons claiming the office is a dispute as to the succession to such office. There may be a dispute as to the right of succession where the contest is whether the office is hereditary or elective or goes by nomination.

Joint managers—Dispute.

Suppose in the case of joint managers for a single office, one of the joint managers dies and a dispute arises as to the succession to such person, but the dispute does not relate to the other surviving managers, the question is whether there is a vacancy in the office and a dispute as

1. See also *Khajah Ashruf Hossein* v. *Mussamat Hazara Begum*, (1872) 18 W. R. C. R. 396.

to the succession to such office? The question is not free from difficulty. In *Somasundara Mudaliar* v. *Vythilinga Mudaliar*[1] their Lordships *Collins*, C. J., and *Benson*, J., held that where one of the joint managers should die and a dispute should then arise as to the succession to such deceased joint managers, there was such a vacancy as to clothe the District Judge with jurisdiction under S. 5. In support of this it may be said that where one of several managers dies and a question arises as to the right of his heirs to take his place (the other managers denying the right of the heirs altogether) there is a dispute as to the right of succession to such office. If there are joint managers and the management is by turns and upon the death of one there is a dispute among *others* as to the person entitled to the turn of the deceased member, why is there not a dispute as to the succession to such office? At any rate the mischief which the section intends to remedy is equally apparent in this case. The section applies to a case in which a question has arisen with reference to the person who is to succeed to the office. That is a dispute respecting the right to succession[2]. Otherwise no effect will be given to the words "any dispute." If, however, a person is appointed temporarily then there is no vacancy. But if there is an office there may arise a vacancy though the actual incumbent is appointed temporarily. The judge is competent to find whether the appointment is temporary or otherwise.

Antecedent dispute.

The dispute referred to must be antecedent to the proceedings that may be taken under this section[3]. A contest between rival applicants for appointment as temporary manager is not such a dispute as will satisfy the condition precedent which the section requires as shown above[3]. There is a dispute within the meaning of the section notwithstanding that nobody can establish his right (successfully in a court of law)[3]. The temporary manager may resign and then a new one may be appointed, provided the dispute continues and is not settled[3].

"*Such office*" means office of "any trustee" &c., to whom property has been transferred.

The appointment by the judge of a temporary man is in his discretion[1] and his discretion cannot be lightly interfered with[4].

1. (1896) I. L. R., 19 M. 285; See also *Somasundara Mudaliar* v. *R. Twigg* C. R. P. 97 of 1900.
2. *Gopala Ayyar* v. *Arunachallam Chetty*, (1902) I. L. R., 26 M. 85.
3. *Somasundara Mudaliar* v. *R. Twigg*, C. R. P. 97 of 1900.
4. *Somasundara Mudaliar* v. *Vythilinga Mudaliar*, (1896) I. L. R. 19 M. 285; *Somasundara Mudaliar* v. *R. Twigg*, supra. Cf. *Shri Vishwambhar Pandit* v. *Vasudev Pandit*, (1888) I. L. R., 13 B. 37.

[5]. "**Any person interested**":—Any interest will do having regard to the terms of S. 15[1].

[6]. "**Civil Court.**"—The principal court of original civil jurisdiction in the district, *i. e.*, the court of the District Judge as a judicial tribunal and not simply the District Judge for the time being[1]. The order of the Judge under this section is a judicial act and an adjudication[1].

[7]. "**To appoint a manager, &c.**"—Any qualified person may be appointed. He may not be of a different creed or religion, but he need not be of the same sect or caste. A mohant or head of a mutt may be appointed.

Minor's appointment.—A minor may not be appointed, but it cannot be illegal. If the guardian of the minor is appointed to act for such minor that may be sufficient. Can a High Court interfere with the discretion exercised by the District Judge in appointing a minor? Apparently not, unless it be *perverse* in the particular case[2].

The Collector as agent to the Court of Wards may be legally appointed notwithstanding S. 21 as temporary manager[2]. Whatever doubt there may be as regards this at one time, it is now expressly provided for by S. 63 of the Madras Court of Wards Act (I of 1902). But there is no similar provision in the Court of Wards Acts of the other Presidencies.

[8]. "**May appoint such manager to act until some other person shall have established his right of succession to such office.**"—Here again the language used is very defective. For if, after the appointment under this section of the Collector as guardian for a minor it should be established in a suit that the minor's ancestor who claimed to be a hereditary manager jointly with others had no hereditary right and that, therefore, the said minor had no right to act as joint manager with the others could the latter be said to establish their *right of succession* to such office? The contention in such cases may be, that upon the death of one the others as survivors are entitled to manage. In that case they may be said to have established their right of succession. Even otherwise, it cannot be said that there may be no remedy. A suit may be filed by the others for restraining the temporary manager from interfering or for declaring that the latter has no *locus standi.*

1. *Gopala Ayyar* v. *Arunachallam Chetty*, (1902) I. L. R., 26 M. 85.
2. *Somasundara Mudaliar* v. *R. Twigg*, C. R. P. 97 of 1900.

In a case where the ward succeeds in establishing his right, then the authority of the said temporary manager *ipso facto* ceases. Where the temporary manager is guilty of misfeasance, he may be removed by suit under S. 14[1].

[9]. **" All the powers which under this or under any other Act the former trustee shall have."**—But suppose the former trustee has powers given to him by custom or by the common law, can the temporary manager exercise them ? It cannot have been intended that he is not to exercise such powers, though apparently the wording of the section, if taken strictly and literally, may seem to negative it, unless the enactment in S. 6 which declares that the right of managers to whom the land is transferred under S. 4 " shall be the same as if this Act had not been passed" be taken to confer rights upon the manager. We do not know of any provision in this or any other Act conferring rights upon managers of religious endowments, excepting the last portion of S. 6 which enables managers to sue for the recovery of rent or other land so transferred ; but even this exception confers no new right.

Nature of Proceeding :—An application is enough. No suit is necessary[2]. No sanction under S. 18 is necessary. The proceeding under S. 5 is of a summary character and hence no particular and formal inquiry need be made. It is sufficient if some *prima facie* case is made out. The judge need not inquire into all the evidence relating to the hereditary right of the particular deceased office-holder[3]. The fact that the deceased and his father acted as managers would be sufficient evidence that it was hereditary[4] and that the deceased did not hold temporarily.

Appeal and Revision.—An order under S. 5 appointing a person as manager is not appealable[5]. But the High Court may

1. *Chinna Rangaiyangar* v. *Subbraya Mudali*, (1867) 3 M. H. C. 334 (337).
2. The effect of this section is misconceived in *Sheik Abdool Khalek* v. *Poran Bibee*, (1876) 25 W. R. C. R. 542.
3. *Somasundara Mudaliar* v. *Vythilinga Mudaliar*, (1896) I. L. R., 19 M. 285 ; *Somasundara Mudaliar* v. *R. Twigg*, C. R. P. 97 of 1900.
4. *Khajah Ashruf Hossein* v. *Mussamat Hazara Begum*(1872), 18 W.R. C. R. 396 ; and *Gopala Ayyar* v. *Arunachallam Chetty*, (1902) I. L. R., 26 M. 85. See also Introduction.
5. *Somasundara Mudaliar* v. *Vythilinga Mudaliar*, supra ; and *Somasundara* v. *Twigg*, C. M. A. 27 of 1900.—In the first case the Privy Council decision in *Meenakshi Naidoo* v. *Subramaniya Sastri*, (1887) I. L. R., 11 M. 26 : S. C. L. R., 14 I. A. 160 (which, however, was an order passed under S. 10 of the Act) was relied on. The case to the contrary in *Sultan Ackeni Sahib* v. *Shaik Bava Malimiyar*, (1879) I. L. R., 4 M. 295, must be treated as overruled. The principle is the same as under S. 18 of the Act. *Kaviraja Sundara Murtiya Pillai* v. *Nalla Naikan Pillai*, (1866) 3 M. H. C. 98 ; *Hajee Kalub Hossein* v. *Ali Hossein* (1872), 4 N. W. P. 3 ; *Venkateswara, In re*, (1886) I. L. R., 10 M. 98 ; and C. R. P. 101 of 1882, (1883) I. L. R., 10 M. 98 note. Cf. also *Raja* v. *Srinivasa*, (1888) I. L. R., 11 M. 319.

revise the order under S. 622, C. P. C.[1], or under the Charter Act, S. 15[2].

Rights, powers, and responsibilities of Trustees, &c., to whom property is transferred under S. 4.

VI. The rights, powers, and responsibilities of every Trustee, Manager, or Superintendent, to whom the land and other property of any mosque, temple, or other religious establishment is transferred in the manner prescribed in S. IV of this Act, as well as the conditions of their appointment, election, and removal, shall be the same as if this Act had not been passed, except in respect of the liability to be sued under this Act[1], and except in respect of the authority of the Board of Revenue, and local agents, given by the Regulations hereby repealed, over such mosque, temple, or religious establishment, and over such Trustee, Manager, or Superintendent, which authority is hereby determined and repealed[2].

Appointment of committees.*

All the powers which might be exercised by any Board, or local agent, for the recovery of the rent of land or other property transferred under the said S. IV of this Act may, from the date of such transfer, be exercised by any Trustee, Manager, or Superintendent to whom such transfer is made[3].

NOTES.

[1]. "**Except in respect of the liability to be sued under this Act**" :—*i. e.*, under S. 14 which applies to all cases of public religious trusts to which the Regulations were applicable.

[2]. "**Which authority is hereby determined and repealed**" —Vide S. 4, last portion and S. 22.

[3]. "**Be exercised by any trustee......to whom transfer is made.**" :—This creates no new right. As manager he has a right of suit in respect of endowed property and if he is one out of several joint mangers he can sue with the others. But the section may,

---

* This marginal note is obviously a mistake.

1. *Somasundara Mudaliar* v. *Vythilinga Mudaliar*, (1896) I. L. R. 19 M. 285 *Somasundara* v. *Twigg* C.R.P. 97 of 1900; and *GopalaAyyar* v. *Arunachellam Chetty*, (1902) I. L. R., 26 M. 85.

2. *Khajah Ashruf Hossein* v. *Mussumut Hazara Begum*, (1872) 18 W. R. C R. 396.

at first sight, seem to enable one of several joint managers to whom property has been transferred to sue (without joining the others) for rent or other property. But this cannot prevent the others from exercising their rights nor can it operate as a bar to the exercise of such rights if others wish to exercise the same. Of course if property is transferred to all managers all of them must sue. Moreover, under S. 4 the transfer must be to all the managers[1]. The successors in office of the persons to whom property had been transferred may also exercise this right though the section seems to be narrowly worded.

Appointment of Committees

VII. In all cases described in S. III of this Act, the local Government[1] shall once for all[2] appoint one or more Committees in every Division, or District[3], to take the place, and to exercise the powers, of the Board of Revenue and the local agents under the Regulations hereby repealed.

Such Committee shall consist of three or more persons, and shall perform all the duties imposed on such Board and local agents, except in respect of any property which is specially provided for under S. XXI of this Act.

NOTES.

[1] **"Local Government"**:—*i.e.*, the person authorised by Law to administer executive Government in Madras or Bengal (*i.e.*, in the part of British India in which the Act containing such expression shall operate).

[2] **"Once for all"**:—This shows that the moment the Local Government appoints a committee it has no further authority to appoint another. The appointment must be made once for all by the Local Government[2]. There must be nothing left for a future occasion. Any default on the part of the Local Government to appoint a committee will not entitle the Collector or other executive officer to appoint a manager or to exercise the powers given by Regulations[3].

[3] **"One or more committees in every Division or District"**:—Can the Local Government appoint more than one committee for the same Division or District? From the express language of the section it may do so. But curiously enough no provision is made

1. See p. 28 [2].
2. G. O. J. D. No. 2275, dated 18th September 1880 (Madras Government).
3. *Mahomed v. Ganapati*, (1889) I. L. R., 13 M. 277.

as to the jurisdiction to be exercised by such committees or as to their rights *inter se*.

Jurisdiction in case of plurality of committees.

The section only empowers the Local Government to appoint one or more committees in a District. Is it to be for the whole District or for a particular place in a District or for particular institutions? From the language of the section it will seem that if more than one committee is appointed for a single District all such committees can jointly exercise the rights exercised by the Board and shall jointly perform also the duties imposed on the Board. Of course it may be said that with reference to the conduct of their internal affairs such committees may arrange among themselves. But if any suit is to be brought all must join in suing[1]. Even where a single committee is appointed and arrangement is made for different members managing different institutions if any suit is to be brought the whole committee must join.

Committees for sub-districts.

Where a district is divided into sub-districts, and one committee is appointed for such sub-district, then such committee is independent of and has apparently no connection with the others. We find in the Reports instances in which Government have appointed committees for particular sub-divisions in a district[2]. The Divisions or Districts mentioned in the section are pre-existing Divisions or Districts; and the Act does not contemplate the creation of a division or district for its own purposes. Hence if a new Division or District be created after the appointment of committees, the Local Government has no power to appoint a new committee for the new Division and the old committee must continue to exercise its power. This is also the effect of the expression "once for all." Ss. XI and XII also suggest that the Legislature contemplated the case of an appointment by the Local Government of a single committee for the management separately of each mosque, temple, or other religious establishment as well as for that of a plurality of mosques, temples, or other religious establishments collectively. No doubt those sections must be read with the present section which clothes the Local Government with

1. *Virasami Nayudu* v. *Arunachella Chetti*, (1880) I. L. R., 2 M. 200.
2. *Chinna Rangaiyangar* v. *Subbraya Mudali*, (1867) 3 M. H. C. 334 (committe for Kumbaconam Circle); *Pandurungy Annachariyar* v. *Ayathory Mudaly*, (1869) 4 M. H. C. 443, (committee for the Tanjore circle); *K. Venkatabalakrishna Chettiyar* v. *Kaliyanaramaiyangar*, (1869) 5 M. H. C. 48 (committee for the Negapatam Circle).

authority to appoint committees. The power conferred on the Local Government by this section is the power to appoint one or more committees in every division or district. It may be inconvenient to appoint one committee for each religious establishment in a district. But is it illegal? The Act is particularly vague at the very outset when it wants to provide a machinery as substitute for the Government control which is withdrawn. There is nothing in the express provision of the Act making such appointment illegal.

Committee for each sectarian religious establishment.

The question remains whether under the section the appointment of a committee for the establishments of each sect or religion is contemplated. The wording of the section may be susceptible of the construction, that the appointment of one or more committees is only for a division or district which may contain mosques, temples and other religious establishments and not separately for the establishments founded for the purposes of the different religions. The result will then be that there can be no separate committees for Sivite or Vaishnavite temples and for Mahomedan religious establishments. But this absurd result can scarcely have been contemplated[1]. Moreover, the expression "*one or more*" occurring in this section, suggests the construction that the Local Government may be empowered to appoint a committee for Vaishnavite temples in a division, a committee for the Sivite temples in the same division and a committee for the mosques in the same divisions. But it may be said that it is consistent with this construction to hold that all such committees have jurisdiction over the whole district and all the religious establishments in such district. But this can scarcely be the intention of the Legislature. It is impossible to suppose that the Legislature would not have contemplated a provision for the separate management of the establishments of the different religions. It may be true that there is nothing particularly objectionable in appointing a single committee to superintend both Vaishnavite and Sivite temples. The same may be the case with other religious establishments devoted for one or other of the deities forming the Hindu Pantheon or even the lower sort of deities contemplated in the later Puranas and other legends. But surely it could not have been intended that a single committee consisting, say, of Hindus should have the right of superintendence

1. *Gandavathara* v. *Devanayaga*, (1883) I. L. R., 7. M. 222 (224).

over mosques. Similarly it could not have been intended that a committee consisting of Mahomedans should have control over Hindu temples, &c. Was it intended that a Hindu should have control over the religious establishments of the Mahomedans or *vice versa*? It may be urged that if the decisions of the Courts that the committee have no authority to interfere in the internal management of the religious establishments be correct[1], then there is nothing incongruous in appointing a committee consisting of both Hindus and Mahomedans for all the religious establishments in a district. But, as will be seen later on[1], these decisions are not supported by the language of the Act. S. 8 which provides for the qualifications for a member of a committee has also some bearing on the matter in hand though it is difficult to understand the exact meaning of the language employed in that section.[2].

It may be observed here that as a matter of fact committees have been appointed by the Government not merely for the establishments of the different religions but also for those of the different sects of the same religion. Instances of such are to be found in the Reports[3]. As to the jurisdiction of such committees no express provision is made. But in consonance with the object of their creation, they can have no jurisdiction over the whole district or the other religious establishments in the district. Otherwise there will be no object gained in making the appointments.

"**Such Committee**":—The singular includes the plural. So that, where more than one committee is appointed in a district, all the committees have the powers of the Board of Revenue.

"**Not less than 3 or more persons**":—So that each committee appointed by the Local Government must consist of not less than *three*, which is the minimum number provided for by the section. If the Local Government should appoint one committee for a district, the nomination of three persons will do and all the three will form the committee for the whole district. If the Government should appoint a committee for each of the different sectarian religious establishments in a district, then each of such committees to have a valid existence must consist of not less than three persons.

The question may arise whether artificial persons (such as corporations) may be appointed as members of a committee. The

1. See (*g*) and (*h*) below, pp. 46 and 47. 2. See p. 58.
3. *Appasami* v. *Nagappa*, (1884) I. L. R., 7 M. 499 (Siva Committee in the Tinnevelly District); *Ponduranga* v. *Nagappa*, (1889) I. L. R. 12 M. 366 and *Tiruvengadath Ayyangar* v. *Srinivasa Thathachariar*, (1899) I. L. R., 22 M. 361 (Vishnu Devastanam Committee in the Tinnevelly District).

word "persons" includes natural and artificial persons unless there is anything repugnant in the context[1]. From S. 8 and the subsequent sections it will appear that there is something repugnant in the context if we take the word person as including an artificial person. S. 8 says that a member of the committee "shall be appointed from among persons professing the religion", &c. How can a corporation be said to profess a religion? But the office of hereditary manager of a temple is said to be a corporation[2]. Such manager professes a religion. So also is the office of the head of a mutt a corporation sole professing a religion[3]. There can be no objection if the head of a mutt or hereditary manager is appointed as a *persona designata*.

Rights and Duties of Committees:—It is singular that when the Legislature was providing a machinery for the control of religious institutions in lieu of the one existing before and expressly taken away by the Act, it was thought sufficient to state vaguely that the committee should have all the powers of the Board of Revenue without setting forth such rights and duties in detail. The Act does not provide for the management of the different committees, for the necessity for holding meetings for conducting business, or for the procedure to be observed in such meetings. In short no provision is made about the internal management of the committee.

The powers of committees though discussed in some of the cases have not been set forth in any detail in the Act. It is, therefore, necessary to mention some of these powers. These may be considered under *three* headings:—*Firstly*, the rights and duties of committees generally. *Secondly*, their rights and duties as against trustees. And *thirdly*, the rights and duties among the members *inter se*.

I. We shall first of all consider the *rights* and *duties* of *Committees* generally.

General superintendence.

(*a*). It must be remembered at the outset that members of the committee and managers constitute the different parts of the machinery provided by the Act for the due administration of the affairs of the religious

1. Maxwell, pp. 400, 401.
2. *Rajah Vurmah* v. *Ravi Vurmah*, (1876) L. R., 4 I. A. 76 (81): S. C. I. L. R., 1 M. 235.
3. *Vidyapurna Thirtha Swami* v. *Vidyanidhi Thirtha Swami*, (1904) 14 M. L. J. R. 105.

institutions falling under S. 3. Of these two parts members of the committee are persons in whom the general superintendence and control of such institutions are vested[1].

Duty to see endowments not wasted.

(b). It is the duty of the committee to see that endowments are appropriated to their legitimate purposes and are not wasted[2].

II. We shall now proceed to consider the *rights* and *duties* of *Committees* against *trustees*.

Right to appoint trustee.

(c). Committees have the right to appoint a trustee, manager or superintendent[3] for a religious establishment falling under S. 3. There is no objection in appointing a Sivite manager for a Vishnu temple[4] or *vice versâ*.

Right to add trustees.

(d). Committees have power to *add* to the number of existing managers, *i.e.*, to appoint new managers for religious establishments under their control in addition to the old, provided the same is for the beneficent management of the temple or other religious establishment[5]. The committee must exercise this power reasonably and in good faith in furtherance of the beneficial administration of the trust. If it is not so exercised, the appointment of additional members will not be given effect to. The power to add, therefore, though discretionary is not absolute and can be controlled by a Civil Court. This principle is also embodied in S. 49 of the Trusts Act which is said to be equally applicable to public trusts[6].

---

1. *Kaliyanaramayyar* v. *Mustak Shah Saheb*, (1896) I. L. R., 19 M. 395.

2. *Chinna Rangaiyangar* v. *Subbraya Mudali*, (1867) 3 M. H. C. 334; *Puddolabh Roy* v. *Ramgopal Chatterjee*, (1882) I. L. R., 9 C. 133; *Ponduranga* v. *Nagappa*, (1889) I. L. R., 12 M. 366; *Kaliyanaramayyar* v. *Mustak Shah Saheb*, (1896) I. L. R., 19 M. 395; *Tiruvengadath Ayyangar* v. *Srinivasa Thathachariar*, (1899) I. L. R., 22 M. 361.

3. *Syed Amin Sahib* v. *Ibram Sahib*, (1868) 4 M. H. C. 112; *Sethu* v. *Subramanya*, (1887) I. L. R., 11 M. 274 (277).

4. *Gandavathara* v. *Devanayaga*, (1883) I L. R., 7 M. 222.

5. *Shaik Davud Saiba* v. *Hussein Saiba*, (1893) I. L. R., 17 M. 212 following the decision in R. A. 31 of 1888 unreported. In *Virasami Nayudu* v. *Subba Rau*, (1882) I. L. R., 6 M. 54, one of the grounds of dismissal of the trustee was general insubordination on his part in refusing to join with him 3 others appointed by the committee to help him and this dismissal was upheld by the High Court.

6. *Sheik Davud Saiba* v. *Hussein Saiba*, supra. See also *Purmanundass Jeevundass* v. *Venayekrao Wassoodeo* (1882) L. R. 9 I. A. 86: S. C. I. L. R., 7 B. 19, where the Judicial Committee held that a Court had power to appoint in its discretion additional trustees and *Thackersey Dewraj* v. *Hurbhum Nursey*, (1884) I. L. R., 8 B. 432 (464) where *Scott*, J. held that the main rules laid down in the Trusts Act as applicable to trusts were part of the common law. But see per *Bhashyam Aiyangar*, J. in *Vidyapurna Thirtha Swami* v. *Vidyanidhi Thirtha Swami*, (1904) 14 M. L. J. R., 105 (117).

(e). Committees have a right to maintain suits to establish their right of control without any preliminary sanction of the Civil Court[1], *i.e.*, they may sue for a declaration that a temple falls under S. 3 and is subject to their control[2]. Suits by committees to enforce their right of control against the officers of the temple subordinate to them may also be maintained without sanction of Court[1]; *e. g.*, committees have an inherent right of suit against persons subject to their control and bound to account to them for misapplication of the trust funds[3].

Suit to establish control—no sanction.

(f). Although committees may have control it has been held that they are not entitled to possession of the temple and its properties[4]. According to the decisions it is only the trustee (though appointed by the committee) that is entitled to the possession of the temple and its properties and to the receipt of the income accruing from such properties[5]. This position, it is submitted, is, however, not strictly correct[6]. The property is vested in the idol and it is a misnomer to call the person who is managing its temporal affairs as the trustee in the sense of a person in whom the property is vested. He is at best an agent of the idol appointed by the committee[6]. He has simply the custody and it is difficult to see why such committee should not have this custody or at any rate sue third parties and hand over the custody to the manager. Moreover, under the Act committees take the place of the Board of Revenue and are appointed to manage the affairs of the mosques &c., under their control. The power to have possession or custody of the endowed properties is one of the powers of management[7]. Under the old Regulations, the manager was deemed to sue on

Possession of endowed properties.

1. *L. Venkatasa Naidu* v. *Sadagopasamy*, (1869) 4 M. H. C. 404, following *Agri Sharma Embrandri* v. *Vistnu Embrandri*, (1866) 3 M. H. C. 198.

2. *L. Venkatasa Naidu* v. *Sadagopasamy*, supra; *Ponduranga* v. *Nagappa*, (1889) I. L. R., 12 M. 366.

3. *Chinna Rangaiyangar* v. *Subbraya Mudali*, (1867) 3 M. H. C. 334; *Puddolabh Roy* v. *Ramgopal Chatterjee*, (1882) I. L. R., 9 C. 133.

4. *Ponduranga* v. *Nagappa*, (1889) I. L. R., 12 M. 366; *Kaliyanaramayyar* v. *Mustak Shah Saheb*, (1896) I. L. R., 19 M. 395; Per *Shephard*, J, in *Seshadri Ayyangar* v. *Nataraja Ayyar*, (1898) I. L. R., 21 M. 179. But see *L. Venkatasa Naidu* v. *Sadagopasamy*, supra, and (1872) 7 M. H. C. 77 where, however, no objection was taken on this score.

5. *Ponduranga* v. *Nagappa*, supra; *Sankaramurti Mudaliar* v. *Chidambara Nadan*, (1893) I. L. R., 17 M. 143.

6. See Introduction, Chapter XII.

7. See also notes to Ss. 11 and 12.

behalf of his procurator the Government[1]. There can be no doubt that the Government may sue for possession and custody. It is difficult to see why a committee which is the substitute for the Board of Revenue is disentitled to sue[2]. An exception[3] is expressly made by S. 12. If the Committee should take leases in the interests of the institution it is not an illegal or a void act[4]. Upon the principle laid down in the cases that the manager is the only person entitled to possession, the Board has directed that tasdik allowances should be received by the manager[5].

Interference in internal management.

(g). According to the decisions a committee will not be entitled to interfere with trustees or managers in matters of ritual or in the internal management of the religious establishments under the control of the committees[6]. In *Seshadri Ayyangar* v. *Nataraja Ayyar*[6] *Davies*, J., expressed a contrary opinion and his reasoning was that the Board of Revenue had absolute and unqualified powers and had the fullest control including even the internal arrangements of the institution, and that such powers and control devolved upon the committee which had taken the place of the Board. No doubt, as pointed out by *Collins*, C. J., in the same case, the Board of Revenue possessed no arbitrary powers under the Regulations. It may also be true as observed in *L. Venkatasa Nayudu* v. *Shri Shadagopa Swami*[7] that the interference by the Board of Revenue though beneficial was in most cases irregular and the fact of interference could not be treated as evidence of a strictly legal right to interfere. Such interference might be referable to the action of the Government or Board of Revenue or Local Agents in their executive capacity[8]. An act done in the exercise of the executive functions of Government would not be an act of itself legalised by the Regulations and, therefore, such act could not be exercised by the committees although they might have taken the place of the Board. However this may be, there is no question of

1. *Jewun Doss Sahoo* v. *Shah Kubeer-ood-deen* (1840) 2 M. I. A. 390.
2. See further notes to S. 11.
3. *Syed Amin Sahib* v. *Ibram Sahib*, (1868) 4 M. H. C. 112; *Sankaramurti Mudaliar* v. *Chidambara Nadan*, (1893) I. L. R., 17 M. 143.
4. *Kaliyanaramayyar* v. *Mustak Shah Saheb*, (1896) I. L. R., 19 M. 395. See further notes to S. 11.
5. Proceedings of the Madras Board of Revenue, No. 2645, dated 19th September 1879. Vide B. S. O. Ch. VI, No. 78, p. 263 (Madras Edition of 1900).
6. Per *Shephard*, J., in *Seshadri Ayyangar* v. *Nataraja Ayyar*, (1898) I. L. R., 21 M. 179; *Tiruvengadath Ayyangar* v. *Srinivasa Thathachariar*, (1899) I. L. R., 22 M. 361.
7. (1872) 7 M. H. C. 77 (81); see also *Ponduranga* v. *Nagappa*, (1889) I. L. R., 12 M. 366.
8. *Ramiengar* v. *Gnana Sambanda Pandara Sannada*, (1867) 5 M. H. C. 53.

an act done by a sovereign in his executive capacity in the appointment of a pag.da servant. Such appointment relates to the internal management. So also questions of ritual relate to the internal management. But if the so-called trustee should be only an agent of the idol appointed by the committee and the Board was dealing with all questions of internal management, the committee appointed in the place of the Board would be entitled to interfere in the internal management when that should be to the interest of the institution or idol. All the powers of the Board have devolved upon the committee. S. 11 does not amount to a prohibition of the internal management by the committee. Its only effect is that the committee cannot appoint one among themselves to be the agent of the idol. See further notes to S. 11.

Appointment of pagoda servants.

(*h*). Following the principle referred to in (*g*) it has been held that the committee can neither appoint nor dismiss a pagoda servant and that the latter can only be appointed or dismissed by the trustee or manager[1].

Accounts.

(*i*). The committee will be entitled to call for accounts from the trustee or manager of the temple under the control of such committee[2] though not from a hereditary trustee or manager[3].

Trustees no servants.

(*j*). Trustees or managers appointed by the committee are responsible to the latter for their conduct[4], but they are not mere servants of the committee[5]. Where trustees want to enforce their right no sanction of the committee is necessary[6].

1. See S. A. 1078 of 1901, Jud. Ind. for 1902, (Madras High Court) p. 263. But see *Gopinadha Panda* v. *Ramachandra*, (1896) 6 M. L. J. R. 255 where, the committee dismissed a person who held the hereditary office of temple treasurer. The point, however, was not apparently argued. From our remarks in (*g*) pp. 46 and 47 it will appear that the view stated in the text (*h*) as the effect of the decisions is erroneous. The other view will not disentitle a dharmakarta from removing a temple servant though hereditary for good and sufficient case. In fact the dharmakarta had this right under the old Regulations. See *Raghavacharry* v. *Yavaluppa*, Mad.Sadr. Decs. of 1849, p. 37. But in this case the dharmakarta's nomination was apparently not subject to the control of Government.

2. See S. 13.

3. *Ramiengar* v. *Gnana Sambanda Pandara Sannadu*, (1867) 5 M. H. C. 53; *K. Venkatabalakrishna Chettiyar* v. *Kaliyanaram Aiyangar*, (1869) 5 M. H. C. 48; *Fakurudin Sahib* v. *Ackeni Sahib*, (1880) I. L. R., 2 M. 197 (198). But see *Jan Ali* v. *Ram Nath Mundul*, (1881) I. L. R., 8 C. 32 contra. See further notes to S. 13.

4. *Chinna Rangaiyangar* v. *Subbraya Mudali*, (1867) 3 M.H.C. 334; *Ranga Pai* v. *Baba*, (1897) I. L. R., 20 M. 398.

5. *Sethu* v. *Subramanya*, (1887) I. L. R., 11 M. 274; *Seshadri Ayyangar* v. *Nataraja Ayyar*, (1898) I. L. R., 21 M. 179 (Per *Collins*, C. J., and *Shephard*, J. *Davies*, J. dissenting).

6. *Agri Sharma Embrandri* v. *Vistnu Embrandri*, (1866) 3 M. H. C. 198.

Dismissal of trustees for just and sufficient cause.

(*k*). Committees may, without recourse to any suit or the sanction of a Civil Court, dismiss for just and proper cause the trustee or manager appointed by them over religious institutions under their control[1]. The leading case upon the subject is that of *Chinna Rangaiyangar* v. *Subbraya Mudali*[2] and the decision in this case has now become the established law. The High Court in this case observed: "The effect of the enactments is to confide to the committee the same duties and responsibilities and to enable them to exercise the same powers as the Board of Revenue; and, assuming for the present that the sections which relate to the bringing of a suit do not apply to the committee, we think the dismissal from office of Panchayats of Pagodas under their general superintendence is within the powers so transferred, but subject, of course, to the right which the person dismissed no doubt has to seek redress in a suit for dismissal on improper or insufficient grounds." And after referring to the Regulations and the powers of the Board of Revenue, the High Court observed: "We think the authority to suspend or remove for just cause was properly incident to the principal duties and responsibilities of the Board of Revenue and was impliedly given." The committee can have no higher rights than those possessed by the Board. It is, therefore, not necessary to consider the soundness of the reasoning adopted in some of the cases that the trustee or manager appointed by the committee has a freehold in his office[3].

Onus.

The onus is on those who rely on the dismissal to make out that there is good and sufficient cause for the dismissal and to establish that the manager's right has ceased[4].

---

1. *Chinna Rangaiyangar* v. *Subbraya Mudali*, (1867) 3 M. H. C. 334; *Syed Amin Sahib* v. *Ibram Sahib*, (1868) 4 M. H. C. 112; *Ramiengar* v. *Gnana Sambanda Pandara Sannada*, (1867) 5 M. H. C. 53; *Virasami Nayudu* v. *Subba Rau*, (1882) I. L. R., 6 M. 54; *Seshadri Ayyangar* v. *Nataraja Ayyar*, (1898) I. L. R., 21 M. 179; *Tiruvengadath Ayyangar* v. *Srinivasa Thathachariar* (1899) I. L. R., 22 M. 361; *Anantanarayana Ayyar* v. *Kuttalam Pillai*, (1899) I. L. R., 22 M. 481; *Dorasami Ayyar* v. *Annasami Ayyar*, (1899) I. L. R, 23 M. 306; and *Thandavaraya Pillai* v. *Subbayyar*, (1899) I. L. R., 23 M. 483.

2. (1867), 3 M. H. C. 334. This case was remitted to the Lower Court for finding upon an issue whether the dismissal was for sufficient cause. The finding was that the dismissal was without just cause. And this finding, was confirmed by the Hight Court in a judgment reported in 3 M.H. C. 338.

3. *Seshadri Ayyangar* v. *Nataraju Ayyar*, (1898) I. L. R., 21 M. 179. See also Introduction, Ch. X.

4. *Dorasami Ayyar* v. *Annasami Ayyar*, (1899) I. L. R., 23 M. 306.

The question what is a just and proper cause for dismissal is one of greater difficulty. The principles which guide courts in dismissing hereditary managers for misconduct[1] &c., will, to a certain extent, hold good in the case of committees dismissing managers appointed by them. What is a just cause for dismissing a hereditary manager will equally be a just cause for dismissing a manager appointed by the Committee. But what is just cause for dismissing the latter may not be a just cause for dismissing a hereditary manager. Again, committees may dismiss a manager appointed by them upon grounds which may not commend themselves to a Court when moved to remove a hereditary manager or even a manager appointed by such committees. The Court may think that the manager may be put upon terms under such circumstances[2]. In *Kristnasamy Tatacharry* v. *Gomatum Rangacharry*[3], however, the Madras High Court held that the question whether there was a sufficient ground for dismissal of a pagoda hereditary servant by a dharmakarta was one of degree and not of principle and must depend upon the circumstances of each case. In this case, the Court set aside the dismissal. If the principle laid down in this case be correct it must equally extend to the matter on hand. A mere error of judgment will not be sufficient to disqualify an office-holder such as a manager. To justify removal from such office it must be shewn that the further holding of it is incompatible with the interests of the temple or religious establishment[4]. The question is whether there is proof of such misconduct as to render his removal from office necessary in the interests of the institution under the control of the Committee[5].

What is just and proper cause?

Some valid grounds of dismissal may here be stated.

(i). A failure on the part of the manager to render accounts to the Committee will be a breach of one of the most important duties cast upon him by law and will be sufficient to justify his dismissal[6].

Not rendering accounts.

1. *Damodar Bhatji* v. *Bhat Bhogilal Kasandas*, (1896) I. L. R., 22 B. 493. See also Introduction, Ch. XII.
2. *Sivasankara* v. *Vadagiri*, (1889) I. L. R., 13 M. 6; *Natesa* v. *Ganapati*, (1890) I. L. R., 14 M. 103. The committee may also impose terms.
3. (1868) 4 M. H. C. 63.
4. *Tiruvengadath Ayyangar* v. *Srinivasa Thathachariar*, (1899) I. L. R., 22 M. 361.
5. *Tiruvengadath Ayyangar* v. *Srinivasa Thathachariar*, supra. See further introduction and notes to S. 14 and *Annaji Raghunath Gosavi* v. *Narayan Sitaram*, (1896) I. L. R., 21 B. 556, (a decision with reference to a hereditary manager.)
6. *Anantanarayana Ayyar* v. *Kuttalam Pillai*, (1899) I. L. R., 22 M. 481.

(ii). If the manager should defy the authority of the committee and refuse to act in conjunction with persons whom the committee may appoint expressly to act with him or set up an hereditary right of managership he may be removed[1]. So also general insubordination and obstruction to the committee will entail dismissal.

Disobedience to committee's authority.

(iii). He may also be removed for neglect in the discharge of his duties[2].

Neglect.

(iv). He may also be dismissed for misappropriation of temple funds or for wrongful alienation of the temple endowments[3] or for setting up a title in himself with reference to the trust properties[4].

Misappropriation.

But in all such cases the committee must give the manager reasonable notice. A dismissal of the manager without giving him an opportunity to be heard in defence and without making any enquiry is invalid and is liable to be set aside at the suit of the manager[5]. But if, upon notice, the manager does not attend the dismissal will be valid though the charges may be proved to be unfounded[6].

(*l*). Pending enquiry as to dismissal the committee may, after giving reasonable notice and after enquiry, suspend the manager for good cause[7]. Suspension is only a temporary removal, whereas dismissal is a permanent removal, and it is extremely unlikely that the Legislature should have armed the committee with a higher power

Power of suspension.

1. *Virasami Nayudu* v. *Subba Rau*, (1882) I. L. R., 6 M. 54.

2. *Fakurudin Sahib* v. *Ackeni Sahib*, (1880) I. L. R., 2 M. 197 (a decision with reference to a hereditary manager); *Virasami Nayudu* v. *Subba Rau*, supra; *Thackersey Dewraj* v. *Hurbhum Nursey*, (1884) I. L. R., 8 B. 432 (466).

3. *Fakurudin Sahib* v. *Ackeni Sahib*, supra.

4. *Chintaman Bajaji Dev* v. *Dhondo Ganesh Dev*, (1888) I. L. R., 15 B. 612; *Huseni Begam* v. *The Collector of Moradabad*, (1897) I. L. R., 20 A. 46 (both being decisions with reference to a hereditary manager). But see *Muhammad Jafar* v. *Muhammad Ibrahim*, (1900) I. L. R., 24 M. 243.

5. *Seshadri Ayyangar* v. *Nataraja Ayyar*, (1898) I. L. R., 21 M. 179. This principle is founded on natural justice and is one applicable to all voluntary societies. *Gompertz* v. *Goldingham*, (1886) I. L. R., 9 M. 319; *Krishnasami Chetti* v. *Virasami Chetti*, (1886) I. L. R., 10 M. 133; *Jagannath Churn* v. *Akali Dassie*, (1893) I. L. R., 21 C. 463. *Lalji Shamji* v. *Walji Wardhman*, (1895) I. L. R., 19 B 507 (525); *Appaya* v. *Padappa*, (1898) I. L. R., 23 B. 122 (129); *Keshavlal* v. *Bai Girja*, (1899) I. L. R., 24 B. 13 (22); *Nathu* v. *Keshawji*, (1901) I. L. R., 26 B. 174 (186). But see *The Advocate-General of Bombay* v. *David Haim Devaker*, (1886) I. L. R., 11 B. 185.

6. *Narasimha Chariar* v. *Muthukumarasamy*, (1901) 11 M. L. J. R., 236.

7. *Seshadri Ayyangar* v *Nataraja Ayyar*, supra. Mr. Justice *Shephard*, however, expressed a contrary opinion in this case. But in *Chinna Rangaiyangar* v. *Subbraya Mudali*, (1867) 3 M. H. C. 334, the authority to suspend for just cause was treated to be on the same footing as the authority to remove and was held to be a proper incident to the principal duties and responsibilities of the Board whose place was taken by the Committee Cf. *Natesa* v. *Ganapati*, (1890) I. L. R., 14 M. 103.

but not with the lesser one. No doubt a power to appoint a manager does not carry with it a power to dismiss the manager so appointed[1]. But where with the power to appoint there is a power to dismiss such power must include the lesser power of suspension. In support of the view that there is no power of suspension, it is said that the committee cannot manage and that no provision is made in the Act about the management of the temple in the interval. But these are mere assumptions. S. 12 of the Act contemplates management by the committee. It is said that S. 11 has the effect of incapacitating the committee from managing. As will be seen from the notes to that section it has no such effect. S. 11 only enacts that the committee cannot appoint one of themselves to be a trustee or manager either permanently or temporarily. It is also not correct to say that no provision is made in the Act about interim management. No doubt S. 5 of the Act will not enable the committee to apply to the Civil Court for the appointment of a temporary manager, for that section only applies to institutions falling under S. 4 and not to those under S. 3. But the committee may appoint a person as manager temporarily, and if, on the ultimate enquiry, they should dismiss the former manager, they may confirm the temporary person. So also the committee may, without dismissing the former manager, suspend him after enquiry, if there is any just cause for doing so and may re-instate him afterwards. But even assuming the above assumptions to be correct, this cannot negative the power of the committee to suspend. So has the Act made no provision about other matters affecting the committee.

III. The last matter that has to be considered is with reference to the *rights* and *duties* of the *members* of the committee *inter se*.

Whole committee must sue.

(*m*) If any suit is to be brought it must be by the whole committee. Some, though a majority, of the members are not entitled to sue without joining the others[2]. So where the Local Government appointed a single committee for a district as was the case in South Arcot, and the members thereof for convenience of management divided themselves into committees for the several taluqs of the district, such self-constituted taluq committees would have no independent existence apart from the committee for the whole district, and such

1. *Gajapati v. Bhagavan Doss*, (1891) I. L. R., 15 M. 44.
2. *Bangaru Aiyar v. Siva Subrahmania Pillai*, (1900) 10 M. L. J. R., 397.

sub-committees would not be entitled to sue for any right of management[1]. In the case in which this point was decided, the Court observed : " It may be assumed that, for the more convenient discharge of the duties confided to it, the committee entrusted the immediate supervision of the religious institutions of particular taluqs to certain members of the committee who were specially interested therein, or had special facilities for discharging the functions of the committee; but *the committee could not divest itself of its rights in favour of some of its members.* The *superintendence* of the pagoda appertains to *the whole committee* * * * and similarly the right to appoint or discharge dharmakartas, and the right to recover possession of the property, belongs, if to any of the members as such members, to the whole committee." The Court accordingly held that the plaintiffs had no *status* as members of a taluq committee as distinct from the District Committee and that the fact that the old dharmakarta had correspondence with the members of the taluq committee could not estop him from questioning the right of the taluq committee to sue.

But where the individual right of any member or members is violated by the others such member or members may sue. For instance where some of the members exclude the others from management and appoint a manager without consulting the others the latter will be entitled to sue for a declaration that the person so appointed as manager is not the rightful manager[2].

Corporate Act.

(*n*). Any act of the committee must be its corporate act[3]. The corporate act is required not merely for binding the committee but also for rendering the act itself valid. The committee should be regarded in the light of a corporation for this purpose so that unanimity on the part of the members is not required[4]. The decision of a majority of the committee with reference to a particular matter discussed in a meeting will be good as being the act of the committee[5]. This is equally

Decision of majority.

1. *Virasami Nayudu* v. *Arunachella Chetti*, (1880) I. L. R., 2 M. 200.

2. *Lakshminarayana Aiyar* v. *Thandavaraya Pillai*, (1899) 10 M. L. J. R., 100.

3. *Thandavaraya Pillai* v. *Subbayyar*, (1899) I. L. R., 23 M. 483.

4. *Anantanarayana Ayyar* v. *Kuttalam Pillai*, (1899) I. L. R., 22 M. 481 (483).

5. *Cooper* v. *Gardner*, (1869) L. R., 8 Eq., 249 followed in *Lalji Shamji* v. *Walji Wardhman*, (1895) I. L. R., 19 B. 507. See also *Pandurungy Annachariyar* v. *Iyathory Mudaly*, (1869) 4 M. H. C. 448.

the case when there are several trustees, and the question arises with reference to their acts[1]. The decision of the majority is only valid and binding on the minority only with reference to acts within their jurisdiction. But if the act is unauthorised or illegal or amounts to a breach of trust, the decision of the majority will not bind the minority, and the latter will be entitled to question it in a suit[2].

What is a majority?

It is almost a truism if it is said that if out of six persons three vote in one way and the rest in another there is no majority either way, and yet this was seriously in question in an early case[3]. There a committee consisted of 6 members, of whom three were for dismissing the old dharmakarta and appointing the plaintiff as dharmakarta (of Sri Rajagopalaswamy temple at Mannargudy) and the other three were against such dismissal (whether at a meeting or not it does not appear). The High Court (*Innes* and *Collatt*, JJ.) held that as the three did not then form the majority of the committee they could not validly dismiss the old dharmakarta and could not validly appoint a new one, and that the fact that one of those who voted against the dismissal had since died could not make the three who were for dismissal a majority. The High Court observed: "Three might perhaps have been sufficient to form a quorum in the absence of other members; but as the case is stated every member of the committee voted. Without deciding whether the committee must not be unanimous in dismissing or appointing a manager or trustee of a temple, we are of opinion that at least there must be a majority of the committee assenting to such dismissal or appointment and that consequently the appointment of the plaintiff was invalid."

Casting vote of Chairman.

At common law there is no casting vote for the chairman and the right to a casting vote must be specially conferred[4]. So that if the votes are equally divided there is no majority.

---

1. *Charavur Teramath* v. *Urath Lakshmi*, (1883) I. L. R., 6 M. 270. But see Yajnawalkya, Ch. II vv. 188 and 192 (Mandlik 230).

2. *Attorney-General* v. *Calvert*, (1857) 23 Beav. 248 approved in *In re Perry Almshouses*, (1898) 1 Ch. 391 and (1899) 1 Ch. 21; *Attorney-General* v. *Welsh*; (1844) 4 Hare 572: S. C. 67 R. R., 152 referred to in *Venkatachalapati* v. *Subbarayadu*, (1890) I. L. R., 13 M. 293; *The Advocate-General* v. *Muhammad Husen Huseni*, (1866) 12 B. H. C. 323; *Lalji Shamji* v. *Walji Wardhman*, (1895) I. L. R., 19 B. 507. See the decision of a Full Bench of the Madras High Court in a recent case not yet reported. L. P. A. 58 of 1902, 13 M. L. J., (Recent Cases) 64.

3. *Pandurungy Annachariyar* v. *Iyathory Mudaly*, (1869) 4 M. H. C. 443.

4. *Rex* v. *Blyth*, (1697) 5 Mod. 404; *Anonymous*, (1697) 12 Mod. 232; *Nell* v. *Longbottom*, (1894) 1 Q. B. 767.

Generally all acts of a corporation must be performed at a meeting convened after due notice to all the members of the body, and this rule is specially enforceable in a case in which the matter to be decided involves the rights of third parties and a decision to their prejudice is to be arrived at[1]. So a committee in cases where the question is as to the removal of a trustee from office must hold a meeting after giving due notice and consider the question[1]. In the case in which the above principles were upheld, the facts were that there were five members of the committee (Musiri), one of them initiated an inquiry into the conduct of the dharmakarta received petitions, &c., and reported the result of his work to two others. Thereupon all three signed and sent an yadast that the dharmakarta (the plaintiff in the case) should present himself at the office for the purpose of an enquiry into certain charges laid against him, but no date was fixed, but the other two members did not take any part in the passing of such an order. The plaintiff took no notice of this yadast and did not attend. Thereupon the three members passed a resolution dismissing the plaintiff from office and sent it over to the other two who, however, did not sign. It was held that the dismissal was not valid.

Acts to be done in meetings

(o). The committee as a body resembling a corporation, has, in the absence of any provision in Act XX, implied powers to make rules or bye-laws with reference to the procedure in the matter of meetings, including the fixing of quorums, and they are valid provided they do not contravene the law of the land and are not unreasonable[2]. As there must at least be two persons to form a meeting[3], a bye-law fixing that one person may form a quorum will be unreasonable and invalid.

Power to make bye-laws.

Where a committee for the whole district consists of about 30 members and they make a rule that 11 of them should have the management over certain institutions including the power of appointment and dismissal of dharmakartas, the Madras High Court held that such of the eleven could dismiss a trustee for reasonable cause[1]. This proceeds upon the principle that the committee in effect passed a resolution that 11 of their number should form a

Nature of bye-law—Quorum or delegation.

1. *Thandavaraya Pillai* v. *Subbayyar*, (1899) I. L. R., 23 M. 483.
2. *Thandavaraya Pillai* v. *Subbayyar*, supra. See Manu, Ch. VIII v. 41. The Mayukha, Ch. XII, S. 1, (Mandlik 130) and Yajnawalkya, Ch. II, v. 192 (Mandlik 230) which refer to the law of guilds or *ganas*.
3. *Sharp* v. *Dawes*, (1876) 2 Q. B. D. 26.
4. *Virasami Nayudu* v. *Subba Rau*, (1882) I. L. R., 6 M. 54.

quorum for transacting business. The Court observed[1]: "It is further contended that the dismissal should have been the act of the majority of the whole committee, and not the mere majority of a portion of such committee. We cannot agree with this contention. The dismissal was the act of a fully convened meeting of eleven members of the temple committee...... ... ...; nor do we see anything unreasonable upon the part of a large committee like that connected with this case, consisting of thirty members, passing a rule, as it is in evidence has been done, for the purpose of transacting business, that eleven of their members shall form a *quorum*." Whether this is the real effect of the rule seems, however, not to have been contested. There can be no objection to a committee passing a resolution that 11 of their number should form a *quorum*. In such a case all and not merely the eleven have a right to attend. But a resolution that certain specified members of the general committee should transact a particular business amounts to a delegation of the rights of the whole committee to a lesser body and is not a resolution merely affecting *quorum*. This was the *dictum* of the High Court at an earlier stage of the same case[2].

A resolution by a committee consisting of 7 passed at a meeting by a majority of those then present (*i. e.*, 5) to the effect that three should form a *quorum* is a valid resolution[3]. Such a *quorum* was held competent to vote for the dismissal of a manager for misconduct and a resolution for removing the manager passed at a meeting consisting of 3 members was held to be valid[3].

The leading case upon the subject is that of *Anantanarayana Ayyar* v. *Kuttalam Pillai*[3] and the following principles may be deduced from it :—

(1). In the case of a body such as the committee under the Pagoda Act unanimity is not necessary, since it is elementary law that in the case of persons called upon to exercise powers and functions of a more or less public character, unanimity is dispensed with for the obvious reason that if it were insisted upon, the power of willing and acting on the part of such persons would become impossible.

(2). Though committees under the Act are not strictly corporations, there can be no doubt that, with reference to their powers

---

1. *Virasami Nayudu* v. *Subba Rau*, (1882) I. L. R., 6 M. 54 at pp. 57 and 58.
2. *Virasami Nayudu* v. *Arunachella Chetti*, (1880) I. L. R., 2 M. 200.
3. *Anantanarayana Ayyar* v. *Kuttalam Pillai*, (1899) I. L. R., 22 M. 481.

to pass a resolution binding on their body in general and to other matters relating to their procedure in the management of properties and trustees under their control, such committees ought to be looked upon in the light of, and be governed by, the rules applicable to regular corporations.

(3). The acts of the majority, in cases within the charter powers, bind the whole. Here majority means, the major part of those present at a corporate meeting.

(4). In the case of a corporate act to be done by the *constituent members*, a majority of those who appear may act.

(5). But in the case of a corporate act to be done by a select and definite body, as by a board of directors, a majority of the definite body must be present and then a majority of the *quorum* may decide. This principle is a peculiarity of English law and is not a principle of general jurisprudence. It is not recognized by the Roman Law.

(6). There is no inflexible rule, as a matter of law, that a majority of all the members of a select body should be present at a meeting of theirs.

(7). A meeting is the ordinary and natural mode of ascertaining the corporate will as it secures the advantages and safeguards arising from personal consultation.

The *fifth* principle, however, seems to be of doubtful application to committees under the Pagoda Act. It may be good with regard to corporations which have a statutory or other recognized select body to represent them. *Lyster's case*[1] referred to by Mr. Justice *Subramania Iyer* was such a case. Even in cases where an act is authorized to be done by a deputy but none is employed it has been held that the act must be done by all the members[2]. The case of committees which are not empowered to do their duties by deputy must be stronger[3]. The actual decision would seem to be correct, notice having been given to all.

Whether there should be unanimity where business is done otherwise at a meeting as by circulation is an open question. *In re Great Northern Salt and Chemical Works—Ex parte Kennedy*[4] Mr. Justice *Stirling* held that the members of a company need not

1. *In re Tavistock Ironworks Company—Lyster's case*, (1867) L. R. 4 Eq. 233.
2. *Cook* v. *Loveland*, (1799) 5 R. R. 533.
3. *Grindley* v. *Barker*, (1798) 4 R. R. 787 followed in *Anantanarayana Ayyar* v. *Kuttalam Pillai*, (1899) I. L. R., 22 M. 481.
4. (1890) 44 Ch. Div. 472 (480).

meet to appoint their directors as no provision to that effect was made in the articles of the company, but that there should be a determination in accordance with the wishes of the majority. Where the business is not such as to require the meeting of a committee the same principles ought to be applicable.

Liability of committee for acts of a member.

(p) Where one member does a particular act on behalf of the committee and the rest ratify such act, the whole committee will be responsible. So that where it is in dispute whether a particular institution falls under S. 3 or S. 4 and one member enters the temple under an assertion of title in favour of the committee and the rest ratify his act, the members of the committee are all responsible[1] for the trespass if the institution falls under S. 4 and not under S. 3.

Costs.

As regards the question of costs where committees sue on behalf of a religious institution under their control and the suit is necessary in the interests of such institution they will be entitled to be reimbursed the costs of the litigation. But if the suit be whether a particular institution is subject to their control and it is found that the institution does not fall under S. 3, they have themselves to pay the costs. The costs of an unsuccessful appeal by the committee cannot be charged to the funds of the temple, &c., under the control of the committee[2].

"Except in respect of any property which is specially provided for under section 21 of the Act":—S. 21 provides for cases in which the purpose of the trust is partly religious and secular in which case the Board may apportion the property to be transferred and transfer the same to the committee or hereditary manager as the case may be.

Provision as to qualifications for member of such Committee.

VIII. The members of the said Committee shall be appointed from among persons professing the religion for the purposes of which the mosque, temple, or other religious establishment, was founded, or is now maintained [1] and in accordance, so far as can be ascertained, with

1. *L. Venkatesa Nayudu* v. *Shriran Shatagopa Shri Shatagopa Swami*, (1872) 7 M. H. C. 77.

2. *Alagirisami Naickar* v. *Sundareswara Ayyar*, (1898) I. L. R., 21 M. 278 (287).

the general wishes[2] of those who are interested in the maintenance of such mosque, temple, or other religious establishment[3].

The appointment of the Committee shall be notified in the Official Gazette[4].

Ascertaining wishes of persons interested.

In order to ascertain the general wishes of such persons, in respect of such appointment, the local Government may cause an election to be held, under such rules (not inconsistent with the provisions of this Act) as shall be framed by such local Government.

NOTES.

[1]. "**The Members of the said Committee shall be &c., or is now maintained**" :—This section provides for the qualifications for the membership of a committee. It says "members shall be appointed from among persons professing the religion for the purposes of which, the mosque, temple, or other religious establishment was founded or is now maintained."

We do not understand this provision. If one committee is appointed for a single district or division and there are various establishments founded for the purposes of different religious persuasions are, persons professing different religious persuasions eligible to sit in that committee? If they are, a committee consisting of persons of different religious persuasions will have the control of mosques, temples, &c., within the District. But we have already said that this cannot be[1] and apparently the Government have taken care not to constitute the Committee in this way.

If the appointment of a Committee for the religious establishments of each religion be contemplated and S. 7 be taken to confer upon the Local Government the right to appoint such Committee, then the words may be taken in a distributive sense, and a Committee for looking after the mosques and other religious establishments of theMahomedans must consist of Mahomedans. while a Committee for superintending temples and other Hindu establishments must consist of Hindus.

Where a Committee is appointed separately for the religious establishments of one particular religion persons belonging to

1. See notes to S. 7, pp. 41 and 42.

different sects in the same religion may be appointed. For instance, a Sivite may be legally appointed to a Committee which has under its control Vaishnavite temples. The word "religion" occurring in this section cannot be construed[1] as meaning "sect".

"Said Committee," *i. e.* committee appointed by Local Government *once for all* under S. 7.

[2]. **"In accordance, so far as can be ascertained with the general wishes"**:—In appointing members duty is imposed on Government to consult the wishes of the people interested, and to do so Government may cause an election to be held and frame rules therefor.

Supposing the general wishes are not consulted at all, or if consulted, they are not heeded to by the Local Government who appoint somebody else is that appointment invalid? The Act makes no provision, but we suppose the appointment by the Local Government would not have given to any difficulties of this sort.

[3]. **"Of those who are interested in the maintenance of such mosque, temple, or other religious establishment"**:—Where one Committee is to be appointed for the whole district which may contain mosques, temples and other religious establishments, all persons interested in all of them will together be entitled to vote for the appointment of a Committee member.

[4]. **"The appointment shall be notified in the Official Gazette"**:—But it is not stated what the consequence will be if this is not done. It cannot, we suppose, vitiate the appointment.

Tenure of office.

IX. Every member of a Committee appointed as above shall hold his office for life[1], unless removed for misconduct or unfitness; and no such member shall be removed[2] except by an order of the Civil Court as hereinafter provided*.

Removal.

NOTES.

Tenure of office.

[1]. **"Every member of a committee appointed as above shall hold his office for life"**:—Two constructions are possible. One is that a member appointed by Local Government under S. 8 shall hold office for life. S. 7

---

* See S. 14.

1. *Alwar Ayyangar* v. *Krishnamachariar*, (1899) 9 M. L. J. R., 173.

confers the right upon the Local Government to appoint a committee. S. 8 gives the qualifications of the members to be appointed and the procedure to be adopted. According to this construction the words "appointed as above" qualify "every member" and not the immediately preceding word "committee". The words "as above" naturally must refer to the preceding section (8) and not the one preceding the latter (S. 7). A second construction is that the words "appointed as above" qualify the word "committee." Two things may be said against adopting this latter construction. First of all in S. 8 we find the expression "said commitiee" so that if the Legislature had intended any qualification for the word "committee" the same expression "said committee" would have occurred. *Secondly*, it may be said that in such a case, the word "such" in "no suchmember" becomes a surplusageand the section should have read well if there should be only "no member."

Two views are possible according as we adopt the constructions above stated. The prevailing opinion is that the office of a committee member generally is held for life[1]. This is by adopting the construction that the expression "appointed as above" qualifies "committee." Even then we fail to see why the other view is not possible. Adopting this construction the expression may also be construed to mean "member of a committee appointed by Local Government once for all" and such member is the one appointed by Local Government. If we adopt the other construction, then S. 9 will only apply to members appointed by Local Government in the first instance, (*i.e.*, immediately after the passing of the Act). When there is a vacancy among such members and new members are appointed, there will then be no warrant for stating that such new members also hold their office for life. If follows that no other provision is made as to the tenure of office in cases where members are appointed to fill up vacancies arising among the members appointed by Local Government[2]. At the same time the Act does not say that the appointment enures only for a term of years. Hence until death, resignation, or removal, a member can hold office. But if there is no limitation in the Act that the office is to be for life, then a member may be appointed for a definite term.

1. We don't say this is the effect of decided cases and the observations in *Meenakshi Naidoo* v. *Subramaniya Sastri*, (1887) L. R. 14 I.A. 160 (163) : S.C. I. L. R., 11 M. 26, if strictly taken do not amount to any decision.

2. See also notes to S. 10.

It is competent to a person before election not to accept. It is likewise competent to him after acceptance to resign as the provision as to membership being for life under S. 9 is intended to be a right in favour of such member. It is not a trust which he can vacate only on good cause being shown[1].

[2]. "**No such member shall be removed**":—The effect of this is to make the member liable to be removed by an order of court under S. 14. The common law rule in the case of corporations is that a member may be removed by the others for sufficient cause and after due n tice to such member. If the expression "such member" should only refer to a member appointed by Local Government under S. 8 the question arises as to the rule applicable for the removal of members not so appointed. No doubt S. 14 is general in its terms and will apply to all members, but whether the common law rule is also applicable in such a case is a question deserving of consideration[2].

Provision for filling up vacancies.

X. Whenever any vacancy [1] shall occur among the members of a Committee appointed as above[2], a new member shall be elected to fill the vacancy, by the persons interested as above provided.[3]:

Procedure.

The remaining members of the Committee shall, as soon as possible, give public notice of such vacancy, and shall fix a day, which shall not be later than three months from the date of such vacancy, for an election of a new member[4] by the persons interested as above provided, under rules for elections which shall be framed by the local Government[5];

and whoever shall be then elected, under the said rules, shall be a member of the Committee to fill such vacancy.

When court may fill vacancy.

If any vacancy as aforesaid[6] shall not be filled up by such election as aforesaid within three months after it has occurred[7], the Civil Court[8], on the application

---

1. *Tiruvengada Ayyangar* v. *Rangayyangar*, (1882) I. L R., 6 M. 114. It does not appear in this case whether the member was appointed by Local Government or otherwise under S. 10. See Bill No. 8 of 1866 *Gazette of India*, p. 472, dated the 24th March 1866, referred to in the above case.

2. See notes to S. 10 pp. 63, 64.

of any person whatever[9], may appoint a person to fill the vacancy, or may order that the vacancy be forthwith filled up by the remaining members of the Committee, with which order it shall then be the duty of such remaining members to comply, and if this order be not complied with, the Civil Court may appoint a member to fill the said vacancy.

NOTES.

[1]. "**Any vacancy**":—The vacancy may arise from any cause, *i. e.*, by death, resignation or dismissal[1].

[2]. "**Appointed as above**":—Here again two constructions are possible. The above words either qualify "committee" or "members." If the former construction be correct then S. 10 may be said to apply to all vacancies irrespective of the fact that the members have been appointed by the Local Government or otherwise. Even then it is a question whether the expression does not convey[2] the idea only of a member appointed by Local Government under S. 8. But if the second construction be correct, then S. 10 is inapplicable to a case of vacancy arising among the members appointed under this section upon a vacancy arising among the members appointed by the Local Government.

[3]. "**As above provided**":—What is meant is that the filling up of the vacancy arising among the members shall be by election by the persons mentioned in S. 8 as being interested in the mosque, temple or other religious establishment. These had to be consulted by Government when members of a committee had to be appointed under S. 8.

[4]. "**The remaining members &c., for an election of a new member**":—If a vacancy occurs duty is imposed on the remaining members of a committee to fix a day (not later than 3 months from the date of the vacancy) for election of a member by election by the persons interested.

Rules for election.

[5]. **Under rules for elections which shall be framed by the Local Government**:—Under this section rules have been framed by the different Local Governments[3]. The appointment to a vacancy in the way pointed out by this section is not vitiated by the fact that the register

1. *Gopinadha Panda v. Ramachandra*, (1896) 6 M. L. J. R., 255.
2. See p. 60.
3. See the last three Appendices in this book.

of voters kept under the rules does not contain all the voters. It is the duty of the persons entitled to vote to get their names entered in the register, and if they do not do this, the register is not bad.[1] Where a vacancy arising among members appointed by Local Government is filled up and persons are appointed under this section and a fresh vacancy arises among the persons so appointed, what is the procedure to be adopted? Two views are possible as already stated. Either S. 10 applies to such a case or it does not. S. 10 may be said to apply if the words "appointed as above" qualify "committee" subject to the qualification stated already[2]. If so, the rules framed by the Local Governments will govern such cases. It must be stated that many elections must have been held as a matter of fact and these rules applied. On the other hand S. 10 will not apply if the said words "appointed as above" qualify "members." Moreover the words "*the vacancy*", "*such vacancy*", and "*vacancy as aforesaid*" point also to the conclusion that S. 10 is applicable only to a case where a vacancy arising among the members appointed by the Government under S. 8 has to be filled up. If so, there is no provision in the Act for filling fresh vacancies arising among the persons appointed under S. 10 and the rules framed by the Local Governments and found in the Standing Orders of the Board of Revenue will only be applicable to the filling up under S. 10 of vacancies arising among members appointed under Ss. 7 and 8 and will have no application to vacancies arising among persons appointed under S. 10 Any appointments made under these rules in such cases will in this view be illegal and *ultra vires*. Difficulty then arises as to the right to fill up vacanciesand S. 14 of the Act will not solve it as that section only refers to cases of misfeasance, breach of trust, or neglect of duty and does not apply to a simple case of the filling up of a vacancy. If the office of membership of committee should resemble that of trustee, (and we should think it does) then there is some solution of the difficulty. Under S. 539, C.P.C., new trustees may be appointed although there is no allegation of breach of trust. But this must be by suit which is necessarily expensive. If the correct view should be that a committee appointed under S. 7 is a statutory corporation aggregate then it may be contended that the power to fill up vacancies must be expressly given or looked to in the statute creating the corporation

1. *Tiruvengada Ayyangar* v. *Rangayyangar*; (1882) I.L. R., 6 M. 114.
2. See pp. 60 and 62.

and that S. 539, C. P. C., should not be so construed as to perpetuate a corporation when under the statute creating it there is no means of perpetuating it. But it has been observed that committees are not corporations although they may resemble corporations and be governed by the procedure relating thereto[1]. Again it is a rule of the common law that where no other mode of succession is pointed out, corporations aggregate have necessarily the implied powers of electing members in the room of such as are removed by death or otherwise[2]. But it may be doubted whether this rule will apply to the case on hand even assuming committes to be corporations. This is not a case where no mode is pointed out at all but one where some mode is pointed out by the Legislature which unfortunately does not meet all cases and, therefore, the principle *expressio unius est exclusio alterius* may be said to apply[3].

In deciding which of the two constructions above pointed out is correct, courts must consider whether by adopting one of them the apparent purpose of the enactment is frustrated and a result which can never have been intended is arrived at. If so, that construction must not be adopted[4]. No apparent purpose of the enactment is frustrated by adopting either of these constructions though it may be, some inconvenience will result in adopting the construction that the words "appointed as above" qualify "members."

As we had occasion to point out in more than one place the Act is full of these ambiguities of construction, and it is regretable to find that they have not been remedied by the Legislature. It is sincerely to be hoped that the Government will remedy these defects in the near future. An amendment of the Act to remedy these defects will surely not affect the Government policy of non-intervention in religious matters.

Where persons have been appointed under the rules to fill up the vacancies arising among persons appointed under S. 10 and such persons have been controlling and managing the institutions falling under S. 3 for more than the statutory period, such persons may, according to the decisions, acquire a right by prescription which cannot be defeated by any defect in their appointment.[5]

---

1. *Anantanarayana Ayyar* v. *Kuttalam Pillay*, (1899) I. L. R., 22 M. 481.
2. *Rex* v. *Mayor of West Looe*, 3 B. & C. 685.
3. Maxwell 461.
4. Ibid p. 112. *Bhagawan Das* v. *Har Dei*, [1903] I. L. R., 26 A. 227 [232].
5. *Balwant Rao* v. *Purun Mal*, (1883) L. R. 10 I. A. 90 : S. C. I. L. R. 6 A. 1 *Gnanasambanda* v. *Velu Pandaram*, (1899) L. R. 27 I. A. 69 ; S. C. I. L. R., 23 M 271

[6]. **"If any vacancy as aforesaid"** :—*i. e.*, a vacancy which shall occur among the Members appointed as above by the Local Government under S. 8 if the construction that the words "appointed as above" qualify "members" be correct. But if the other construction be adopted the "vacancy" referred to here may be a vacancy among the members however appointed.

[7]. **"Shall not be filled &c., has occurred"**:—If, at the elecion of which notice is given by the committee, no member is filled or elected for some cause or other (it may be the votes are equally divided among more than one person for a single vacancy, or, the election turns out to be invalid and three months elapse from the date of the vacancy) application may be made to the District Judge who is then competent *himself* to appoint a person to fill the vacancy, or to order the remaining members to fill up the vacancy forthwith. But it has been held that where the judge passes an order that the remaining members do fill he vacancy forthwith, such order will not entitle the other members of the committee to nominate a person but only to elect a person as trustee or manager (in accordance with the rules)[1]. We, however, doubt whether this is correct. The Act says that the District Judge may order the other members of the committee to fill up the vacancy. No doubt the Act does not say expressly that such members may nominate. But neither does it say that they should fill up the vacancy "by such election." Unless some such words are introduced there is no justification for this view. Even if the construction adopted in the case referred to be correct it is only on being ordered by the District Judge that the remaining members have the right to fill up the vacancy by election and it is also their duty to comply with such order of the District Judge. If they fail to comply with such order the District Judge may himself appoint[1]. It has been held that they fail to comply with such order where instead of electing according to the rules they themselves nominate a person for the vacancy[1].

District Judge to fill up.

But should the committee not fix a date for election and it was the fault of the committee and not of the persons interested that no election was held, it would seem that in that case too, the District Judge would have jurisdiction for if the three months had

1. *Ramanuja Aiyangar v. Anantaratnam Aiyar*, (1895) 6 M. L. J. R. 1.

expired before the election, the power and duty of appointing a successor would devolve on the District Judge. It seems to be a great hardship that the persons interested should thus lose their right of election without any fault of theirs. Surely provision should have been made for such a case by stating that the District Judge should, on application or complaint from the persons interested, call for an election and could not exercise his right of appointment before the result of such election.

It would appear, however, that under S. 14 the committee might be compelled to fix a day and that if the committee unreasonably delay in fixing a day for the election they might be removed.

The District Judge has power to appoint only if the vacancy is not filled up by election as mentioned in the first part of S. 10 and even then only on application. But under S. 10, the judge will have jurisdiction to fill a vacancy not only when there is a single vacancy in the committee but also when there are more vacancies than one or when there is a vacancy among all the members of the committee[1].

[8]. "**Civil Court**":—*i. e.* The Principal Court of original jurisdiction in the District in which the temple &c., is situate. Their Lordships of the Judicial Committee have held that the power of appointment is conferred on the Civil Court not as a matter of ordinary civil jurisdiction but because the officer who constitutes the Civil Court is sure to be one of weight and authority, and with the best means of knowing the movements of local opinions and feelings[2]. But such officer is conferred the power not as a *persona designata*[3], as otherwise the expression "Civil Court" will not occur. It is purely a discretion vested in the District Judge, and there is no appeal provided for from an order appointing a person as member of commitee[4]. The judge may ask the persons interested to hold an election and recommend a person to him, but he is not bound to appoint the person so recommended[5].

---

1. *Syed Mahomed* v. *Sultan Khan*, (1900) 4 C. W. N. 527.

2. *Meenakshi Naidoo* v. *Subramaniya Sastri*, (1887) L. R., 14 I. A. 160: S. C. I. L. R., 11 M. 26.

3. *Gopala Ayyar* v. *Arunachellam Chetty*, (1902) I. L. R., 26 M. 85.

4. See cases cited in notes (2) and (3) supra.

[9]. **"The application of any person whatever"**:—Here the expression "interested person" referred to in the former part of this section and S. 9 does not occur. The section does not say "any person interested" may apply but "any person whatever." The section does not also say that the judge is entitled to act *suo motu*. If this be the case, is a Judge entitled to act upon an application made by the Judge's sheristadar or attender who may be a Christian? he answer may be in the affirmative if the section confers a *right* upon the officer presiding over "the Civil Court" as a *persona designata*. There will also be nothing incongruous in giving such persons a right to apply as the judge having the right may also be a Christian. But it has been already stated that jurisdiction is conferred upon the District Judge not as a *persona designata*[1]. The Judge is exercising judicial functions[2] when he acts under S. 10 because he must be satisfied that the circumstances entitling him to exercise jurisdiction do exist in the particular case. For instance, he is to be satisfied that there is a vacancy which has not been filled up by election as mentioned in the first part of the section. The fact that there is no appeal does not show that when the judge acts under S 10 he does not act judicially[2]. There is no appeal merely because appeal is only the creature of statute and S. 10 does not give a right of appeal[3]. Moreover "it is a canon of interpretation that all words, if they be general and not express and precise, are to be restricted to the fitness of the matter. They are to be construed as particular if the intention be particular; that is, they must be understood as used in reference to the subject-matter in the mind of the Legislature, and strictly limited to it[4]." Hence the words "any person whatever" should be construed as "any person having any interest whatever."

Appeal, Revision and Suit:—It has been already observed that there is no right of appeal. In *Meenakshi Naidu* v. *Subramania Sastri*[3] their Lordships of the Judicial Committee observed: "In the opinion of their Lordships the tenth section places the right of appointing

Appeal.

1. See notes under heading [8] p. 66.

2. *Gopala Ayyar* v. *Arunachellam Chetty*, (1902) I. L. R., 26 M. 85.

3. *Meenakshi Naidoo* v. *Subramaniya Sastri*, (1887) L. R., 14 I. A. 160: S. C. I. L. R., 11 M. 26.

4. Maxwell p. 85. See also *Bhagwan Das* v. *Har Dei*, (1903) I. L. R., 26 A. 227 (232).

a member of the committee in the Civil Court, not as a matter of *Ordinary Civil Jurisdiction*, but because the officer who constitutes the Civil Court is sure to be *one of weight and authority*, and with the best *means of knowing the movements of local opinions and feeling*, and one can hardly imagine a case in which it would be more desirable that the discretion should be exercised by a person acquainted with the District and with all the surroundings. The exercise of their discretion being so placed in the District Judge their Lordships are unable to find any thing in the tenth section which confers a right of appeal."

Revision.

With reference to revision under S. 622 or S 15 of the Charter Act, it has been already observed that the Judge acts under this section judicially[1]. Therefore a revision will lie[1] where there is a material irregularity or failure to exercise jurisdiction or illegal exercise of jurisdiction.

Suit

With reference to a suit to set aside an appointment although the question was left open, the Privy Council in the case already cited[2] observed: "Mr. Doyne in the course of his argument contended that if a person, very improper and unfit by reason of his religious qualification or moral conduct was appointed, there must be a right either by appeal against the Judge's order or by suit or in some other way to remove the person so appointed. There is force in this argument, but whether a person so improperly appointed could, as has been suggested, be removed by proceedings equivalent to *quo warranto* in England, or whether, upon a full consideration of the merits, the appellant could be considered as a person improperly appointed are questions which their Lordships are not called upon to express an opinion. In their opinion it is clear that there is no *appeal* from that which was a pure discretion vested in the District Judge."

Of course there is no provision as in some other Acts (for instance, the Guardian and Wards Act) that orders under the Pagoda Act are final and not liable to be set aside by a suit. But this of itself will not be entitled to much weight. In a case where the

1. *Gopala Ayyar* v. *Arunachellam Chetty*, (1902) I. L. R., 26 M 85.
2. *Meenakshi Naidoo* v. *Subramaniya Sastri*, (1887) L. R., 14 I. A. 160: S. C. I. L. R., 11 M. 26. See also *Alwar Ayyangar* v. *Krishnamachariar*, (1899) 9 M. L. J. R. 173.

appointment is filled by election by the committee and there is some flaw in such filling up, a suit will lie to set aside the appointment on the ground of such defect. The fact that the District Judge fills up the vacancy will, it is submitted, not make any difference. Where the circumstances conferring jurisdiction upon the District Judge to exercise the power do not exist, an appointment made in the absence of those circumstances is liable to be set aside by suit and the fact that the act of the District Judge is a judicial act and liable to be set aside in revision does not take away the remedy by suit which the persons interested may possess.

No member of a committee to be trustee, &c., of the mosque, &c., under charge of such committee.

XI. No Member of a Committee appointed under this Act [1] shall be capable of being, or shall act, also as a trustee, manager, or superintendent, of the mosque, temple, or other religious establishment [2], for the management of which such Committee shall have been appointed.

NOTES.

[1]. "**No member of a committee appointed under this Act**":—Here the Legislature has not adopted the language used in Ss. 8, 9 and 10 which has given rise to the ambiguities of construction pointed out in those sections.

[2]. "**Shall be capable of being &c., trustee**":—A member of committee shall not be qualified to become a Trustee, Manager or Superintendent of the mosque, &c., under the management of such committee as otherwise the policy of the law in making the control by the committees over the religious establishments in their charge effective will be frustrated. But this does not prevent a member of the committee from being an hereditary manager for an institution coming under S. 4 if he is so entitled to it by succession or other lawful right. A member of the committee may also be a hereditary servant in the temple, &c., under the management of the committee of which he is a member although he cannot be the manager[1]. There may be hereditary offices attached to a temple

1. An instance of a pagoda servant being a member of the committee of the pagoda under the control of such committee is to be found in *Kristnasamy Tatacharry* v. *Rangacharry*, (1868) 4 M. H. C. 63. There the member of the committee was also the 5th Thirtham Arulapadu of Shri Devarajaswami temple in Little Conjevaram subject to the control of the committee.

though the same may fall under S. 3. Such office-holders are servants of the pagoda.

Right of committee to the possession of endowed properties.

It is also provided by this section that a member of committee *shall not act as trustee*, &c., for the management of which such committee shall have been appointed. The effect of these words simply appears to us to be that a committee cannot appoint one of themselves either *permanently* or *temporarily* to be a manager. A member of committee cannot even *act* as trustee. But the construction placed upon these words by the Madras High Court is that they disqualify members of committee from exercising the rights of a trustee and that members of a committee cannot sue for possession of temple properties from a wrong-doer or from a manager whom they have dismissed for misfeasance[2]. It is also said that they cannot sue for rents and collect the income when the trustee neglects to collect the same and use it for the purposes of the trust and thus prevent a breach of trust. It cannot, however, be gainsaid that under S. 12 power is given to the committee for recovering rent of land or other property transferred to the committee as a matter of fact by the Board. But why this distinction is to be made is not known. It is not known why the committee can exercise rights over one class of property but not over another. The Act says that the committee should exercise the rights and take the place of the Board. Surely the Board were giving leases and managing the properties under their control and as one of the incidents of management were receiving and collecting rents. But the powers which have devolved upon the committee are said to be mere powers of supervision and control[3].

Ponduranga v. Nagappa.

In *Ponduranga* v. *Nagappa*[1] which is regarded as the leading case upon the subject their Lordships *Muthusamy Iyer* and *Parker*, JJ., observed: "We agree with the subordinate Judge that the appellants representing the committee would not be entitled to possession of the temple and its properties even if it were found to be subject to their jurisdiction. It is provided by S. 11 of Act XX o

1. *Ponduranga* v. *Nagappa*, (1889) I. L. R., 12 M. 366; *Sankaramurti Mudalia* *Chidambara Nadan*, (1893) I. L. R., 17 M. 143; Per *Shepard* J in *Seshadri Ayyang* *Nataraja Ayyar*, (1898) I. L. R., 21 M. 179.

2. *Ponduranga* v. *Nagappa*, (1889), I. L. R., 12 M. 366. But see cases cited in note (5) p. 45.

1863 that no member of a committee shall be capable of being or shall act as trustee of a temple for the management of which such committee shall have been appointed, and as it is the lawful trustee or the manager of the temple for the time being that is entitled to possession of its properties and to the receipt of its income, the appellants are not at liberty to claim to be put in his place * * * *. The appellant's counsel draws our attention to S. 12 of Act XX of 1863 but it appears to us to be limited to such property as was actually in the possession of the Board of Revenue when the Act was passed. Under that enactment, the committee has, subject to the restrictions imposed by S. 4, the same powers that the Board of Revenue had under Regulation VII of 1817, but those powers were primarily powers of supervision and control designed to ensure due appropriation by the existing trustees of temple endowments to the purposes for which they were destined."

Case discussed.

Apparently the learned Judges would draw a distinction between property transferred by the Board to the Committee and property not so transferred. But even with regard to the property so transferred the learned judges would seem to suggest that although the Committee might possess the powers of the Board of Revenue such powers were merely powers of supervision and control. It is, however, difficult to maintain this latter view in the face of the express provision in S. 12. The committee could collect rents of the land transferred to them by the Board. That supposes they may give leases and manage the property. When property is transferred to them by the Board there is nothing in the Act which compels them to make over the management of the same to the manager[1]. That means the committee may manage. Moreover, we know that the Board of Revenue and Local Agents gave leases of the endowed land and in many cases treated leases granted by the manager &c., as not binding[2]. S. 12 further shows that the committee is appointed for the *superintendence* of the mosque, temple or religious establishment and for the *management* of its affairs. After this it is submitted that it is idle to contend that the powers of the committee are merely powers

1. Either under a mistaken impression of their powers or for sake of convenience committees, it appears, have in most cases transferred to the manager even the property made over to them by the Board.

2. See *Mayandi Chettiyar v. Chokkalingam Pillai*, (1904) 14 M.L.J.R., 200.

of supervision and control whatever these words may mean. Further, even a manager can have strictly no *possession*. The property is vested in the deity or idol. The manager has no legal property vested in him and is only an agent or servant of the deity or idol[1]. He is only entitled to the custody or management of the property. The committee can take over such custody and management from such a person in a proper case or provided the comm ittee act *bonafide* in the interests of the institution. When the committee sue for such taking over of the custody or management they are not really suing for possession. It is submitted that the correct view is that the committee can exercise the powers of management vested in them by the Act provided they act *bonafide* in the interests of the institution and that the mere fact that they appoint a manager will not prevent them from exercising such rights. At any rate it is submitted that so far as regards property transferred by the Board is concerned powers of management are expressly given to the committee by S 12[2].

Taking of rent deeds.

If, as a matter of fact, the Committee take rent deeds from tenants a question arises whether such action on the part of the Committee is illegal or is merely irregular. If the act is illegal the lease itself will be void and no obligation can arise so as to be enforceable by the manager. If it is merely irregular then the lease itself will be good. So far as regards property transferred to the committee the lease is good and even enforeable by the committee. From the observations made in the previous paragraphs it follows that it makes no difference if the lease is with respect to property not so transferred. Even if the correct view be that committees have no right to manage endowed properties no made over to them by the Board their action in taking leases in thei names can at the most only be irregular. This was the view take in *Kalianaramayyar* v. *Mustak Sha Sahib*[2]. His Lordship Mr Justice *Subramania Iyer*, while holding that muchilikas taken i the names of a committee member with respect to property n transferred to the committee were not void and that the tenant mu pay the rent, observed: "Members of committees are th persons in whom the general superintendence and control of suc institutions (*i. e.*, falling under S. 3) are vested. In exercisin

1. See notes to S. 7. under heading (*f*) and Introduction Chapter XII.
2. *Kaliyanaramayyar* v. *Mustak Shah Saheb*, (1896) I. L. R., 19 M. 395. Bombay where Act XX of 63 does not apply Committees have apparently the rig to manage. *Rambabu* v. *Committee of Rameshwar*, (1899) 1 Bom. L. R. 667.

such general control it is an unquestionable duty of theirs to see that the rents payable to the institution are punctually collected and all steps legally necessary for their collection are duly taken. In the performance of this duty, however, the procedure to be observed by them is to get the managers to make the collection and perform all acts necessary for this purpose. Now, if in deviation from this course they take upon themselves to obtain muchilikas in their own names, what is it but an act done in the discharge of their duty to see to the realisation of rents? Such an act done *prima facie* in the interests of the institution can hardly be said to be illegal or wrongful so as to make it void as is contended on behalf of defendant. In my view it is an act which falls within their powers as the controlling authority though, in performing it, they acted in a manner which is not in strict conformity with the procedure prescribed by the law. Moreover, in the face of the provisions of S. 12 of Act XX of 1863, it is scarcely possible to contend that there is anything *in the nature of the act* of collecting rents considered by itself which renders such an act inconsistent with the proper performance by members of committees, of their duties as the supervising authority. For, by the last part of that section, committees are empowered *to collect rents directly* in the case of lands transferred to them by or under the authority of the Board of Revenue. This provision, though confined to the case of such lands, shows that in the opinion of the framers of the Act, direct participation in actual management by collecting rents is not so outside the legitimate functions of committees as to compel courts to decide that an act perfectly valid, if done by them with reference to that portion of the endowments consisting of lands transferred by the Board, is utterly void when it is done with reference to the other portion of the landed endowments. It seems to me more reasonable to hold that, though the members of the committee in the present case deviated from the strict procedure in taking the muchilikas in their own names instead of having them taken by the manager in his own name, yet their action is not illegal." The learned judge then referred to the cases[1] of corporations taking or giving loans for purposes not specified by the charter in which it was held that the loans

1. *Silver Lake Bank* v. *North*, 4 Johnson, Ch. 370; *Coltman* v. *Coltman*, (1881) 19 Ch. D. 64.

were not illegal though it would be a case for the Government to forfeit the charter.

On appointment of Committee, Board and local agents to transfer property.

XII. Immediately on the appointment of a committee as above provided, for the superintendence of any such mosque, temple, or religious establishment, and for the management of its affairs, the Board of Revenue, or the local agents acting under the authority of the said Board, shall transfer to such committee all landed or other property[1] which at the time of appointment shall be under the superintendence, or in the possession, of the said Board or local Agents, and belonging to the said religious establishment, except as is hereinafter provided for,

Termination of powers and responsibilities of Board and agents.

and thereupon the powers and responsibilities of the Board and the local Agents, in respect to such mosque, temple, or religious establishment, and to all land and other property so transferred, except as above, and except as regards acts done and liabilities incurred by the said Board or agents previous to such transfer, shall cease and determine[2].

Commencement of powers of committee.

All the powers which might be exercised by any Board or local agent, for the recovery of the rent of land or other property transferred under this section, may from the date of such transfer be exercised by such committee to whom such transfer is made[3].

NOTES.

[1]. "**Shall transfer to such committee all landed or other property**":—Under this section duty is imposed on the Board and local agents to transfer to the committee all landed or other property, which shall be under the superintendence or in the possession of the Board or such local agents at the date of the appointment of

the committee. Supposing the Board would not transfer would the committee have a right to compel the Board to do so? There is no right without a remedy[1]. So that the Board would be compelled to transfer. But the question is whether the Board could be compelled at the suit of the committee. As the transfer was to be to the committee, it would seem that the latter might sue and compel the Board to transfer the properties in the possession of such Board to the committee.

[2]. "**The powers and responsibilities of the Board and Local Agents, &c., shall cease and determine**":—Upon transfer, the rights and responsibilities of the Board and local agents shall cease. But the section does not in terms say that all such powers and duties shall devolve upon the committee.

[3]. "**All the powers which might be exercised by any Board or local agent for the recovery of rent of land * * may * * be exercised by such committee**":—The powers which the committee can exercise relate by the express language of the section to recovery of rent[2]. It may also be stated that the section does not say that all the powers exercised by the Board with reference to the property transferred to the committee shall devolve upon the latter. But then the *first* part of S. 7 states that the committee shall take the place and exercise the powers of the Board. In the *second* part of S. 7 it is stated that the committee shall perform all the duties imposed on such Board except in respect of any property specially provided for under S. 21. According to *Chinna Rangaiyanyar* v. *Subbraya Mudali*[3] the effect of the enactments in Ss. 7 and 12 is to confide to the committee the same duties and responsibilities and enable them to exercise the same powers as the Board of Revenue, and that S. 14 provides a remedy by suit for the due performance by committees of their duties of superintendence and management. The decisions in later cases that these duties are primarily duties of supervision and control[4] can be no authorities against the view that with respect to the land transferred to the committees the latter have full powers of management. These cases do

Right of committee to sue.

1. *Ashby* v. *White*, (1703) 2 Ld. Raym. 938: S. C. 1. Smith's Leading cases 248.
2. *Ponduranga* v. *Nagappa*, (1889) I. L. R., 12 M. 366. *Sankaramurti Mudaliar* v. *Chidambara Nadan*, (1893) I. L R, 17 M. 143.
3. (1867) 3 M. H. C. 334 (335 and 337).
4. *Ponduranga* v. *Nagappa*, (1889) I. L. R., 12 M. 366 (368); Per *Collins*, C. J. and *Shephard*, J., in *Seshadri Ayyangar* v. *Nataraja Ayyar*, (1898) I. L. R., 21 M. 179.

not consider the language in the *second* part of S. 7. Where land transferred under this section is under the management of the committees who are subsequently dispossessed of such land they can sue for the recovery of such land from the trespasser. When land is transferred to a corporation which is capable of holding land it has the incidental right of suit with respect to such property and this right need not be expressly mentioned[1]. The right to collect the rents also implies the right to take muchilikas. If they take muchilikas from the tenants they may eject the tenants also. It can hardly be supposed that they have no right to eject a trespasser. Within six months of their dispossession they may bring a suit under S. 9 and no question of their right to sue can arise under that section[2]. No doubt it may be said that there can be no real hardship by holding that the committees have no right to sue as the manager has the right to sue. But assuming that there exists no hardship which is more than doubtful why does the Act give committees the power or the right to collect the rent? The cases of *Ponduranga* v. *Nagappa*[3] and *Sankaramurti Mudaliar* v. *Chidambara Nadan*[4], hold that committees are not entitled to possession in any case. In the former the language of S. 7 was not considered. Moreover, the question arose in that case with reference to property not transferred, and the High Court held that the committee had no right of suit with reference to such property. The Court had not to consider the question whether the committee had a right to sue with reference to the property transferred[5]. So also in the latter case the Court had to consider only the question whether the committee had a right to sue with reference to the property not transferred The observations with reference to S. 12 made in these cases can only be *obiter dicta,* and with all respect to the learned judges who made those observations, they are not warranted by the language of Ss. 7 and 12 taken together. In the beginning of S. 12 it is expressly stated that committees are appointed for the *superintendence* of the mosque, &c., and for the *management* of its affairs. W

1. See Coke Litt 325 b and Cf. *Mayor of Colchester* v. *Lowten*, (1813) 1. & 246 : S. C. 12 R. R. 216.

2. See *Ghelabhai Jivanram* v. *Dajibhai Vasonjee*, (899) 1 Bom L. R. 199.

3. (1889) I. L. R., 12 M. 366.

4. (1893) I. L. R., 17 M. 143.

5. See also notes to S. 11, pp. 68 to 72.

have already stated that under S. 7 the committees take the place and exercise the powers of the Board and shall perform all the duties imposed on such Board except in respect of property specially provided for in S. 21. So that these provisions take away the force of any reasoning based upon the fact that S. 12 while declaring that the powers and responsibilities of the Board are determined upon the transfer referred to in the section *does not say that all the powers generally of the Board devolve upon the committee.* We have already observed that S. 11 does not amount to a prohibition against the exercise by the committee of the rights of manager. Moreover S. 13 imposes a duty on the committee to keep accounts of their management and favors the view that the committee may manage property. In Bombay to which, however, Act XX of 1863 does not apply temple committees appear to have the right of management[1].

Duty of trustee, &c., as to accounts.

XIII. It shall be the duty of every trustee, manager, and superintendent of a mosque, temple, or religious establishment to which the provisions of this Act shall apply[1],to keep regular accounts of his receipts and disbursements, in respect of the endowments and expenses of such mosque, temple, or other religious establishment;

And of committees.

and it shall be the duty of every committee of management, appointed or acting under the authority of this Act, to require from every trustee, manager, and superintendent of such mosque, temple, or other religious establishment[2], the production of such regular accounts of such receipts and disbursements at least once in every year; and every such Committee of management shall themselves keep such accounts thereof[3].

NOTES.

[1]. "**It shall be the duty of every trustee, &c., to which the provisions of this Act shall apply.**"—The *first* part of the section imposes a duty on managers of religious institutions to keep regular accounts of the receipts and disbursements whether such institutions fall under S. 3 or S. 4. The provisions of the

1. *Rambabu* v. *Committee of Rameshwar*, (1899) 1 Bom. L. R. 667.

Act apply to both classes of institutions. It will, therefore, seem to be the duty of an hereditary manager to keep regular accounts under this section just as much as it is the duty of a manager appointed by the committee. This is only declaratory of the common law[1] so that even if the whole section be held to be applicable only to a manager of an institution falling under S. 3 the common law rule will apply to the hereditary managers. The particle "*and*" after "manager" and before "superintendent" is apparently a mistake for "*or*" the latter word having occurred up till now. But no provision is made in the Act for inspection of accounts or, if the construction placed by the Madras High Court referred to below be correct, for checking the accounts of a manager &c., of a religious establishment falling under S. 4. It is only by charging the manager with breach of trust and on the application of a person interested for leave to file a suit against such manager that inspection may be ordered by the judge under Ss. 18 and 19.

[2]. "**And it shall be the duty of every committee of management, * * * to require from every trustee, * * of such mosque, temple or other religious establishment**":—This language clearly covers the case of a manager nominated by the committee, for as the said manager is under the jurisdiction and control of the committee, it is but reasonable that he should account his management to the committee. The duty is just as much upon the committee to require the manager to produce his accounts[2] as it is the latter's duty to produce such accounts when called upon by the committee, at least once a year or periodically[2].

The question is whether the language is also applicable to the case of an hereditary manager. It may seem unreasonable to enact that an hereditary manager should submit his accounts to the committee which has no jurisdiction over him. A literal reading of the section seems to suggest the view that a manager of an institution falling under S. 4 is bound to produce his accounts to the committee and that an obligation is imposed on the committee to require such hereditary manager to produce his accounts. A strict

---

1. *Fakurudin Sahib* v. *Ackeni Sahib*, (1880) I. L. R., 2 M. 197.

2. Per *Shephard, J.*, in *Seshadri Ayyangar* v. *Nataraja Ayyar*, (1898) I. L. R., 21 M. 179 (183).

construction of the section also leads to the same result. The words in the *first* part are "every trustee..............of a mosque .... *to which the provisions of this Act shall apply*" is under a duty "to keep regular accounts of his receipts . ...in respect of the endowments and expenses of such mosque." In the *second* part the words are :—"It shall be the duty of every committee .... to require from every trustee .... of *such* mosque .... the production of *such* regular accounts of such receipts. In the *second* part though the words "every trustee" may be explained away as meaning only such trustee as is under the control of the committee (as the words are simply "*every trustee*" and not "every such trustee"), the words "*such mosque,*" &c., cannot be so explained away. The expression "*such mosque,*" &c., refers to the *mosque,* &c., mentioned in the *first* part, *i.e.*, a mosque to which the provisions of this *Act* shall apply and that will refer to both the classes mentioned under Ss. 3 and 4.

According to the literal meaning of the words, therefore, whatever construction is placed on the *second* part must also be placed on the *first* part. If the words "*such mosque,*" &c., had not occurred in the *second* part, it is possible to place a different construction upon the two parts.

But this interpretation, it is said, imputes an absurd intention on the part of the Legislature. The Act draws in other sections a distinction between the different classes of institutions falling under Ss. 3 and 4 and does not place the managers of institutions under S. 4 under the control of committee. The committee had under the prior sections nothing to do with managers of institutions falling under S. 4. The object of the Legislature seems to be to make the managers falling under S. 4 independent of any committee. If S. 13 applies to all trustees, then the object of the Legislature is frustrated. Bearing some such considerations as these in mind, the Madras High Court has not adopted the literal construction pointed out above. In *Ramiengar* v. *Gnanasambanda*[1] their Lordships, *Scotland,* C. J., and *Innes,* J., observed : "The general language of the 13th section did seem on first reading to give the district committee special power to call for such accounts from the trustee of

1. (1867) 5 M. H. C. 53.

pagoda without distinction, but on looking attentively at the Act, we think it has not that operation. Construed with the provisions in the other sections, we have now no doubt that the power extends only to the trustees or managers of the pagodas described in S. 3 over whom the district committee exercise their general powers of superintendence." This case was adopted in the later case of *K. Venkatabalakrishna Chettiar* v. *Kaliyanaramaiyungar*[1], where the point about the right or duty of the committee to require the production of proper accounts directly arose for decision. The view laid down in these cases receives some support also from the fact that in S. 6, which deals with the powers of trustees, it is stated that the powers and responsibilities of the hereditary trustees shall be the same as if they were before the Act was passed except with only one substantial reservation, *i. e.*, the liability to be sued under S. 14.

It, therefore, seems now to be settled at any rate so far as the Madras High Court is concerned, that the section has no application to hereditary managers though a provision of the sort will be highly useful in their case as it will serve as a check on their conduct or management.

It may be noticed that this view is not in accordance with the view taken by the same court as regards S. 14, which is in terms similar to S. 13 (the language used in both sections being in substance very similar). The only difference in the language is that the expression "to which the provisions of this Act apply" which occurs in S. 13, is not to be found in S. 14. As regards S. 14 it is now settled in all the High Courts that effect should be given to the language used and that, therefore, it is applicable to all endowments which are public religious endowments.

The Calcutta High Court has, however, taken a different view as regards S. 13. In the case of *Jan Ali* v. *Ram Nath Mundul*[2], the Calcutta High Court held that the same view must be taken as regards both Ss. 13 and 14. After dealing with the sections of the Regulation, and the sections of the Act up to

1. (1869) 5 M. H. C. 48. See also *Fakurudin Sahib* v. *Ackeni Sahib*, (1880) I. L. R., 2 M. 197.

2. (1881) I. L. R., 8 C. 32.

12, they observed : "Then comes S. 13 (they quote the section)...... Who are the trustees, managers, or superintendents of the religious establishments to whom the provisions of this Act apply? It appears to us that if we read the language of Ss. 3 and 4, it is impossible to come to any other conclusion than *that the trustee, manager or superintendent to whom the provisions of the Act apply* is *a trustee, manager, or superintendent of a mosque, temple, or other religious establishment to which the provisions of Regulation XIX* of 1810 *apply*; and, as I have already pointed out, the mosque, temple, or other religious establishment to which the provision of Regulation XIX of 1810 applies is a mosque, temple, or other religious establishment, for the *support of which endowments have been granted in land by Government or by individuals*. The conclusion then, to which we are led is that the same construction must be placed on Ss. 13 and 14 of the Act, and that the mosque, temple, or other religious establishment there mentioned is not *any* mosque, temple, or other religious establishment *whatever*, but any mosque, temple, or religious establishment for the support of which endowments in land have been made by the Government or private individuals."

Even if this view should prevail (and it accords with the literal interpretation of the section) the section does not enable the committee to remove the hereditary manager. The duty to produce accounts does not make the committee the controlling authority.

As to the question of liability of the hereditary mananger to keep regular accounts, it is now settled that he is bound to keep proper accounts under the common law quite independent of the section and the omission to keep such accounts will entail dismissal[1]. Notwithstanding this, it is frequently the case that no accounts are kept, and heads of institutions regard the endowments and their income more as their private property than as property for which they are liable to account.

It has been held that a manager appointed by the committee who failed to submit accounts is guilty of such misfeasance as to justify the committee in dismissing him[2].

1. *Fakurudin Sahib* v. *Ackeni Sahib*, (1880) I. L. R., 2 M. 197.
2. *Anantanarayana Ayyar* v. *Kuttalam Pillai*, (1899) I. L. R., 22 M. 481.

[3]. "**Every such committee of management shall themselves keep such accounts thereof**":—This imposes a duty on the committee to keep accounts. S. 19 also contemplates filing of accounts by the committee by order of the Judge on an application under S. 18, and this is only justifiable upon the view that under S. 13 the committee is bound to keep accounts[1].

Any person interested may singly sue in case of breach of trust, &c.

XIV. Any person or persons interested in any mosque temple, or religious establishment, or in the performance of the worship or of the service thereof, or the trusts relating thereto, may, without joining as plaintiff any of the other persons interested therein, sue before the Civil Court the trustee, manager, or superintendent of such mosque, temple, or religious establishment, or the member of any Committee appointed under this Act, for any misfeasance, breach of trust, or neglect of duty, committed by such trustee, manager, superintendent, or member of such Committee, in respect of the trusts vested in, or confided to them respectively;

Powers of Civil Court.

and the Civil Court may direct the specific performance of any act by such trustee, manager, superintendent, or member of a Committee,

and may decree damages and costs against such trustee, manager, superintendent, or member of a Committee,

and may also direct the removal of such trustee, manager, superintendent, or member of a Committee.

NOTES

This section is important and a crop or net work of decisions has arisen under this section.

1. *Syed Amin Sahib v. Ibram Sahib*, (1868) 4 M. H. C., 112 (113).

Objects of the section:—The objects of the legislature in enacting this section are (1) to throw facilities to prevent breaches of trust[1], and (2) to provide a remedy to persons who before the Act had no right to sue or whose right to sue before the Act was more than doubtful[2].

[1] "**Any person or persons interested**":—Three kinds of interest are stated in the section:—(1) An interest which a person may possess in the mosque &c; (2) an interest in the performance of the worship or service in such mosque, &c; and (3) an interest which a person may possess in the trusts relating to such mosque &c.

As to the nature of the interest required reference may be made to S., 15, and the notes thereon.

[1a] "**Any Mosque, Temple or religious establishment**":—

Nature of mosques, &c., to which S. 14 applies.

These words are wide. It may be noted that in this section the expression '*to which the provisions of this Act shall apply*" which finds a place in S. 13 does not occur. But notwithstanding this, the construction placed upon the section by judicial decisions is that it has application not to *any* mosque &c. *whatever* but *only* a mosque &c. for which Regulations VII of 1817 and XIX of 1810 would have been applicable. According to the decision in *Jan Ali* v. *Ram Nath Mundal*[3] these Regulations would be applicable to a mosque, temple or religious establishment *for which endowments had been made either by Government or by private individuals*. This, however, is not strictly correct for two reasons:—*Firstly*, it is not strictly correct to say that endowments have been made for a temple. Endowments are made for the deity or idol. It is, therefore, doubtful whether there is any temple without an endowment for the idol. The walls of the temple and even the site may constitute an endowment[4]. *Secondly*, no distinction is drawn by the judges in this case between public and private temples, &c. The Judges take note of only one circumstance and give exclusive prominence to it. The preamble

1. *Syed Amin Sahib* v. *Ibram Sahib*, (1868) 4 M.H.C. 112; *Sabapathi* v. *Subraya* (1878) I. L. R., 2 M. 58 (60); *Dhurrum Singh* v. *Kissen Singh*, (1881) I.L. R., 7 C. 767 (771).

2. *Hidait-Oon-Nissa* v. *Syud Afzul Hossein*, (1870: 2 N. W. P. 420; *Hajee Kalub Hossein* v. *Mussumat Mehrum Beebee*, (1872) 4 N. W. P. 155. *Cf. Nellaiyappa Pillai* v. *Thangama Nachiyar*, (1897) I. L. R., 21 M. 406 (409).

3. (1881) I. L. R, 8 C.32.

4. *Muhammad Siraj-ul-Haq* v. *Imam-ud-din*, (1896) I. L. R., 19 A. 104.

to the Regulations recites that considerable endowments have been granted in money or by assignments of land, or of the produce or portions of the produce of land by former Governments of this country as well as by the British Government and by individuals, for the support of mosques &c. and in S. 2, it is stated that the general superintendence of all endowments in land or money granted for the support of mosques &c. shall be vested in the Board of Revenue. The Regulations are intended to prevent endowments from being converted to the private use of individuals &c.(S.5). But S. 9 of the Regulations seems, in our opinion, to refer to *all* endowments, establishments, and buildings of the nature before described and by the term "establishment of the nature before described" we must understand mosques &c. as contradistinguished from endowments. S. 10 imposes a duty on the local agents to ascertain and report to the Board, the names of the trustees &c., of such religious establishments. It is one thing to say that the Board did not care to take up the management of mosques &c., for the *maintenance and support* of which no endowments might exist and did not, therefore, assume the management of such mosques &c., and quite another thing to say that the Board had no jurisdiction over such mosques &c. *Thirdly*, in most cases temples &c., are supported by voluntary contributions. More strictly speaking the maintenance of the idol is made out of funds raised by voluntary contributions. No reason is pointed out to exclude these religious establishments from the operation of the Act[1].

Actual control by Board not necessary.

The question is whether S. 14 will apply notwithstanding the Board may not have in fact taken charge under the Regulations. The language of the section is general[2]. It is not a condition precedent under the section which is general in its application[3] that the Board should actually take charge of the temple, mosque, &c., although the latter may fall under the Regulations. The words are "*any trustee*" &c. The utmost that can be

1. In *Muhammad Siraj-Ul-Haq* v. *Imam-ud-din*, (1896) I. L. R., 19 A. 104 it has been held that the fact that a mosque is supported by voluntary subscriptions and that lands are purchased out of the same will not prevent the mosque from falling under the Act.

2. *Pancheowrie Mull* v. *Chumroolall*, (1878) I. L. R. 3 C. 563 ; *Kalee Churu Giri* v. *Golabi*, (1878) 2 C. L. R., 128 (131); *Fakurudin Sahib* v. *Ackeni Sahib*, (1880) I. L. R. 2 M. 197; *Jan Ali* v. *Ram Nath Mundul*, (1881) I. L. R., 8 C. 32 (36).

3. *Dhurrum Sing* v. *Kissen Singh* (1881) I. L. R., 7 C. 767 ; *Muhammad Siraj-Ul-Haq* v. *Imam-ud-din* (1896) I. L. R., 19 A. 104.

said is that taken with the context these words must be qualified by some such words as these :—"of a mosque &c. to which the Regulations of 1810 and 1817 would have been applicable." This is the effect of the several cases cited below[1]. Whether even this limitation should be introduced into the section is a question which will be considered later on.

The case of *Muthu* v. *Gangathara*[2] has been supposed to lay down a contrary view so that actual control may be necessary for the application of S. 14. This case, however, cannot really be taken to lay down any such view. The contention in the case was whether the institution was public. The defendant denied that the institution was a common place of worship. The court below without taking any evidence decreed the plaintiff's suit. The High Court in setting aside this decree observed: "Unless, therefore, the endowment was one which would have fallen under the provisions of Regulation VII of 1817 it will not fall under the provisions of Act XX of 1863." This does not mean that the actual control of the Board is necessary.

This was the view of the case taken by *Benson J.* in the more recent case of *Saturluri Seetaramanuja Charyulu* v. *Nanduri Seetapati*[3]:

The case of *Hajee Kalub Hossein* v. *Mussumat Mehrum Beebee*[4] may also seem at first sight to lay down that S. 14 does not apply unless it is shewn that the management of the trust estate had been under the control of the Government. But this case might be explained on the footing that the absence of control was regarded by the judges as a piece of evidence from which one might infer that the institution was a private and not a public one.

---

1. *Ganesh Sing* v. *Ramgopal Singh*,(1870) 5 B. L. R. app 355 ; *Dhurrum Singh* v. *Kissen Singh* 1881) I L. R. 7 C. 767 ; *Jan Ali* v. *Ram Nath Mundal*,(1881) I. L. R. 8 C. 32 where it was held that S 14 had application to institutions coming under Regn. XIX of 1810 ; *Protap Chandra Misser* v *Brojonath Misser*,(1891) I. L R. I C 275 *Sheoratan Kunwari* v *Ram Pargash*, (1896) I. L. R. 18 A. 227 (231) ; *Muhammad Siraj-Ul-Haq* v. *Imam-ud-din*, (1896: I. L. R. 19 A 104 (109) ; *Saturluri Seetaramanuja Charyulu* v. *Nanduri Seetapati*, (1902) I. L. R. 26 M. 166. But see *Bibee Kuneez Fatima* v. *Bibee Saheba Jan*, (1867) 8 W. R. C. R. 313 ; *Hajee Kalub Hossein* v. *Mussumat Mehrum Beebee*, (1872) 4 N. W. P. 155 ; *Fakurudin Sahib* v. *Ackeni Sahib*, (1880) I. L. R., 2 M. 197 ; and *Muthu* v. *Gangathara Mudaliar*, (1893) I. L. R. 17 M. 95.

2. (1893) I. L. R. 17 M. 95.

3. (1902) I. L. R. 26 M. 166.

4. (1872) 4 N. W. P. 155 where the endowment was created in 1851. See also *Bibee Kuneez Fatima* v. *Bibee Saheba Jan*, (1867) 8 W. R. C. R. 313 ; *Delroos Banoo Begum* v. *Nawab Syud Ashgur Ally Khan*, (1875) 15B. L. R. 167 : S. C. 23 W. R. 453 affirmed on appeal to the Privy Council (1877) I. L. R., 3 C 324. See, however, *Kalee Churn Giree* v. *Golabi* (1878) 2 C. L. R. 128. The question is noticed but not decided in *Jan Ali* v. *RamNath Mundul*, (1881) I. L. R. 8 C. 32.

Applicability of section to institutions after Act or Regulations.

If all that is necessary to consider is whether a particular institution might have been under the control of the Board by reason of its coming under the Regulations and not whether the institution was actually under the control of the Board, the section (and the Act) will be applicable to institutions coming into existence after Act XX of 1863[1]. The section will also have application to institutions which came into existence before Act XX of 1863 but after the Regulations[2]. In *Sheoratan Kunwari* v. *Ram Pargash*[3], *Edge. C. J.* held differing from the view he had expressed in a previous case[4] that S 14 of the Act applied whether or not the Board of Revenue had, under Regulation XIX of 1810 exercised or had vested in it the right to nominate the trusteeship or managership of the temple and that, therefore, S. 14 applied notwithstanding that an endowment might have come into existence after Act XX of 1863. Mr. Justice *Shephard* however, in *Sivayya* v. *Rami Reddi*[5] took a broader ground and held that S. 14 was not intended to be restricted to such institutions as came within the purview of the Regulations or even to institutions founded before the Act itself came into force. The soundness of this view will be considered later on[6].

---

1. *Sheoratan Kunwari* v. *Ram Pargash*, (1896) I. L. R. 18 A 227 overruling *Raghubar Dial* v. *Kesho Ramanuj Das*, (1888) I. L. R., 11 A. 18; Per *Shephard* and *Subramania Iyer*, JJ. in *Sivayya* v. *Ram Reddi*, (1899) I. L. R, 22 M 223.

2. Per *Shephard*, and *Subramania Iyer*, JJ. in *Sivayya* v *Rami Reddi*, (1899) I. L. R., 22 M 223. The institution that was in question in *Delroos Banoo Begum* v. *Syed Ashgur Ally Khan*, (1875) 15 B. L. R. 167: S. C. 23 W. R. 453 came into existence after the Regulation but there was no objection raised on that score. Noverthless, the High Court stated that tho Collector could have taken charge if the institution was a public one. The High Court whose reasoning was adopted by the Privy Council (see I. L. R., 3 C 324) only considered the question about the control of the Board and held that the absence of such control showed that the endowment was a private one. See also notes to S. 2 and 5 of the Regulation. In *Jan Ali* v. *Ram Nath Mundul*, (1881) I. L. R., 8 C. 32 the endowment was one made in 1834 but the High Court did not consider the year material as affecting the question of the jurisdiction under the Regulation or Act).

3. (1896) I. L. R. 18 A. 227. The other judge agreed with *Edge*, C. J.

4. *Raghubar Dial* v. *Kesho Ramanuj Das*, (1888) I. L. R., 11 A 18 (26).

5. (1899) I L. R., 22 M 223.

6. See below under heading "Applicability of section to private endowments." pp. 87 to 89.

Applicability of Act and section to private religious endowments.

There remains the question whether the Act is applicable to private endowments for religious purposes. We have already pointed out that the words in this section are more general[1] and that we do not find in it even the qualification stated in S. 13 viz., that the mosque, &c., must be one to which "the provisions of the Act are applicable." It may also be observed that the Act is only dealing with public religious endowments in the preamble and in Ss. 7 to 13.

Looking at the terms of the section and comparing it with S. 13, however, it may be said that the language of S. 14 should be understood as we find it and effect given to the section to its full est extent seeing that its terms are general in its application and will even include private religious endowments. The word "other" in "or other religious establishment" only includes of course one *ejusdem generis* to those stated before *i. e.*, akin to a mosque or temple. But there are no qualifying words before "mosque" or "temple" and the term "*any*" occurring before "mosque", &c., is not restrictive in significance. But general words and phrases, however, wide and comprehensive in their literal sense, must be construed as strictly limited to the actual objects of the Act and as not altering the law beyond[2].

In *Sivayya* v. *Rami Reddi,*[3] Mr. Justice *Shephard* held that S. 14 of the Act was not intended to be restricted to such institutions as came within the purview of the Regulations. If this be so, the Act might have application to private religious endowments although the Regulations were not applicable to the same. But this point was not in question there and the observations of *Shephard* J. must be taken with the facts of that case.

Nor can we state that the case of *Fakurudin Sahib* v *Ackeni Sahib*[4] is authority for the view that S.14 should be understood so as to include even private endowments. The question in that case was whether the court had authority to remove an hereditary trustee for

1. *Punchcowrie Mull* v. *Chumroo Lall,* (1878) I. L. R., 3 C. 563; *Fakurudin Sahib* v. *Ackeni Sahib,* (1880) I. L. R., 2 M. 197. Cf. also *Dhurrum Singh* v. *Kissen Singh,* (1881) I. L. R., 7 C. 767; and *Muhammad Siraj-Ul-Haq* v. *Imam-ud-din,* (1896) I. L. R. 19 A 104. See also p. 84.
2. Maxwell p. 118.
3. (1899) I. L. R., 22 M. 223, (226 and 227).
4. (1880) I. L. R., 2 M. 197.

misconduct under S. 14. The Court in holding that S. 14 applied observed: "Although it has been held that the provisions of S. 13 of the Act relating to rendition of accounts by the trustees and managers to the committee constituted by the Act apply only to the institutions mentioned in S. 3 we can find nothing to control the generality of the terms of S. 14 which empower any person interested in any mosque, temple or religious endowment * * * to sue the trustee * * * for misfeasance." These observations must only be taken as negativing any distinction between the trustees of religious institutions falling under S. 3 and the trustees of religious institutions falling under S. 4 with respect to their liability under S. 14. The question whether S. 14 applied to private trusts was neither raised nor discussed in that case[1].

The weight of authority is certainly in favour of the view that S. 14 of the Act generally has no application to the case of private religious trusts. The case of *Delroos Banoo Begum* v. *Syud Ashgur Ally Khan*[2] is the earliest authority bearing upon the point. *Glover* and *R. C. Mitter* JJ., while holding that the endowment in question was not of a public character and did not, therefore, fall under the Act, observed: "Now Act XX of 1863 was passed as appears from its preamble to relieve the Boards of Revenue and Local Agents of the duties imposed upon them by Regulation XIX of 1810 which Regulation so far as related to endowments for the support of mosques, Hindu temples or other religious purposes was by it repealed. The endowments, &c., referred to in the Act Ss. 3, 4 and 5 are declared to be the same as those to which the Regulation of 1810 was applicable and S. 15 of that Regulation specifies the kind of endowment which should be made subject to its control and supervision. The words of the section are:—'It is to be clearly understood that the object of the present Regulation is solely to provide for the due appropriation of lands granted for public purposes'".

The above case was appealed to the Privy Council[3] and the Judicial Committee while affirming the judgment of the High Court upon another point observed: "Their Lordships having come to this conclusion upon the main facts of the case, it is not

1. This case is discussed in *Protap Chandra Misser* v. *Brojonath Misser*, (1891) I. L. R., 19 C. 275.
2. (1875) 15 B. L. R. 167: S. C. 23 W. R. 453.
3. (1877) I. L. R., 3 C. 324.

necessary for them to determine the other point which the High Court decided,—viz., that this endowment was not of such a public character as would sustain a suit under Act XX of 1863 but their Lordships desire to say that they see no reason for disagreeing with that part of the judgment." Later decisions have adopted the view that the Act has application only to public religious endowments and not to private religious endowments[1].

The case of *Jan Ali* v. *Ram Nath Mundul*[2], however, lays down a somewhat different principle. The judges there observed: "The conclusion to which we are led is that the same construction must be put upon Ss. 13 and 14 of the Act and that the mosque, temple, or religious establishment there mentioned is not *any* mosque, temple, or religious establishment whatever, but any mosque, temple or religious establishment for the support of which endowments in land have been made by the Government or private individuals[3]". We have already discussed the soundness of this view and stated as our opinion that the Regulations are not to be so restricted[4]. It is also not consistent with the observations of *Shephard*, J., in *Sivayya* v. *Rami Reddi*[5] where he held that S. 14 was not intended to be restricted only to such institutions as came within the purview of the Regulations. If the observations of *Shephard*, J., are not taken as extending to private trusts, we think they lay down a sound principle of law consistent with the decisions.

Applicability of Act to Presidency Towns.

Actual control of a religious institution by the Board not being necessary, the question arises whether the Act is applicable to the Presidency Towns. This question has been already considered[6] in the notes to S. 1. It could not be said that the Board exercised no control under the Regulations over religious institutions in the Presidency Towns. From the papers relating to the withdrawal of

---

1. Per *Muthusawmy Iyer* and *Best*, JJ. in *Sathappayyar* v. *Periasami*, (1890) I. L. R., 14 M. 1; *Natesa* v. *Ganapati*, (1890) I. L. R., 14 M. 103 in which the contention was raised that the Chidambaram temple was a private one but was negatived; *Protap Chandra Misser* v. *Brojonath Misser*, (1891) I. L. R., 19 C. 275; *Sajedur Raja* v. *Baidyanath Deb*, (1892) I. L. R., 20 C. 397. See also *Bibee Kuneez Fatima* v. *Bibee Saheba Jan*, (1867) 8 W. R. C. R. 313; *Hajee Kalub Hossein* v. *Mussumat Mehrum Beebee*, (1872) 4 N. W. P. 155; *Muthu* v. *Gangathara*, (1893) I. L. R., 17 M. 95.
2. (1881) I. L. R., 8 C. 32.
3. See also *Natesa* v. *Ganapati*, (1890) I. L. R., 14 M. 103.
4. See beginning of note [2] pp. 83 and 84. See also notes to Ss. 2, 5, 9 and 10 of the Regulations.
5. (1899) I. L. R., 22 M. 223 (226 and 227).
6. See p. 9.

Government connection it would appear[1] that in Fort St. George, "the supervision" not only of the pagoda at Triplicane, but of all others was "vested in the Collector, although excepting in the case of the Triplicane Pagoda, direct interference in the internal affairs of the pagodas" had not been exercised to any great extent. However, in cases of breach of trust &c , resort was usually had to the Supreme Court who also nominated dharmakartas for the town pagodas. The trend of judicial decisions is to the effect that the Act has no application to the Presidency Towns[2]. In the latest case upon the subject *Subramania Aiyar*, J., observed[3]: "This Court, as the successor to the late Supreme Court, possesses a jurisdiction similar to that exercised by the Court of Chancery in England over charities. Within the original jurisdiction of this Court persons interested in charities have all along been allowed, as relators, to take legal proceedings in reference to the due administration of charities. According to the analogy of the procedure applicable to similar cases in England, the Advocate-General should be a party to proceedings like the present. But a different practice has long prevailed....... Following the view taken by *Garth*, C. J., and *Markby*, J., in *Panchcowrie Mull* v. *Chumroolall*[4] we hold that Act XX of 1863 was not intended to apply to a suit such as this brought under the ordinary original jurisdiction of this Court inherited from the Supreme Court." The same result was arrived at in a previous case[5] decided by the same learned Judge as a single judge setting on the original side and not referred to either in the arguments or in the judgment in the later case. In the Calcutta case[6] referred to by the learned judge *Garth*, C. J., and *Markby*, J., observed: "The first thirteen sections of the Act clearly do not apply, and although the language of S. 14 which empowers any person interested in a religious endowment to sue a trustee, is general in its terms, yet we do not consider that the legislature had in its

1. Letter from Collector to the Board of Revenue, dated 4th January 1843, Paper No. 86 in the Blue book of 1849 "Idolatry" pp. 131 to 137. See also *Mr. Melville's* note, dated 1st July 1844, Paper No. 141 at p. 445.

2. *Panchcowrie Mull* v. *Chumroolall*, (1878) I. L. R., 3 C. 563; *Srinivasa Appangar* v. *Raghavachariar*, (1896) 6 M. L. J. R. 239; *Annasami Pillai* v. *Ramakrishna Mudaliar*, (1900) I. L. R., 24 M. 219. In *Sabapathy* v. *Subraya*, (1897) I. L. R., 2 M. 58 (61) the question was raised but not decided.

3. *Annasami Pillai* v. *Ramakrishna Mudaliar*, (1900) I.L.R., 24 M. 219 at pp. 231 and 232.

4. (1878) I. L. R., 3 C. 563.

5. *Srinivasa Appangar* v. *Raghavachariar*, (1896) 6 M. L. J. R. 239.

6. *Panchcowrie Mull* v. *Chumroolall*, (1878) I. L. R., 3 C. 563 overruling the decision of *Norman*, J. in *Ganes Sing* v. *Ramgopal Sing*, (1870) 5 B. L. R app. 55 and reversing the decision of *Kennedy*, J. on appeal.

contemplation to interfere with the procedure of the Supreme Court in reference to trusts concerning property, which could not, under any circumstances, come under the direct control of Government."

The expediency of extending the application of the Act to the Presidency Towns is more doubtful though *Garth*, C. J., and *Markby*, J., throw out a suggestion[1], that a procedure similar to that which is provided by Act XX of 1863 for suits to which that Act extends may usefully be applied to all suits of that nature. We are doubtful if the learned judges will stick to their remarks even at the present day after the experience we have of the committees in the mofussil (at any rate of the Madras Presidency).

Disappearance of temple walls.

The fact of the disappearance of the temple walls will not prevent the application of the Act. The Thakurji is the owner and so long as he is there, the Court has jurisdiction. Otherwise, the only thing that the trustee has to do is to pull down or dismantle the walls so as to escape jurisdiction[2].

"**Religious establishment**" :—This will include a mutt, and it has been held that heads of mutts can be proceeded against under the Act[3]. In *Jusagheri Gosamiar* v. *The Collector of Tanjore*[4] it was held that the Nadiem mutt in Tanjore was an institution coming under S. 4 *A darga*[5] or *Khankah* is also included.

Nature of remedy.

[2]. "**May &c., sue**":—The Section is merely enabling or is only permissive[6]. It does not take away rights which persons had prior to the Act[7] to

1. *Panchcowrie Mull* v. *Chumroo Lall*, (1878) I. L. R., 3 C. 563 (572).
2. *Sheoratan Kunwari* v. *Ram Pargash*, (1896) I. L. R., 18 A. 227.
3. *Kolandai Mudali* v. *Sankara Bharadhi*, (1881) I.L.R., 5 M. 302 where it was held that a mutt was a religious endowment and that the Pensions Act was not applicable. In *Mahalinga Rau* v. *Venkoba Ghosami*, (1881) I. L. R., 4 M. 157 there was no contention that the Act would not apply to a *mutt* but the court held that the suit was not of the nature contemplated in S. 14. In *Sathappayyar* v. *Periasami*, (1890) I. L. R., 14 M. 1 the contention was not that the Act would not apply to any *mutt* but that the Act did not apply to a private mutt or trust. See *In the matter of the Petition of Mohun Dass* v. *Lutchmun*, (1880) I. L. R., 6 C. 11; *Gyananda Asram* v. *Kristo Chandra*, (1901) 8 C. W. N. 404 (mohunt of a temple).
4. (1870) 5 M. H. C. 334. See also *Ram Churn* v. *Chuttur Bhoje*, (1845) 7 B. S. D. A. 205, (mohunt of a temple).
5. *Fakurudin* v. *Ackeni Sahib*, (1880) I. L. R., 2 M. 197. Cf. *Jewun Doss* v. *Shah Kubeer*, (1841) 2 M. I. A. 390.
6. *Chinna Ranguiyangar* v. *Subbraya Mudali*, (1867) 3 M. H. C. 334; *Jeyangarulavaru* v. *Durma Dossji*, (1868) 4 M. H. C. 2; *Syed Amin Sahib* v. *Ibram Sahib*, (1868) 4 M. H. C. 112; *Hidait-Oon-nissa* v. *Syud Afzul Hossein*, (1870) 2 N. W. P. 420; *Hajee Kalub Hossein* v. *Mussumat Mehrum Beebee*, (1872) 4 N. W. P. 155; *Kishore Bon Mohunt* v. *Kalee Churn Giree*, (1874) 22 W.R.C.R., 364 (365); *Puddolabh Roy* v. *Ramgopal Chatterjee*, (1882) I. L. R., 9 C. 133; *Sathappayyar* v. *Periasami*, (1890) I.L.R., 14 M. 1 (14); *Narayana Ayyar* v. *Kumarasami Mudaliar*, (1899) I. L. R., 23 M. 537.
7. *Agrisharma Embrandri* v. *Vistnu Embrandri*, (1866) 3 M. H. C. 198; *Jeyangarulavaru* v. *Durma Dossji*, supra. See *Hajee Kalub* v. *Mussumat Mehrum*, supra and the last three cases in note (6).

bring suits in the ordinary Courts. The provisions of the Act are clearly intended to extend and not to restrict the remedy by suit for breaches of trust and neglect of duty by the trustees &c.[1] It empowered persons whose right of suit was or was believed to be doubtful before the Act to institute a peculiar class of suits[2]. As observed by the Madras High Court in *Syed Amin Sahib* v. *Ibram Sahib*[3], "the enactments in Ss. 14 and 15 are enabling and intended to give to the persons described and who are individually not interested otherwise than in connection with others, the right to sue individually before the Civil Court the member of any committee appointed under this Act." In *Dhurrum Singh* v. *Kissen Singh*[4], however, *Maclean*, J., observed: "S. 14 is generally applicable to all religious endowments and while it in one sense restrains the ordinary Courts from dealing with cases against trustees of religious endowments, it gave special facilities for suits in the Principal Civil Court of the District by any of the persons interested in these endowments." These observations must not be taken as favoring the view that the Act has imposed any restraint upon pre-existing rights. It gives a right of suit to certain persons (and these are some of the special facilities the Act affords[5]) and when giving such right appoints a special *forum* for the enforcement of such right[6].

We shall here mention some pre-existing rights which still can be enforced unrestricted by S. 14:—

Some pre-existing rights.

(1). The right of a dharmakarta to bring suits to recover property or to sue for damages caused by neglect of a previous dharmakarta is a right vested under the ordinary law. This right can be enforced quite independent of the Act[7].

(1) Suit by manager for endowed property.

(2). The inherent right of committees which are vested under the Act with the powers of superintendence and control previously exercised by the

(2) Suit by Committee.

---

1. *Jeyangarulavaru* v. *Durma Dossji*, (1868) 4 M. H. C. 2. See also the cases cited in notes (1) and (2) p. 83.
2. *Hidait-Oon-Nissa* v. *Syud Afzul Hossein*, (1870) 2 N. W. P. 420; *Hajee Kaluh Hossein* v. *Mussumat Mehrum Beebee*, (1872) 4 N. W. P. 155.
3. (1868) 4 M. H. C. 112 (113).
4. (1881) I. L. R., 7 C. 767.
5. See *Sabapathi* v. *Subraya*, (1878) I. L. R., 2 M. 58.
6. See *Hidait-Oon-Nissa* v. *Syud Afzul Hossein*, (1870) 2 N. W. P. 420.
7. *Jeyangarulavaru* v. *Durmu Dossji*, (1868) 4 M. H. C. 2; *Manally Chenna Kesavaraya* v. *Vaidelingu*, (1877) I. L. R., 1 M. 343; *Virasami Nayudu* v. *Subba Rau*, (1882) I. L. R., 6 M. 54. See also notes under heading [4] "The trustee, manager &c." pp. 96 to 98.

Board to enforce such right of control[1] as well against the managers appointed by them as against the officers of the temple subject to the control of such committees[2] or the right of a committee to sue for a declaration that the defendant is not a hereditary dharmakarta and that the temple belongs to the class[1] described in S. 3 or to prevent the manager dismissed from office from assuming the same or to sue for sums misappropriated by the manager[3] may be enforced independent of the Act.

(3) Suit by dismissed dharmakarta for reinstatement.

(3). The right of a dharmakarta dismissed from office by the committee to sue for a declaration that the dismissal is wrongful or for restoration to office[4].

(4) Suit for share in management.

(4). The right of a manager whether hereditary or appointed by the committee to share in the management or for recovery of the property belonging to the religious establishment of which he is the manager[5]. Here the manager may allege that he is the only person lawfully entitled to the office and that the defendant is not the rightful manager[6] or that he is a co-dharmakarta along with the defendant[7].

(5) Worshipper's right of suit.

(5). The right of a worshipper to sue when he is obstructed in the performance of his devotions to the Deity is a right personal to such worshipper and may be enforced independently of the Act.[8]

---

1. *L. Venkatasa Naidu* v. *Sadagopasamy Iyer*, (1869) 4 M. H. C. 404.

2. *Chinna Rangaiyangar* v. *Subbraya Mudali*, (1867) 3 M. H. C. 334 (where the Court held that a committee can dismiss a trustee of an institution falling under S. 3 without filing a suit under the Act); *L. Venkatasa Naidu* v. *Sadagopasamy Iyer*, (1869) 4 M. H. C. 404; *Syed Amin Sahib* v. *Ibram Sahib*, (1868) 4 M. H. C. 112; *Puddolabh Roy* v. *Ramgopal Chatterjee*, (1882) I. L. R., 9 C. 133.

3. *Puddolabh Roy* v. *Ramgopal Chatterjee*, (1882) I. L. R., 9 C. 133.

4. *Syed Amin Sahib* v. *Ibram Sahib*, (1868) 4 M. H. C. 112; *Virasami Nayudu* v. *Subba Rau*, (1882) I. L. R., 6 M. 54. In *Chinna Rangaiyangar* v. *Subbraya Mudali*, (1867) 3 M. H. C. 334 the suit was instituted independent of the Act but no question was raised that it was not maintainable.

5. *Agri Sharma Embrandri* v. *Vistnu Embrandri*, (1866) 3 M. H. C. 198; *Hajee Kalub Hossein* v. *Mussumat Mehrum Bibee*, (1872) 4 N. W. P. 155; *Kishore Bon Mohunt* v. *Kalee Churn Giree*, (1874) 22 W. R. C. R. 364; *Kalee Churn Giri* v. *Golabi*, (1878) 2 C. L. R., 128; *Mahalinga Rau* v. *Vencoba Ghosami*, (1881) I. L. R., 4 M. 157; *Athavulla* v. *Gouse*, (1888) I. L. R., 11 M. 283 (which was a suit by a manager to enforce his vested rights against his co-manager).

6. *Kishore Bon Mohunt* v. *Kalee Churn Giree*, supra.

7. *Athavulla* v. *Gouse*, (1888) I. L. R., 11 M. 283. *Miya Vali Ulla* v. *Syud Bava Saheb Santi Miya*, (1896) I. L. R., 22 B. 496 a decision under S. 539, C. P. C.

8. *Abdul Rahman* v. *Yar Muhammad*, (1881) I. L. R., 3 A. 636; *Radhabai* v. *Chimnaji*, (1878) I. L. R., 3 B. 27. See also *Kalidas Jivram* v. *Gor Parjaram Hirji*, (1890) I. L. R., 15 B. 309. See also Introduction Ch. XV.

(6) Suit by founder.

(6). The right of the founder or his heirs to see that his intention is properly carried out, to enforce the trusts if not carried out, to sue for removal of trustee on the ground of misconduct and to appoint somebody else may be enforced independent of the Act[1]. That the founder has such a right under the Hindu Law is clear[2].

(7) Suit by committee member against others for exclusion.

(7). The right of a member of the committee to sue if he should be excluded in the management which is vested by the Act in the whole committee as where a majority of the members passed on their own responsibility a resolution dismissing the temple trustee and appointing another without convening a meeting and against the opinions of the other members and proceeded to enforce such order by directing the new trustee to be put in possession. If it had stopped with a mere resolution, there might be no cause of action[3]. There would be also no cause of action where the committee expressed an opinion in answer to a communication that a will made by the manager appointing his successor was invalid[4].

(8) Suit by dharmakartas against special managers.

(8). The right of a general manager (dharmakarta) of a temple to see that endowments managed by special managers are properly managed is one that can be enforced independent of the Act[5].

But the fact that such rights can be enforced in the ordinary courts does not prevent the persons possessing such rights from bringing suits under the Act after the necessary sanction if the suit is for the purposes mentioned in S. 14[6].

---

1. *Hidait-Oon-Nissa* v. *Syud Afzul Hossein*, (1870) 4 N. W. P. 420; Per Be... J. in *Sathappayyar* v. *Periasami*, (1890) I. L. R., 14 M. 1 (14). The question was n... decided in *Balwant Rao* v. *Purun Mal*, (1880) L. R., 10 I. A. 90; S. C. I. L. R., ... A. 1. In *Sheoratan Kunwari* v. *Ram Pargash*, (1896) I. L. R., 18 A. 227 the founde... representative brought his suit under S. 14.

2. See Introduction Ch. XV. See also *Gossamee Sree Greedharreejee* v. *Rumalolljee Gossamee*, (1889) L. R., 16 I. A. 137 : S. C. I. L. R, 17, C. 3; *Sheoratan Kunwari* v. *Ram Pargash*, (1896) I. L. R., 18 A. 227.

3. *Lakshminarayana Aiyar* v. *Thandavaraya Pillai*, (1899) 10 M. L. J. R. 100.

4. *Hakeem Hisam-Ood-Deen* v. *Khaleefa*, (1870) 2 N. W. P. 400 Cf. All. L. J.

5. *Nellaiyappa Pillai* v. *Thangama Natchiar*, (1897) I. L. R., 21 M. 406; *Chidambaram Chetty* v. *Minammal*, (1898) I. L. R., 23 M. 439.

6. *Narayana Ayyar* v. *Kumarasami Mudaliar*, (1899) I. L. R., 23 M. 537. S... also *Sheoratan Kunwari* v. *Ram Pargash*, (1896) I. L. R., 18 A. 227.

It was observed in an early case[1] that after the enactment of S. 30 in the Civil Procedure Code of 1877 the retention of S. 14 was not at all necessary in the Statute Book as it was said that the persons mentioned in the section had no right to bring a representative suit under Act VIII of 1859[2] and that S. 30 of the Code of 1877 for the first time made a provision for enabling persons to bring representative suits.

We, however, wish that the provision instead of being omitted altogether from the Statute Book will be mended, so that the present defects may be remedied by extending the scope of the Section to all private religious endowments, to suits against strangers (*i. e.*, alienees from trustees and persons in unlawful possession) &c. Nor is it correct to say that S. 30 of the Code of 1877 laid down any new principle of law. S. 30, C. P. C.,[3] is only regulative and confers no rights much less any new rights. It is merely a rule of procedure[4]. Moreover it is not correct to say that the remedy by a suit instituted under S. 30, C. P. C., is the same as the remedy by a suit instituted under S. 14 of the Act. As observed by their lordships *Sir S. Subramania Iyer* and *Benson*, JJ. in *Narayana Ayyar* v. *Kumarasami Mudaliar*[5]: "The second plaintiff being a mere worshipper, could not sue in the Subordinate Judge's Court. It is only the provisions of Ss. 14 and 15 of Act XX of 1863 which give him a right to maintain a suit for the removal of a trustee, and such a suit by a worshipper lies only in a District Court." In *Kishore Bon Mohunt* v. *Kalee Churn Giree*[6] the Calcutta High Court with reference to Act VIII of 1859 observed: "That Section (14 of Act XX) does not preclude a party from suing under Act VIII of 1859." Thus it seems to be hardly correct to say that S. 14 may be deleted out of the Statute Book at any rate for the reasons given by *Maclean*, J. Further, if the case

1. Per *Maclean*, J. in *Dhurrum Singh* v. *Kissen Singh*, (1881) I. L. R., 7 C. 767 (770).
2. Per *Maclean*, J. in *Dhurrum Singh* v. *Kissen Singh*, (1881) I. L. R., 7 C. 767 (770). The case of *Rup Narain Singh* v. *Junko Bye*, (1878) 3 C. L. R., 112 having been decided in 1878 after the passing of the Code of 1877 may not be an authority under the code of 1859. Cf. also *Panchcowrie Mull* v. *Chumroo Lall*, (1878) 2 C. L. R. 121; S. C. I. L. R., 3 C. 563.
3. *Anandrav Bhikaji Phadke* v. *Shankar Daji Charya*, (1883) I. L. R., 7 B. 323 (328).
4. *Srinivasa Chariar* v. *Raghava Chariar*, (1897) I. L. R., 23 M. 28 (31).
5. (1899) I. L. R., 23 M. 537 (539).
6. (1874) 22 W. R. C. R. 364 (365).

of *Sajedur Raja* v. *Baidyanath Deb*[1] wherein it was held that the "numerous parties" referred to in S. 30, C. P. C., meant parties capable of being ascertained and not the public entitled to worship should be taken to lay down a sound principle of law, the basis of Mr. Justice *Maclean's* observation would be entirely taken away.

In what Court the suit lies.

[3]. **"The Civil Court"**:—A special *forum* is constituted by the section for the institution of suits under S. 14. This is "the Civil Court" which by force of the Interpretation Clause means the Principal Court of Original Civil jurisdiction in the District in which the mosque, temple or religious establishment is situate, relating to which, or to the endowment whereof, any suit shall be instituted &c., *i. e.*, the District Court. Under the Civil Procedure Code, every suit shall be instituted in the Court of the lowest grade competent to try it (S. 15). The suit under S. 14 of the Act is not triable in the ordinary Civil Courts but only in the District Court[2] (or "the Civil Court" as defined in S. 2 of this Act). But the District Court is the proper *forum* only with reference to the special classes of suits mentioned in the section. What these suits are will be mentioned later on.

Against whom the suit lies—Only as against manager &c. not as against strangers.

[4]. **"The trustee, manager, superintendent of such mosque &c., or the member of any committee appointed under this Act"**:—The persons against whom a suit may be brought under S. 14 is a trustee, manager or superintendent or member of committee. The Court has jurisdiction under this section both as against a manager appointed by the committee[3] but also as against a hereditary manager or other person whose nomination is not vested in the committee[4]. No prior application to the committee is necessary[5]. The suit under S. 14 will lie only as against *the* trustee of a mosque

1. (1892) I. L. R., 20 C. 397. But see Introduction Chs. XV and XVI.
2. *Narayana Ayyar* v. *Kumarasami Mudaliar*, (1899) I. L. R., 23 M. 537.
3. *Shanmugam Pillai* v. *Sankaramurti Mudaliar*, (1899) 10 M. L. J. R. 109.
4. *Fakurudin Sahib* v. *Ackeni Sahib*, (1880) I. L. R., 2 M. 197; *Dhurrum Singh* v. *Kissen Singh*, (1881) I. L. R., 7 C. 767; *Natesa* v. *Ganapati*, (1890) I. L. R., 14 M. 103; *Sheoratan Kunwari* v. *Ram Pargash*, (1896) I. L. R., 18 A. 227. The case of *Muthu* v. *Gangathara*, (1898) I. L. R., 17 M. 95 must not be taken to lay down the contrary. It simply states a fact in that case that "the trustee was not nominated by nor subject to the confirmation of Government." But this must not be taken as a decision that S. 14 only applies to trustees under S. 3.
5. *Agri Sharma Embrandri* v. *Vistnu Embrandri*, (1866) 3 M. H. C. 198. See also *Ponnambala Mudaliyar* v. *Varaguna Rama Pandia Chinnatambiar*, (1872) 7 M. H. C. 117 (a case under the Regulation with reference to a charitable trust).

or *the* member of a committee *while holding office* as such[1]. A suit against a dismissed manager or as against the representatives of a deceased manager[2] will not fall under S. 14. A suit against a person who is not admitted to be a manager *i. e.*, a suit against a trespasser cannot be brought under this section[3]. Hence in a suit under S. 14 against the trustee &c., no relief can be claimed against a stranger[4]. In a suit under S. 14 for misfeasance or for wrongful alienation by the trustee &c., the alienee from the trustee &c., cannot be a party and no relief can be claimed as against him[5]. If the plaintiff admits that the defendant is a manager, that is enough to bring his suit under S. 14, although the defendant may only be a *defacto* manager[6]. If the defendant says and proves that he is not a manager, then there is an end of the suit which is thus disposed of on the merits. But the Section has no application to constructive trustees[7] nor to persons who are the mere agents of trustees[8]. The reason for the view that in a suit under S. 14

---

1. *Jeyangarulavaru* v. *Durma Dossji*, (1868) 4 M. H. C. 2; *Manally Chenna Kesavaraya* v. *Vaidelinga*, (1877) I. L. R., 1 M. 343 (348); *Sabapathi* v. *Subraya*, (1878) I. L. R., 2 M. 58; *Virasami Nayudu* v. *Subba Rau*, (1882) I. L. R., 6 M. 54; *Sivayya* v. *Rami Reddi*, (1899) I. L. R., 22 M. 223.

2. *Jeyangarulavaru* v. *Durma Dossji*, (1868) 4 M. H. C. 2; *Manally Chenna Kesavaraya* v. *Mangadu Vaidelinga*, (1877) I. L. R., 1 M. 343; *Sabapathi* v *Subraya*, (1878) I. L. R., 2 M. 58; *Virasami Nayudu* v. *Subba Rau*, (1882) I. L. R., 6 M. 54. Cf. *Nellaiyappa Pillai* v. *Thanguma Nachiyar*, (1897) I. L. R., 21 M. 406 (409).

3. *Kishore Bon Mohunt* v. *Kalee Churn Giree*, (1874) 22 W. R. C. R., 364; *Sabapathi* v. *Subraya*, (1878) I. L. R., 2 M. 58; *Mahalinga Rau* v. *Vencoba Ghosami*, (1881) I. L. R., 4 M. 157; *Virasami Nayudu* v. *Subba Rau*, (1882) I. L. R., 6 M. 54; *Muhammad Siraj-ul-Haq* v. *Imam-ud-din*, (1896) I. L. R., 19 A. 104; *Sivayya* v. *Rami Reddi*, (1899) I. L. R., 22 M. 223. The same principle has been held applicable in the case of suits under S. 539 C. P. C. See also Introduction Ch. XV.

4. *Mahalinga Rau* v. *Vencoba Ghosami*, (1881) I. L. R., 4 M. 157; *Sivayya* v. *Rami Reddi*, (1899) I. L. R., 22 M. 223; *Muhammad Jafar* v. *Muhammad Ibrahim*, (1900) I. L. R., 24 M. 243. But see *Sajedur Raja* v. *Baidyanath Deb*, (1892) I. L. R., 20 C. 397; and *Sheoratan Kunwari* v. *Ram Pargash*, (1896) I. L. R., 18 A. 227.

5. *Sabapathi* v. *Subraya*, (1878) I. L. R., 2 M. 58; *Mahalinga Rau* v. *Vencoba Ghosami*, (1881) I. L. R., 4 M. 157; *Jan Ali* v. *Ram Nath Mundul*, (1881) I. L. R., 8 C. 32; *Virasami Nayudu* v, *Subba Rau*, (1882) I. L. R., 6 M. 54; *Sivayya* v. *Rami Reddi*, (1899) I. L. R., 22 M. 223; *Muhammad Jafar* v. *Muhammad Ibrahim*, (1900) I. L. R., 24 M. 243 (245). But see *Sheoratan Kunwari* v. *Ram Pargash*, (1896), I. L. R., 18 A. 227. Cf. *Bibee Kuneez Fatima* v. *Bibee Saheba Jan*, (1867) 8 W. R. C. R. 318 where this point was not raised.

6. *Ganes Sing* v. *Ram Gopal Sing*, (1870) 5 B. L. R., App. 55 followed by *Kennedy* J. in *Panchcowrie Mull* v. *Chumroo Lall*, (1878) I. L. R., 3 C. 563 at pp. 567 and 568, (The appellate court in the latter case reversed the decision of *Kennedy* J., on another point); *Muhammad Siraj-ul-Haq* v. *Imam-ud-din*. (1896) I. L.R., 19 A. 104.

7. *Sabapathi* v. *Subraya*, (1878) I. L. R., 2 M. 58.

8. *Venkatappayya* v. *Venkatapathi*, (1899) 9 M. L. J. R., 105.

only *the trustee* &c., can be impleaded as a defendant and that *no stranger* such as an alienee or trespasser in possession can be impleaded is stated to be that the section creates a special jurisdiction and that the provisions for compulsory reference to arbitration are only explicable upon the footing that the suit is against the manager but are inexplicable with reference to persons other than managers[1]. If this be the correct law, and we have no reason to suppose it can be otherwise as the section at present stands, it goes against all admitted principles of procedure. Processual law must be framed in such a way as to enable a party to obtain justice without further litigation. S. 28 of the Civil Procedure Code, has been enacted with this object. When parties litigate a question that question must be completely determined in the presence of all the parties interested in the same. In the matter on hand what is the use of a declaration[2] against a manager which does not bind the alienees? If a manager alienates trust property wrongfully, it serves no purpose of the person interested if he is only allowed to sue the manager. His object is to get a verdict that the alienation is not binding and how is this object satisfied if he is allowed only to bring a suit against the manager[3] and get a declaration as against him which does not bind the alienee. If trespassers are in possession of trust property and the manager does not take steps to recover it for the trust even then the persons interested can only sue the manager. What purpose does this serve? The persons interested want to recover the property for the trust or to state more accurately want that the property should be recovered for the trust, and yet this cannot be done in a suit under S. 14. If all persons claiming an interest in the property, who can be impleaded in an ordinary suit under S. 28, C. P. C., cannot be impleaded under S. 14 of this Act, what is the use of a suit under S. 14? The result is that the alienee or trespasser is allowed to take advantage of his own wrong and the property cannot be recovered from such alienee

1. See *Sabapathi* v. *Subraya*, (1878) I. L. R., 2 M. 58; *Sivayya* v. *Rami Reddi* (1899) I. L. R., 22 M. 223.

2. As to whether even such declaration is maintainable without a prayer for removal of the manager, see *Mahalinga Rau* v. *Vencoba Ghosami*, (1881) I. L. R., 4 M 157 and *Muhammad Jafar* v. *Muhammad Ibrahim*, (1900) I. L. R., 24 M. 243 (245). See further note under heading [6] pp. 111 to 113.

3. See cases cited in last note.

or stranger until the defaulting manager is removed and a new one is appointed who will then have to take steps to bring a suit for possession against the person in possession. In the meantime limitation will be running and the property may be irretrievably lost for the trust. The person having the interest specified in this section is helpless and the section does not help him as in a suit under this section he can only get a declaration that the property belongs to the trust[1] and that the alienation, if any, relied upon is invalid, but this declaration can only be against the manager and not against the stranger who cannot be impleaded in such a suit. The ordinary law also will not help him as it has been held in the decided cases that, under the ordinary law, he is not entitled to sue for possession[2], that not even the committee in cases where the latter appoint a manager will be entitled to sue for such possession[3] and that it is only the manager who is entitled to sue for possession[3]. No doubt these cases cannot be said to negative the right, if any, of the worshippers to sue under S. 30 C. P. C., and their right in such suit which is a representative one to ask for possession[4]. But the Calcutta High Court seems to hold that worshippers have no right to bring a suit under S. 30 C. P. C[5]. As it is, the remedy given, under S. 14, is worse than useless, and it is sincerely to be hoped that in the interests of these religious endowments the section will be amended by the Legislature so as to enable the persons interested to sue in one suit both the manager and the persons in possession of the trust property who may either claim under an alienation from the manager or claim hostilely to him. There can be on two opinions upon the question whether it is expedient that strangers, be they alienees from the manager or trespassers, should be joined in the suit against the manager. If authority were wanting it is to be found in the very case of *Sivayya* v. *Rami Reddi*[6], where a Full Bench of the Madras High Court held that

1. As to whether a suit for such declaration will lie, see p. 98 note (2) and notes under heading [6] pp. 111 to 113.

2. *Subbarayadu* v. *Asanali Sheriff*, (1899) I. L. R., 23 M. 100 (note); *Kamaraju*, v. *Asanali Sheriff*, (1899) I. L. R., 23 M. 99. But see *Zafaryab Ali* v. *Bakhtawar Singh* (1883) I. L. R., 5 A. 497; and *Kazi Hassan* v. *Sagun Balkrishna*, (1899) I. L. R., 24 B. 170 (175, 176 and 180).

3. *Ponduranga* v. *Nagappa*, (1889) I. L. R., 12 M. 366; *Muthusami Pillai* v. *The Queen Empress*, (1895) I. L. R., 26 M. 243 (note): S. C. 6 M. L. J. R., 14. See also cases cited in note (4) p. 45.

4. At any rate the question had not to be considered in those cases. See also Introduction Ch. XV.

5. *Sajedur Raja* v. *Baidyanath Deb*, (1892) I. L. R., 20 C. 397.

6. (1899) I. L. R., 22 M. 223.

alienees could not be proper parties in a suit under S. 14. Mr. Justice *Shephard* there observed[1]: "With the view to obviating further litigation it is clearly expedient that they should be joined and that the property should be recovered from them in the same suit.........Perhaps it might have been convenient to give the Court the jurisdiction exercised by the Allahabad High Court in the case of *Sheoratan Kunwari* v. *Ram Pargash*[2], but I cannot agree with that court that the jurisdiction has been given." If it be objected—and no person who has the well-being of these endowments at heart will object to the amendment itself—that the provisions in the Act as to compulsory reference ought not to be extended to persons other than the managers, we say that persons who claim under alienations from managers can not be in a better position than their alienors. But, however this may be, it does not matter much if these provisions as to compulsory reference are repealed provided a remedy under the Act is given against strangers.

Suit is in substance for breach of trust.

[5]. "**For any misfeasance, breach of trust or neglect of duty**:"—The suit under S. 14 against the trustee, manager or superintendent or member of committee must be for *misfeasance, breach of trust* or *neglect of duty*. A suit which does not charge the trustee, &c., with misfeasance, breach of trust or neglect of duty, does not lie under S. 14. This and the following sections (15 to 20) provide for the interference of the court by way of suit in certain cases, but they are entirely confined to cases which may be classified as breaches of trust or neglect of duty[3]. To sum up in one word the suit against the trustee is in substance one for breach of trust[4] and without an allegation of that sort there can be no exercise of jurisdiction under the section[5].

Misfeasance is a familiar term in the law of torts. It is there used as distinguished from *malfeasance* and *non-feasance*

1. (1899) I. L. R., 22 M. 223 at p. 227.
2. (1896) I. L. R., 18 A. 227.
3. *Meenakshi Naidoo* v. *Subramaniya Sastri*, (1887) L. R. 14 I.A. 160: S.C.I.L.R., 11 M. 26.
4. *Agri Sharma Embrandri* v. *Vistnu Embrandri*, (1866) 3 M. H. C. 198; *Syed Amin Sahib* v. *Ibram Sahib*, (1868) 4 M. H. C. 112; *Manally Chenna Kesavaraya* v. *Vaidelinga*, (1877) I. L. R., 1 M. 343 (348); *Muhammad Siraj-Ul-Haq* v. *Imam-ud-din*, (1896) I. L. R., 19 A. 104 (106).
5. *Kishore Bon Mohunt* v. *Kalee Churn Giree*, (1874) 22 W. R. C. R. 364.

According to the Century Dictionary it has the following meanings. "*In law*: (*a*) a wrong done. (*b*) In modern use, more specifically the misuse of power; the wrongful and injurious exercise of lawful authority, as distinguished from *malfeasance* and *nonfeasance*." It is also there stated that this term is often carelessly used in the sense of *malfeasance*. *Malfeasance*, according to the Century Dictionary, is "evil-doing; the doing of that which ought not to be done; wrongful conduct; specifically the doing of an act which is positively unlawful or wrongful in contradistinction to misfeasance or the doing of a lawful act in a wrongful manner." *Non-feasance*, according to the Century Dictionary, is "the omission of some act which ought to have been performed by the party." Malfeasance is a positive wrong or the commission of some evil or unlawful act. It is an active wrong-doing. But a misfeasance is the improper performance of some lawful act. The latter term occurs in the English Companies Act of 1862. By *misfeasance* is there meant misfeasance in the nature of a breach of trust resulting in some actual loss to the Company[1] concerned. The same term occurs in the Indian Companies Act VI of 1882, S. 214. The words in this section are "any misfeasance or breach of trust in relation to the Company." The present section goes further and adds neglect of duty. Whether the law is wider under the Religious Endowments Act than under the Indian Companies Act need not be considered.

Suit to cancel deed of endowment.

The term "misfeasance" has been the subject of judicial consideration in several cases. Before proceeding to consider these cases we may observe that a suit by an endower to cancel the deed of endowment executed by him on the ground that it has been fraudulently obtained from him, is not a suit for misfeasance, &c., within the meaning of the section[2]. Then again, the

1. *Coventry and Dixon's Case*, (1880) 14 Ch. Div. 660 (670).

2. *Hidait-Oon-Nissa* v. *Syud Afzul Hossein*, (1870) 2 N. W. P. 420. Such a suit is not a suit for a mere declaration but a suit in which consequential relief is asked for within the meaning of S. 7 cl. iv (c) of the Court Fees Act. See *Samiya Mavali* v. *Minammal*, (1899) I. L. R., 23 M. 490 dissenting from *Karam Khan* v. *Daryai Singh*, (1883) I. L. R., 5 A 331 (F.B.). See also *Valambal Ammal* v. *Vythilinga Mudaliar*, (1900) I. L. R., 24 M. 331 which is also reported again by oversight in I. L. R., 25 M. 380; and C. M. A. 77 of 1903, 13 M. L. J. (Rec. Cas). 59. Cf. also *Guruvajamma* v. *Venkatakrishnama Chetti*, (1900) I.L. R. 24 M. 34. But if the endower wants also possession of the properties, than Court fee ought to be paid as in the case of other suits for recovery of property. See *Mahomed Masik* v. *Malkai Mukhadraj Uzwa Badshah Mehal Saheba*, (1883) I.L.R., 10 C. 380.

misfeasance, breach of trust, or neglect of duty must be in respect of the trusts vested in or confided to the manager or committee as the case may be, although such misconduct may be with reference to the affairs of the establishment. If, therefore, a manager becomes insolvent or otherwise impecunious a suit to remove such manager[1] (assuming that the same will be a valid ground for removal) is not a suit falling under S. 14 charging misfeasance.

In *Syed Amin Sahib* v. *Ibram Sahib*[2], the earliest case where the meaning of this term was in question the facts were that a manager who was the Khatib of a mosque was removed by the committee. He thereupon sued the committee for restoration and for damages. The High Court observed: "We think *misfeasance* in this provision was simply used with reference to *wilful acts of breaches* of trust, *acts of a criminal nature*; and that the provision applies to personal misconduct amounting to a breach of trust or neglect of duty by any member of the committee in respect of the property and endowments vested in the committee by S. 12 and of which they are by S. 13 required to keep regular accounts. * * * There may be a removal from office on insufficient grounds, without any misfeasance, on the part of the committee, and an improper removal occasions an injury and loss in respect of which redress can be obtained only by the person dismissed and to a suit for such redress, S. 14 has no application."

Mere error of judgment.

Where there is only an error of judgment the same will not entail removal from membership of the committee. The question what conduct will justify removal from membership of a committee is different from the question whether the committee can be sued in a suit under S. 14 in respect of an act of dismissal which is wrongful as against the manager though there may be no such misconduct as will justify removal of the manager. If the manager is removed on insufficient grounds, can the manager bring a suit under S. 14 to set

1. In *Thackersey Dewraj* v. *Hurbhum Nursey*, (1881) I.L. R., 8 B. 432, *Scott*, J., observed at p. 470 that insolvency would be a ground for removal, though it would not necessarily imply misconduct. See *Adam's Trust, In re* (1879) 12 Ch. Div. 634 and Trusts Act, S. 73. Cf. also *Rajendronath Dutt* v. *Shaik Mahomed Lal*, (1881) L.R. 8 I. A. 135 (139): S. C. I. L. R. 8 C. 42 (47).

2. (1868) 4 M. H. C. 112.

aside such dismissal? The action of the committee may not be justifiable and the committee may be liable in damages. There may be the violation of a right possessed by the manager for which the latter is entitled to redress. If it is not a misfeasance, is this not a neglect of duty committed by the committee in respect of the trusts vested in or confided to the committee[1]? If a suit lies in such a case two assumptions are made. *First*, that a suit for damages in respect of the trust will lie under S. 14. The case of *Srinivasa* v. *Venkata*[2] holds that such a suit will lie, but *Shephard*, J., doubts the soundness of this view (see *Sivayya* v. *Rami Reddi*[3]). *Secondly*, a redress personal to the manager is a redress in respect of the trusts of the institution[4]. But a further consideration of this question becomes unimportant in view of the fact that the section is merely enabling and the manager is not bound to proceed under the section. He may proceed under the general law for redress for such wrongful removal for the manager has not merely a bare interest as is provided in S. 15 of the Act[5].

In *Elayalwar Reddiar* v. *Namberumal Chettiar*[6] it was held that where a manager who did not receive certain voluntary contributions and perform certain festivals for the expenses of which such voluntary contributions were made, he was guilty of a breach of trust or neglect of duty. According to Mr. Justice *Subramania Iyer*, the dharmakarta was bound to receive the contributions and perform the festivals if such performance was not inconsistent with the usage of the institution. According to Mr. Justice *Moore*, the manager would be liable only when there being a custom for him to receive the contributions and perform the festivals from the same he should fail to observe such custom or usage.

1. In *Syed Amin Sahib* v. *Ibram Sahib*, (1868) 4 M. H. C. 112, it was held that a suit for such redress did not lie under S. 14.

2. (1887) I. L. R., 11 M. 148.

3. (1899) I. L. R., 22 M. 223 (227). It is submitted that this doubt is not warranted. See p. 106.

4. *Syed Amin Sahib* v. *Ibram Sahib*, (1868) 4 M. H.C. 112 (114) holds that such a redress is only personal and does not concern the trusts of the institution and that S. 14 does not, therefore, apply. But see *Elayalwar Reddiar* v. *Namberumal Chettiar*, (1899) I. L. R., 23 M. 298.

5. *Athavulla* v. *Gouse* (1888) I. L. R., 11 M. 283.

6. (1899) I. L. R., 23 M. 298.

Circumstances which will justify removal of manager &c.

Here we have to consider what misconduct will justify removal of the manager &c. The principles guiding courts in this matter have been more fully stated in the introduction[1]. But we shall here refer to a few circumstances, the existence of which has been held to constitute a sufficient ground for such removal.

(*a*). Failure to keep accounts on the part of managers of institutions coming under both Ss. 3 and 4[2] or on the part of the committee is a neglect of duty which will entail the person concerned with forfeiture from his office.

(*b*). The failure on the part of the manager of an institution coming under S. 3 to submit accounts to the committee is a breach of one of the most important duties cast upon the manager by the law and will justify his dismissal[3].

(*c*). Wilful obstruction of the public worship by the manager as by closing the temple at the time of the festivals is a breach of trust or misfeasance and will justify the manager's dismissal[4].

(*d*). The opposition by a minority of the managers as against the majority with reference to the repairs of the institution, (the usage of the institution being that when there is a minority the latter should act in accordance with the resolutions of the majority) will justify dismissal of the minority or at least the taking of security from such minority[5].

(*e*). The refusal by the manager to receive voluntary subscriptions offered by the votaries and perform festivals especially when there should be a custom to receive such contributions and perform the festivals.[6]

There are again other circumstances which will not be sufficient to justify the dismissal of the manager or member of a committee.

---

1. Chapter XIV. See also pp. 49 and 50.

2. *Fakurudin Sahib* v. *Ackeni Sahib*, (1880) I.L.R., 2M. 197. Here the manager was a hereditary manager and there were also other circumstances in the case which were said to amount to a neglect of duty. See also notes to S. 18.

3. *Anantanarayana Ayyar* v. *Kuttalam Pillai*, (1899) I. L. R., 22 M. 481.

4. *Natesa* v. *Ganapati*, (1890) I. L. R., 14 M. 103.

5. See *Natesa* v. *Ganapati*, supra. In *Dhurrum Singh* v. *Kissen Singh*, (1881) I. L. R., 7 C. 767, where the trustee or mahant of the temple of *Harmandir* tried to remove a cradle which was reputed to be that of Guru Gobind and a Granth which was reputed to have been sent by him to the temple and to contain a gold leaf on which the Guru himself inscribed some words. The cradle and the Granth were objects of great veneration among the Sikhs. See also *Sivasankara* v. *Vadagiri*, (1889) I. L. R., 13 M. 6.

6. *Elayalwar Reddiar* v. *Namberumal Chettiar*, (1899) I. L. R. 23 M. 298.

(a). The appointment by the committee of a Sivite as Dharmakarta for a Vishnu temple is not illegal and is not such misconduct as will justify the dismissal of the committee[1].

(b). The sanctioning of expenditure from temple funds by a Tengalai member of a committee in respect of fines paid and costs incurred in disputes between Tengalais and Vadagalais only shows the partiality of the member; but is not sufficient to justify his dismissal[2].

(c). The interference of the committee with the trustee in matters of ritual although unwarranted may be ascribed to a mistaken understanding on the part of the committee of the scope of the duties devolving on such committee and is not such misconduct as will justify removal of the committee members[3].

We shall next advert to certain classes of suits which do not fall under S. 14 as not being suits for *misfeasance*, &c. Two of these suits are mentioned in heading [3][4] and in the beginning of this heading[5] but for convenience we shall mention all in this connection :—

(1) A suit by an endower to cancel the deed of endowment made by him[6].

(2). A suit by a manager or co-manager for management or for a share in management[7].

---

1. *Gandavathara Ayyangar* v. *Devanayaga Mudali*, (1883) I. L. R., 7 M. 222. The suit as brought is difficult to understand. Sanction was also asked as against the Sivite appointed as dharmakarta. It is difficult to comprehend the acts of misconduct alleged against him. If the contention was that there was no valid appointment and that, therefore, the person purported to be appointed was not the dharmakarta one could understand the same. But a suit involving that contention will not fall under S. 14. See cases referred to in p. 97, note (4).

2. *Tiruvengadath Ayyangar* v. *Srinivasa Thathachariar*, (1899) I. L. R., 22 M.361.

3. *Tiruvengadath Ayyangar* v. *Srinivasa Thathachariar*, (1899) I. L. R., 22 M. 361. (where the facts were that the committee stopped the Desikar festival in the Srivilliputhur temple unless the Vadagalais should consent to a *Tengalai Namam* being affixed on the forehead of the Desikar and to certain hymns not being recited at such festival). See notes under S. 7, pp. 46 and 47.

4. p. 93. 5. p. 101.

6. *Hidait-Oon-nissa* v. *Syed Afzul Hossein*, (1870) 2 N. W. P. 420.

7. *Agri Sharma Embrandri* v. *Vistnu Embrandri*, (1866) 3 M. H. C. 198; *Hajee Kalub Hossein* v. *Mussumat Mehrum Bibee*, (1872) 4 N. W. P. 155; *Kishore Bon Mohunt* v. *Kalee Churn Giree*, (1874) 22 W. R. C. R., 364; *Kalee Churn Giri* v. *Golabi*, (1878) 2 C. L. R., 128; *Mahalinga Rau* v. *Vencoba Ghosami*, (1881) I. L. R., 4 M. 157; *Athavulla* v. *Gouse*, (1888) I. L. R., 11 M. 283; *Miya Vali Ulla* v. *Sayed Bava Santi Miya*, (1896) I. L. R., 22 B. 496 (case under S. 539, C. P. C).

(3). Suit by members of a committee to enforce their right of control[1].

(4) The question whether a suit for damages personal to the trustee will lie under S. 14 is a more difficult one. We have already referred to this in a slight degree when considering the case of *Syed Amin Sahib* v. *Ibram Sahib*[2]. A suit for damages against the manager for breach of trust is a suit for breach of trust in respect of the trusts confided in the manager. We hardly fail to see what otherwise such a suit is. The court under S. 14 may decree damages and costs. How can a court under S. 14 decree damages if no suit for damages can lie under S. 14. The case of *Srinivasa* v. *Venkata*[3] is authority for the view that a suit for damages against the manager will lie under S. 14. The doubt thrown upon this case by Mr. Justice *Shephard*[4] is hardly borne out either by authority or principle. But this is with respect to damages recoverable for the institution. But when the act of the manager or committee amounts to a personal wrong from which damage ensues to a person whether he be a subordinate officer of the temple or manager a suit may not lie. The person affected has, of course, a remedy independent of the Act.

[6] "**May direct the specific performance, &c. and may also direct the removal of such trustee, manager, superintendent or member of a committee**":—Under this section the court can do either one or all of three things.

(i) It can direct the specific performance of any act by the trustee, &c.

(ii) It may decree damages and costs against the trustee, &c.

(iii) It may direct the removal of such trustee, &c.

We should observe that these words strike the key-note to the classes of suits falling within the scope of the section. They must be considered when the question arises whether a particular suit is or is not outside the scope of the section. It has been observed by the Allahabad High Court in ***Muhammad Siraj-ul-Haq*** v. ***Imam-ud-din***[5] that a person suing under S. 14 can only sue for mis-

1. *L. Venkatasa Naidu* v. *Sadagopasamy Iyer*, (1869) 4. M. H. C. 404; *Puddolabh Roy* v. *Ramgopal Chatterjee*, (1882) I. L. R., 9 C. 133; *Pondurunga* v. *Nagappa*, (1889) I. L. R., 12 M. 366. See also cases cited in notes (1, 2 and 3), p. 45.
2. (1868) 4 M. H. C. 112.
3. (1887) I. L. R., 11 M. 148.
4. *Sivayya* v. *Rami Reddi*, (1899) I. L. R., 22 M. 223.
5. (1896) I. L. R., 19 A. 104.

feasance or breach of trust or neglect of duty, but that it is not necessary to state what the court may do on its finding a breach of trust. It has also been observed in the same case that if a plaintiff under S. 14 states what the court ought to do, it is merely burdening the plaint. It is difficult to understand these observations. A plaintiff must state definitely in his plaint all the reliefs he wants and we can never conceive of a plaint without a prayer column (S. 50, clause (*e*) C. P. C.). A plaint under S. 14 of Act XX of 1863 is no exception to this general rule. A suit charging the trustee with misfeasance but asking for no reliefs is unmeaning.

Directing specific performance of any act. Decree mandatory not prohibitory.

We shall now proceed to consider the decree that may be passed under this section. First of all, the section says that the Civil Court may direct the *specific performance* of any *act* by the trustee, &c. These words are very general. It is said that these words show that a proper decree under S. 14 should be mandatory rather than prohibitory[1]. The trustee should do certain affirmative acts with reference to the trust. These are his duties. Such duties should be enforced specifically by a mandatory decree, *i. e.*, the trustee should be directed to do his duty specifically. There should be no prohibitory decree. This may seem a jugglery of language. If a person who is directed to do a specific act tries to do an exactly contrary act, why should he not be restrained from doing that act? And yet that will be the effect of recognising the validity of the distinction pointed out. However this may be, we think, the same result may be arrived at. In the case of a mandatory decree, the decree should direct that the act should be done specifically. Such a decree can be enforced under the provisions of S. 260, C. P. C. Why is it to be assumed that a trustee has only affirmative acts to perform? Negatively, he may also be under a duty not to perform certain acts (Cf. S. 54 ill. (*f*) of the Specific Relief Act). In case he is committing a breach of trust, why should he not be prevented from committing such a breach? We should rather think that S. 55 of the Specific Relief Act will apply to such cases and that a mandatory and restrictive injunction may be a proper decree that may be passed under S. 14. The greater power of the Court to award a mandatory injunction given under S. 14 must include the lesser power to award a restrictive injunction.

1. *Dhurrum Singh* v. *Kissen Singh*, (1881) I. L. R., 7 C, 767.

We shall then advert to some instances in which the performance of specific acts may be directed by the Court under S. 14:—

Compelling dharmakarta to hold festivals.

(1). If the dharmakarta omits to perform or hold any festival which according to long usage has been performed then he may be compelled to perform or hold the festival[1]. Even if there be no such usage, where voluntary contributions are offered to the dharmakarta for certain festivals or other acts of public worship not inconsistent with the usage of the institution, the dharmakarta is bound to receive the contributions and to celebrate the festivals or other acts of public worship. If he refuses he will be compelled specifically to perform the festival or other acts of public worship[2] unless such refusal is in the *bonafide* interests of the institution. In *Protap Chandra Misser* v. *Brojonath Misser*[3]. it was held that a decree that the shebaits should perform the sheba according to certain rules, that they should repair the temple within six months, and that, if they should neglect to act according to the rules and to repair the temple within the prescribed time, the plaintiffs or the members of their family would be competent to sue for the appointment of a manager was outside the scope of S. 14 of the Act No reasons were assigned for this but the objection taken by the appellants was that the decree was declaratory and that it could not be passed under S. 21 of the Specific Relief Act (apparently Cl. (*b*).) We fail to see the force of this objection.

Directing manager to perform acts.

(2). Directing the manager to perform the acts of the wakf and to defray the expenses incidental to such acts out of the income accruing from the wakf properties is within the scope of the Section[4] and is covered by the expression "may direct," &c. So also directing the manager to perform certain rites, ceremonies or worship, out of the trust properties, is within the scope of the Section[5].

---

1. *Elayalwar Reddiar* v. *Namberumal Chettiar*, (1899) I. L. R., 23 M. 298.
2. Per *Subramania Iyer*, J., in *Elayalwar Reddiar* v. *Namberumal Chettiar*, (1899) I. L. R., 23 M. 298.
3. (1891) I. L. R., 19 C. 275 at pp. 281 and 286.
4. *Jan Ali* v. *Ram Nath Mundul*, (1881) I. L. R., 8 C. 32 (36).
5. *Elayalwar Reddiar* v. *Namberumal Chettiar*, (1899) I. L. R., 23 M. 298.

[redacted]

(3). Where certain things are objects of great veneration among a portion of the public and are objects of worship and the manger tries to remove them from the place in which they are to another place that will constitute an obstruction to the public worship. The manager will be directed to retain the things in their accustomed place[1]. In *Dhurrum Singh* v. *Kissen Singh*[1], the Court held that the public had a right to worship at all times, the Granth and the cradle in the place where they were used to be without let or hindrance and that the removal of the cradle and the Granth even though temporary was an infringement of the said right of the public and that, consequently, (though there may be a pecuniary advantage to the institution) it was a breach of trust to remove them. The decree passed by the Court was for the specific performance of the following act, *i. e.*, the keeping of the cradle and the Granth in the temple by the mohunt.

Directing manager to keep Granth.

(4). Where the misconduct is not so serious as to entail forfeiture of office, the Court may simply direct the manager to keep accounts in bound books instead of in cadjan[2] and file them in Court half-yearly or monthly as the case may be and to give notice to the plaintiff or other person or persons to be named by the Court that the accounts have been filed and are open for the inspection of the plaintiff or other interested persons[3].

Directing manager to keep accounts.

(5). A suit for a scheme of management is maintainable under the general law. It is because of this that persons having a "direct interest" or a bare interest are allowed to sue under S. 539, C. P. C., among other things for a scheme. In the famous *Ranchhod Temple case*[4] cited in the Introduction the Privy Council has treated this as undoubted law. Mr. Mayne, the Counsel who argued for the appellant in this case admitted that where there was a religious foundation there must be a scheme. The Privy Council held that

Directing scheme.

1. *Dhurrum Singh* v. *Kissen Singh*, (1881) I. L. R., 7 C. 767. Here the objects of veneration and worship were Guru Govind's cradle and granth in the temple of Harmandir, a great Sikh temple at Patna. The trustee wanted to send them to the capital of the Raja of Jind a leading Sikh Chief in order that the Ranis may pay their respects in consideration of which the Raja promised considerable presents to the temple.

2. App. I of 1902 M. H. Ct. Jud. Ind. 1903, p. 71.

3. *Syud Imdad Hossein* v. *Mahomed Ali Khan*, (1874) 23 W. R. C. R. 150. See also case cited in note (2.)

4. *Chotalal Lakhmiram* v. *Manohar Ganesh Tambekar*, (1899) L. R., 26 I. A. 199 S. C. I. L. R., 24 B. 50. See Introduction, Chapter I, pp. vii and viii.

as before the trust funds could be ascertained it would be impossible to settle a scheme the decree of the Indian Courts directing an account to be taken of the trust property was correct[1].

The only question is whether such a suit is maintainable, under S. 14, the only suit provided for under S. 14 being a suit for misfeasance or breach of trust or neglect of duty. But though the object of the legislature is to provide a remedy for misfeasance or breach of trust, and although the framing of a scheme is generally and primarily intended for the benefit of the institution and is calculated to prevent breaches of trust or misfeasance by the trustee, a suit for a scheme is not maintainable under S.14 *without misfeasance* alleged and found against the trustee[2]. A suit simply for a scheme of management on the ground that it will be more beneficial to the institution or on the ground that the direction of the Court is necessary is not maintainable under S. 14. It is maintainable of course under S. 539, C. P. C., where the language used is quite different. The case of *Narayana Ayyar* v. *Kumararasami Mudaliar*[3] assumes that no suit for a scheme is maintainable under S. 14 but only under S. 539, C. P. C. The learned Judges in that case were only stating what was a fact in that case, *viz.*, that the reliefs (settling a scheme, appointing new trustees &c.,) were not claimed to be under Act XX but under S. 539, C. P. C., or in a suit instituted under that section. Where a scheme is framed and the trustee is directed to observe that scheme, is he not directed the specific performance of an act within the meaning of the section? Where there is a charge against the trustee for misfeasance, breach of trust, &c., &c., it is a suit for misfeasance &c., and upon proof of such misfeasance &c., a scheme may be framed. It may be that even where such charge is negatived the decree may direct simply a scheme without awarding anything more. But the recent case of *Karedla Vijayaraghava Perumalayya Naidu* v. *Vemavarapu Sitaramayya*[4], however is authority for the

1. See *Barrett* v. *Kemp Brothers*, (1904) 1 K. B. 517, where it was held that the judgment of a Court as to a point of law based upon an admission of counsel was nevertheless the decision of the Court and would be binding as such.

2. In *Muhammad Siraj-ul-Haq* v. *Imam-ud-din*, (1896) I.L.R., 19 A. 104, the suit was under S. 14 charging the trustee with misconduct and there was a prayer for a scheme. But no objection was taken.

3. (1899) I. L. R., 23 M. 537.

4. (1902) I. L. R., 26 M. 361.

[redacted]

view that a District judge had no power to frame a scheme under S. 14 of the Act. If this should be the correct view, we must regret the language adopted by the Legislature in S. 14 and the policy of the Government in hesitating to amend the Act for remedying these defects.

Suit for declaration.

(6). Another question arises whether a plaintiff can sue under S. 14 for a declaration that certain specific properties belong to the religious establishment or idol or that certain alienations made by the manager are not binding and liable to set aside. Where misfeasance &c., is charged against the manager and is proved and such misfeasance consists in the wrongful alienation of the trust property, the court may declare in a suit under S. 14 for such misfeasance, that the property belongs to the temple and that the alienation of the same is not binding and valid against the temple, &c. Otherwise there is no meaning in a *suit for misfeasance.* Where the misfeasance charged is the assertion of a hostile title, the suit may be for a declaration that the hostile title set up by the trustee is not valid and cannot hold good. Of course the assertion of a hostile title together with other circumstances may also be a ground for removal when a suit for removal may be laid and in such suit a declaration that the hostile title set up is not valid may also be asked and decreed. But where there is no charge for misfeasance can a suit for a declaration lie? The assertion of a hostile title by the trustee is a breach of trust. We should have thought that there can be no doubt as to the entertainment of a suit under S. 14 for a declaration that such hostile title is not valid and yet we find the Calcutta High Court[1] holding that such a prayer is outside the scope of a suit under S. 14.

There is an apparent warrant for this view of the Calcutta High Court from the defective and ambiguous language employed by the Legislature in enacting S. 14. The section empowers the court to decree *three* classes of relief (1) directing specific performance of an act by the manager, (2) directing payment of damages and costs, and (3) directing removal of the manager. Awarding a declaration that certain property belongs to the temple, idol or trust

1. (1881) I. L. R., 8 C. 32 (40). See also *Protap Chandra Misser* v. *Brojonath Misser*, (1891) I. L. R., 19 C. 275. See p. 108.

and that any hostile title set up by the manager or any alienation made by the manager is not directing specific performance of any act by the manager &c. Nor is it decreeing damages and costs. But we conceive that the section does not exhaust all the reliefs which can be awarded by a Civil Court in a suit instituted under the section. The section only mentions some of the reliefs that may be awarded but does not confine the power of the Court to award these reliefs only. The words "may direct" &c., "may decree" &c., "may remove" &c., and "also direct" &c., are consistent with the view that the Civil Court is not confined to the award of the reliefs mentioned in the section. The remedy must be commensurate with the disease. So that the misfeasance charged or found must determine the nature of the reliefs to be awarded. In some cases the language employed may amount both to a declaration and a direction for the specific performance of any act. Where a trustee is directed to perform certain rites and ceremonies out of the endowed properties there is in effect a declaration that the endowed properties are liable for the expenses of such rites and ceremonies.

The case of *Sivayya* v. *Rami Reddi*[1] held that a declaration against a dharmakarta that certain property belonged to the temple of which he was the dharmakarta and that his alienation was null ought to stand in a suit instituted under S. 14. But the point was not taken nor did the trustee appeal against such declaration. The trustee was charged with misfeasance and we think the declaration was properly made. The Court might have removed the trustee (the plaint did not ask for such removal too) but the fact that it did not do so did not affect the matter and did not prevent the Court from granting the declaration[2].

The case of *Muhammad Jafar* v. *Muhammad Ibrahim*[3], is however, a direct authority upon the point. It was there held that the prayer for declaration was ancillary to the prayer for removal of the trustee and that a Civil Court had jurisdiction under S. 14 to grant a declaration.

1. (1899) I. L. R., 22 M. 223 (228).
2. But see *Mahalinga Rau* v. *Vencoba Ghosami*, (1881) I. L. R., 4 M. 157.
3. (1900) I. L. R., 24 M. 243. See also *Sheoratan Kunwari* v. *Ram Paragash* (1897) I. L. R., 18 A. 227 where a declaration was made that certain alienations of endowed property did not affect the religious establishment.

The case of *Mahalinga Rau* v. *Vencoba Ghosami*[1] which is distinguished in the above case is, rather difficult to understand. The plaintiff alleging himself to be a disciple of a mattam brought a suit to recover the mattam properties on behalf of the mattam and for a declaration that the properties are those of the mattam. He alleged by way of misfeasance and breach of trust that the defendants colluded together and got up certain documents to show that the property was the private property of some of the defendants. The High Court held that the suit was not one falling under S. 14 of the Act as there was no prayer for the removal of the managers or for damages or for the specific performance of any act by the managers and the object of the suit was only for the recovery of the property for and on behalf of the mattam. We do not understand how the property can be recovered by the plaintiffs from the managers when the latter are not removed. That may have weighed much with the Judges. If the case should be construed to be an authority for the position that a prayer for possession is not maintainable under S. 14 it would be difficult to accept the soundness of that view. The Judges do not consider the question whether a person having a bare interest is entitled to sue for possession. Nor do we think that this case even as distinguished by the Madras High Court in *Muhammad Jafar* v. *Muhammad Ibrahim*[2] can be said to lay down any correct principle of law. Why is a Court prevented from entertaining under S. 14 a suit for declaration in which misfeasance is charged against the trustee merely because the suit does not contain a prayer for removal[3] ?

It is equally difficult to understand the decision of the Calcutta High Court in *Protap Chandra Misser* v. *Brojonath Misser*[4] which held that a declaratory decree of the nature passed in that case by the Lower Court was outside the purview of S. 14.

Directing manager to hand over possession.

(7). It has been held by the Madras High Court that a suit for possession by a person having a bare interest under S. 15 is not maintainable against strangers in possession[5]. We do not think that this view proceeds upon the ground that a

1. (1881) I. L. R., 4 M. 157.
2. (1900) I. L. R., 24 M. 243.
3. See *Sivayya* v. *Rami Reddi*, (1899) I. L. R., 22 M. 223.
4. (1891) I. L. R., 19 C. 275. The argument of counsel in this case was that it was a declaratory decree. See also page 108 post.
5. Per *Shephard* J. in *Sivayya* v. *Rami Reddi*, (1899) I.L.R., 22 M. 223 (227); *Subbarayadu* v. *Asanali Sheriff*, (1899) I.L.R., 23 M. 100 (note); *Kamaraju* v. *Asanali Sheriff* (1899) I.L.R., 23 M. 99. But see *Zafaryab Ali* v. *Bakhtawar Singh*, (1883) I.L.R., 5 A. 497.

suit for possession is outside the scope of S. 14. As already observed[1] no suit will lie against strangers under this section and consequently no relief can be awarded under the section against strangers. But the cases already cited as showing that a suit for possession will not lie are with the exception of *Sivayya* v. *Rami Reddi*[2] not cases under S. 14. So that the question still remains whether a person having only a bare interest under S. 14 can still maintain a suit against the manager for the recovery of possession on the ground of the latter's misfeasance &c. For this purpose it may be assumed that the manager has possession and not merely custody and that, under the general law, a person having a bare interest is not entitled to maintain a suit for possession either against the manager or against strangers though it will be then difficult to conceive how a suit will lie for possession without removal of the manager. It may also be assumed that a suit for removal will lie under the general law by a person having a bare interest without having recourse to the provisions of Ss. 30 and 539, C. P. C. The case of *Kamaraju* v. *Asanali Sheriff*[3] seems to suggest that worshippers suing under S. 30, C. P. C., may sue to recover possession from strangers and we suppose also from the manager after removing him. However this may be, we fail to see why a prayer for possession may not be included in the special suit prescribed under S. 14. If the manager has only custody, *a fortiori* it will follow that a person having a bare interest may sue for removal of the manager and for recovery of the custody from such manager. A suit under S. 14 is representative suit[4].

Where the manager deals wrongfully with trust property or sets up an hostile title there is a breach of trust by the manager and a person having the interest provided for under S. 15 may sue for removing the manager from management and for recovering possession of the trust property on behalf of the trust (or on behalf of the person to be newly appointed as manager)[5]. Directing the manager to give over possession is directing the specific performance of an act by the manager. But as the manager is to be removed and then only the possession or custody is to be recovered from him it may be said that the words "may direct the specific performance of an act by the trustee" refer only to a manag

1. See note under heading [4] pp. 96 to 100.
2. (1899) I. L. R., 22 M. 223.
3. (1899) I. L. R., 23 M.
4. See p. 125.
5. *Sheoratan Kunwari* v. *Ram Pargash*, (1896) I. L. R., 18 A. 227. But *Bhurruck Chunder Sahoo* v. *Golam Shuruff*, (1868) 10 W. R. C. R. 458.

holding office as such and not removed and that such words may not thus help us much. This is, however, putting a very narrow construction upon these words[1]. Moreover as observed by us already the Civil Court is not confined to awarding only the reliefs mentioned in S. 14. When the manager is removed on the ground of misfeasance he should not be allowed to remain in possession or to have the custody of the endowed properties. It seems hardly possible to suppose that the Legislature ever intended that the defaulting manager should be allowed to remain in possession or custody notwithstanding his removal from office. What is the use of removing the manager from office if the court has no power to protect the trust properties from waste or maladministration in the same suit or to pass a decree with reference to the same for better and efficient management? It may be said that the court may order a Receiver under S. 503, C. P. C., but that can only be when the property is the subject of a suit. Property is the subject of a suit when the suit is for recovery of the property. We also think that it is the subject of a suit when the suit is for a declaration of title to such property. So that if the Civil Court is to appoint a Receiver in a suit under S. 14 there must at least be a prayer for a declaration. But this appointment of a Receiver is only a discretionary matter and if the court cannot grant possession or custody to the plaintiff in the suit or if the plaintiff is not entitled to any possession or custody the discretion will be sparingly if at all exercised. According to *Maclean*, C. J., there is no power for the Civil Court in a suit under S. 14 to appoint a receiver[2]. This is rather an extreme view and can only be justified upon the ground that a suit for declaration or for possession will not lie under S. 14. It may be that no receiver can be appointed in cases under the Guardians and Wards Act[3] and in cases governed merely by the Probate Act though in the latter class of cases courts have held otherwise[4]. In all such cases the ground must be that there is no property the subject of a pending suit. But this can hardly govern the present case[5].

---

1. *Subbayya* v. *Krishna*, (1890) I. L. R., 14 M. 186.

2. *Gyananda Asram* v. *Kristo Chandra Mukherji*, (1901) 8 C. W. N. 404. Mr. Justice *Banerjee* expresses no opinion on this point.

3. Woodroffe on Receivers 142. See also *Abdul Rahiman Saheb* v. *Ganapathi Bhatta*, (1900) I. L. R., 23 M. 517.

4. Woodroffe on Receivers, pp. 106 to 112 and the cases cited therein.

5. *Sham Chand Giri* v. *Bhaya Ram Pandey*, (1894) 5 C. W. N. 365 where a receiver of a shrine was appointed. See also *Sia Ram Das* v. *Mohabir Das*, (1899) I.L.R., 27C.279, where a receiver of a matt was appointed. But these cases were under the ordinary law. See also *Juggodumba Dossee* v. *Puddumoney*, (1875) 15B.L.R. 318 (330).

(8). The damages claimable under the section is damages in respect of the trust[1]. Damages may be given for misfeasance, breach of trust or neglect of duty. Where the manager misappropriates temple moneys, a plaintiff under S. 14 may sue the manager for damages for the sums so misappropriated and which cannot be traced specifically in the latter's hands[2]. If the property can be traced to the manager the plaintiff may bring a suit for following the specific property in such manager's hands but for sums misappropriated and otherwise utilised there is no specific property to be followed and the plaintiff will be entitled to damages on behalf of the trust. Where a manager does not collect the outstandings due to the temple and loss is occasioned thereby he is liable for neglect of duty or for breach of trust. But a mere neglect without consequential damage or loss to the temple does not give any cause of action against the manager[3].

Awarding damages.

(9). The plaintiff may no doubt ask for the removal[4] of the manager in a suit under S. 14 but can he also ask for the appointment of a new manager in the same suit? No doubt the section does not state expressly that the court has power to appoint new managers but as pointed out by us already the mention of some of the reliefs which the court may award does not negative the power of the court to award further reliefs especially when the latter are ancillary to the primary reliefs asked for[6]. The tendency of decisions

Appointing new managers.

1. See notes under heading (5) pp. 102, 103 and 106.

2. *Chinna Jiyan Garula Varu* v. *Sri H. M. Mahant Durma Dossji*, (1870) 5 Ma. Jur. 214; *Srinivasa* v. *Venkata*, (1887) I. L. R., 11 M. 148; *Perumal Naik* v. *Saminatha Pillai*, (1896) I. L. R., 19 M. 498.

3. *Tiruvengadath Ayyangar* v. *Srinivasa Thathachariar*, (1899) I. L. R., 22 M. 3 (363.)

4. *Fakurudin Sahib* v. *Ackeni Sahib*, (1880) I. L. R., 2 M. 197; *Jan Ali* v. *Ram Nath Mundul*, (1881) I. L. R., 8 C. 32; *Natesa* v. *Ganapati*, (1890) I. L. R., 14 M. 10; *Subbayya* v. *Krishna*, (1890) I. L. R., 14 M. 186; *Rangasami Naickan* v. *Varadappa Naickan*, (1894) I. L. R. 17 M. 462 (466 and 467); *Gyananda Asram* v. *Kristo Chandra Mukherji*, (1901) 8 C. W. N. 404. This is also the express language of the section.

5. The case of *Jan Ali* v. *Ram Nath Mundul*, (1881) I. L. R., 8 C. 32 proceeding upon this ground has stated that a prayer for the appointment of new trustees is outside the scope of the section. See also the *dictum* of *Shephard*, J. in *Sivayya* v. *RamiReddi*, (1899) I.L.R., 22M. 223 (227) and that of *Subramania Iyer*, and *Benson*, JJ. in *Narayana Ayyar* v. *Kumarasami Mudaliar*, (1899) I. L. R., 23 M. 537 where their Lordships observed that the reliefs by way of appointing new trustees, vesting property in the latter and settling a scheme are claimable under S. 539, C. P. C.

6. *Sheoratan Kunwari* v. *Ram Pargash*, (1896) I. L. R., 18 A. 227. See also *Muhammad Siraj-Ul-Haq* v. *Imam-ud-din*, (1896) I. L. R., 19 A. 104 and notes p. 11

is against awarding this relief in a suit under this section[1]. When a suit is provided for, though specially, why should it be supposed that the Legislature intended that the plaintiff should only sue for removal under S. 14 and should be driven to a new suit for the appointment of new managers[2] ? No doubt the enactment in S. 539, C. P. C., enables a plaintiff to combine in one suit the reliefs for removal of trustee, for appointment of fresh trustees, for vesting property in them and for scheme[3] even assuming that the last three reliefs fall outside the scope of S. 14. But S. 539, C. P. C., was only introduced in 1877 and we must refer to the intention of the Legislature in 1863. The absurdity is that but for S. 539 there must be one suit for removal under S. 14, a second suit for the appointment of new managers and if the view that persons having a bare interest are not entitled to ask for possession or custody even in a suit under S. 14 be correct a third suit by the new managers for possession. This is due to the defective language employed by the Legislature and yet there is no attempt to remedy these defects. There may be no difficulty in cases falling under S. 3. The committee may appoint a manager. But in cases falling under S. 4 difficulty is likely to arise. Where the office devolves by hereditary succession the next heir will be the manager[4]. But where the succession is by appointment the necessity for the judge's appointment is sure to arise.

Costs :—Where by reason of some formal defect not due to any fault of the parties a suit brought under S. 14 by a person interested fails the Court has power to order his costs to be paid out of the trust estate[5]. But the mere fact of having obtained sanction will not entitle an unsuccessful plaintiff to get such costs[6].

---

1. See cases cited in note (5) p. 116. But see cases cited in note (6) p. 116. In *Fakurudin Sahib* v. *Ackeni Sahib*, (1880) I.L. R., 2M. 197 *Veerasami* v. *Chokkappa*, I. L.R., 11M. 149 (note), *Srinivasa* v. *Venkata*, (1887) I. L. R., 11 M.148, and the High Court decision referred to in *Ramalingam Pillai* v. *Vythilingam Pillai*, (1893) I. L. R., 16 M. 490 no prayer for appointing new managers was asked as a matter of fact. The old managers were removed and in the first case separate applications were made for appointing new managers apparently under S.5. (*Sultan Ackeni Sahib* v. *Shaik Bava Malimiyar*, (1879) I. L. R., 4 M. 295). See *Kishore* v. *Kalee*, (1874) 22 W. R. 364.

2. In *Delroos Banoo Begum* v. *Nawab Syud Ashgur Ally Khan*, (1875) 15 B. L. R. 167: S. C. 23 W. R. C. R.453 the suit was under S. 14 and there was a prayer not only for removal of the old trustee but also for the appointment of new trustees. See also *Chinna Jiyan Garula Varu* v. *Durma Dossji*, (1870) 5 Mad. Jur. 214.

3. *Narayana Ayyar* v. *Kumarasami Mudaliar*, (1899) I. L. R., 23 M. 537.

4. Provisions similar to S.11 of Madras Regulation XXV of 1802 and Ss.6 and 7 of Madras Regulation XXIX of 1802 should have been made. See Introduction Ch. XIV.

5. See S. 18 and *Ramakissoor Dossji* v. *Sriranga Charlu*, (1898) I.L.R., 21M.421: S.C. 8M.L.J.R., 74 where the plaintiff withdrew the suit as the manager sought to be removed died and the District Judge allowed the withdrawal and directed the plaintiff's costs to be paid out of the devastanam funds. There was an appeal against this but the High Court held that there was no appeal.

6. *Chinnasami Mudali* v. *Advocate-General*, (1874) I. L. R., 17 M. 406.

Order granting sanction under S. 18:—As will be pointed out in S. 18 an order granting sanction is not conclusive on the question of title[1]. The manager will not be precluded from raising in the suit the question that the sanction is *ultra vires* either on the ground that the Act has no application to the religious establishment in dispute or on the ground that the granting of the sanction is otherwise illegal[2].

Jurisdiction under S. 14 not taken away by clause in deed of endowment:—Where there is a clause in a deed of endowment to the effect that the manager is not subject to the liability under S. 14 such clause cannot be given effect to and cannot take away the jurisdiction conferred upon the Civil Court under this section[3]. This is upon the principle (which has been referred to in the Introduction[4]) that where there is maladministration the same is a public wrong and there can be no condonation of it by the persons interested. The manager of a religious endowment is subject to the jurisdiction of the Civil Courts though he is not liable to be removed by the Government[5].

Applicability of Pensions Act:—It has been held in a series of cases by the Madras High Court that the Pensions Act is not applicable to religious endowments or to yeomiah or other allowances granted to religious institutions[6] so that it will not be necessary to obtain the certificate referred to in that Act in any suit against the manager under S. 14 regarding the said allowances and the Government will not be entitled to remove the manager for not properly carrying out the trust[7]. But the Bombay High Court holds that the Pensions Act is applicable to religious endowments and that, therefore, a suit in the Civil Courts without the certificate required under the Pensions Act is not maintainable[8]. But according to the Pensions Act, production of a certificate is not a

1. *Venkatasa Naiker* v. *Srinivassa Chariyar*, (1869) 4M. H. C. 410 (421); *Protap Chandra Misser* v. *Brojonath Misser*, (1891) I. L. R., 19 C. 275. See also *Syed Amin Sahib* v. *Ibram Sahib*, (1868) 4 M.H.C.112 (where, however, the point was not raised).
2. *Protab Chandra Misser* v. *Brojonath Misser*, (1891) I. L. R. 19 C. 275. See p. 141 post.
3. *Syud Imdad Hossein* v. *Mahomed Ali Khan*, (1874) 23 W. R. C. R. 150.
4. Introduction Ch. VI pp. lxxx and lxxxi and Ch. VII p. lxxxiii.
5. *The Secretary of State for India* v. *Abdul Hakkim*, (1880) I. L. R., 2 M. 294.
6. *The Secretary of State for India* v. *Abdul Hakkim*, (1880) I. L. R., 2 M. 294; *Kolandai Mudali* v. *Sankara Bharadhi*, (1882) I. L. R., 5 M. 302 (303) which refers also to an unreported decision in A. S. 126 of 1881; *Subrahmanya Aiyar* v. *The Secretary of State for India*, (1883) I. L. R., 6 M. 361; *Athavulla* v. *Gouse*, (1888) I. L. R., 11 M. 283.
7. *The Secretary of State for India* v. *Abdul Hakkim*, (1880) I. L. R., 2 M. 294.
8. *Vyankaji* v. *Surja Rao Apaji Rao*, (1891) I. L. R., 16 B. 537; *Miya Vali Ulla* v. *Sayad Bava Santi Miya*, (1896) I. L. R., 22 B. 496.

condition precedent to the institution of the suit so that the certificate may be produced at any time before the hearing[1] or the Court may adjourn the suit to enable the plaintiff to produce the certificate[2].

Suit must correspond with the Sanction :—A suit under S. 14 must be filed only with the leave of the Court obtained under S. 18. The suit filed under S. 14 with such leave must be in strict conformity with the terms of the sanction granted by the Civil Court under S. 18 which requires, a person to obtain leave for the institution of the suit under the Act as against the manager. The application should, therefore, state definitely what the plaintiff wants against the manager and the judge may grant sanction for all or any of the reliefs prayed for in the application. The sanction is a condition precedent to the suit under S. 14 and the suit instituted under S. 14 must be one for the institution of which sanction has been accorded[3]?. In *Srinivasa* v. *Venkata*[3], the facts were that the plaintiffs (two worshippers of the Srirangam temple) obtained leave under S. 18 for removal of the manager and for damages for a large amount stated to have been misappropriated by him but in their suit under S.14 they merely asked for his removal without praying for damages. The Court held that such a suit was not maintainable. The reason for this was stated to be that the character of the suit which the applicant proposed to institute was one of the circumstances which the judge was entitled to take into consideration in granting an application under S. 18. The character of the suit proposed to be instituted would show in some measure the *bona fides* of the applicant and if the latter, without leave of the court granting the sanction, should file a different suit, *i.e.*, omit to ask for any particular relief (accorded by the sanction) it may be that the judge would have refused sanction for the suit with such reliefs omitted, For aught it may be, the judge may not consider under such circumstances the misconduct to be serious and may take action under S. 19. The object of the sanction is to prevent vexatious suits and enforcing the terms of the sanction strictly is the only way to prevent such vexatious suits.

---

1. In *Vyankaji* v. *Surja Rao Apaji Rao*, (1891) I. L. R., 16 B. 537 the certificate was produced in appeal and the objection on the ground of want of certificate was disallowed.
2. *Miya Vali Ulla* v. *Sayad Bava Santi Miya*, (1896) I. L. R., 22 B. 496.
3. *Srinivasa* v. *Venkata*, (1887) I. L. R., 11 M. 148.

As in most other cases where a rule is strictly enforced, the enforcing of this rule carries with it both its own advantages and disadvantages. If an immaterial relief asked for in the application under S. 18 and sanctioned by the judge is omitted, that omission is also bad and the suit will be liable to be dismissed on that ground. Or suppose the applicant finds that upon subsequent inquiry he cannot in fact maintain a particular charge or that *in law* he cannot maintain a particular relief is he still bound to bring a suit in terms of the sanction notwithstanding some of the reliefs may be unsustainable or is he to be told that his suit will be liable to be dismissed because he may only ask for such reliefs as may be substainable either in law or in fact?

Amendment of sanction.

There is, however, one remedy which the learned judges suggest in the case of *Srinivasa* v. *Venkata*[1] and that is we think a sufficient protection against the evils which otherwise will exist from the strict observance of the rule. The plaintiff under such circumstances may ask for leave to amend the original sanction and the same may be amended[1]. The plaintiff may also, on finding, in the course of the enquiry in the suit, that he cannot maintain the suit with reference to certain reliefs or that he cannot maintain the suit by reason of not having given details of the charges against the manager may withdraw the suit, get the original sanction amended and file a fresh suit in accordance with the amended sanction. This may be treated as a fresh sanction[2].

The question is the same in a suit under S. 539 and the sanction necessary under S. 539 must be strictly followed in filling the suit under S. 539[3]. It has even been held that the court is not competent to grant reliefs other than those referred to in the sanction[3].

Forma Pauperis:—A suit under S. 14 may be brought in *forma pauperis*. The restrictions for bringing a suit in *forma pauperis* are contained in Chapter XXVI of the Code of Civil Procedure and particularly in Ss. 402 and 407. The Religious

1. *Srinivasa* v. *Venkata*, (1887) I. L. R., 11 M. 148.

2. C. R. P. 363 of 1900, dated 24th September 1901. M. H. Ct. Jud. Ind. for 1901, p. 144.

3. *Sayad Hussein Miyan Dada Miyan* v. *The Collector of Kaira*, (1895) I. L. R., 21 B. 257 where the case of *Srinivasa* v. *Venkata*, (1887) I. L. R., 11 M. 148 is referred to with approval.

Endowments Act does not contain any restriction that a person suing under the Act should not sue as a pauper[1]. The same principles will apply to a suit under S. 539, C. P. C.

Suit for removal, possession and damages.

Court Fee :—A suit for the removal of a manager without any further relief is a suit incapable of valuation, and the court-fee is Rupees ten (10) only under Sch. II, Art. 17, cl. vi of the Court Fees Act (VI of 1870)[2]. But if damages are claimed in addition against the manager, then the claim for damages must be separately valued and court-fee (*ad valorem*) must be paid also on the amount of damages claimed[3]. A suit for removal of the managers and for appointment of new managers in the place of those removed is one incapable of valuation and a stamp of Rs. 10 is payable under Sch. II, Art. 17, cl. vi[4]. Upon a similar principle it has been held[5] that a suit for removal of managers, for appointment of new managers and for vesting the property in such new managers is not a suit capable of being estimated at a money value and falls under Sch. II, Art. 17, cl. vi. Where in addition to the prayer for removal of the manager there is a prayer for the recovery of the trust property (assuming such a prayer is maintainable in a suit under S. 14) court-fee must be paid on the value of the trust property sought to be recovered[6]. In *Delroos Banoo Begum* v. *Nawab Syud Ashgur Ally Khan*[7] it was held by the Calcutta High Court that a suit for the removal of the trustee in which the plaintiff asked for the appointment of himself as trustee in the place of the person to

1. *Gurusami Chetti* v. *Krishnasami Naikar*, (1901) I. L. R., 24 M. 419.
2. R. A. Nos. 89 of 1881 and 65 of 1884 [the former being reported in I. L. R., 11 M. 149 (note)] approved in *Srinivasa* v. *Venkata*, (1887) I. L. R., 11 M. 148 (150); *Muhammad Siraj-ul-Haq* v. *Imam-ud-din*, (1896) I. L. R., 19 A. 104. But see *Mohun Singh* v. *Sukka Singh*, (1853) B. S D. A. 888, a case under Bengal Regulation X of 1829, Sch. B, Art. 8.
3. *Srinivasa* v. *Venkata*, (1887) I. L. R , 11 M. 148. See also S. 7, cl. i.
4. *Thakuri* v. *Bramha Narain*, (1896) I. L. R., 19 A. 60, which was a case under S. 539, C. P. C. In this case the plaintiffs themselves prayed for being appointed.
5. *Girdhari Lal* v. *Ram Lal*, (1899) I. L. R., 21 A. 200, which was also a suit under S. 539, C. P. C.
6. See S. 7, cls. iii, iv (a), and v. See also *Mohamed Masik* v. *Badshah Mehal Saheba*, (1883) I. L. R., 10 C. 380. The High Court of Madras held in *Sonachala* v. *Manika*, (1885) I. L. R., 8 M. 516, that a suit for removal of an existing trustee, for appointing the plaintiff in his stead and placing the latter in possession of trust property is a suit falling under S. 7 of the Court-Fees Act.
7. (1875) 15 B. L. R., 167. This case was distinguished in *Thakuri* v. *Bramha Narain*, (1896) I. L. R., 19 A. 60, on the ground that in the former emoluments were attached to the office of trustee so that though plaintiffs prayed in that case for their being appointed to the office, a different result was arrived at.

be removed was not properly stamped with a fee of 10 Rs. The trustee was entitled to a certain share in the profits of the trust estate and as the plaintiff had asked that he should be appointed a trustee it was held that he must pay court-fees calculated on the amount of his share of the profits as appurtenant to the office of trustee. *Ashgur Ally's case* was explained in *Omrao Mirza* v. *Jones*[1] differently by each of the two judges who took part. Mr. Justice *Prinsep* held that the suit was for removal of trustee, that the subject-matter of the suit was the right to retain control over the trust property and not the corpus itself, that such a suit would fall under Sch. II, Art. 17, cl. vi, but that as plaintiff had fixed the valuation at Rs. 7,000 he need not be made to pay court-fee upon any higher sum. Mr. Justice *O'Kinealy* was of opinion that the suit should be valued according to the interest of the plaintiff in the subject-matter of the suit, that this was the basis of the decision in the earlier case[2], and that as the plaintiff had fixed Rs. 7,000 as the valuation that sum must be taken as the interest of the plaintiff in the subject-matter of the suit. We should think that Rs. 7,000 was given by the plaintiff as valuation for the purposes of jurisdiction and that only Rs.10 was payable for the purpose of the court-fee. In fact this was admitted by Mr. Justice *Prinsep*, but as plaintiff was willing to pay stamp duty on Rs. 7,000 he thought that that was amply sufficient and that the decision of the lower court that stamp duty on a higher sum was payable was wrong[3].

According to the Allahabad High Court[3] a suit under S. 14 is a suit for misfeasance so that such suit must only charge the manager with misfeasance and the plaintiff must not dictate to the court what it should do when misfeasance is found and if a plaintiff asks for reliefs it is merely burdening the plaint with unnecessary allegations. The same court has held[4] that in such a case, the proper court-fee is Rs. 10 according to Sch. II, Art. 17, cl. vi. We have already discussed this case when considering the scope of the suit under S. 14. We think that the proper court-fee in that case has to be paid with reference to S. 7 of the

1. (1884) I. L. R., 10 C. 599.
2. *Delroos Banoo Begum* v. *Nawab Syud Ashgur Ally Khan*, (1875) 15 B. L. R. 167.
3. See this case explained in *Muhammad Siraj-Ul-Haq* v. *Imam-ud-din*, (1896) I. L. R., 19 A. 104.
4. *Muhammad Siraj-Ul-Haq.* v. *Imam-ud-din*, (1896) I. L. R. 19 A. 104.

Court-Fees Act and that the decision upon the question of court-fee is erroneous. The case of *Sonachala* v. *Manika*[1] is a distinct authority for the view that S. 7 of the Court-Fees Act will apply. No doubt that case was not under the Religious Endowments Act (the institution in question being only charitable and not religious) nor was it under S. 539, C. P. C[a]. It was a suit filed under the ordinary law. But as pointed out in an Allahabad case[2], the suit was for removal of a trustee in possession, and it was sought to oust the trustee also from possession. But if possession cannot be asked in a suit under S. 14 the suit can only be for removal of the trustee, and such suit is incapable of valuation so that court-fee is payable under Sch. II, Art. 17, cl. (vi) of the Court-Fees Act[3]. The case of *Sonachala* v. *Manika*[1] distinguished the earlier case of *Govindan Nambiar* v. *Krishnan Nambiar*[3] upon the ground that in the latter case both the karnavan and anandravan were beneficiaries and that the possession of either was the possession of both. If the distinction were sound and if all worshippers were beneficiaries, a suit by such worshippers for removal of the trustee and for possession might be governed by the decision in the earlier case. But if the trustee has possession and worshippers have to sue not merely for removal of the old manager but also for recovery of possession (at any rate on behalf of the person to be newly appointed as manager) the suit is for ejectment and it is difficult to see on what principle such a suit is not governed by S. 7 of the Court-Fees Act. If the worshippers are to be deemed as entitled to joint possession[4] or if the trustee is to be deemed as not having any possession, that may be different. Notwithstanding that the true theory ought to be that the manager is only entitled to *custody*, the word "possession" may have been used by the Legislature as including such custody[5]. No special provision is made in the Court-Fees Act as to the court-fee payable in suits filed under Act XX. It is very desirable that the Legislature should make a special provision for the class of suits to be filed under the Act. A considerably lesser court-fee ought to be

1. (1885) I. L. R., 8 M. 516.
2. See *Thakuri* v. *Bramha Narain*, (1896) I. L. R., 19 A. 60.
3. *Govindan Nambiar* v. *Krishnan Nambiar*, (1881) I. L. R., 4 M. 146.
4. See *Athavulla* v. *Gouse*, (1888) I. L. R., 11 M., 283, where the court held that persons in joint possession may bring a suit for declaration. But see *Panga* v. *Unnikutti*, (1900) I. L. R., 24 M. 275; *Raman .diodi* v. *Unni*, (1901) 11 M. L. J. R. 338.
5. Pollock and Wright on possession, pp. 55, 122; Wilberforce, 122 to 124; Maxwell, 77; Lightwood, 180 to 182, 185, 219. Cf. cases under S. 9, Specific Relief Act.

insisted upon and if this were so there will be an effective check upon the managers.

Suit for account.

If the suit be for an account, court-fee is payable according to the amount at which the relief sought is valued by the plaintiff[1]. This will not prevent the court from decreeing a larger sum, but the decree can be executed only on the plaintiff paying the excess stamp[2].

Suit for scheme

If the plaintiff adds a prayer for a scheme with the prayer for removal, no additional stamp need be paid. But if the suit be only for a scheme (assuming such a suit will lie under S. 14) such suit is also incapable of valuation and Rs. 10-0-0 under Schedule II, Article 17, clause vi, is the proper court-fee to be paid.

Suit for declaration and injunction.

Where the suit is for a declaration that the property belongs to a particular religious establishment and we have seen that such a suit will lie under S. 14 when it is alleged that the trustee is wrongfully alienating the same or asserting a hostile title to it then a court-fee of Rs. 10-0-0 is leviable[3] under Sch. II, Art. 17, cl. iii. When a mandatory injunction is sought[4] court-fee shall be payable on the amount at which the relief is valued by the plaintiff in his plaint[5] although the injunction is sought with reference to the property of the religious establishment[6].

1. S. 7, cl. iii (f). But in *Girdhari Lal* v. *Ram Lal*, (1899) I. L. R., 21 A. 200, it was held that the mere fact that the plaintiffs while praying in a suit under S. 539, C. P. C., for removal of the old trustees, for appointment of new trustees and for vesting the properties in the latter asked also for an account would not take the case out of the purview of Sch. II, Art. 17, cl. vi. But this must not be supposed as authority for the position that no court-fee is payable with reference to a prayer for an account in such a suit. On the other hand the reference to S. 50, C. P. C., and to Ss. 7, cl. iv (f) and 11 of the Court Fees Act, shows that the plaintiff must value such relief and must pay the stamp on such valuation in addition to the stamp duty payable on the reliefs for removal of the old trustees, &c.

2. See *Arogya Udayan* v *Appuchi Rowthan*, (1901) I. L. R., 25 M. 543.

3. In *Girijanund Datta Jha* v. *Sailajanund Datta Jha*, (1896) I. L. R., 23 C. 645, the suit was for a declaration that some maintenance was a charge on the "Charo" (offerings to idol) and it was held that the proper stamp was Rs. ten under Sch. II, Art. 17, cl. iii of the Court Fees Act. The suit, however, was not under the Act.

4. Such an injunction can be given under S. 14. See *Dhurrum Singh* v. *Kissen Singh*, (1881) I. L. R., 7 C. 767.

5. See S. 7, sub-sec iv (c). See *Raghunath Ganesh* v. *Gangadhar Bhikaji*, (1885) I L. R., 10 B. 60. See also *Thakuri* v. *Bramha Narain* (1896) I. L. R., 19 A. 60 which was, however, a suit under S. 539, C. P. C.

6. Such a suit is not one relating to moveable or immoveable property within the meaning of S. 7, cls. i, iii, iv (a), v and vi. See *Thandavaraya Pillai* v. *Subbayyar*, (1899) I. L. R., 23 M. 483 which was a suit not under the Act being one by a dharmakarta for wrongful dismissal and injunction. See also *Thakuri* v. *Bramha Narain*, (1896) I. L. R., 19 A. 60.

Declaration and consequential relief.—Under the ordinary law a suit for a bare declaration is not maintainable when the plaintiff is entitled to further relief as by way of possession[1]. A declaratory decree should not be made when the object of the plaintiff is to evade the stamp laws or to eject the defendant under the color of a mere declaration of title[2]. If no suit for declaration will lie under S. 14, then no difficulty arises. But if such a suit is maintainable (and we have tried to show that it is so) the question arises whether the plaintiff must not ask in his suit for removal of the defendant from office a prayer for removing the defendant from possession of trust properties. If such prayer for possession is not maintainable under S. 14, then the suit cannot be bad for merely asking for a declaration. But if such prayer is maintainable (and we think that where the manager is in possession or custody and it is sought to remove the manager, a prayer for possession or custody is also maintainable, then the plaintiff is bound to ask that the defendant do give up possession or custody, at any rate, to the person to be newly appointed as manager. A pujari entitled to enter the temple for doing service cannot sue for possession butmay sue for injunction[3].

Nature of suit by worshipper :—We think the suit by the worshippers under S. 14 is a representative suit binding on the trust and is not a personal suit binding only on the parties to that suit[4]. The fact that sanction of court is necessary under S. 14 also favors this view. This is also the nature of the suit under S. 539, C. P. C[5]. In fact it is the sanction that gives a title to the plaintiff in a suit either under S.14 of this Act or under S. 539, C. P. C., to represent the public.

Execution :—Where the decree directs the specific performance of any act by the manager, *i.e.*, where the decree directs particular acts to be performed by the manager in the management of the temple, such decree may be enforced by the imprisonment of the manager or by attachment of his property or both under S. 260, C.P.C[6]. So that where a decree directs the filing of accounts an application for execution is maintainable[6] The application for execution must

1. See S. 42 of the Specific Relief Act.
2. *Chockalingapeshana Naicker* v. *Achiyar*, (1875) I. L. R., 1 M. 40.
3. *Vengan Poosari* v. *Patchamuthu*, (1908) 14 M. L. J. R. 290.
4. Per *Best*, J., in *Sathappayyar* v. *Periasami*, (1890) I. L. R., 14 M. 1 (14).
5. *Lakshmandas* v. *Jugalkishore*, (1896) I. L. R., 22 B. 216.
6. *Damodharbhat* v. *Bhogilal Karsondas*, (1899) I. L. R., 24 B. 45.

specify the mode in which the assistance of the court is sought; otherwise it will be bad under Ss. 235, cl. (*g*) and 260, C. P. C.[1] A decree for settling a scheme of management and for appointment of managers[2] may also be executed and the application must specify the mode in which the assistance of the court is sought under S. 235, cl. (*j*) and 260, C. P. C[1]. Liberty to apply for further directions may be reserved by the decree[3] and when further directions are wanted application must be made to the court[4]. If the decree should direct that the manager should continue only so long as he should manage properly and was removable on proof of misconduct, such a decree would only be a declaratory decree. But the Bombay High Court has ruled otherwise[5]. A decree may direct that in default of the trustee doing certain acts the trustee shall be deemed to have been removed or upon the trustee doing the acts the suit shall stand dismissed. Here the question whether the trustee has committed default is one arising in execution under S. 244, C. P. C.

A decree for injunction must be executed. If any party bound by the decree commits a breach he is guilty of contempt and the decree can also be enforced against him in execution[6].

If under S. 14 a decree for possession of endowed property can be passed against the manager, then the liability to deliver possession carries with it the liability to hand over the account-books and other documents relating to the management of the endowed property[7]. So that the decree-holder may ask for the said documents in execution[7]. But it is doubtful whether the liability to deliver possession carries also with it the liability to hand over the title-deeds relating to the estate without an express direction in the decree to that effect[8]. It is said that the rule is that when the principal thing is awarded the subsidiary or accessory is also implicitly

1. *Sha Karamchand* v. *Ghelabhai*, (1893) I. L. R., 19 B. 34.

2. As to whether such a decree can be passed under S. 14, see notes, pp 109 to 111.

3. *Damodar Bhatji* v. *Bhat Bhogilal Kasandas*, (1896) I. L R, 22 B. 493.

4. *Damodharbhat* v. *Bhogilal Karsondas*, (1899) I. L. R., 24 B. 45.

5. *Madhavrao* v. *Ramrao*, (1896) I. L. R., 22 B. 267 following *Ranganasary* v. *Shappani Asary*, (1870) 5 M. H. C. 375. In the Bombay case it was held that the question of misconduct or mismanagement would fall under S. 244, C. P. C.

6. See *Ram Saran* v. *Chatur Singh*, (1901) I. L. R., 23 A 465; *Sadagopachari* v. *Krishnamachari*, (1889) I. L. R., 12 M. 356; *Sakarlal* v. *Bai Parvatibai*, (1901) I. L R 26 B. 283. But see *Dahyabhai* v. *Bapalal*, (1901 I. L. R., 26 B. 140.

7. *Shri Bhavani Devi of Fort Pratabgad* v. *Devrao Madhavrao*, (1887) I. L. R 11 B. 485.

8. The case of *Shri Bhavani Devi of Fort Pratabgad* v. *Devrao Madhavrao*, (1887) I. L. R., 11 B. 485, will seem, however, to suggest the other way.

ordered. But the analogy suggested by the Bombay High Court does not seem to hold good. It may be admitted as a familiar principle in the construction of statutes that a principal command implies and includes the incidental minor commands *necessary for giving it effect*. But in the case on hand the decree for possession may be given effect to and executed notwithstanding the title-deeds or other accounts of management are not handed over. If the plaint asks specially for the title-deeds, &c. and the decree awards the same that is a different thing.

Nature of interest entitling person to sue.

XV. The interest required in order to entitle a person to sue under the last preceding section need not be a pecuniary, or a direct or immediate, interest, or such an interest as would entitle the person suing to take any part in the management or superintendence of the trusts[1].

Any person having a right of attendance, or having been in the habit of attending, at the performance of the worship or service of any mosque, temple, or religious establishment, or of partaking in the benefit of any distribution of alms, shall be deemed to be a person interested[2] within the meaning of the last preceding section.

NOTES.

[1]. "**The interest required ...... in the superintendence of the trusts**":—It is negatively stated that certain kinds of interest are not necessary. The interest which will entitle a person to sue under S. 14 need not be (*a*) pecuniary, (*b*) direct, (*c*) immediate, or (*d*) such as to entitle the person suing to take part in the management or superintendence of the trusts.

"*Pecuniary interest*" is such interest as entitles a person to receive some share of the offerings or some money etc., out of the income of the trust estate by reason of his holding some office in the temple or otherwise.

"*Direct interest*" is an interest apparently different from the interest which a person has as a mere worshipper &c., about which, however, see heading [2] below. It was held in *Jan Ali* v. *Ram Nath Mundul*[1] that a bare worshipper or a person having merely a

1. (1881) I. L. R., 8 C. 32. See also *Lutifunnissa Bibi* v. *Nazirun Bibi*, (1884) I. L. R., 11 C. 33; *Narasimha* v. *Ayyan Chetti*, (1888) I. L. R., 12 M. 157 (160) which held that a general manager had not a *direct interest*.

right of attendance or having been in the habit of attending the performance of any worship was not aperson having a "*direct interest*" as used in S. 539, C. P. C., of the code of 1877 or, S. 539, C. P. C., of the code of 1882 before the amendment by Act VII of 1888 and was therefore not entitled to maintain a suit under that section even with the sanction of the Advocate-General. Whether that decision be right or wrong this decision can no longer hold good after the amendment introduced by Act VII of 1888 and this has been pointed out in the later cases[1]. So that the decisions under S. 539 of the code of 1882 as amended by Act VII of 1888 (the language being "having an interest in the trust") will also guide us in arriving at a correct construction of S. 15 of the Pagoda Act.

"*Immediate interest*" is an interest which is not contingent. An interest which a person may acquire hereafter upon a certain contingency is not an immediate interest so that the mere possibility of interest or the mere possibility of succession will not be an immediate interest[2]. So that a person who belongs tothe family of the founder but who is not the founder's heir has not an immediate interest[3] nor has the wife of a hereditary manager an immediate interest[4]. But as the section states that the interest need not be immediate the persons last mentioned have a right of suit under S. 14 after obtaining leave on the ground of their being worshippers[5]. The founder's heir has a direct interest within the meaning of the section[6]. Is a person who as an archæologist interests himself in an institution by reason of its antiquity, ancient history, architecture or inscriptions, entitled to sue under S. 14? It may be that such a person has no "direct or immediate

1. *Mohiuddin* v. *Sayiduddin*, (1893) I. L. R., 20 C. 810 at p. 816 following *Zafaryab Ali* v. *Bakhtawar Singh*, (1883) I. L. R., 5 A. 497 and *Jawahra* v. *Akbar Husain*, (1884) I. L. R., 7 A. 178. See also *Subbayya* v. *Krishna*, (1890) I. L. R., 14 M. 186 (188,189). But see *Wajid Ali* v. *Dianat-ul-lah Beg*, (1885) I. L. R., 8 A. 31.

2. *Mohiuddin* v. *Sayiduddin*, (1893) I. L. R., 20 C. 810. This is a decision under S. 539, C. P. C., which now requires that a person should have *an interest*.

3. App. 101 of 1901, dated 25th September 1902. M. H. Ct. Jud. Ind. for 1902, p. 260.

4. *Suppammal* v. *The Collector of Tanjore*, (1889) I. L. R., 12 M. 387 (391). In *Bibee Kuneez* v. *Bibee Saheba*, (1867) 8 W. R. C. R. 313 (314) a sister was held to have no interest but this was merely an *obiter*.

5. See heading [2] and *Radhabai* v. *Chimnaji*, (1878) I. L. R., 3 B. 27. *Lutifunnissa Bibi* v. *Nazirun Bibi*, (1884) I. L. R., 11 C. 33 is not against this view.

6. *Lakshmandas Parashram* v. *Ganpatrav Krishna*, (1884) I. L. R., 8 B. 365; *Thackersey Dewraj* v. *Hurbhum Nursey*, (1884) I. L. R., 8 B. 432; *Chintaman Bajaji Dev* v. *Dhondo Ganesh Dev*, (1888) I. L. R., 15 B. 612; *Sheoratan Kunwari* v. *Ram Pargash* (1896) I. L. R., 18A. 227. But see *Narasimha* v. *Ayyan*, (1888) I. L. R., 12 M. 157.

interest". But such an interest is not wanted under S. 15. But if such person is a Christian or a person who is the follower of a religion other than the one for the purpose of which the mosque, temple &c., may have been founded it can be hardly contended that the Legislature intended to give such persons a right which they did not possess before the Act. If the Legislature had any such intention, more explicit language would have been used. The words of a statute are to be restricted to the nature of the subject and the object the Legislature has in view[1]. If the person be of the religion for the purpose of which the mosque &c., was founded then he has an interest within the meaning of S. 15 even without reference to the interest which he may possess as an archæologist &c.

"*Such an interest as would entitle the person suing to take any part in the management or superintendence of the trusts:*"— A manager has the interest that is referred to here. He may, therefore, get the permission of the court under S. 18 and sue under S. 14. But then S. 14 is only enabling so that a manager is not obliged to sue under S. 14[2]. His right to sue under the general law is not taken away by S. 14. But if he elects to sue under S. 14 he has to observe the formalities prescribed by the Act. But if after obtaining leave, he sues in the ordinary Courts and not in the *District Court,* the reference in the plaint to the sanction under S. 18 may be treated as a surplusage. But if he wants the special forum created by S. 14 he must obtain leave of the Civil Court under S. 18 and can only bring the suits and as against the persons referred to in S. 14.

Where a person has the interest mentioned in S. 15, such interest is not taken away by the fact that he belongs to a sect different from the one to which the author or founder of the trust belongs[3]. So where the endowment is made by a Sunni, a Shiah may, as a person interested, sue under S. 14[3]. So also where a person who is a Mahomedan occupies a very conspicuous position amongst the Mahomedans as the muttawalli of a large Mahomedan establishment he is competent to bring a suit under S. 14 with reference to a public appropriation made by a fellow Mahomedan[3].

1. Maxwell on the Interpretation of Statutes, 74.
2. *Athavulla* v. *Gouse*, (1886) I. L. R., 11 M. 283 (286).
3. *Doyal Chand Mullick* v. *Keramut Ali*, (1869) 12 W. R. C. R. 382.

It is said in *Kishore Bon Mohunt* v. *Kalee Churn Giree*[1] that a person who alleges himself to be a Mohunt by nomination by the will of the former Mohunt and by election by respectable people of the District is not a person having any interest such as is mentioned in S. 15. But we do not think that this is sound. A person who alleges himself to be a Mohunt is a person who has such an interest as entitles him to take part and that a prominent one in the management of the trusts. A Mohunt of a Mutt is entitled to manage the Mutt. What better interest can be found than that of a manager? But the decision itself is right in the particular case on the facts arising before it. The suit was by a person alleging himself to be the lawful Mohunt against a trespasser. Such a suit is clearly not maintainable under the Act.

[2]. "**Any person...... shall be deemed to be a person interested**":—A worshipper is expressly referred to in the section as having an interest which will entitle him to sue under the Act[2]. Before S. 539 of the Civil Procedure Code of 1882 was amended by Act VII of 1888 there was a conflict in the Indian Courts[3] as to whether there was any difference in the enactment in S. 539, C. P. C., and the enactments in Ss. 14 and 15 of this Act but the amendment introduced by Act VII of 1888 has set this at rest[4]. A wife of a worshipper is also a worshipper[5]. But there must be some interest[6].

Reference to arbitrators.

XVI. In any suit or proceeding instituted under this Act[1], it shall be lawful for the Court before which such suit or proceeding is pending, to order any matter in difference[2] in such suit[3] to be referred for decision to one or more arbitrators.

---

1. (1874) 22 W. R. C. R. 364.

2. *Jeyangarulararu* v. *Durma Dossji*, (1868) 4 M. H. C. 2.

3. The Calcutta Court held that a worshipper had not a direct interest within the meaning of S. 539, C. P. C. *Jan Ali* v. *Ram Nath Mundul*, (1881) I. L. R., 8 C. 32 (35). See also *Lutifunnissa Bibi* v. *Nazirun Bibi*, (1884) I. L. R., 11 C. 33. The Madras High Court followed the Calcutta view. *Narasimha* v. *Ayyan*, (1888) I. L. R., 12 M. 157 (160). But a different view was taken by the Bombay and Allahabad High Courts. *Radhabai* v. *Chimnaji*, (1878) I. L. R., 3 B. 27; *Phate Sahib Bibi* v. *Damodar Premji*, (1879) I. L. R., 3 B. 84; *Manohar Ganesh Tambekar* v. *Lakhmiram*, (1887) I. L. R., 12 B. 247; *Chintaman Bajaji Dev* v. *Dhondo Ganesh Dev*, (1888) I. L. R., 15 B. 612. For Allahabad see *Jawahra* v. *Akbar Husain*, (1884) I. L. R., 7 A. 178. But see *Wajid Ali* v. *Dianat-ul-lah Beg*, (1885) I. L. R., 8 A. 31.

4. *Subbayya* v. *Krishna*, (1890) I. L. R., 14 M. 186; *Mohiuddin* v. *Sayiduddin*, (1893) I. L. R., 20 C. 810; *Sajedur Raja* v. *Gour Mohun Das*, (1897) I. L. R., 24 C. 418. See also Introduction, Ch. XV.

5. *Radhabai* v. *Chinnaji*, supra; *Lutifunnissa Bibi* v. *Nazirun Bibi*, supra.

6. *Bibee Kuneez Fatima* v. *Bibi Saheba Jan*, (1867) 8 W. R. C. R. 313 (314).

Whenever any such order shall be made, the provisions of Chapter VI of the Code of Civil Procedure shall in all respects apply to such order and arbitration[4], in the same manner as if such order had been made on the application of the parties under Section 312 of the said Code.

Civil Procedure Code applies.

NOTES.

Special Provision :—This is a special provision by which the Civil Court is empowered to refer compulsorily and without the consent of the parties any matter in difference in any suit or proceeding under the Act to one or more arbitrators for decision. The existence of this provision is one of the considerations which have induced courts to hold that suits against alienees or strangers are not maintainable under S. 14[1].

[1.] "**In any suit or proceeding under this Act**" :—This refers to a suit under S. 14 or proceeding under S. 18. So that, there can be a compulsory reference even when leave is asked for instituting a suit under S. 14.

[2.] "**Any matter in difference**":—The question has been discussed whether the judge has power to refer the whole suit for decision by the arbitrator. The Madras High Court has held in *Vijayaraghava Perumalayya* v. *Sitaramayya*[2] that under S. 16 it is not open to the Civil Court to refer the whole suit for decision though the court may refer any matter in difference in the suit. Apparently the court in this case was induced to adopt this construction by reason of the language of S. 16 which only refers to "any matter in difference" and not "all or any of the matters in difference." But the words in S. 506, C. P. C., corresponding to S. 312 of the old Code of Civil Procedure (Act VIII of 1859) are also similar. That section also refers to "any matter in difference" and it has never been doubted that under S. 506, C. P. C., and under S. 312 of the old Code the whole suit cannot be referred. We should, therefore, think that the decision in *Vijayaraghava*

Can the whole suit be referred?

1. *Sabapathi* v. *Subraya*, (1878) I. L. R., 2 M. 58; *Sirayya* v. *Rami Reddi*, (1899) I. L. R., 22 M. 223.
2. (1902) I. L. R, 26 M. 361.

Perumalayya v. *Sitaramayya*[1] is erroneous and does not lay down a correct rule of construction. The singular number will include the plural so that the section must be read as authorising any matter or matters in difference to be submitted to the decision of the arbitrator. The decision of Mr. Justice *Subramania Iyer* in *Perumal Naik* v. *Saminatha Pillai*[2] favors the view that the whole suit may be referred under S. 16.

Legality of referring question of manager's removal from office.

The jurisdiction to remove trustees exercised by the Civil Court has no reference to their crimes or the punishment of crimes. Although removal from office is often decreed when misconduct is proved it is not decreed as a punishment. A manager may be removed even when no misconduct is established provided the court is satisfied that the further continuance of the manager in office will prevent the due execution of trusts[3]. So that the jurisdiction to remove a manager is purely a civil jurisdiction which is exercised by the court as ancillary to its principal duty to see that the trusts are properly executed[4]. The question of removing the manager may be referred under S. 16 to an arbitrator for decision, and no objection can be raised upon the ground that such a question involves one of punishment[5].

[3]. "**In such suit**" :—By a clerical mistake the words "or proceeding" are omitted.

[4]. "**The provisions of Chapter VI of the Code Civil Procedure shall in all respects apply to such order and arbitration**" :—Chapter VI refers to the old Code (Act VIII of 1859). The corresponding Chapter of the present Code (Act XIV of 1882) is Chapter XXXVII. S. 312 of the old Code referred to in heading [2] and in S. 17 is S. 506 of the present Code. So that, the provisions contained in Ss. 507 to 522 shall, so far as they go, apply[6] to compulsory references under S. 16. The award may be modified

1. (1902) I. L. R., 26 M. 361.
2. (1896) I. L. R., 19 M. 498 followed by a Division Bench of the Madras High Court in *Nambi Aiyangar* v. *Yajnanarayana*, (1901) 12 M L. J. R., 431.
3. *Letterstedt* v. *Broers*, (1884) L. R., 9 A. C. 371 (386).
4. *Perumal Naik* v. *Saminatha Pillai*, (1896) I. L. R., 19 M. 498.
5. *Perumal Naik* v. *Saminatha Pillai*, (1896) I. L. R., 19 M. 498 followed in *Nambi Aiyangar* v. *Yajnanarayana*, (1901) 12 M. L. J. R., 431. But no reference can be made under S. 16 when the question is as to the removal of the shebait of an idol which is private as the Act has no application to private religious endowments. *Protap Chandra Misser* v. *Brojonath Misser*, (1891) I. L. R., 19 C. 275.
6. See S. 3 of Act XIV of 1882.

or corrected on any of the grounds referred to in S. 518, C. P. C., or remitted for reconsideration under S. 520 or set aside under S. 521, C. P. C.

Where the arbitrators framed a scheme on a reference under S. 14 the award may be modified by omitting the scheme or remitted to the arbitrators as it has been held that the District Court itself has no jurisdiction[1] to frame a scheme in a suit under S. 14. The fact that the arbitrators awarded interest prior to suit and not claimed in the plaint would not vitiate the award provided the amount awarded including principal and interest did not exceed the amount claimed in the plaint[2]. The averment in a plaint as to the amount of damages is not a material one except as fixing a limit beyond which recovery cannot be had[3]. Moreover if the suit be for an account the court or the arbitrator has jurisdiction to award interest prior to date of suit on sums found due though such interest be not claimed provided of course the plaintiff be made to pay before-hand the proper court fee on the sums so awarded in excess.

Appeal or Revision :—It is said that Chapter VI of the old Code of Civil Procedure shall apply in all respects to the order and arbitration made under S. 16. S. 588, C. P. C., clauses 25 and 26, provide for an appeal in cases where the award is modified or set aside but that section is in a separate Chapter. No special procedure is laid down in the Act and we have to look to the Civil Procedure Code in respect of appeals &c. Under the Code of 1859 there was no appeal from a judgment "given according to the award" (S. 325) and there was no appeal generally from orders prior to decree (S. 363). The latter section is in Chapter VIII which is not made applicable according to this section. But this will not affect the result as an appeal must be expressly conferred by statute. There is no section in Ch. VI of the old Code conferring any right of appeal. The question whether an appeal will lie has been left open in *Perumal Naik* v. *Saminatha Pillai*[4]. Where the award is set aside on any of the

1. *Karedla Vijiaraghava Perumalayya* v. *Vemavarapu Sitaramayya*, (1902) I. L. R., 26 M. 361 where, however, there was a reference of the whole suit and the award was set aside as a whole.

2. *Perumal Naik* v. *Saminatha Pillai*, (1896) I. L. R., 19 M. 498.

3. Sedgwick on Damages (8th Edition), Vol. III, p. 1260, approved in *Perumal Naik* v. *Saminatha Pillai*, supra.

4. (1896) I. L. R., 19 M. 498. A revision petition under S. 622, C. P. C., was filed in that case.

grounds mentioned in S. 324 (corresponding to the present S. 521) C. P. C., and the suit is tried and decreed by the Judge there is no "judgment given according to the award" within the meaning of S. 325 of the old Code and hence there will be an appeal from that decree and the validity of the order setting aside the award may be questioned in such appeal[1]. Where the award is illegal as where the arbitrators award reliefs outside the scope of S. 14 or where the reference is illegal[2] then there is an appeal as the validity of the award itself is in dispute and S. 325 (corresponding to present S. 522) does not prohibit an appeal in such cases[3]. But there can be no appea lfrom an order setting aside the award as S. 588 is in a separate chapter and is not referred to in this section.

Reference under S. 312 of Civil Procedure Code.

XVII. Nothing in the last preceding Section shall prevent the parties from applying to the Court, or the Court from making the order of reference, under the said S. 312 of the said Code of Civil Procedure.

NOTES.

Scope of Section :—This section enacts that the fact that the Civil Court can compulsorily refer a suit does not take away the right of both parties by mutual consent to enter into a reference.

Where in a suit under S. 14 of the Act parties by mutual consent agreed to refer the matters in difference between them to more than one person for arbitration under S. 506 (corresponding to S. 312 of the old Code) but did not provide as a term of the contract of reference that in case of difference between the arbitrators, the decision should be in accordance with that of the majority or that the decision should be in accordance with that of an umpire, it was held in an early case[4] that it would be open to the District Judge to say that the decision should be in accordance with that of the majority or otherwise. The reasoning was that the District Judge might have inserted such provision even without the consent of the parties at the time of the order and that his subsequent ratification would amount to a previous command.

1. *George* v. *Vastian*, (1898) I. L. R., 22 M. 202 and the cases therein cited.

2. *Vijiaraghava Perumalayya* v. *Sitaramagya*, (1902) I. L. R., 26 M. 461. See also *Nambi Aiyangar* v. *Yajnanarayana*, (1901) 12 M. L. J. R., 431.

3. *Indur Subbarami Reddy* v. *Kandadai Rajamannar Ayyangar*, (1902) I. L. R., 23 M. 47. See other cases under S. 522, C. P. C.

4. *Immedy Kanuga Ramaya Gaundan* v. *Ramaswami Ambalam*, (1872) 7 M.H. C. 173.

XVIII. No suit shall be entertained under this Act [1] without a preliminary application being first made to the Court [2] for leave to institute such suit. [*The application may be made upon unstamped paper*[a]].

Preliminary application for leave to institute suit.

The Court, on the perusal of the application [3], shall determine whether there are sufficient *prima facie* grounds for the institution of a suit, and if in the judgment of the Court there are such grounds, leave shall be given for its institution.

[*In calculating the costs at the termination of the suit, the stamped duty on the preliminary application shall be estimated, and shall be added to the costs of the suit*[a]]. If the Court shall be of opinion that the suit has been for the benefit of the trust, and that no party to the suit is in fault [4], the Court may order the costs, or such portion as it may consider just, to be paid out of the estate.

Costs.

NOTES.

Object of the Section :—The object of insisting upon sanction is to prevent vexatious suits against the manager &c[1]. The Court will have to consider whether the application is *bona fide* and not vexatious and the character of the suit proposed to be instituted may be an element in the determination of this question[1]. The provision is also intended to protect managers &c., from a multiplicity of suits[2] and to dispense with the necessity of joining all the persons interested[3].

[1]. "**No suit shall be entertained under this Act**" :—Sanction under this section is a condition precedent to the institution of a suit under the Act[4] but such sanction is not necessary for suits not coming under the Act or not brought under

a. The words in closed brackets have been repealed by the Court Fees Act VII of 1870).

1. *Srinivasa* v. *Venkata*, (1887) I. L. R., 11 M. 148.
2. Per *Best*, J., in *Sathappayyar* v. *Periasami*, (1890) I. L. R., 14 M. 1 (14).
3. *Rangasamy Naickan* v. *Varadappa Naickan*, (1894) I. L. R., 17 M. 462 (466). See also note (2).
4. C. R. P. 101 of 1882, (1883) I. L. R., 10 M. 98 note : *Venkateswara, in re* (1886) I. L. R., 10 M. 98.

it[1]. According to the Madras High Court the Pensions Act is not applicable to religious endowments and hence no certificate under that Act is necessary in addition to the sanction required under this section but it will be otherwise if the Bombay decisions lay down the correct law[2]. In what cases of religious establishments sanction may be given reference may be made to the notes to S. 14. Sanction may be asked even against a manager appointed by Committee and the District Judge will not be right if he refers the party in the first instance to the committee[3].

[2]. "**A preliminary application being first made to the court**" :—The application under S.18 must be verified and presented either in person or by pleader as in the case of plaints[4]. S. 647, C.P.C., provides for certain formalities of procedure being observed even in miscellaneous applications like the one under consideration[4]. Hence where leave was granted on an unverified letter enclosing a mahazarnamah purporting to be from certain persons of the Mussulman community of Kurnool and sent by post to the District Judge, it was held that such letter should not be treated as an application under S. 18, and the order granting leave must be set aside[4]. Where an application is made for leave to file a suit against several joint managers for breach of trust the application must contain specifically the charges against each and an order granting leave based upon an application defective in this respect is liable to be set aside[5].

[3]. "**On the perusal of the application**" :—Stress must be laid upon these words[6]. Two consequences follow:—(1) no evidence is necessary and (2) no notice to the manager &c., is necessary. On a mere perusal of the application filed under S. 18 the judge may grant sanction. He need not take any evidence at all[7]. It may no

1. *Ayri Sharma Embrandri* v. *Vistnu Embrandri*, (1866) 3 M. H. C. 198; *Chinna Rangaiyangar* v. *Subbraya Mudali*, (1867) 3 M. H. C. 334; *Jeyangarulavaru* v. *Durma Dossji*, (1868) 4 M. H. C. 2; *Syed Amin Sahib* v. *Ibram Sahib*, (1868) 4 M. H. C. 112; *Haidait-Oon-Nissa* v. *Syud Afzul Hossein*, (1870) 2 N. W. P. 420; *Hajee Kalub Hossein* v. *Mussumat Mehrum Beebee*, (1872) 4 N. W. P. 155; *Kishore Bon Mohunt* v. *Kalee Churn Giree*, (1874) 22 W. R. C. R. 364; *Sabapathi* v. *Subraya*, (1878) I.L.R., 2 M. 58; *Mahalinga Rau* v. *Vencoba Ghosami*, (1881) I. L. R., 4 M. 157; *Puddolabh Roy* v. *Ramgopal Chatterjee*, (1882) I. L. R., 9 C. 133; *Virasami Nayudu* v. *Subba Rau*, (1882) I. L. R., 6 M. 54; Per *Best*, J., in *Sathappayyar* v. *Periasami*, (1890) I. L. R., 14 M. 1 (14).

2. See notes to S. 14, pp. 117 and 118.

3. *Shanmugam Pillai* v. *Sankaramurti Mudaliar*, (1899) 10 M. L. J. R., 109; Appeal 205 of 1899 dated 1st November 1900 M. H. Ct. Jud. Ind. 1900, p. 77.

4. *Amdoo Miyan* v. *Muhammad Davud Khan*, (1901) I. L. R., 24 M. 685.

5. C.R.P. 487 of 1900, dated 9th November 1903, M. H. Ct. Jud. Ind. 1903; p. 70.

6. C. R. P. 101 of 1882 (1883), I. L. R., 10 M. 98 (note); *Venkatappayya* v. *Venkatapathi*, (1896) 7 M. L. J. R., 84; S. C. I. L. R. 24 M. 687 (note); C. R. P. 487 of 1900, supra. See also *Waris Ali* v. *Amiruddin*, (1896) A. W. N. 200.

7. *Kishore Bon Mohunt* v. *Kalee Churn Giree*, (1874) 22 W. R. C. R. 364 (365); *Venkatappayya* v. *Venkatapathi*, (1896) 7 M. L. J. R., 84; S. C. I. L. R., 24 M. 687 (note); C. R. P. 487 of 1900, supra.

doubt be a judicial proceeding, but the words of the section expressly authorize the judge to grant the sanction upon a mere *perusal* of the application without hearing any evidence[1] and without hearing the parties[2]. Upon the same principle no notice need be given by the judge to any of the parties and a sanction granted without giving notice to the other party or without hearing the other party is not bad[3]. But the court must be satisfied that there are sufficient *prima facie* grounds although such grounds may appear from the application itself[4]. If no sufficient *prima facie* grounds exist, then leave ought not to be granted. The appointment by the committee of a Sivtie as manager of a Vishnu temple is not illegal and is no ground for granting sanction for filing a suit to remove members of the committee from office[5]. Much less, can it be a ground for *removing* the manager. The character of the suit proposed to be instituted is one of the elements which the judge may take into consideration before granting the sanction[6]. The judge must also be satisfied about the interest of the plaintiff to maintain the suit and may require him to prove the interest before granting the sanction[7].

Effect of Sanction:—The effect is to dispense with the necessity of joining the others interested and to enable the person who has obtained leave to bring the suit under S. 14[8]. The sanction must no doubt be that of the District Court[9], but this does not mean that there can be no power of supervision over the order of the District Judge[10]. The judge may amend the sanction[11].

---

1. *Kishore Bon Mohunt* v. *Kalee Churn Giree*, (1874) 22 W. R. C. R. 364. See C. R. P. 101 of 1882 (1883) I. L. R., 10 M. 98 (note).
2. *Venkatappayya* v. *Venkatapathi*, (1896) 7 M. L. J. R. 84; S. C. I. L. R., 24 M. 687 (note).
3. *Venkatappayya* v. *Venkatapathi*, supra; *Amdoo Miyan* v. *Mahomed Daood Khan*, (1901) I. L. R., 24 M. 685.
4. *Kishore Bon Mohunt* v. *Kalee Churn Giree*, (1874) 22 W. R. C. R. 364; C. R. P. 101 of 1882, (1883) I. L. R., 10 M. 98 (note); *Srinivasa* v. *Venkata*, (1887) I. L. R., 11 M. 148 (150). *Waris Ali* v. *Amiruddin*, (1890) A. W. N. 200.
5. *Gandavathara Ayyangar* v. *Devanaya Mudali*, (1883) I. L. R., 7 M. 222. The appointment in that manner to a committee is not illegal. *Alwar Ayyangar* v. *Krishnamachariar*, (1899) 9 M. L. J. R., 173. But see *Soobbramaniya Sastri* v. *Meenakshi Naidu*, (1882) 6 Ind. Jur. 128 affd. on review, ibid 264 and reversed on another point by P. C. in L. R., 14 I. A. 86; and *Gandavathara* v. *Devanayaga*, supra.
6. *Srinivasa* v. *Venkata*, (1887) I. L. R., 11 M. 148.
7. *Bibee Kuneez Fatima* v. *Bibee Saheba Jan*, (1867) 8 W. R. C. R. 313. See *Gopal Dei* v. *Kanno Dei*, (1903)) I. L. R., 26 A. 162 (165) and other cases under S. 539, C. P. C.
8. Per *Best*, J. in *Sathappayyar* v. *Periasami*, (1890) I. L. R., 14 M. 1 (14); Per *Best* and *Weir*, JJ. in *Subbayya* v. *Krishna*, (1890) I. L. R., 14 M. 186; Per *Shephard* J. in *Rangasami Naickan* v. *Varadappa Naickan*, (1894) I.L.R., 17 M. 462 (466).
9. C. R. P. 101 of 1882 (1883) I. L. R., 10 M. 98 (note).
10. See cases cited in notes 1, 3, 4 and 5, p. 142.
11. *Srinivasa* v. *Venkata*, (1887) I. L. R., 11 M. 148. C. R. P. 363 of 1900, dated 24th September 1901, M. H. Ct. Jud. Ind. for 1901, p. 144.

[4]. "**And no party to the suit is in fault.**":—In order that costs may be validly paid out of the estate under this section, *two* conditions must be satisfied :—(*a*) The suit should have been for the benefit of the trust and (*b*) no party to the suit must be in fault. The effect of this is that where *any* of the parties to the suit is in fault, no order can be made under S. 18 for costs to be paid out of the estate[1]. The object of this provision appears to be that suits which may be for the benefit of the estate although no person can be said to be in fault, should not be discouraged or prevented by there being no provision for costs. The example of a suit falling within this provision and given in *Sookram Doss* v. *Nund Kishore*[2] is, however, not correct. It is there said that where the right of succession is disputed and it is necessary to secure the property belonging to the endowment and to provide for the performance of worship or service by a suit, costs may be given out of the estate if the provisions of S. 18 are satisfied[2]. But we fail to see how a suit in such a case will lie under S. 14. Where the succession is disputed and the person in possession is not admitted to be the trustee, no suit can lie under S. 14 as has already been pointed out in that section[3]. S. 5 is the only section which applies to cases of disputed succession, and even that section is only applicable to a limited class of cases[4]. But for proceeding under that section no sanction is necessary. But in a suit under S. 14 charging the trustee with misfeasance in most cases one party must be in fault. Where the trustee is removed for misfeasance the plaintiff succeeds. The trustee may be a pauper and the suit may be for the benefit of the estate. But S. 18 does not authorize the successful plaintiff to get costs out of the estate. If so, its scope is very limited and no provision is made for the great majority of cases. The word "and" after the expression "the suit has been for the benefit of the trust" and before "no party to the suit is in fault" cannot be construed as meaning "or"[1].

Costs.

The question whether the court has power to order costs be paid out of the estate in cases not covered by S. 18 is mo

1. *Sookram Doss* v. *Nund Kishore Doss*, (1874) 22 W. R. C. R. 21.
2. Ibid at p. 22.
3. Page 97 note (3). See also *Sheik Abool* v. *Poran Bibee*, (1876) 25 W. R. C. R. 542 (545).
4. See *Gyanananda Asram* v. *Kristo Chandra Mukerji*, (1901) 8 C. W. N. See other cases referred to in notes to S. 5, pp. 31 to 35.

difficult. Chief Justice *Couch* in *Sookram Doss* v. *Nund Kishore Doss*[1] was inclined to doubt the existence of this power. We are also constrained to think that in a suit under S. 14 the ordinary rule should not be applied. This rule is stated in Tudor on Charitable Trusts[2] as follows:—"As a rule, the relator in a charity information, where there is nothing to impeach the propriety of the suit, and no special circumstances to justify a special order, is, upon obtaining a decree for the charity, entitled to have his costs as between solicitor and client, and to be paid the difference between the amount of such costs and the amount of the costs which he may recover from the defendants, out of the charity estate." In the case already referred to[1] it was also said that costs should fall at least in the first instance upon the property recovered by the proceedings. But should justice to the relator or the interests of the charity render it necessary, costs should be ordered to be paid out of the charity funds generally. No doubt in the case of a breach of trust the trustees not merely will be ordered to pay their own costs personally but will also be liable for the costs of the plaintiff[3]. This principle is stated in Lewin on Trusts[4]. The learned author there says: "If any particular instance of misconduct or a general dereliction of duty in the trustee or even his mere caprice and obstinacy be the immediate cause why the suit was instituted, the trustee, on the charge being substantiated against him, must pay the costs of the proceedings which his own improper behaviour occasioned; and of course if the trustee be decreed to pay the costs personally, he cannot afterwards deduct them from the trust fund in his hands." A suit under S. 14 by a worshipper is similar to a suit by a relator. S. 14 provides that the Civil Court may decree costs against the trustee &c., and according to this the manager may be ordered to pay out of his own pocket the successful plaintiff's costs. Then S. 18 provides that under certain circumstances costs may be awarded to be paid out of the estate. The provision in S. 18,

---

1. (1874) 22 W. R. C. R. 21 (22).

2. Page 345 (3rd Edn.) citing Lord *Langdale*, M. R. in *Attorney-General* v. *Kerr*, (1841) 4 Beav., 297 at p. 303: S. C. 55 R. R. 85 and *Attorney-General* v. *Mercers Co.*, (1834) 2 My. & K. 654.

3. *The Haberdashers Company* v. *Attorney-General*, (1702) 2 Bro. P. C. 370; S. C. 1 Eng. Rep. (H. L.) p. 1003.

4. Pages 989 and 990.

however, does not go to the extent to which provision is made under the ordinary law. Hence the common law rule as to costs does not apply to suits under S. 14. This is a great hardship upon worshippers who bring suits under the Act. If the manager is impecunious or insolvent and the suit is for the benefit of the trust, they cannot recover any costs from the manager or from the trust funds under S. 18 if the manager is in fault. The trust gains an advantage at the expense of others without reimbursing the latter for sums spent for the trust. This will certainly act as a deterrent against suits being filed against misconducting managers. While the section must afford a safeguard to the manager against vexatious suits, it must not be so framed as to have the effect of acting as a deterrent upon persons who are interested in the efficient management of the trusts by the managers. The Act provides for suits against managers, and whether those provisions are effective checks upon mismanagement or otherwise, the persons bringing suits for the benefit of the trust have not even the satisfaction of feeling that they will be able to recover costs if the trustee is insolvent.

If the suit under S. 14 is withdrawn owing to some technica[l] defect, the Civil Court has jurisdiction to order costs out of th[e] trust estate[1].

S. 14 does not say under what circumstances the judge wi[ll] be justified in awarding costs against the manager personally. Fo[r] this we have to look to the common law. The ordinary rule wher[e] trustees are concerned, is that they obtain their costs out of th[e] trust funds. But when they are in the wrong and the suit has bee[n] made necessary by their wrong-doing they are made to pay th[e] costs personally, just as if they were an ordinary losing party[2] The suit under S. 14 being a special suit for misfeasance, th[e] latter part of the rule will ordinarily apply where the judge find[s] misfeasance.

Nature and effect of order:—An order under this sectio[n] granting leave does not preclude the manager &c., from contendin[g] in the suit under S. 14 either that the Act has no applicati[on] to the temple or religious establishment in question or that, othe[r]

1. *Ramakissoor Doss* v. *Sreerangacharlu*, (1898) I. L. R., 21 M. 421 whe[re] however, it was only held that there was no appeal from the order of withdrawal

2. Lewin on Trusts (8th Edition), pp. 989 and 990 approved in *Thacker[sey] Dewraj* v. *Hurbhum Nursey*, (1884) I. L. R., 8 B. 432 (473). See *Brinklow* v. *Singlet[on]* [1904] 1 Ch. 648.

wise, the leave obtained is illegal[1]. So also an order refusing leave on the ground that the temple falls under S. 4 is not conclusive on the question of title[2]. An order granting or refusing sanction is not an adjudication of any matter *inter partes* on any right claimed[3]. The order can only be either granting or refusing leave so that the judge has no jurisdiction to dispose of the matter in dispute at once[4]. The effect of the order is to dispense with the necessity of joining the others interested[5].

Appeal and Revision:—No appeal lies against an order granting or refusing sanction[6]. The Act itself does not provide for any appeal. It is not a decree within the meaning of the Civil Procedure Code as it is not an adjudication of any matter *inter partes* on any right claimed[7]. This method of stating the principle seems to be unobjectionable. But in C. R. P., 101 of 1882[8], the principle is stated differently. It is there stated that it is to be inferred from the language of the Act that leave has to be granted or refused by the Court mentioned in the Act, that if leave has been given by that Court the condition imposed by the Legislature has been satisfied and that, therefore, such grant or refusal cannot be interfered with by an Appellate Court. This, however, proceeds against all approved principles relating to the nature of orders passed in appeals. When the Appellate Court passes an order it passes the same as the one which ought to have been passed by the Lower Court. That is why in the Civil Procedure Code where a decree is passed on appeal such decree is to be executed by the Court of First Instance[9].

---

1. *Protap Chandra Misser* v. *Brojonath Misser*, (1891) I. L. R., 19 C. 275. See also *Syed Amin Sahib* v. *Ibram Sahib*, (1868) 4 M. H. C. 112. The Judge's decision on the question of the applicant's interest to sue will also not be decisive in the suit under S. 14. See *Delroos Banoo Begum* v. *Ashgur Ally*, (1875) 15 B. L. R., 167.
2. *Venkatesa Naiker* v. *Srinivassa Chariar*, (1869) 4 M. H. C. 410 (421).
3. C. R. P. 101 of 1882, (1883) I. L. R., 10 M. 98 (note).
4. *Kaviraja Sundara Murtiya Pillai* v. *Nalla Naikan Pillai*, (1866) 3 M. H. C. 93 (94).
5. *Rangasami Naicker* v. *Varadappa Naickan*, (1894) I. L. R., 17 M. 462 (466). See cases cited in note (8), p. 137.
6. *Khudeeram Singh* v. *Sham Singh*, (1864) W. R. Sp. Mis. 25; *Kaviraja Sundara Murtiya Pillai* v. *Nalla Naikan Pillai*, (1866) 3 M. H. C. 93; *Hajee Kalub Hossein* v. *Ali Hossein*, (1872) 4 N. W. P. 3; *Delroos Banoo Begum* v. *Kazee Abdur Ruhman*, (1874) 21 W. R. C. R. 368; C. R. P. 101 of 1882 (1883) I. L. R., 10 M. 98 (note); *Venkateswara, in re* (1886) I. L. R., 10 M. 98; *Karemal* v. *Azim Ali Khan*, (1891) I. L. R., 18 C 382; *Protap Chandra Misser* v. *Brojonath Misser*, (1891) I. L. R., 19 C. 275. Cf. *Jagobindo Nath* v. *Surutsundari Devi*, (1891) I. L. R., 18 C. 322, a decision under S. 375, C. P. C.
7. C. R. P. 101 of 1882, (1883) I. L. R., 10 M. 98 (note); *Venkateswara, in re* (1886) I. L. R., 10 M. 98.
8. (1883) I. L. R., 10 M. 98 (note). *Protapchandra Misser* v. *Brojonath Misser*, (1891) I. L. R., 19 C. 275.
9. See S. 583, C. P. C.

Moreover if this second principle be adopted the logical consequence of it will be that no revision too will lie and the order granting or refusing sanction cannot be interfered with in revision either under S. 622, C. P. C., or S. 15 of the Charter Act. In fact an argument to that effect was founded upon these observations by the respondents' vakil in *Amdoo Miyan* v. *Mahomed Davood Khan*[1] but the Court apparently overruled this contention although the judgment as reported does not refer to this point[2]. The order under this section is, however, a judicial order[3] and as such must be subject to revision either under S. 622, C. P. C., or S. 15 of the charter Act[4]. As pointed out by Chief Justice *Edge* and *Burkitt*, J., in *Waris Ali* v. *Amiruddin*[5] the granting or withholding of leave is not a matter within the uncontrolled discretion of the Civil Judge. The Judge is bound to grant the leave if there are sufficient *prima facie* grounds for the institution of the suit[5], and if the judge does not determine this question in an application under S. 18 his order is liable to revision under S. 622, C. P. C.[6] or the Charter Act.

Revision.

Amendment of sanction :—A sanction once granted may be amended subsequently[7]. S. 19 enables the Court to direct the manager to file accounts. If on seeing the accounts any definite act of mal-administration is found which cannot be known to an ordinary worshipper before the filing of accounts, the sanction may be amended in order to include the act of mal-administration as a charge against the manager. So also if upon seeing the accounts certain charges against the manager have to be given up there is no use in insisting upon the worshipper to bring his suit on the original sanction. He may get the sanction amended by getting these charges which are unsustainable omitted from or struck out of the sanction and such amended sanction may be treated as a fresh one[8].

1. (1901) I. L. R., 24 M. 685.

2. From the fact that the Court set aside the order in revision it must be inferred that the Court thought that a revision lay.

3. *Gopala Ayyar* v. *Arunachellam Chetty*, (1902) I. L. R., 26 M. 85.

4. *Karemali* v. *Azim Ali Khan*, (1891) I. L. R., 18 C. 382. See also *Kishor Bon Mohunt* v. *Kalee Churn Giree*, (1874) 22 W. R. C. R. 364; C. R. P. 101 of 1882 (1883) I. L. R., 10 M. 98 (note); *Venkateswara, in re* (1886) I. L. R., 10 M. 98 C. R. P. 487 of 1900, dated 9th November 1903. M. H. Ct. Jud. Ind. for 1903, p. 70.

5. (1896) A. W. N. 200. See also *Kishore Bon Mohunt* v. *Kalee Churn Giree* (1874) 22 W. R. C. R. 364 (365).

6. *Waris Ali* v. *Amiruddin*, supra; C. R. P. 487 of 1900, supra.

7. *Srinivasa* v. *Venkata*, (1887) I. L. R., 11 M. 148.

8. C. R. P. 363 of 1900, dated 24th September 1901, M. H. Ct. Jud. Ind. for 1901, p. 144.

Court may require accounts of trust to be filed.

XIX. Before giving leave for institution of a suit, or after leave has been given, before any proceeding is taken, or at any time when the suit is pending, the Court may order the trustee, manager, or superintendent, or any member of a committee, as the case may be, to file in Court the accounts of the trust, or such part thereof as to the Court may seem necessary.

NOTES.

Reasons for enacting the section :—Power is given under this section to the Court (*i. e.*, Civil Court) to direct accounts to be filed so that by a judicious use of this power the Court may be enabled to prevent vexatious suits against managers[1].

Scope of section :—The Court may order the trustee &c., to file in Court (*i. e.*, Civil Court) the accounts of the trusts or such part thereof as to the Court may seem necessary in the following three cases mentioned in the section :—

(1) Before giving leave under S. 18 for the institution of a suit. But an application for leave must be pending[2].

(2) After leave has been given under S. 18 and before any proceeding is taken (*i. e.*, apparently under S. 14). So that after leave and before suit, the Civil Court may direct the trustee, &c., to file accounts.

(3) At any time when the suit (instituted under S. 14) is pending.

The manager may be directed to file accounts although no suit is pending provided an application for leave is either pending or disposed of against the manager. The power given to direct accounts to be filed includes, it is submitted, the power to order inspection. There is no use in directing accounts to be filed unless the worshipper is enabled to inspect the accounts. It cannot be said that the accounts are the private property of the manager and that, therefore,

1. *Srinivasa* v. *Venkata*, (1887) I. L. R., 11 M. 148.
2. *Kishore Bon Mohunt* v. *Kalee Churn Giree*, (1873) 22 W. R. C. R. 364 (365).

unless there is a charge made against the manager in a Civil Court the accounts ought not to be directed to be filed. But the provision is really intended for the benefit of innocent managers. It enables the Judge to see whether there is any foundation for all or any of the charges brought against the managers. The accounts are not the private property of the managers. Of course this may be a powerful weapon against miscalcitrant managers.

Worshippers who are interested only in the efficient management of the trust are also enabled to give up charges which may have no foundation and which may turn out to be extravagant on a perusal of the accounts.

This section does not enable the Civil Court to direct the manager to file accounts periodically although it may refuse leave to institute any suit. But in a suit under S. 14, the Civil Court has such power as we have already seen[1]. This is some check upon any abuse of power by the managers.

No civil suit to bar proceedings for criminal breach of trust.

XX. No suit or proceeding before any Civil Court under the preceding sections, shall in any way affect or interfere with any proceeding in a Criminal Court for criminal breach of trust.

NOTES.

The effect of this provision is that the jurisdiction of the ordinary Criminal Courts is not taken away by any proceedings taken under Act XX of 63 and that no sanction is necessary for the institution of criminal proceedings[2]. The ordinary operation of the Criminal Law is not excluded either by Regulation VII of 1817 or Act XX of 1863.

Cases in which the endowments are partly for religious and partly for secular purposes.

XXI. In any case in which any land or other property[1] has been granted for the support of an establishment partly of a religious and partly of a secular character[2],

---

1. *Syed Imdad Hossein* v. *Mahomed Ali Khan*, (1874) 23 W. R. C. R. 150. See Appeal I of 1902, dated 2nd November 1903, M. H. Ct. Jud. Ind. for 1903, pp. 70 and 71 and notes to S. 14, p. 109.

2. Proceedings of the High Court, dated 22nd February 1876, I. L. R., 1 M. 55

or in which the endowment made for the support of an establishment is appropriated partly to religious and partly to secular uses[3],

the Board of Revenue, before transferring to any trustee, manager, or superintendent or to any committee of management appointed under this Act, shall determine[4] what portion, if any, of the said land or other property shall remain under the superintendence of the said Board for application to secular uses,

and what portion shall be transferred to the superintendence of the trustee, manager, or superintendent, or of the committee,

and also what annual amount, if any, shall be charged on the land or other property which may be so transferred to the superintendence of the said trustee, manager, or superintendent, or of the committee, and made payable to the said Board or to the local agents, for secular uses as aforesaid.

In every such case the provisions of this Act shall take effect only in respect to such land and other property as may be so transferred[5].

NOTES.

Object of Section :—As the jurisdiction of the Government or the Board of Revenue over charitable as distinguished from religious endowments is not taken away by this Act, necessary provision is made with respect to such charitable endowments.

[1]. "**Land or other property**" :—Where land or other property is not endowed for a religious establishment or for an establishment partly of a religious and partly of a secular character but there is only a charge of a portion of the profits for religious uses and the land itself is endowed for charitable as distinguished from religious uses, the section has apparently no application. The

land may be retained by the Board and the latter may be giving a fixed proportion of the profits to the trustee &c.

[2]. "**Granted for the support of an establishment partly of a religious and partly of a secular character**":—The establishment itself may be partly of a religious and partly of a secular character and land or property may have been granted for the support of such establishment as a whole. In such cases power is given to the Board of Revenue under this section to apportion the land to be retained by the Board for appropriation to secular uses and the land to be transferred to the trustee &c., for appropriation to religious uses.

[3]. "**Or in which the endowment made for the support of an establishment is appropriated partly to religious and partly to secular uses**":—The establishment may be of a religious character. But the endowment made in support of such establishment may be made partly for religious and partly for secular uses. In such a case also apportionment should be made by the Board of Revenue.

[4]. "**The Board of Revenue &c., shall determine**":—It cannot be supposed that the determination of the Board is final. The manager or other person interested in the religious establishment may question the same in a regular suit. The last sentence in the section "in every such case &c., transferred" is only intended to guard against the supposition that the Regulations have ceased to be applicable to such land and not to make the determination of the Board final.

[5]. "**The provisions of this Act shall take effect only in respect to such land and other property as may be so transferred**":—Under Ss. 3 and 12 and S. 4 duty is imposed on the Local Government to transfer property either to the Committee or to the manager as the case may be and it is also declared that upon such transfer, the duties and responsibilities of the Board and the local agents cease and determine. This provision only reiterates that the duties and responsibilities of the Board cease with respect to the land or other property transferred and not with respect to other lands so that the Board and local agents have duties and responsibilities with respect to land or other property endowed for secular uses or retained by the Board for such uses.

XXII. Except as provided in this Act, it shall not be lawful [*after the passing of this Act*[a]], for any Government in India[1], or for any Officer of any Government in his official character,

Government not to hold charge henceforth of property for support of any mosque, temple &c.

to undertake or resume the superintendence of any land or other property granted for the support of, or otherwise belonging to, any mosque, temple, or other religious establishment, or

to take any part in the management or appropriation of any endowment made for the maintenance of any such mosque, temple, or other establishment, or

to nominate or appoint any trustee, manager or superintendent thereof, or

to be in any way concerned therewith.

NOTES.

Extent of application :—This section applies to the whole of India.

[1]. "**Any Government in India**" :—This does not of course refer to the Governments of the Native States. The expression only includes the Government of India or the several Local Governments of the different Provinces in India belonging to or vested in His Majesty. See S. 24.

Effect of the section :—Its effect is to prohibit the Government in India or any officer of any Government (Madras, Bombay, Bengal &c.,) in his official character from (1) undertaking or resuming the superintendence of any land or other property endowed for any mosque or other establishment, or (2) taking any part in the management or appropriation of any endowment made for the maintenance of such mosque or other establishment, or (3) nomi-

---

a. The words in closed brackets have been repealed by the Repealing Act XVI of 1874.

nating or appointing any trustee &c., of such mosque or other establishment, or (4) being in any way concerned with such mosque or other establishment. Hence, after Act XX of 1863, the Government cannot remove any manager of any religious establishment from office[1] and cannot equally nominate a manager[2] for such religious establishment. Such appointment and dismissal will be illegal and *ultra vires*. Even a temporary appointment of an officer of Government in his official capacity will be invalid[3] and this provision must equally be applicable to the case of an appointment made under S. 5. The Advocate-General as representing the public (the founders of an institution) has no right to dismiss a mohant[4].

The question whether the Collector as Agent to the Court of Wards is an officer of the Government within the meaning of the section is more difficult. If a minor's estate is in the charge of the Court of Wards and the Collector as Agent to the Court of Wards is appointed as such Agent and as guardian to his ward[5] a manager under S. 5, is he an officer of the Government appointed in his official character as manager ? The Court of Wards is a statutory body having a separate existence with distinct rights and liabilities. It is just like the Universities of Madras, Calcutta, Bombay &c., or the several Municipal Councils established under the Acts relating to Municipalities. The Collector may be an officer of Government. But is he an officer of Government when he exercises the powers conferred on him by the Court under S. 8 of the Court of Wards Act (Madras) ? There can be no legal objection if he is appointed in his individual capacity. The case of *Somasundara* v. *Vythilinga*[5] is authority for the position that such appointment is valid. Any difficulty that may exist is removed by the express provision in the New Court of Wards Act for Madras (Madras Act I of 1902) S. 63 which enacts that the Court may in cases where the ward is the hereditary manager of a religious establishment, make such arrangements as it thinks fit for the due discharge of the ward's

---

1. *The Secretary of State for India* v. *Abdul Hakkim*, (1880) I. L. R., 2 M. 294.
2. *Mahomed* v. *Ganapati*, (1889) I. L. R., 13 M. 277. See also *Balwant Rao* v. *Puran Mal*, (1883) L. R. 10 I. A. 90 (93).
3. *Sayad Hussein Dadumian* v. *The Collector of Kaira*, (1895) I. L. R., 21 B. 48.
4. *Dhuncooverbai* v. *The Advocate-General*, (1899) 1 Bom. L. R., 743 (747).
5. (1896) I. L. R., 19 M. 285. See *Somasundara* v. *Twigg*, C. R. P. 97 of 1900.

duties as manager &c., provided that for the direct and personal management of the *religious affairs* of any such institution &c., the Court shall appoint suitable persons other than officers of Government and that the Court shall as far as possible restrict its superintendence to the preservation of the property belonging to the religious establishment &c.

If a person is not appointed in his official capacity, then there is no objection under this section. There are numerous officers of Government who in their individual capacity are under no prohibition to take up the management and are best fitted for taking up the management. If the management is in the hands of any of these, we will not have heard of the mismanagement of our religious endowments. It is to be sincerely hoped that the Government will not view with disfavor the native officers under their employ taking up the management of these religious endowments.

Effect of Act in respect of Regulations therein mentioned, and of buildings of antiquity, &c.

XXIII. Nothing in this Act shall be held to affect the provisions of the Regulations mentioned in this Act, except in so far as they relate to mosques, Hindoo temples, and other religious establishments; or to prevent the Government from taking such steps as it may deem necessary, under the provisions of the said Regulations, to prevent injury to and preserve buildings remarkable for their antiquity, or for their historical or architectural value, or required for the convenience of the public.

NOTES.

This section reiterates that the provisions of the Regulations are not affected by this Act except so far as they relate to mosques &c.

A saving clause is also added that even with respect to such mosques or religious establishments if the buildings attached thereto have an historical or architectural value or are remarkable for their antiquity or are required for the convenience of the public, the Government may take steps to prevent injury to those buildings and preserve them. (See now the Ancient Monuments Preservation Act VII of 1904).

"India."

XXIV. The word "India[a]" in this Act shall denote the territories which are or may become vested in Her Majesty by the Statute 21 and 22 Vic., c. 106, entitled "An Act for the better Government of India[b]."

NOTES.

"**India**:"—This term so far as we know only occurs in S. 22.

The whole Act has been extended to the district of Canara in the Bombay Presidency by Bombay Act VII of 1865.

It has been extended to the following Scheduled Districts. The Act has been declared by notification under S. 3 (*a*) of the Scheduled Districts Act, 1874 (XIV of 1874, printed in General Acts, Vol. II) to be in force in the following Scheduled Districts, namely :—

The Districts of Hazaribagh, Lohardaga and Manbhum, and Pargana Dhalbhum and Kolhan in the District of Singbhum ... See Gazette of India, 1881, Pt. 1, p. 504.

The Scheduled portion of the Mirzapur District ... ... Ditto 1879, Pt. 1, p. 383

Jaunsan Bawar ... ... Ditto 1879, Pt. 1, p. 382.

The Districts of Hazara, Peshawar, Kohat, Bannu, Dera Ismail Khan and Dera Ghazi Khan ... ... Ditto 1886, Pt. 1, p. 361

The Chief Commissionership of Assam (except the North Lushai Hills) ... ... Ditto 1897, Pt. 1, p. 20

It has been extended by notification under S. 5 of the last mentioned Act, to the following Scheduled Districts, namely :—

Kumaon and Garhwal... ... ... See Gazette of India, 187 Pt. 1, p. 60

The North-Western Provinces Tarai .. Ditto 1876, Pt. 1, p. 50

Ajmere and Merwara ... ... Ditto 1877, Pt. 1, p. 60

---

a. i. e., British India Cf. Definitions of British India and India in S. 3 (7) a S. 3 (27) respectively of the General Clauses Act (X of 1897).

b. i. e., The Government of India Act, 1858.

APPENDICES.

APPENDIX I.

The Madras Endowments and Escheats Regulation, 1817.*

REGULATION VII OF 1817

(*Passed on the 30th of September* 1817.)

A Regulation for the due appropriation of the rents and produce of lands granted for the support of mosques, Hindu temples and colleges, or *other* public *purposes; for the maintenance and repair of bridges,* choultries, or chuttrams *and other public buildings; and for the custody and disposal of escheats.*

Preamble.

WHEREAS considerable endowments[1] have been granted in money, or by assignments of land, or of the produce, or portions of the produce of land by former Governments of this country as well as by the British Government, and by individuals for the support of mosques[2], Hindu temples [3], colleges[4], and choultries, and for other pious and beneficial purposes; and whereas there are grounds to believe that the produce of such endowments is in many instances appropriated, contrary to the intentions of the donors, to the personal use of the individuals in immediate charge and possession of such endowments; and whereas it is the duty of the Government to provide that all such endowments be applied according to the real intent and will of the grantor; and whereas it is moreover *expedient* to provide for the maintenance and repair of bridges, choultries [5], chuttrums and other buildings, which have been erected, either at the expense of Government or of individuals, for the use and convenience of the public; and also to establish proper rules for the custody and disposal of escheats:—the following rules have been enacted, to be in force from the date of their promulgation throughout the provinces immediately dependent on the Presidency of Fort St. George.

*** See the Repealing and Amending Act, 1901 (Act XI of 1901).**

The Bengal Charitable Endowments, Public Buildings and Escheats Regulation.*

REGULATION XIX OF 1810.

(Passed on the 14th December 1810).

A Regulation for the due appropriation of the rents and produce of lands granted for the support of [mosques, Hindu temples[a]], *colleges and other purposes; for the maintenance and repair of* [bridges, Sarais, Kattras and other[a]] *public buildings; and for the custody and disposal of* nazul property *or escheats.*

Preamble.

1. WHEREAS considerable endowments [[1]]. have been granted in land by the preceding Governments of this country and by individuals for the support of [*mosques, Hindu temples*[a]], colleges[[4]] and for other [*pious and*[a]] beneficial purposes; and whereas there are grounds to suppose that the produce of such lands is in many instances appropriated, contrary to the intentions of the donors, to the personal use of individuals in immediate charge and possession of such endowments; and whereas it is an *important* duty of *every* Government to provide that all such endowments be applied according to the real intent and will of the grantor; and whereas it is moreover *essential* to provide for the maintenance and repair of [*bridges, Sarais*[[6]], *Kattras*[[7]] *and other*[a]] buildings which have been erected either at the expense of Government or of individuals for the use and convenience of the public and also to establish proper rules for the custody and disposal of *nazul property*[[3]] or escheats, the following rules have been enacted to be in force from the period of their promulgation throughout the Provinces immediately dependent on the Presidency of Fort William.

NOTES.

Preliminary:—For the sake of convenience the sections of both the Regulations are given underneath one another. The section of the Madras Regulation appears first and then the section of the Bengal Regulation. Above each section of the Bengal Regulation

---

* See the Repealing and Amending Act, 1903 (I of 1903).

a. The words in closed brackets have been repealed by Act I of 1903 (The Repealing and Amending Act).

the figures B. R. are given. The difference in the sections are pointed out in italics except in the title and where closed brackets appear. In the latter case it is meant to indicate that the portion in such closed brackets has been repealed.

Regulations compared :—The provisions of the Bengal Regulation are substantially similar to those of the Madras Regulation In fact the latter Regulation was framed on the model of the Bengal Regulation. With the exception of S. 16 of the Madras Regulation which is not contained in the Bengal Regulation and S. 6 of the latter Regulation which is not found in the Madras Regulation, all other sections are similar. The Bengal Regulation as it originally stood instead of saying "Board of Revenue" simply as in the Madras Regulation, stated *Board of Revenue* and *Board of Commissioners.* But as the Bengal Board of Revenue Regulation, 1822, has been amended, there is a single Board of Revenue and hence the Repealing Act of 1903 has made the necessary changes in the Bengal Regulation. Then certain Hindustani terms, such as Serais, Kattras and Nazul are used in the Bengal Regulation which do not appear in the Madras Regulation, but some of these terms have been repealed. Lastly, the Bengal Regulation speaks of "endowments in land" only and not of other endowments.

Extent :—The Madras Regulation applies to the whole of the Madras Presidency except the Scheduled Districts by the Laws Local Extent Act, 1874 (XV of 1874), S. 4.

It has since been extended by India Government Notifications under S. 3(*a*) of the Scheduled Districts Act, 1874, Nos. 1150 and 1151, dated 3rd October 1879, to Badrachellam and Rekapalli Taluqs and the Rampa country (See Gazette of India, 1879, Part I, p. 630, and Fort St. George Gazette, 1879, p. 722).

It has been declared by notification under S. 3(*b*) of the said Act not to be in force in the Scheduled Districts in Ganjam and Vizagapatam. (See Fort St. George Gazette, 1898, Part I, p. 667 and Gazette of India, 1898, Part I, p. 872).

The Bengal Regulation has been declared to apply to the whole of Bengal except the Scheduled Districts (See Act XV of 1874, S. 6).

Under S. 3 of the Scheduled Districts Act, 1874 (XIV of 1874), the Bengal Regulation has been declared to be in force in the following Scheduled Districts :—West Jalpaiguri, Hazaribagh, Lohardaga, Manbhoom, Pergunnah Dhalbhoom and Sylhet. (See Bengal Code, Vol. I, Edition 1889, Appendix, pp. 627 and 651).

Object :—The object is, as stated in S. 15 of the Madras Regulation (S. 16 of the Bengal Regulation), to provide for the due appropriation of endowments and not to resume the same. The objects as stated in the preamble are three-fold :—

(1) to provide for the due appropriation of endowments,

(2) to provide for the due appropriation, maintenance and repair of bridges, choultries, &c., and

(3) to provide for the custody and disposal of escheats.

To effectuate the *first two* objects, the Regulations provide that the superintendence of all endowments and public buildings do vest in the Board of Revenue though Act XX of 1863 has repealed the provisions of the Regulations so far as religious endowments are concerned (and in Bengal, Regulation XVII of 1816, S. 16, has repealed so much of the Bengal Regulation XIX of 1810 as requires the Board of Revenue and Commissioners to provide for the due repair of public edifices, such as bridges, Sarais and Khattras).

Ss. 3 to 5, and Ss. 9 to 15 of the Madras Regulation, and Ss. 3 to 6 and Ss. 10 to 16 of the Bengal Regulation, further deal with the mode in which the above objects may be more effectually carried out. Ss. 7 and 8 of the Madras Regulation (corresponding to Ss. 8 and 9 of the Bengal Regulation) are general and enable the Board of Revenue to appoint local agents for carrying out these and other provisions.

As regards the last object provision is made in Ss. 6 and 9 of the Madras Regulation, corresponding to Ss. 7 and 10 of the Bengal Regulation.

Repeal :—The Regulations recognise the admitted duty of Government to provide that all public endowments be applied according to the real intent and will of their respective grantors[1]. It is a duty undertaken by all Governments, which at all claim to be civilized and rational. Even before the Regulations, the Government were discharging similar duties towards these endowments. These duties devolved upon the British Government from the Hindu Kings and the Mahomedan Government. But as regards superintendence of native religious endowments, conscientious scruples at last are said to have prevailed with the result that through the intervention of the Legislature so much of these Regulations as relates to endowments for the support of mosques, Hindu temples or other religious purposes has been repealed by Act XX of 1863. After the Act, the Collector has no jurisdiction to appoint[2] or to remove managers of religious endowments[3] or to carry out trusts relating thereto.[4]

Under Bengal Regulation XVII of 1816, S. 16, so much of this Regulation (XIX of 1810) as requires the Boards of Revenue and Commissioners to provide for the due repair of public edifices, such as bridges, Sarais and Kattras has been repealed, and S.17 transfers the general control over these to the superintendents of police.

Applicability :—The Regulations only applies to public endowments and not to private endowments[5]. This is clear from S. 15 of the Madras Regulation (corresponding to S. 16 of the Bengal Regulation) which speaks only of endowments granted for public purposes. In *Jan Ali* v. *Ram Nath Mundul*[6] it was observed by the Calcutta High Court

Public endowments.

---

1. See preamble.

2. *The Secretary of State for India* v. *Abdul Hakkim*, (1880) I. L. R., 2 M. 294 *Mahomed* v. *Gunapati*, (1889) I. L. R., 13 M. 277.

3. *The Secretary of State for India* v. *Abdul Hakkim*, supra; *Balwant Rao Bishwant Chandra Chor* v. *Purun Mal Chaube*, (1883) L. R., 10 I. A. 90 (93) : S. C. I. L. R. 6 A. 1 (6).

4. *Balwant Rao Bishwant* v. *Purun Mal*, supra.

5. *Bibee Kuneez Fatima* v. *Bibee Saheba Jan*, (1867) 8 W. R. C R. 313; *Delroos Banoo Begum* v. *Nawab Syud Ashgur Ally Khan*, (1875) 28 W. R. C R. 457 : S. C. 15 B. L R. 167 affirmed on appeal to P. C., in *Ashgar Ali* v. *Delroos Banoo Begum*, (187 I. L. R., 3 C. 324 (330); *Satnappayyar* v. *Periasami*, (1890) I. L. R., 14 M. 1; an *Protap Chandra Misser* v. *Brojonath Misser*, (1891) I. L. R., 19 C 275. See also cas cited in pp. 83 to 85.

6. (1881) I. L. R., 8 C. 32.

that the Regulations would be applicable only to a mosque, &c., for which endowments had been made either by former Governments or by this Government or by private individuals. Whether this view be right or wrong (and Ss. 9 and 15 of the Madras Regulation may seem to throw doubt upon this view[1]) it is immaterial for our present purpose[2]. No question of endowments arises with reference to the maintenance and repair of public buildings.

Endowments made after Regulations.

A question has been raised whether the Regulations are applicable only to endowments existing at the time of the Reglations and not to endowments made after the Regulations. S. 2 of the Regulations is general and makes no distinction between endowments made before the Regulations and made after them. Where a mosque or other religious establishment is in existence at the time of the Regulations and there are endowments attached to it, there can be no reason to suppose that the Regulations meant to draw a distinction between such endowments and endowments made after the passing of the Regulations to the same establishment and to say that the Board has no control over the latter class of endowments. In *Sivayya* v. *Rami Reddi*[3], Mr. Justice *Shephard* raised but did not decide this question. Mr. Justice *Subramaniya Iyer* took the view that the Regulations applied to all endowments whether made before or after the Regulations. It cannot be said that any difference is made by the Regulations with regard to escheats and all the sections in the Regulations are consistent with the view that the Regulations apply to all endowments irrespective of the date when they might have been made. In *Delroos Banoo Begum* v. *Syud Ashgur Ally Khan*[4] and *Jan Ali* v. *Ram Nath Mundul*[5] although the institutions themselves came into existence after the Bengal

---

1. See the discussion of this case at pp. 83 and 84

2. The Regulations having been repealed by Act XX of 63 so far as religious endowments are concerned.

3 (1899) I. L. R., 22 M. 223.

4. (1875) 15 B. L. R. 167; S. C. 23 W. R. C. R. 457. In this case the Court expressly stated that the Bengal Regulation would apply to such an endowment. This case was affirmed by the Privy Council in *Ashgar Ali* v. *Delroos Banoo Begum*, (1877) I. L. R., 3 C. 324 (330).

5. (1881) I. L. R., 8 C. 32.

Regulation the year was not considered material as regards the applicability or otherwise of the Regulation[1].

Other remedies not excluded by Regulations:—The Regulations are only supplementary of existing remedies[2] A suit will lie in the ordinary civil courts for removal of a trustee of a charitable endowment[3]. No prior application to the Board of Revenue will be necessary[2]. The ordinary Criminal Law is also not excluded[4]. This is expressly reserved by S. 16 of the Madras Regulation though there is no corresponding section in the Bengal Regulation.

[1]. "**Endowments**":—As to the meaning of this word see Introduction, Ch. II, pp. xi and xii. The Regulations do not use this term as synonymous with "establishment", but a distinction is drawn between "endowment" and "establishment". This latter term occurs in Ss. 3, 9 and 10 of the Madras Regulation, corresponding to Bengal Ss. 3, 10 and 11.

---

1. See p. 86 and note (2) to that page. See also *Suppammal* v. *The Collector of Tanjore*, (1889) I. L. R., 12 M. 387 (389); *Mohiuddin* v. *Sayiduddin*, (1893) I. L. R., 20 C. 810 (818, 819). In *Seshadri Ayyangar* v. *Nataraja Ayyar*, I. L. R., 21 M. 179, *Collins*, C. J., and *Davies*, J., stated at pp. 219 and 195 respectively that the general superintendence of *all* endowments vested in the Board by Ss. 2, 3 and 15 of the Madras Regulation, but no question of date arose. See also *Kassyvassy Kristna Putter* v. *Vangala Shangaranat Josser*, (1858) M. S. D. A. p 39 (where, the endowment was one of 1845); and *Wasik Ali Khan* v. *The Government*, (1834) 5 B. S.D.A. 363 : S. ., (1836) 6 B. S. D. A. 110 (where, however, the endowment was in 1806). In *Ganapati Ayyan* v. *Savithri Ammal*, (1897) I. L. R., 21 M. 10 (15), *Shephard*, J., directed in the decree that a charity established shortly prior to 1878 should be subject to the superintendence of the Tanjore District Board (The Board of Revenue being authorized under S. 51(2) of the Madras Local Boards Act V of 1884 to make over to the Local Boards, on certain requisites being complied with, the management of charitable endowments). This decree was concurred in by *Subramania Aiyar*, J. In *Subbayya* v. *Krishna*, (1890) I. L. R., 14M. 186, the endowment was one of 1820. The Madras Government has also acted on the view that the Regulation will be applicable in such a case with regard to choultries. Maskell, p. 523. But see the opinion of the District Judge in *Narasimha* v. *Ayyan*, (1888) I. L. R., 12 M. 157 (159). It is admitted that the section applies to escheats subsequent to the Regulation. See the opinion of the District Judge in *Narasimha* v. *Ayyan*, (1888) I. L. R., 12 M. 157 (159). Standing Orders of the Board of Revenue (Madras) Edn. of 1900, No. 179 (ii, 3), p. 758. See also Ss. 6 and 9 of the Madras Regulation, correspondiug to Ss 7 and 10 of the Bengal Regulation. There is no difference drawn between escheats and endowments so far as regards the vesting of superintendence is concerned. The choultry of Kalla Singanna Chetty in *Benares* apparently founded and endowed after 1810 was taken charge of by the Local Agents. See Parliamentary Return printed in 1860 (East India, Hindoo Shrines), p. 21.

2. *Ponnambala Mudaliyar* v. *Varaguna Rama Pandia Chinnatambiar*, (1872) 7 M. H. C. 117. See also *Kassyvassy Kristna Patter* v. *Vangala Shangaranat Josser*, (1858) M. S. D. A. p. 39 followed in *Narasimma Charry* v. *Tundree Comara Tata Charry*, (1858) M. S. D. A. p. 141.

3. *Ponnambala* v. *Chinnatambi*, supra; *Subbayya* v. *Krishna*, (1890) I. L. R., 14 M. 186 (197, 220, 221); *Rangasami Naickan* v. *Varadappa Naickan*, (1894) I. L. R., 17 M. 462 (466).

4. Proceedings of the High Court, dated 22nd February 1876, I. L. R., 1 M. 55.

[2]. "**Mosques**" :—These represent the Mahomedan religious institutions which the Board of Revenue had control of under the Regulations. The nature of a mosque has been discussed in the Introduction, Chapter II. pp. xviii to xx, and Chapter IX, pp. cxvi to cxviii. But the mention of the expression "mosques" does not exclude other Mahomedan religious establishments. Khankas and dargas also came under the purview of the Regulations[1].

[3]. "**Hindoo temples**" :—No express mention is made of the religious establishments of the Jains, Sikhs and other classes. For the meaning of the term "Hindoo" see Introduction (Chapter II, pp. xiii and xiv). The Regulations apparently use the term in a loose sense. "Jain" and "Sikh" would come under the term "Hindoo[2]". It was the general belief that Christian religious establishments did not come under the Regulations. We never heard of the Regulations having been so applied[3]. There must have been some endowments made for these establishments even by the former rulers of the country. Some inams must have been granted and some of these are to be found in Tinnevelly and Tanjore Districts. If the theory be that the duties of superintendence formerly exercised by the native rulers devolved upon the British Government upon their assumption of sovereignty and that the Regulations only intended to provide for these duties, then there is reason for restricting the scope of the Regulations to native endowments and for not applying them to the Christian establishments and endowments as the native rulers would not have exercised control over the same. The mention of Hindoo temples does not exhaust the category of Hindoo religious establishments. The Regulations were applied to mutts[4].

1. *Shah Imama Buksh* v. *Moosummat Beebee Shahee*, (1835) 6 B.S.D.A. 22; *Jeiwun Dass Sahoo* v *Shah Kubeer-Ood-Deen*, (1840) 2 M. I. A. 3. 0.

2. *Rani Bhagwan Kuar* v. *Jogendra Chandra Bose*, (1903) L. R. 30, I.A. 249 (253 to 257): S. C. I. L. R., 31 C. 11 (29 to 32).

3. Letter from Secretary to Government of Bengal to Secretary to the Government of India, dated 8th August 1844, Parliamentary Return 1849, Idolatry (India) p. 321 and Note of Senior Member, p. 322. But the Christians never asked for the extension of the Regulations to their endowments but agitated for a repeal of the Regulations.

4. *Ram Churn Das* v. *Chutter Bhoje*, (1845) 7 B. S. D. A. 205; *Greedharee Doss* v. *Nund Kishore*, (1863) 1 Marsh 578; *Jusagheri Gosamiar* v. *The Collector of Tanjore*, (1870) 5 M. H. C. 334. Cf. *Narain Das* v. *Bindrabun Das*, (1815) 2 B. S. D. A. 151; *Mohant Rama Nooj Doss* v. *Mohunt Debraj Doss*, (1839) 6 B. S. D. A. 262. But in most of these early cases the words "mutt" and "temple" are used indifferently. See Eliott's Report, Parliamentary Return, 1849, Idolatry (India), p.410; note by Under Secretary, Ibid, p. 443. But see letter from Ag. Secretary to Board of Revenue to the Chief Secretary to Government, dated 17th July 1843, Ibid, p.194 (case of Poonje Mattam in North Arcot District).

[4]. "**Colleges**" :—These are universities or institutions which have for their object the pursuit of literary studies. A common instance of this is to be found in the Sanskrit schools or colleges in which Vedic or other instruction is taught with free board and lodging for students in most cases. These schools for Vedic instruction must be distinguished from the Agama schools which exist all over the country, many of them as attached to the great Hindu temples. The latter schools may be solely concerned with theological study and hence may fairly be thought to be outside the pale of Government superintendence. The Madras Board of Revenue in S. O. No. 75[1] expressly states that it is the duty of the Collectors to prevent the appropriation of the proceeds of an endowment, and that in the case of these schools this duty should be exercised but only no further than is absolutely necessary to secure these results. Then there are the Vedic and Sanskrit schools. The Tanjore Rajas and the Tinnevelly Chieftains founded many choultries attached to a great majority of which were these Vedic or Sanskrit schools. These Vedic schools are also apparently regarded as schools for religious instruction. But there is a marked difference between these schools and the Agama schools. In these schools instruction in Sanskrit literature, grammar, &c., may be and is more often given. Then again there were schools attached to some of the mutts. The institution of tolls in Northern India is a counterpart of these schools. Whereas in Bengal considerable sums are expended by the Government for Sanskrit studies besides the numerous endowments already existing it is regrettable to find that in the Madras Presidency, which boasts of its being ahead of the other Presidencies in other matters, the Government is indifferent to the promotion of Sanskrit study. No contributions worth the name are made. More strenuous endeavours must be made to enforce the provisions of these Regulations in order to see that endowments made for the purposes of Sanskrit instruction are appropriated according to the intent of the grantors. In some cases, it is said that the income accruing from these endowments is diverted for roads, bridges, dispensaries or is spent otherwise. A part of the income of the mutts used to be devoted to Sanskrit instruction in former times. We do not hear of Sanskrit instruction in these mutts

---

1. (1900) Edn. p. 260. See also Maskell, p. 298.

now. If the Government is not willing to spend anything from the public revenue for the cause of Sanskrit studies the Government may at any rate prevent the diversion of the existing endowments and take steps to improve the existing schools to suit modern circumstances. The modern system of university education, the necessity for English education and the poor prospects of a person versed only in Sanskrit studies are standing menaces to the development if not to the existence of the indigenious Sanskrit Schools. If we add to this, the diversion of the funds properly available for the maintenance of these schools their fate in Madras at any rate is sealed.

[5]. "**Choultries**":—It is a large shed used as a village hall or assembly or it is a khan or caravansary or inn for the resting of travellers. The vernacular name is chavadi (Tam. and Tel.) and Chanti (Mal.) meaning a public lodging place or shelter for travellers[1]. When refreshments are given gratuitously or provisions distributed *gratis* in such a place it is called chuttram. A *chuttram* is a place where refreshment is given gratuitously, especially to Brahmins[2]. Formerly liberal grants were made for the erection and maintenance of these choultries. Waste lands were given freely by the Government for sites[3]. But latterly Government aid was not so overflowing, the reason being that choultries had been erected sufficient enough to meet the wants of the travellers[4]. Then stricter rules were made and the liberality of the Government could only be expected if the choultry proposed to be established was intended for all classes of inhabitants and not for any particular class of the public[5]. Now the grant of waste lands in aid of choultries erected by private individuals is prohibited and the circumstances must be so exceptional as to warrant the grant of a special concession[6].

[6]. "**Sarai**":—A building for the shelter and accommodation of travellers or a caravenserai. It is similar to a choultry. This term occurs in the Bengal Regulation.

1. Wilson's Glossary, p. 108.
2. Wilson's Glossary, p. 104.
3. See Madras B. S. O. 74 (3), p. 260 (Edn. 1900).
4. Railway communication all over the country was another reason.
5. Maskell, pp. 445 to 447 and 523.
6. Madras B. S. O. No. 74 (3), Edn. (1900), p. 260.

[7]. "**Kattra**":—A market place or a market town belonging to a fort. This term also occurs only in the Bengal Regulation.

[8]. "**Nazul**" :—Lit. descent.—In Revenue language an escheat, escheated property in gardens and houses; any property that is considered to have lapsed to the State (Wilson's Glossary, 269).

General superintendence of endowments for support of mosques, &c.

2. The general superintendence of all *endowments*[1] *in land or money* granted for the support of mosques, Hindu temples, or colleges, or for other pious and beneficial purposes[2], and of all public buildings, such as bridges, *choultries, or chuttrums,* and other edifices, in the several Provinces dependent on the Presidency of Fort St. George is hereby vested in the Board of Revenue.

B. R.

Superintendence of lands granted for support of mosques, &c.

2. The general superintendence of all *lands* [1] granted for the support of [*mosques, Hindu temples,*[a]] colleges and for other [*pious and*[a]] beneficial purposes[2], and of all public buildings, such as bridges, Sarais, Kattras, and other edifices is hereby vested in the Board of Revenue [*and Board of Commissioners in the several districts subject to the control of those Boards respectively*[a]].

NOTES.

Control prior to Regulations :—Even before the Regulations the British Government by virtue of its sovereign power, asserted as the former rulers of the country had done, the right to visi endowments of a public nature and to prevent and redress abuse in their management[1]. There can also be little doubt that thi superintending authority was exercised by the old rulers[1]. Th British Government not only assumed long before the Regulations the power to superintend the management of the pagodas throughou

(*a*) The words in closed brackets have been repealed by the Repealing a Amending Act, 1903 (I of 1903).

1. *Ramiengar* v. *Gnanasambanda Pandarasannada*, (1872) 5 M. H. C. 53 (57 *Rajah Muttu Ramalinga Setupati* v. *Periyanayagam Pillai*, (1874) L. R. 1, I. A., 2 (232, 233); *Seshadri Ayyangar* v. *Nataraja Ayyar*, (1898) I. L. R., 21 M., 179 (1 218).

2. *Rajah Muttu Ramalinga* v, *Periyanayagam Pillai*, supra.

the Peninsula but exercised its authority through the agency of the Collectors. The Regulations merely defined the manner in which the power of superintendence and control was thenceforth to be exercised[1].

[1]. **"The general superintendence of all endowments":—** The Bengal Regulation uses the term "*lands*" instead of the term "*endowments in land or money.*" The power of superintendence entrusted by the Government to the Board of Revenue and the Collectors is vested by the Madras Regulation in the Board of Revenue and by the Bengal Regulation in the Board of Revenue and Commissioners and Ss. 7 and 8 of the Madras Regulation corresponding to Ss. 8 and 9 of the Bengal Regulation authorize the Governor-in-Council or the local Government[2] to appoint local agents[1]. The general management of all endowments is made a legal obligation[3] on the Board of Revenue[4]. One thing that has to be observed is that what was vested by the section in the Board of Revenue or the Board of Revenue and Board of Commissioners as the case might be[4], was the general superintendence of *all endowments* of religious and charitable institutions but not the superintendence of the *institutions* themselves. Ss. 9 to 13 of the Madras Regulation, corresponding to Ss. 10 to 14 of the Bengal Regulation, deal with certain duties relating to the institutions. But beyond these, the Regulations speak of no duties of the Board with reference to the institutions. Hence it might be said that the Board could not have interfered with managers in matters of ritual affecting the institution and that the committees which took the place of the Board could equally not so interfere (even assuming that managers had any right to interfere in matters of ritual). Hence it might also be said that the Government did not intend to take up the direct internal management of the native religious establishments but it must be remembered that the Regulations did not confer any new rights on Government[5].

Interference in matters of ritual.

1. *Rajah Muttu Ramalinga Setupati* v. *Perianayagum Pillai*, (1874) L. R., 1 I. A., 209 (235).
2. Originally it was the Governor General in Council in Bengal that had this right.
3. See notes to Preamble of Act XX of 1863 under heading "Government control," pp. 5 and 6, notes to S. 1, pp. 7 and 8.
4. In the Bengal Regulation it was originally the Board of Revenue and Board of Commissioners.
5. See Chapter XVII from which it will appear that there was some interference,

Renunciation by Government of rights vested in Regulations:—According to the decision in *Venkatesa Nayudu* v. *Shrivan Shatagopa Shri Shatagopa Swami*[1] there was nothing in the Regulations to prevent the Government from renouncing the rights vested under the Regulations. This position was doubted in a later case[2]. We have already discussed this matter in connection with religious endowments[3] and the conclusion we came to was that the Government might have framed a scheme for the better management of the institution, but could not have diverted the usage of the institution and could not have given up absolutely the duty of superintendence imposed upon the Government by the Regulations except under statutory authority.

Superintendence in the Board not in Court:—Under this section the general superintendence is vested in the Board[4] and not in the Sudder Court[5], but the Regulations as already observed are only supplementary of existing remedies[6].

[2]. "**Or for other pious and beneficial purposes**":—This is rather a very vague expression. A "pious purpose" is not the same as a "superstitious purpose[7]." By a "beneficial purpose" it is meant, we suppose, a purpose, beneficial to the public or any class of the public. This is a "charitable purpose" as understood in English Law. If there is no intention by any endowment to confer a benefit either upon the people in general or upon any class of sectarians, then there is no "pious and beneficial purpose" within the meaning of the Regulations[8]. A public purpose is a charitable purpose and what is beneficial to the public is a public purpose. This expression then indicates that the Regulations apply only to endowments for public purposes.

---

1. (1872) 7 M. H. C 77. See *Nallathambi Battar* v. *Nellakumara Pillai*, (1873) 7 M. H. C. 306 (310) where the High Court observed that the Government assuming to act within the law could not create a valid title to more than they themselves possessed.

2. *Appasami* v. *Nagappa* (1884) I. L. R., 7 M. 499 (509).

3. See notes to S. 3 of Act XX of 1863 pp. 14 to 16.

4. *Wasiq Uli Khan* v. *The Government*, (1836) 6 B. S. D. A. 110; *Greedharee Doss* v. *Nundkishore Dutt Mohunt*, (1863) 1 Marsh 573.

5. *Greedharee Doss* v. *Nundkishore*, (1863) 1 Marsh 573 (588).

6. See p. 158. See also pp. 182 and 183.

7. See Introduction, Ch. VI, p. lxviii and Ch. VII, p. lxxxviii.

8. *Sathappa yar* v. *Periasami*, (1890) I. L. R., 14 M. 1 (6).

Effect of Section :—The effect of vesting this right of superintendence in the Board is to take away the powers of managers of endowed property and to confer upon the Board the right to sanction the revision of existing appropriations if unduly made[1].

Effect of Act XX:—The effect of Act XX of 1863 is to determine the right of superintendence vested under this section in the Board of Revenue so far as religious endowments are concerned[2].

Board to provide for appropriation of such endowments and for repair of public buildings.

3. It shall be the duty of the Board of Revenue to take *such measures as may be necessary to ensure* that all endowments made for the maintenance of establishments of the description above-mentioned are duly appropriated to the purpose for which they were destined by the Government or the individuals by whom such endowments were made. In like manner it shall be the duty of that Board to provide, with the sanction of Government, for the due repair and maintenance of all public edifices which have been erected at the expense either of the former or present Government, or of individuals, and which either are, or can be, rendered conducive to the convenience of the community.

B. R.

Appropriation of endowments.

3. It shall be the duty of the Board of Revenue [*and Board of Commissioners*[a]] to take *care* that all endowments made for the maintenance of establishments of the above description be duly appropriated to the purpose for which they were destined by the Government or individual by whom such endowments were granted. In like manner it shall be the duty of *the Board of Revenue*[b] to provide, with the sanction of Government, for the due repair and maintenance of all public edifices which have been erected,

---

a. The words in closed brackets have been repealed by the Repealing and Amending Act (I of 1903).

b. Substituted for '*those Boards*' by Act I of 1903 (the Repealing and Amending Act).

1. See S. 9 and *Seena, Pena, Reena, Seena Mayandi Chettiyar* v. *Chokkalingam Pillay*, (1904) L. R. 31 I. A. 83 (88): S. C. I. L. R., 27 M. 291 (295).

2. See pp. 155, 156 and notes to S. 1 of Act XX of 1863 pp. 8, 9 and 10.

either at the expense of the former or present Government, or of individuals, and which either at present are or can conveniently be rendered conducive to the convenience of the community.

NOTES.

Duties of Board.—S. 2 having stated the right of the Board this section states the duties. Two duties are mentioned in this section. (1) The duty of taking necessary measures to ensure that all endowments made for the maintenance of religious and charitable establishments are duly appropriated towards their proper or destined purposes. (2) The duty of providing with the sanction of Government for the maintenance and repair of all public edifices.

So far as Bengal is concerned this duty is taken away from the Board of Revenue (and Board of Commissioners) by Bengal Regulation XVII of 1816, S. 16.

Duty of Manager to send accounts:—To carry out the first duty managers are directed to send monthly, quarterly, and annual statements to the local agents[1].

Buildings fallen to decay or not calculated to be useful if repaired, how to be disposed of.

4. In those cases, however, in which any of the buildings *specified in the preceding section*[1] have fallen to decay, and cannot be conveniently repaired, or are not calculated, if repaired to afford any material accommodation to the public[2], the Board of Revenue shall *submit to Government their opinion as to the most expedient mode of disposing of such buildings*; and they shall be sold on the public account, or otherwise disposed of, *as the Governor in Council may determine.*

B. R.

Disposal of ruined buildings.

4. In those cases, however, in which any of the buildings *in question* have fallen to decay, and cannot, *from that other causes*, be conveniently repaired, or not calculated if repaired to afford any material accommodation to public, [a] the *Board* shall *recommend* that they be sold on the public account, or otherwise disposed of, *as may appear most expedient.*

---

a. Substituted for the word "Boards" by The Repealing and Amending I of 1903.

1. *Syud Keramut Ali* v. *Moonshee Abdool Wahab*, (1872) 17 W. R. C. R. 131

NOTES.

[1]. "**Buildings specified in the preceding section**":—*i. e.*, public edifices which have been erected at the expense either of the former or present Government, or of individuals. The Bengal Regulation has "any of the buildings in question."

[2]. "**Have fallen to decay** ...... **to the public**":—Duty is imposed on the Board to submit their opinion as to the most expedient mode of disposing of public edifices in 2 cases:—(1) when the public edifices have fallen to decay and cannot be conveniently repaired; or (2) when the public edifices have fallen to decay and are not calculated, if repaired, to afford any material accommodation *i. e.*, use, or enjoyment or convenience to the public.

The Governor in Council may then direct the sale of such edifices on the public account or may otherwise dispose of the same.

Board to prevent endowments from being appropriated to private uses.

5. Under the foregoing rules it *may* be incumbent on the Board of Revenue to prevent any *endowments in land or money*, which have been granted for the support of establishments of the above description, *or any public edifices*, from being converted to the private use of individuals or *otherwise misappropriated*.

B. R.

Lands or public edifices not to be appropriated by individuals for private uses.

5. Under the foregoing rules it *will of course* be incumbent on the Board of Revenue [*and Board of Commissioners*a] to prevent any *lands* which have been granted for the support of establishments of the above description from being converted to the private use of individuals, *or appropriated in any other mode contrary to the intent and will* [*of the donor; and likewise to prevent all public edifices from being usurped by individuals and falling into the possession and exclusive use of private persons.*

NOTES.

This section only sums up the effect of the preceding sections. Duty is imposed under this section upon the Board of Revenu

---

a. The words in closed brackets have been repealed by the Repealing and Amending Act I of 1903.

to prevent endowments and other public edifices from being converted to the private use of individuals or otherwise misappropriated. For the due discharge of this duty the Board is empowered under S. 13 of the Madras Regulation (corresponding to S. 14 of the Bengal Regulation) to appoint trustees or managers in certain cases. For the due discharge of this duty trustees or managers were before Act XX of 1863 directed to send monthly, quarterly and annual statements to the Board or local agents[1].

B. R.

Estimates of necessary repairs to be submitted to Government.

6. *Whenever the Board of Revenue [and Board of Commissioners[a]] may be of opinion that any of the above-mentioned edifices require repair, they shall obtain the necessary estimates of the expense required for the execution of the work, and forward them to Government for its approval.*

NOTES.

Bengal Regulation XVII of 1816, S. 16, having repealed so much of this Regulation as requires the Board to provide for the due repair of public edifices such as bridges, sarais and kattras, the retention of the section seems to be no longer necessary.

This section is not to be found in the Madras Regulation but it will follow from Ss. 3 and 4 which impose a duty on the Board to make repairs with the sanction of Government that the Board must submit estimates.

General superintendence of escheats.

6. The general superintendence of all escheats[1] is likewise hereby vested in the Board of Revenue, who will, through the channel hereafter mentioned, inform themselves fully of all property of that description, and *submit* to Government their *opinion as to the most expedient mode of disposing thereof; and the same shall be sold on the public account, or otherwise disposed of, as the Governor in Council may determine.*

---

a. The words in closed brackets have been repealed by the Repealing and Amending Act (I of 1903).

1. *Syud Keramut Ali* v. *Moonshee Abdool Wahab*, (1872) 17 W. R. C. R., 13[illegible] (135).

B. R.

7. The general superintendence of all *nazul property or* escheats[1] is likewise hereby vested in the Board of Revenue [*and Board of Commissioners respectively*[a]] who will inform themselves fully through the channel hereafter mentioned of all property of that description, and *report* to Government *whether it should in their opinion be sold on the public account, or in what other mode it should be disposed of.*

Superintendence of Nazul property.

NOTES.

[1]. "**All escheats**" :—Lands or any property falling to the State through want of heirs or forfeiture by rebellion. The Regulations do not purport to define the cases in which Government will be entitled by escheat to any property but only to vest the property escheated to them under the superintendence of the Board. This section and S. 9 corresponding to Ss. 7 and 10 of the Bengal Regulation do not limit the operation of the Regulations to property already vested in Government by escheat. Future escheats also come within the scope of the Regulations. This is one argument to show that the Board is also vested with the superintendence of endowments made since the Regulations for religious and charitable purposes. The Regulations deal with all these in the same way.

Right of Crown.

Escheat can be claimed only by the Crown. There being no feudal law in India a Zemindar who has carved out an alienable and hereditary subordinate tenure cannot claim such tenure on the failure of the heirs of the derivative holder.[1] But the Crown can lay claim to a property as an escheat only on failure of all heirs.[2] This principle cannot obviously apply in the case of religious and charitable endowments. The laws of inheritance do not apply to such property[3]. If the property is a religious endowment, it is regarded

a. The words in closed brackets have been repealed by the Repealing and Amending Act (I of 1903).

1. *Ranee Sonet Kowar* v. *Mirza Himmut Bahadoor*, (1876) L. R. 3 I. A. 92 : S. C. I.L.R.,1 C. 391 ; *Nil Madhub Sikdar* v. *Narattam Sikdar*, (1890) I.L.R., 17 C. 826 (828).

2. *The Collector of Masulipatam* v. *Cavaly Vencata Narrainapah*, (1860) 8 M. I. A. 500 ; *Gridhari Lall* v. *The Bengal Government*, (1868) 12 M. I. A. 448.

3. *Elder widow of Raja Chutter Sein* v. *Younger widow of Chutter Sein*, (1807) 1. B. S. D. A. 180 ; *Shah Imam Bukhsh* v. *Moosummat Beebee Shahee*, (1835) 6 B. S. D. A. 22. See Chapter IX p. cxxi. See also Chapters XII and XIII.

as belonging to the Deity[1]. The fact that services are not performed or that the pagoda is abandoned will not entail a forfeiture of the endowed property for the benefit of the Crown or will not entitle Government to claim the same by escheat[2]. It is clear that the Crown cannot resume the same on failure of the services unless there is a condition to that effect at the time of the original grant. A private endower cannot resume the same and a similar condition in his favor will probably be regarded as void as opposed to the rule of perpetuities[3]. It is not clear how endowed property will escheat[4]. If the purposes for which the property is endowed fail, *i.e.*, if there is a failure of objects, the rule of *cypres* may be applied and the Court will apply the funds *cypres*[5]. An equitable court applying the doctrine of *cypres* no doubt applies it by virtue of a power vested in the Sovereign which power is exercised through the Courts. But this is different from the doctrine of escheat. Notwithstanding this there were several orders of the Madras Board of Revenue[6] to the effect that all lapses in pagoda and mosque endowments should be reported to the Board as they would escheat to the Crown, the Board being vested under this section with the general superintendence of all escheats. If only a money allowance was granted annually, the Government might, perhaps, stop the payment on the failure of the object for which the allowance was made. But this is not on the ground of escheat.

Local agents.

7. To enable the Board of Revenue the better to carry into effect the duties intrusted to them by this Regulation, local agents shall be appointed in each Zila, subject to the authority, control and orders of that Board.

B. R.

Appointment of local agents.

8. To enable the Board of Revenue [*and Board of Commissioners*[a]] the better to carry into effect the duties intrusted to them by this Regulation, local

a. The words in closed brackets have been repealed by the Repealing and Amending Act I of 1903.

1. *Ram Sundar Rey* v. *Heirs of Raja Udwant Singh*, (1832) 5 B. S. D. A. 210. See Chapters VIII and IX, pp. xcvi, xcvii, xcix, cvii, cvvii, cxxi, cxxii.

2. See *The Secretary of State for India* v. *Haibatrao Hari* (1903) I. L. R., 28 B. 276 where the Bombay High Court held that there could be no escheat to the Crown of corporate property on the dissolution of the corporation.

3. A custom to resume under such circumstances may be valid. Cf. *Perkash Lal* v. *Rameshwar Nath Singh*, (1904) I. L. R., 31 C. 561 (569).

4. W. and B. Dig of H. L. p. 741 note (*d*) and Steele p. 235.

5. *The Incorporated Society* v. *Price*, (1884) 1 Jo. Lat. 498: S. C: 68 R. R. 329.

6. Maskell's Standing Orders of the Madras Board of Revenue, p. 499 (under date 23rd August 1849). This is not repeated in the authorized edition now issued and the definition of escheat there given will not cover this case.

agents shall be appointed in each Zila subject to the authority, control and orders of *the Boards*.

NOTES.

Local agents are appointed to facilitate the Board in the discharge of the duties imposed upon them by the Regulations. The appointment does not rest with the Board but with the Governor in Council (see S. 8) corresponding to S. 9 of the Bengal Regulation. Prior to the Regulations it was only through the executive officers of the District, the Government was exercising similar rights of superintendence and just as this Regulation imposed a legal obligation upon the Board to exercise these duties the old manner in which such duties were being discharged was at the same time recognised by statute by Ss. 7 and 8 (corresponding to Ss. 8 and 9 of the Bengal Regulation)[1].

Ex-officio agents.

8. The Collector of the Zila shall be *ex-officio* one of those agents, and the Governor in Council, when he deems it necessary, may appoint any other public officer or officers from the civil, military or medical branch of the service, to act in conjunction with him.

B. R.

Collector to be *ex-officio* agent with others.

9. The Collector of the Zila shall be *ex-officio* one of those agents, with whom the *Local Government*[b] will unite such other public officers, whether in the civil, military or medical branch of the service, as may from time to time be judged expedient.

NOTES.

The Bengal section was modified by Act XXXVIII of 1837 (Bengal Local Agent) which ran thus :—" It is hereby enacted, in modification of the provision contained in S. 9, Regulation XIX of 1810 of the Bengal Code, that no person shall, by reason of his not being in the civil, military or medical branch of the service,

---

a. Substituted for the expression "those boards respectively" by Act I of 1903 (The Repealing Amending Act 1903).

b. By Act I of 1903 (The Repealing and Amending Act) the words "Governor General-in-Council" used originally should be read as if the words "Local Government" were substituted therefor.

1. *Rajah Muttu Ramalinga* v. *Perianayagum*, (1874) L. R. 1 I. A. 209 (235).

be incapable of being appointed a Local Agent." This Act has been repealed by the Repealing Act VIII of 1868.

The Collector of the Zillah (*i. e.*, the District Collector) shall be *ex-officio* (*i. e.*, by virtue of his office as Collector of the District) one of the local agents and to act in conjunction with, or to assist him, other local agents may be appointed by the Governor in Council or local Government. A field for selection is thus given and apparently it will not be legal to appoint anybody as a *local agent* unless the person selected be a public officer in the civil, military or medical branch of the Government service. During the period of Government connection with religious endowments this was true only in the Madras Presidency. In Bengal, however, Act XXXVIII of 1837 already referred to provided that the appointment by the Governor in Council of a person who was not in any of the three branches of service mentioned in this section was nevertheless good and as a matter of fact even native local agents were appointed[1].

Agents to ascertain particulars of endowments &c., and report to Board ;

9. Under the provisions of the present Regulation, it will be the duty of the local agents to obtain full information from the public records and by personal inquiries, respecting all endowments, establishments and buildings of the nature of those *before* described, and *respecting* all escheats, [¹] and to report to the Board of Revenue any instance in which they may have reason to believe that lands or buildings, *or the rent or revenues derived from lands*, are unduly appropriated, [²] being in all cases careful not to infringe any private rights, or to occasion unnecessary trouble or vexation to individuals.

B. R.

Agents to ascertain and report particulars of endowments, &c :

10. Under the provisions of the present Regulation, it will *of course* be the duty of the agents to obtain full information from the public records, and by personal inquiries, respecting all endowments, establishments and buildings of the nature of those *above* described, and *of* all *nazul property or* escheats[¹], and to report to the Board [*to whose authority those agents are respectively subject*[a]] any instnces in which they may have

a. The words in closed brackets have been repealed by the Repealing and Amending Act I of 1903.

1. Parliamentary return 1849, Idolatry (India) p. 416.

reason to believe that the lands or buildings are improperly appropriated[2]: being in all cases careful not to infringe any private rights, or to occasion unnecessary trouble or vexation to individuals.

NOTES.

This and the following three sections, *i. e.*, Ss. 10 to 12 (corresponding to Ss. 11 to 13 of the Bengal Regulation) detail the duties imposed on the *local agents.* They are :—(1) the ascertainment of particulars of *all* endowments, establishments, buildings (of the nature before described) and escheats (S. 9 corresponding to S. 10 of the Bengal Regulation) ; (2) reporting to the Board if revenues are unduly appropriated (S. 9 corresponding to S. 10 of the Bengal Regulation) ; (3) reporting to the Board the names of the present managers &c., and the authority of their appointment &c. (S. 10 corresponding to S. 11 of the Bengal Regulation) ; (4) reporting to the Board all vacancies and casualties together with all circumstances to enable the Board to judge of the claims of the several claimants (S. 11 corresponding to Bengal S. 12) ; and (5) recommending fit persons for nomination by the Board in cases where the nomination rests with Government. (S. 12 corresponding to Bengal S. 13.)

[1]. "**All endowments......all escheats**" :—This *prima facie* includes endowments coming into existence after the Regulation. The same is the case with escheats.

[2]. "**Lands or buildings or the rent or revenues derived from lands are unduly appropriated**":—The judicial committee has held in a recent case[1] that the effect of this section is to do away with the powers of lease possessed by the manager before theRegulations. This section imposes a duty on the local agents similar to the one imposed on the Board by S. 5. This section also takes care to protect private rights[2]. What the exact significance of this protection

---

1. *Sena, Pena, Reena, Seena Mayandi Chettiyar* v. *Chokkalingam Pillay*, (1904) L. R. 31 I. A. 83 ; S. C. I. L. R., 27 M. 291.

2. See *Raghavacharry* v. *Yavaluppah*, (1841) M. S. D. A. p. 37 where it is observed that the entire management of the pagoda affairs rests with the Dharmakarta and in the exercise of this power he is left unrestricted by the Hindu Law and the Regulations. But the Regulations here referred to are the Regulations which deal with the law to be applied by courts in given cases. See notes to S. 14 of the Madras Regulation.

is has not been considered in the Privy Council case[1]. If it is said that the local agents have the power not to affirm leases made by managers in case they find it not beneficial to the religious or charitable institutions, that is a different matter. But according to the decision of the Privy Council[1] the effect of the Regulations was to supersede the powers of managers to alienate charitable (including religious) property and to sanction the revision of existing appropriations if unduly made. If this be the effect of the Regulations, the repeal of the Regulations as regards religious endowments will not of itself restore the old law[2]. So that in cases falling under S. 3 of Act XX of 1863, managers appointed by committees will not have the powers of leasing endowed property but as the Act in Ss. 7 and 12 states that the duties of the Board will devolve upon the committee the latter will have the right to alienate for purposes binding upon the institution under the control of the committee. S. 4 of the Act declares that the duties of Board will fall upon the manager to whom property is transferred under that section. So that, managers of institutions falling under S. 4 of the Act will have the right to alienate for purposes binding on the institutions under their control.

to report names, &c., of present trustees or managers and by what authority appointed ;

10. The said local agents shall further ascertain and report *to the Board of Revenue* the names of the present trustees, managers or superintendents [[1]] of the several institutions, foundations or establishments [[2]] above described, *together with other particulars respecting them,* and by whom and under what authority they have been appointed or elected, and whether in conformity to the special provisions of the original endowment and appropriation by the founder, or under any general rules or maxims applicable to such institutions and foundations.

B. R.

also names &c., of present trustees or managers :

11. The said agents will further ascertain and report the names together with other particulars, of the present trustees, managers or superintendents of the several institutions, foundations or establish-

1. *Mayandi Chettiyar* v. *Chokkalingam Pillay,* (1904) L. R. 31 I. A. 83 ; S. C. I. L. R., 27 M. 291.

2. Maxwell, pp. 585, 586.

ments above described, *whether under the designation of mutawali or any other*, and by whom and under what authority appointed or elected, and whether in conformity to the special provisions of the original endowment and appropriation by the founder, or under any general rule or maxim applicable to such institutions and foundations.

NOTES.

It is the duty of the local agents to see that the institutions are under the management of the rightful persons. The appointment of a manager must be in conformity with the rule laid down by the founder or the general rules and maxims applicable to such institutions[1].

[1]. "**Trustees, Managers, or Superintendents**":—These words have been indifferently used. This is also the terminology adopted in Act XX of 1863.

[2]. "**Institutions, foundations or establishments**":—These are not the same as endowments. Endowments are made for the institutions &c. For the meaning of these words, see Ch. II, pp. xi and xii.

Evidence:—The reports made by collectors or local agents in pursuance of this and the next succeeding section being made by public officers in the course of duty and statutory authority are admissible as evidence under S. 35 of the Evidence Act although such reports may express opinions on the private rights of parties.[2] But, such opinions must not be regarded as having judicial authority[3].

to report to Board vacancies or casualties, and pretensions of claimants;

11. The local agents shall also report to the Board of Revenue all vacancies [1] and casualties which may occur, with full information of all circumstances, to enable that Board to judge of the pretensions of the person or persons claiming the trust, particularly whether the succession has been heretofore by inheritance in the line of descent, or whether the successor has been in former instances elected, and by whom, or whether he has been nominated by the founder, or his heir or

1. *Wasiq Uli Khan* v. *The Government*, (1836) 6 B. S. D. A. 110.

2. *Rajah Muttu Ramalinga Setupati* v. *Perianayagum Pillai*, (1874) L. R. 1 I. A. 209 (238, 239).

3 *Ibid*, 238.

representative, or by any other individual patron of the foundation, or by any officer or representative of Government, or directly by the Government itself [2].

B. R.

and all vacancies or casualties with full information as to pretensions of claimants :

12. The local agents will also report to the *Board of Revenue*[a] all vacancies [1] and casualties which may occur, with full information of all circumstances, to enable the *Board*[b] to judge of the pretensions of the person or persons claiming the trust ; particularly whether the succession have (sic) been heretofore by inheritance in the line of descent, or whether the successor have (sic) been in former instances elected, and by whom, or whether he have (sic) been nominated by the founder or his heir or representative, or by any other individual patron of the foundation, or by any officer or representative of Government, or directly by the Government itself [2].

NOTES.

[1]. " **All vacancies** ":—The vacancy may arise from any cause, *i. e.*, death, resignation or removal[1]. The vacancies and casualties which the local agents are required to report are, we presume, with reference to the offices of trustee, manager, or superintendent. That is the proper construction, to be placed having regard to the subsequent language in this section and the language of the preceding section.

[2]. " **Whether the succession.........Government itself** ":— In the case of a vacancy, the report of the local agents should state whether the office of trustee &c. devolves (1) by right of inheritance, (2) by election, or (0) by nomination (a) by the founder or his heirs or (b) by any other individual patron or (c) by any officer or representative of Government or (d) by the Government directly. Where the office devolves by nomination by Government or by any public officer, the local agents are required under S. 12 to propose competent persons for the approval of the Board. The Board has

---

a. Substituted for " Superior Boards" by Act I of 1903 (The Repealing and Amending Act).

b. Substituted for " Boards" by the above Act.

1. *Gopinadha Panda* v. *Ramachandra*, (1896) 6 M. L. J. R. 255.

a right to see that the proper managers are in charge of the charitable institutions and in cases where there is no proper election to direct a fresh election[1].

Power of Local agents to dismiss :—In a case where the office devolves by nomination upon the Government or any public officer the local agents have, according to the decisions, a power as incidental to their duties to remove managers &c., for misconduct[2]. But this does not disentitle such managers to dismiss subordinate servants of the institutions[3]. If such subordinate servants hold hereditary offices then the dismissal must be for sufficient cause[3]. Whether the local agents have such rights has not so far as we are aware been raised in any case. But we do not see why they have no such rights[4]. The local agents have, however, no right to dismiss hereditary managers for misconduct[5] although they have the power to take away the management from them and assume the management themselves[6] or provide for such management in any other way.

After Act XX of 1863 the Board or local Agents have no right to dismiss a manager of a religious endowment upon any ground[7] just as much as they have no right to appoint a manager[8].

---

1. *Narain Das* v *Bindrabun Das*, (1815) 2 B. S. D A: 151 ; *Ram Churn Das* v. *Chuttur Bhoje*, (1845) 7 B. S. D. A. 205 where an assembly was directed to be held by the local agents on account of the disqualification of a person previously elected.

2 *Wasik Ali Khan* v. *The Government*, (1834) 5 B. S. D. A. 363: S. C. (1836) 6 B. S. D. A. 110 ; *Ram Churn Das* v. *Chuttur Bhoje*, (1845) 7 B. S. D. A. 205 ; *Kassyvassy Kristna Putter* v *Vangala Shangaranat Jesser* (1858) M. S. D. A p. 39 ; *Chinna Rangaiyungar* v. *Subbraya Mudali*, (1867) 3 M. H. C. 334 (336). Cf. *Moohummad Sadik* v. *Moohummud Ali*, (1798) 1 B. S. D. A. 17.

3. *Ragharacharry* v. *Yavaluppa*, (1849) M. S. D. A. p. 37 ; *Subturshy Goorookul* v. *Tambia Pillay*, (1854) M. S. D. A. p. 81 ; *Vadachella Goorookul* v. *Sabapaty Chetty*, (1855) M. S. D. A. p. 78 ; *Ranee Purvata Vurdhany Nauchear* v. *Mungalasuara Goorookul*, (1856) M. S. D. A p. 165. The dismissal is liable to revision in Civil Courts.

4. See Parliamentary Return 1849, Idolatry (India), pp. 132, 133, 199, 217 and 409.

5. *Local Agents of Zillah Hooghly* v. *Krishnanund Dundee*, (1848) 7 B. S. D. A. 476. But see *Wasik Ali Khan* v. *The Government*, (1834) 5. B. S. D. A. 363: S. C. (1836) 6 B. S. D A. 110 explained in *Chinna Rangaiyangar* v. *Subbraya Mudali*, (1867) 3 M. H. C. 334 (336). See the other decisions referred to in note (2). But see the case of *Poonjc Matam* in North Arcot District referred to in the letter from the Secretary, Revenue Board, to the Chief Secretary to Government, dated 7th July 1843. Parliamentary Return 1849, Idolatry (India) p. 194.

6. *Jusagheri Gosamiar* v. *The Collector of Tanjore*, (1870), 5 M. H. C. 334 (343). See also *Wasik Ali Khan* v. *The Government*, (1834) 5 B. S. D. A. 363 : S. C. (1836) B. S. D. A. 110 ; and *Local Agents of Zillah Hooghly* v. *Krishnanund Dundee*, (1848) B. S. D. A. 476.

7. *The Secretary of State for India* v. *Abdul Hakkim*, (1880) I. L. R., 2 M. 294 ; *Balwant Rao* v. *Purun Mal*, (1883) L. R. 10 I. A. 90 (93) : S. C. I. L. R., 6 A. 1. (6).

8. *The Secretary of State for India* v. *Abdul Hakkim*, (1880) I. L. R., 2 M. 294 ; *Mahomed* v. *Ganapati*, (1889) I. L. R., 13 M. 277.

12. In those cases in which the nomination has usually rested with the Government, or with a public officer, or *in which* no private person *may be* competent and entitled to make sufficient provision for the succession to the trust and management[1] it will be the further duty of the local agents to propose, for the approval and confirmation of the Board of Revenue, a person or persons for the charge of trustee, manager or superintendent, *strictly* attending to the qualifications of the person *or persons* selected, [2] and to any special provisions of the original endowments and foundation, and to the general rules or the known usages of the country applicable to such cases.

to recommend fit persons where right of nomination rests with Government.

B. R.

13. In those cases in which the nomination has usually rested with the *present or former* Government, or with a public officer, or *of right appertains to Government*, *in consequence of* no private person *being* competent and entitled to make sufficient provision for the succession to the trust and management [1], it will be the further duty of the local agents to propose, for the approval and confirmation of the *Board of Revenue*a a *fit* person or persons for the charge of trustee or manager and superintendent, *duly* attending to the qualifications of the person selected[2] and to any special provisions of the original endowment and foundation, and to the general rules or the known usages of the country applicable to such cases.

to recommend fit persons in cases where nomination vests in Government

NOTES.

The local agents are required under this Section to propose a person fit and proper according to the established rules or usage for approval by the Board in the following cases :—(1) where the nomination has usually rested with the Government or with a public officer or (2) where there is no private person competent and entitled to make sufficient provision for the succession.

[1]. **"Or in which no private person...and management":—** This will arise in a case where the private person entitled t nominate dies without nomination and there is no other privat

---

a. Substituted for "Superior Board" by Act 1 of 1903 (The Repealing ar Amending Act).

individual entitled to nominate. Generally the actual incumbent of the office has the right of nominating his successor. He need not exercise his right with the previous knowledge and consent of the revenue authorities *i. e.*, the local agents[1]. If he dies without nominating any body or his nomination is void[2], then if the case is governed by the Hindu Law the management will vest in the founder and his heirs[3]. In the absence of the founder and his heirs, the right of nomination will devolve upon the Court in the absence of the Regulation. Under this section and S. 13 it will devolve upon the Board.

Where the right of nomination rests with the founder and his heirs but the founder and his line is extinct the right to nominate will under Ss. 12 and 13 rest with the Board.

If there is a person entitled to manage or to nominate, the fact that a report is made to the effect that there is no person entitled to manage and to nominate and that such report is acted upon will not debar the person entitled from bringing a suit to establish his right[4]. Where the Board appoints a person in the belief that he is hereditarily entitled and a suit is brought by the rightful person, the person so appointed cannot claim that he has been appointed under S. 12 and that thus he has a title which cannot be displaced.

The Board has no power to appoint if the two conditions mentioned in the begining of this note are not satisfied[5]. The Board under the Regulations has no authority to interfere in the appointment of a manager except where the right of appointment rests with, or has been solely exercised by, the ruling power[6].

[2]. "**Qualifications of the person or persons selected**" :— Under the Mahomedan Law, a female may manage the temporal affairs of an endowment but not the spiritual affairs. So that the

---

1. But see *dictum* of *Money* in *Wasik Ali Khan* v. *The Government*, (1836) 6 B. S. D. A. 110.

2. See *Sayad Muhammad* v. *Fatteh Muhammad*, (1894) L. R. 22 I. A. 4 : S. C. I. L. R., 22 C. 324.

3. *Jagannath Prasad Gupta* v. *Runjit Singh*, (1897) I. L. R., 25 C. 354. See also Chapters XII and XV. For Mahomedan Law, see Chapter XIII.

4. *Nallathambi Battar* v. *Nellakumara Pillai*, (1873) 7 M. H. C. 306 (311, 312). See notes to S. 14 of the Madras Regulation.

5. *Local Agents of Zillah Hooghly* v. *Krishnanund Dundee*, (1848) 7 B. S. D. A. 76

6. *Agri Sharma Embrandri*, v. *Vistnu Embrandri* (1866) 3 M. H. C. 198 (199).

person proposed must not be a female in the case of a vacancy in the office of Sajjadanashin but may be a female in the case of a vacancy in the office of Mutwalli[1]. Under the Hindu Law a female may be a *Dharmakarta*[2] or an *Archaka*[3] but cannot be an *Acharia Poroosha*[3]. Express regard should be had to the conditions of the deed of appropriation, the intentions of the appropriator and the particular law or usage applicable[4].

It has been held[5] that under the Regulations misappropriation will be a sufficient disqualification although it will not be so under the ordinary law or usage.

Board to appoint persons, or make other provisions for trust with reference to conditions of endowment.

13. On the receipt of the report and information required by the preceding clause, the Board of Revenue *shall* either appoint the person or persons nominated for their approval, or *shall* make such other provision for the trust, management or superintendence, as may *to them seem* right and fit, with reference to the nature and conditions of the endowment, having previously called for any further information from the local agents *that may appear to them to be requisite.*

B. R.

Board to appoint such persons, or make other provision for trust.

14. On the receipt of the report and information required by the preceding clause the Board of Revenue [*or Board of Commissioners*[a]) *will* either appoint the person or persons nominated for their approval, or *will* make such other provision for the trust, superintendence and management as may be right and fit with reference to the nature and conditions of the endowment, having previously called for any *requisite* further information from the local agents.

---

a. The words in closed brackets have been repealed by the Repealing and Amending Act (I of 1903).

1. *Shah Imam Bukhsh* v. *Moosummat Beebee*, (1835) 6 B. S. D. A. 22; *Hussain Beebee* v. *Hussain Sherif*, (1868) 4 M. H. C. 23. See further Chapter IX, p. cxvi and Chapter XIII.

2. *Sashammal* v. *Parker*, (1853) M. S. D. A. 237; *Parker* v. *Seshammal*, (1854) M. S. D. A. p. 182; *Sadagopa Charry* v. *Sadagopa Charry*, (1854) M. S. D. A. p. 55; See Chapter XII, pp. clvii to clxi.

3. *Seshammal* v. *Soondararajiengar*, (1858) M. S. D. A. p. 261. See further Chapter XII.

4. *Wasiq Uli Khan* v. *The Government*, (1836) 6 B. S. D. A 110.

5. *Ram Churn Das* v. *Chuttur Bhoje*, (1845) 7 B. S. D. A. 205. But criminal conviction for house-trespass or other offence may be no disqualification. *Mohunt Ram Nooj Doss* v. *Mohunt Debraj Doss*, (1839) 6 B. S D. A. 262; *Local Agents of Zillah Hooghly* v. *Krishnanund Dundee*, (1848) 7 B. S. D. A. 476.

NOTES.

In making the appointment regard must be had to the rules if any framed by the founder.[1] This section authorises the Board to make provision for the due administration of the endowments. This power though discretionary is not absolute and can be controlled by a Civil Court.[2]

The Board has not this power so far as religious endowments are concerned after the passing of Act XX of 1863.[3]

Effect of this Section:—It was held that by virtue of this section the Board could renounce the duties imposed upon it[4]. But this can hardly be the effect of the section. It only enables the Board in certain cases (mentioned in S. 12) to make provision for the due administration of the endowment. But this does not mean that they can give up the duty of superintendence. The power given by this section to the Board is though discretionary yet not absolute and can be controlled by a Civil Court.[5] It was held that this section would not entitle the Board to remove an incumbent who claimed to hold by virtue of an hereditary right although the Board might prevent misappropriation by appointing temporary curators &c.[6]

Persons feeling injured by orders under Regulation may sue for recovery of rights or for damages.

14. Nothing contained in this Regulation shall be construed to preclude any individual who may conceive that he has just grounds of complaint on account of any orders which may be passed by any of the before-mentioned authorities with respect to the appropriation of any lands or buildings, *or of any rents and revenues from lands*, of the nature of those before described, from suing in the mode and form prescribed by the Regulations where Government or public officers are parties; or under the general provisions of the Regulations, if the suit be brought against a competitor or other private person, for

1. *Wasiq Uli Khan* v. *The Government*, (1836) 6 B. S. D A. 110.
2. *Sheik Davud Saiba* v. *Hussein Saiba*, (1893) I. L. R., 17 M. 212,
3. *The Secretary of State for India* v. *Abdul Hakkim*, (1880) I. L. R., 2 M. 294; *Balwant Rao* v. *Purun Mall*, (1883) L.R. 10 I.A. 90 (93); *Mahomed* v. *Ganapati*,(1889) I. L. R., 13 M. 277.
4. L. *Venkatesa Nayudu* v. *Shrivan Shatagopa*, (1872) 7 M. H. C. 77. But this case is doubted in *Appasami* v. *Nagappa*, (1884) I. L. R., 7 M. 499. See further notes to S. 1, of the Regulations p. 164, and S. 3 of Act XX, pp. 14 to 16.
5. *Sheik Davud Saiba* v. *Hussein Saiba*, (1893) I. L. R., 17 M. 212.
6. *Local Agents of Zillah Hoogly* v. *Krishnanund Dundee*, (1848) 7 B. S. D.A. 476.

the recovery thereof in the regular course of law, or for compensation in damages for any loss or injury supposed to have been unduly sustained by him.

B. R.

15. Nothing contained in this Regulation shall be construed to preclude any individual who may conceive that he has just grounds of complaint on account of any orders which may be passed by any of the above-mentioned authorities, with respect to the appropriation of any lands or buildings of the nature of those described, from suing [*in the mode and form prescribed by the Regulations, where Government or public officers are parties; or under the general provisions of the Regulations if the suit be brought against a competitor or other private persons*] for the recovery thereof in the regular course of law, or for compensation in damages for any loss or injury supposed to have been unduly sustained by him.

Saving of private rights.

NOTES.

Scope and object of Section :—It is not intended by this section to limit the jurisdiction of Courts to cases contemplated by it[1]. The object of the section is to provide against the finality of erroneous orders passed by Board of Revenue[2]. The Regulation is only supplementary of existing remedies so that such remedies may be resorted to although suits relating to such remedies may not be exactly covered by this section[1].

Suits not barred by the Regulation :—A suit by a dharmakarta that his dismissal is wrongful and for restoration to office is not barred by this section[3]. So also a suit by a person holding

(*a*) The words in closed brackets have been repealed by the Repealing and Amending Act 1903 (I of 1903).

1. *Ponnambala Mudaliyar* v. *Varaguna Rama Pandia Chinntambiar*, (1872) 7 M. H. C. 117.

2. Ibid; *Nallathambi Battar* v. *Nellakumara Pillai*, (1873) 7 M. H. C. 306 (311). See also *Raghavacharry* v. *Yavaluppa*, (1849) M. S.D. A., p. 37; *Subturshy Goorookul* v. *Tambia Pillai*,(1854)M.S.D. A.81; *Vadachella Goorookul* v. *Sabapathy Chetty*,(1855) M. S. D. A. p. 78; *Kassyvassy Kristna Putter* v. *Vanyala Shangaranat Josser*, (1858) M. S. D. A. p. 39. See also note (3).

3. *Wasik Ali Khan* v. *Government*, (1834) 5B.S.D.A.363: S. C. (1836) 6 B.S. D. A. 110; *Ram Churn Das* v. *Chutter Bhoje*, (1845) 7 B. S. D. A. 205; *Local Agents of Zillah Hooghly* v. *Krishnanund Dundee*, (1848) 7 B. S. D. A. 476: *Casee Syed Ali* v. *Khadir Ali*, (1850) M. S. D. A. p. 80 (where a suit for establishing a personal right of superintendence was held not barred); *Kassyvassy Kristna Patter* v. *Vungala Shangaranat Josser*, (1858) M. S. D. A. p. 39; *Chinna Rangaiyangar* v. *Subbraya Mudali*, (1867) 3 M. H. C. 334. See also *Doddacharyar* v. *Paroomal Naicken*, (1850) M. S. D. A. 98.

an hereditary office in a temple and subordinate to the Dharmakarta is not barred[1]. Any person alleging himself to be aggrieved by orders passed by the local agents under the Regulations has his remedy in a Civil Court[2]. Suits for removal of managers for misconduct and for appointment of new managers may be brought under the ordinary law and are not barred by the Regulations[3].

A suit by the grantees to contest the right of Government to resume an inam granted for the support of a chattram can be brought in the Civil Courts[4].

Powers of a manager:—It has been held that a manager appointed by Government may sue himself for recovery of endowed lands and that the Government need not sue[5]. He is a procurator of Government[6]. But the Judicial Committee decided recently that the Regulation took away the rights of the managers to alienate endowed property even for necessity[7]. So that the decision in *Raghavacharry* v. *Yavaluppa*[8] which held that the manager was unfettered by the Regulations in the exercise of his duties with reference to the charitable or religious institutions[8] must now be explained as not being applicable to the manager's powers of lease or other alienation.

15. It is to be clearly understood that the object of the present Regulation is solely to provide for the due appropriation of lands *or other*

Object of Regulation.

1. *Raghavacharry* v. *Yavaluppa*, (1849) M. S. D. A. p. 37; *Subturshy Goorookul* v. *Tumbia Pillay*, (1854) M. S. D. A. p. 81; *Vadachella Goorookul* v. *Sabapathy Chetty*, (1855) M. S. D. A. p. 78.

2. *Doddacharryar* v. *Paroomal Naicken*, (1850) M. S. D. A. p. 98; *Nallathambi Battar* v. *Nellakumara Pillai*, (1873) 7 M. H. C. 306.

3. *Kassyvassy Kristna Patter* v. *Vungala Shangaranath Josser*, (1858) M. S. D. A. p. 39 (F.B.) [overruling in effect *Ranee Purvata Vurdhany Nauchear* v. *Mungalaswara Goorookul*, (1856) M. S. D. A. p. 165; *Daseekaniengar* v. *Singamiengar*, (1857) M. S. D. Ap. 5; and *Vurdacharry* v. *Ahobilum Veeraghava Aiyar*, (1857) M. S. D. A p. 161]; *Ponnambala Mudaliyar* v. *Varaguna Rama Pandia Chinnatambiar*, (1872) 7 M. H. C. 117; *Subbayya* v. *Krishna*, (1890) I. L. R., 14 M. 186 (197, 205, 206, 209, 220 and 221). See also Chapter XV.

4. *Subramanya Ayyar* v. *The Secretary of State for India*, (1883) I. L R. 6 M. 361.

5. *Jewun Doss Sahoo* v. *Shah Kubeer-Ood-Deen*, (1841) 2 M. I. A 390.

6. Ibid. After XX of 1863, a manager of a religious endowment is not a procurator of Government. See note (5) to p. 10 of the notes to S. 1 of Act XX of 1863.

7. See notes to S. 9 of the Madras Regulation, pp. 173 and 174.

8. *Raghavacharry* v. *Yavaluppa*, (1849) M. S. D. A. p. 37 (38). See note (2) p. 173.

endowments granted for public purposes [1] agreeably to the intent of the grantor, and not to resume any part of them, *or of their* produce, for the benefit of Government. In like manner it is fully intended that all buildings erected by any former or the present Government, or by individuals, for the convenience of the public, should be exclusively appropriated to that purpose, with the exception of such as have fallen to decay and cannot be conveniently repaired, or which can no longer contribute to the accommodation of the community.

B. R.

Object of Regulation.

16. It is to be clearly understood that the object of the present Regulation is solely to provide for the due appropriation of lands granted for public purposes[1] agreeably to the intent of the grantor, and not to resume any part of the produce of them for the benefit of Government.

In like manner it is fully intended that all buildings erected by the former or present Government or by individuals for the convenience of the public should be exclusively appropriated to that purpose, with the exception of such as have fallen to decay and cannot *from that or any other cause* be conveniently repaired, or which, *under existing circumstances*, can no longer contribute to the accommodation of the community.

NOTES.

Care is naturally taken to disabuse the belief, if any, of any person that the object of the Government is only to make provisions for the due appropriation of endowments but not to resume them.[1] The section was only intended to remove any suspicion that might lurk among the Hindus or Mahomedans. But so much concern was taken in the management of their religious endowments and the Government connection or interference proved so effective a check upon mismanagement that as a matter of fact the measure was greatly popular and it was only the withdrawal of the superintendence that was looked upon with great regret.

[1] "**Endowments granted for public purposes**":—These sections[2] chiefly determine the question as to the nature of endowments applicable according to the Regulations. The Regulations apply only to endowments for public purposes and this may no

1. *Subramanya Ayyar* v. *The Secretary of State for India*, (1883) I. L. R., 6 M. 361.

2. S. 15 of the Madras and S. 16 of the Bengal Regulations. See also p. 164.

be taken to be settled law.[1] The decisions which hold that the Regulations apply only to endowments for public purposes mainly rely upon this section[2]. Some also refer to the preamble and the general provisions of the Regulations[3]. The case of *Jan Ali* v. *Ram Nath Mandul*[4] simply states that the Regulation is applicable to a particular class of endowments viz., endowments in land (or money) granted by former rulers of this country or by British Government or by individuals. The remarks which I have already made regarding this case in the notes to Act XX must be borne in mind.[5] As to what is a public or charitable purpose, see Chapter VI[6].

Native servants and others guilty of fraud or embezzlement, be punished.

16. *The legislative provisions now in force,* [1] *or which may hereafter be enacted, for the punishment of fraud or embezzlement in the Native servants of Government employed under the Collector in the Department of land revenue, shall be held applicable to all Native servants and to all trustees, managers or superintendents, employed in or charged with, the settlement, custody or appropriation of the revenues, funds, or other property of the public institutions referred to in this Regulation.*

NOTES.

This section is not be found in the Bengal Regulation.

[1] "**The legislative provision now in force**":—These are the Madras Revenue Malversation Regulation (IX of 1822), its amendment Regulation (III of 1823) and the Madras Subordinate Collectors and Revenue Malversation (Amendment Regulation VII of 1828).

But after Act XX of 1863, these Regulations will not apply to native religious endowments.

1. *Delroos Banoo Begum* v. *Nawab Syed Ashgur Ally Khan*, (1875) 15 B. R. 167: S. C. 23 W. R. 457; *Sathappayyar* v. *Periasami*, (1890) I. L. R., 14 M: 1; *Protap Chandra Misser* v. *Brojonath Misser*, (1890) I. L. R., 19 C. 275. See also *Bibee Kuneez Fatima* v. *Bibee Saheba Jan*, (1867) 8 W. R. C. R. 313.
2. *Delroos Banoo Begum* v. *Nawab Syed Ashgur Ally Khan*, (1875) 15 B. L. R. 167; *Protap Chandra Misser* v. *Brojonath Misser*, (1891) I. L. R., 19 C. 275.
3. *Sathappayyar* v. *Periasami*, (1890) I. L. R., 14. M. 1.
4. (1881) I. L. R., 8 Cal. 32.
5. See notes to S. 14 pp. 83 and 84.
6. Ch. VI pp. lxv to lxxxi.

PAPENDIX II.

THE COORG TEMPLE FUNDS MANAGEMENT REGULATION, 1892.

Contents.

REGULATION No. IV OF 1892.

(Received the Governor General's assent on the 14th November, 1892, published in the Gazette of India of 3rd December, 1892, Part I, p. 702, and in the Coorg District Gazette of 2nd January, 1893, Part I, p 1).

A REGULATION FOR THE MANAGEMENT OF TEMPLE FUNDS IN COORG.

Whereas certain temples and religious institutions in Coorg are in receipt of annual cash allowances from the Government;

And whereas it is necessary to provide for the due application of such allowances, and of certain other moneys of which the said temples and religious institutions are in receipt or possession;

It is hereby enacted as follows :—

Title, application and commencement.

1 (1). This Regulation may be called the Coorg Temple Funds Management Regulation, 1892.

(2). It applies to the temples and institutions named in the schedule and to such other temples or institutions as the Chief Commissioner, with the previous sanction of the Governor General in Council, may, by notification in the Coorg District Gazette, from time to time direct; and

(3). It shall come into force on such day* as the Chief Commissioner may, by a like notification, appoint.

Interpretation clause.

2. In this Regulation the words "funds" and "said funds" mean the Muzarayi funds, that is to say :—

(*a*) the cash allowances for the time being paid by the Government for the maintenance of the said temples and institutions;

(*b*) all bequests, gifts and offerings to or for the said temples and institutions;

(*c*) all funds invested or in hand to the credit of the said temples and institutions at the commencement of this Regulation; and

(*d*) the income accruing from all lands which have been or may hereafter be granted either partially or wholly rent-free for the said temples and institutions.

---

* The 15th January 1893—See Coorg District Gazette, 1893, part I, p. 3.

3. The said funds shall be under the management and control of a committee, which shall consist of fifteen members appointed or elected as hereinafter provided.

Committee of management and its constitution.

4. The Chief Commissioner shall appoint the members of the first committee from among the persons qualified for election as hereinafter provided, and shall divide the members so appointed into three groups of five members each, and shall so fix the term of office of each member that one member from each of such groups shall retire annually commencing from the end of the first year. All vacancies so caused and all other vacancies shall be filled by election.

Appointment and election of members of committee.

5. The Chief Commissioner shall from time to time, as occasion may require, make rules regulating—

Power of Chief Commissioner to make rules.

(a) the division of the said temples and institutions into three groups for the purpose of electing five members each;

(b) the protection of Coorgs to non-Coorgs in the representatives to be elected for each group;

(c) the qualifications of electors and candidates for election;

(d) the registration of electors;

(e) the times of election and the mode of recording votes; and

(f) all other matters necessary for carrying this Regulation into effect:

Provided that no person shall be qualified for election who—

(1) is not a male Hindu of not less than twenty-five years of age, and a native of or a settled resident in Coorg;

(2) is unable to read and write Kanarese;

(3) is an insolvent;

(4) has been convicted of any such offence, or has been subjected by a Criminal Court to any such order, as implies, in the opinion of the District Judge, a defect of character which unfits him to be a member:

Provided also that no one shall be qualified to be an elector who is not a male Hindu of not less than twenty-five years of age and a native of or a settled resident in Coorg:

Provided also that, for the purposes of this section, all Hindus who have resided in Coorg for five years immediately before election shall be taken to be settled residents therein.

Eligibility of members of committee for election or re-election.

6. Except as provided in S. 4, the term of office of members of committee shall be five years; but an outgoing member shall, if otherwise qualified, be eligible for election or re-election.

Resignation of members of committee.

7. Any member of committee may resign his office by letter to the District Judge, and on his resignation being accepted in writing by the District Judge he shall be deemed to have vacated his office.

Removal of members of committee.

8. The District Judge may from time to time remove any member who refuses or without sufficient excuse neglects to act, or has absented himself from three consecutive meetings of the committee, or who is or has become incapable of acting, or has been declared an insolvent or been convicted of any such offence, or subjected to any such order, as is referred to in clause (4) of the first proviso to S. 5.

Casual vacancies.

9. Upon the occurrence of any vacancy by the resignation, removal or death of a member, a new member shall be elected to fill the place, and shall hold office for the time for which it was tenable by the member whose place he fills.

Incapacity of member of committee to have personal interest.

10. No member of committee shall be capable of being or acting as manager of, or shall hold any paid office connected with, any of the said temples and institutions.

President of committee.

11. The committee shall elect one of their own body as president.

Quorum.

12. The quorum necessary for the transaction of business at a meeting of the committee shall not be less than five.

President of meetings of committee.

13 At every meeting of the committee the president, if present, shall preside. In his absence the committee shall elect a president for that meeting.

Decision of question by majority of votes.

14. All questions coming before the committee shall be decided by a majority of the votes of the members present. In the case of an equality of votes the president of the meeting shall have a second or casting vote.

Appointment of managers.

15. (1) The committee shall from time to time appoint one or more suitable person or persons to be manager or managers of the said temples and institutions respectively, and may for sufficient cause fine or remove any person so appointed.

(2). Nothing in sub-section (1) shall be held to empower the committee to refuse without sufficient cause to appoint as manager or managers the person or persons (if any) possessing hereditary or other rightful claims to be so appointed.

(3). The amount of fine imposable under sub-section (1) shall not exceed one month's pay of the person fined.

Duties of manager, and accounts to be submitted by him.

16. The committee shall prescribe the duties to be performed by such manager or managers respectively, and shall require the production at least once a year of full, complete and separate accounts of receipts and disbursements on behalf of such temples and institutions respectively, in such form as the committee may direct.

Audit of accounts.

17. The District Judge may from time to time call for the accounts of all or any of the said temples and institutions; and may from time to time appoint one or more auditor or auditors to audit the said accounts; and the auditor or auditors so appointed shall receive such remuneration out of all or any of the said funds as the District Judge may direct. The audited accounts shall be published in the Coorg District Gazette, and in such other manner, if any, as the District Judge may direct.

18. The committee may institute legal proceedings in any Civil or Criminal Court in the name of its president, and the cost of such proceedings may, unless the Court shall otherwise order, be debited to the said funds; and any person interested in any of the said temples and institutions, or in the performance of the worship or service thereof, or of the trusts relating thereto, may sue in the District Court the committee in the name of the president, or any particular member or members thereof by name, or any such manager or managers as aforesaid, for any misfeasance, breach of trust or neglect of duty committed in respect of such temple, institution, worship, service or trusts by the committee or by any member or members thereof, or by any person or persons holding office as manager or managers thereunder, as the case may be; and the said court may direct the specific performance of any act by the committee, and may decree damages with or without costs against the committee, or against such member, members, manager or managers as aforesaid and may also direct the removal of any member, members, manager, or managers; and no person removed by any such order shall be afterwards capable of being elected a member of committee or appointed a manager (as the case may be) without the permission in writing of the District Judge.

Legal Proceedings.

19. Every person having a right of attendance or having been in the habit of attending at the performance of the worship or service, or having the right or being in the habit of partaking in the benefit of any distributions of alms, at any of the said temples or institutions shall be deemed to be a person interested within the meaning of the last foregoing section.

Supplement to the last foregoing section.

20. In any civil suit or proceeding under this Regulation, it shall be competent for the District Judge, with or without the consent of either party, to order any matter in dispute in such suit or proceedings to be referred for decision to one or more arbitrator or arbitrators. Whenever any such order shall be made, the provisions of Chapter XXXVII of the Code of Civil Procedure* shall (except as herein provided) apply to such order and arbitration.

Arbitration.

XIV of 1882.

* i. e., Act XIV of 1882.

21. (1). No suit shall be entertained under this Regulation except in accordance with an order of the District Court to be made upon a preliminary application to that court for leave to institute such suit.

Leave for institution of suits.

(2). The District Judge after perusing the application, may either require the attendance of the parties, or may, without hearing the parties, give or refuse leave, or grant leave subject to such conditions as he may deem fit.

22. All rules made under this Regulation, and every appointment or election of a member and every vacancy in the office of a member, shall be notified in the the Coorg District Gazette.

Notification of rules, appointments, elections and vacancies.

23. Except as provided in this Regulation, it shall not be lawful for the Government, or for any officer of the Government in his official capacity, to take any part in the management or control of the said funds or of the said temples and institutions.

Exclusion of Government servants from taking part in management of temples or funds.

24. Except as hereinbefore otherwise provided, all disputes arising in respect of any matter provided for by this Regulation or by any rules made thereunder shall be referred to the District Judge, whose decision thereon shall be subject to appeal to the Judicial Commissioner within the prescribed period and subject thereto shall be final.

Reference disputes to District Judge with appeal to Judicial Commissioner.

The Schedule.

		Present annual allowance		
		Rs.	A.	P.
1.	Onkareshwara pagoda at Merkara	4,435	6	0
2.	Onkareshwara Choultry	380	0	0
3.	Rajah's tombs	2,000	0	0
4.	Tavunad Pagoda	2,320	7	5
5.	Tavunad Choultry	3,956	10	7
6.	Brahmadaya at Subrahmania paid at Merkara ...	48	0	0
	Total ...	13,140	8	0

APPENDIX III.

THE CHARITABLE ENDOWMENTS ACT

Act No. VI of 1890*.

(Received the assent of the Governor General on the 7th March, 1890).

An act to provide for the Vesting and Administration of Property held in trust for charitable purposes.

Whereas it is expedient to provide for the vesting and administration of property held in trust for charitable purposes. It is hereby enacted as follows :—

Title, extent and Commencement.

1. (1). This Act may be called the Charitable Endowments Act, 1890.

(2). It extends to the whole of British India, inclusive of[a] * * * * British Baluchistan ; and

(3). It shall come into force on the first day of October 1890.

Definition.

2. In this Act " Charitable purposes " includes relief of the poor, education, medical relief and the advancement of any other object of general public utility, but does not include a purpose which relates exclusively to religious teaching or worship.

Appointment and incorporation of Treasurer of Charitable endowments.

3. (1). The Governor-General in Council may appoint an officer of the Government by the name of his office to be Treasurer of Charitable Endowments for the territories subject to any Local Government[b].

*For statement of Objects and Reasons, see Gazette of India, 1889, Part V, p. 137. The Act has been declared in force in Upper Burma (except the Shan States) by the Burma Laws Act, 1898 (XIII of 1898).

It has been declared to be in force in the Santhal Parganas under S. 3 of the Santhal Parganas Settlement Regulation (III of 1872) as amended by the Santhal Parganas Laws Regulation (III of 1886). See Calcutta Gazette 1892, Pt. I, p. 448.

(a). The words " Upper Burma, and " after "inclusive" were repealed by Sch. V to the Burma Laws Act 1898 (XIII of 1898).

(b). For officers appointed under the powers conferred by this section, see Gazette of India, 1890, Part I, p. 755.

(2). Such treasurer shall, for the purposes of taking, holding and transferring moveable or immoveable property under the authority of this Act, be a corporation sole by the name of the Treasurer of Charitable Endowments for the territories subject to the Local Government, and, as such Treasurer, shall have perpetual succession and a corporate seal, and may sue and be sued in his corporate name.

Orders vesting property in Treasurer.

4. (1) Where any property is held or is to be applied in trust for a charitable purpose, the Local Government, if it thinks fit, may, on application made as hereinafter mentioned, and subject to the other provisions of this section, order, by notification in the Official Gazette, that the property be vested in the Treasurer of Charitable Endowments on such terms as to the application of the property or the income thereof as may be agreed on between the Local Government and the person or persons making the application, and the property shall thereupon so vest accordingly.

(2). When any property has vested under this section in a Treasurer of Charitable Endowments, he is entitled to all documents of title relating thereto.

(3). A Local Government shall not make an order under sub-section (1) for the vesting in a Treasurer of Charitable Endowments of any securities for money, except the following, namely :—

(*a*). Promissory notes, debentures, stock and other securities of the Government of India, or of the United Kingdom of Great Britain and Ireland ;

(*b*). Bonds, debentures and annuities charged by the Imperial Parliament on the revenues of India ;

(*c*). Stock or debentures of, or shares in, Railway or other Companies, the interest wheron has been guaranteed by the Secretary of State for India in Council ;

(*d*). Debentures or other securities for money issued by or on behalf of any local authority in exercise of powers by an Act of a legislature established in British India ;

(*e*). A Security expressly authorised by any order which the Governor General in Council may make in this behalf.

(4). An order under this section vesting property in a Treasurer of Charitable Endowments shall not require or be deemed to require him to administer the property, or impose or be deemed to impose upon him the duty of a trustee with respect to the administration thereof.

Schemes for administration of property vested in the Treasurer.

5. (1). On application made as hereinafter mentioned, and with the concurrence of the person or persons making the application, the Local Government, if it thinks fit, may settle a scheme for the administration of any property which has been or is to be vested in the Treasurer of Charitable Endowments, and may in such scheme appoint, by name or office, a person or persons, not being or including such Treasurer, to administer the property[a].

(2). On application, made as hereinafter mentioned, and with the concurrence of the person or persons making the application,theLocal Government may, if it thinks fit, modify any scheme settled under this section or substitute another scheme in its stead.

(3). A scheme settled, modified or substituted under this section, shall come in to operation on a day to be appointed by the Local Government in this behalf, and shall remain in force so long as the property to which it relates continues to be vested in the Treasurer of Charitable Endowments or until it has been modified or another such scheme has been substituted in its stead.

(4). Such a scheme, when it comes into operation, shall supersede any decree or direction relating to the subject-matter thereof in so far as such decree or direction is in any way repugnant thereto,and its validity shall not be questioned in any Court nor shall any Court give, in contravention of the provisions of the scheme or in any way contrary or in additon thereto, a decree or direction regarding the administration of the property to which the scheme relates.

(a). For schemes settled under this section

(1) in the Bombay Presidency, see Bombay List of Local Rules and orders Vol. I, Ed. 1896, pp. 531, 532, 538 to 540;

(2) in the Madras Presidency, see Madras List of Local Rules and orders Vol. I. Ed. 1898, p. 240;

(3) in the United Provinces, see the North-Western Provinces and Oudh List of Local Rules and orders, 1894, pp. 142 to 148.

(5). In the settlement of such a scheme effect shall be given to the wishes of the author of the trust so far as they can be ascertained, and, in the opinion of the Local Government, effect can reasonably be given to them.

(6). Where a scheme has been settled under this section for the administration of property not already vested in the Treasurer of Charitable Endowments, it shall not come into operation until the property has become so vested.

Mode of applying for vesting orders and schemes.

6. (1). The application referred to in the two last foregoing sections must be made,—

(*a*) if the property is already held in trust for a Charitable purpose, then by the person acting in the administration of the trust, or, where there are more persons than one so acting, then by those persons or a majority of them; and.

(*b*) if the property is to be applied in trust for such a purpose, then by the person or persons proposing so to apply it.

(2). For the purposes of this section the executor or administrator of a deceased trustee of property held in trust for a Charitable purpose shall be deemed to be a person acting in the administration of the trust.

Exercise by Governor General in Council of powers of Local Government.

7. (1). The Governor General in Council may exercise all or any of the powers conferred on the Local Government by Ss 4 and 5.

(2). When the Governor General in Council has signified to the Local Government his intention of exercising any of those powers with respect to any property, that Government shall not, without his previous sanction, exercise them with respect thereto.

Bare trusteeship of Treasurer.

8. (1). Subject to the provisions of this Act, a Treasurer of Charitable Endowments shall not, as such Treasurer act in the administration of any trust whereof any of the property is for the time being vested in him under this Act.

(2). Such Treasurer shall keep a separate account of each property for the time being so vested in so far as the property consists of securities for money, and shall apply the property, or the income thereof in accordance with the provision made in that behalf in the vesting order under S. 4 or in the scheme, if any, under S. 5, or in both those documents.

(3). In the case of any property so vested other than securities for money, such treasurer shall, subject to any special order which he may receive from the authority by whose order the property became vested in him, permit the persons acting in the administration of the trust to have the possession, management and control of the property, and the application of the income thereof, as if the property had been vested in them.

Annual publication of list of properties vested in Treasurer.

9. A Treasurer of Charitable Endowments shall cause to be published annually in the local official Gazette, at such time as the Local Government may direct, a list of all properties for the time being vested in him under this Act and an abstract of all accounts kept by him under sub-section (2) of the last foregoing section.

Limitation of functions and powers of Treasurer.

10. (1). A Treasurer of Charitable Endowments shall always be a sole trustee, and shall not as such Treasurer, take or hold any property otherwise than under the provisions of this Act, or, subject to those provisions, transfer any property vested in him except in obedience to a decree divesting him of the property, or in compliance with a direction in that behalf issuing from the authority by whose order the property became vested in him.

(2). Such a direction may require the Treasurer to sell or otherwise dispose of any property vested in him, and with the sanction of the authority issuing the direction, to invest the proceeds of the sale or other disposal of the property in any such security for money as is mentioned in S. 4, sub-section (3), clause (a), (b), (c), (d) or (e), or in the purchase of immoveable property.

(3). When a Treasurer of Charitable Endowments is divested by a direction of the Local Government or the Governer General in Council under this section, of any property, it shall vest in the person or persons acting in the administration thereof and be held by him or them on the same trusts as those on which it was held by such Treasurer.

Provision for continuance of office of Treasurer in certain contingencies.

11. If the office held by an officer of the Government who has been appointed to be a Treasurer of Charitable Endowments is abolished or its name is changed, the Governor General in Council may appoint the same or another officer of the Government by the name of his office to be such Treasurer, and thereupon the holder of the latter office shall be deemed for the purposes of this Act to be the successor in office of the holder of the former office.

Transfer of property from one Treasurer to another.

12. If by reason of an alteration of the limits of the territories subject to a Local Government, or for any other reason, it appears to the Governor General in Council that any property vested in a Treasurer of Charitable Endowments, should be vested in another such Treasurer, he may direct that the property shall be so vested, and thereupon it shall vest in that other Treasurer and his successors as fully and effectually for the purposes of this Act as if it had been originally vested in him under this Act.

Powers to frame forms and make rules.

13. The Governor General in Council may frame forms for any proceedings under this Act for which he considers that forms should be provided and may make such rules[a] consistent with this Act as he may deem expedient for—

(a) prescribing the Local Government which is to exercise the powers conferred by this Act in the case o[f] property which is, or is situated, in territories subjec[t] to two or more Local Governments;

(b) prescribing the fees to be paid to the Government i[n] respect of any property vested under this Act in [a] Treasurer of Charitable Endowments.

(c) regulating the cases and mode in which schemes [or] any modifications thereof are to be published befo[re] they are settled or made under S. 5;

---

a. For rules and forms, see Gazette of India, 1890, Part I. p. 757. The Boa[rd] of Revenue in Allahabad is appointed to be the public servant to whom annu[al] abstract of accounts is to be submitted. N. W. P. and Oudh Local Rules (1898) 1[…]

(*d*) prescribing the forms in which the accounts are to be kept by Treasurers of Charitable Endowments, and the mode in which such accounts are to be audited; and

(*e*) generally, carrying into effect the purposes of this Act.

Indemnity to Government and Treasurer.

14. No suit shall be instituted against the Government in respect of anything done or purporting to be done under this Act, or in respect of any alleged neglect or omission to perform any duty devolving on the Government under this Act or in respect of the exercise of, or the failure to exercise, any power conferred by this Act on the Government, nor shall any suit be institutued against a Treasurer of Charitable Endowments except for divesting him of property on the ground of its not being subject to a trust for a charitable purpose, or for making him chargeable with or accountable for the loss or misapplication of any property vested in him, or the income thereof, where the loss or misapplication has been occasioned by or through his wilful neglect or default.

Saving with respect to Advocate General and Official Trustee.

15. Nothing in this Act shall be construed to impair the operation of S. 111 of the statute 53 George III, Chapter 155*a*, or of any other enactment for the time being in force, respecting the authority of an Advocate-General at a presidency to act with respect to any charity, or of Ss. 8, 9, 10 and 11 of Act No. XVII of 1864*b* (an Act to constitute an Office of Official Trustee) respecting the vesting of property in trust for a charitable purpose in an Official Trustee.

General Controlling authority of Governor General in Council.

16. A Local Government shall, in the exercise of its powers under this Act, be subject to the control of the Governor General in Council.

---

a. The East India Company Act 1813.

b. The Official Truestees Act which is now amended by Act V of 1902.

APPENDIX IV.

Bombay Act No. VII of 1865.

(The assent of the Governor-General of India to this Act was first published by the Governor of Bombay on the 5th December 1865.)

An Act to extend the provisions of Act of the Governor General of India in Council No. XX of 1863 to the district of Canara in the Bombay Presidency.

Preamble.

Whereas it is expedient to extend the provisions of Act No. XX of 1863 (An Act to enable the Government to divest itself of the management of religious endowments) to the district of Canara in the Bombay Presidency; It is enacted as follows:—

Act XX of 1863 extended to Canara.

1. The provisions of Act No. XX of 1863 are hereby extended to the district of Canara in the Bombay Presidency.

Notice of appointment of Committee.

2. A notice of appointment of the Committee referred to in S. 7 of Act XX of 1863 shall, if posted at the Mamlatdar's office, be equivalent to a notification of such appointment in the official Gazette.

Interpretation-clause.

3. The words "Board" and "Board of Revenue" as used throughout Act XX of 1863 shall, for the purposes of this Act, be held to mean the Revenue Commissioner of the division.

APPENDIX V.

The Religious Endowments Bill with the Statement of Objects and Reasons.

The following Bill was introduced into the Council of the Governor-General of India for the purpose of making Laws and Regulations on the 26th February 1862, and was referred to a Select Committee who will make a report thereon after the 1st of June next.

A Bill to enable the Government to divest itself of the management of Religious Endowments.

Preamble.

WHEREAS it is expedient to relieve the Boards of Revenue, and the Local Agents, in the Presidency of Fort William in Bengal, and the Presidency of Fort Saint George, from the duties imposed on them by Regulation XIX, 1810, of the Bengal Code (*for the due appropriation of the rents and produce of lands granted for the support of mosques, Hindoo temples, colleges and other purposes; for the maintenance and repair of bridges, serays, kuttras, and other public buildings; and for the custody and disposal of Nuzzal property or escheats)* and Regulation VII, 1817, of the Madras Code (*for the due appropriation of the rents and produce of lands granted for the support of mosques, Hindoo temples, and colleges or other public purposes; for the maintenance and repair of bridges, choultries, or chuttrums, and other public buildings; and for the custody and disposal of escheats*), so far as those duties embrace the superintendence of lands granted for the support of mosques or Hindoo temples, and for other religious uses; the appropriation of endowments made for the maintenance of such religious establishments; the repair and preservation of buildings connected therewith and the appointment of trustees or managers thereof; or involve any connexion with the management of such religious establishments and whereas is is expedient for that purpose to repeal so much of Regulation XIX, 1810, of the Bengal Code, and Regulation VII, 1817, of the Madras Code, as relate to endowments for the support of mosques, Hindoo temples, or other religious purposes, it is enacted as follows :—

Regulations repealed.

I. So much of Regulation XIX, 1810 of the Bengal Code, and so much of Regulation VII, 1817 of the Madras Code, as relates to endowments for the support of mosques, Hindu temples, or other religious purposes, are repealed.

A—26

Government to determine as to the mosques, temples &c., which it shall relinquish.

II. As soon as possible after the passing of this Act the Government shall determine, in respect to each and every such mosque, temple, or religious establishment mentioned in the preamble to this Act and now under the superintendence of the Board of Revenue, whether the said mosque, temple, or establishment shall be left to the management of the present trustees, managers, or superintendents, or whether special provision shall be made for the management thereof.

On such determination notification to be made on which Board of Revenue and Local Agents shall act.

III. Whenever the Government shall determine that any such religious establishment shall be left to the management of the present Trustees, Managers, or Superintendents, it shall declare the same by notification in the Official Gazette, and thereupon the Board of Revenue or the Local Agents acting under the authority of the said Board, shall transfer to the said Trustees, Managers, or Superintendents all landed or other property now under the superintendence or in the possession of the said Board or Local Agents, and belonging to such religious establishment, except as provided in Ss.13 and15 of this Act, and the powers and responsibilities of the Board and Local Agents in respect to such religious establishment and to all lands and other property so transferred, except as above, and except as regards acts done and liabilites incurred by the said Board or Agents previous to such transfer shall cease and determine.

Rights, &c., of Trustees to be same as if this Act had not passed.

IV. The rights, powers, and responsibilities of Trustee Managers, or Superintendents to whom th superintendence of the lands and othe property of any such religious establishmen is transferred in the manner prescribed in the preceding section o this Act, as well as the conditions of their appointment, electio and removal, shall be the same as if this Act had not been passed except in respect of the liability to be sued under S. 10 of this Ac and except in respect of the authority of the said Board and Loc Agents given by the said Regulations over such establishment an over such Trustees, Managers, or Superintendents, which authori is hereby determined and repealed.

When special provision to be made, Government shall appoint a committee to act in place of the Board and Local Agents.

V. Whenever the Government shall determine that speci provision shall be made for the superinte dence of any such religious establishment shall once for all appoint for that purp a committee of management consisting o or more persons who, in respect to su religious establishment and to all the lands and other prope belonging thereto and to all persons employed in connexion therew except as provided in Ss. 13 and 15 of this Act, exercise all powers vested by the said Regulations in the Board of Reve and the Local Agents and shall perform all the duties now imposed by law on the said Board and Local Agents.

Provision as to qualifications for Member of such Committee.

VI. The Members of the said Committee shall be appointed from among persons professing the religion for the purposes of which the establishment, was founded, or is now maintained and in accordance, so far as can be ascertained, with the general wishes of those who are interested in the maintenance of such establishment. The appointment of the Committee shall be notified in the Official Gazette.

Every Member to be appointed for life, unless removed for misconduct, &c.

VII. Every Member of a Committee appointed as above shall hold his office for life, unless removed for misconduct or unfitness, and no such Member shall be removed except by an order of the Civil Court as hereinafted provided.

How vacancies filled up.

VIII. Any vacancy which may occur among the Members of a Committee of management appointed as above shall be filled up by the remaining members, and if any vacancy shall not be filled up within 3 months after it has occurred, the Civil Court, on the application of any person whatever, may order that the vacancy be forthwith filled up by the remaining members, and if this order be not complied with, may appoint a member to fill the said vacancy.

On appointment of Committee Board and Local Agents to transfer property.

IX. Immediately on the appointment of a committee as above provided, for the superintendence of any such religious establishment, and for the management of its affairs, the Board of Revenue, or the Local Agents acting under the authority of the said Board, shall transfer to such committee all landed or other property which at the time of appointment shall be under the superintendence, or in the possession, of the said Board or Local Agents, and belonging to the said religious establishment, except as provided in Ss. 13 and 15 of this Act, and thereupon the powers and responsibilities of the Board and the Local Agents, in respect to such religious establishment and to all land and other property so transferred, except as above, and except as regards acts done and liabilities incurred by the said Board or Agents previous to such transfer, shall cease and determine.

Termination of powers and responsibilities of Board and Agents.

Any person interested may sue in case of Breach of Trust, &c.

X. Any person or persons interested in any Mosque, Temple, or religious establishment, or in the performance of the worship or of the service thereof, or the Trusts relating thereto, may, without joining as plaintiff any of the other persons interested therein, sue before the Civil Court the Trustee, Manager, or Superintendent of such Mosque, Temple, or religious establishment, or the Members of any Committee appointed under this Act, or any of them, for any misfeasance, breach of Trust, or neglect of duty, committed by such Trustee, Manager, Superintendent, or Member of such Committee, in respect of the Trusts vested in, or confided to, them respectively; and the Civil Court may direct the specific performance of any act by all or any of such Trustees, Managers, Superintendents or any of such Members of a Committee and may decree damages and costs against them and may also direct the removal of all or any of such Trustees, Managers, Superintendents, or any of such Members of a Committee.

Powers of Civil Court.

XI. The interest required in order to entitle a person to sue under the last preceding section need not be a pecuniary, or a direct or immediate, interest, or such an interest as would entitle the person suing to take any part in the management or superintendence of the Trusts. Any person having a right of attendance, or having been in the habit of attending, at the performance of the worship or service of any mosque, temple, or religious establishment or of partaking in the benefit of any distribution of alms shall be deemed to be a person interested within the meaning of the last preceding section.

Nature of interest entitling person to sue.

XII. No suit or proceeding before any Civil Court under this section, shall in any way affect or interfere with any proceeding in a Criminal Court for Criminal Breach of Trust under the Indian Penal Code.

No Civil suit to bar proceedings for Criminal Breach of Trust.

XIII. In any case in which lands have been granted for the support of establishments partly of a religious and partly of a secular character or in which the endowments made for the support of an establishment are appropriated partly to religious and partly to secular uses, the Board of Revenue, before transferring to any Trustees, Managers, or Superintendents or to any Committee of management appointed as aforesaid, shall determine what portion, if any, of the said land or other property shall remain under the superintendence of the said Board for application to secular uses, and what portion shall be transferred to the superintendence of the said trustees, managers, or superintendents, or of the said committee, and also what annual amount, if any, shall be charged on the land or other property which may be so transferred to the superintendence of the said trustees, managers, or superintendents or of the said committee, and made payable to the said Board or to the local agents, for secular uses as aforesaid. In every such case the provisions of this Act shal

Cases in which the endowments are partly for religious and partly for secular purposes.

take effect only in respect to such land and other property as may be so transferred.

Government henceforth not to undertake charge of property for support of any Mosque, Temple, &c.

XIV. After the passing of this Act it shall not be lawful for the Government or for any officer of the Government to undertake or resume the superintendence of any lands or other property granted for the support of or otherwise belonging to any Mosque, Hindoo Temple, or other religious establishment, or to take any part in the management or appropriation of endowments made for the maintenance of any such establishment or to nominate or appoint any Trustees, Managers, or Superintendents thereof, or to be in any way connected therewith.

Effect of Act in respect of Regulations therein mentioned, and of buildings of antiquity, &c.

XV. Nothing in this Act shall be held to affect the provisions of the Regulations mentioned in this Act, except in so far as they relate to Mosques, Hindoo Temples, and other religious establishments; or to prevent the Government from taking such steps as it may deem necessary, under the provisions of the said Regulations, to prevent injury to and preserve buildings remarkable for their antiquity, or for their historical or architectural value, or required for the convenience of the public.

Statement of Objects and Reaons.

It has long been the avowed policy of the Government of India to divest itself of all direct concern with the management of religious endowments, but the obligations imposed on its officers by law in the Presidencies of Bengal and Madras present difficulties which have hitherto, as far as regards those Presidencies, prevented the full accomplishment of this purpose.

The subject has given rise to much correspondence to which it is not necessary more particularly to advert. It may suffice to state that the Secretary of State in his Despatch, dated the 16th July 1860, reviewing the more recent proceedings of the Government of India relative to "the repeal of those provisions of the Bengal and Madras Codes by which the general superintendence of the endowments for the support of Mosques and Temples is vested in the Revenue Officers of Government," expressed an opinion "that all that is requisite is an Act on the principle of Act No X of 1840 in regard to the temple of Juggernath, repealing the existing enactments on the subject, and transferring the entire superintendence of the institutions to their respective trustees, provision being made for an appeal by suit in the ordinary way to the established Courts of Justice in all disputes relating to the control and application of their funds."

Previous to this expression of opinion by the Secretary of State, a Bill had been brought into the Legislative Council early in 1860, simply repealing Regulation XIX of 1810 of the Bengal Code and Regulation VII of 1817 of the Madras Code, and reserving the jurisdiction now exercised, or which but for those Regulations might have been exercised, by Courts of Justice, in enforcing the due execution or administration of any trust or endowment, and in securing the due appointment or succession to the management thereof.

To this proposed measure two objections have been made. *First*, that by the repeal of the Regulations above cited, the Government is relieved of all concern in the management, not only of all religious endowments, but also of other trusts not of a religious character, which those Regulations impose upon it and which it is not desirable that it should be relieved of. *Second*, that a sudden and abrupt relinquishment by Government of the guardianship of the property of religious and charitable endowments which it has so long managed on behalf of the public, without making due provision for their future management, would be unjust.

Concurring in these objections, I have endeavoured to frame this Bill so as to carry out the object proposed by the Secretary of State, without interfering with the provisions of the existing law so far as they define the duty of Government and its officers in respect to public property not connected with religious endowments and at the same time to provide for due supervision of religious endowments which are now managed by the Government and its Officers, but from which they will henceforth be disconnected*.

(Signed) CECIL BEADON,

---

* The proceedings of the Legislative Council in connection with this Bill (dated 5th February 1862, 26th February 1862 and 25th February 1863) are reported in the Calcutta Gazette, 1862, Supplement, p. 28 and 1863, p. 105.

APPENDIX VI.

Rules framed by the N. W. P. and Oudh Government for election of Temple Committee Members.

Under S. 10, Act XX of 1863, the Hon'ble the Lieutenant Governor is pleased to prescribe* the following rules for filling any vacancy which may hereafter occur among the Members of a Committee appointed under the Act abovenamed to superintend the maintenance of any mosque, temple or other religious establishment.

All persons who may be hereafter appointed to such Committee shall be elected by the male residents of the vicinity, such electors being not less than eighteen years of age and professing the religion in the interests of which the endowment was founded, and having their permanent residence at a distance of not more than five miles from the institution.

Whenever any vacancy shall occur among the Members of a Committee appointed as above, the remaining Members of the Committee shall, as soon as possible, affix a notice, if the establishment be Mahomedan, in Persian and Urdu, or if it be Hindu, in the Hindi language and character, conspicuously and in front of the main entrance to such mosque, temple, or other religious establishment, declaring the occurrence of the vacancy and calling on all qualified electors to assemble at noon on a day which shall be specified in the notice, and which shall not be later than three months from the date of the vacancy, at some convenient place, which shall also be specified, for the purpose of electing a new member.

The remaining Members of the Committee, or one or more of them, shall attend at the specified time and place for the purpose of conducting the election, which shall be made as follows:—

Every voter shall be questioned separately. A separate paper shall be provided for each proposed member, whose name shall be written at the head of the paper. Every voter shall sign his name, or cause his name to be signed f r him, on the paper provided for the member for whom he votes

The signatures shall be numbered consecutively as they are made, and as each signature is affixed, the name of the person voted for and the number of votes that have been recorded shall be called out.

The person who may obtain the largest number of votes shall be held to have been duly elected.

---

* Notification No. 602 A, 22nd February 1865, Allahabad Gazette 1865, p. 120.

APPENDIX VII.

Rules framed by the Bengal Government for election of Devastanam Committee Members, Bengal.

The following Rules are published for general information*, for the election of a new Member of any Committee appointed under Ss. 7 and 10, Act XX of 1863, to exercise the powers of the Board of Revenue and the Local Agents under the repealed Regulation XIX of 1810, in regard to any mosque, temple, or other religious establishment.

Register of those interested to be kept.

The Members of every Committee appointed under S. 7, Act XX of 1863, shall keep a Register of all those who are interested in the maintenance of the mosque, temple, or other religious establishment superintended by the Committee.

In a public place and open to public inspection.

2. This Register shall be open to public inspection, and a copy shall be affixed to some public place within the limits of the said temple, mosque, or religious establishment.

Whose names are to be entered in the Register.

3. The Committee shall, as soon as possible after its appointment, enter in this Register the name of every male person having the interest in the Temple, Mosque or Establishment described in S. 15 of Act XX of 1863, *i. e.*, of every male person "having a right of attendance or having been in the habit of attending at the performance of the worship or service of the Mosque, Temple, or Religious Establishment, or of partaking in

* Calcutta Gazette Notification, the 2nd December 1835—*Vide* Calcutta Gazette 1865, p. 2096.

the benefit of any distribution of alms, with his residence and the date of the entry of his name in the Register".

Question of doubt as to entry or removal of names how to be decided.

4. If any doubt arises as to the eligibility of any individual to be included in the Register thus prescribed, or if any person whose name is not spontaneously entered in the Register by the Committee shall claim to have his name so entered, or if there be a doubt as to whether the name of any person shall be removed from the Register, the question whether in each case the name shall be entered or not, or removed or not, shall be decided by the votes of the majority of the Committee.

Name of person acquiring an interest to be immediately entered, and Register to be revised every six months.

5. The Committee shall be bound to enter in this Register the name and residence of any person as soon as he acquires the interest defined in Rule 3, together with the date of the entry, and the Register shall be revised by the Committee at least once in every six months, in order to ascertain that it is correctly kept up, and that the name of no person not interested, as defined in Rule 3, is kept on the Register.

No name to be registered or removed during vacancy in the Committee.

6. No name is to be entered on the Register, or removed from it during the existence of any vacancy among the Members of the Committee.

Rights of those registered.

7. The persons whose names are entered in the Register thus prescribed are to be accepted as the persons interested in the maintenance of the Mosque, Temple, or Religious Establishment, as described in S. 8 of Act XX of 1863, and entitled therefore to vote at the election of any new Member of the Committee under S. 10 of Act XX of 1863.

Day of election how to be notified.

8. Immediately upon the occurrence of a vacancy among the Members of the Committee, the remaining Members shall fix an early convenient day for the election of a new Member to fill the vacancy, giving notice thereof with all possible publicity, by beat

of drum, and by a written proclamation suspended at the door of the Mosque, Temple, or Religious Establishment.

Election to be held publicly in the presence of candidates and of Members of the Committee.

9. The election shall be held upon the day thus notified in the most public manner possible, all candidates being invited to be present. The members of the Committee are to be, one or more of them, present at the election throughout the day.

Election to be by poll. Rule for its conduct.

10. The election shall be by poll. A separate list shall be taken of the votes recorded for each candidate for the vacancy; such of the electors as are able to write shall sign their own names in the list to which they wish their names to be appended, and the Committee shall cause to be recorded the names of those electors who cannot write in the list to which they wish their names attached.

Hours of election.

11. The lists will be kept open on the day of election from sunrise to 10 A. M., and from 1 P. M., to sunset, and any elector shall be entitled to have his vote recorded during those hours. At 10 A. M., and again at sunset, the Member or Members of the Committee present, and likewise any of the candidates present, shall affix their signature immediately below the name of the last elector whose vote is recorded on each of the lists.

Precaution for integrity of lists.

Declarations of the result of the election.

12. As soon as the sun sets, the remaining Members of the Committee shall reckon up the votes taken and declare the candidate who has received the most votes to be duly elected to fill the vacancy in the Committee.

Poll lists how to be kept.

13. The poll lists shall be carefully kept and deposited among the records of the Temple, Mosque, or Religious Establishment, and shall be open to public inspection in the same manner as the Register of Electors.

APPENDIX VIII.

Rules framed by the Madras Government for the Election of Temple Committee Members, Madras.

Rules for the supply of vacancies in Managing Committees appointed under S. 7, Act XX of 1863*:—

I. On the occurrence of a vacancy, the remaining members of the Committee shall forthwith give public intimation of such vacancy by advertisement in the District Gazette, and by causing a written or printed notice thereof to be affixed to some conspicuous place in each religious institution under their management.

II. The advertisement and notice shall set forth the name of the member in whose stead a new member is to be elected; the date on which the vacancy occurred; and the place, day and hour fixed for the election by the remaining members of the Committee.

III. The place of the election shall be the principal religious institution under the management of the Committee, or the KASBA town of the district, or of the taluk, in which the institution where the vacancy occurs is situated.

IV. The day to be fixed for the election shall not be earlier than one month, nor later than three months, from the date on which the vacancy occurred, and within those limits shall as far as practicable, be so fixed as to enable persons living within the jurisdiction of the Committee, and entitled to vote at the election under clause XIII INFRA to attend and vote for a new member.

V. The voting shall commence at 6 P. M., and close at 5 P. M., of the day fixed for the election.

VI. The remaining members of the Committee shall appoint a sufficient number of respectable and trustworthy persons as tellers to receive and register the votes of the electors. No person shall be appointed a teller who is himself a

---

* B. P. No. 3055, 7—6—1865.

candidate for the vacant office, or the agent of such candidate.

VII. The remaining members of the Committee shall make such arrangements for taking the votes of the electors, as will admit of all voters having reasonable time and opportunities to register their votes within the hours fixed, and shall appoint not less than two tellers to each office where the votes may be given. Each elector shall declare to the tellers, in writing, the name, residence occupation, or other description of the persons for whose appointment he votes, as well as his own.

VIII. The tellers shall immediately enter the names &c., of the elector and his nominee in a book which shall be provided for the purpose by the Committee, and shall require the voter to attest the register by signature or mark. The voting papers shall also be duly filed by the tellers.

IX. The books of registry shall be in the prescribed form, and at the close of the voting shall be signed by the tellers who took the votes therein registered.

X. The result of the election shall be declared by the remaining members of the Committee within twenty-four hours after the closing of the voting.

XI. A notice containing the result of the election and signed by the remaining members of the Committee and the tellers shall without delay be published in three successive issues of the District Gazette and affixed to some conspicuous place in each religious institution under the management of the Committee.

XII. After the result of the election has been declared, the registry book of votes and files of voting papers shall be kept open for the inspection of the electors for a fortnight, in a convenient place at the town where the election took place, and shall be carefully preserved by the Committee among their records.

XIII. The following persons will be entitled to vote at elections of members of Committee :—

1. Owners of lands, situated within the jurisdiction of the Committee, and paying an annual revenue to Government of not less than Rs. 20.

2. Owners of landed property, situated as aforesaid, wholly or partially exempted from the payment of revenue to Government, but which if not so exempt would be liable to an annual payment of Rs. 20.

3. Owners of house property, situated as aforesaid, of the estimated value of Rs. 250 and upwards.

4. Occupiers of houses, situated as aforesaid, of the annual rental of Rs. 50* and upwards.

5. Persons in the employment of Government on salaries of Rs. 150 per annum and upwards, or in the receipt of pensions from Government of the like amount.

6. Possessors of private income to the amount of Rs. 150 and upwards.

7. Persons supporting any religious endowment under the management of the Committee by annual payments of not less than Rs. 50, or a donation of Rs. 500.

8. Graduates of any University who have resided for six months prior to the election within the jurisdiction of the Committee.

9. Any person not qualified as aforesaid and claiming to vote must establish his right to the satisfaction of the Committee.

Provided always that no person shall be entitled to vote at any election unless he professes the religion for the purposes of which the religious institution under the management of the Committee was founded or is maintained, and is interested in its maintenance and is not a minor:

* B. P. No. 847, 10-12-89.

Provided also that no person shall be entitled or allowed to vote unless he has been registered as a voter at least seven days before the occurrence of the vacancy at which he desires to vote.

XIV. Every Committee shall keep a register of voters, in which shall be entered the name, occupation or other description and qualification of every person entitled to vote at their elections; and every person satisfying the Committee that he possesses the qualifications hereinbefore mentioned shall be entitled to be registered as a voter, and be furnished with a copy of the entry of his name, &c., in the register.

XV. No person shall be entitled to more than one vote for each vacancy.

XVI. Voting by proxy shall be allowed only in the case of absentees supporting institutions under the management of the Committee by annual payment of Rs. 500 or upwards, or donations of Rs. 5,000. The authority produced by the proxy must have been executed before a public officer not below the grade of Sub-Magistrate and attested by him.

XVII. Voters proved to have wilfully registered more than one vote for each vacancy shall thereby be disqualified for again voting, and their names shall be removed from the register.

XVIII. The person who receives the largest number of votes shall be declared duly elected as a member of the Committee, and in the event of two or more persons having an equal number of votes, the selection shall be determined by lot.

XIX. Any person proved to have given, directly or indirectly, any valuable consideration whatever in return for a vote shall be thereby disqualified from being elected.

XX. The election of any person, except in conformity with these rules shall be null and void.

INDEX.